FAIR FIGHT

Legal Ethics for Litigators

LAWRENCE J. FOX & SUSAN R. MARTYN

AMERICAN BAR ASSOCIATION
Litigation Section

Cover design by Elmarie Jara/ABA Design

Printed in the United States of America.

24 23 22 21 20 5 4 3 2 1

A catalog record for this book is available from the Library of Congress.

Discounts are available for books ordered in bulk. Special consideration is given to state bars, CLE programs, and other bar-related organizations. Inquire at Book Publishing, ABA Publishing, American Bar Association, 321 N. Clark Street, Chicago, Illinois 60654-7598.

www.shopABA.org

Dedication

For Paulette and Peter
Our spouses who supported and encouraged us.

Brief Contents

Contents

Preface

The authors first met as advisors to the American Law Institute's Restatement of the Law Governing Lawyers, a project only ethics geeks can appreciate—sitting in windowless conference rooms for dozens of meetings over 13 years of debate and compromise before the final volumes were launched. Next came a sojourn on the American Bar Association's Ethics 2000 Commission, where we served as commissioners debating and updating the contours of the Model Rules of Professional Conduct.

Following these developments in the law, we soon began a wonderful and unique collaboration, combining the perspectives of a longtime practitioner (Larry Fox) with those of a longtime academic (Susan Martyn). We began by writing books for law students, *Traversing the Ethical Minefield*, first published by Aspen in 2004 and now in its fourth edition, and *The Law Governing Lawyers: Model Rules, Standards, Statutes and State Rules of Professional Conduct*, also published by Aspen annually with a third author, W. Bradley Wendel. Most recently we completed a short volume entitled *Representing Clients: An Ethics Guide for Clinical Law Students and Emerging Lawyers*, published this year by Foundation Press.

We also authored several versions of a legal ethics guide for clients, the most recent being *How to Deal with Your Lawyer: Answers to Commonly Asked Questions*, published by Oxford University Press in 2008. And we are so pleased to have spent time on making legal ethics accessible to practicing lawyers as well. We began with our first volume, *Red Flags: Legal Ethics for Lawyers*, published by The American Law Institute in 2005 and 2010. Next came *The Ethics of Representing Organizations: Legal Fictions for Clients*, published by Oxford in 2010. And now, we have completed this volume for litigators.

Fair Fight follows the course of a litigation-client representation, fleshing out the lawyer's fiduciary obligations and some of the bodies of law that limit client advocacy (crime, fraud, procedural, and evidentiary rules). The book then digs into a number of specifics in representing clients pretrial, at trial, and on appeal. We conclude with a chapter on judicial ethics. Each chapter includes text addressing the basic law that governs a topic, followed by engaging Q & A's that detail the issues in specific contexts. Footnotes add hundreds of cites to relevant legal authority.

You will find that this book confronts you, the conscientious lawyer, with a myriad of rules and cases that must govern your conduct as an ethical lawyer. Some of these essential legal obligations also grant you a measure of discretion under specific circumstances. As you represent your clients zealously within the bounds of the law, please remember that just because you *may* file a lawsuit, rely on an oral fee agreement, speak to the press, or advertise on your website does not mean you should. Similarly, if proceeding with a representation *requires* you to seek a confidentiality or conflicts waiver, you can choose instead to decline or withdraw from the representation. Our clients rely on us for our competence but also for all of our other qualities, including conscientious exercise of our discretion that serves to make us loyal and trusted advocates and advisors.

We envision *Fair Fight* as a useful and somewhat entertaining legal ethics resource. You can use it in at least three ways. First, consider this volume an introduction and refresher to the field of professional responsibility. Use a chapter-by-chapter approach, as you would with any book. Second, you might use *Fair Fight* as a reference to assist you in identifying, exploring, and resolving ethics issues as they arise in representing litigation clients. We recommend you begin by reading Chapter 1 to understand the layout and the topics covered in the book. Then we invite you to use the table of contents and the index to search for issues or topics you encounter when you represent clients. Third, you might view *Fair Fight* as a series of stories designed to help you understand typical ethics issues that arise in litigation practice. You can do this by reading the Q & A's throughout the volume and then referring to the footnotes and adjacent text material for more information.

As we refined and completed this volume, we realized how much we owe hundreds of lawyers like you for sharing your needs, your points of view, and your hypotheticals with us. We hope you will enjoy *Fair Fight* and find it a useful resource in your practice.

Larry Fox and Susan Martyn
February 2020

Acknowledgments

In addition to the hundreds of lawyers and students who have taught us and refined our understanding of the law governing lawyers over the past 30 years, we thank our colleagues at Yale and the University of Toledo Law Schools and Mitchell Hamline School of Law for sharing their sage wisdom.

We are also grateful to colleagues who have read or commented on this volume, Harry S. Bryant, Elizabeth McCuskey, Lee Pizzimenti, and Douglas Richmond. Susan thanks Mark Squillace and Maureen Ryan for inviting her to Boulder, where she used part of a summer as a research scholar to complete some of the work on this volume, and Emily Morrison for her research assistance.

We owe a special debt of gratitude to Bea Cucinotta, whose cheer, patience, and organization helped make this book possible.

Author Biographies

Lawrence J. Fox

Lawrence J. Fox is the George and Sadella Crawford Lecturer at Yale Law School, teaching professional responsibility and the Ethics Bureau at Yale (EBaY), a clinic that provides assistance and counseling on a pro bono basis to nonprofit legal service providers, courts, and law schools.

Mr. Fox formerly served as a managing partner of Drinker Biddle & Reath LLP, then a general practice law firm of approximately 650 lawyers with its principal office in Philadelphia and branch offices in New Jersey, New York, California, Delaware, the District of Columbia, Illinois, and Wisconsin.

Mr. Fox has spent his entire career as a trial lawyer, first at Community Action for Legal Services in New York City and, from 1972 until 2017, at Drinker Biddle & Reath LLP. As a partner at Schoeman Updike Kaufman & Gerber LLP, he now specializes in representing lawyers regarding their professional responsibilities.

Mr. Fox has taught professional responsibility at Yale, Harvard, and the University of Pennsylvania Law Schools and lectured at more than 35 law schools throughout the country, as well as abroad in Russia, China, Argentina, Austria, and the United Kingdom. He has produced and participated in hundreds of continuing legal education seminars and written extensively in the professional responsibility field. This is his seventh book with co-author Susan Martyn. He also has written *Legal Tender: A Lawyer's Guide to Professional Dilemmas* and is the editor and contributing author of *Raise the Bar: Real World Solutions for a Troubled Profession* (2007) and *A Century of Legal Ethics: Trial Lawyers and the ABA Canons of Professional Ethics* (2009), all published by the American Bar Association.

Mr. Fox is a former member and Chair of the ABA Standing Committee on Ethics and Professional Responsibility, a former Chair of the ABA Section of Litigation, and a Fellow in the American College of Trial Lawyers. He was an advisor to the American Law Institute's 13-year project, The Restatement of the Law Governing Lawyers, and the founder and a member of Ethics 2000, the ABA Commission established to update and redraft the Model Rules of Professional Conduct.

Susan R. Martyn

Susan Martyn is Distinguished University Professor and Stoepler Professor of Law and Values Emeritus at the University of Toledo College of Law. She teaches Legal Ethics at Mitchell Hamline School of Law and is Visiting Professor of Law at Yale Law School.

Professor Martyn has been instrumental in developing the Law Governing Lawyers. She acted as an advisor to the American Law Institute's Restatement of the Law Governing Lawyers (1987–2000) and was a member of the American Bar Association's Ethics 2000 Commission, which redrafted the Model Rules of Professional Conduct (1997–2002). She is a member of the Michigan, Ohio, and Supreme Court Bars and served on the Ohio Supreme Court's Task Force on the Rules of Professional Conduct (2003–2006). She is a contributor to continuing legal education programs and served as a member of the ABA Standing Committee on Ethics and Professional Responsibility from 2007–2010. She is a life member of the American Law Institute and a Fellow in the American Bar Foundation.

PART ONE

The Big Picture

The Daunting Task

This is a book about trial lawyer ethics. But like the litigation process itself, this book considers to a far greater extent matters outside the courtroom, much of it addressing topics common to all representations, such as obligations to clients and the limits of the law, and much of it addressing pleadings, answers, motion practice, depositions, settlement, and appeals. But before we focus on the trial, we should address ethical advocacy at the level of 25,000 feet.

We trial lawyers have erected as the apotheosis of our work, the lawyer who is dealt a sow's ear and who turns it, by virtue of the lawyer's charm, credibility, good humor, powerful rhetoric, and withering cross-examination, into a silk purse or, better yet, membership in the American College of Trial Lawyers.

There is only one problem with the foregoing: that is, the lawyer starts believing she possesses such power and that there are no consequences to her taking on or advocating for lost causes. Lawyers face two formidable impediments. First, there are court rules, such as Civil Rule 11, that limit frivolous court filings. Second, there are Model Rules of Professional Conduct, such as Model Rule 3.1, that renders it a disciplinary violation to bring or defend a proceeding or assert or controvert an issue unless there is a non-frivolous basis in both law and fact for doing so. The only exceptions are a good faith argument for an extension, modification, or reversal of the law and the right of a lawyer for a criminal defendant to provide the client a constitutional defense. So in chasing such an elusive goal, keep in mind that your long shot may be considered frivolous advocacy by those who are both likely to be more objective and have the power to sanction lawyers who stray.

This is just one example that illustrates how your practice can seem so simple, yet so daunting. You earn fees by representing clients, but you are also subject to limits that can put the brakes on a client representation. We call this a "fair fight" because it requires zealous advocacy within the bounds of the law.

The law that governs the conduct of lawyers in litigation and elsewhere includes each jurisdiction's Rules of Professional Conduct, common law (such as agency and malpractice law), a few statutes (such as fee-shifting provisions), and court rules (such as Rules of Civil Procedure). Your license to practice and your income depend on your understanding of all these bodies of law, as adopted in each jurisdiction. In this volume, we refer collectively to all this law as "the law governing lawyers."

Rules of Professional Conduct govern the conduct of all lawyers admitted to law practice. Violation of your jurisdiction's Rules of Professional Conduct subjects you to professional discipline, with sanctions ranging from disbarment, suspension from practice, and fines to public and private reprimands. Because nearly every jurisdiction has patterned its Rules of Professional Conduct on the American Bar Association's Model Rules, we cite to the ABA Model Rules, noting some significant departures where relevant.[1]

Most of the common law governing lawyer conduct has been collected in the Restatement (Third) of the Law Governing Lawyers. When we refer to this common law, we rely on the Restatement. We do so because it is fairly recent (2000), does an admirable job of restating and organizing both the Rules of Professional Conduct and the common law, and has been cited and relied on in hundreds of court opinions.[2]

Perhaps most familiar to litigators is the organic law that governs the litigation process, such as the procedural or evidence rules. We will refer to that law, but we will primarily focus on the vast body of law and ethical discretion that shapes your professional obligations to all clients, including litigation clients. All of which leads us to one final

1. State rules of professional conduct generally adopt the numbering and most of the substance of the American Bar Association's MODEL RULES OF PROFESSIONAL CONDUCT, available in law libraries and at http://www.abanet.org/cpr/mrpc/mrpc_toc.html. We cite the 2019 ABA Model Rules in this volume as "MR __." In footnotes, we refer to a particular state rule of professional conduct as "Rule [#]." You can find the most recent iteration of your state rules of professional conduct at http://www.abanet.org/cpr/links.html.

2. The American Law Institute's RESTATEMENT (THIRD) OF THE LAW GOVERNING LAWYERS (2000) is available in law libraries and on Westlaw and Lexis. We cite the RESTATEMENT as "RLGL § ___."

observation: DO NOT RELY ON THIS BOOK FOR LEGAL ADVICE. We have used a Q & A, or dialogue, format here to invite you into a conversation about your professional responsibilities, not to offer you answers to any specific legal problem. As every lawyer knows, the exact requirements of all of the legal rules will differ jurisdiction to jurisdiction. Further, a slight change in facts can make a huge difference in outcome. With these caveats in mind, we hope to engage you in a fascinating subject, and by citing Model Rules, Restatement sections, and relevant portions of the Model Code of Judicial Conduct,[3] we hope to facilitate your further research.

3. States generally follow the template of the American Bar Association's Model Code of Judicial Conduct in crafting their own judicial rules. We cite to the 2011 ABA Code of Judicial Conduct as "MCJC Rule ___."

CHAPTER 1

Five Steps to a Fair Fight

Representing clients in litigation can be a real challenge. You must deal with a client or clients, opposing parties, witnesses, and, of course, the court. Although these issues may seem unique to your litigation practice, in fact most of them correspond to professional responsibility obligations that exist in every kind of client representation.

For this reason, to get us started, in this chapter we summarize our five-step approach to legal ethics issues generally, an approach that dictates the order of topics in this volume. We will refer to these issues often throughout this book. Along the way, we will focus specifically on the application of these rules and obligations to your litigation practice.

§ 1.01 Step One: Identify Your Client Obligations—The Six Cs

Lawyers assume six ethical obligations—what we call the six Cs—when an actual or implied client-lawyer relationship is established. These obligations rest on a key agency law insight now restated in the law governing lawyers: You derive your power from clients, but your superior knowledge and skill also allow you to overpower your client's interests. You assume fiduciary duties of client identification, competence, proper deference to client control, communication, confidentiality, and conflict of interest resolution to prevent underidentification with clients and to ensure that the client's best interests are promoted in a representation.[4]

The first C, client identification, requires you to properly recognize your clients, an inquiry that can produce unanticipated results.

In most situations, lawyers know who their clients are because they have expressly agreed to represent them. Increasingly, however, the law governing lawyers also has recognized what lawyers may think of as "accidental" clients, those a lawyer did not expect, but those recognized by law as being owed the same fiduciary duties that lawyers owe clients they intend to represent.

General rules of contract and tort govern the creation of client-lawyer relationships.[5] If you provide or agree to provide legal advice or services in response to a request for either, you have a client. If you are asked to provide legal advice or services, fail to say "no," and the person who asked reasonably relies on you to provide services, you have a client. Courts approach discrepancies in remembering what occurred from the viewpoint of the reasonable prospective client.[6]

These legal principles can create accidental clients when a lawyer does not intend them. Accidental clients lurk in all prospective client situations. They also can be created by court appointments[7] and by imputation.[8] Identifying some clients can be complicated by their organization, such as entities that act only through agents.[9] They also can change, such as by merger, reorganization, bankruptcy, or death. Accommodating a client may create an accidental joint client. Accidental clients also can materialize as quasi-clients if your client designated them as third-party beneficiaries.[10]

Once you identify accidental as well as intended clients, you will be in a position to avoid client-lawyer relationships you do not wish to create and embrace those you do. When you know your clients, you will be able to know whom to bill and to whom you owe your other five C fiduciary duties.

§ 1.02 Step Two: Clarify Your Fee

Lawyers are fiduciaries and, therefore, they owe clients certain precontractual duties of fairness in bargaining for fees. Model Rule 1.5

4. RLGL § 16.
5. MR Scope ¶ [17]; RLGL § 14.
6. RLGL §§ 14(1)(b), 14 cmt. e.
7. *Id.* § 14(2).
8. MRs 1.8(k), 1.10, 1.11, 1.12.
9. MR 1.13.
10. RLGL § 51 cmt. f.

articulates this premise by providing that you may not agree to, charge, or collect an unreasonable fee or expense.[11] Factors determining reasonableness include the time and difficulty of the matter, the fee customarily charged, the amount involved, results obtained, your experience and ability, and the kind of fee. You are free to charge an hourly, flat, contingent, or blended fee, but it must be reasonable. Contingent fees and agreements to split fees must meet specific written requirements. All other fees should be communicated to the client, preferably in writing, along with the scope of representation and the basis or rate at which expenses are charged. Failure to clarify the basis for expenses in such an agreement leaves you with the only option of passing on the actual cost.

In an increasing number of situations, courts determine a reasonable fee. Often this occurs in a statutory fee shifting case, but it also can occur where a court has jurisdiction to consider the fee as part of its general obligations, for example, in approving the reasonableness of amounts owed by an estate or trust to a lawyer for the personal representative or trust.

Courts also become involved in common-fund cases, especially class actions, by virtue of judicial obligations under court rules. And of course, whenever litigation over a fee occurs, courts look to the reasonableness of the fee in deciding the matter.

Once you take on a representation and agree to a fee, fiduciary duties attach, making any attempt to modify a fee after the initial agreement subject to a presumption that you unduly influenced the client. To rebut this presumption, you should recommend that clients have outside legal advice before agreeing to a fee modification. Clients also have the right to fire lawyers at any time for any reason, or no reason at all, and you must withdraw from a matter if this occurs. You also must withdraw when, if you continue a representation, any of your other ethical obligations will be violated.

§ 1.03 Step Three: Attend to the Six Cs

Client Identification

We introduced the first "C," client identification, in § 1.01. But knowing you represent a "client" also requires attention to the precise identification of that client. When you represent entities, you must know who is empowered by the entity to direct your services.[12] In all client

11. *Id.* § 34.
12. MR 1.13(a); RLGL § 96(1).

representations, you also need to clarify whether you represent more than one client, including any constituent of the entity.[13] You also must identify whether you do or do not represent a prospective client[14] or a third-party payer.[15] Once identified, you must remain alert to the possibility that client identity can change during the representation due to reorganization, death, or disability, among others.

Competence

The second "C," competence, focuses on why you were hired in the first place: to provide competent and diligent service in a complex legal system that clients are not able to navigate themselves. Both tort law and the Rules of Professional Conduct require "reasonable" competence and diligence.[16] You do not have to be perfect, but you do have to meet or exceed the standard of practice in your jurisdiction. A violation of the Rules of Professional Conduct may be evidence of a lapse from the appropriate standard of care.[17]

In both malpractice and disciplinary matters, reasonable care can be established by expert testimony, although disciplinary agencies typically do not proceed against lawyers for isolated instances of incompetence or lack of diligence. Some errors are deemed so obvious that they are within the common knowledge of a fact finder. These include the failure to file within a mandatory time period and the failure to perform legal or factual research. Most courts also recognize another obvious error, often labeled breach of fiduciary duty, which includes a failure to fulfill the obligations just identified.[18]

Malpractice requires not only that a client prove a lawyer violated the appropriate standard of care, but also that the violation caused the client harm. The same is true of suits for breach of fiduciary duty, which typically allege violation of a well-defined core professional duty, such as communication, confidentiality, or conflict of interest.

If you make a mistake, notify your client as well as your carrier. You do not need to fall on your sword, but you do need to explain the facts that led to your error, the conflict of interest you now face, and your need to withdraw. Do not attempt to settle the matter yourself; your now former client needs independent representation before deciding

13. MRs 1.7, 1.13(f); RLGL § 96 cmt. h.
14. MR 1.18.
15. MR 1.8(f).
16. MRs 1.1, 1.3; RLGL §§ 16(2), 48–54.
17. MR Scope ¶ [20].
18. *Id.*

what to do about your mistake. Moreover, the law of undue influence is likely to invalidate any agreement you negotiate solely with your client, and the potential for serious discipline also should not be overlooked. Above all, avoid any deceit or cover-up of any relevant facts. That constitutes breach of fiduciary duty and often fraud, which brings additional adverse tort and disciplinary consequences.

Lawyers also need to think about competence in a limited but growing class of cases where third-party nonclients seek relief. In most jurisdictions, third parties who are intended beneficiaries or who are invited to rely on your representation of a client may sue for malpractice. Third parties also may sue for fraud, which includes intentional as well as reckless misstatements of material fact, as long as the third party reasonably relies on the misstatement and can prove damages. Some courts also recognize a cause of action against lawyers for negligent misrepresentation and for aiding and abetting a client's breach of fiduciary duty, but only if the lawyer gives substantial assistance to the client's breach, for example, by engaging in fraud, a crime, or statutory breach.

Control

Unlike competence, the other Cs are measured by a client's reasonable expectations, not a lawyer's sense of professional practice. These Cs are aspects of your basic loyalty obligation to clients. They keep you focused on your client's objectives and prevent your inadvertent shift to the competing interests of others, including yourself.

The third "C," control, assumes that, like other agents, you have a duty to act on the client's behalf, subject to the client's right to control the objectives of the representation. The law governing lawyers divides client-lawyer authority into three spheres. Clients have sole authority to determine the objective or goals of the representation. Lawyers have sole authority to take actions required by law before tribunals and to refuse to engage in unlawful conduct. Clients and lawyers share authority and are free to negotiate control in the vast middle sphere that governs all other aspects of the representation.[19]

The client's ambit of authority includes the goals of the representation and specific decisions where clients retain sole authority, including whether to settle or appeal a matter, and, in criminal cases, how to plead, whether to waive a jury trial, and whether to testify.[20] Clients may authorize you to make a particular decision within this area,

19. MR 1.2; RLGL §§ 21–23.
20. MR 1.2(a); RLGL § 22(1).

but the ultimate authority of clients to decide may not be delegated completely.

The lawyer's sphere of sole authority includes refusing to perform, counsel, or assist a client's unlawful act. Despite client preferences that might be to the contrary, the lawyer also has sole authority to bind clients by actions taken before tribunals that are required by law or court order.

The third sphere, where your clients and you share authority, often is labeled the means to accomplish the client's objectives. Tactics are part of this vast middle ground, where your client and you are free to agree to a strategy. You may bargain for authority in this middle sphere before a client engages you, and if you do not feel comfortable with your client's later requests, you may withdraw from the representation. This sphere also includes the scope of the representation, which you may limit only if the limit is reasonable and secured with the client's informed consent.

All three spheres of authority require that you initiate communication during a representation. When a client decision arises, you must promptly inform and consult with your client, and then clarify your client's decision. When a client insists on illegal conduct, you must inform the client that the conduct is not permitted and explain why. When a client has decided on an objective, you should consult with the client about the means to accomplish it.

The outcome of these consultations creates your actual authority and empowers you to act on behalf of the client. Clients also can be legally bound by apparent authority, which requires their own holding out to a third party that you are duly authorized, even if you in fact are not.[21]

Communication

The fourth "C," communication, is essential to every aspect of the client-lawyer relationship.[22] It defines the initial terms of the representation and is necessary to make each of your fiduciary duties work properly. Clients cannot control the goals of a representation without understanding feasible legal options. You cannot act competently without understanding what your client hopes to accomplish and knowing how to get there. You need facts sufficient to permit you to apply the law to your client's situation, and confidentiality helps you gather research for the client's benefit. And you must search for and resolve conflicts of interest to avoid favoring your own or some other person's interest over that of your client.

21. RLGL §§ 25–28.
22. MR 1.4; RLGL § 20.

The key to fulfilling the scope of this duty: Lawyers cannot wait for client inquiries; lawyers must initiate the conversation. Seven specific events trigger this obligation. First, when you initially agree to a fee, you should define the scope of a representation and craft an engagement agreement. Second, throughout the representation, you should explain the matter to enable the client to determine the objectives of the representation. Third, you should keep the client reasonably informed about the status of the matter throughout the representation, including changes in your practice, such as a serious illness or a law firm merger. Fourth, you must inform the client when you make a material mistake in a matter. Fifth, you should promptly respond to your client's requests for information. Sixth, you must inform your client whenever the law imposes limits on conduct the client expects you to undertake. Finally, you must specifically obtain your client's informed consent to important decisions, including placing limits on the scope of a representation, obtaining exceptions to fiduciary duties (especially confidentiality and conflicts of interest), and before providing an evaluation for use by third parties that is likely to adversely affect the client's interests.

Like other fiduciary duties, informed consent is viewed from the client's perspective. To obtain informed consent, you must first disclose and explain the risks of the proposed course of conduct and, second, inform the client of alternatives to that option. When considering litigation, disclosure of ADR options could be one such alternative.

Confidentiality

The fifth "C," confidentiality, assures that clients are encouraged to share all relevant information with their lawyers. Without relevant facts, you can mistake what your client wishes to accomplish, the law that is relevant to your client's circumstance, and other legal options that might be available to fulfill your client's needs. Breaching confidentiality can result in serious harm to client interests.

Modern confidentiality obligations originated in both agency law and the attorney-client privilege, an evidentiary doctrine. Today, the agency fiduciary duty can be found in both the Rules of Professional Conduct as well as agency law. It protects all information relating to the representation of a client, from the initial prospective client communication, throughout the representation, and beyond, even after your client's death or reorganization.[23] The evidentiary privilege is narrower, and may be invoked only before a tribunal to block offering or disclosure of confidential communications between client and lawyer or the

23. MRs 1.6, 1.8(b), 1.9, 1.18; RLGL §§ 59–68.

agents of either for the purpose of seeking legal advice.[24] The law of evidence also immunizes from discovery lawyer work product, which includes the lawyer's opinions and mental impressions formed in representing the client in anticipation of litigation.[25]

Both fiduciary duty and the evidence-based privilege recognize parallel exceptions whose exact dimensions nevertheless may differ substantially, even within the same jurisdiction. Exceptions to the fiduciary duty of confidentiality usually grant lawyers discretion to disclose, and if you choose to do so, you must only disclose to the extent reasonably necessary to accomplish the narrow purpose of the exception. Once privilege exceptions are established, courts may order lawyers to testify on pain of contempt if they refuse to do so.

Express or implied client consent allows disclosure or use of client confidences. Most jurisdictions also recognize a confidentiality exception to prevent future client crime or fraud. Whether criminal or not, the Rules of Professional Conduct also recognize future threats of serious bodily harm as an additional sufficiently weighty reason to permit disclosure, even without client consent.

Two exceptions grant you some measure of self-protection. One allows you to employ confidential information to collect fees and to defend yourself against charges of misconduct by clients or others. The other allows you to seek guidance about how to comply with your ethical obligations by sharing otherwise confidential information with another lawyer.

Most jurisdictions also recognize an exception "to comply with other law or a court order." "Other law" includes the Rules of Professional Conduct, statutory legal requirements, and court rules. In the context of the evidentiary privilege or work-product protections, this exception requires you first to claim the privilege (or the client will lose it) and then, if the other side prevails, either to appeal the order to testify or produce documents, or to obey it if no appeal or collateral attack is available.

Conflicts of Interest

Your sixth "C" requires you to identify and avoid or resolve conflicts of interest.[26] This obligation is based on your fiduciary duty of loyalty, which imposes the obligation to seek client consent whenever, from the client's point of view, your judgment might reasonably be called into

24. RLGL §§ 68–86.
25. *Id.* §§ 87–93.
26. MRs 1.7–1.12; RLGL §§ 121–135.

question. It also prevents client harm by imposing on you the obligation to recognize and respond to any influences that may interfere with your ability to act in the client's best interests as defined by the client.

Both agency law and the Rules of Professional Conduct recognize that conflicts of interest can arise from several sources, including the lawyer's own personal interests, the interests of other clients, third persons, and former clients. Pursuing the client's best interests requires you to remain vigilant throughout the representation so that you can recognize conflicts when they arise. Once identified, a conflict must be disclosed to your client(s), unless doing so would violate another client's confidentiality. If confidentiality obligations intrude, you should resolve the conflict by not proceeding in the matter.

A lawyer's conflicts are imputed to the lawyer's "firm," a defined term that includes any law office, practice, department, or organization. This imputation is premised on the fiduciary principle that all firm lawyers owe loyalty to all firm clients and lawyers readily interact with each other in firms. Imputation also requires a conflict of interest system to check for conflicts whenever a firm takes on a new lawyer, new matter, or new client.

If conflict disclosure will not violate the lawyer's duty of confidentiality, such disclosure is the beginning of the informed-consent process, which allows your client to consent to continuing the representation in spite of the conflict. In some situations, conflicts are so serious that client consent cannot vitiate them. When this occurs, you may not seek an exception to the loyalty requirement and must turn down a prospective client or withdraw from representing the current client(s) to avoid the conflict.

Failure to recognize and properly respond to conflicts creates overlapping remedies for clients. If harm is caused, the client may seek tort relief. If harm is threatened, the client may seek disqualification or injunctive relief ordering you to end the representation of the conflicting interest. If you have proceeded in a representation without disclosing a conflict, your client also can seek fee forfeiture, disgorgement of fees already paid, or a constructive trust of other property that is implicated.

§ 1.04 Step Four: Observe the Limits of the Law

Every agency and client-lawyer relationship is subject to one significant limitation: Neither your client's power of control nor your obligation of loyalty allows either of you to violate the limits or bounds of the law. Both of you remain responsible for the consequences of your conduct as autonomous legal persons.[27] The limits or bounds of the law remind us not to overidentify with clients.

The limits of the law include several familiar bodies of law that are explicitly incorporated into lawyer code provisions. This means that straying over the line can result in both professional discipline as well as other legal consequences, such as procedural sanctions, civil and criminal accountability, or equitable relief.

The most obvious legal limits are created by the criminal law, and today's thousands of criminal statutes can create legal limits that go unrecognized. Tort law, and in particular the law of fraud, create similar limitations. The law of evidence, which recognizes the client-lawyer privilege and the work-product doctrine, is enforced by contempt orders and sanctions when orders are violated. Courts also impose monetary sanctions for violations of procedural rules, such as Rules 11 and 26. Tribunals further exercise their inherent power when they disqualify, disbar, or discipline lawyers, or hold lawyers in contempt.

The Rules of Professional Conduct impose additional limits on client advocacy. Specific rules govern ex parte contact with opponents, define improper inducements to settle a matter, and regulate lawyers who serve as witnesses in client matters.

All of these bodies of law impose limits or bounds that restrain unfettered client allegiance. If you violate these legal limits or fail to identify them to avoid violation by clients, you also may face professional discipline. Taken together, these limits remind us that client-lawyer relationships do not exempt either client or lawyer from general legal requirements, some of which impose limits on client advocacy. This is not an unfamiliar role, because lawyers have long advised clients about how to avoid illegality. Many of these limits seek to provide a fair and accessible justice system. Others seek to avoid serious wrongdoing.

§ 1.05 Step Five: Recognize Remedies

Lawyers owe agency-based fiduciary duties to clients, the violation of which can trigger equitable as well as legal remedies. These fiduciary duties are the foundation for many of the provisions in the Rules of Professional Conduct, violation of which also can trigger professional discipline. Lawyers who fail to understand a legal limit imposed on unrestrained client advocacy also may be accountable to third-party nonclients.

---

27. MRs 1.2(d), 8.4; RLGL §§ 6, 23(1), 30.

Client legal remedies include claims for breach of contract, malpractice, and breach of fiduciary duty. Equitable remedies for breaches of fiduciary duty also grant clients presumptions of undue influence and allow them to seek a constructive trust, disqualification, injunctive relief, fee forfeiture, or restoration of pre-contractual rights.[28]

Nonclients can seek relief against you if they are identified third-party beneficiaries, invited by your client or you to rely on your legal services, or if you commit crimes or intentional torts against them. In an increasing number of situations, nonclients also seek relief for negligent misrepresentation or aiding and abetting a client's breach of fiduciary duty. Nonclients involved in litigation also can seek procedural sanctions for filing frivolous actions or discovery abuse.

Both client and nonclient remedies have been created to support lawyer fiduciary duties or the limits on advocacy imposed by other law. If you understand and observe your six C obligations, you should not create grounds for client relief. Identifying and staying within the limits of the law also should keep you out of third-party trouble.

All of this legal regulation demands careful attention to your six C professional responsibilities, and proper identification of the limits of the law. It also requires that you understand a range of distinctive remedies created by the Rules of Professional Conduct, statutes, and common law. We hope this book will help heighten your understanding of this law governing lawyers, so that you will serve your clients well. If you do not, keep in mind you may confuse your client's identity, or worse, misunderstand your own obligations created by the Rules of Professional Conduct or other legal regulation.

§ 1.06 Our Problem Approach

To appreciate our methodology, let's get started with a typical problem:

LinkedIn

Q. You know about LinkedIn?

A. A little.

Q. That's another tool our CMO loves. She wants each of us to be on there.

A. Why?

Q. It's the social media site for professionals. When people go on our individual LinkedIn site, CMO tells us they should be

28. RLGL § 6.

greeted by a detailed description of our successes. You know. Big suits. Big deals. No time for false modesty.

A. There she goes again. Certainly would promote your brand.

Q. That's the word she uses. This is all about branding.

A. Ugh! Madison Avenue destroys a profession. You must be very careful. You are talking about confidential information.

Q. But most of our engagements are a matter of public record.

A. Makes no difference. It's still confidential for our purposes. If you want to ask the client to consent—give informed consent after you have explained that it is the client's choice and fully described the risks involved—okay. But without that, your CMO is setting a trap. And that's not all. What you put on LinkedIn could make you more vulnerable to malpractice claims.

Q. How could that be?

A. Because, if you describe your superior expertise, you might be setting your firm up for a malpractice claim where the standard of care is not your firm's mediocrity, but the superlative suggested by a press agent.

Q. Is that it?

A. No, there's more. First, depending on your jurisdiction, if you have a conversation in real time with a nonlawyer, such as a live chat or comment to an individual post, that could be considered impermissible direct solicitation of business. Further, anything you speak of to acquire business is likely to be considered advertising, which requires compliance with local advertising rules.[29]

Q. You finished?

A. At least one more. If you are a Texas lawyer and you give legal advice to a New York client, that would be UPL, unauthorized practice of law. A crime in most states.

Q. Well, you must admit LinkedIn is great for securing endorsements and testimonials. What could have more credibility?

A. We admit it might be helpful. The question is whether it is permissible. Again, you have to know the local rules. And whatever you do, if a judge says something nice about you on the record, do not post it on the web.

29. MRs 7.1–7.3; W. Va. Legal Ethics Op. 2015-02, Social Media and Attorneys.

PART TWO

Who Is Your Client?

Why Identifying Your Client Matters

Your role as an officer of the legal system creates primary obligations to clients, as well as responsibilities to courts and third parties. All of these obligations require you to identify your clients, an inquiry that can produce unanticipated results.

In most situations, you know who your clients are because you have expressly agreed to represent them.[30] Increasingly, however, the law governing lawyers also has recognized implied or "accidental" clients—those you may think of as unexpected but nevertheless are recognized by law as being owed the same fiduciary duties lawyers owe intended clients.[31]

Once a legally recognized client-lawyer relationship begins, the law governing lawyers obligates you to fulfill six fiduciary duties, which we call the six Cs: client identification, competence, client control over the goals of the representation, communication, confidentiality, and conflict-of-interest resolution.[32] Lawyers who ignore the presence of any legally recognized clients easily can ignore one or more of these obligations. If this occurs, you set yourself up for trouble, because the law governing lawyers provides for multiple and overlapping

30. RLGL § 14(1)(a).

31. Lawrence J. Fox & Susan R. Martyn, Red Flags: A Lawyer's Handbook on Legal Ethics 1–28 (2d ed. 2010); Susan R. Martyn, *Accidental Clients*, 33 Hofstra L. Rev. 913 (2005).

32. RLGL § 16.

remedies[33] for the breach of these duties—remedies such as professional discipline,[34] malpractice,[35] breach of fiduciary duty,[36] fee forfeiture,[37] and disqualification.[38]

In Part Two, we identify several situations where you can take on an incidental, accidental, or even unintended representation that binds you legally. We explore express and implied client-lawyer relationships (created by conduct from the viewpoint of the reasonable client), prospective clients (those who discuss the possibility of creating a client-lawyer relationship), pro bono and court-appointed clients, multiple clients, former clients, third-party payment or direction (including insurance defense, government clients, and entity clients), joint clients, clients who change or morph (such as by merger, reorganization, or bankruptcy), imputed clients, and quasi-clients (such as third-party beneficiaries).

Throughout Chapters 2 through 8, it will become clear that you cannot recognize or solve any legal ethics issue until you first learn to identify your clients, including those you may consider to be "accidental" clients. Once you understand the necessity of properly identifying clients, you will be in a position to avoid client-lawyer relationships that you do not wish to create, and to recognize the moment when fiduciary duties attach to client-lawyer relationships that you intend to undertake. In other words, the first step to addressing any legal ethics issue is to know your clients, so that you will be able to observe the other five Cs for all legally recognized clients and avoid interference by those who are not.

---

33. *Id.* §§ 5, 6.
34. *Id.* § 5.
35. *Id.* §§ 48, 50, 52–54.
36. *Id.* § 49.
37. *Id.* § 37.
38. *Id.* § 6 cmt. i.

CHAPTER 2

Beginning a Client-Lawyer Relationship: Actual, Implied, and Prospective Clients

§ 2.01 Introduction: When Does It All Begin?

Many provisions of the Rules of Professional Conduct assume that a prospective or actual client-lawyer relationship has been established, but do not explain how that occurred. General legal principles found in contract and tort law fill this gap.[39]

Prospective clients are those who consult or discuss with you the possibility of obtaining legal services, whether or not they in fact become clients.[40] Actual clients result when a prospective client requests legal assistance or advice (offer), a lawyer provides the service or agrees to provide it (acceptance), and the client pays for the service or agrees to pay for it (consideration). Courts hold that a prospective client's reasonable reliance on a lawyer's advice or assistance suffices as an alternative for consideration (promissory estoppel).[41]

Some courts prefer a tort analysis, which leads to similar results: A lawyer who renders legal service or advice to a person under circumstances that make it reasonably foreseeable that harm will occur to that person if the services are rendered negligently will be accountable to that person, even absent any overt agreement to provide services or promise to pay.[42]

39. MR Scope ¶ [17].

40. MR 1.18(a); RLGL § 15.

41. Togstad v. Vesely, Otto, Miller & Keefe, 291 N.W.2d 686 (Minn. 1980).

42. RLGL § 14.

Courts look back on the matter from the perspective of a reasonable client's belief that the lawyer was protecting that person's interest.[43] As a result, your memory of who said what when may not be the version that ultimately prevails.

You can clarify what you intend with an engagement or non-engagement letter. Use a non-engagement letter when you do not intend to take on a representation. An engagement letter should make clear your client's identity as well as the scope of the matter you intend to undertake. Both can plant the seeds of goodwill for future representations.

§ 2.02 Marketing

Modern Marketing

Q. We know you think this social media stuff is a passing fad. The hula hoop of the 2010s. But it is the wave of the present. And the tsunami of the future. Email? Passé: Like carbon paper, the only thing left will be those who did not get it.

A. So?

Q. So, we lawyers have to jump on the bandwagon. Take advantage of what's happening every which way.

A. And you want our take?

Q. Until they repeal those antediluvian Rules of Professional Conduct as outdated as well, we better learn what that intersection looks like.

A. With visions of IBM Selectric typewriters, we are all ears.

Q. Our marketing department says every lawyer should have a blog. Without one you don't exist. With one, they beat a path to your door.

A. I've read a few of them. The first casualty is modesty.

Q. And the second is truth. But our CMO tells us the real way to make them effective is to be responsive to your groupie's questions. A little free advice is like chum in the ocean.

A. Let's stop right there. Your CMO is obviously right. Start answering questions for free from all your "so-called" admirers, and there is no end to the number that will line up.

---

43. *Id.* § 14 cmt. a; Nelson Bros. Prof'l Real Estate, LLC v. Freeborn & Peters, LLP, 773 F.3d 853 (7th Cir. 2014) (lawyer owed duty to company members of an LLC as well as company client when lawyer's undisclosed conflict of interest created individual liabilities for members; malpractice verdict of more than $1 million affirmed).

Q. I can't wait to tell her. You of all people, endorsing her approach.
A. And she is dead wrong.
Q. You just gave me whiplash.
A. Don't you see? You give advice that way and you run the risk of creating a client-lawyer relationship with none of the upside: a reasonable fee, and all of the downside: a malpractice claim. A disciplinary complaint. And it's even worse than that.
Q. How can that be?
A. Because you don't know who is receiving the advice. You could have a conflict giving advice contrary to the interests of a present or former client of your firm.
Q. Ouch!

§ 2.03 Engagement Agreements

You are so delighted to have new business; translate that enthusiasm into a gracious epistle that actually states your hourly rate or other fee agreement and otherwise tells the client the terms of the engagement. That way there will be no dispute as to the scope of the representation, the basis for the fee, or the way in which disbursements and other expenses will be handled. How much better is such a letter than something mumbled by the lawyer at that first interview regarding all of these matters, a conversation the client may well remember, if the client remembers it at all, quite differently from the lawyer.

Although there are critical items that should be addressed in the engagement letter, there are others that should be avoided no matter how helpful the lawyer may think they might be. For example, an engagement letter is no place for business development, no place for the lawyer to expand this assignment from handling one lawsuit into a scope description that sounds like you plan to provide legal services for all future matters as well, an undertaking on which your client will rely.

Similarly, no matter how expert or experienced you are in the matters to be undertaken, this is no time to translate your pride in your accomplishments into a higher standard of care, or to brag about your special expertise or experience. For if you do, and if then your work should ever be challenged by your now disgruntled former client (heaven forbid), some court may conclude that a higher standard should apply to your work because of the wording in your letter. Finally, your engagement letter should not promise the client any particular result. If the letter addresses this topic at all, it should be to remind the client of the vagaries of legal engagements that lawyers and clients confront together in an uncertain if not treacherous world.

§ 2.04 Crafting an Engagement Letter

The Engagement Letter

Q. We've got a problem. I wish we had never hired that consultant.

A. Yes, when law became a business, we started losing our dignity and our control. What's the problem?

Q. Well, Legal Sales came in and reviewed our operation. They were brutal. Said we were firmly stuck in the twentieth century. I took that as a compliment. So they changed everything. Down to our engagement letters, logos, a firm color, a slogan ("We have your back"). It's this letter that brings me to your door.

A. Don't tell me.

Q. Yes. They told us our engagement letter was too bland, too formal. That it would not appeal to the millennials. So we revamped it. And now we face litigation.

A. What does it say?

Q. The letter tells the client how capable we are. That we are cutting edge. We promise great results. And how we are prepared to handle all the client's legal needs.

A. How enthusiastic.

Q. Oh, the letter is that alright. And now it is Exhibit A in a malpractice complaint. Says we lost this lawsuit after promising great results. Alleges we failed to warn them about some new EPA regulations that had nothing to do with the Superfund case we were handling. Refuses to pay our fees, which it alleges are so unreasonable we were unwilling to reveal them in our engagement letter. That was another one of our so-called consultant's ideas.

A. I told you years ago we did not want law firms run by nonlawyers. Now you see why. Your consultant had you break every rule in the book.

Engagement letters are essential. Even though the Model Rules do not require them (i.e., the failure to use such a writing will not result in discipline), they not only protect the client, they also protect the lawyer. But the engagement letter is a place to be circumspect. Define with precision what you will do and what you won't do. Tell the client the exact amount of the fee and how it will be calculated. If you can't announce your hourly rate, maybe you should reduce it. If you agree on a contingent fee, the Rules of Professional Conduct require a definitive writing.

The engagement letter is no place to boast of your expertise, or you run the risk that has now turned into a reality—that you will be held to a higher standard of care. And an engagement letter is no place to seek new business. Don't tell the client how happy you are to become the client's outside general counsel when all they asked was for you to serve a subpoena, that is, unless you are prepared to anticipate the client's every need.

Q. Now you tell me.

§ 2.05 Engagement Letters: Wrap-Up

Use engagement letters to prevent misunderstandings by clarifying the scope and basis for your fee in undertaking a client representation. Client letters also can be used to address other issues that might arise during the course of the matter, such as:

- Identifying the client and related parties;
- Identifying the goals of the representation;
- Defining the scope of the engagement;
- Describing the fee agreement and billing schedule;
- Describing responsibilities of lawyer and client;
- Specifying methods of communication;
- Identifying proposed staffing as well as agents of client or lawyer;
- Identifying third-party neutrals;
- Identifying and obtaining informed consents to conflicts of interest;
- Identifying what will occur if you must withdraw from a joint representation;
- Determining confidentiality ground rules in joint representations;
- Specifying grounds for withdrawal or termination;
- Describing law-firm policy about file retention; and
- Specifying methods of dispute resolution between lawyer and client.[44]

---

44. Ronald E. Mallen & Jeffrey M. Smith, Legal Malpractice § 2:12 (5th ed. 2000); Gary A. Munneke & Anthony E. Davis, The Essential Formbook: Comprehensive Management Tools for Lawyers 141–44 (2000).

§ 2.06 Non-engagement Letters

Just as engagement letters can help you clarify duties to a new client, a non-engagement letter can help you clarify the absence of any such duty to a prospective client. Use them to decline a specific request for representation, to clarify that you represent some but not all of the parties to a matter, to prevent reliance by unrepresented third parties who may or may not be beneficiaries of your client, or to prevent a claim for negligent misrepresentation.[45]

Prospective clients are those who consult or discuss with lawyers the possibility of obtaining legal advice or services.[46] To the extent a lawyer offers legal advice and gains information from such a person, two duties, however limited, attach: competence in any advice you offer and confidentiality that cloaks anything you learn.[47]

With respect to competence, be careful to say what you mean. "You have no case" is legal advice, and if offered to a prospective client it means that you have accepted that person's offer or request for legal services. Add consideration (any payment for the consult) or detrimental reliance and you have a client-lawyer relationship, the first of six Cs appropriate to the scope of the representation. If you mean, "I don't want to waste my time determining whether you have a case," "I don't ever handle matters like this one," or "I can't take your case because I currently represent the other side" make that clear, or run the risk that a prospective client will remember the conversation differently after the statute of limitations expires.[48]

Determining whether to retain a lawyer requires a prospective client to disclose some information. To facilitate this exchange, the law governing lawyers cloaks the initial prospective client consult with the same confidentiality protection clients receive. If you decide not to represent the prospective client, that person or entity becomes a "former client" for purposes of the confidentiality rules. The result: Even if you never open a client file, you must enter the prospective client's identity into your conflicts database, and refrain from using or disclosing the information shared in the discussion.[49]

---

45. MUNNEKE & DAVIS, *supra* note 44, at 280.

46. MR 1.18(a).

47. MR 1.18(b)–(d); RLGL § 15.

48. Flatt v. Superior Court, 885 P.2d 950 (Cal. 1994) (lawyer who informed prospective client she could not represent her due to a conflict has no duty to warn prospective client about relevant statute of limitations).

49. MR 1.18(b); RLGL § 15.

§ 2.07 The Meaning of the Initial Meeting

The Nonexistent Non-engagement Letter

Q. I just got a call from Mrs. Togstadt.

A. So?

Q. She is the woman who came in a month ago to talk about a possible medical malpractice claim. I think we chatted about it for a few minutes.

A. Not that I remember.

Q. Well I didn't remember the name. But I do recall her issue. Something about a misdiagnosis. Anyway, I distinctly remember telling her I didn't think we were interested but would chat with you. She doesn't remember it that way. Her first words were "How's my case coming?"

A. Why don't you just remind her we agreed not to proceed.

Q. Oh, you are clever. The problem is I just checked my notes. And, if they are accurate, her statute of limitations ran two weeks ago. Her claim is now time-barred. It's a good thing I remember what I told her.

A. That may be good, but not good enough. When it comes to a contest between you and Mrs. Togstadt, whom do you think the jury will favor?

Q. But I am telling the truth.

A. I believe you. So may the jury. But what you said was, at best, ambiguous and, at worst, misleading. What you should have done was send her a non-engagement letter that clearly stated we are not taking her case and warned her to act quickly if she wanted to bring a claim because of the statute of limitations.

Q. I guess you are right. But doing so is such a pain. The good news is I don't think she has a very good claim.

A. Well that will be a defense. In order to collect from us she will have to prove more than that we took on her case. She'll have to prove that, if she became a client, we breached the standard of case by missing the statute of limitations, and that she would have won that case and not only would have won but would have collected damages from the doctor. But our defense puts us in the awkward position of trashing her claim, something that will cause a jury to look askance because, at that point, the jury will have already concluded we took the case.[50]

---

50. Togstad v. Vesely, Otto, Miller & Keefe, 291 N.W.2d 686 (Minn. 1980) (upholding $649,500 jury verdict against lawyer who advised prospective client he did not wish to represent her, based on prospective client's testimony that lawyer also gave her negligent legal advice by advising her she had no medical malpractice case).

Q. All that for want of a one-page letter?
A. Precisely.
Q. One thing's for sure: We won't do that again.

§ 2.08 Implied Clients

The Speech

Q. The Chamber of Commerce sponsored a "Defending Your Company" forum. I was lucky enough to be one of the presenters. My topic: avoiding personal liability. At the beginning and at the end I gave my usual disclaimer. "This was not legal advice. For that you need to consult your own lawyer . . . or me." I thought I was pretty good that day.
A. Did you get any business?
Q. Two follow-up calls. And one lawsuit.
A. A lawsuit?
Q. Yep. A guy in the audience claims he followed my advice. Then his company endured a class action. They lost, the business went south and he's personally liable for the business's debts. Had to declare personal bankruptcy. And it's all my fault.
A. What a shame. The disclaimers should protect you—as long as you did what they said. So we hope you offered legal information, but not legal advice tailored to this fellow's individual situation. If so, this guy has no claim to be an accidental client.[51] Was your disclaimer in writing?
Q. Not on my slides. But the Chamber had a disclaimer on the registration page.
A. That'll be helpful. As with all protective actions, to the extent they are in writing you are far more likely to be able to rely upon them. People's memories fade . . . perhaps conveniently.

51. RLGL § 14(1); Md. Op. 2007-18 (2008) (lawyer conducting domestic relations law seminars for the lay public who wants to avoid creating a client-lawyer relationship must offer only general legal information as opposed to advice targeted to a particular attendee's situation).

§ 2.09 Social Meetings

Casual Advice

Q. One of those long airplane flights to San Diego. Lucky to get an upgrade. My seat companion is lost in his spreadsheets for the first hour. Then he says, "Damn board," loud enough for the whole cabin to hear. "You a CEO?" I ask, figuring I'll flatter him. Turns out he is. What an opportunity. And he starts spinning this tale of woe. He thinks things are under control. Turns out they're not. But he wants to solve the problem himself, not aggravate the board. Not jeopardize his bonus. Or the stock price. I listen carefully. I know some SEC stuff. Our firm has done a lot of work in that area. So I advise him that he's okay. And I wish him good luck. When I tell my partner the story at lunch the next day, he is horrified. "You gave him bad advice," he says, and you better call him promptly. My answer: The advice is worth what he paid for it. And if he's ever going to hire us, that chance will evaporate if I admit error. I don't owe him a call, right?

A. Your colleague has it right. This fellow did not become a client. But he was a prospective client.[52] And while you had no obligation to give him any advice, once you offered it, it had better be right.[53] We call these folks accidental clients and the absence of a fee, a conflicts check, and an engagement letter doesn't absolve you of responsibility. It's time to make that call. You can couch it in a positive way. Tell him how you were so concerned you did some further research.

Q. Easy enough for you to say.

§ 2.10 E-lawyering

Website Advertising

Q. Our firm just came up with a great idea. We'll use our website to advertise our services to small businesses, complete with an email feature that invites readers to "ask the lawyer." We'll call the service "BizHelp."

52. MR 1.18; RLGL § 15.

53. Nelson v. Nationwide Mortgage Corp., 659 F. Supp. 611 (D.D.C. 1987) (lawyer who volunteered to answer questions and explain document to opposing party in transaction undertook a client-lawyer relationship and a duty of care to opposing party).

A. What a great idea. Everyone's online today. You can be as accessible as anyone. Just three things to worry about.

Q. Worry?

A. First, be as careful on your website as you would be if you were advertising—because that's what the discipline folks will say you are doing. This means no false, fraudulent, or misleading communications.[54] No promotionals, no promises about results, no boasting about prior victories, no superlatives you cannot substantiate.[55] Just because your target audience is businesses does not change the rules.

Q. We won't mislead—no problem there.

A. Second, businesses present a far wider and, in many cases, far more specialized range of problems than individual clients. If you are offering soup to nuts legal services to these businesses you better be in a position to provide them (1) because of your own experience, (2) by getting yourself a quick but sufficient tutorial, or (3) by associating yourself with or referring these clients you've caught in your web to someone who has the necessary expertise.[56]

Q. Don't worry, we know what we are doing.

A. Third, we worry about "Ask the Lawyer." We know, we know, you thought, lure 'em in with a little free advice, and they'll beat a track to your paying door. Almost a public service. But how does it look to your visitors? Like you are acting as their lawyer. Forming a client-lawyer relationship. Providing free legal services. Offering legal advice to someone who asks is enough to bind you to a client-lawyer relationship, even if you don't know who they are, the nature of their matters, whether they present a potential conflict of interest, or how the advice you are providing fits into their needs.[57] All opportunities for

54. MR 7.1; Fla. Bar v. Went for It, Inc., 515 U.S. 618 (1995); Shapero v. Ky. Bar Ass'n, 486 U.S. 466 (1988); Bates v. State Bar of Ariz., 433 U.S. 350 (1977).

55. MR 7.1 cmts. [2]–[3].

56. MR 1.1; RLGL § 48; Horne v. Peckham, 158 Cal. Rptr. 714 (Cal. Ct. App. 1979) (lawyer who acknowledged need for tax expertise had a duty to refer client to an expert in the field or to comply with the specialized standard of care); State *ex rel.* Counsel for Discipline of the Neb. Supreme Court v. Orr, 759 N.W.2d 702 (Neb. 2009) (lawyer subject to discipline for making repeated mistakes over a long period of time in establishing and representing a client's business franchise, causing client's business to be shut down by federal regulators).

57. RLGL § 14; Ariz. Op. 97-04 (just as lawyers should not answer specific legal questions in giving a legal seminar to lay people, lawyers should not answer specific legal questions from lay persons through the Internet unless the question presented is of a general nature and the advice given is not fact specific); Vt. Op. 2000-04 (the more email responses to website inquiries address specific facts, the greater the risk a client-lawyer relationship will be formed; website disclaimer does not necessarily preclude client-lawyer relationship).

you to get sued[58] and worse yet, disciplined[59]—with no income to show for your efforts. A risky proposition to be sure.

Q. What if we just tell them not to rely on us?

A. If you are going to offer free advice, you must remember to treat the people who are to receive it exactly like you treat full-fledged paying clients. And you should expect to be held to the exact same standard of care regarding client identification, control, communication, competence, confidentiality, and conflict of interest resolution as if you had entered into a formal engagement agreement after consultation. So make sure you know what you are saying, that the client understands the scope of your undertaking,[60] you are not violating the conflict of interest rules[61] in taking on this "albeit informal" representation, and you maintain confidential everything you learn in the course of your work.[62]

§ 2.11 Prospective Clients

Beauty Contests

Q. Those damn companies. They don't just call a lawyer up and hire her. No. They have to hold beauty contests. Gives the general counsels something to do. And makes 'em feel real important. So there's this big class action suit. Sued everybody—the company, its officers, its auditors, its banks. Yesterday my partner went to the swimsuit competition. Thinks it went well, but the company's interviewing ten, count 'em, ten law firms. Today I get a call from the accountants. They want to hire us . . . me. What a great deal. Since we won't hear from the company for a week, the case is mine, right? A bird in the hand and all that.

A. Not so fast. It all depends on what happened yesterday. Or the day before. Did your colleague have any understanding with the company before he met with them?

Q. How do you mean?

A. Did they agree you could represent another defendant if they didn't choose your firm?

---

58. Togstad v. Vesely, Otto, Miller & Keefe, 291 N.W.2d 686 (Minn. 1980).
59. MR 1.1.
60. MR 1.2(c); RLGL § 19.
61. MRs 1.7–1.12; RLGL §§ 121–135.
62. ABA Comm. on Ethics & Prof'l Responsibility, Formal Op. 10-457 (2010) Lawyer Websites.

Q. I doubt it. That would be a helluva way for a lawyer to start the talent show. "You don't mind if we represent someone else, do you?" Doesn't sound warm and fuzzy and my colleague was so desperate for this new matter I'd be shocked if he started off that way. Would it have worked?

A. Know what you mean. Hard question to ask. But if the question were asked and the prospective client agreed, the consent the lawyer received would likely be enforceable, especially in the case of a sophisticated client and assuming the meeting progressed as the client anticipated.[63]

Q. But how 'bout me? Assume no agreement.

A. Then the question is whether the company will object to your firm's representing the accountants.

Q. How could they? They aren't a client. Just another one of those highfaluting companies that makes a big deal about selecting counsel.

A. That may be true. But no matter how highfaluting they are, they are still a prospective client who provided a prospective lawyer with all kinds of confidential information. Didn't you say your colleague met with them for three hours?

Q. Something like that.

A. Anyway, whatever the length, the company is entitled to protection of that confidential information. And not have it fall into the hands of the accountants.[64]

Q. I promise not to talk to our pageant team.

A. That promise won't solve the problem. Whatever they learned is imputed to you.[65] And we are afraid that three-hour meeting can't bring you within Model Rule 1.18.

Q. What's that?

A. It's a Model Rule that came out of the ABA Ethics 2000 project that rewrote the Model Rules around the turn of the century. It provides a reminder and a little gift.

Q. The reminder?

A. You won't want to hear this. It reminds lawyers of the existing law. What we just discussed. Prospective clients are entitled to confidentiality and that obligation—to keep the prospective clients' confidences—can disqualify the prospective lawyers from taking on another representation, particularly in the same matter.

---

63. MR 1.18 cmt. [5]; RLGL § 15 cmt. c.
64. MR 1.18(b); RLGL § 15(1)(a).
65. MR 1.10; RLGL § 123.

Q. And the gift?

A. The rule provides that if a prospective client provides confidential information to a lawyer but then does not retain the lawyer, the lawyer's law firm may take on a conflicting representation with two conditions: (1) that the lawyer or lawyers who participated in the initial conversation "took reasonable reassures to avoid exposure to more disqualifying information than was reasonably necessary," and (2) the lawyer who learned confidential information is screened from the firm's representation of the second client.[66]

Q. So, if my buddy just had a short phone call with the company, I'd be home clear?

A. If your jurisdiction has adopted Rule 1.18 that's generally correct; but I'm afraid with a three-hour song and dance you only have one life raft, with apologies for the mixed metaphor.

Q. What's that? Tell me. Tell me.

A. Your colleague can call the company to determine whether the company will consent to the conflict and permit your firm to take on the representation.[67] But don't make that call quite yet.

Q. Why not?

A. Because you need the permission of the accounting firm to clear the conflict.[68] Without that permission, you cannot start the process.

Q. All because my friend got called first?

A. And went to the beauty contest.[69]

---

66. MR 1.18(d); RLGL § 15(2).

67. MR 1.18(d)(1); RLGL § 15(2)(b).

68. MRs 1.18(b), 1.6(a); RLGL §§ 15(1)(a), 60.

69. Miness v. Ahuja, 762 F. Supp. 2d 465 (E.D.N.Y. 2010) (despite lack of formal discussion, under the totality of the circumstances, including a long personal relationship, several conversations on social occasions, and lawyer's offer to represent friend, a prospective client relationship existed); Poly Software Int'l, Inc. v. Su, 880 F. Supp. 1487 (D. Utah 1995) (lawyer who gave prospective client choice between introductory meeting or longer session not disqualified where client selected first option, even though meeting took over an hour due to need to translate client's foreign language); Cascades Branding Innovation, LLC v. Walgreen Co., No. 11-C-2519, 2012 WL 1570774 (N.D. Ill. May 3, 2012) (law firm disqualified due to law firm lawyer's email with prospective client which disclosed core business and litigation strategies); Laryngeal Mask Co. v. Ambu A/S, No. 07-CV-1988-DMS (NLS), 2008 WL 558561 (S.D. Cal. Feb. 25, 2008) (law firm disqualified due to previous interview of firm lawyer by opposing party which had considered firm for same lawsuit); Bays v. Theran, 639 N.E.2d 720 (Mass. 1994) (lawyer disqualified where one telephone conversation with prospective client included discussion of the merits of the case); Mayers v. Stone Castle Partners, 1 N.Y.S.3d 58 (App. Div. 2015) (law firm not disqualified due to telephone conversation with prospective client that involved confidential information but did not have the potential to be significantly harmful under Rule 1.18(c)).

CHAPTER 3

Ending a Client-Lawyer Relationship: Former Clients

§ 3.01 Introduction: Completing a Representation

When you complete a client matter, or voluntarily or involuntarily withdraw from a representation, your current client becomes a former client. At this point, you lose all but two of the fiduciary duties you assumed when you took on the representation. You no longer represent a "client," and you no longer owe duties of control, competence, and communication. But your fiduciary obligation of loyalty remains to the extent that you cannot undermine what you have accomplished, including switching sides in the same matter or subsequently attacking your own former work product.[70] And your full fiduciary obligation of confidentiality lasts forever, even after the death of the client. As with current clients, you may not reveal any information relating to the representation of your former client or use the information to the former client's disadvantage.[71]

The "substantial-relationship" test has been formulated by courts to protect former client confidentiality in subsequent adverse representations. The substantial-relationship test prohibits a lawyer from undertaking these representations when there is a substantial risk that

70. MR 1.9 cmt. [1]; RLGL § 132 cmts. d(i), d(ii); Boies, Schiller & Flexner LLP v. Host Hotels & Resorts, Inc., 603 Fed. App'x 19 (2d Cir. 2015) (upholding $271,063 in sanctions against a firm for its willful refusal to recognize an obvious conflict caused by firm's suit against former client which would inevitably require firm to attack its own work product).

71. MR 1.9(c); MRs 1.6(a), 1.8(b) (current clients).

confidential factual information that would normally (not actually) have been obtained in the former representation would materially advance a new, current client's position in the subsequent matter.[72] This conflict might be consentable and, like other conflicts, requires that you obtain their informed consent before you represent any subsequent clients whose interests are materially adverse to those of the former client in a substantially related matter.[73] You can be disqualified or disciplined if you take on a new matter when you should not. To clarify this change in status and obligation, be sure to do two things whenever you complete a matter or your representation otherwise ends: Send the former client a disengagement letter that clarifies the fact that the representation has ended and move the client's entry in your conflicts database from your current-client conflicts file to your former-client conflicts file.

§ 3.02 Disengagement Letters

Disengagement letters are essential to clarify that you no longer represent a client. Use them when you complete a matter, decide to withdraw, are fired by the client, or when you leave a law firm and do not intend to continue work on a matter. The letter should make clear the reason the relationship has ended, and include appropriate warnings about unfinished work and time deadlines.[74] You may want to address whether the client wants you to communicate with successor counsel, and how you intend to provide for the orderly transfer of client files

72. MR 1.9 cmt. [3]; RLGL § 132 cmt. d(iii); Fla. Bar v. Dunagan, 731 So. 2d 1237 (Fla. 1999) (lawyer suspended for 91 days for representing husband and wife in acquiring a business and shortly thereafter representing husband in a dissolution); R & D Muller, Ltd. v. Fontaine's Auction Gallery, LLC, 906 N.E.2d 356, 358 (Mass. App. Ct. 2009) (earlier representation incorporating client's business and later advice reminding her to observe corporate formalities to help "maintain a barrier against personal liability" substantially related to subsequent adverse suit against same former client that claimed personal liability on the basis of piercing the corporate veil); Hurley v. Hurley, 923 A.2d 908 (Me. 2007) (trial court properly disqualified lawyer from representing husband in divorce where lawyer had represented wife in personal injury action four years earlier); Niemi v. Girl Scouts, 768 N.W.2d 385 (Minn. Ct. App. 2009) (although representation in employment discrimination suit may be relevant to a subsequent defense of an employment discrimination action brought by the same person, the passage of 25 years since former representation renders the two matters not substantially related); *In re* Hostetter, 238 P.3d 13 (Or. 2010) (lawyer suspended for 150 days for representing client in obtaining a series of loans and subsequently suing his former client's estate to recover debt on behalf of lender; interests of former client survive client's death); Kanaga v. Gannett Co., No. 92C-12-182, 1993 WL 485926 (Del. Super. Ct. Oct. 21, 1993) (lawyer who represented physician in contested medical malpractice case involving a hysterectomy disqualified from subsequent representation against former client in defamation action which involved allegations that physician performed unnecessary hysterectomies).

73. MR 1.9; RLGL § 132.

74. Gilles v. Wiley, Malehorn & Sirota, 783 A.2d 756 (N.J. Super. Ct. App. Div. 2001) (former client stated cause of action against lawyers who withdrew at the last minute without adequately warning her by certified mail that the statute of limitations was about to run out on her medical malpractice case).

and documents. You also can use this opportunity to convey a willingness to serve in additional matters in the future.

When you hope for future business in a disengagement letter, be careful to clarify your lack of continuing obligation in the matter for which you no longer assume any responsibility. Otherwise, the client may reasonably believe you stand ready to be the client's continuing counsel and may rely on your lack of communication as legal advice that all is well, or that nothing else needs to be done.[75]

§ 3.03 Staying In or Getting Out

Completing a Case

Q. I cannot believe it. We represented Excelsior three years ago. Nasty employment discrimination claim at the Savannah plant. Got them a great settlement. Now we brought a Superfund case for Acme. Sued Excelsior for its contribution to the pollution of the Quinnipiac River. No possible connection between the matters. Excelsior admits that. What they are claiming is they are a current client of our firm. Says if they had another discrimination claim we would be their firm. Ridiculous.

A. When was the last service?

Q. Thirty-eight months ago.

A. Are they still in your database?

Q. What do you mean?

A. Are you sending them client updates?

Q. Of course. Our consultants told us to. We call them "Hot off the Press." Great title, don't you think?

A. And how are those addressed?

Q. I think they start "Dear Valued Client." Uh, oh. I see what you mean.

A. And do you invite them to firm sponsored CLEs?

Q. Of course. We've been told the best source of new business is former clients. And that turns out to be correct.

A. Now let us ask you the $64,000 question.

Q. $64,000?

A. That was an old TV quiz show. Anyway, did you send a disengagement letter?

75. Spence v. Wingate, 684 S.E.2d 188 (S.C. Ct. App. 2009) (lawyer who previously represented wife concerning disposition of her dying husband's estate may have a continuing fiduciary duty to wife to protect wife's interests in husband's life insurance proceeds despite later becoming counsel to the husband's estate).

Q. What's that?

A. That's the hardest letter I'll bet you never write. It can convert a present client into a former client while at the same time sending the message that you love the now former client and hope they will call you the next time they need a law firm.

Q. How the hell do you do that?

A. Not an easy assignment. But if there is no disengagement letter and the former client has wastebaskets full of client alerts, you will find yourself in a dog fight over the present/former distinction with one guaranteed result.

Q. What's that?

A. I guarantee that if the client is found to be a present client you'll be knocked out of the adverse representation that started this madness and . . . you'll never receive any new business from your "former" client.

§ 3.04 What Do You Intend?

The Ambiguous Disengagement Letter

Q. I must admit we were very happy to secure some lender liability cases from First Union Bank. There were three in total and when we closed out the last I composed the cover letter quite carefully. I wrote, "We were so pleased to represent the bank in these difficult cases." A little boast. "We hope should you require additional services in the human resources area, you will think of Caldwell & Moore for those engagements." A little nudge.

A. So far, so good. Why have you called us?

Q. Because, five or six months ago, we got a call from Wolf Homebuilders. They have a lender liability claim against First Union. Conflict checks correctly revealed that First Union is a former client. So we sue away.

A. And First Union moved to disqualify.

Q. Precisely. They say that we are their outside general counsel in employment cases. They were so pleased with our work and never expected our firm to be turncoats. What do you think?

A. This is a hard one.

Q. Didn't need you to tell us that.

A. Lawyers sit permanently on the pointy horns of a dilemma. As each representation ends, the lawyer wants the departing client to call the firm with the next matter. Simultaneously, the lawyer wants the client to recognize it is a mere former client, only entitled to Rule 1.9 protection. As we all know, it is extremely difficult to simultaneously hold two conflicting thoughts in your head. So too here. As a result, it is impossible to predict what will happen. One thing's for sure.

Q. What's that?

A. Your firm has received its last new matter from First Union. At least for a long while.

§ 3.05 Keeping Confidences

The Wrong Use

Q. I was so proud of our work. We brought a lawsuit against the City of Pasadena to challenge its refusal to rezone an undeveloped parcel on the wrong side of town so that our client could develop a high-end shopping center. Our constitutional argument won the day, but it took four years and more than a mil to get there.

A. Congratulations. Real victories on appeal are hard to come by in land use cases.

Q. Agreed. But here's the thing. One of my partners lives nearby. He has opposed the shopping center from the beginning. Urged the firm not to take the case. When we did, he refused to work on it. Now he's leading opposition on a new front, claiming the runoff from the parking lot will cause environmental damage.

A. I'll bet that has your client pleased.

Q. Former client. And besides that bad news, we just got more. The client has sued the firm and our partner for breach of fiduciary duty. Says we owed him loyalty. As a former client.

A. Oh no!

Q. Our colleague tells us not to worry. Says he has a First Amendment right to do what he was doing. Is he right?

A. We doubt it. Lawyers do not lose all free speech rights when they take the oath. But they lose some. Take the obvious: You have no free speech right to disclose confidential client information unless you can identify a good faith exception in the applicable rule.

In this case then there are two issues at stake. The first involves confidentiality. What your colleague is doing is directly related to the zoning representation. If anyone in your firm knows confidential information relating to this client that could be used by your colleague as part of his environmental attack, he would be barred from proceeding because all of that confidential information is imputed to all your firm's lawyers.

Q. Oh, we got him there. He did not help us at all with the Pasadena Center. But I know for a fact he reviewed our electronic files on a regular basis, hoping to watch firsthand our project's untimely demise.

A. But even if there were no connection between the representation with regard to zoning and the environmental issues, your colleague and your firm still could lose this suit. While there admittedly is some debate on the topic, the protection afforded former clients is not limited to nondisclosure of confidential information. We also owe former clients a certain level of loyalty. This means we cannot "foul the nest" by engaging in conduct that thwarts the very objectives the client paid us to achieve. And this is a classic example of that.[76]

Q. So, there is good news and bad news.

A. Yep. The good news, your colleague better get out of the "oppose the shopping center" business. The bad news is your partner and your firm may be subject to a claim for breach of fiduciary duty.[77]

§ 3.06 Lawyers Changing Jobs

Departing General Counsel

Q. We hired the General Counsel of Northampton Hospital to beef up our health-care practice. She is a former litigator, and we hope she will do trial work for us, but we are already running into problems. We have this great medical malpractice case against Northampton Hospital. The events took place after she left Northampton and joined our firm. We thought there would be no problem.

A. But now?

---

76. RLGL § 132 cmt. d(ii).

77. Oasis West Realty, LLC v. Goldman, 250 P.3d 1115 (Cal. 2011) (lawyer's use of client confidential information to oppose client's project after lawyer ended the representation establishes cause of action for breach of fiduciary duty, professional negligence, and breach of contract); Disciplinary Counsel v. Ward, 34 N.E.3d 74 (Ohio 2015) (lawyer suspended for one year due to use of client's confidences to solicit new client to sue former client's estate).

Q. The other side has moved for disqualification. They say this representation, adverse to Northampton Hospital, is substantially similar to work she did for the hospital. But it is a completely different case.

A. This is not an uncommon problem. As you know, lawyers are free to take positions directly adverse to their former clients the day the client becomes a former client. When you think about it, it is a strange rule. On day 374 you are representing the client. On day 375 you are suing the hell out of the former client. But unless the matters are substantially related, that is what the rule says. Of course, that standard is a trial lawyer's dream.

Q. What does that mean?

A. It gives plenty of ammunition to both sides; they can litigate the substantial-relationship question endlessly.

Q. Well, what about this playbook stuff they keep raising?

A. When the matters are entirely different, often the argument will be made that because the former lawyer knows the personalities and the procedures of the former client, the representation is barred. Generally, the courts are not buying. They say there has to be more of a nexus between the two representations (the one for, and the one against) for the former lawyer to be disqualified. But if Northampton Hospital can point to something more specific—like the fact that this case is just like others or involves the same procedure, or the exact same personnel—they may have a case. One of these days your former general counsel will be far enough removed temporally to not face this barrage,[78] but it is a risk when the former lawyer has just recently departed or otherwise ended the former representation.[79]

---

78. MR 1.9 cmt. [3].

79. United States *ex rel.* Fair Lab. Practices v. Quest Diagnostics Inc., 734 F.3d 154 (2d Cir. 2013); Mitchell v. Metro. Life Ins. Co., No. 01-CIV-2112(WHP), 2002 WL 441194 (S.D.N.Y. Mar. 21, 2002) (lawyer personally disqualified in subsequent suit and conflict imputed to new law firm for defending Met Life in a number of lawsuits while employed at her former firm, learning company policies, playbook information, and personally interviewing managers whose testimony would be relevant in subsequent action); *In re* Carey, 89 S.W.3d 477 (Mo. 2002) (en banc) (lawyers who billed Chrysler over 500 hours on products liability and consumer fraud matters and later formed a new law firm that took on plaintiffs in a national products liability class action against Chrysler violated Rule 1.9 and were indefinitely suspended, because (1) the subsequent matters involved the same former client and the same type of case; (2) the lawyers deposed several of Chrysler's expert witnesses in the past; (3) the lawyers knew Chrysler's roadmap in defending and settling similar products liability cases; (4) the lawyers had access to detailed confidential information about a government investigation that was the subject of the litigation); *In re* Basco, 221 S.W.3d 637 (Tex. 2007) (disqualification of hospital's lawyer required because lawyer would have to challenge advice given by former partner in a previous case).

CHAPTER 4

Court Appointments, Pro Bono, and Unpopular Clients

§ 4.01 Introduction: Clients Who Have Difficulty Finding a Lawyer

Access to lawyers and to formal justice remains elusive for most of the poor and much of the middle class. Moreover, lawyers are free to take on any client they wish, so that unpopular clients or those who can afford to pay also can find it difficult to retain a lawyer. This concern is not new. In 1919, Reginald Heber Smith wrote that without equal access to the law, "[t]he system not only robs the poor of their only protection, but it places in the hands of their oppressors the most powerful and ruthless weapon ever invented."[80]

Three different approaches have been employed to address these needs. The first accepts public responsibility for access to justice, a goal that can be accomplished by creating legal rights to representation, publicly funding legal services programs, and simplifying legal procedures. The second approach focuses on a duty of individual lawyers to serve as court-appointed counsel or provide free or reduced rate services

80. Reginald H. Smith, Justice and the Poor: A Study of the Present Denial of Justice to the Poor and of the Agencies Making More Equal Their Position Before the Law with Particular Reference to Legal Aid Work in the United States (1919).

pro bono publico, for the common good.[81] The third approach stresses deregulation, such as Washington and Utah's recent licensing of legal assistants.[82] To date, none of these strategies has gone far enough in its implementation to alleviate the lack of access to justice in civil cases.

Today we are left with three realities: The judicial branch of government defines and regulates the "practice of law," prohibits unauthorized practice, and has used this power to find some legislative intrusions unconstitutional.[83] Second, government funds remain inadequate to pay for civil or criminal defense legal services, both of which fall far short of those necessary for clients who need lawyers. Third, these realities mean that lawyers are left to shoulder the responsibility for the public's access to justice. We benefit financially from our market-driven system and should not avoid the reality of the unequal access it creates.

The Model Rules acknowledge the lawyer's pro bono obligation, but only as a "should." Model Rule 6.1 defines various kinds of pro bono services and recommends 50 hours of pro bono services per year. Model Rule 6.2 makes it difficult but not impossible to decline a court appointment. Model Rules 6.3 through 6.5 offer lawyers various incentives to assist legal services, law reform organizations, and limited legal services programs. Together, these carrots encourage most lawyers to give back, but the reality remains that few offer enough pro bono to meet the need.

§ 4.02 Court Appointments in Criminal Cases

The Obstinate Defendant

Q. We thought we were doing the truly patriotic thing. We agreed to represent a Guantanamo defendant. No matter how despicable these folks might be, we know they are entitled to a defense and as it turns out, many of these individuals were wrongfully incarcerated for years.

A. You mean you did the patriotic, controversial thing.

Q. That is for sure, but now we are in a professional responsibility quandary. Our client insists on representing himself. The rules of the Tribunal prohibit that. But my client insists that working

81. N.Y. R. Ct. App. § 520.16 (2015) (pro bono requirement for bar admission); Bothwell v. Republic Tobacco Co., 912 F. Supp. 1221 (D. Neb. 1995) (to preserve the credibility of the courts as a legitimate civil justice system, court has inherent power to appoint counsel to serve without pay in a civil case when necessary to achieve justice in a particular case).

82. See, e.g., https://www.utcourts.gov/utc/limited-legal/.

83. Campbell v. Asbury Auto., Inc., 381 S.W.3d 21 (Ark. 2011).

with a lawyer only gives legitimacy to what he considers a deeply flawed process. We actually agree with him on that.

A. You have remonstrated with the client?

Q. Of course, we have explained how helpful we can be and the risks of representing oneself in a proceeding like this.

A. Then you should refuse to represent him. He should have the right to represent himself, the rules of the Tribunal notwithstanding. But at the end of the day, if the Tribunal refuses to agree to his representing himself, and you have exhausted every reasonable opportunity to challenge that ruling, then you have the responsibility to the court to provide the best representation you can, regardless of your client's direction to the contrary.[84]

§ 4.03 Court Appointments in Civil Cases

Appointed Pro Bono

Q. I don't believe it! I'm in a medical malpractice defense firm. Represents both individual docs and hospitals. Another firm in town represents a different insurer, arguing that they have no duty to pay a judgment against a doc who skipped the jurisdiction and refused to cooperate in the defense of his case. Plaintiff asked the court to appoint a lawyer to represent the absent doc. You can guess who got appointed? Surely, I cannot be conscripted to provide civil pro bono.

A. Although such appointments in civil cases are rare, judges have the inherent authority to appoint lawyers when necessary to ensure a fair and just proceeding and the credibility of the justice system.[85] We're sorry to tell you that yours just might be such a case. The court needs the absent doc's interests to

---

84. ABA Comm. on Ethics & Prof'l Responsibility, Formal Op. 07-448 (2007) Appointed Counsel's Relationship to a Person Who Declines to Be Represented (A lawyer whose "client" has never accepted the client-lawyer relationship . . . does not have such a relationship, because the client-lawyer relationship requires mutual assent. The lawyer's responsibility arises from the authority of the appointing tribunal and includes whatever obligations the tribunal may identify.).

85. Bothwell v. Republic Tobacco Co., 912 F. Supp. 1221 (D. Neb. 1995) (denying appointment by applying a "market" analysis); Hanson v. Morton, 67 A.3d 437 (Del. 2013) (lack of malpractice insurance does not excuse in-house lawyer's court appointment to represent indigent parent in child dependency and neglect matter).

be fairly represented in determining whether the plaintiff is entitled to the insurance coverage.[86]

Q. But don't I have some right to claim that I'm not the right lawyer for the job?

A. You could. But would that happen if this were a paying client?

Q. Well, I'm not sure I know that much about insurance law.

A. When was the last time you confessed ignorance to someone who would pay your hourly rate?

Q. What if I feel conflicted?

A. You could assert an ethical objection but the burden rests on you to show good cause, which requires a demonstration that you would in fact violate the rules by taking on the case, say by a conflict of interest.[87]

Q. How about poverty? This case could take way too much of my time.

A. That works only if the financial burden is unreasonable.[88] The same is true if the matter is repugnant to the lawyer. Absent a real showing, you must accept the appointment, even though the court has created an actual, albeit involuntary, client-lawyer relationship.[89]

§ 4.04 Pro Bono Clients

The Legal Services Hotline

Q. The local legal services office has asked our firm to staff a hotline one night per month. We will either give quick advice over the telephone or make an appointment for the person with a staff lawyer for more difficult questions. These folks aren't clients, right?

A. You (and the legal service program and its clients) are fortunate. You are making good on your pro bono commitment under Model Rule 6.1 and helping people who really need your services. Whether you agree to staff a hotline, "Ask a

86. Pruitt v. Mote, 503 F.3d 647 (7th Cir. 2007) (failure to appoint counsel in federal civil litigation prejudicial under 28 U.S.C. § 1915(e)(1) because district court considered only the complexity of the case and neglected to take into account pro se litigant's competence to litigate his own claims); Burke v. Lewis, 122 P.3d 533 (Utah 2005).

87. MR 6.2.

88. Synergy Assocs., Inc. v. Sun Biotechnologies, Inc., 350 F.3d 681 (7th Cir. 2003) (court could not reappoint lawyer on pro bono basis where lawyer was owed nearly $100,000 in fees and costs and previously allowed by court to withdraw from the representation).

89. RLGL § 14(2).

Lawyer" night at a local television station, or at the local courthouse kiosk once a month, when you answer questions about legal problems, you do have clients, albeit for a limited time and purpose.[90] You have assumed the six Cs, which means that you must identify your client, give competent advice, accept client control, communicate adequately, keep the client's confidences, and resolve conflicts.

Q. So how can we handle the conflict of interest issues?

A. Here, running a conflicts check before you answered any question would make short-term legal services virtually impossible to provide. Yet without such a check, the potential exists for you to give a person legal advice adverse to the interests of a current client of your law firm. Model Rule 6.5 was drafted with these considerations in mind. It facilitates your pro bono service by making you responsible for conflicts only when you know about them on the spot. Under this rule, lawyers serving pro bono hotlines such as the one you describe will be free to take on any matter that does not involve an obvious conflict of interest without making the elaborate check that would so obviously destroy the very purpose that the hotline was designed to fulfill. If your caller wants to sue your law firm's biggest client, Big Bank, you must excuse yourself from answering the question. But if you don't know the name of the caller or the name of the potential adversary, or if you do but do not know that the adversary is currently a client of your firm, then the rule protects you by suspending the need for conflicts checks in short-term pro bono representations. We hope this encourages you to assist nonprofit pro bono projects. With that good news, maybe you will do it once a week.

Q. With this good news, maybe I can convince the firm to help out more often!

A. We hope so. But one more thing: This rule only applies to short-term legal advice. Any more services and you must determine whether there are any conflicts and address any that are found.

90. MR 6.1; RLGL § 38 cmt. c.

§ 4.05 Unpopular Clients

But They Can Pay

Q. I know we should not be so flattered. We are the tenth firm Fribourg Trust approached. But we did make the top ten.

A. For what?

Q. The bank's been sued for failing to return to their families the money the bank received as deposits from Holocaust victims.

A. What would you do?

Q. Defend them. Some of the banks may be entitled to keep the money because these folks were not able to determine whether their ancestors sought safe haven in Switzerland. It is not exactly as if anyone received notice of what money was being held.

A. I understand that.

Q. Well, it's actually worse. Some at the bank want the lawyers to argue that the Holocaust never happened.

A. You are not going to do that!

Q. Actually, it's worse. Fribourg Trust wants to argue the Holocaust never occurred. They want to bring in that nut job from Iran to so testify.

A. Well, you know Rule 3.1 bars the use of frivolous defenses with equal fervor as the bar to frivolous claims.

Q. Then how 'bout if we say we'll defend, but not on this basis.

A. You could do that. You also could agree to negotiate a fair settlement but not to engage in litigation for your client. These are both examples of limited-scope legal services.[91]

Q. But that is no solution to another problem. Many of our colleagues say "pass it on to law firm 11." Some are related to Holocaust victims. Others are Jewish. And ten firms have already rejected the case.

A. But is not Fribourg Trust entitled to representation? Even Fribourg Trust?

Q. An interesting question. Our firm has represented the right of Nazis to march through towns with large numbers of descendants of Holocaust victims, as unpopular as they are. But there the principle behind the march was the First Amendment. Maintaining free speech almost invariably requires the representation of those who espouse unpopular views.

---

91. MR 1.2(c).

And we represent the alleged (and likely) perpetrators of horrible murders on the independent grounds: opposition to the death penalty or the need to rectify the consequences of the violation of Constitutional protections. Fribourg Trust seems different.[92]

A. Is it because you will be paid?

Q. Interesting point. It seems to make a difference. Somehow there is less guilt if the representation is pro bono. But, of course, some of our colleagues will say this is the last client and the last cause that deserves pro bono treatment.

---

92. Monroe H. Freedman & Abbe Smith, Understanding Lawyers' Ethics 73 n.40 (5th ed. 2016); Leonard Orland, A Final Accounting: Holocaust Survivors and Swiss Banks (2010).

CHAPTER 5

Joint Clients

§ 5.01 Introduction: Joint Clients and Joint Loyalty

Joint clients are those that a lawyer represents at the same time in the same legal matter. Each of the six Cs due each client can be affected by a joint representation. Competence necessitates an understanding of the law governing the matter, including the legal rights and legal options of each client. More than one client means more than one source of control over the goals of the representation once these legal options are understood. It also requires communication with each client, not just dependence on one to update the other. Confidentiality necessitates an advanced understanding, usually that the lawyer will share all information learned in the joint representation with the other client(s). All of these issues stem from the sixth C: conflict of interest resolution. More than one client means simultaneous loyalty to each. No advice may favor one over the other, often compelling both the lawyer's and the clients' roles and relationships to alter.

The Rules of Professional Conduct and some court opinions prohibit some joint representations.[93] Where allowed, joint representations

93. MRs 1.7–1.8; Pergament v. Ladak, No. 11-CV-2797, 2013 WL 3810188 (E.D.N.Y. July 23, 2013) (law firm disqualified from simultaneous representation of bankrupt company and former CEO who allegedly embezzled from the company); Ky. Bar Ass'n v. Roberts, 431 S.W.3d 400 (Ky. 2014) (lawyer suspended for 61 days due to simultaneous representation of estate of homicide victim and two sons named as heirs, one of whom later was convicted of killing father).

require proper safeguards to protect your fiduciary obligations to each client.[94]

§ 5.02 Marriage Dissolution

Prohibited Joint Clients

Q. I pride myself on being the orneriest matrimonial lawyer in town. Everyone knows it. It's my stock in trade. So imagine my surprise when this couple shows up. I can't figure what both of them are doing here. They each have the same story. They each called different lawyer friends and each recommended me. Even though they said they wanted the proceedings to be amicable; peace in our time is not what I am known for. Anyway, they decided why not have one lawyer. They would save money and each be represented by the recommended counsel. How flattering. So, of course, I said I would do it.

A. Are you sure?

Q. Well they have agreed to alimony and joint custody.

A. If you were representing the wife alone, would you tell her she's struck a great deal?

Q. Hell, no. She's getting screwed. Her alimony ought to be 50 percent higher and she's giving up the house, which I would never recommend.

A. And you told them you'd represent them both?

Q. Sure. They agreed to all this before they crossed my threshold.

A. Do you think you are really "representing" them?

Q. No. To be honest. I'm sort of one of those lawyers for the situation.

A. Precisely. Which is why the ethics rules in almost all states say you cannot represent both husband and wife in a divorce.[95]

Q. Why is that?

A. You just demonstrated it. In representing both you are not able to give either the advice you would give if you only represented one. This is just one example of the rule that prohibits a lawyer from representing both A and B in the lawsuit

94. *Speakers Hash Over Common Problems that Haunt Lawyers in Joint Representations*, 31 Law. Manual Professional Conduct 328 (2015).

95. *In re* Braun, 227 A.2d 506 (N.J. 1967); Matter of Gould, 620 N.Y.S.2d 491 (N.Y. App. Div. 1995); State Bar of Tex. Ethics Op. 583 (2008) (lawyer may mediate a divorce settlement between unrepresented parties, but may not agree to mediate and prepare necessary documents to effectuate the results of the mediation).

A v. B. This is quite simply a non-consentable conflict under the rules.[96]

Q. That is why I thought of myself as the lawyer for the situation.

A. We rather think of it as the lawyer who is guaranteed to suffer at least one, and maybe two, malpractice suits. As the meanest family law lawyer in town you can serve as a mediator for these two under Rule 1.12. There you represent no one and try to help each to reach a satisfactory resolution. But you don't owe either duties of zealous advocacy or confidentiality because being a mediator means you have to make it crystal clear you represent neither.

But the way you are going is not just prohibited by the rules; it is also an example of very bad lawyering because your hands are tied. As soon as you think of a new issue—for example, cost of living adjustments—you are in an impossible trap in which what you are suggesting is good for one client and very bad for the other.

§ 5.03 Group or Aggregate Settlements

The Homeowner's Settlement

Q. We represent a group of homeowners. They all have claims for faulty construction of their dream homes. Mostly windows, but siding, too. Thirty-five clients in all. Quimby Windows has offered $500,000 to settle the whole shooting match. A fair number. So what we thought was we'd send each client a letter, enclosing a release and telling each how much he or she will get. We've already allocated the total, giving more to some, less to others, based on how flawed we thought their windows were.

A. Sounds like a great result. Congratulations. But before you start celebrating, we better keep you out of trouble. You've got to tell each client the total amount and what each of your clients will be receiving.

Q. Not that! If we go there, we'll set off a fight among the clients and we'll never get the 90 percent participation Quimby requires. You know how clients are. They hear a half a mil and they think half should be theirs.

---

96. MR 1.7(b)(3).

A. That may be so. But too many lawyers have run afoul of Rule 1.8(g). That rule is quite explicit as to how these aggregate settlements must be handled. Each client must be informed of (1) the total settlement and (2) the proposed allocation among the multiple clients. Then and only then can an aggregate settlement pass ethical muster.[97]

Q. Well, actually there's more I didn't tell you.

A. Uh oh.

Q. Quimby offered our firm $100,000 if we agreed never to sue them again. Quite a deal. We get one-third of the $500,000 and $100,000 on top of that.

A. And you accepted?

Q Wouldn't you? Pure profit. And we don't have to share it with our clients.

A. How do you figure?

Q. Well, Quimby was worried some ethics guy might call this a bribe.

A. We would.

Q. See. They were right. So, we agreed to "consult," if you get my drift, for that extra money. Then no one can call it a bribe.

A. Where do we begin. First, if there were any legitimate way to proceed here, you would have to tell your clients. At least that way the clients could decide whether they want to seek fee forfeiture for your misconduct. But all that is really irrelevant. You see, Rule 5.6 prohibits the offer or acceptance of any agreement that restricts the right of a lawyer to practice law.[98]

Q. This isn't a restriction. We have plenty of work.

A. But none against Quimby. That's what Rule 5.6 was intended to get at.

Q. What if we had accepted their first offer? They said they would pay our clients an extra $100,000 if we agreed never to sue them again. Now that was a conflict. The clients get extra. And we lose a prime target.

A. That would've been better for your present clients, but still would violate Rule 5.6.

Q. Is there any way we can capitalize on the fear we've sown in the hearts of Quimby's officers?

---

97. MR 1.8(g); RLGL § 128 cmt. d(i).

98. *In re* Hager, 812 A.2d 904 (D.C. 2002) (lawyer suspended for one year for agreeing not to represent any clients against settling defendant); Cardillo v. Bloomfield 206 Corp., 988 A.2d 136 (N.J. Super. Ct. App. Div. 2010) (agreement that violated Rule 5.6 not enforceable).

A. It's too late now. But if after the next case is over—and we mean signed, sealed, and delivered—you can be hired by Quimby to become its lawyer. Then Quimby becomes a current client of your firm and you would need Quimby's informed consent to take any position adverse to the company, consent we bet won't be forthcoming. But if that retention occurs before the matter adverse to Quimby is totally settled, the worst case is bribery and the best, a clear violation of an important rule of professional conduct. So, just keep representing disgruntled homeowners.

§ 5.04 Accommodation Clients

Accommodating the Client's Employee

Q. I've really helped my client. They are a defendant in a 10b-5 case. The claim is securities fraud. Something about off balance sheet financing. Understated the true liabilities. My folks say everyone was doing it. And the accountants gave 'em a clear opinion.

A. What did you do?

Q. Well, the damn class action lawyers—our nemeses who keep us in business—want to take the CFO's dep. Of course. When the CFO finds out, he asks for his own lawyer. Just what my client needs: another expense. So, GC calls me. Asks whether he's got to get this CFO a lawyer. Turns out GC isn't just worried about the cost. He figures if CFO gets his own lawyer, CFO might get scared and abandon the "team." I think GC's being paranoid, but I figure I can earn GC's undying admiration. I tell him we'll represent CFO as an accommodation. He's thrilled, thanks me profusely and agrees to advise CFO to use our firm to represent him at the deposition. Aren't you proud of me for remembering that thing about accommodation clients?

Pretty clever, right?

A. Not so fast. First, you must talk to GC. When he was talking to CFO, CFO was an unrepresented party.

Q. Of course.

A. That meant that the only advice GC was allowed to give CFO was whether to get counsel. But GC went further. He advised CFO to hire you. That might be viewed as just a run-of-the-mill recommendation. But not in this context. When the reason was to "control" CFO.

Q. Ok, ok, but we are where we are.
A. When do you meet with your new "accommodation client?"
Q. Tomorrow. The deposition is next week.
A. And what will you do?
Q. I'm going to tell him that I'm going to prepare him for the deposition and attend the deposition with him. Put him at ease. Make sure he stays on message. I want to do my best for GC and the company.
A. Well, is CFO a client or not?
Q. That's why I'm talking to you. I thought by having him be an accommodation client I didn't really have to worry about those niceties.
A. Well, it is possible to say he's not a client. And you are representing the client, the company, as you prepare and attend CFO's dep. The problem with that analysis is that it makes CFO an unrepresented person. As a result, as we already observed, under Rule 4.3 you cannot give him any advice other than to get a lawyer. This means you will have to warn him that you only represent the company, that anything he tells you will not be kept confidential, and that you will report everything to the company.
Q. Not a good way to start a relationship. And he's going to complain instantly that GC's advice that he look to me for representation was a false promise.
A. Precisely.
Q. But don't I solve that problem by telling him he's an accommodation client?
A. The problem is, the ALI notwithstanding,[99] the Rules of Professional Conduct and the courts do not condone some middle ground, some second-class client status. One is either a client or not a client. There is no authority for this half-baked notion and if there were it would be an impossible recipe for representation disaster as the lawyers for those faux clients grappled—without any standards—for how much representation they can provide.[100]
Q. So I guess I have to treat this CFO as a real client. I certainly want to save the client money and keep CFO on the reservation.

99. RLGL § 132 cmt. i.

100. Universal City Studios, Inc. v. Reimerdes, 98 F. Supp. 2d 449, 453 (S.D.N.Y. 2000) (law firm that took on representation of company as an accommodation to a co-plaintiff client not entitled to drop client like a "hot potato" in order to take on a new adverse representation).

A. Whoa! You have just stated an impossible contradiction. If this person is a client, your obligation is to do what is in the best interests of CFO. And in taking CFO on as a client, you have to assure yourself that you can represent his best interests consistent with what you perceive to be the best interests of the corporate client. Otherwise, you have an impossible conflict of interest. So if you really think the purpose of this representation is keeping CFO in line, and you imagine that will be a difficult task, then you should decline the representation right now. And even if you see no problem now, you have to remain ever vigilant as the matter unfolds and identify any conflict that arises thereafter. If you don't detect a new conflict when it emerges, you can be subject to discipline.[101]

Q. So I can resign the CFO representation and just continue with the company?

A. That could be the result. But any time you take on the representation of a corporate client and one or more of its constituents—employees, officers, directors, agents—in a litigated matter, you should recognize that one of the risks that may arise after a conflict develops is that you won't be able to continue either representation.[102]

Prospective Waivers

Q. Well, we'll put in any engagement letter that if a conflict develops, we are permitted to continue the company representation. After all, that's the biggy.

A. Glad you mentioned engagement letters. Have you prepared one for CFO?

Q. Hadn't even thought about it. But now I see one is necessary. Our jurisdiction requires engagement letters for all new clients.

A. And you can put all the language in there you wish about CFO agreeing to your representing the company if a conflict is identified later. But it may not be worth the paper it's written on.

Q. A deal's a deal.

A. Not when it comes to prospective waivers like this one. You have CFO agreeing long before an as yet unidentified conflict

---

101. Office of Disciplinary Counsel v. Cynthia A. Baldwin, 151 D.B. 2017 (D. Bd. Rpt. Mar. 8, 2019) (counsel for Penn State publicly censured for improper joint representation of several top Penn State employees in Grand Jury proceedings; employees had a conflict of interest with the university in criminal probe of football coach's neglect of sexual abuse by another staff member).

102. MR 1.7 cmts. [4] and [29].

arises and long before CFO knows what confidential information he will have shared with you, to agree that you can drop him and keep the company. Doesn't sound like informed consent to us. And there's one additional problem.

Q. What's that, pray tell.

A. By definition, the CFO will be hiring a new lawyer. And that lawyer will look very carefully at the question whether her new client stands to lose in any way by having his former lawyer representing another party with whom CFO is now in conflict. She might recommend letting it go. But she might not. And if not, in our view the prospective waiver is unlikely to hold up.

Confidential Information and Third-Party Payment

Q. Let's assume the company is willing to run the risk. Can I go forward with the client representation?

A. Well, there are a couple of things you have to worry about. First, how are you going to handle confidential information from your two clients?

Q. Gee, I just assumed I would tell the company everything CFO told me. And the reverse? I'm not so sure. GC is a pretty secretive type.

A. Well, you have to address this issue of confidential information sharing and it cannot be a one-way street; either the clients agree to share all confidential information. Or they don't. But both clients should be on notice so they both know the consequences of their conversations with you. And even if the agreement is they won't share, you should explain to the clients that should the receipt by you of unshared confidential information give rise to a conflict, you will be obliged to withdraw from one or both representations without explanation.

Second, the fact is that you are being paid by the company to represent CFO. You have to make it clear to your CFO client and yourself that you will not let the fact that you are being paid by a third party (even when the third party is a co-client) affect the independence of the advice you will provide. The rules demand client approval when a third party pays the lawyer.[103]

103. MR 1.8(f); RLGL § 134.

Q. Seems like a lot of trouble just to take CFO to a deposition.

A. That certainly is true. Every day in America lawyers take "accommodation" clients to depositions with not a thought about what is in fact occurring from a professional responsibility point of view. And because the witnesses represented at these depositions really have no independent stake in the matter—their jobs, their personal assets, their reputation, and certainly no potential liability is at stake—everything goes smoothly.

But in this matter, a securities fraud case in which the CFO could become the object of regulatory scrutiny, might be added as an additional defendant, could lose his job, might even become the object of unwanted SEC attention, depending, of course, on the facts, it is critical that the lawyer who undertakes the "accommodation" recognize how high the stakes might be not only for the new client but also for the lawyer herself if the deposition prep or the deposition itself turns dicey.

§ 5.05 Employer and Employee

The Company Accident

Q. There was this terrible accident. Our company operates school buses for 45 different municipalities. This one driver must not have done the proper pre-drive inspection of his bus that day. Sure enough, his brakes would not hold, and the result was four tragic deaths and multiple injuries. As general counsel, I went to the hospital to meet the driver, who miraculously survived the crash. I told him I represented the company and that I needed his confidential statement. He admitted no inspection had been made that day, and so I got him to sign an affidavit to that effect. I told him I would help him in any way I could; I felt so sorry for him. Still later, the company decided to defend its conduct, based on the driver's failure to inspect, so we turned over the driver's statement to the police. Now the driver has been indicted for grossly negligent driving.

A. So what is the problem?

Q. The problem is the driver has brought a breach of fiduciary duty claim against me. He claims I said I would represent him, and then I breached confidentiality by turning his statement over to the police. I was supposed to keep it confidential from his employer and anyone else. Am I in trouble?

A. You certainly could be.[104] Even as you describe the conversation, he could have concluded you were representing him. And of course, there is no videotape of what you actually said. Moreover, his recollection of the conversation may be completely different, which is why you should have clarified your representation of the company and your refusal to represent him.[105] If he was your client, then you had a joint representation, a representation that was fraught with conflict, a conflict that is manifest in your employer's direction that you blame the driver. Once that conflict became clear, you had an obligation to withdraw from both representations, the representation of the driver and the representation of the company. But you did not do that.

Q. I never thought I represented the driver.

A. That may be so, but a jury may very well conclude to the contrary. Any time you represent two clients the opportunity for a conflict arises and the need to respond and perhaps withdraw from both representations is high. It becomes higher when two clients are employer and employee.

§ 5.06 Co-plaintiffs

All in the Family

Q. That accommodation question got me more than I bargained for. But there certainly must be room for trial lawyers to represent more than one client.

A. Of course. There are plenty of situations in which a joint representation is ethically proper. Such representations also make sense strategically in certain cases. A unified defense on behalf of similarly situated defendants, all represented by one lawyer, can look more formidable than tables filled with defense counsel. Then there's the little thing called cost. Joint representation can save a bundle of cash; maybe even secure a better law firm for the engagement.

But any time lawyers represent more than one client—on either side of the v.—ethical issues lurk and they lurk for the

---

104. Perez v. Kirk & Carrigan, 822 S.W.2d 261 (Tex. App. 1991) (lawyer breached fiduciary duty of confidentiality by disclosing client's statement to prosecutor).

105. RLGL § 14.

entire period of the representation. Careful analysis at the beginning. Vigilance for the long trip to conclusion.

Q. Well this one's an easy one. Just the other day father and son came calling. Dad's on crutches. Son has a cast on his arm. Turns out they were struck by a speeding driver while son was driving dad to a night of bowling. Other driver's pleaded guilty to driving 15 miles over. Only bad news is the speeder may have a very small insurance policy. But I tell them I'm glad to represent both of 'em. I even gave them a break on the fee. Just charging 'em 30 percent.

A. You have fallen into a too-common trap. That puny liability policy may not cover both claims. How are you going to handle that?

Q. I was so focused on the clear liability that I didn't think about it.

A. Well, how will you handle it?

Q. I'll tell them they have to agree in advance how they will allocate any settlement.

A. Not a bad idea. But not where your approach should start. The first thing you need to do is point out the problem and explain to them that each might want to get his own lawyer who can enhance his damage claim and perhaps disparage the co-plaintiff's. Now this is father and son, so it's unlikely they would want to do that, but they should know. Then you can discuss an approach to settlement. But that is not enough.

Q. Why not?

A. Because the case might not settle. And you may have to try it. You can see how your trial tactics will be affected by your dual duty. You must share that likely awkwardness as well as the potential for a defense motion to disqualify another way of making it clear to the clients how the limited resource conflict might play out.[106]

Q. So then I'm home free. I sure would like to help these deserving folks.

A. Not quite. Let's assume you're preparing son for his deposition. You ask him where he was before he picked up dad. At the local watering hole with his buddies for a little TGIF celebration, he answers unselfconsciously. What do you do then?

Q. It would make no difference; the other driver was speeding.

A. Are you so sure?

---

106. Johnson v. Clark-Gin Services, Inc., Case No. 15-3290, 2016 WL 7017267 (E.D. La.) (law firm that represented Amtrak employees and passengers against third-party truck driver in civil suit for injuries in train collision disqualified due to nonconsentable conflicts).

Q. Well now that you push me, I guess the speeder may make something of that. Arguing that drinking, not speeding, was the actual cause of the accident. I guess I better tell dad.

A. But can you?

Q. Of course. He's my client, too.

A. What do you think son would say?

Q. Oh! This is one of those things where I should've reached an understanding with my clients in advance how I would handle confidential information.

A. You can say that again. We take it you did not.

Q. Frankly, I didn't think of that. I was just looking forward to collecting on an easy liability case.

A. Well, the first thing you should do is try to convince son to allow you to tell dad. If he consents, you can share the information and take it from there.

Q. But what if he prohibits me from doing so?

A. Now you would have to find out what the default rule is on sharing confidential information in your jurisdiction. Failing that, the decision is yours and we wouldn't envy you one bit, having to face that dilemma. In any event, you're also going to be forced to resign at least one representation and probably both, since an informed consent to the potential conflict under these circumstances is likely not available.

Q. Why?

A. Because you cannot share enough information with dad to get his informed consent.

We hope the lesson is clear. When approaching a joint representation, a superficial analysis of the case is not enough. You have to dig deep. That may not unearth all of the landmines. But a thorough review should identify potential traps so that you can decide whether the risk of commencing a joint representation is likely to achieve a reasonably satisfactory result.

Q. So I can't represent dad and son?

A. Of course you can. But only after you pursue a little more due diligence and a lot more informed consent.

§ 5.07 Common-Interest Arrangements

Coerced Cooperation

Q. This case is a big one. Antitrust. Brought by pharmacies against a dozen pharmaceutical companies. We got hired by Big Pharma. A real coup. Just when we were contemplating all the work we would have to do, the judge laid down the law. He does not want 12 motions to dismiss. Twelve briefs why class action status should not be granted. We've got to cooperate. And our client goes nuts.

A. Why? You'd think they'd be pleased that they'll save some money.

Q. Well, that's true. But they don't like the idea that cooperation might be viewed as reinforcing the accusation that the drug companies engaged in actionable conduct.

A. They have a point. And no one can force a party to join a common-interest arrangement. But it is the judge who is insisting on this. Besides, we always want to please the court, don't we? And the common-interest arrangement won't be obvious to the jury.

Q. Now you know that's not true. This judge is not going to allow 12 cross-examinations of the plaintiffs' witnesses.

A. But that would be the case even if there were no common-interest agreement.

Q. My client understands all that, but they still don't like being forced into such an arrangement. They don't want to be under an obligation to share their privileged information.

A. And they won't, because you can identify and limit the information you agree to share. A common-interest arrangement, whether as a matter of common law or written agreement, protects from scrutiny any privileged information of one party that is shared with another. Because, otherwise, sharing privileged information with a co-defendant would represent a waiver of the privilege. You remember the basic rule of privilege. It's a communication only between client and lawyer or the agents of either for the purpose of giving or receiving legal advice. If you have a privileged conversation in a crowded elevator, your client can lose the privilege. But if another party has a common interest with the first party as to the shared privileged information, then sharing it should not waive the privilege. Nothing, however, about the common-interest privilege requires a party to share any given information with the others.

Q. So, I guess I just give my client a long lesson and hope I can calm them down. They sure don't want to cross the judge.

A. There is one more warning you must share with any client when you discuss joint interest agreements.

Q. What is that?

A. The possibility that you might be disqualified.

Q. Me! We have no conflicts. Trust me; we checked very carefully.

A. We're sure you did. But there is a possibility that counsel for one of the other parties could be subject to a disqualification motion. And if that is successful, the next move might be to disqualify all the counsel to parties to the arrangement.[107]

Q. How could that be?

A. Because the claim will be that the disqualified lawyers had confidential information of the present or former client, the client that successfully moved for disqualification, and the disqualified lawyers will be deemed to have shared it with you. Such motions have hardly been common and rarely successful, but it is a risk factor that should be addressed before a client consents to joining such an undertaking. What one party shares is entirely up to the party. And the only penalty for not sharing is having the other members of the group throw you out. The same is true of continuing as a member of the group. Such participation, Her Honor notwithstanding, should be entirely voluntary and revocable at will.

Q. That's another of my client's worries. They really don't trust the other pharmaceutical companies. These are their sworn enemies. You cannot imagine how truly competitive this business is. And so they are convinced the participants will stay part of the arrangement just long enough to learn our client's privileged information, then withdraw and start blabbing it about.

A. Well, anyone can violate the principles behind a joint interest arrangement at any time. But that is not how such agreements work. The participants are barred from sharing any privileged information they learn from any other participant, even after they withdraw. And there can be sanctions imposed if that rule is violated. Moreover, any party that seeks to invade your private space by obtaining your privileged information through a party that withdrew from a common-interest agreement is subject to disqualification or other sanctions for violating Rule 4.4(a).[108]

107. *In re* CMH Homes, Inc., No. 04-13-00050-CV, 2013 WL 2446724 (Tex. App. June 5, 2013) (lawyers disqualified for associating with another lawyer who withdrew from a previous case due to a former client conflict; "associated" lawyers include partners, employees, associates and also individuals working together on a case or issue regardless of their actual status as a member of a firm).

108. MR 4.4(a) states: "In representing a client, a lawyer shall not use means that have no substantial purpose other than to embarrass, delay, or burden a third person, or use methods of obtaining evidence that violate the legal rights of such a person."

CHAPTER 6

Insurance Defense and Other Third-Party Funders

§ 6.01 Introduction: The Triangular Relationship

Insurers are one example of a triangular relationship, where a third person hires or pays a lawyer to provide legal services for another. Lawyers in this world need to identify whether they represent one or more clients, and if one is a third-party nonclient, to inform the client-insured, keep the insured's confidences, and prevent interference by the third party with the lawyer's professional judgment.[109]

The triangular world of a substantial number of lawyers who provide insurance defense representation catches them between the routine demands of insurers, who select the lawyers who will receive large groups of cases, and the individual insureds, whose entire focus is their one lone matter and whose interests may depart from those of the insurer. As a consequence, lawyers in this practice often face pressure from either insured or insurer, or both, to shape, and in some cases cramp, the bounds of fiduciary duty owed clients.

Most of the problems created by insurance defense practice originate in the insurance contract itself. Typical liability policies promise to "defend" when a covered person is sued for a covered event, and to "indemnify" that person up to an insured amount. They also provide that the insured agrees to "cooperate" in the defense of the matter, and usually delegate authority to the insurer "to make such investigation, negotiation, and settlement of any claim or suit as it deems expedient."

109. MR 1.8(f); RLGL § 134.

These contract provisions can create a conflict between the interests of insured and insurer. The obligation to defend necessitates a client-lawyer relationship with the insured, complete with all of the six Cs. Limitations on indemnity and coverage can create battles between the insured and insurer. Delegated settlement authority can conflict with the insured's right to control the goals of the representation.

Both insurance law and the Rules of Professional Conduct address these recurring situations. Insurance law addresses conflicts created by policy language by construing the contract language against the insurer-drafter. Courts read the insurance contract to promote more consistent obligations—for example, to both defend and settle with due consideration for the insured's interests. By requiring due regard for the insured's interests, this insurance law also indirectly supports maintaining the integrity of the lawyers' obligations to their client-insureds. The Rules of Professional Conduct apply all of the six Cs to insurance defense lawyers, which require client identification writ large, by definition in every case referred by an insurance company, competent client service, proper communication, confidentiality, and conflict of interest resolution. The debate about the insured's delegation of control over the matter continues in both bodies of law. Although insurers can depend on some contract language, they cannot put lawyers in an impossible ethical dilemma. You will be the one who has the pleasure of recognizing and responding to these issues. We hope the scenarios portrayed in this chapter get you started in the right direction.

§ 6.02 Third-Party Funders

Professional Independence?

Q. I love these cases. Rich son gets in trouble with the law. DUI. Public drunkenness. You get the idea. Now the son gets charged with a crime. Parents see their precious child—the one who went to science camp at age 12—about to ruin his entire life. After all they did to get him into college. So they'll pay big bucks for a lawyer to get son off. That's where I step in. My specialty. Charging big bucks for staging the best production of teenage contrition that you have ever seen.

A. Sounds like an easy life.

Q. You could say that, but you can imagine how difficult it is to deal with the parents.

A. The parents? They're not your client.

Q. Easy enough for ivory tower academics to say. But the parents are paying; the parents are the nervous ones, and they call daily for an update.

A. And what do you do?

Q. I take whatever time it takes to calm them down. Tell them what progress I am making.

A. With the son's permission?

Q. Hardly. I know where my bread is buttered. Besides, the kid couldn't care less. Or he wouldn't be in such trouble.

A. We hate to bring you up short. But the principle is so important that it's enshrined in the rules twice.[110] No matter who pays you, the client is the person to whom you owe all the fiduciary duties. Which means you must maintain client confidentiality, even as to the person or entity paying you. Unless the real client, in this case "the kid," gives you informed consent. It also means you have to resist the officious intermeddling of dad, even if he threatens to withhold payment.

Q. Nice to state such lofty goals, but you've never sat where I sit. Reality bites.

A. This is why the rules give such clear direction. You have to explain—no matter how painful it might be—that you are not permitted to tell dad what son tells you. And that's because you have to assure son that what he tells you will be kept confidential in order to learn the truth, so you can defend son effectively.

Q. Maybe you're not as unrealistic as I thought. Because you are certainly correct that too often my defense of these precious undergraduates is undone when I learn—way too late and from the other side—how many drinks the bartender will testify were consumed by my "just a couple of beers" client in trouble with the law.

§ 6.03 Insurers

The Eternal Triangle

Q. I might be able to stand up to dad. He's a one-time client. I mean funder. But the same rules can't possibly apply to our insurance company clients.

110. MRs 1.8(f), 5.4(c); RLGL § 134.

A. You defend insurance companies?

Q. Not really. Old Forge Insurance is our biggest client. But it's not Old Forge who is getting sued. It's their insureds. Auto accidents. Homeowner claims. Dozens of cases. All sent to us by Old Forge.

A. Who's the client in that situation?

Q. Never gave it a thought. I know who we care about. We need Old Forge to love us. Their insureds? We barely talk to most. They just want us to leave them alone and make the matter go away without their premiums going up. So, if I had to guess, I'd say we represent both.

A. You may be right. It depends on the law in your jurisdiction. In many the lawyer is deemed to have two clients.[111] In others it's only one.[112]

Q. The insurance company?

A. No. The insured. But your answer speaks volumes. This is an area where the proper application of the rules of professional responsibility comes into a clash with the reality that you describe. Law firms that are hired by insurance companies to represent the insureds will always be beholden to the insurance companies for repeat business. And the insurance companies, whose biggest or second biggest expense is the legal fees they pay, want to control representation costs on a macro basis and be treated like clients (including the right to sue for malpractice and otherwise control lawyer's fees) even if the jurisdiction concludes that the lawyer only has one client, the insured. Put those facts together with the fact that in the great majority of cases the interests of the insurance company and the insured are perfectly aligned and the insured really doesn't want to be treated as a client so much as have the matter go away: you have a reality clash with the ideal construct of the lawyer only owing full fidelity to the insured and not

111. Paradigm Ins. Co. v. Langerman Law Offices, P.A., 24 P.3d 593 (Ariz. 2001) (In some cases the potential for conflict between insured and insurer is strong from the beginning, for example until insurer has committed itself to offering or waiving policy limits. When such a conflict arises, lawyers' duty is exclusively owed to insured and not the insurer.); Gafcon, Inc. v. Ponsor & Assocs., 120 Cal. Rptr. 2d 392, 404 (2002) ("[A]bsent a conflict of interest, an attorney retained by an insurance company to defend its insured under the insurer's contractual obligation to do so represents and owes a fiduciary duty to both the insurer and insured.").

112. Evraz, Inc., N.A. v. Cont'l Ins. Co., No. 3:08-cv-00447-AC, 2013 WL 6174839 (D. Or. Nov. 21, 2013) (law firm hired by company five years before insurer accepted company's tender of defense did not represent insurer); Pine Island Farmers Coop v. Erstad & Riemer, P.A., 636 N.W.2d 604, 609 (Minn. Ct. App. 2001) ("the insured is the sole client of the defense attorneys hired by the insurer").

permitting the insurance company to invade the client-lawyer relationship.

Q. So why do I have to worry about the rules?

A. Let's explore a few situations. First, what happens if the insurance company sends a reservation of rights letter giving six reasons why the insurance company might not pay the insured's claim?

Q. Oh, they just do that as a matter of course. It's just boilerplate.

A. You might be right in the great majority of cases. But not all. Think about a case in which the insurance company suggests that the claim will be defended but the insurance company thinks it has solid grounds for asserting the claim is not covered. Now can you treat the insurance company as the client?

Q. I guess not. There's a conflict between them. The insurance company may not care what kind of a defense they provide if they're not worried about paying the claim. And the insurance company may take a very different view of a possible settlement.

A. You are so correct. Can you think of anything else?

* * *

Q. I guess there are cases where the insurance, even if available, may not be sufficient to cover the insured's exposure.

A. Precisely. Now the insured really needs a lawyer looking out for them. Think about what happens if the lawyer representing both the insurance company and the insured receives an offer to settle within policy limits. Does the insured need their own lawyer then?

Q. I would say so. That's one that gets us all the time. If the insured were our only client, we would do everything in our power to convince the insurance company to settle to remove the threat of an uninsured verdict against the insured. Of course, we do the right thing even with the insurance company as a co-client. But you are right; it's a lot harder to be tough with the insurance company when we depend on them for future business.

A. What about when you learn something from your client, the insured, which suggests the insurance company has grounds to rescind the policy?

Q. Oh, we know how to deal with that one. Years ago we went to a seminar where the boring ethics geek told us that in that situation, even if both the insured and the insurance company are clients, the lawyer is absolutely barred by that confidentiality stuff from sharing that with the insurance company. And if the insured and the insurance company get in a battle royale over coverage, this same instructor told us we were barred from representing either. To us that's a really good rule. We don't need to be in an uncomfortable position with the insurance company any more often than is required. Is that it?

* * *

A. Not quite. What if you're representing an insured and perhaps the insurance company tells you to settle the case for $50,000, the amount of plaintiff's last offer?

Q. I would settle in a New York minute. My client, the insured, will be thrilled.

A. Do you know that?

Q. They are always happy to a make the case go away.

A. Always? We doubt it. Sometimes the insured has a very different interest in a settlement from the insurance company.

Q. I guess you are right.

A. Sure we are. It could be reputational. Think of a physician who seeks vindication by taking the case to trial. Or the insured who doesn't want the enterprise's rates to go up by paying off what the insured believes to be a totally frivolous claim.

Q. Don't I have to settle?

A. Not if your client—or one of your two clients—directs you not to do so. It is the insured's right to direct his or her lawyer not to settle.

Q. Even if the policy says the insurance company gets to decide?

A. Yes, even then. Your job is to represent your client, not to enforce your client's contractual obligations on behalf of the insurance company, even when the insurance company is also a client. Your client, to put it simply, is entitled to relieve the insurer of its obligations.[113]

Q. But the insured may lose its coverage.

A. That is correct. And it is your job to advise the client why it is not in the client's best interests to go along with the settlement. Not doing so could result in real financial pain with no assurance of vindication. But at the end of the day, Rule 1.2 provides that the client gets to decide. And if the client so decides, you—with one client or two—have to abide by the instructions of the insured.

Q. Are we done?

---

113. Rogers v. Robson, Masters, Ryan, Brumund & Belom, 392 N.E.2d 1365 (Ill. App. Ct. 1979), *aff'd*, 407 N.E.2d 47 (Ill. 1980) (although insured's policy gave insurance company the right to settle without insured's consent, the duty of the lawyer could still be breached).

* * *

A. Not even close. Let us assume the insurance company issues rules for its counsel that bar hiring experts until one month before trial, or require insurance company approval to file motions to dismiss or for summary judgment, or require permission to take more than five depositions.

Q. You don't have to assume. The insurance companies we deal with not only chisel us on rates but also have these damn representation guidelines.

A. What do you do about them?

Q. We abide by them unless they are a disaster. I mean these insurance companies are serious.

A. Well, you have to be very careful. You can certainly consider the guidelines as suggestions, but the rules make it clear that you have to exercise independent judgment.[114] That need becomes particularly acute when you are representing an insured whose interests because of a reservation of rights letter, limited coverage, possible disclaimer of coverage, reputational interests, or similar concerns are different from those of the insurance company. If necessary, you must push back against such restrictions and, in appropriate cases, insist on taking whatever steps you deem necessary in your independent professional judgment to be undertaken.[115] Remember, the insurance company has contractually agreed to provide the insured with a defense.

* * *

Q. Easy enough to say, but I wish the reality were so simple. You know these insurance companies keep threatening us to take all their representations in-house if we don't tow their line. Can they really do that?

A. The answer to that question varies. It is certainly a fact that insurance companies have established "law firms" with law firm-sounding names that are made up exclusively of full-time insurance company employees.

Q. Doesn't that create conflicts?

A. It sure does. If those individuals are full-time employees, then they are always representing the insurance company, not

114. MRs 1.8(f)(2), 5.4(c).

115. Petition of Youngblood, 895 S.W.2d 322, 328 (Tenn. 1995) ("The terms of the agreement between the insurer and the attorney whereby the attorney agrees to undertake the representation of the insured must respect the attorney-client relationship between the attorney and the insured. . . . Any policy, arrangement or device which effectively limits, by design or operation, the attorney's professional judgment on behalf of or loyalty to the client is prohibited.").

just being paid by it. This means they should decline taking on any matter in which there is a cognizable conflict of interest between the insured and the insurance company. And they should be barred from disclosing any conflict-creating or affirming information to their full-time employer that they learn from the insured.[116]

Q. Do they?

A. Well, the unlikelihood that they could is but one reason why some jurisdictions have prohibited that approach outright.[117] Since these lawyers are full-time employees of the insurance company, can we really expect them to keep information confidential or push back on the insurance companies' representation guidelines? Again, we have a situation in which the insurance companies understandably are looking at representation standards and economics on a macro basis, when, in situations in which the interests of the insurance company and the insured diverge, the principles of the Rules of Professional Conduct regarding competence, conflict-free representation, and professional independence must take center stage.

Q. Another threat that has been made is that this one insurance company will only hire us if we agree to a fixed fee for each representation: $7,500 a pop.

A. How's that sound to you?

Q. It's on the low side. And for some cases it's a mere fraction of what, even at our pathetic hourly rates, we would charge.

A. You've identified the problem. There is nothing wrong with fixed fees. And a client generally can agree to a fixed fee so long as it is not unreasonably low. But here the client is not agreeing to the fixed fee. And if the real party in interest is being assigned a lawyer under a fixed fee agreement that carries with it such a huge disincentive for the lawyer to provide the essential and independent services the insured requires, the fixed

---

116. Parsons v. Cont'l Nat'l Am. Group, 550 P.2d 94, 99 (Ariz. 1976) ("When an attorney who is an insurance company's agent uses the confidential relationship between an attorney and a client to gather information so as to deny the insured coverage under the policy in the garnishment proceeding we hold that such conduct constitutes a waiver of any policy defense, and is so contrary to public policy that the insurance company is estopped as a matter of law from disclaiming liability under an exclusionary clause in the policy.").

117. Cincinnati Ins. Co. v. Wills, 717 N.E.2d 151 (Ind. 1999) (although insurer's in-house lawyers may represent insured in lawsuits by third parties, lawyers violated professional conduct rule prohibiting the practice of law under a misleading name when they used an independent name for their practice even though they were full-time employees for insurer); Gardner v. N.C. State Bar, 341 S.E.2d 517 (N.C. 1986) (lawyer employed full-time by insurer cannot represent insured because it would violate ban on practice of law by corporations).

fee arrangement will be deemed to interfere with lawyer competence and independence, and be stricken in favor of an alternative fee arrangement that vitiates those disincentives. So the answer to fixed fee arrangements is, very much, it depends.

§ 6.04 Offers to Settle Within Policy Limits

The Unreasonable Insurance Company

Q. I don't know what to do. I am representing the driver of an automobile who was in a serious accident. United Indemnity hired me for this case.

A. What's the problem?

Q. Well, I've got two clients, the driver and the insurance company.

A. Are you sure?

Q. That's the way I see it.

A. Well, let's stop right there. When an insurance company hires you to represent its insured, you don't necessarily have two clients. Though insurance companies—for reasons we have never understood—want to be treated as clients, not every state accepts that proposition. In some states you only represent the insured, not the insurance company, and you can see quite quickly how having two clients complicates things.

Q. That's why I came to you. The insured has a $100,000/$300,000 policy. The plaintiffs have offered to settle for the $300,000. The insured is thrilled with that result because the insured has been worried sick that part of this claim would be uninsured.

A. You are going to settle?

Q. Well, the insurance company says I cannot. They think the claim is a fraudulent one and want me to take the case to trial. What shall I do now? One client wants one result; the other client wants a different one.

A. Precisely why having two clients is so difficult. Even if you have two clients, when a conflict like this arises, your exclusive client is the insured. If you think the settlement is a fair one, your job is to convince the insurance company to settle within the limits.

Q. What if they refuse?

A. If they refuse, then it is your job to make the record—that you recommended this settlement, that you thought it was reasonable, that you urged the insurance company to accept it, and that they refused. But since you are settling with the insurance company's money, you actually can't settle the case. All you and your insured can hope for is that if the case goes to trial and there is a judgment for more than coverage, the insurance company's conduct will be found in bad faith and any excess will have to be paid by the insurance company.

Q. But I hate to get cross-wise with United Indemnity. They send me lots of business.

A. That's where lawyer independence comes in. It is hard to represent your primary client fully when that individual is not a repeat customer. But you have no choice. The Rules of Professional Conduct make that clear. And one more thing . . .

Q. What's that?

A. If the insured and the insurance company get into further litigation over this question, you may not represent either side.

§ 6.05 Policy Defenses

Learning Too Much

Q. Problems in this area of insurance defense abound.

A. What do you mean?

Q. Well, I have been asked by the insurance company to represent this lawyer. It is a malpractice claim. Very big bucks. And very bitter litigation.

A. Sounds like a great challenge.

Q. Oh, it's a challenge alright, but I just got blindsided on this one. Turns out my client admits he was hooked on heroin. It is quite sad really.

A. What's that got to do with the matter you are handling?

Q. Well, the policy provides for no coverage when an insured is found to be taking illegal substances. Heroin is at the top of that list. Then, since I represent the insurance company as well, it seems to me that I have an obligation to tell them that they are off the hook. But if I do so, I have destroyed my client's coverage and, perhaps, my client's career.

A. This is just another reason why the idea of two clients creates disastrous results. In most joint representations the lawyer informs the clients that all confidential information of one will be shared with the other. With those ground rules the clients know how to proceed. But here your client correctly expects confidentiality at least with respect to issues relating to coverage. And your client is entitled to that. You may not get involved in issues that would compromise the coverage the insurance company client is offering your insured client. So you are absolutely forbidden from telling the insurance company that this is the case.[118]

Q. But now I feel so conflicted by being put in this awkward spot because the insurance company is such a good client.

A. If the conflict is so serious that you think it will affect your ability to represent the insured, then your obligation is to withdraw from the representation entirely, without telling anybody the reason for your withdrawal. And you can recommend that separate counsel be hired for the insurer, counsel who does not also represent the insured.

118. Parsons v. Cont'l Nat'l Am. Grp., 550 P.2d 94 (Ariz. 1976) (insurer estopped from denying coverage because it attempted to use insured's statements obtained by lawyer hired by insurer to defend against insured).

CHAPTER 7

Entity and Government Clients

§ 7.01 Introduction: The Legal Fiction

Lawyers who provide legal services to organizations face unique ethical issues because their clients are legal fictions: entities, abstractions, or amalgams of individual interests. These legal fictions range in size from small partnerships, professional corporations, and family companies to large corporations and government agencies. And they range from struggling dance companies and active senior citizen housing sponsors to Fortune 100 companies and universities and their hospitals.

Because organizations are so pervasive, nearly every lawyer will represent one sometime in his or her legal career. In fact, at least half of all lawyers in practice represent organizations on a regular basis, either as outside counsel or inside employees.[119] The in-house counsel lawyer-employee has only one client, the organization, and all financial rewards are provided by that same client, which can make it very difficult to remain objective in the face of client demands.[120]

Model Rule 1.13(a) adopts the entity theory for all organizations. The entity concept assumes that an organization has a distinct legal

119. About 61,000 lawyers (approximately 10 percent of the practicing bar) serve as inside counsel to about 21,000 profit and nonprofit private sector corporations. Ass'n of Corporate Counsel, Profile of In-House Counsel (2006), *available at* https://www2.acc.com/vl/public/Surveys/loader.cfm?csModule=security/getfile&pageid=16297.

120. E. Norman Veasey & Christine T. Guglielmo, Indispensable Counsel: The Chief Legal Officer in the New Reality 10–11 (2012).

personality apart from any individual constituent or aggregate of individual constituents within the whole. It is borrowed from corporate law, which recognizes corporations as distinct legal persons who can contract, sue, and be sued in their own right, and incur liability apart from that of their owners.

Applied to legal representation, the entity theory means that the organization's lawyer represents and has a client-lawyer relationship with the entity only, not with any constituent or group of constituents within the organization.[121] Each constituent is an agent of the whole, who speaks for the organization through a different role and with a distinctive view of the organization's interests, often filtered through a personal lens. The organization must act through its "duly authorized constituents," but these constituents are not clients, and they (and the entity's lawyer) easily can misconstrue the lawyer's role.[122]

When a given constituent or group of constituents propose to engage in unlawful conduct, the lawyer must pursue the matter up the ladder of organizational authority.[123] When the disagreement cannot be resolved by such an appeal, the lawyer faces an especially difficult dilemma.

Lawyers can work their way through this thicket by remembering to identify their entity clients, clarifying this identity to their client's constituents regularly, and, when necessity demands it, providing the six Cs to the organizations they represent.

§ 7.02 Close Corporations

Who Is the Client, Really?

Q. Representing close corporations—particularly family-owned ones—is a constant challenge.

A. Part lawyer; part psychiatrist.

Q. Certainly true; and traps for the wary every step of the way. Here's today's installment. We've been representing Arbor Real Estate for years develop multifamily housing. They've

---

121. D'Andrea v. Epstein, Becker, Green, Wickliff & Hall, P.C., 418 S.W.3d 791 (Tex. App. 2013) (question of material fact whether misuse of a memo prepared by outside counsel at inside counsel's request was foreseeable, rendering outside counsel liable for malpractice); ABA Comm. on Ethics & Prof'l Responsibility, Formal Op. 08-453 (2008) In-House Consulting on Ethical Issues (law firm's ethics counsel usually represents the organization as a whole, not individual firm lawyers).

122. Lawrence J. Fox & Susan R. Martyn, The Ethics of Representing Organizations: Legal Fictions for Clients 8–9 (2009).

123. MR 1.13(b); RLGL § 97 cmt. f.

gotten themselves into a fight with another contractor. Delayed the project a year. Cost 'em a fortune. So we sued.

A. So far, so good.

Q. Not really. From the beginning, it was dad's fight. His son and his nephew thought it was a waste of time. But they relented reluctantly.

A. The problem?

Q. Trial is next week. There's an offer on the table. Dad says reject it. I ask if board agrees. Dad replies, angrily, "I am still CEO around here. We're going to trial." I'm not so sure.

A. You are correct so far. You are supposed to deal with the individual assigned to the matter unless you have doubts about that person's authority, as here. Then you must take steps to ensure that you have authority at the highest level you require. It may upset the CEO, even get you fired, but if this is a board-level matter, you better get your instructions from the board. Let dad and the boys duke it out. Just make sure no innocent bystanders get caught in the cross-fire.[124]

Q. CEO threatened to fire us if we did not follow his chosen path.

A. If he actually goes through with that threat, the rules offer, and even might require, further action by you. Rule 1.13(e) provides that if you are terminated by a corporate official who is not acting consistent with obligations owed to the organization, the lawyer shall proceed as reasonably necessary to inform the organization's highest authority, which in your case is the board. Maybe that'll save your engagement.

Q. But will it save this dysfunctional family?

A. You'll have to go elsewhere for that advice.

§ 7.03 Corporate Families

Do I Have to Tell the Parent?

Q. We have been representing Apex in bitter negotiations against Colossus. No matter how hard we try, our client is almost irrational about this one. They do not view Colossus as a competitor. They view Colossus as the enemy.

---

124. Ky. Bar Ass'n v. Hines, 399 S.W.3d 750 (Ky. 2013) (lawyer suspended from practice for 120 days for violating duty of loyalty in Rules 1.13(a) and 1.7 for suing some of corporate client's board members without the consent of the board's majority); State *ex rel.* Okla. Bar Ass'n v. Perry, 936 P.2d 897 (Okla. 1997) (lawyer disbarred for representing both corporation and constituent who did business with each other without disclosing his serious conflict of interest).

A. Sounds like a difficult client, maybe one that doesn't worry about the budget.

Q. That is true. It is a mixed blessing. But our client is definitely prepared to spend big bucks on this litigation. However, that is not our problem.

A. Tell us more.

Q. It turns out that for the last three years our L.A. office has been representing the parent of Colossus, Excelsior Corporation. Somehow, we missed it in our conflicts check. I suggested we tell the client, but my partners are really worried. The client has already been unhappy with our unwillingness to be as aggressive as they wish. If they learn this fact, there may be hell to pay.

A. And you? Do you think you have to tell them?

Q. Well, one of my partners says it is perfectly okay to sue the subsidiary of your client; there is no conflict. Why should we tell them? What they don't know won't hurt them.

A. We are afraid that is no solution. It is true that there is a comment to Rule 1.7 that permits lawyers to take positions adverse to members of their clients' corporate families, but it is not a hard and fast rule. Whether you get away with it is very fact dependent. Are the two entities in the same line of business? Do they have common management, employ common general counsel, or is there any other reason to treat them both as clients for conflict purposes?[125] In any event, your client is entitled to know this very important fact. It may be that they won't do anything. Or maybe they will object.

Q. My guess is they will. They might even try to fire us and seek repayment of our fees because of the undisclosed conflict.

A. That certainly is possible. But you are forgetting the other side of the equation.

Q. What's that?

A. You now have to tell Excelsior because it is entitled to know you have been adverse to its subsidiary. It, too, may do nothing, but it also may move to disqualify you from continuing the representation. And it won't help one whit that Excelsior is

---

125. GSI Commerce Solutions, Inc. v. BabyCenter, LLC, 618 F.3d 204, 209–11 (2d Cir. 2010) (law firm disqualified from representing a party suing a corporate affiliate of a current client where corporate affiliates shared "operational commonality"); Certain Underwriters at Lloyd's London v. Argonaut Ins. Co., 264 F. Supp. 2d 914, 924 (N.D. Cal. 2003) (parent corporation and its subsidiary, even if wholly owned, are generally regarded as separate entities for conflicts purposes unless an exception applies where the relationship between the entities are such they have a "unity of interests," such as relatively direct financial relationship or common management, including supervision, over the legal affairs of both entities).

learning this important fact after you have been handling this matter adverse to its subsidiary for years.

Q. Don't you think it was up to them to discover this?

A. No, the duty is on the lawyer to communicate with the client. The rules place the burden that way. Blaming the client is not only unflattering; it is unlikely to be viewed sympathetically.

§ 7.04 Entity Client Depositions

Accommodating the CEO, CFO, and the Board

Q. It's a great case. So much at stake. And the key witnesses are the CEO, the CFO, and the board. A chance to represent the great and near great. Show our stuff.

A. It's a journey fraught with peril.

Q. There you go again. Just when I am on top of the world you have to be the ink droplet in the glass of cold milk.

A. Just want you to be careful.

Q. Oh I will be, you can be sure. With clients like these, how can I miss?

A. Let us count the ways. You said clients.

Q. I mean the company and the big cheeses.

A. Do you represent them all?

Q. Well, I represent the company, of course. There are no individual parties in this matter.

A. You only have one client.

Q. Hadn't really thought about it.

A. Start thinking now.

Q. Well, I heard some big ethics expert talk about accommodation clients. I think that's what these other folks are.

A. And what does that mean?

Q. I don't really know. I guess it means you represent these guys at their deps as a favor to your real client.

A. Does that make them clients?

Q. I don't know.

A. Well we suggest you better find out.

Q. There's no time like the present.

A. Our rules say nothing about accommodation clients. Even though the Restatement mentions it,[126] courts have refused to accept the

126. RLGL § 132 cmt. i.

label.[127] We have clients,[128] prospective clients,[129] former clients,[130] adverse parties,[131] and other represented[132] and unrepresented persons.[133] Calling someone an accommodation client does not answer any question whose answer you need to know.

Q. Does it really matter? I'm just taking them to a deposition.

A. And preparing them for that deposition?

Q. Of course. What do you think I am?

A. An effective lawyer. A conscientious lawyer. A well-prepared lawyer. As a result, when you sit in that conference room going over the upcoming deposition, you will not just be representing the company, you may be representing the soon-to-be deponent.

Q. Not really.

A. Ok, let's assume that person is not a client. What does that mean?

Q. It means I don't have a joint representation.

A. True enough. But what else?

Q. That's why I came to you.

A. It means that this person is unrepresented. And under our rules it means that you can't give this person any legal advice. Except for one thing.

Q. What's that?

A. The advice to get a lawyer. That and you have an obligation to correct any misperception the person may have about your role.[134] And then there's the deposition itself.

Q. Is that a problem?

A. Only from the very beginning. When the lawyer on the other side asks the witness if he is represented . . . . And then when you direct the witness not to answer. And the lawyer on the other side turns to the witness and asks whether the witness is going to take your advice, will you be acting as lawyer for the witness?

Q. I . . . I guess so. It certainly doesn't fit my role for me to think of this person as unrepresented. Isn't it better to say I am giving advice to my client through a constituent?

---

127. Universal City Studios, Inc. v. Reimerdes, 98 F. Supp. 2d 449, 453 (S.D.N.Y. 2000) (court criticized expert witness's use of the term "accommodation" client).

128. MRs 1.1–1.8, 1.10–1.17, 2.1–2.4, 3.7; RLGL §§ 14, 16–32, 34–56, 59–97, 104.

129. MR 1.18; RLGL § 15.

130. MR 1.9; RLGL §§ 33, 132.

131. MRs 3.1–3.4, 3.8, 4.1, 4.4; RLGL §§ 98, 105–120.

132. MR 4.2; RLGL §§ 99–102.

133. MR 4.3; RLGL § 103.

134. MRs 1.13(f), 4.3; RLGL § 103 cmt. e.

A. That would be so if you were certain that this individual was in need of no independent legal advice and the individual understood and accepted your view. But that situation may be quite rare.[135] Which leaves one choice.

Q. I represent this person at least for this day and trip.

A. We think so.

Q. What does that mean?

A. You have a joint representation, but with none of the protections.

Q. Not so cryptic.

A. Generally, when you have a multiple representation, the representation of the clients commences at the same time at the beginning of the representation. That gives the lawyer a chance at the earliest possible time to talk about the risks, about how confidential information will be handled, about what happens if conflicts develop. Not to mention confirming it all in writing.[136] Here, you, the lawyer, have been representing the company for a long time, plan to continue to represent the company to conclusion, and view this representation as a punctuation mark in a long paragraph. Which doesn't mean you don't have to contend with these matters.

Q. How am I going to do that?

A. You're going to walk a tight rope, my friend. And explain it to both clients in writing.[137] If you don't, and the company and the employee are now at loggerheads and unwilling to give informed consent to the conflict, your corporate client better start looking for substitute counsel.

Q. Meaning?

A. You probably will be forced to withdraw.[138] We also hope that the entire time you were in accommodation mode you were not aware of any conflict or you might be in trouble for not withdrawing from her representation at a much earlier time. A

---

135. MRs 1.13(f), 1.13 cmt. 2.

136. MR 1.7(b)(4).

137. MR 1.7; RLGL §§ 75, 128, 131.

138. *In re* Rite Aid Corp. Sec. Litig., 139 F. Supp. 2d 649 (E.D. Pa. 2001) (law firm that represented defendant corporation and defendant former chief executive who resigned during the litigation not disqualified where former CEO dealt with law firm solely through corporation and was therefore an accommodation client and consented to law firm's subsequent continued representation of corporation after it had ceased representing former CEO because of conflicts); Miller v. Alagna, 138 F. Supp. 2d 1252 (C.D. Cal. 2000) (county lawyers disqualified from representing police officers in excessive force and wrongful death claim); Yanez v. Plummer, 164 Cal. Rptr. 3d 309 (2013) (cause of action for breach of fiduciary duty stated by former company employee who alleges wrongful discharge against inside company lawyer who represented both company and employee after employee expressed concern about his job due to the fact his disposition testimony would not likely be favorable to the company).

lawyer, for sure, can represent the organization and its officers, partners, or directors at the same time. But as with all joint representations they may only continue so long as no unwaived conflict arises between or among them.[139]

§ 7.05 Identifying a Government Client

The State or the Department?

Q. The governor put out a plea for pro bono help. No one wanted to sue the tobacco companies. They always won. Yet the state had incurred billions—billions with a "b"—paying the Medicaid charges of smokers. We agreed to take the case on a contingency. Figuring we would never win. Still think that. But this is a classic example of no good deed goes unpunished. We were hired by a group of pharmaceutical companies. They want to challenge as discriminatory recent real estate tax increases authorized against domestic corporate manufacturers. We bring the case against the state's revenue office on constitutional grounds. Instantly we get a call from the AG. What the hell are we doing suing our client? We point out our client is the health department. He responds, it's all one enterprise called the State of New Jersey. I respond on bended knee, pointing out how hard we are working pro bono for the Medicaid expense recovery with so little chance of success. Won't he please give informed consent to the apparent conflict, which isn't a conflict anyway, I ask the AG. Gee, he'd love to help us out: He sure appreciates what good public citizens we have been. But no governmental entity is permitted to "waive a conflict." Period. End stop. And he is clear that representing the health department is representing the state. Could this be right?

A. It may well be correct. First, whether representing the health department constitutes representing the state is a function of state law. Look at the New Jersey constitution and other relevant state law. We presume the AG knows who the client is but check to be sure. Second, although a conflict like this would be consentable generally, the rules prohibit consents to conflicts where to seek one would be illegal. And the most

139. Lawrence J. Fox, *Defending a Deposition of Your Organizational Client's Employee: An Ethical Minefield Everyone Ignores*, 44 S. Tex. L. Rev. 185 (2002).

typical example of such an illegal consent is the prohibition by some states against governmental waivers.[140] Sorry. But the law's the law.

§ 7.06 The Government Client

A substantial group of lawyers provide legal services to federal, state, and local government units in the widest variety of matters.[141] Model Rule 1.13, Comment [9] extends the rule's entity concept of organizations to governmental organizations, but cautions that issues related to client identity and fiduciary obligations may be shaped not only by the government lawyer's general and specific ethical obligations but also by the client-government's public obligations imposed by constitution, statute, regulation, or common law.

At various times, government lawyers have identified their client as an agency official, the agency itself, a branch of government, the government itself, or the people served by the government.[142] Lawyers who work for government agencies typically view their client as the agency, with its policy articulated by the agency officer who has the power to decide a particular matter.[143] On the other hand, lawyers who work in a state attorney general's office or the U.S. Department of Justice may define their client as the state or federal government itself, where the public interest is articulated by the person or persons in the office with legitimate authority to direct government policy.[144] Government lawyers such as judge advocate general lawyers or public defenders also

140. MR 1.7 (b)(2), 1.7 cmt. [16]; *In re* Advisory Comm. on Prof'l Ethics, Docket No. 18-98, 745 A.2d 497, 502 (N.J. 2000); State *ex rel.* Morgan Stanley & Co., Inc. v. MacQueen, 416 S.E.2d 55, 60 (W. Va. 1992); Tenn. Ethics Op. 2002-F-146 (2002). Other states, however, permit government waivers of conflicts of interest. Ill. Ethics Op. 95-5 (1995); Iowa Ethics Op. 06-03 (2006); Kan. Ethics Op. 95-11 (1995) (withdrawing prior opinion); Md. Ethics Op. 99-28 (1999) (modifying prior opinions); N.Y. Ethics Op. 629 (1992) (modifying prior opinions); Pa. Ethics Op. 2006-24 (2006).

141. The federal government employed about 34,000 lawyers, state governments about 40,000, and local governments about 52,000 in 2014. Together, these lawyers account for about 20 percent of all U.S. lawyers. Bureau of Labor Statistics, Occupational Employment and Wages, May 2018: Lawyers, *available at* http://www.bls.gov/oes/current/oes231011.htm (last visited July 28, 2015).

142. Richard W. Painter, Getting the Government America Deserves: How Ethics Reform Can Make a Difference 121–22 (2009).

143. *See* D.C. R. Prof'l Conduct 1.6(k) (2015) ("The client of the government lawyer is the agency that employs the lawyer unless expressly provided to the contrary by applicable law, regulation, or order.").

144. Jonathan R. Macey & Geoffrey P. Miller, *Reflections on Professional Responsibility in a Regulatory State*, 63 Geo. Wash. L. Rev. 1105 (1995).

may be assigned to represent individuals.[145] Prosecutors, on the other hand, do not represent individuals, but are "ministers of justice"[146] who represent a sovereign government, which has an obligation to "govern impartially."[147]

Like an organization's lawyer, the government lawyer must take direction from duly authorized constituents of the client. When a given constituent or group of constituents propose to engage in unlawful conduct, the lawyer must pursue the matter up the ladder of government authority.[148] When the disagreement cannot be resolved by such an appeal, the lawyer and constituents may end up asking a court to resolve it.[149]

Some government lawyers have the power to control and decide certain legal matters that ordinarily would be reposed only in the client.[150] When a government lawyer has this responsibility, the lawyer essentially serves as trustee for the government, taking into consideration some version of the public interest in making the decision.

Lawyers working for government clients are subject to both the general conflicts provision in Model Rule 1.7 and the former client conflict provision in Model Rule 1.9.[151] Lawyers currently working for the

---

145. *See* D.C. R. PROF'L CONDUCT 1.6 cmt. (39) (2015); D.C. Ethics Op. 313 (2002) (whether former Navy JAG lawyer now can continue to represent same defendant in post-conviction proceeding in private practice); Kathleen Clark, *Government Lawyering: The Ethics of Representing Elected Representatives*, 61 LAW & CONTEMP. PROBS. 31 (1998).

146. MR 3.8 cmt. [1]; Office of Disciplinary Counsel v. Wrenn, 790 N.E.2d 1195 (Ohio 2003) (prosecutor who failed to disclose relevant, exculpatory, and unprivileged information when asked by both defense counsel and the court suspended for six months, stayed, despite the fact that defendant's eventual conviction and sentence did not change as a result).

147. Berger v. United States, 295 U.S. 78, 88 (1935); Freeport-McMoRan Oil & Gas Co. v. F.E.R.C., 962 F.2d 45 (D.C. Cir. 1992) (the principle in *Berger* applies equally to the government's civil lawyers, who should have dismissed an appeal when the issue became moot).

148. MR 1.13(b); RLGL § 97 cmt. f.

149. Vaughn v. King, 167 F.3d 347 (7th Cir. 1999) (City of Gary Sanitary District had statutory power to hire independent outside counsel without mayor's signature); Salt Lake City Comm'n v. Salt Lake City Attorney, 985 P.2d 899, 907 (Utah 1999) (in the absence of any contradictory statutes, county attorney represents county as an entity, not individual commissioners, who therefore have no power to hire outside counsel when they disagree with county attorney except when county attorney "refuses to act or is incapable of acting or is unavailable for some other reason"; disagreements about whether this exception has occurred may be settled by appeal to the attorney general or by seeking a declaratory judgment from a court); State *ex rel.* McGraw v. Burton, 569 S.E.2d 99 (W. Va. 2002) (in light of long-established statues, practice and precedent, the State executive branch and related entities may in some circumstances employ and use non-employee lawyers).

150. MR Scope ¶ [18]; RLGL §§ 97(1), 97 cmt. g; 28 U.S.C. §§ 516, 519 (2012) (authorizing the Department of Justice to make and control most litigation decisions—this power varies considerably at the state level).

151. MR 1.11(d); *In re* Jackson, 27 So. 3d 273 (La. 2010) (prosecutor disbarred for dismissing drunk driving case after accepting $500 from defendant to represent him in same case); PAINTER, *supra* note 142, at 126–29.

government and those who leave government service also are subject to the specialized conflicts provisions of Model Rule 1.11.[152]

In addition to the applicable Rules of Professional Conduct, state and federal conflict of interest statutes regulate government lawyers during and after their government service. State disciplinary agencies also have relied on these provisions in cases of professional discipline.[153] The goal of both sets of rules is to prevent potential abuses, such as use of confidential governmental information or the risk that a lawyer might misuse a government position to benefit herself in later private practice.

All of this legal regulation demands careful attention, especially to several details that many of these rules share. First, each rule makes the role of the government employee relevant to its reach. Second, many of these rules also define the lawyer's role after leaving government service. Finally, each rule creates a distinctive penalty. Some create criminal penalties, others administrative remedies, such as loss of a government contract or benefit. Federal and state governments have found these additional remedies necessary to curb specific abuses of the public trust. Courts also have used these provisions as a guide to other relief, such as disqualification.[154] To fully understand their obligations, wise government lawyers need to remain aware of both relevant rules of professional conduct as well as other state and federal law.

§ 7.07 Government Consent

For Want of a Writing

Q. I know we should never have taken on the representation of Cheltenham Township. The money is not good enough, and our clients deal with the municipality all the time. But we agreed to do so after I talked to the township solicitor. I explained our predicament, and she assured me that the township would never object to our firm representing clients adverse to the township so long as the matters were unrelated to anything we were handling for the township.

A. What is the problem? Sounds like you have got a reasonable prospective consent that puts the township on notice of the

152. *In re* White, 11 A.3d 1226 (D.C. 2011) (lawyer disbarred for serving as a government lawyer and supervising investigation of a claim and subsequently representing same private client in litigation of same claim).

153. Office of Disciplinary Counsel v. Eilberg, 441 A.2d 1193 (Pa. 1982) (lawyer suspended from practice for five years for violating 18 U.S.C. § 203(a)).

154. Kessenich v. Commodity Futures Trading Comm'n, 684 F.2d 88 (D.C. Cir. 1982); *In re* Rest. Dev. of P.R., Inc., 128 B.R. 498 (Bankr. D.P.R. 1991).

matters you would likely handle where the township was on the other side.

Q. That is what I thought. But when the township objected to our handling a zoning appeal for this shopping center developer based on a conflict of interest, I reminded the solicitor of her promise. Her response: She does not remember making such a deal and besides, she asserts, the consent would have to be in writing. Whatever happened to a handshake agreement?

A. Her rejoinder sorry to say, is correct. Informed consents to conflicts of interest—and, one would say, a fortiori, prospective waivers of conflicts of interest—must be in writing.[155] It is not only important so that memory loss cannot come into play, but a strict requirement for all informed consents to conflicts. It protects the client, but it also protects the lawyer. Even if you had it in writing, the township could challenge it because it was prospective. But here you relied on an oral agreement. One more thing . . .

Q. What's that?

A. Be very careful when dealing with governmental clients. In some states those clients are prohibited by legislation from waiving conflicts.

§ 7.08 The Departing Government Lawyer

Ordinary Former Lawyers?

Q. We hired the general counsel of the Food and Drug Administration. We do a lot of pharmaceutical defense work, and he is a perfect hire. So, we immediately assign him to handle the defense of one of our giant pharmaceutical clients in multiple cases across the country relating to its drug for diabetes. Now the plaintiffs' lawyers have moved to disqualify him on the grounds that the FDA was working on this drug at the time he was general counsel. He had nothing to do with this work, but it did take place while he was in that supervisory position. They might even dig up some pleadings where his name appears as general counsel of the FDA. If they are right, I think we made a huge blunder hiring this fellow.

A. The good news is you made no blunder. But the rule applicable to former government lawyers is narrower than the rule

155. MRs 1.0(b), 1.7(b)(4).

for private lawyers; those departing lawyers are only prohibited from getting involved in matters in which they were personally and substantially involved. So, even though his name might appear on every pleading filed by the agency during his tenure, that does not mean he is barred from this work if, in fact, he was not personally and substantially involved. Even if he were personally and substantially involved, your firm could have continued to be involved in this matter, but only if he were screened from participating in it, that is, he played no role at your firm and was barred from participating in the case. But I am afraid it is too late because he has already been involved. Let us hope that he was not personally and substantially involved while at the FDA.

There is one other thing you should know about this case. When a lawyer leaves the government and goes to work in a private law firm, the lawyer may be barred from participating in a case even if the lawyer's client is pursuing a case that looks very much like what the government agency was trying to accomplish. Let us give you an example. Say, this same lawyer at the FDA was doing an investigation of the diabetes drug that you just mentioned. Now he goes to work for a law firm that is suing the manufacturer of the diabetes drug. The FDA is not a party to the matter. But even though that lawyer would appear to be on the same side of the issue relating to that drug, the lawyer is not free to work on the matter at plaintiffs' law firm unless the FDA gives him permission to do so.

Q. That sounds like a crazy rule.

A. Actually, it is not. When working for the government, lawyers have special investigative powers. As a matter of public policy, this rule gives the particular agency the authority to decide whether one of its lawyers may leave the agency to go to work for any litigant in the same factual underlying matter, armed with the special knowledge that lawyer may possess. It is, in fact, a sound policy.

CHAPTER 8

Clients Who Morph

§ 8.01 Introduction: Clients Can Change

Like the law, clients are rarely static. Individual clients can marry, divorce, lose or gain mental capacity, and die. Entity clients can dissolve, change management, merge, split into or purchase affiliates, and be sold. Clients in debt can file for bankruptcy. Prospective clients can become clients, clients can become former clients. Each of these changes triggers a reorientation for the client's lawyer, and may mean that the lawyer now represents a new client.

§ 8.02 Clients Who Die

Disappearing Damages

> Q. I had a very significant plaintiff's personal injury case. My client was injured in a boating accident and sadly enough, ended up crippled for life. We brought a personal injury claim against the owner of the other vessel, and we have been engaged in settlement discussions. You can imagine the significance of my client's special damages. He will need extra care the rest of his life. As a result, I received a settlement offer in mid-seven figures last week. But, even more tragic, my client died last night from an unexpected heart attack. I think I should accept the

offer before they find out he has passed away. That's because any settlement offer they made while he was alive will be withdrawn immediately once they learn this very sad news.

A. Who is your client?

Q. The guy that was hurt.

A. But he is deceased.

Q. Oh, I hadn't thought of that. I guess I represent his estate.

A. Did you file a pleading to that effect?

Q. No, I called you.

A. You see the problem. Once your client passed on, you have no client. It may be that his estate will hire you. But, at the moment, you don't have someone to call and if you accept the offer, you will be misrepresenting your status. The other side will think you are someone's lawyer, but you are not. As a result, you can take no action except to notify the other side.[156]

Q. What a shame.

A. It is tragic all around, but that is the correct result.

§ 8.03 Clients with Diminished Capacity

Getting Old

Q. I feel terrible. I've represented this client for years. Wills, trusts, starting a couple of businesses. Great fellow. Four years ago he was in an auto accident. The truth is he's never been the same since. Don't know whether it's the accident, dementia, or the loss of his wife of 54 years. Anyway, I have a chance to settle his case. Finally, we got a decent offer.

A. Sounds good.

Q. It would be but when I went to tell him, he did not recognize me. I talked about the accident and got no reaction. I know it's the client's decision, but I am not sure how to proceed.

A. You are doing the right thing. Model Rule 1.6(b)(4) now recognizes consulting another lawyer to discuss how to resolve a difficult ethics question as an exception to confidentiality.

Q. You mean I did the right thing for the wrong reason.

---

156. Virzi v. Grand Trunk Warehouse & Cold Storage Co., 571 F. Supp. 507 (E.D. Mich. 1983) (settlement set aside due to lawyer's failure to disclose client's death during pretrial settlement conference); *In re* Forrest, 730 A.2d 340 (N.J. 1999) (lawyer's failure to disclose client's death violated Rules 3.3(a)(1) and 3.4(a), resulting in six-month suspension from practice); *see also* § 26.05 in this book.

A. You could say that. There is an argument that consultation would be impliedly authorized. But now it is in the rules. To encourage lawyers not to solve problems on their own.

Q. But what do I do now?

A. Rule 1.14 is the applicable rule. It tells us that when dealing with clients with diminished capacity the lawyer should maintain a client-lawyer relationship to the greatest extent possible. Given that, you should revisit your client. Maybe he was having an off day. You might find him in good shape the next time.

Q. And if not?

A. Then you are free to consult others—his family, his doctor—to determine how to proceed. Rule 1.14 mirrors the exception for consulting another lawyer under Rule 1.6(b)(4) in that way. They may have a solution. Maybe he needs his medication changed. Or his daughter can help you establish communication.[157]

Q. That would be ideal. But suppose that doesn't work?

A. Then you have no alternative but to seek to have a guardian ad litem appointed to give you a client to consult.

Q. I hate to do that. What a loss of dignity.

A. Of course you do, but as a last resort it can solve a challenging problem.[158]

§ 8.04 Children

Client Testimony Versus Client Best Interests

Q. We agreed to represent the child in proceedings before the Family Court to determine whether the child should be placed in foster care. There are clearly issues relating to the fitness of the parents. But notwithstanding those, our client, the child, now 14, insists she will be so much better off at home than being placed with strangers. If we were deciding, we would think her best interests were otherwise. On the other hand, we

157. *In re* Runge, 858 N.W.2d 901 (N.D. 2015) (lawyer did not violate Rule 1.14 by helping elderly client to revoke power of attorney formerly given to client's daughter so that client could leave an assisted-living facility).

158. Dunn v. Patterson, 919 N.E.2d 404 (Ill. App. Ct. 2009) (lawyer who placed a provision in a trust document that would not allow clients to amend or revoke their trust documents without either meeting with him or petitioning a court acted properly under Rules 1.14 and 1.2, because he reasonably believed that clients could not act adequately in their own interest, consulted with clients, and clients agreed to provision for third-party consent, which is a recognized method of protecting principals from making changes based on mental incompetency or undue influence).

worry that going home will put the client in serious jeopardy. What do we do?

A. Your client is the child, and the child is 14. And we assume of the sound mind and full capacity of a typical 14-year-old.

Q. That's how she appears.

A. Then Rule 1.14 tells us that, absent some undisclosed infirmity, you should be client-directed, an advocate for the client's wishes. You are her lawyer. Others may claim they are acting in the best interests of the child, but the proceedings are only legitimate if the client's wishes are also presented and presented fully and enthusiastically. The whole idea behind Rule 1.14 is to respect the dignity of the client, even when the client is somewhat impaired. That is your situation. And that means you are the one true champion of the 14-year-old.[159]

§ 8.05 Class Action Clients

The Uncertified Class

Q. The power of a class action! I have a client who has been terminated in clear violation of the age discrimination laws. From what he told me, there were dozens in his position. I brought it as a class action just last week. Now the company's lawyer has called me up. Offered an extra $100,000 to my client if we settle now and the only condition is that I promise not to sue 'em again. When I asked whether they thought the court would approve this deal, they told me the best news of all: The settlement doesn't require court approval. Who knew?

A. It is true that Rule 23 of the Federal Rules of Civil Procedure only requires court approval of a settlement after the class is certified.[160] Obviously, your worthy opponent is relying on this provision. The problem is, you will be sorry to learn, the rules of civil procedure do not have the ability to change the Rules

159. Gross v. Rell, 40 A.3d 240 (Conn. 2012) (lawyer who represented impaired client in conservatorship proceeding not protected by quasi-judicial immunity applicable to conservators who act as agents of the court because primary role of lawyer is to serve as client's zealous advocate, not to protect client's best interests); R.L.R. v. State, 116 So. 3d 570 (Fla. Dist. Ct. App. 2013) (court-appointed lawyers not required to disclose location of runaway dependent child, child would likely run away again if location disclosed and child would be less likely to seek legal advice); People v. Austin M., 975 N.E.2d 22 (Ill. 2012) (hybrid representation by lawyer who confused his roles as defense counsel and guardian ad litem caused per se conflict of interest requiring reversal of delinquency adjudication, even without any showing of adverse impact on lawyer's performance); Branham v. Stewart, 307 S.W.3d 94 (Ky. 2010) (lawyer retained by minor's best friend to pursue lawsuit represents the minor and owes the client ordinary professional obligations).

160. Fed. R. Civ. P. 23 (e).

> of Professional Conduct. You filed a lawsuit as a class action. When you did so you undertook to represent the class. At that moment you accepted a fiduciary duty to the class that you cannot so easily jettison simply because suddenly you wish to put the interests of your initial individual client or your own interests in the driver's seat.[161]

Making the offer contingent on your agreeing never to sue the company again, as noted elsewhere, is another ethics violation.[162] Lawyers are banned from offering or accepting as part of a settlement any restriction on their right to practice law. The rule, Model Rule 5.6, is designed to save lawyers from the trap that would be created by it being in the best interests of the present client to accept the limitation even though the lawyer, and more important the public, would want the lawyer experienced in these matters to be able to take on new representations against the company. If the company wants to prevent the lawyer from suing it again it may do so by hiring the lawyer to represent the company; any such engagement, however, must come after the first matter is settled and not even be hinted at as part of the settlement process.

§ 8.06 Companies That Fail

Company Bankruptcy

Q. My former client company went bankrupt. Now the trustee is waiving the privilege, something the former board would never have considered. This can't be happening. My treasured (and intemperate) memo's seeing the light of day?

A. Yes, it is. Your former client has morphed into a new entity, the bankrupt company, which is now legally controlled by a new "CEO": the trustee. Remember, entities can merge, be bought or sold, or, as in your case, go under. In all these situations, control transfers to new managers who may not see the issues for the "new" enterprise from the same perspective as your former client representatives did.[163]

---

161. Schick v. Berg, No. 03-cv-5513(LBS), 2004 WL 856298 (S.D.N.Y. Apr. 20, 2004); Janik v. Rudy, Exelrod & Zieff, 14 Cal. Rptr. 3d 751 (Cal. Ct. App. 2004) (class member could allege legal malpractice for failure to pursue cause of action not specifically approved in class certification order as long as cause of action arose out of the same facts and class members would reasonably expect it to be considered).

162. *See* § 5.03 and § 25.15 in this book.

163. Antioch Litigation Trust v. McDermott Will & Emery LLP, 738 F. Supp. 2d 758 (S.D. Ohio 2010) (bankruptcy trustee succeeded to all litigation claims of bankrupt company, including malpractice and aiding and abetting breaches of fiduciary duty by former board members against its former lawyers).

§ 8.07 Changes in Management

The New CEO

Q. I thought that privilege was sacrosanct. I always am so careful to make sure that my communications will withstand scrutiny by our adversaries. And I teach my colleagues that as well. I make sure the only advice they put in their memos is legal advice. I also make sure that nobody distributes any memoranda with our clients to anyone who will break the privilege.

I certainly did that here. I just reviewed the requested documents and every one of them is privileged. But I have been asked to produce them by the new CEO of my old client, Colossus. I am sick about that. Some of what I wrote should never see the light of day.

A. You have identified an important issue. You are correct that we have an obligation to maintain the privilege to the greatest extent possible. That is our job. But the privilege belongs to the client. And guess what?

Q. I give up.

A. Our clients can morph. One day your client's CEO is George, and the next day it is Sarah. There is nothing to prevent Sarah from waiving the organization's privilege if she decides it is in the best interests of the organization or she wants to look better than George.[164] Your privileged communications are always at risk of seeing the light of day, which means you have an extra responsibility when dealing with privileged documents.

Q. What's that?

A. You have to assume that privileged documents will someday be disclosed and act accordingly. Ask yourself, does this really have to be put in writing? And if the answer is yes, then ask yourself a second question: Do I have to state this in such an embarrassing or unflattering way? Assume one day every memorandum you write will appear on the front page of *The Wall Street Journal*. Then ask yourself whether you would be proud to have it revealed. If not, rewrite it and instruct your clients to write to you in the same cautious way.[165]

---

164. Great Hill Equity Partners IV, LP v. SIG Growth Equity Fund I, LLLP, 80 A.3d 155 (Del. Ch. 2013) (corporation that survives a merger maintains control of attorney-client privilege regarding negotiation communications prior to the merger agreement).

165. RLGL § 73 cmt. k.

PART THREE

Representing Clients

Lawyers and Clients: Fiduciary Duty

When you enter into a client-lawyer relationship, courts hold that you have expressly or impliedly agreed to carry on the matter to conclusion.[166] To do this, both agency law and the Rules of Professional Conduct (together, the law governing lawyers) recognize that you have assumed six fiduciary obligations (what we call the six Cs):

1. **C**lient identification (Chapters 2 through 8)
2. **C**ompetence (Chapter 10)[167]
3. Deference to **C**lient **C**ontrol over the goals of the representation (Chapter 11)[168]
4. **C**ommunication (Chapter 12)[169]
5. **C**onfidentiality (Chapters 13 and 14)[170]
6. **C**onflict-of-interest resolution (Chapter 15)[171]

These fiduciary duties originated and reside in agency law, forming the basis for similar requirements in the Model Rules of Professional

166. Maples v. Thomas, 565 U.S. 266 (2012) (lawyer who abandons client without notice severs principal-agent relationship; client cannot be charged with acts or omissions of such a lawyer); Disciplinary Counsel v. Hoff, 921 N.E.2d 636 (Ohio 2010) (lawyer indefinitely suspended for accepting $5,000 fee from client to resolve federal income tax deficiencies but failing to perform any work, including contacting the IRS, or refunding the fee).

167. MRs 1.1, 1.3; RLGL §§ 16(2), 48–54.

168. MR 1.2; RLGL §§ 21–23.

169. MR 1.4; RLGL § 20.

170. MRs 1.6, 1.8(b), 1.9; RLGL §§ 59–68.

171. MRs 1.7–1.12; RLGL §§ 121–135.

Conduct. They rest on a key agency insight about all client-lawyer relationships: client-principals empower and control lawyer-agents. The lawyer-agent's superior knowledge, skill, and experience can allow a lawyer to steer a course away from a client representation as defined by the client. To ensure that the client's best interests are respected, fiduciary duty imposes on the lawyer affirmative obligations of proper deference to client control, communication, competence, confidentiality, and conflict-of-interest resolution. When these duties are met, clients properly determine their own best interests within the bounds of the law. When they are breached, a lawyer usually has underidentified with a client's interests.

The key to understanding these foundational fiduciary duties is to remember that the law governing lawyers imposes an affirmative obligation on the lawyer to initiate all conversations about the six Cs. Failure to do so leaves the lawyer vulnerable to a myriad of remedies, including civil liability, fee forfeiture, disqualification, injunctive relief, constructive trusts, and professional discipline.[172]

172. RLGL § 6.

CHAPTER 9

Fees, Glorious Fees

§ 9.01 Introduction: Reasonable Limitations on Fee Contracts

The fiduciary duty you assume when agreeing to represent a client does not attach until the client-lawyer relationship is established. However, because clients often repose trust in lawyers before this official starting point (assuming that point is clear), Rules of Professional Conduct and cases (where judges set, supervise, or decide disputed fees) impose four different obligations that limit your ability to charge whatever you choose.

First, every fee agreement, every invoice for professional services, and every effort to collect fees and expenses is subject to an objective standard of reasonableness, measured by the range of reasonable fees other reasonable lawyers would charge for the same or similar representation.[173] Courts look to the same factors lawyers do: the time, labor, and skill involved; the fee customarily charged by similarly situated lawyers; the amount involved and results obtained; limitations put on a lawyer's time or acceptance of other employment; and the kind of fee, whether fixed, contingent, or hourly. With respect to disbursements and expenses, it is perfectly proper to agree in advance to the basis on which you will charge for such services (again, subject to the reasonableness standard). Absent such an explicit agreement, you may

173. MR 1.5(a); RLGL § 34.

bill only the actual cost of these expenses.[174] If you bill more, you have turned disbursements into a "profit center" in violation of Model Rule 1.5's reasonableness requirement.

If another lawyer would consider it unreasonable to charge the fee or expense you anticipate, that lawyer could be the source of expert testimony in a later disciplinary action or fee dispute should the client object. And client challenges to fee arrangements—whether warranted or not—are not rare.

Second, Rules of Professional Conduct and some statutes require special and specific writing obligations for many fee agreements. All contingent-fee arrangements, for example, require a written agreement,[175] and some jurisdictions regulate the amount of the contingency or require specific language in engagement agreements.[176] In a growing number of jurisdictions, as the chart in § 9.02 indicates, *all* fee contracts must be reduced to a written format.[177] Written fee agreements enable you to establish the basis for your fee as well as your disbursements and expenses. You can add that one of the obligations of the client, the breach of which might provide a basis for withdrawal, is that the client makes timely payment of fee bills rendered.

Third, in certain circumstances some fee contracts are not permitted at all. For example, most jurisdictions do not allow contingent fees in divorce or dissolution matters or in criminal cases. Nonrefundable "retainers" also may be banned completely.[178]

Fourth, because clients can fire lawyers at any time for any reason or no reason at all, most courts hold that when this occurs, lawyers lose their right to a contract fee and can recover only in quantum meruit.[179] You should reduce all fee agreements to a writing and keep track of billable hours in all representations. If you do not complete the matter, the burden of proof will be on you to establish the basis for quantum meruit, which a court may well decide should be measured by

174. ABA Comm. on Ethics & Prof'l Responsibility, Formal Op. 00-420 (2000) Surcharge to Client for Use of Contract Lawyer (If contract lawyer is billed as an expense, in absence of contrary understanding, the client may be charged only the direct cost of the lawyer. If contract lawyer is billed as legal services or fees, a surcharge may be added without client consent, as long as rate charged is reasonable.).

175. MR 1.5(c).

176. CAL. BUS. & PROF. CODE § 6146 (2019) (actions against health care providers); FLA. R. PROF'L CONDUCT 1.5(f) (2018); N.Y. JUD. LAW § 474-a (2018) (Contingent Fees in Medical, Dental and Podiatric Malpractice Actions).

177. *E.g.*, ALASKA R. PROF'L CONDUCT 1.5(b) (2009); COLO. R. PROF'L CONDUCT 1.5(b) (2019); CONN. R. PROF'L CONDUCT 1.5(b) (2019); D.C. R. PROF'L CONDUCT 1.5(b) (2015); N.J. R. PROF'L CONDUCT 1.5(b) (2018); PA. R. PROF'L CONDUCT 1.5(b) (2019); CAL. BUS. & PROF. CODE § 6148 (2018) (all fees over $1,000).

178. *E.g.*, COLO. R. PROF'L CONDUCT 1.5(g) (2019).

179. RLGL § 40.

the "lodestar" method: reasonable number of hours times a reasonable hourly rate. In some cases, the client purports to fire a lawyer "for cause." If this occurs and a court finds a clear and serious violation of professional duty, total or partial fee forfeiture also becomes a real possibility.[180]

§ 9.02 Chart: Written Fee Agreements Requirements by State

Jurisdiction	Contingent Fees	Other Fees
ABA Model Rules	1.5(c): Writing required	1.5(b): Writing preferred to communicate the scope of representation and the basis or rate of the fee and expenses for which the client will be responsible
Alabama	1.5(c): Writing required	1.5(b): Writing required
Alaska	1.5(c): Writing required	1.5(b): Writing consistent with Rule 1.4(c) required if fee >$1,000
Arizona	1.5(c): Writing required	1.5(b): Writing required
Arkansas	1.5(c): Writing required	1.5(b): Writing preferred
California	Cal. Bus. & Prof. Code § 6147: Writing required	Cal. Bus. & Prof. Code § 6148: Writing required if fee > $1,000 and client not a corporation
Colorado	1.5(c): Writing required	1.5(b): Writing required
Connecticut	1.5(c): Writing required	1.5(b): Writing required, except public defenders or when the lawyer will be paid by the court or a state agency
Delaware	1.5(c): Writing required	1.5(b): Writing preferred
District of Columbia	1.5(c): Writing required	1.5(b): Writing required
Florida	4-1.5(f): Writing required	4-1.5(e): Writing preferred
Georgia	1.5(c): Writing required	1.5(b): Writing preferred
Hawaii	1.5(c): Writing required	1.5(b): Writing preferred

180. *Id.* § 37.

Jurisdiction	Contingent Fees	Other Fees
Idaho	1.5(c): Writing required	1.5(b): Writing preferred
Illinois	1.5(c): Writing required	1.5(b): Writing preferred
Indiana	1.5(c): Writing required	1.5(b): Writing preferred
Iowa	1.5(c): Writing required	1.5(b): Writing preferred
Kansas	1.5(d): Writing required	1.5(b): Writing preferred
Kentucky	1.5(c): Writing required	1.5(b): Writing preferred
Louisiana	1.5(c): Writing required	1.5(b): Writing preferred
Maine	1.5(c): Writing required	1.5(b): Writing preferred
Maryland	1.5(c): Writing required	1.5(b): Writing preferred
Massachusetts	1.5(c): Writing required	1.5(b): Writing required if > $500
Michigan	1.5(c): Writing required	1.5(b): Writing preferred
Minnesota	1.5(c): Writing required	1.5(b): Writing preferred; required for non-refundable availability or special service retainers
Mississippi	1.5(c): Writing required	1.5(b): Writing preferred
Missouri	4-1.5(c): Writing required	4-1.5(b): Writing preferred
Montana	1.5(c): Writing required	1.5(b): Writing required if >$500
Nebraska	1.5(c): Writing required	1.5(b): Writing preferred
Nevada	1.5(c): Writing required	1.5(b): Writing preferred
New Hampshire	1.5(c): Writing required	1.5(b): Writing preferred
New Jersey	RPC 1.5(c): Writing required	RPC 1.5(b): Writing required
New Mexico	16-105(D): Writing required	16-105(B): Writing required

Jurisdiction	Contingent Fees	Other Fees
New York	1.5(c): Writing required	1.5(b): Writing required
North Carolina	1.5(c): Writing required	1.5(b): Writing preferred
North Dakota	1.5(c): Writing required	1.5(b): Writing preferred
Ohio	1.5(c): Writing required	1.5(b): Writing preferred
Oklahoma	1.5(c): Writing required	1.5(b): Writing preferred
Oregon	ORS § 20.340: Writing required for personal injury and property damage claims	1.5: No writing required
Pennsylvania	1.5(c): Writing required	1.5(b): Writing required
Rhode Island	1.5(c): Writing required	1.5(b): Writing required
South Carolina	1.5(c): Writing required	1.5(b): Writing preferred
South Dakota	1.5(c): Writing required	1.5(b): Writing preferred
Tennessee	1.5(c): Writing required	1.5(b): Writing preferred
Texas	1.04(d): Writing required	1.04(c): Writing preferred
Utah	1.5(c): Writing required	1.5(b): Writing preferred
Vermont	1.5(c): Writing required	1.5(b): Writing preferred
Virginia	1.5(c): Writing required	1.5(b): Writing preferred
Washington	1.5(c)(1): Writing required	1.5(b): Writing preferred; upon the request of the client in any matter, writing required
West Virginia	1.5(c): Writing required	1.5(b): Writing required
Wisconsin	20:1:5(c): Writing required	20:1.5(b): Writing required
Wyoming	1.5(c): Writing required	1.5(b): Writing preferred

§ 9.03 Reasonable Hourly Fees

Hourly fees should provide the client with an itemized basis for evaluating your service and mirror the way many lawyers work. But anyone who works at a law firm that depends on hourly fees knows there can be subtle and not so subtle pressures to bill hours. Like fee-for-service medicine, the more you do, the more you get paid. Although hourly fees certainly provide an incentive to cover all bases, exploitation of such an agreement can lead to unnecessary professional services. Your agreement to bill implicitly includes an agreement to bill only for hours actually spent on the matter. As one federal judge put it: "Billing for hours not worked is fraud."[181]

Though your engagement agreement provided the client would pay for every hour dedicated to the matter, your total fee also must yield a reasonable fee.[182] Best practice is to periodically check the entire bill and measure it against the reasonableness standard.

Accurate time records are important, even if you never intend to use them. You need to keep track of billable hours for at least four reasons:

1. If you charge on the basis of hours worked, you must be able to document what you have done.
2. If your client becomes a prevailing party entitled to statutory fees, judges often award a fee based on your lodestar (reasonable hourly rate times reasonable number of hours actually worked).
3. If you win a sanctions motion, you must be able to document the time spent on the matter caused by the sanctionable conduct.
4. If your client fires you, you lose your contract rights and can recover only for quantum meruit, where you bear the burden of establishing the amount to which you are entitled, a task made far easier if you can identify the services you performed and know the number of hours you worked.

---

181. Kelly v. Hunton & Williams, No. 97-CV-5631JG, 1999 WL 759972 (E.D.N.Y. Sept. 21, 1999).

182. MR 1.5(a); RLGL § 34; *In re* Fordham, 668 N.E.2d 816 (Mass. 1996) (lawyer disciplined for accurately charging client $50,000 for 227 hours of billed time in obtaining an acquittal on a drunk driving charge, based on expert testimony that a reasonable lawyer would charge no more than 40 billable hours).

§ 9.04 Calculating and Charging Hourly Fees

The Honest Hour

Q. At least once a decade there are declarations that the billable hour is dead. But that method of billing clients persists. Few clients recall that it was their general counsel who invented the idea. They wanted more accountability and an end to the use of "For professional services" billing with a number picked out of thin air. They wanted descriptions; time kept in tenths of an hour, making almost every lawyer in America a liar. Keep time in tenths and that's all you do all day. Anyway, we're stuck with that billing method, so we'd better focus on the ethics of the arrangement. The problem is there are only so many hours in the week. But we've come up with some creative ideas to improve our billables.

A. Why? Are we worried?

Q. No. No. This is all legitimate. Our lawyers spend their lives traveling around the country. That's the bad news. But the good news is most of our clients let us bill travel time. As they should. If we have to be in Los Angeles for a deposition, it's not our fault it takes us eight hours or more to get there.

A. You are right. There is nothing wrong with billing for travel time.

Q. That's good news. You see, we've told all our lawyers that unless there's an emergency, they should work on a different client's matter as they travel. That way they can turn a six-hour trip into 12 billable hours. The first client gets its lawyer where the client wants him to appear. The second gets six hours of uninterrupted time dedicated to the second client's work.

A. Modern alchemy. What an accomplishment. I suppose you've told the clients what you are doing.

Q. Of course not. Why should we? The first client would pay for the travel time if our lawyer slept, watched a movie, or had two martinis. The second gets quality time. What's to disclose?

A. Because double billing, unless approved by the client, is a fraud. A fraud on your clients. If you have the temerity to tell the affected clients what you are doing, it may be acceptable. So, if you got an explicit agreement up front, you have a few more hours to yourself to relax this month. But absent that, the ethics opinions prohibit such clever accounting.[183]

---

183. ABA Comm. on Ethics & Prof'l Responsibility, Formal Op. 93-379 (1993) Billing for Professional Fees, Disbursements and Other Expenses; Cal. Formal Op. 1996-147. *See also* William G. Ross, The Honest Hour: The Ethics of Time-Based Billing by Attorneys (1996).

Q. Well, what if we're traveling for client A and our lawyer works on a pro bono matter when she could be sleeping. Can she bill the paying client for that time?

A. This is a much closer question. After all, you are not double billing. The pro bono matter is more like reading a book.

Q. I guess you won't like our other ideas. When we have to go to motion court for multiple clients, we were going to charge each client for the full time spent at the courthouse. And if we recycle old work product, we were going to bill the second client the same amount we billed the first.

A. Clever. Real clever. But impermissible. When we tell clients we are going to bill the time dedicated to the matter, we'd better do just that. If you are in court six hours for three clients you better do some simple division, not multiplication, to determine the amount each is to be billed. And when our client is fortunate enough to benefit from our storehouse of knowledge, we do not do a qualitative review of the time spent with the idea of increasing our billable hours. The economies generated by our prior experience must be passed on to the client, not upwardly adjusted to the number of hours it would have taken if we didn't have the perfect memorandum of law already in our database courtesy of our efforts on behalf of an earlier client.[184]

§ 9.05 Disbursements

Contract Lawyers as Profit Centers

Q. We got this huge case for Excelsior. It is an electronic discovery dream, that is, tens of thousands of documents that have

184. Updike, Kelly & Spellacy, P.C. v. Beckett, 850 A.2d 145 (Conn. 2004) (clients stated cause of action for misrepresentation against lawyers who grossly underestimated amount of lawyer's hourly fee and never adjusted initial estimate when it became clear it was no longer valid); *In re* Myers, 127 P.3d 325 (Kan. 2006) (lawyer censured for regularly rounding up ¾-hour increments to 1 hour for billing purposes; unreasonable to bill in one hour increments for work not performed); *In re* Hellerud, 714 N.W.2d 38 (N.D. 2006) (lawyer who billed $15,000 in hourly fees for an estate totaling $65,000, charging the same rate for his own time and that of his legal assistant, reprimanded and subject to partial fee disgorgement for charging both an unreasonable rate and an unreasonable number of hours despite probate court's approval of fees); Disciplinary Counsel v. Johnson, 835 N.E.2d 354 (Ohio 2005) (lawyer suspended for one year despite acquittal on criminal charges for often appearing in juvenile court on behalf of two or more clients at the same time and failing to apportion billing, charging clearly excessive fees ranging from a total of 14 to 33 hours per day); *In re* Paulson, 71 P.3d 60 (Or. 2003) (lawyer publicly reprimanded for charging an excessive fee for billing former client $67.50 for time spent answering former client's complaint about her conduct to the bar; lawyer performed the work but not for the benefit of the client); *In re* Dorothy, 605 N.W.2d 493 (S.D. 2000) (lawyer publicly censured for charging client a total hourly fee of $62,000 and collecting $47,000 by complicating and extending child custody proceedings).

to be reviewed. Frankly, we cannot handle the workload in the time allowed, so we hired temporary lawyers to assist us. They are doing a fine job, but now it is time to send our first bill to the client. One of our partners says we can only bill the exact amount the agency is charging us for these lawyers. I say we can mark that number up so that we make a little profit on these folks. Who is correct?

A. You both are. There are some opinions that say this is like any other disbursement, and you cannot make a profit on the expenditure. But others recognize that (1) you are supervising these folks, and (2) you are responsible for their work, even if they are temporary employees. Their misdeeds become your liability. The majority view is with you. As long as the surcharge is disclosed and reasonable, you should have no trouble defending it, that is, unless there is contrary authority in your jurisdiction.[185]

Q. Well, how about things like photocopying? Do we have to charge the client no more than our exact cost?

A. ABA Opinion 93-379 says that so long as you disclose the amounts that you charge your clients for things like photocopying and that charge is reasonable it does not have to be the exact cost. But it has to be fully disclosed. Otherwise, if there is no disclosure, then you must charge based on the actual cost as calculated by a cost accountant which might include some small amount of overhead for copying a page. One more thing.

Q. What's that?

A. When you are contracting with outside services whose cost you are going to pass on to the client, you are permitted to help the client choose a provider and even recommend a preferred provider. But the client must be told in advance that you are going to incur this expense and should be given an opportunity to decide how the client wishes to proceed. And whatever you do, do not accept any rebates from the service provider without passing that savings back to the client. Similarly, do not cause the client to hire an ancillary business of your law firm (e.g., lobbying or public relations) without full disclosure and an opportunity for the client to consider other vendors for

---

185. ABA Comm. on Ethics & Prof'l Responsibility, Formal Op. 00-420 (2000) Surcharge to Client for Use of a Contract Lawyer (If the contract lawyer's charge is billed as an expense, absent an understanding to the contrary, the client may be charged only the direct cost of the contract lawyer's services. If contract lawyer services are billed as legal fees, the amount charged is governed by MR 1.5(a)'s reasonableness requirement, which could include a surcharge as long as client is informed and the total charge represents a reasonable fee.).

the services involved. A lawyer's stock in trade is lawyering, not making money on ordering tuna fish sandwiches.[186]

§ 9.06 Reasonable Contingent Fees

Contingent fees offer clients risk-free access to the courthouse. They are allowed in a vast number of situations as long as the client has been advised of alternative fee options and there is some genuine risk of non-recovery.[187] Some contingent-fee agreements are blended with other fees, such as an hourly fee up to a certain amount combined with a contingent fee above a specified recovery amount.

Generally, contingent fees align the interests of the lawyer with those of the client. As the client's recovery goes up, so does the lawyer's. You also may reasonably charge a contingent fee when no real risk of non-recovery exists, but only so long as your efforts bring value to the client, such as when the question of the *amount* of recovery is subject to a good faith dispute.[188]

Courts and the Rules of Professional Conduct nevertheless recognize conflicts of interest inherent in contingent fees with several clear provisions. First, contingent fees are prohibited in several circumstances,

---

186. *In re* Wright, 290 B.R. 145 (Bankr. C.D. Cal. 2003) (under FED. R. BANKR. P. 2016(a), law firm for Chapter 13 debtors not allowed to recover fees paid to a contract lawyer as fees or expenses unless debtors agreed to the use and billing rate of the contract lawyer); *In re* Green, 11 P.3d 1078 (Colo. 2000) (en banc) (lawyer publicly censured for seeking an unreasonable fee as a matter of law by charging hourly rate for faxing documents, calling the court clerk's office, and delivering documents to opposing counsel); Guerrant v. Roth, 777 N.E.2d 499 (Ill. App. Ct. 2002) (computer research expenses were not separately recoverable as cost or out-of-pocket expense pursuant to contingent-fee contract, but must be included as part of the attorney fee award); *In re* Guste, 118 So. 3d 1023 (La. 2012) (lawyer suspended for two years for, after completing legal work, continuing to charge regular rate for personal services such as running errands for client).

187. *In re* Sulzer Hip Prosthesis & Knee Prosthesis Liab. Litig., 290 F. Supp. 2d 840 (N.D. Ohio 2003) (contingent-fee agreements unenforceable when entered into with plaintiff class members after both sides had signed memorandum outlining full settlement because there was no significant risk of nonrecovery); *In re* Merry-Go-Round Enters., Inc., 244 B.R. 327, 334 (Bankr. D. Md. 2000) (40 percent preapproved contingent fee that resulted in $71.2 million to lawyers reasonable because case was "imaginatively conceived, skillfully staged, thoroughly prepared, aggressively pursued, and timely and successfully resolved for the great benefit" of the bankrupt estate, even though contingent fee was 20 times hourly fee in the case); Anderson v. Kenelly, 547 P.2d 260 (Colo. App. 1975) (contingent-fee contract unreasonable and unconscionable where little skill or effort was required to obtain correct information that resulted in immediate payment of life insurance proceeds); Attorney Grievance Comm'n v. Ashworth, 851 A.2d 527 (Md. 2004) (25 percent contingent fee not unreasonable even though matter settled within days because lawyers with excellent skills and reputations often can expend less time and effort to obtain satisfactory results).

188. *In re* Powell, 953 N.E.2d 1060 (Ind. 2011) (lawyer suspended for 120 days for collecting contingent fee, despite arguable reasonable belief that the matter or amount would be contested at the outset, because lawyer learned within a few days that neither was in dispute and took advantage of the emotional vulnerability of his client); ABA Comm. on Ethics & Prof'l Responsibility, Formal Op. 94-389 (1994) Contingent Fees.

essentially because the conflict is deemed uncontestable. In domestic relations matters, the clients must feel free to reconcile, so you are not allowed to take on such matters on a contingency. On the other hand, once the divorce or dissolution occurs, some courts distinguish collection of past-due child support and allow contingent fees in those matters.[189]

Contingent fees are prohibited in criminal matters for the reason that no res exists from which to determine the fee. Inventive lawyers who wish to charge negative or reverse contingent fees, such as $X for each year or month saved from a potential sentence, have been disciplined for violating this rule. The risk of overestimating the potential penalty to a client in desperate circumstances is simply too great.[190] On the other hand, reverse contingent fees outside of criminal practice, where client and lawyer reasonably base the fee on a realistic exposure to liability, are consistent with the Model Rules.[191]

Second, regardless of whether a jurisdiction requires all fee contracts to be in writing, all jurisdictions require contingent-fee contracts to be in writing to fully communicate to the client the nature of the fee and its collection.[192] Some jurisdictions require extensive disclaimers and regulate the percentage of the contingent fee as well, often stipulating that the percentage should go down as the recovery increases,[193] though it is totally ethical in most jurisdictions to have the percentage go up as the recovery increases on the theory that the last dollar is the hardest

189. MR 1.5(d)(1); RLGL § 38(1)(b); King v. Young, Berkman, Berman & Karpf, P.A., 709 So. 2d 572 (Fla. Dist. Ct. App. 1998) ("bonus" fee provision in hourly fee contract in divorce case void because contingent on securing the divorce; bonus provision also renders entire fee contract unenforceable).

190. MR 1.5(d)(2); RLGL § 38 (1)(a).

191. ABA Comm. on Ethics & Prof'l Responsibility, Formal Op. 93-373 (1993) Contingent Fees in Civil Cases Based on the Amount of Money Saved for the Client.

192. United States v. 36.06 Acres of Land, 70 F. Supp. 2d 1272 (D.N.M. 1999) (oral contingent-fee contract not enforceable due to unclean hands for failure to obtain a written agreement but lawyers could recover in quantum meruit with appropriate reduction for withdrawal in the middle of the case); Gagne v. Vaccaro, 766 A.2d 416 (Conn. 2001) (oral contingent-fee contract not enforceable, but lawyer may be able to recover for unjust enrichment); Schumacher Law Corp. v. Taylor, 667 So. 2d 1121 (La. Ct. App. 1995) (contingent-fee contract unenforceable because not clearly explained to client and because the contract failed to distinguish in writing the personal injury contingency fee from the domestic relations hourly fee).

193. *See, e.g.*, Fla. R. Prof'l Conduct 1.5(f) (2018), N.J. Ct. R. 1:21-7 (2009). Some states also require a closing statement that regulates the actual calculation of the contingent fee. *See, e.g.*, Ohio Rev. Code § 4705.15 (2015).

to recover.[194] Agreeing to or charging more than this regulated amount violates the reasonableness standard of Model Rule 1.5.[195]

Third, issues regarding settlement also produce potential conflicts of interest. Sometimes the client will insist on going to trial when the lawyer believes that is imprudent; sometimes the client will want to snare an early low-ball settlement offer as a sure thing when the lawyer's best judgment is that the client should take the matter to trial to achieve a fair recovery. Though there is no perfect remedy when such a conflict occurs, you must be mindful that the decision to settle or go to trial is the client's, and, therefore, although you owe the client your best advice, you must avoid overreaching by disclosing your competing interest.[196]

Accordingly, every settlement offer must be relayed to your client, and every settlement decision is the client's. If you have a different point of view, especially one colored by your need for a certain payoff now or later, you must explain that view to the client under the rubric of "conflict of interest." Failure to identify your conflicting interest could be grounds for an allegation of breach of fiduciary duty, which, if found, could suffice to support total or partial forfeiture of your fee.[197]

Finally, before you collect your fee, be sure to provide an accounting at the end of the representation. Some jurisdictions require a specific form or regulate how you calculate the contingency. The general rule provides that unless your contract specifies otherwise, you are not entitled to a percentage of items not generally considered damages, such as costs and attorney's fees, and the amount of the client's recovery should be computed "net of any offset, such as a recovery by an opposing party on a counterclaim."[198]

---

194. Alioto v. Hoiles, 531 F. App'x 842 (10th Cir. 2013) (lawyer's $16 million contingent fee reduced to quantum meruit $1 million due to absence of a statutorily required statement in fee contract that rendered contract voidable); Am. Home Assurance Co. v. Golomb, 606 N.E.2d 793 (Ill. App. Ct. 1992) (fee contract that exceeded maximum contingent fee allowed under state statute void; quantum meruit recovery also barred because lawyer engaged in illegal conduct).

195. ABA Comm. on Ethics & Prof'l Responsibility, Formal Op. 94-389 (1994) Contingent Fees.

196. Lofton v. Fairmont Specialty Ins. Managers, Inc., 367 S.W.3d 593 (Ky. 2012) (lawyer who withdrew from representation because he disagreed with client about settlement value of the case forfeited all right to contingent fee; good cause for withdrawal does not equate with good cause for quantum meruit recovery).

197. RLGL § 37.

198. *Id.* § 35 cmt. d.

§ 9.07 Contingent-Fee Look Backs

20-20 Hindsight

Q. I knew we should've never taken that contingent-fee case. But we were all so envious of the incomes of those trial lawyers. We sell hours and there are only so many of them in a year. But contingent fees can give you some real punch.

Anyway, Colossus had this claim against Progressive. Progressive supplied a new production line for Colossus' engine business. But the line was 18 months late and never met the contractual requirement to manufacture 200 engines per day; not even close.

Colossus claimed damages of $50 million including lost profits, lost contracts with its customers, and retrofitting the line to meet its needs. Asked us if we would take the case on a contingent fee. We asked to be paid our hourly rate to investigate the merit of the claim. Our conclusion: risky (Progressive would argue they built it to Colossus's design) but worth a try. We offered to handle the case for one-third if settled before trial, 40 percent if we had to try it. Colossus to pay all expenses and disbursements.

A. And you lost?

Q. Hell no. We settled on the eve of trial for $60 million. The client was thrilled. I remember them saying when we agreed to take the case how happy they'd be if they got a chance to pay us $4 million. Now they have an opportunity to pay us almost $20 million.

A. What could be wrong?

Q. They're refusing to pay us anything. Say the fee is unreasonable, unethical.

A. Such gratitude.

Q. You have no idea how askance our partners looked at the three of us who wanted to take the case as we logged thousands of hours, uncompensated hours. They even cut my compensation last year. And now it's even worse. The joy of victory has turned into the agony of defeat. You think they are right?

A. Well, what are they arguing?

Q. First, they say if they paid us the contract fee it would work out to thousands an hour.

A. That should be irrelevant. A contingent-fee agreement pays for results. The idea behind the arrangement is to align the interests of the lawyer with that of the client. Instead of the client worrying about how many hours the lawyer is dedicating to that matter, overstaffing, too many depositions, the client knows that the lawyer will take all steps necessary to maximize the recovery for both client and lawyer. Think of it this way. Which client is better off? The one whose lawyer spent 50 hours and got the client $1 million or the lawyer who spent 500 hours and got the client $500,000?

Q. That's what I told them. But they came back and said we should have capped our fees. No more than $5 million regardless of recovery.

A. Well, the rules of our profession certainly don't require that. And why would a client want a contingent fee capped? Certainly removes the lawyer's incentive to put in extra time and energy just when they might be rewarded.

Q. Then they argue that we were required to have the percentage of our fee go down as the recovery went up.

A. That idea is as crazy as a fee cap. In fact, it's upside down. Take your case. You could probably have settled it early for a million dollars. That recovery would represent low hanging fruit. Indeed, the client might've gotten that amount without a lawyer.

But getting $60 million; that represents a real accomplishment. And you should get particularly well-earned kudos (and a higher percentage) for the last $10 million the client received. The ABA Standing Committee on Ethics and Professional Responsibility has unanimously endorsed a sliding scale where the percentage increases as the recovery to the client goes up.[199]

Q. But they say when we entered into the agreement, we had a fiduciary duty to make the fee lower for our long-time client and make sure the client got independent representation to advise the client regarding the fee.

A. First, lawyers are not fiduciaries when it comes to fee arrangements. The ethical obligation is to neither charge nor collect an unreasonable fee. And a one-third contingent fee, depending on when the case ends, is certainly consistent with the standard in the profession. Second, there is no authority we know of that requires the lawyer to recommend, let alone require, the client to retain another lawyer.

199. ABA Comm. on Ethics & Prof'l Responsibility, Formal Op. 94-389 (1994) Contingent Fees.

Q. Well, they said when we entered into a contingent fee it was a case of the lawyer doing business with the client. Something about Rule 1.8(a).

A. It is true that Rule 1.8(a) gives special requirements for when a lawyer enters into a business relationship with the lawyer's client. And that rule requires the arrangement be in writing, the client be urged to consult another lawyer, and the transaction must pass muster as entirely fair to the client. The rule would apply in the fee context if the lawyer took a lien on the client's property to secure payment of a fee.[200] Or if the lawyer agreed to be paid in the client's stock. But contingent-fee agreements are governed by Rule 1.5 and other than the charging of a reasonable rate, the only other requirement is that the fee agreement be in writing, as we are sure yours was.[201]

Q. Absolutely. Next, they say it was improper for us to charge them a contingent fee since they could've afforded to pay us on an hourly basis.

A. Again, Colossus is wrong. It is true contingent fees have been a boon to those who couldn't get into court any other way. The contingent fee is pure genius in that respect. But that does not mean the wealthiest corporations cannot take advantage of the benefits of a contingent fee.

Q. That's what we thought when we took the case. I remember explaining to the CFO how there would be no more auditing of our bills. There would be no bills at all, except for disbursements. And how our interests and theirs were perfectly aligned. Most important, I told him how this arrangement would help his cash flow concerns, which he told me were quite serious at the time. Thinking back on that reminds me of another of their objections.

A. What's that?

Q. They say if we were going to charge a contingent fee, our firm should have paid all these expenses—more than $1 million—and that we ran up too much in disbursements.

---

200. Van Horn v. Van Horn, 2 A.3d 401 (N.J. Super. Ct. App. Div. 2010) (disqualification not a proper remedy for opposing party who alleges that lawyer violated Rule 1.8(a) by taking mortgage in opponent's house to secure lawyer's fee; client could seek invalidation of transaction or discipline, if appropriate); Cotton v. Kronenberg, 44 P.3d 878 (Wash. Ct. App. 2002) (lawyer disqualified from the case and liable for breach of fiduciary duty, ordered to fully disgorge fee, and potentially liable under state consumer protection act for accepting conveyance of client's property in lieu of a fee in a criminal defense case).

201. MR 1.8(a) & cmt. [1].

A. The only way you could've gotten into trouble is if you had paid those expenses. The rules are clear: Lawyers may advance that money for the impecunious client, but at the end of the day, the client must be responsible for those disbursements. Is that it?

Q. No. Sadly, they have more. They argue that when we took the case on a contingency, we already had two expert opinions that attributed the failure to Progressive. And they remember one of our lawyers saying this was a very solid case. Under those circumstances, they say a one-third fee was way too high for what was essentially a no-risk case.

A. Hindsight is 20-20. We are sure your experts were going to be matched, expert for expert, by the other side.

Q. Of course. Our experts said it was Progressive's fault. We wouldn't have brought the case if we hadn't lined them up. But the other side got this professor from MIT and a retired engineer from Boeing. They blamed Colossus. And we did tell the client it was a solid case. But that hardly meant it was a lay down. Or anything close to that.

A. That's just the beginning of the risks you undertook. Just think about it. First, the client can drop the case at any time and for any reason. Second, the client controls settlement entirely and can settle for a nominal sum or some non-monetary term that might not be contemplated by your contingent-fee agreement. Third, the client can fire the lawyer at any time for no reason at all. Fourth, how many times have clients not told you everything you need to know or misremembered some initial facts of the case? Fifth, there is always the risk of a change in the law that wipes out your client's claim or dramatically diminishes the potential damages that can be achieved. Sixth, every real trial lawyer has won cases she should have lost or lost cases she should have won. No matter how strong one thinks one's client's matter is, that is no guarantee that the case will be won or, if won, will result in the hoped-for damage award. Seventh, some of the biggest trial victories have been lost on appeal. Indeed, really large verdicts are clearly subject to special scrutiny and if the appeal results in a new trial, the contingent-fee lawyer will be required to retry the case, an obligation that must be fulfilled even as the chance of a successful result seems to diminish materially.

Q. The way you put it, it's a wonder we took the case at all.

A. That is true. Our experience suggests that contingent-fee practice is not for the faint of heart. And the firm that dabbles in contingent-fee litigation runs real risks because such firms do not have enough contingent-fee cases to compensate for the risks inherent in each case. We guess that describes your firm.

Q. I'll say. But the one risk we never thought of was the one we face now. Who thought Colossus would renege on our deal?

A. We're sure you didn't. And as a public policy matter, let us hope they do not succeed. The reasonableness of contingent-fee agreements should be judged at the outset, but Rule 1.5 has been amended to assess reasonableness at the time of collection of the fee as well.

If the risk at the time was fairly reflected in the arrangement, the fact that the result turns out to award the law firm a huge fee, maybe an "hourly rate" in four figures, ought to be something that is celebrated. If not, if we are going to allow a look-back in every contingent-fee case, if a court or jury is going to reset the fee after expensive look back litigation, then the genius of the contingent fee will be destroyed. Lawyers willing to take on a contingent-fee matter will add ten or more points to the percentage charged to reflect yet one more very serious risk, the risk that perversely increases as the lawyer's success on behalf of the client improves.

Q. Are you telling us that a one-third contingent fee will always pass muster, what with all those risk factors?

A. Generally, that is the case. But there are exceptions.[202] For example, charging a client a contingency fee when the client's claim is certain to succeed. Think of a lawyer preying on estate beneficiaries who will receive the deceased's bequest without the help of a lawyer. Similarly, if a client has a claim against an entity that always settles early and for large sums, charging 30 percent may not reflect the level of contingency. On the other hand, even if the putative defendant has conceded liability, this does not mean a full contingent fee would not be appropriate if causation and/or damages are contested and there is real risk that a substantial damage recovery can be secured.

---

202. *In re* Powell, 953 N.E.2d 1060 (Ind. 2011) (lawyer suspended for 120 days for collecting contingent fee, despite arguable reasonable belief that the matter or amount would be contested at the outset, because lawyer learned within a few days that neither was in dispute and took advantage of the emotional vulnerability of his client); Okla. Bar Ass'n v. Flaniken, 85 P.3d 824 (Okla. 2004) (one-third contingent fee from probate estate not unreasonable despite the fact that an anticipated will challenge never occurred; court rejects proposed hindsight test where a lawyer has otherwise lawfully contracted for a percentage of a client's recovery).

§ 9.08 Reverse Contingent Fees

Avoiding the Billable Hour

Q. All this discussion of how risky our contingent-fee case really was gives me an idea. As you note, we do mostly defense work. Save our clients a bundle with our no holds barred litigation style. If those damn plaintiffs are going to whip us, they will have to work hard for it. But our clients are always grousing about our hourly rates. And how many of our lawyers attend depositions or meetings. Claim our only goal is to run up the hours. Not true, but that's what they think. What if we took their cases on a reverse contingent fee? They get sued for $50 million to be trebled. We agree to handle the case for one-third of anything they save from $150 million. Our fortunes are tied to theirs and we have no obligation to keep time records, let alone hear carping about our staffing decisions.

A. Pretty good idea. Reverse contingent fees are ethically proper. The ABA Standing Committee wrote several opinions endorsing them.[203] And many Fortune 500 companies have experimented with that approach. They are not free from ethical concerns, however.

Q. Why is that?

A. Well, first, the benchmark has to be set fairly. Just because a client is sued for 500 mil doesn't mean that should be the number from which the fee is calculated. In the best of all worlds, you would have an in-house counsel or another lawyer represent the client in helping to select the number. That way no one argues later that you overstated the client's risk.

Q. Is that all?

A. Not really. It may be that the standard percentages used for regular contingent fees should not be employed here. Again, without knowing more about the underlying case it's hard to judge what would be reasonable. The profession doesn't have enough experience with reverse contingent fees to conclude that numbers in the range of 25 to 40 percent will automatically be viewed as

203. ABA Comm. on Ethics & Prof'l Responsibility, Formal Op. 94-389 (1994) Contingent Fees; ABA Comm. on Ethics & Prof'l Responsibility, Formal Op. 93-373 (1993) Contingent Fees in Civil Cases Based on the Amount of Money Saved for the Client.

reasonable. But don't let that deter you. Using such fee arrangements could provide you with a bevy of happy clients.[204]

§ 9.09 Reasonable Fixed Fees

Fixed or flat fees offer your client certainty about cost but create a perverse incentive. Like managed care, you get more the less you do, subject only to the threat of malpractice. To make sure your fixed fee is reasonable, think about the other lawyers in your jurisdiction. Would they charge that much? That little? If you estimate a fixed fee on the basis of your experience with other similar cases, using it as a kind of average fee, you have the right idea. If you intend to undercut the competition, you may risk a charge of incompetence or unreasonable interference with your professional judgment in violation of Model Rule 5.4(c) if the compensation is not adequate to ensure competent representation. To prevent such an abuse, some jurisdictions prohibit fixed fees for insurance defense work.[205] Remember, you can blend a fixed fee with another fee, such as an hourly rate. Many clients will be willing to pay an hourly fee but want the assurance of a fixed-fee ceiling.

One last caveat: There is no such thing as a nonrefundable fixed fee. A client who decides to fire you the day after hiring you is entitled to a refund of the portion of the fee you have not yet earned. And if some unforeseen circumstance occurs, like a complaining witness in a criminal case retracts her testimony, causing the charges to be dropped the next day, you also may owe your client a refund, because the total fee you charged has now become unreasonable.[206]

---

204. Brown & Sturm v. Frederick Rd. Ltd. P'ship, 768 A.2d 62 (Md. Ct. Spec. App. 2001) (reverse contingent fee contracts are permissible, but lawyers' use of their dominant position to take advantage of clients renders contract unenforceable).

205. Am. Ins. Ass'n v. Ky. Bar Ass'n, 917 S.W.2d 568 (Ky. 1996).

206. *In re* Sather, 3 P.3d 403 (Colo. 2000) (lawyer disciplined for failing to return unearned portion of client's flat fee and for falsely labeling it as a "non-refundable"); *In re* Kutner, 399 N.E.2d 963 (Ill. 1979) (lawyer disciplined for charging $5,000 flat fee for defense of criminal battery case where complainant asked judge one week later to drop charges and case was dismissed); Columbus Bar Ass'n v. Halliburton-Cohen, 832 N.E.2d 42, 43 (Ohio 2005) (lawyer charged clearly excessive fee to divorce client by charging a "lost opportunity" non-refundable retainer because lawyer was already barred from representing others in the case and she did not agree to be available for any future representation; excessive fee combined with failure to refund unearned portion resulted in six months suspension).

§ 9.10 Limits on Fixed Fees

Flat-Fee Insurance Defense

Q. Clients always want us to work on a fixed fee. But every time we've tried it, we've been burned. No matter how many contingencies we try to factor into our estimate, the litigation always takes longer and uses more lawyer hours than we estimated. But now we have an offer from an insurance company. They want us to take more than 100 files. And pay us $10,000 per file. Flat fee. One million bucks. Sure is tempting. But somehow, it doesn't seem right.

A. Your instincts are correct. In the context of insurance defense—an insurance company having a lawyer to defend its insureds—you have to remember that the insured is either your only or your primary client. You cannot let the entity that pays you interfere with your professional independence. The question is whether the amount you are being paid per case is so small in relation to some or all of the cases assigned to your firm that the likelihood is that you cannot provide effective counsel. If so, then you must reject the arrangement. In fact, in some states fixed fees in this situation are per se impermissible.[207]

§ 9.11 Fee Splitting

Earning That Referral Fee

Q. We are a corporate law firm. And we never get involved in anything that looks like personal injury, unless it is on the defense side. Sadly, the CEO of one of our clients was in an automobile accident. She suffered pretty severe injuries and huge medical bills, and the other driver was speeding. So, she asked us if we could handle her case. We told her that would be malpractice. But we did recommend a wonderful firm. At the time of the referral, the plaintiff's personal injury firm agreed to pay us a referral fee of 25 percent.

---

207. Am. Ins. v. Ky. Bar Ass'n, 917 S.W.2d 568, 572 (Ky. 1996) ("[P]ressures exerted by the insurer through the set fee interferes with the exercise of the attorney's independent professional judgment . . . quite simply, in easy cases, counsel will take a financial windfall; in difficult cases, counsel will take a financial loss."); Fla. Ethics Op. 98-2 (collecting authorities); Utah Ethics Op. 02-03 (2002) (flat-fee arrangements are not per se prohibited for insurance defense lawyers, but lawyer may not permit insurer's directive to interfere with lawyer's independent professional judgment).

A. Sounds terrific!

Q. Well, it would be, but when we went to collect the referral fee—$875,000—the referring firm balked, pointing out there was no written agreement, something about fee-sharing arrangements having to be in writing. Can that be correct?

A. Virtually every jurisdiction requires fee-sharing agreements to be in writing. They also require various levels of disclosure and approval by the clients. Finally, many jurisdictions insist that the firm share full responsibility for the case in order to receive a referral fee. We don't know what the situation is in your state. But a careful review of Rule 1.5 (e) will help you.

Q. But we have nothing in writing.

A. We understand. In some jurisdictions you nevertheless can collect the fee; in others you would have lost the fee by not following the protocol set forth in the rule. This will require some research on your part. Find out where your state stands in terms of exact requirements and then determine whether the courts in your state are willing to give you some or all of the referral fee, even though it was not in writing. A lot will depend on how your original client responds when it becomes known that you failed to fulfill the requirements of Rule 1.5 (e).[208]

§ 9.12 Changing Fee Agreements

Owning the Store

Q. Our client has this great claim. So good our firm agreed to take it on a contingency. Little did we think we'd be victims of a hometown verdict for the defense that looked with scorn on our overpaid New York investment-banker clients.

---

208. Wagner & Wagner LLP v. Atkinson, Haskins, Nellis, Brittingham, Gladd & Carwile PC, 596 F.3d 84 (2d Cir. 2010) (fee division agreement that violated N.Y. ethics rule invalid; court ordered share of fees to injured child); Eng v. Cummings, McClorey, Davis & Acho PLC, 611 F.3d 428 (8th Cir. 2010) (lack of writing in fee-sharing agreement renders any division unenforceable); Chambers v. Kay, 56 P.3d 645 (Cal. 2002) (referral fee agreement that did not comply with Rules of Professional Conduct void and quantum meruit not allowed); Saggese v. Kelley, 837 N.E.2d 699 (Mass. 2005) (oral agreement to split fee enforceable against lawyer where client consents because 1.5(e) intended to protect clients, not lawyers; in future cases, referring lawyer must disclose fee split to client in writing and lawyer to whom referral is made should confirm client consent); N.Y. State Bar Ass'n Op. 745 (2001) (lawyer who is disqualified due to a nonconsentable conflict of interest may not collect a referral fee; a lawyer disqualified due to a consentable conflict who refers the matter to another lawyer may collect a referral fee).

A. One of the risks.
Q. That's true. But the good news is the judge's charge was filled with error. We've got great issues on appeal.
A. Good luck.
Q. Not so fast. Our contingent-fee agreement only requires us to work through trial and post-trial motions. And my partners think I should do some billable-hour work for a change. But what I thought was I'd tell our client we'd stay with the contingent fee, but up the percentage to 60 percent. Since they are ready to walk away, I think they'll take the deal.
A. Your reasoning might be sound, but we urge extreme caution. Rule 1.8(i) provides that a lawyer shall not acquire a proprietary interest in a cause of action. The rule is designed to prevent the client from losing control of the claim. The rule does contain an exception for "a reasonable contingent fee."
Q. This one is certainly that. The risk is that high.
A. It may be a fair measure of the risk. And your clients are grown-ups. But 60 percent looks like the lawyers, not the client, will be in control. And remember, Rule 1.5(a) and many courts give the client a "look-back" and if you win and seek 60 percent of the recovery as a fee, you will certainly be vulnerable to a "look-back" and subject to a disciplinary complaint as well.

§ 9.13 Fee Modification

You've taken on a client, provided a written fee agreement, and one or both of you want to modify the fee. At this point, you have assumed the six Cs, so you have taken on fiduciary obligations, which require that you protect your client with a fair and reasonable modification of the original agreement. If you do not, you will be unable to rely on the modification because courts presume undue influence when examining changes made to client-lawyer contracts, including fee agreements, when made much after the lawyer has begun the representation.[209] You can rebut such a presumption only by showing a combination of these

209. RLGL §§ 18(1)(a), 38(2); *In re* Thayer, 745 N.E.2d 207 (Ind. 2001) (lawyer suspended for 30 days for, after settlement of the case, presenting client with a higher contingency fee than initially agreed to); Ky. Bar Ass'n v. Basinger, 53 S.W.3d 92 (Ky. 2001) (lawyer suspended for 60 days for agreeing to hourly fee and attempting to charge contingent fee); *In re* Curry, 16 So. 3d 1139 (La. 2009) (lawyer suspended for six months for modifying firm's fee agreement with client during ongoing litigation in ways that favored firm's interest violated Rule 1.8(a)); Brown & Sturm v. Frederick Rd. Ltd. P'ship, 768 A.2d 62 (Md. Ct. Spec. App. 2001) (reverse contingent fee contract entered into one year after lawyers began providing legal services to clients resulting in nearly $5 million fee invalid); *In re* Marshall, 217 P.3d 291 (Wash. 2009) (lawyer disbarred for demanding additional fees after agreeing to a flat fee).

factors: Unanticipated circumstances arose that led to a change, the client asked for the change, the client benefited from the change, the client was aware of (because you disclosed) the advantages and disadvantages of the change, and the client consulted an independent lawyer before deciding to accept the modification.[210]

Courts carefully scrutinize fee modifications much like they carefully regulate business deals with clients. You should provide a writing to modify any fee agreement and use it to articulate the factors just listed that benefit your client. If you are unable to do so, you may have stepped into unreasonable territory, making the modified fee uncollectible and perhaps subjecting you to professional discipline as well.

§ 9.14 Lawyer Hindsight

The Bad Deal

Q. I convinced the CFO of Magna Corporation our firm would take on Magna's dispute with the engineer who designed the new product line on a contingent-fee basis. Case looked like a lay down. The production line was supposed to produce 50 microchips a minute; current production isn't half that. We've been in discovery for months. The case is costing us a fortune. And we're not close to finished. But we now know there's a good argument that it's not the production line but the use of inferior raw materials that's causing the problems. I'm ready to either throw in the towel or insist we get paid on an hourly basis, at premium rates.

A. We sympathize with your plight. But there is a reason why they call these fee agreements contingent. Because there is an element of risk. Will the client recover? If so, how much? Maybe the client will drop the suit. Or settle for non-monetary relief not contemplated by the agreement. Lawyers try to minimize the risk before signing on by researching as much as possible the strengths and particularly the weaknesses of the case, and by rejecting those that carry high levels of risk. But once the contingent-fee agreement is signed, the lawyer is on the hook. The client gets to decide whether and when to settle, or

210. *In re* Lawrence, 23 N.E.3d 965 (N.Y. 2014) (where long-time client complained about hourly fee and demanded contingent fee after an adverse court ruling, firm entitled to $44 million contingency fee after unexpected settlement offer materialized a few months after fee modification).

to force the matter to trial, and unless the contingent-fee agreement says otherwise, even to appeal.[211]

Q. I see a theme developing here. The client gets to decide. I'll have a heart-to-heart with my client. As long as the CFO agrees, I can shift to an hourly fee, correct?

A. Except for one problem.

Q. What's that?

A. You may have to convince a court as well. Your client Magna can avoid any modification to a fee contract made after the client-lawyer relationship begins.[212] The courts presume undue influence once your fiduciary duty attaches.[213] That leaves you with the burden of proof to establish that the modification was "fair and reasonable to the client."[214] If the modification results in a larger fee for you, you probably won't be able to keep it. If your client has independent counsel in deciding whether to modify, you're in better shape, but still not completely home free. You will have to show that the modification made sense from the client's perspective when made, and that you properly disclosed the details of both arrangements.[215]

§ 9.15 Fees on Termination

"You're fired." Words no lawyer wants to hear (unless the lawyer has been searching for a way to get rid of this client). If the client fires you, you lose the right to a contract fee, because courts imply a term in the contract that the client should be free to end the agency relationship at any time for any reason.[216] If the firing is without cause, you gain a fee based on quantum meruit or fair value, usually measured by a reasonable hourly rate times a reasonable number of hours expended on the matter.[217] If you bargained badly and quantum meruit happens to be greater than your contract fee, most jurisdictions will limit you to the lesser of quantum meruit or your contract fee.[218]

The reality of these rules dictates that you must always keep track of billable hours, whether you charge monthly retainers, fixed, or

211. ABA Comm. on Ethics & Prof'l Responsibility, Formal Opinion 94-389 (1994).
212. RLGL §§ 18, 38(2).
213. Vaughn v. King, 167 F.3d 347 (7th Cir. 1999).
214. RLGL § 18(1)(a).
215. *Id.* § 18 cmt. e.
216. MR 1.16(a)(3); RLGL § 32(1).
217. RLGL § 39.
218. *Id.* § 40.

contingent fees. If you do not, you will lack the documentation necessary to meet your burden to prove quantum meruit, or fair value of your provided services.

If a client fires you for cause (a serious and clear breach of fiduciary duty) then you may forfeit all or part of the fee. You have the burden to separate out the portion of the fee justified by loyal, competent, and confidential service. The rest is lost because of the breach.[219]

If you fail to communicate material facts to a client, violate a conflicts rule, or breach confidentiality, you may be subject to fee forfeiture. To prevent this, know your six C fiduciary obligations and be prepared to respond immediately when a conflict or potential breach of confidentiality develops.

§ 9.16 The Client's Power to Terminate

Fired!

Q. You know our firm. A bunch of stick in the muds. Grinding out the hours. Limited only by the fact that our lawyers get exhausted. Then some of our corporate clients pushed back. Asked us if we'd take matters on a contingent fee. They claimed cash flow problems. And getting bleary eyed reading endless time sheets filled with meaningless entries. We got a little excited. Maybe we'd hit. Get a big pay day. We took one on as an experiment. A suit against the manufacturer of a new run-flat tire line. Blowouts occurred at a frightening rate. Our client claimed millions in damages. We sign up for 25 percent. We agree to upfront the costs too. Not everyone was happy. Such a big case screwed up our billable-hours budget. But the cohort with visions of sugar plums prevailed.

We worked our collective tails off. Hired experts. Depositions galore. And the electronic discovery! Then the client gets a new CEO. He doesn't know us. But he decides we're too conservative. He's got a pilot friend who is, as he says, "a real plaintiffs' lawyer." We're fired. And the new guy is going to trial next week. On our work product.

219. Fracasse v. Brent, 494 P.2d 9 (Cal. 1972) (client has the right to discharge lawyer with or without cause, and lawyer can recover in quantum meruit in either situation if contingency occurs); Teichner v. W & J Holsteins, Inc., 478 N.E.2d 177 (N.Y. 1985) (lawyer's fee forfeited whenever client discharges lawyer "for cause," but lawyer can recover quantum meruit if discharge was without cause).

A. Now you know yet another reason they call these contingent fees. The client can fire you at any time and for no reason.[220]

Q. So unfair. And you know we never even thought about that. We've represented the client for 27 years. We still do.

A. Now you want to know what fee you get?

Q. Exactly. 2,700 mostly boring hours. Disbursements of $200,000 or so. And our client's fate in the hands of someone else.

A. With your fee, if your client loses, you'll get nothing. Maybe reimbursement of the expenses.

Q. We're not even thinking about that possibility. What happens when the client wins?

A. You'll be entitled to the lesser of your contract fee or quantum meruit.[221]

Q. Is that ethics speak for a few dollars?

A. Could be. In many jurisdictions, quantum meruit is defined as your hours times a reasonable rate.[222]

Q. But we didn't even keep time records. Our folks loved that.

A. Well, some courts are kind. Others not so kind absent time records.[223]

Q. But we should get a percentage. A big percentage. We did all the work.

A. Some jurisdictions agree. For them, quantum meruit could easily mean that your firm should get a significant percentage, perhaps from successor counsel.[224] But be prepared for a dog fight with CEO's high-flying friend who will argue he had to start all over, and without his formidable trial skills the company would never have collected a dime.[225]

Q. There goes our firm's contingent-fee practice.

A. At least you learned one lesson.

Q. What's that?

---

220. MR 1.16(a)(3); RLGL § 32(1).

221. RLGL § 40.

222. Malonis v. Harrington, 816 N.E.2d 115 (Mass. 2004).

223. Badillo v. Playboy Ent. Group, Inc., 302 F. App'x 901 (11th Cir. 2008).

224. Olsen v. Harbison, 119 Cal. Rptr. 3d 460 (2010) (discharged contingent-fee lawyer entitled to quantum meruit recovery from former client but not from former co-counsel for payment); *Malonis v. Harrington*, 816 N.E.2d 115 (Mass. 2004) (discharged contingent-fee lawyer entitled to quantum meruit from successor counsel unless successor counsel otherwise agrees with client).

225. Augustson v. Linea Aerea Nacional-Chile S.A., 76 F.3d 658 (5th Cir. 1996) (court approval of lawyer's withdrawal over client's objection not enough to justify any fee recovery where client eventually got a settlement twice what lawyer had urged client to accept).

A. The essence of a contingent fee is risk. If you're going to do contingent-fee cases, you should pursue many of them. Having only one contingent case in the inventory is risky business.

§ 9.17 Statutory Fee-Shifting Agreements

Our Contract

Q. Client company wanted to pursue an environmental action against a former property owner but didn't want to take on the cost of an hourly fee. I agreed to a 40 percent contingent fee. We won. The client is receiving $100,000 in damages. We also petitioned for statutory attorney fees and the court awarded the client $80,000. I say I'm entitled to 40 percent of $100,000, plus the $80,000. The client says I get the $40,000 and that's it. What an ingrate.

A. Under your fee agreement, which we are sure you crafted, your client could be correct. Let's start with whether your fee is reasonable. In many jurisdictions, this would depend on the Rule 1.5(a) factors, such as the difficulty of the matter, the results achieved, and the customary fee in your locality. But in some jurisdictions, contingent fees are more specifically regulated. For example, in Florida, your 40 percent contract would subject you to discipline.[226]

Now, assuming you contracted for a reasonable fee, if the fee agreement provides that you will receive 40 percent of your client's recovery, your contract fee is $40,000. If, however, you were smart enough to contract for 40 percent of any money received by the client from the opposing party, including statutory fee awards, you should get 40 percent of your client's total $180,000, or $72,000.

Absent a statute, the American Rule (unlike the English) does not provide for fee shifting to a prevailing party. But fee shifting statutes, often called private attorneys general provisions, can create a right to a "reasonable attorney's fee" to a

226. Fla. R. Prof'l Conduct 1.5(f) (2018).

"prevailing party."[227] Hundreds of statutes, including environmental, securities, civil rights, and consumer provisions provide for fee shifting. When this occurs, the statute governs the entitlement.[228] But typically, these provisions pay your client (the prevailing party), not you. You are free to contract for a reasonable fee, be it contingent, hourly, or fixed.[229] Many lawyers blend provisions, providing in the fee contract that any contingent fee owed the lawyer will be offset by the statutory fee award. We hope you carefully read the statute and the cases construing it to create a fee contract that benefits both you and your client.

Q. But the fee award was $80,000. I should at least get that! Otherwise the client keeps my fee.

A. Not so fast. As we have already explained, statutory fee-shifting provisions provide for a fee to the prevailing party, not the prevailing party's lawyer. Unless your fee agreement with the client contemplated that result, you are limited to your own bargain.

§ 9.18 Court-Awarded Fee Enhancements

No Good Deed Goes Unpunished

Q. We took on a pro bono case for a children's organization. They were challenging the way the state of Missouri runs its foster care system. The facts were outrageous, and by the end, a very skeptical judge made findings of fact that were stunning. The neglect and underfunding he found to be profound. The state AG immediately offered to settle and, after we refused to waive our entitlement to our fees (which we plan to contribute to the organization), we entered into a consent decree that should improve the lot of the foster children of Missouri dramatically.

---

227. Buckhannon Bd. & Care Home, Inc. v. W. Va. Dep't of Health & Human Res., 532 U.S. 598 (2001) (parties who receive a judgment on the merits, or a court-ordered consent decree are "prevailing parties," but a party who recovers because of a defendant's voluntary change in conduct not caused by the underlying lawsuit is not); Loggerhead Turtle v. City Council, 307 F.3d 1318 (11th Cir. 2002) (*Buckhannon* applies only to "prevailing party" statutes, not to "whenever appropriate" fee award statutes such as the Clean Water and Clean Air Acts).

228. City of Burlington v. Dague, 505 U.S. 557 (1992) (requires lodestar calculations under federal fee shifting statutes); Walker v. Giuffre, 35 A.3d 1177 (N.J. 2012) (contingency fee enhancements valid under state fee-shifting statutes despite *Purdue*).

229. Gobert v. Williams, 323 F.3d 1099 (5th Cir. 2003) (upholding validity of fee contract that provided for contingent fee in addition to any statutory fees awarded plaintiff).

A. Congratulations!

Q. Not quite yet. We are now litigating our fee. The organization depends on it. And what a strong case. $300,000 in disbursements. A lodestar of over $1 million. And the judge says he has never seen a better prepared case. I'll bet he gives us a huge premium.

A. We hate to burst your bubble. But the Supreme Court has made it almost impossible to get more than the lodestar.[230]

Q. How could that be? The entire fee is contingent. We risked it all.

A. The Court says that in "extraordinary situations" an enhancement might be allowed but found all factors such as risk calculable in the lodestar.

Q. And the outstanding presentation?

A. The Supreme Court says that is what justifies your billing rate.

Q. But the result. The trial judge was so impressed.

A. Again, that is what you were expected to do for your hourly rate. The truth is the new standard is so high it is unlikely anyone will ever achieve it. And if you get a chance to seek a premium, you will do so knowing you are facing odds that makes the chance of the Jamaica team's winning the bobsled at the next Olympics a lay down.

Q. Sure will discourage bringing these suits.

A. The dissenters were concerned about this. We would not be surprised if that was the Court's real motivation, to wit, discouraging the filing of public law-reform litigation.

§ 9.19 Statutory Fees

State and federal statutes limit or shape all kinds of lawyers' fees. Limitations on contingent fees in certain classes of cases (worker's compensation and tort reform provisions) commonly are found in state law. Likewise, federal statutes control the size of a contingent fee in social security disability claims and appeals.[231] General provisions such as state probate and federal bankruptcy codes often grant or require judicial review of lawyers' fees because they are expenses against an estate

230. Perdue v. Kenny A., 559 U.S. 542 (2010) (lodestar calculation cannot be enhanced except in extraordinary circumstances, requiring a reasonably specific explanation for the enhancement, which was not given in this case).

231. Gisbrecht v. Barnhart, 535 U.S. 789 (2002) (Social Security Act provision that limits attorney fees to 25 percent of past-due benefits does not displace contingent-fee agreements that are within such statutory ceiling).

subject to the power of a court.[232] Similar provisions grant judges the power to supervise fees when lawyers represent minors. Although a few courts have interpreted their state constitutional separation of power provisions to limit the legislative branch's ability to regulate fees,[233] most courts defer to legislative power reasonably exercised in this area.[234]

When fee shifting occurs pursuant to statute, the cases construing the statute govern the entitlement.[235] Usually, these provisions pay your client (the prevailing party), not you. At the same time, you are free to contract for a reasonable fee, be it contingent, hourly, or fixed.[236] Many lawyers blend provisions, providing in the fee contract that any contingent fee will be offset by the statutory amount. Enjoy your newfound source of income. But remember competence: Carefully read the statute and the cases construing it to create a fee contract that benefits both you and your client.

§ 9.20 Class Action Fees

The Justified Settlement

Q. We've been defending our government client against a ridiculous class action suit alleging police brutality. I think we can offer the named plaintiffs a great settlement of their claims. We'll give them minimal injunctive relief if they agree not to seek an award of fees from the court.

A. Class action fees are subject to two bodies of law: first, any relevant statutory fee-shifting provision and, second, the

---

232. *In re* ASARCO, LLC, 751 F.3d 291 (5th Cir. 2014) (two law firms entitled to a fee enhancement of $4 million plus their regular fees and expenses of $120 million for obtaining the largest fraudulent transfer judgment in Chapter 11 bankruptcy history, but not entitled to any fee for time litigating their fee applications); *In re* Market Ctr. E. Retail Prop., Inc., 730 F.3d 1239 (10th Cir. 2013) (bankruptcy courts have discretion in awarding fees but must follow factors set in statute and case law).

233. Maas v. Olive, 992 So. 2d 196 (Fla. 2008) (construing a state statute that created an absolute cap on fees in post-conviction proceedings to require retention of inherent court authority to order additional compensation in cases justified by unusual or extraordinary circumstances); Irwin v. Surdyk's Liquor, 599 N.W.2d 132 (Minn. 1999) (statute that set a maximum permissible fee in worker's compensation cases invalid).

234. Samuel v. W.C.A.B., 814 A.2d 274 (Pa. Commw. Ct. 2002) (statutory provision that set standard and enhanced fees in worker's compensation actions constitutional because it was similar to Pa. Rule 1.5, in that it acted simply as a guide to a Worker's Compensation Judge in determining the reasonableness of fee agreements but did not limit a higher fee where appropriate).

235. *Perdue*, 559 U.S. 542 (lodestar calculation cannot be enhanced except in extraordinary circumstances, requiring a reasonably specific explanation for the enhancement, which was not given in this case); Walker v. Giuffre, 35 A.3d 1177 (N.J. 2012) (contingency fee enhancements valid under state fee-shifting statutes despite *Perdue*).

236. Gobert v. Williams, 323 F.3d 1099 (5th Cir. 2003) (upholding validity of fee contract that provided for contingent fee in addition to any statutory fees awarded plaintiff).

court's common-law obligation to supervise common-fund settlements.[237]

Q. That's just great, you mean I have to justify this settlement to the court?

A. Yes, and you probably will only get this sweet result for this client once. But, you will be relieved to know that the Supreme Court has blessed a settlement similar to the one you suggest. Since the suit was no doubt brought pursuant to relevant civil rights statutes that grant the fee shift to the "prevailing party," the Court has held that fee waivers by parties can be approved by courts as long as the defendants do not have a policy, practice, or law that requires waiver as a condition of settlement.[238]

Q. That is so unfair. Creates a huge conflict between lawyer and client, which can save my client a fortune. We will just make sure not to adopt a "policy." Take each case on its merits.

A. Or so you will assert.

---

237. Pearson v. NBTY, Inc., 772 F.3d 778 (7th Cir. 2014) (settlement approval reversed due to agreement that selfishly maximized attorney's fee and minimized cost to defendants at the expenses of class members who received only meager recovery for alleged misrepresentations); Rodriguez v. Disner, 688 F.3d 645 (9th Cir. 2012) (court may consider misconduct of lawyers in determining reasonable fees under the common-fund doctrine; lawyers' entering into incentive agreements without informed consent made total fee forfeiture reasonable, despite lawyers' efforts and notable success in case).

238. Evans v. Jeff D., 475 U.S. 717 (1986); Bernhardt v. City of Los Angeles, 279 F.3d 862 (9th Cir. 2002) (*Evans* justifies successful challenge to settlement agreement where governmental unit exhibits a pattern or practice of requiring lawyer fee waiver or when such agreements have the effect of deterring lawyers from representing plaintiffs in civil rights cases).

CHAPTER 10

Competence

§ 10.01 Introduction: Why You Were Hired in the First Place

Clients hire lawyers for competent service precisely because they are not able to navigate a complex legal system themselves. Lawyers know that the nature of law and the legal system means that not every client can be satisfied by the services the client receives or the result the lawyer achieves. Model Rules 1.1 and 1.3 mimic the malpractice standard of care by requiring "reasonable" competence and diligence. This means you do not have to be perfect, but you do have to meet or exceed the standard of practice in your jurisdiction. In a malpractice case, reasonable competence and diligence can be established by expert testimony, which also can provide the basis for discipline, although disciplinary agencies typically do not proceed against lawyers for isolated instances of incompetence or lack of diligence.[239]

Agents who breach competence or fiduciary duties may be liable in both contract and tort. The contract remedy usually is reserved for cases where a lawyer disobeys a clear and legal instruction of the client

239. State *ex rel.* Counsel for Discipline of the Neb. Sup. Ct. v. Orr, 759 N.W.2d 702 (Neb. 2009) (lawyers not subject to discipline for isolated mistakes, but lawyer who made repeated mistakes over a long period of time in establishing and representing a client's business franchise reprimanded).

or acts contrary to the client's clear interests.[240] Tort remedies include intentional torts, such as fraud[241] and conversion,[242] and more typically, negligence based on allegations of breach of fiduciary duty or malpractice. Violation of a rule of professional conduct does not automatically give rise to a tort action against a lawyer but may provide "evidence of breach of the applicable standard of conduct."[243]

In situations where the client has been deprived of a core fiduciary duty—such as control, communication, confidentiality, or loyalty (failure to identify or resolve a conflict of interest)—or, as some courts put it, the lawyer has acted "outside the scope of authority granted by the client,"[244] courts identify a breach of fiduciary duty remedy. Other courts describe this cause of action as constructive fraud,[245] or assume that breach of fiduciary duty is a species of malpractice that does not require expert testimony to show duty and breach.[246]

Most of the situations where clients seek a tort remedy do not involve such clear breaches of fiduciary duty. Instead, the client alleges a breach of the duties of care or competence—that the lawyer should have known more, should have had more experience, or should have exercised better judgment or care in accomplishing the client's goals. These situations commonly allege legal malpractice and usually require expert testimony to prove that the lawyer did not use reasonable care or "exercise the competence and diligence normally exercised by lawyers in similar circumstances."[247]

Reasonable care usually depends on evidence of professional custom, or expert testimony that defines what a reasonably prudent lawyer

---

240. Interclaim Holdings, Ltd. v. Ness, Motley, Loadholt, Richardson & Poole, 298 F. Supp. 2d 746 (N.D. Ill. 2004) (upholding compensatory damages of $8.3 million and punitive damages of $27.7 million on breach of contract theory against law firm that settled claims and released frozen assets without client's consent).

241. Baker v. Dorfman, 239 F.3d 415 (2d Cir. 2000) (lawyer who lied about the extent of his legal experience to client liable for fraud, including compensatory, emotional distress, and punitive damages); Johnson v. Proskauer Rose, LLP, 9 N.Y.S.3d 201 (N.Y. App. Div. 2015) (client's suit against law firm for self-dealing and fraud cannot be defended by the sophisticated investor doctrine).

242. Barbara A. v. John G., 193 Cal. Rptr. 422 (1983) (lawyer who told client he "can't possibly get anyone pregnant" liable for battery and fraud after client suffered a tubal pregnancy, which resulted in permanent sterility); ERA Realty Co. v. RBS Props., 586 N.Y.S.2d 831 (N.Y App. Div. 1992) (lawyer who used invalid legal process liable for conversion).

243. MR Scope ¶ [20]; dePape v. Trinity Health Systems, Inc., 242 F. Supp. 2d 585 (N.D. Iowa 2003) (violation of Model Rule 1.4, the "minimum communication" that should have been maintained, sufficient to establish standard of care in malpractice suit against law firm without expert testimony because Rule violation provides "guidance in determining the fiduciary duty owed to a client by an attorney").

244. Kilpatrick v. Wiley, Rein & Fielding, 909 P.2d 1283, 1290 (Utah Ct. App. 1996).

245. RLGL § 49 cmt. a; Restatement (Second) of Torts § 551(2)(a) (Am. Law Inst. 1965).

246. Estate of Fleming v. Nicholson, 724 A.2d 1026 (Vt. 1998) (no expert testimony necessary to establish negligence as a matter of law against lawyer who failed to inform client about a permit violation discovered during a title search on land the client wished to purchase, despite lawyer's claim that state had a nonenforcement policy concerning that type of violation).

247. RLGL § 52.

in your jurisdiction would know and do in the same or similar circumstances. If you aren't sure what similarly situated lawyers need to know in providing a specific legal service and if your client suffers harm as a result of deficiencies in your services, you are risking an after-the-fact judgment that you have not met the requisite standard of care. Remember that any lawyer in your jurisdiction can testify to what you should have done.

Specifically, lawyers must know relevant law and facts, must possess the requisite skill to be able to use this information throughout a representation, and must take the time to prepare diligently for the matter. If you do not know enough or have enough experience to handle a matter, you can become competent by studying or associating with another lawyer with more experience. If you wonder whether you know enough, but aren't sure, you are well advised to find out. There is no such thing as an ignorant, inexperienced, or error-in-judgment defense to a claim of malpractice supported by expert testimony.[248] Your license to practice holds out to clients and to courts that your agreement to handle a matter means you possess the skill and ability to do so. And don't forget specialization. Just as a family practice physician who delivers babies is held to the standard of an expert ob-gyn, so also will you be held to the expert standard of care if you dabble in an area of practice that your jurisdiction deems specialized.[249]

Courts also recognize some limited legal duties to nonclients when doing so will foster the client's intent and not harm the client-lawyer relationship.[250] Clients should receive frank advice untainted by lawyer concerns about liability to others. But at the same time, lawyers cannot escape generally applicable law that creates responsibility to nonclients (such as fraud and other intentional torts).[251] Courts also find lawyers liable for economic harm on a negligence theory when a client invites

---

248. Togstad v. Vesely, Otto, Miller & Keefe, 291 N.W.2d 686 (Minn. 1980) (defense to legal malpractice based on error in judgment does not exist where lawyer's breach of the standard of care supported by expert testimony); *see also In re* Johnson, 32 P.3d 1132 (Kan. 2001) (lawyer's inexperience in the practice of law and lack of a mentor, which may have led to his failure to pursue discovery to appropriately respond to a summary judgment motion and to his frivolous filing of an appeal to avoid malpractice, created no defense to professional discipline for lack of competence and diligence).

249. Horne v. Peckham, 158 Cal. Rptr. 714 (1979) (lawyer who acknowledged the need for expertise in tax had duty to refer client to an expert practitioner or to comply with the specialty standard of care); Jerry's Enters. v. Larkin, Hoffman, Daly & Lindgren, Ltd., 711 N.W.2d 811 (Minn. 2006) (negligent failure to research or raise relevant issue in property transaction); Ziegelheim v. Apollo, 607 A.2d 1298 (N.J. 1992) (negligent settlement advice in divorce case).

250. Greycas, Inc. v. Proud, 826 F.2d 1560 (7th Cir. 1987) (lender who required opinion letter from borrower's lawyer was third-party beneficiary with standing to sue borrower's lawyer for malpractice); Sickler v. Kirby, 805 N.W.2d 675 (Neb. Ct. App. 2011) (owners of closely held business were third-party beneficiaries of lawyer who represented the corporation); *but see* Doe v. Bernabei & Wachtel, PLLC, 116 A.3d 1262 (D.C. 2015) (witness to client's lawsuit had no cause of action against client's lawyers for posting her mobile phone video of the incident on the Internet to assist client's claim).

251. RLGL § 56 cmt. b.

third-party reliance or creates a third-party beneficiary of the lawyer's services, or when the lawyer engages in a negligent misrepresentation or aids and abets a client's fraud or breach of fiduciary duty.[252]

§ 10.02 Reasonable Competence

Expanding Your Practice

Q. How hard can it be?
A. How hard can what be?
Q. We have always wanted to expand our practice to more glamorous engagements.
A. You mean lucrative?
Q. That too. And we finally have our chance. We received a call asking us to defend one of our existing clients in an international arbitration. It will take place in London, and our litigation colleagues are salivating at the prospect of taking on this desirable new work.
A. Congratulations. Sounds wonderful.
Q. There is just one problem. We have never done an international arbitration, but I figure if we just assume the Federal Rules of Civil Procedure apply, we will be able to get through the day.
A. That may be an unwarranted assumption.
Q. I doubt it. But, in any event, we are going to get one of our associates to attend a CLE, and somebody told us there is a book you can purchase that explains international arbitration.
A. I would not rush into this quite so quickly. Think of the malpractice pitfalls.[253]
Q. You're telling us we cannot undertake this matter? I can't tell you how disappointed our folks will be.

---

252. *Id.* § 51.

253. Peterson v. Katten Muchin Rosenman LLP, 792 F.3d 789 (7th Cir. 2015) (malpractice cause of action for failing to advise client about risks of business scheme, distinction between business and legal advice a question of fact); L.D.G., Inc. v. Robinson, 290 P.3d 215 (Alaska 2012) (lawyers not immune from malpractice liability even when mistake involves unsettled legal questions because standard of care may require lawyer to advise client of course of action in light of the uncertainty); Iowa Attorney Disciplinary Bd. v. Wright, 840 N.W.2d 295 (Iowa 2013) (lawyer violated Rule 1.1 by failing to do a cursory Internet search that would have revealed client's dream of a Nigerian inheritance was probably based on a scam); Miranda v. Said, 836 N.W.2d 8 (Iowa 2013) (bad legal advice about immigration that caused family to be separated for a decade stated cause of action for legal malpractice, including mental anguish and punitive damages); Delgado v. Bretz & Coven, LLP, 967 N.Y.S.2d 371 (N.Y. App. Div. 2013) (law firm's erroneous advice that caused client to be deported stated cause of action for malpractice).

A. We are not saying that. But we are warning you that as you enter a new area of practice, you and your firm have to meet the competency standard under Rule 1.1 in order to fulfill your professional obligations.

Q. Well, our firm certainly knows its way around the courthouse. That's for sure.

A. The question is whether that skill is totally transferrable. Rule 1.1 tells us that you are certainly entitled to enter new fields of litigation. But in order to get yourselves up to speed, you may have to pursue a more elaborate course of study. Alternatively, the rule permits you to associate with an experienced lawyer in international arbitration.[254] But either way you go, it is essential you explain to your client your present limitations and, if you choose to associate with another lawyer, the client must approve of that association before you begin sharing confidential information with another law firm and, perhaps, incurring additional expenses for the client. For everybody there is always the first time. The first time, however, cannot be jumping into the deep end of the pool without any swimming lessons.[255]

Q. Thanks. I guess we will follow what you say, but I sure hope we don't lose this opportunity. Of course, the next time we get a call we will be able to tell the second client how experienced we are.

§ 10.03 Reasonable Diligence

Diligence: Not to Worry

Q. I'm a new associate. About a month into the job, I finally get to the bottom of a stack of subrogation cases on my desk. Left by the last disgruntled associate. Turns out the statute of

254. MR 1.1 cmt. [2].

255. *In re* Kaszynski, 620 N.W.2d 708 (Minn. 2001) (lawyer disbarred for having no experience but holding himself out as an expert in immigration law and for failing to supply documentation of clients' claims, putting them in danger of deportation); State *ex rel.* Counsel for Discipline of the Neb. Supreme Court v. Orr, 759 N.W.2d 702 (Neb. 2009) (lawyer publicly reprimanded for inexcusably violating Rule 1.1 by engaging in repeated incompetence for one client over a long period of time, undertaking franchise agreement drafting without ascertaining the law governing the matter); *In re* Richmond's Case, 872 A.2d 1023, 1028 (N.H. 2005) (lawyer suspended for six months for violating Rule 1.1 for incompetently issuing unregistered securities, because rule "mandates that a general practitioner . . . identify areas in which the lawyer is not competent"); *In re* Dumke, 635 N.W.2d 594 (Wis. 2001) (lawyer suspended for two years for undertaking specialized legal representation in sexual predator proceedings and failing to seek expert opinion to evaluate state's case).

limitations had expired on the claim. My boss told me not to worry, insurers never raise the defense. Should I quit?

A. We sympathize. Your boss should have given you better guidance and should have established policies and procedures that prod all lawyers in the firm to comply with this obligation.[256] But even if you didn't realize that any of the claims were approaching the limitations period, you should have reviewed the files first with that in mind, or asked someone who could help.

Model Rule 1.3 requires that lawyers act with reasonable diligence and promptness. Diligence requires commitment and dedication to the client's interests; something called zealous representation.[257] Promptness should speak for itself: You must manage the workload imposed by the rest of your practice so that you can give reasonable and timely attention to each client matter. If you have supervisory authority in a law firm, you have the same obligation to watch the workload of those you supervise. Simple procrastination in a matter may or may not be serious, depending on the time deadlines imposed and the exigencies of the situation. But anytime "being behind" causes harm to your client, you may face malpractice or disciplinary consequences.

Both you and your boss are responsible to the client, who could file a grievance. You have no defense of reasonable reliance on your boss, because Model Rule 5.2 only provides that excuse to "subordinate lawyers" when the issue presents an arguable question of professional duty.[258] We think your boss, not you, deserves the discipline for failure to supervise.[259] As for malpractice, you are both on the hook. Maybe the last disgruntled associate, too.

---

256. MR 5.1; RLGL § 11.

257. MR Preamble [2]; RLGL § 52 cmt. c; MODEL CODE OF PROF'L CONDUCT Canon 7 (AM. BAR ASS'N 1983) (A Lawyer Should Represent a Client Zealously Within the Bounds of the Law).

258. People v. Casey, 948 P.2d 1014 (Colo. 1997) (lawyer who assisted client in crime of criminal impersonation by not correcting court record of client's name not relieved of responsibility because he consulted with senior partner); Daniels v. Alander, 844 A.2d 182 (Conn. 2004) (associate reprimanded for failure to correct supervisory lawyer's false statement to a court made when associate was present).

259. *In re* Cohen, 847 A.2d 1162, 1166 (D.C. 2004) (partner who had "no system in place to impart rudimentary ethics training to lawyers in the firm" suspended for 30 days because the discreet nature of the case, extended length of the representation, and small law firm size meant he reasonably should have known of associate-son's ethics violations and intervened to mitigate or avoid them); *In re* Anonymous Member of S.C. Bar, 552 S.E.2d 10 (S.C. 2001) (law firm partners and other lawyers who directly or indirectly supervise other lawyers can be sanctioned and subject to discipline for failing to mitigate known misconduct of another lawyer in discovery and depositions, failing to make reasonable efforts to supervise, even without knowledge of misconduct, or failing to put systematic procedures in place to prevent misconduct).

§ 10.04 Chart: Legal Malpractice and Breach of Fiduciary Duty

Common-Law Elements
1. Client-lawyer relationship (foreseeable plaintiff) a. Offer b. Acceptance c. Consideration or detrimental reliance 2. Duty = Expert testimony usually required except common knowledge 3. Breach a. Expert testimony generally required b. No expert testimony for common knowledge i. Breach of a core fiduciary duty (compliance with reasonable client instructions, communication, confidentiality, serious conflicts of interest) ii. Missed deadlines iii. Failure to research applicable law 4. Causation a. Actual = but for = case within a case b. Proximate = foreseeable consequences 5. Damages a. Economic loss b. Emotional distress c. Punitive

§ 10.05 Obvious Errors

In malpractice cases, some errors are so obvious that they trigger the "common knowledge" exception to the expert-testimony requirement, which deems some breaches of duty clear enough that a lay juror can recognize them without the aid of an expert witness.[260] In the same way that physicians can be found liable for leaving surgical instruments in a person's body or operating on the wrong wrist, lawyers can be found liable without expert testimony for three obvious errors:

260. RLGL §§ 16, 49.

1. Failing to file within a mandatory time period;[261]
2. Failing to do legal or factual research;[262] and
3. Failing to observe core fiduciary duties such as obedience to client control and instructions, communication, confidentiality, or conflict of interest resolution.[263]

Even though these are obvious, insurers know they are far too common.

§ 10.06 Obvious Negligence

Missing a Deadline

Q. I didn't worry, because I believed my boss that the defendant insurer would not raise the statute-of-limitations defense. But they did and the trial judge just dismissed my case. Our client is furious. Now am I in trouble?

A. If you miss a time period and cannot secure an extension, you will face a potential malpractice claim, though disciplinary agencies will seldom impose sanctions unless you exhibit a pattern of such behavior. As for malpractice, juries don't need an expert to know that promptness requires you to file a case or appeal on a timely basis. In evidentiary terms, the common-knowledge exception to the expert-testimony requirement applies because deadlines are obvious and lawyers should know and comply with them on behalf of clients,[264] all of which translates into your need for an appropriate tickler system to remind you about dates.

261. Barnes v. Turner, 606 S.E.2d 849 (Ga. 2004) (statute requiring renewal of security interest five years after sale of a business); George v. Caton, 600 P.2d 822 (N.M. Ct. App. 1979) (statute of limitations).

262. Smith v. Lewis, 530 P.2d 589 (Cal. 1975) (legal research which would have indicated a potential though unclear change in law); Schmidt v. Crotty, 528 N.W.2d 112 (Iowa 1995) (factual research regarding property descriptions).

263. RLGL § 49; DePape v. Trinity Health Sys., Inc., 242 F. Supp. 2d 585 (N.D. Iowa 2003) (law firm breached duty of communication by failing to provide necessary information to client); Bayview Loan Servicing, LLC v. Law Firm of Richard M. Squire & Assocs., LLC, No. CIV.A.10-1451, 2010 WL 5122003 (E.D. Pa. Dec. 14, 2010) (lawyer breached fiduciary duty by failing to inform client he had missed a filing deadline); Maritrans GP Inc. v. Pepper, Hamilton & Scheetz, 602 A.2d 1277 (Pa. 1992) (law firm breached fiduciary duty of loyalty by taking on adverse substantially related representation); Perez v. Kirk & Carrigan, 822 S.W.2d 261 (Tex. App. 1991) (lawyer breached fiduciary duty of confidentiality by disclosing client's statement to prosecutor); Olfe v. Gordon, 286 N.W.2d 573 (Wis. 1980) (lawyer breached agency duty of obedience by disregarding client's instructions to draft a first rather than second mortgage).

264. Cammarota v. Guerrera, 87 A.3d 1134 (Conn. App. Ct. 2014) (common knowledge sufficient to understand handing a check to the wrong person, the wrong person also being a co-client and business partner).

§ 10.07 How to Respond to Errors

When you err, don't trust your instincts. You are too embarrassed, angry, or, at the very least, lacking in objectivity to trust yourself. Instead, follow these steps:

First, you should inform your client of the relevant facts that led to your error,[265] explain the nature of your conflict of interest (that you must withdraw because your client may have a claim against you, most likely a nonconsentable conflict),[266] and advise your now former client in writing of the desirability of seeking the advice of independent legal counsel.[267]

Second, do not lie, conceal, or attempt to cover up any relevant facts. Answer client questions as honestly as you can. Do not offer any opinion about the merits of your client's underlying matter or any other relief your client may now seek against you. That constitutes legal advice that could be faulty due to your conflict of interest.

Third, remember that you are subject to discipline if you settle your former client's complaint against you unless you have notified your former client in writing of the need for independent counsel and given that person or entity a reasonable opportunity to seek such advice.[268] Even then, if your former client was not independently represented, the law of agency will presume undue influence, putting the burden of proof on you to prove that the settlement was fair and reasonable to the client.[269] Send the client a disengagement letter complete with the disclosures listed in the last paragraph.[270]

Fourth, if a claim is made, call your liability carrier and turn the matter over to it. If you don't have malpractice insurance, retain other counsel or call yourself a fool.

Following these steps enables you to meet your fiduciary obligation of competence and communication. It also may help you reduce the chance of a lawsuit or disciplinary complaint, or if either occurs, can

---

265. MR 1.4; RLGL § 20; ABA Comm. on Ethics & Prof'l Responsibility, Formal Op. 481 (2018) A Lawyer's Duty to Inform a Current or Former Client of the Lawyer's Material Error.

266. MR 1.7(b); RLGL § 122 cmt. g; Leonard v. Dorsey & Whitney LLP, 553 F.3d 609 (8th Cir. 2009) (lawyer has a duty to disclose potential malpractice claim if claim creates a conflict of interest that would disqualify lawyer from representing the client because the lawyer's interest in avoiding liability conflicts with client's interest to seek recovery for harm caused by the lawyer's error); *In re* Tallon, 447 N.Y.S.2d 50 (N.Y. App. Div. 1982) (lawyer has a professional duty to promptly notify his client of his failure to act and of the possible claim his client may have against him); Williams v. Joynes, Crean v. Chozick, 714 S.W.2d 61 (Tex. App. 1986) (failure to disclose malpractice to client tolls the statute of limitations); N.Y. State Bar Ass'n Op. 734 (2000) (legal services organization is bound by the same ethical standards as other lawyers and, therefore, must inform a client when a significant error giving rise to a possible malpractice claim has been made and withdraw from the representation).

267. MR 1.8(h)(2); RLGL § 54.

268. MR 1.8(h)(2); RLGL § 54.

269. RLGL § 54 cmt. c.

270. *See* § 3.02 in this book.

reduce the severity of the outcome, because your client understands that you did the right thing once a mistake was uncovered. If you fail to inform the client, he or she reasonably may suspect that you have more to hide, and many jurisdictions toll the statute of limitations on your client's malpractice claim until the time that person or entity reasonably should have known about the problem. Admit your error, start the clock ticking, and get on with your practice.

§ 10.08 Chart: Lawyer Tort Liability to Nonclients

1. Malpractice:
   a. Third-party beneficiaries of clients, RLGL § 51(3),
   b. Those invited to rely by the lawyer (prospective clients, RLGL § 51(1)), and
   c. Those invited by lawyer or client to rely, if not too remote from the lawyer to be entitled to such protection (RLGL §§ 51(2), 95).
2. Misrepresentation:
   a. Intentional or reckless misstatements (fraud): Lawyer is liable to all those who reasonably relied on the false information.[271]
   b. Negligent misstatements: Lawyer is liable to those in a limited class of persons "for whose benefit and guidance he intends to supply the information or knows the recipient intends to supply it."[272]
3. Aiding and abetting a client's tort:
   a. Lawyer knows of client's tortious acts,
   b. Lawyer knows client's conduct constitutes a tort, such as fraud or breach of fiduciary duty,
   c. Lawyer provides substantial assistance to client's tort, not just to the client, and lawyer commits a
      - Statutory violation,
      - Crime,
      - Fraud, or
      - Acts in a self-interested or conflict-of-interest manner
   d. Breach causes harm to third parties.

271. RLGL §§ 56 cmt. f, 98; RESTATEMENT (SECOND) OF TORTS § 531 (AM. LAW INST. 1965).
272. RLGL §§ 56, 98; RESTATEMENT (SECOND) OF TORTS § 552(2) (AM. LAW INST. 1965).

§ 10.09 Lawyer Liability to Third Persons

Third-Party Obligations

Q. I hate preparing auditors' letters. You spend hours gathering the information. You can never bill the time. And the whole idea is to say nothing. We don't make predictions. Not in our business. You win cases you should lose and vice versa.

A. Is there a question? Or just a speech?

Q. A question. Because we are on the horns of a dilemma. Our client has been sued for patent infringement. Big case. The patent in question is the key feature of the clients' new product line. We dutifully send the meaningless auditors' letter identifying the case and refusing to express any opinion. That was last week. The audit is likely to be completed next week.

A. So far, so good.

Q. So far. But we just learned that our client's CEO deleted from the patent application prior art that could invalidate the patent based on a fraud on the patent office. We obviously did not know that when we wrote the letter.

A. This is just another example of why it is so important to avoid, if possible, overstating any lawyer duties to anyone other than the client. When that occurs, conflicts become a real possibility. As here. If there were no auditors' letter, you still would have problems, but they would be one-dimensional. Here you have undertaken duties to the auditors, admittedly for the client's benefit.

Q. Must we withdraw the letter? Disclose the reason?

A. That depends on two things. First, did you make any representations in the letter that you now know are incorrect?

Q. We tried to avoid that. We just said the chances of success are neither likely nor remote.

A. Well, are they now remote?

Q. Probably not. Just materially diminished.

A. Then the second issue is whether you are committing a fraud or aiding and abetting a client fraud by standing silent in the face of new material information.

Q. How do we do that?

A. The rules do not define "fraud," except by telling you to look at the law of the applicable jurisdiction.[273] You certainly did not engage in fraud as you wrote the auditors' letter. But if it

273. MR 1.0(d).

is fraud and your state has adopted Model Rules 1.6(b)(2) and 1.6(b)(3), those exceptions would permit, but not require, disclosure. And with that permission to disclose, some other positive law might require some disclosure if that is necessary to prevent further fraud.

Q. Damn accountants!

A. Well, they are doing their jobs; we have to do ours.

§ 10.10 Third-Person Obligations: The Law of Deceit

The law of fraud, deceit, and misrepresentation creates a definitive legal boundary to your own conduct and that of your clients and is incorporated into your professional obligation by rule of professional conduct provisions as well. Here, we address the tort of misrepresentation, which forms the basis for understanding the potential for liability far beyond a client-lawyer relationship. The Restatement (Second) of Torts §§ 525–552C lay out the basic elements of a cause of action for misrepresentation:

1. Making a false representation (by words or actions), or failing to speak when:
   a. fiduciary obligation exists, or
   b. previous statements made have become untrue, misleading or material;
2. Concerning a presently existing material fact;
3. Which the representor knows to be false or is made recklessly, knowing that there is insufficient knowledge upon which to base the representation, or which is made negligently;
4. For the purpose of inducing another to act;
5. The other party reasonably relies on the representation;
6. To the other's injury or damage.

In tort, "fraud" includes both intentional as well as reckless misstatements. To be liable, the defendant does not have to intend harm to the plaintiff, but only has to know he is lying, or recklessly ignoring the truth.[274] This distinction is important, because the lawyer's liability for fraud extends to all foreseeable third persons who reasonably rely on

274. Slotkin v. Citizens Cas. Co. of N.Y., 614 F.2d 301 (2d Cir. 1979) (insurance defense lawyer who settled medical malpractice case liable for fraud for stating that "to the best of his knowledge" there was no excess insurance coverage, when lawyer's file indicated otherwise); Fire Ins. Exch. v. Bell, 643 N.E.2d 310 (Ind. 1994) (plaintiff's counsel had right to rely on insurance defense counsel's representation of policy limits even though plaintiff's lawyer could have used discovery to ascertain limits).

the false information.[275] If the lawyer's material misrepresentation is merely negligent, liability usually extends to a more limited group of persons identified at the time the statements were made.

Although the tort of misrepresentation usually requires an affirmative misrepresentation, there are a few occasions when failure to speak can create liability as well. Fiduciary duties create obligations to disclose, which means that lawyers, who owe fiduciary duties to clients, have affirmative duties to disclose material information to them.[276] A duty to disclose also may arise when previous statements have become untrue, misleading, or material.[277] For example, a lawyer may have a duty to disclose tax liens to a prospective purchaser at a foreclosure sale if the buyer was induced to bid by the lawyer's incomplete prior representations.[278]

Whenever you state a fact orally or in writing that you expect another will rely on, do not depend solely on your client for determining the truth of the matter.[279] Lawyers have been held liable for fraud and negligent misrepresentation to third parties when they believed their client's lie and innocently (they thought) repeated it.[280]

§ 10.11 Third-Person Obligations When Opining

The Opinion Boilerplate

Q. My firm gave an opinion to help our client, an Internet sensation, to secure a bank line of credit. We inserted the usual boilerplate about reviewing all pending litigation against client and finding no substantial likelihood that any pending suit

275. RLGL § 56 cmt. f; Restatement (Second) of Torts § 531 (Am. Law Inst. 1977); Ultramares Corp. v. Touche, Niven & Co., 174 N.E. 441 (N.Y. 1931).

276. Bayview Loan Servicing, LLC v. Law Firm of Richard M. Squire & Assocs., LLC, No. CIV.A.10-1451, 2010 WL 5122003 (E.D. Pa. Dec. 14, 2010).

277. Restatement (Second) of Torts § 551 (Am. Law Inst. 1965); *see also In re* Alcorn, 41 P.3d 600, 610 (Ariz. 2002) (trial lawyers who made a secret agreement with opposing counsel to dismiss action against their client fined and disciplined for failing to disclose agreement to trial judge who indicated he did not want any sweetheart deals or anything "crafted" that "would be misleading" to him); People v. Rolfe, 962 P.2d 981 (Colo. 1998) (lawyer censured for violating Rule 3.3(a)(1) for stating that a social worker had "begun" her investigation of the matter, but failing to inform the court about the existence of social worker's letter that concluded no abuse could be substantiated).

278. Gerdin v. Princeton State Bank, 371 N.W.2d 5 (Minn. Ct. App 1985).

279. *See* Comm. on Legal Opinions, *Guidelines for the Preparation of Closing Opinions*, 57 Bus. L. 875 (2002); Comm. on Legal Opinions, *Legal Opinion Principles*, 53 Bus. L. 831 (1998).

280. ESG Capital Partners, LP v. Stratos, 828 F.3d 1023 (9th Cir. 2016) (cause of action stated for common-law fraud, and primary violation federal securities law against lawyer who made multiple false statements in the sale of securities apart from those of his client); Thomas Lee Equity Fund V, L.P. v. Mayer Brown, Rowe & Maw, LLP, 612 F. Supp. 2d 267 (S.D.N.Y. 2009) (cause of action stated for common-law aiding and abetting a fraud against law firm for partner's repeating of client's intentional misstatements during due diligence in a leveraged buyout).

will result in substantial damages. But the partner working on the opinion trusted a law student who forgot to check one of the pending lawsuits, a significant patent infringement case. Turns out substantial damages are not only alleged; they are more than likely. But no harm, no foul. We figure it's the client's fault because the CEO told us there was no problem with the infringement at all. Besides, why did the bank have us—whose fees our client had to pay—provide an opinion if the bank wasn't going to check it?

A. Not so fast. Let's start with malpractice to your client. If your partner (or her law student assistant) didn't look at the proper records at all, that's a breach of the standard of care, no expert testimony required.[281] If she did, but misread them, expert testimony that no lawyer should delegate this job to a law student or that proper supervision would have uncovered the problem could create the same basis for establishing a breach of the standard of care.

Once you discovered the correct situation, you breached another fiduciary obligation. You should have consulted with your client about the adverse effect of your findings, and not released the letter disclosing the sensitive lawsuit unless your client gave informed consent to the proper disclosures.[282] Perhaps other collateral was available, or perhaps the bank would have loaned your client less money knowing the actual facts. If the client might lose money on the loan due to this breach, you should notify your carrier.

But your troubles don't end there. You also might be liable to the bank. Courts generally require privity with the lawyer and reject the idea that lawyers owe malpractice duties to undifferentiated third parties. Here, however, the bank was the intended third-party beneficiary of this information, and, therefore, you again need to notify your carrier of this exposure.[283]

Q. But I already told you the bank had its own lawyers.

A. True, but the bank had no obligation to duplicate your work.[284] And, we're sorry to say, it gets worse. Your partner represented that she had reviewed all pending litigation, when in fact, she

281. RLGL § 52 cmt. g; Schmitz v. Crotty, 528 N.W.2d 112 (Iowa 1995) (lawyer failed to investigate property descriptions of predecessor counsel in valuing estate taxes).

282. MR 2.3; RLGL § 95.

283. RLGL § 51(2).

284. Greycas, Inc. v. Proud, 826 F.2d 1560 (7th Cir. 1987) (lender had no obligation to conduct its own UCC search and acted reasonably in relying on borrower's lawyer to do so).

had not. If she knew that, she intentionally lied. If she honestly believed the law student would follow through but failed to supervise, she's negligent. If she deliberately disregarded a high risk of harm, say, by not teaching the law student how to perform due diligence, then it may be characterized as reckless. Where the misrepresentation is intentional or reckless, most courts label it as "fraud" and hold that all foreseeable third parties (here, the bank) can recover, even if not in privity, as long as they reasonably relied on a misrepresentation of material fact.[285] Most jurisdictions do not extend liability for negligent misrepresentation to the group of all those who might foreseeably rely, but only to those "in a limited group of persons for whose benefit and guidance" the speaker intends to supply the information.[286] Some jurisdictions might find a group of lenders or bond holders too large to qualify,[287] but all would extend liability here.[288] And we think you know that many plaintiff's lawyers will "underplead" fraud so they can trigger your carrier's coverage of negligence,[289] not to mention professional discipline.[290]

§ 10.12 Lawyer Legal Accountability to Nonclients

Lawyers accustomed to the six Cs easily can assume that their only responsibility is to their clients. However, no agent or principal can evade general legal obligations.

For courts, the cases that have the easiest path to finding liability to nonclients involve intentional torts. Thus, lawyers who commit fraud,[291]

285. Restatement (Second) of Torts § 531 (Am. Law Inst. 1965); Ultramares Corp. v. Touche, Niven & Co., 174 N.E. 441 (N.Y. 1931).

286. Restatement (Second) of Torts § 552(2) (Am. Law Inst. 1965).

287. *Id.*

288. Denney v. Deutsche Bank AG, 443 F.3d 253 (2d Cir. 2006) (law firm's $81 million class action settlement of fraud claims for providing opinion letter used to market tax shelter later disallowed by IRS); Mehaffy, Rider, Windholz & Wilson v. Cent. Bank Denver, N.A., 892 P.2d 230 (Colo. 1995) (lawyer who issued a legal opinion in connection with a municipal bond offering may be liable to third-party investors under Restatement (Second) of Torts § 552 for negligent misrepresentation).

289. *Greycas*, 826 F.2d at 1560.

290. MRs 4.1(a), 8.4(c); *Greycas*, 826 F.2d at 1560.

291. Hartford Accident & Indem. Co. v. Sullivan, 846 F.2d 377 (7th Cir. 1988) (lawyer liable for fraud in helping client obtain fraudulent bank loan); Bonavire v. Wampler, 779 F.2d 1011 (4th Cir. 1985) (lawyer liable for fraud for knowingly misrepresenting client's honesty and experience); Fire Ins. Exch. v. Bell, 643 N.E.2d 310 (Ind. 1994) (lawyer liable for fraud for misrepresenting policy limits).

abuse of process,[292] malicious prosecution,[293] or conversion[294] do not escape liability simply because they did so in the act of providing services to a client. And do not forget that agreeing to assist a client's tortious act, such as fraud or breach of fiduciary duty, generally constitutes a concert of action or civil conspiracy.[295]

When negligence is alleged, courts generally recognize that antagonists do not have standing to seek enforcement of the Rules of Professional Conduct outside of a disciplinary context.[296] So, for example, nonclients probably should not be able to complain that you negligently advised a client to take action contrary to the nonclients' interests.[297] This limitation on duty dovetails with the general requirement in negligence that liability depends on a client-lawyer relationship.

But if your client or you invite a third party to rely on your work, and if you neglect or negligently produce it causing harm to the third party, you can be held liable to both your client and the third party.[298] One example is an invitation to rely on your legal opinion (which may

---

292. Givens v. Mullikin, 75 S.W.3d 383 (Tenn. 2002) (cause of action stated against lawyer for abuse of process (as well as insured client and insurer who directed the lawyer's conduct) for barraging opposing party with subpoenas, interrogatories, and a deposition seeking information that had already been turned over).

293. Zamos v. Stroud, 87 P.3d 802 (Cal. 2004) (cause of action for malicious prosecution stated against lawyer who properly commenced a lawsuit but continued to prosecute it after learning it was not supported by probable cause); Raine v. Drasin, 621 S.W.2d 895 (Ky. 1981) (lawyer liable for malicious prosecution for joining two physicians in malpractice case after reviewing records which clearly showed they had treated patient only after his injury had occurred).

294. ESG Capital Partners, LP v. Stratos, 828 F.3d 1023 (9th Cir. 2016) (cause of action stated for conversion by third party against lawyer who placed third-party funds in an unauthorized client trust account for a stock purchase and then issued checks from unauthorized account to client and lawyer for other purposes without third-party's knowledge or permission); ERA Realty Co. v. RBS Props., 586 N.Y.S.2d 831 (N.Y. App. Div. 1992) (lawyer liable for conversion for using void process to acquire funds).

295. Banco Popular N.A. v. Gandi, 823 A.2d 809 (N.J. Super. Ct. App. Div. 2003) (lawyer who handled transfers of assets from client to his wife that assisted client in obtaining bank loan made no actual misrepresentations to the bank and was not liable for common-law fraud nor for negligence; bank did state a claim, however, for conspiracy to defraud a creditor as long as lawyer actively participated in the client's fraud); Tensfeldt v. Haberman, 768 N.W.2d 641 (Wis. 2009) (client's violation of divorce judgment by executing will makes client's lawyer who drafted documents liable to children for intentionally aiding and abetting client's unlawful act as a matter of law).

296. MR Scope ¶ [20].

297. RLGL §§ 66(3), 67(4); Reynolds v. Schrock, 142 P.3d 1062 (Or. 2006). *See also* Hays v. Page Perry, LLC, 26 F. Supp. 3d 1311 (N.D. Ga. 2014) (lawyer has duty to report company agent's regulatory violations to the company's owner and obligation to advise owner of legal obligations, but no duty independent of service performed for client to report violations of a client company to regulatory authorities); Cruze v. Hudler, 267 P.3d 176 (Or. Ct. App. 2011), *modified*, 274 P.3d 858 (Or. Ct. App. 2012) (same lawyer who was privileged to advise client in *Reynolds* to act contrary to third-party's interests jointly liable with client for rendering substantial assistance to client's efforts to fraudulently induce third-party investment; causes of action also stated for state securities law violations, elder abuse, and racketeering).

298. RLGL § 51.

be required by the third party as part of a transaction).[299] You may avoid this reliance by making clear that your opinion or representation is intended for the client only, or by making clear that you are relying on the client's provision of facts without an independent investigation.[300] Similarly, if you invite a nonclient to rely on your services, for example, by offering to file a court document, and the opposing party suffers harm as a result of deficient performance by you, that party will have a cause of action against you if you fail to follow through competently with the task you undertook.[301]

You also owe duties of competence to third-party beneficiaries of your client (such as intended beneficiaries of your client's will or trust), regardless of their reliance on your work.[302] Here, everything depends on the clarity of your client's intent. When the parties are potential adversaries or incidental rather than intended beneficiaries, courts refuse to find a duty of care.[303] For example, courts have refused to impose a duty on the lawyer for a personal representative to the estate beneficiaries.[304] On the other hand, courts have imposed liability on

---

299. MR 2.3; RLGL § 95; Crews & Assocs., Inc. v. City of Port Gibson, No. 5:14-cv-37-DCB-MTP, 2014 WL 6069320 (S.D. Miss. Nov. 13, 2014) (company that requested a legal opinion from city may sue city's lawyers for malpractice).

300. RLGL § 51 cmt. e.

301. Nelson v. Nationwide Mortgage Corp., 659 F. Supp. 611 (D.D.C. 1987) (lawyer volunteered to answer questions and explain document); Kremser v. Quarles & Brady, L.L.P., 36 P.3d 761 (Ariz. Ct. App. 2001) (corporation's lawyers undertook responsibility to perfect nonclient creditor's security interest).

302. Lucas v. Hamm, 364 P.2d 685 (Cal. 1961) (intended beneficiaries of a will could recover from lawyer whose negligence in drafting document caused them to lose their testamentary rights); Fabian v. Lindsay, 765 S.E.2d 132 (S.C. 2014) (intended beneficiary named in a will may sue will drafter for malpractice that prevented fulfilling testator's intention); *In re* Guardianship of Karan, 38 P.3d 396 (Wash. Ct. App. 2002) (minor child has cause of action against mother's lawyer who set up child's trust to allow pilfering of the estate).

303. Capitol Indem. Corp. v. Fleming, 58 P.3d 965 (Ariz. Ct. App. 2002) (surety who posted bond for an estate's conservator incidental, not intended beneficiary of services provided by conservator's lawyer); MacMillan v. Scheffy, 787 A.2d 867 (N.H. 2001) (buyers in real estate transaction unable to prove that seller's lawyer, who drafted the deed, had the purpose to benefit them; mere fact they were grantees under the deed was not enough); Kilpatrick v. Wiley, Rein & Fielding, 37 P.3d 1130 (Utah 2001) (law firm's representation of a limited partnership does not create implied client-lawyer relationship with individual limited partners unless the latter reasonably believe the firm represents their discrete interests); Bovee v. Gravel, 811 A.2d 137 (Vt. 2002) (bank shareholders were not beneficiaries of law firm's representation of bank).

304. Trask v. Butler, 872 P.2d 1080 (Wash. 1994) (lawyer owed no duty of care to estate or heirs, who were only incidental rather than intended beneficiaries of attorney-client relationship); Neal v. Baker, 551 N.E.2d 704 (Ill. App. Ct. 1990) (income beneficiary pursuant to the will was not a third-party beneficiary of the lawyer-client relationship between the lawyer and the executor, where beneficiary contested lawyer's claim that the beneficiary should have paid the inheritance tax).

a fiduciary's lawyer when the latter assisted his client in breaching a fiduciary duty.[305]

Beyond cases where your client intends to benefit a third party, most courts impose a duty to prevent economic harm only when liability for misrepresentation or its statutory equivalents, such as securities fraud, can be established.[306] This duty stems from the fact that once you have undertaken a duty to speak, you must do so with care. If you make the misrepresentation intentionally or recklessly, your liability extends to all persons who might foreseeably rely on it.[307] Although a few jurisdictions extend liability for negligent misrepresentation this far as well,[308] most hold lawyers liable for negligent misrepresentation only to those in a limited class of persons for whose benefit and guidance the lawyer intends to supply the information, or to those third persons to whom the lawyer knows the recipient intends to supply the information.[309]

§ 10.13 Third-Person Obligations When Representing Fiduciaries

You Can Break the Contract

Q. I represented one of two partners in a single asset partnership, which owned an apartment house. The litigation finally settled and the partners agreed that the property would be transferred

305. Chem-Age Indus. Inc. v. Glover, 652 N.W.2d 756 (S.D. 2002) (lawyer can be liable for assisting a client in breaching a fiduciary duty to a third person if fiduciary was lawyer's client, lawyer knew fiduciary was breaching a fiduciary duty to plaintiff, and lawyer substantially assisted the breach causing damages).

306. Rubin v. Schottenstein, Zox & Dunn, 143 F.3d 263 (6th Cir. 1998) (en banc) (lawyer who represented seller in a securities transaction assumes a duty to provide complete and nonmisleading information with respect to subjects on which he undertakes to speak under 17 C.F.R. § 240, 10b-5); Orshoski v. Krieger, No. OT-01-009, 2001 WL 1388037 (Ohio Ct. App. Nov. 9, 2001) (prospective buyers who relied on negligent misrepresentations of lawyer for developer concerning subdivision's restrictive covenants could sue for negligent misrepresentation, but not for legal malpractice).

307. Restatement (Second) of Torts § 534 (Am. Law Inst. 1965); First Ark. Bank & Trust v. Gill Elrod Ragon Owen & Sherman, P.A., 427 S.W.3d 47 (Ark. 2013) (state statute governing lawyer liability creates fraud exception that allows third-party nonclients to seek recovery).

308. Molecular Tech. Corp. v. Valentine, 925 F.2d 910 (6th Cir. 1991) (Michigan law imposed duty with respect to any negligent misrepresentations to all foreseeable third parties who defendant knew would reasonably rely on information); Cromeans v. Morgan Keegan & Co., 1 F. Supp. 3d 994 (W.D. Mo. 2014) (bondholders may sue lawyers who included incorrect facts in offering statement; national trend is to allow nonclients to bring negligent misrepresentation claims against lawyers); Mehaffy, Rider, Windholz & Wilson v. Cent. Bank Denver, N.A., 892 P.2d 230 (Colo. 1995) (lawyer may be liable to third-party investors under Restatement (Second) of Torts § 552 for negligent misrepresentation by issuing a legal opinion in connection with a municipal bond offering).

309. RLGL § 51; Restatement (Second) of Torts § 552(2) (Am. Law Inst. 1965).

to my client who would market it and, once sold, turn over half the proceeds to my guy.

A. So far, so good.

Q. Yeah. I hate these "family" disputes. Bitter. Irrational. I recommended this arrangement to both of them.

A. I thought you only represented one of them.

Q. I did. The other fella was unrepresented. Anyway, my client sold the place. Got a great price.

A. Still okay.

Q. That's true. But then my client tells me that he and the partner have another investment. On that one, my guy claims he is owed more than his former partner is due on the sale of the property we litigated. He asks if it is okay to withhold the one-half because of the second dispute.

A. And you said?

Q. Of course. I know I am privileged to advise a client to breach an agreement. I gotta warn him of the consequences, but the client can make that decision.

A. You are absolutely right.

Q. Well that opinion did not stop the disappointed partner from suing my client and ME!

A. If it were simply your advice, you would be in the clear.

Q. But . . .

A. But there are two issues of concern. First, because your client was arguably acting as a fiduciary for his former partner in selling the property, mixing in another dispute might be actionable. Second, if the disgruntled one thinks you were acting as his counsel as well, then he could claim you were acting in breach of your fiduciary duty to HIM.

Q. Sounds tough.

A. Could be. Could be.[310]

---

310. Cruze v. Hudler, 267 P.3d 176 (Or. Ct. App. 2011), *modified*, 274 P.3d 858 (Or. Ct. App. 2012) (lawyer jointly liable with client for rendering substantial assistance to client's efforts to fraudulently induce third-party investment; causes of action also stated for state securities law violations, elder abuse, and racketeering); Chem-Age Indus. Inc. v. Glover, 652 N.W.2d 756 (S.D. 2002) (lawyer can be liable for assisting a client in breaching a fiduciary duty to a third person if fiduciary was lawyer's client, lawyer knew fiduciary was breaching a fiduciary duty to plaintiff, and lawyer substantially assisted the breach, thereby causing damages).

CHAPTER 11

Control

§ 11.01 Introduction: Who's in Charge?

Like other agents, lawyers have a duty to act on the client's behalf, subject to the client's right to control the objectives of the representation.[311] At the same time, many clients defer to and rely on their lawyers' expertise regarding the means to accomplish client goals. The Rules of Professional Conduct and the law of agency recognize three spheres of authority between client and lawyer. In the first two, clients and lawyers each retain sole authority to make certain decisions that cannot be overridden by the other.[312] In the third, client and lawyer decision-making authority overlap.[313] The scope of a client's control and the lawyer's authority also impact the client's and the lawyer's relationship with third parties.[314]

In the first sphere, clients retain sole authority to make decisions concerning the goals of the representation, including specifically whether and when to settle or appeal a matter, and in criminal cases, how to plead, whether to waive a jury trial, and whether to testify.[315] Clients may authorize their lawyers to make a particular decision within this

311. RLGL § 16; Restatement (Third) of Agency § 1.01 (Am. Law Inst. 2006).
312. RLGL §§ 22, 23.
313. *Id.* §§ 20, 21.
314. *Id.* §§ 25–30.
315. MR 1.2(a); RLGL § 22(1).

sphere, but the ultimate authority of clients to decide may not be completely ceded to their lawyers.[316]

In the second sphere, lawyers retain sole authority to refuse to perform, counsel, or assist a client's unlawful act.[317] Lawyers also may take actions in tribunals they reasonably believe to be required by the law or by court order, despite client preferences to the contrary.[318]

In all other decisions not reserved exclusively to clients or lawyers, clients and lawyers share authority.[319] Your clients and you are free to bargain about any lawful means that will be used to pursue the clients' objectives. If you do not want to engage in the scorched-earth tactics your client insists on, you may withdraw from the representation,[320] just as the client may discharge you if the client is unhappy with your approach to the matter.

All three spheres of authority place affirmative duties of communication on lawyers during a representation. Whenever a client decision arises, you must promptly inform and consult with the client about the decision.[321] Whenever a client insists on illegal conduct, you must promptly inform the client that the conduct is not permitted, and must explain why.[322] Once the client has decided on an objective, you must act to implement it,[323] reasonably consulting with your client as to the means by which the objective is to be accomplished.[324]

The outcome of this consultation creates the express terms of the engagement or, in agency terminology, actual authority, which obligates you to obey the client's lawful instructions and empowers you to act on behalf of the client.[325] Actual authority includes implied authority, which encompasses the authority to act in a manner that will further the client's objectives, as long as the lawyer reasonably believes the

---

316. Abbott v. Kidder Peabody & Co., 42 F. Supp. 2d 1046 (D. Colo. 1999) (lawyers representing 200 individual plaintiffs disqualified because of contract that gave settlement authority to a select group of plaintiffs; each individual client's approval is essential); Mattioni, Mattioni & Mattioni, Ltd. v. Ecological Shipping Corp., 530 F. Supp. 910 (E.D. Pa. 1981) (provision in contingent-fee contract that required lawyer's consent before settling case invalid and voided entire fee contract; lawyer reduced to quantum meruit recovery for fee).

317. MR 1.2(d); RLGL § 23(1).

318. MR 3.3; RLGL § 23(2).

319. MRs 1.2(a), 1.4; RLGL §§ 20, 21.

320. MRs 1.2 cmt. [2], 1.16(b)(4).

321. MRs 1.2(a), 1.4(a)(1); RLGL § 20(3).

322. MR 1.4(a)(5); RLGL § 20(1).

323. Vandermay v. Clayton, 984 P.2d 272 (Or. 1999) (lawyer liable for breach of fiduciary duty without expert testimony for drafting ambiguous indemnity agreement that did not include the protections client insisted upon); Olfe v. Gordon, 286 N.W.2d 573 (Wis. 1980) (lawyer liable without expert testimony for failure to effectuate client's instruction to secure a first mortgage in sale of her home).

324. MR 1.4(a)(2).

325. RLGL § 21 cmt. d; Restatement (Third) of Agency § 8.09 (Am. Law Inst. 2006).

client desires such action.[326] Once reasonable consultation has occurred, you are impliedly authorized to take lawful measures to advance the client's objectives.[327] A lawyer agent who acts within this scope legally binds the client principal.[328] A client also can be bound by a lawyer's apparent authority, that is, authority "traceable to the principal's manifestations" that causes another reasonably to believe the lawyer agent had the requisite authority to act on behalf of the client.[329]

§ 11.02 Chart: Authority Between Client and Lawyer

Client's Sole Authority	Negotiated Authority Delegated Discretion	Lawyer's Sole Authority
Objectives, goals, and specific decisions	Means	Refuse unlawful conduct and take action before tribunals
MR 1.2(a) [objectives, decisions to settle and appeal; in criminal cases, pleas, jury trial waiver, and whether client will testify]	MR 1.2(a) [means and implied authorization]; MR 1.2(b), 2.1 [moral views]; MR 1.2(c) [scope of the representation]; MR 1.4 [initiate communication]	MR 1.2(d) [client criminal or fraudulent activity] MR 1.4(a)(5) [consult about relevant limitations]; MR 3.3 [candor to the tribunal]
RLGL § 22	RLGL §§ 20, 21	RLGL §§ 23, 25

§ 11.03 Client Control

Lawyer agents are empowered by clients and obligated by fiduciary duty to obey a client-principal's lawful instructions regarding the objectives of the representation.[330] When clients act through duly-authorized agents, lawyers must communicate with agents about the goals, but only within the initial bounds of authorization set by the client.[331]

326. RLGL § 21 cmt. b; Restatement (Third) of Agency § 2.01 (Am. Law Inst. 2006).
327. MR 1.2(a); RLGL § 21(3).
328. RLGL § 26.
329. *Id.* § 27; Restatement (Third) of Agency § 2.03 (Am. Law Inst. 2006).
330. MR 1.2(a); RLGL § 16(1).
331. Machado v. Statewide Grievance Comm., 890 A.2d 622 (Conn. App. Ct. 2006) (lawyer reprimanded for failing to abide by client's directive to seek bankruptcy when client's duly-authorized agent sought to change the scope of the representation without authorization).

Because clients may not know or understand the range of available legal alternatives, lawyers have an affirmative obligation to explain legal options sufficiently so that clients are able to make informed choices about how to reach their objectives. In addition to the client's right to determine the goals of the representation, both Model Rule 1.2(a) and the Restatement identify several specific client decisions that may not be irrevocably delegated to a lawyer in both civil and criminal cases.[332]

These specific events—client objectives, decisions to settle and appeal, plea bargains, jury trial waiver, and whether client will testify—trigger a lawyer's duty to communicate with a client because of their finality in determining a client's rights. Although your client generally can delegate settlement authority, such a delegation is always revocable. If you do not disclose a specific offer, you run the risk of making or rejecting a settlement without the client's actual authority, subjecting you to liability to your client,[333] as well as to the third party (if the third party reasonably relies on your tortious misrepresentation of authority).[334] In both civil and criminal cases, clients decide after lawyers fulfill their obligation to communicate relevant information about whether to appeal a matter.[335]

Any decision that disposes of a client's rights is within your client's sole authority to make decisions concerning the goals of the representation and subject to revocable delegation. If you contemplate a stipulation, consent judgment, waiver of a cause of action or defense, or any other action that will foreclose or limit a client's rights, be sure to seek and obtain specific authorization before acting.

§ 11.04 Settlement Authority

Who Decides?

Q. We've been defending a personal injury claim that is as bogus as it is aggravating to our client. Worse yet, there is no insurance. So, my guy is on his own. But it's one of the blessed cases. Client says he'd rather pay me $50,000 than to pay the plaintiff $25,000. Doesn't want to set a precedent. So, all along I've been under instruction. Settle for $7,500; not a penny more. In the

332. RLGL § 22.

333. *Id.*; Moores v. Greenberg, 834 F.2d 1105 (1st Cir. 1987) (lawyer liable for the difference between offer and eventual jury verdict for failing to relay a $90,000 settlement offer).

334. RLGL § 30.

335. *Id.* § 22; Garza v. Idaho, 139 S. Ct. 738 (2019); Roe v. Flores-Ortega, 528 U.S. 470 (2000).

beginning I brought him settlement demands, and he almost took my head off. Yesterday, plaintiff's counsel called. His client will settle for $15,000. After all that. But, of course, I turned the offer down. As fast and as firmly as I could. I have my marching orders.

A. You could be right.

Q. Could! Of course I am right. My client could not be more clear.

A. That is certainly true. But let us warn you about two things. First, whatever your client told you, there's really no way to know how he will react when he actually confronts a firm offer in hand. Second, let's assume you try the case, lose to the tune of 100k, and your client finds out about the offer at 15. You think your now disgruntled client might misremember his instructions and wonder why you didn't tell him?

Q. I should hope not.

A. Of course. But better to act now than spend the rest of the representation on tenterhooks that your client's unequivocal stance gets amended with the benefit of hindsight. Remember, all of this will arise in the context of Model Rule 1.2(a), which makes it clear that one of the matters totally allocated to the client for decision making is whether to settle.[336] As a result, our recommendation to you is to call the client, explain the new offer, and prepare yourself for the tirade, an impassioned onslaught of a few minutes' duration that could save you a year of aggravation. Or, you could explain this in the beginning so that your client knows he will get these communications as a routine matter.

§ 11.05 Settlement Offers

A Client's Change of Mind

Q. I know I was right on this one. My client sued for medical malpractice with really serious repercussions. His special damages alone were over $500,000. Time and again he told me he would never accept a dime less than $3 million. So, when the other side offered to settle for $1.5 million, I knew what to do.

---

336. *In re* Grievance Proceeding, 171 F. Supp. 2d 81, 84 (D. Conn. 2001) ("Implicit in Rule 1.2(a)'s requirement that a lawyer 'shall abide by a client's decision whether to accept an offer of settlement' is both a requirement to communicate all settlement offers to the client and a requirement that the client be permitted to decide whether to accept or not to accept any such offer."); Estate of Falco, 188 Cal. App. 3d 1004, 1013 (1987) ("A client's right to reject settlement is absolute.").

I turned the offer down flat. A year later we try the case. And while we put some gigantic numbers up on the blackboard, the jury came in with a verdict of $1 million, barely covering the out-of-pocket costs. As my client walked out of the courtroom, defense counsel blurted out, "You should have taken our offer." My client turns to me and asks me what that was about. So, I tell him how I rejected $1.5 million because it was not close to $3 million. Now I have been sued for failing to communicate with my client.

A. We feel your pain. You thought you had a clear basis for rejecting the offer. The problem is your client has buyer's remorse now that there is a jury verdict. More importantly, you did not convey the $1.5 million offer.

Q. I thought that was the right thing to do.

A. Not really. Despite what clients tell you in the abstract, when an actual offer is received, the rules require that you relay that offer to the client. A concrete offer of $1.5 million might spur the client into making a counteroffer, or re-evaluating the client's position, or simply instructing you to reject the offer out of hand. But the offer is a new fact, and it is an important one. You can offer a defense here, but there is no guaranty jurors won't find that they would have wanted to know about the offer, even if that view is prompted by 20-20 hindsight.[337]

§ 11.06 Aggregate Settlements

The Union Members' Agreement

Q. So, we had this great idea. A group of union members asked us to sue for age discrimination. Company had huge layoffs. We didn't want to go through the class action rigmarole so we got each client to sign the same agreement. They agreed to be bound by a vote of a majority of the group to any group settlement offer that the company made. And not to accept any offer by the company that didn't include something for everyone. They wanted to prevent cherry picking by the employer. All for one and one for all and all that.

337. Patrick v. Williams, 402 S.E.2d 452 (N.C. Ct. App. 1991) (lawyer liable for punitive damages for failing to inform client of settlement offer, accepting inadequate settlement without client's consent, and failing to appeal a trial court order); Abadir v. Dellinger, 709 S.E.2d 743 (W. Va. 2011) (lawyer who was apparently authorized to settle case can be sued for malpractice for lack of actual authority to settle).

A. The flags are waving in the breeze. What an imaginative idea.
Q. That's what we thought. Just like a company that's governed by a majority vote of the directors. Or a partnership, by a majority of the partners. We figured this group came together to form a new organization for the purpose of pressing the litigation.
A. Imaginative, yes? In fact, one of the authors opined years ago that this could be an ethically proper way to proceed. Alas, the courts have not been buying. As for the majority vote provision, the case law concludes that a client's right to decide whether and when to settle is so enshrined in Rule 1.2(a) of the Model Rules as an exemplar of client autonomy that this important right may not be waived prospectively. The only valid settlement approval is a contemporaneous one.[338]

The same is also true of an agreement not to settle unless an offer is made for all plaintiffs in the matter. Any client at any time is entitled to accept a lone settlement offer even if the client agreed otherwise. Defendants are free to cut one or more clients from the pack with offers, which must be conveyed by the lawyer to each client individually and which each client is absolutely free to embrace. They do not have to; they just have to be allowed to.

§ 11.07 Plea Bargains

Buyer's Remorse

Q. I was representing a criminal defendant. From the beginning, he wanted to testify in his own defense. I tried everything to persuade him that was not a good idea, but to no avail.
A. He ended up testifying?
Q. Yes, and it was a disaster. His alibi fell apart completely on cross-examination. There is no doubt in my mind that he sealed his own conviction by taking the stand.
A. Well, you tried your best.
Q. I certainly thought so, but now I am being sued for malpractice for letting him take the stand. How can that be?
A. Well, anybody can sue anybody. There is no way of stopping that. But the good news is that you certainly have a complete

338. Abbott v. Kidder Peabody & Co., 42 F. Supp. 2d 1046 (D. Colo. 1999) (lawyers representing 200 individual plaintiffs disqualified because of contract that gave settlement authority to a select group of plaintiffs; each individual client's approval is essential).

defense. Two things: First, you certainly gave your client the best advice you could, trying to persuade the client not to testify. Second, the decision to testify is exclusively that of the client. That is the way the rules are written. As a result, the jury will be charged that you are obliged to follow your client's instructions. If you had done otherwise, you would then be in trouble.

Q. But do I have to wait until trial?

A. That is not clear. But it seems to us that motion practice based on Rule 1.2(a) may end this lawsuit before trial.

§ 11.08 Client Instructions

Don't Talk to Mama

Q. We are handling a habeas case for a capital defendant. We are doing it pro bono, and sometimes I think this representation is the living embodiment of "no good deed goes unpunished." Our review of the record demonstrates ineffective assistance of counsel. Particularly at the penalty phase. The original lawyers spent all their time worrying about guilt/innocence. They were completely unprepared for a guilty verdict. They had done no investigation of the client's past. They had not even interviewed his mother.

When we told the client of all these deficiencies, the client seemed excited about our proposed course of action. In every respect but one: The client instructed us not to talk to his mother. "She has suffered enough with me as a son," is what we were told. If we don't talk to Mom, we will be as ineffective as the earlier counsel.

A. We are sure you did the good-lawyering thing. Try to explain to the client why he should change his mind.

Q. We certainly did. It is only after days of trying that we came to you.

A. Well, this is one of the hardest ones. The client gets to determine the objectives of the representation. The objective here is, of course, to get the client off death row, maybe even out of prison. But a specific direction like this, based on important issues to the client, is different from a judgment call on cross-examination. The right answer under the rules has to be to abide by the client's instructions. At least until you have done all your other investigation, when the topic might be revisited.

But there is another way of looking at it. Rule 1.2, the rule that allocates authority between lawyer and client, has a middle ground. While the client sets the objectives, the lawyer is generally in charge of the means, in consultation with the client.

Q. But what if you get a direct order? This is what we have here.

A. We think if you want to persuade the client that the client is in error, that is obviously the best solution. But in another context, if the client were to tell you not to do something that you thought should be done, you would probably follow the direction of the client. However in this case, with the death penalty on the line, maybe we need special rules to address that difficult situation.

Q. Can we argue that it is one of those things that is exclusively in our control?

A. Well, there is an argument that the Rules of Professional Conduct require you to be diligent and competent. And so when the client is telling you not to talk to mom, he is really telling you to act in violation of the rules, not usually what we think of as falling into that category, but it is a possibility.

This is why some lawyers would go talk to mom. Totally respectable members of our profession take the view that they will not permit their client to commit suicide, that not talking to mom is tantamount to that result, and their job is to save the client—at all costs. One can hardly say those lawyers are unethical. But they certainly are flying in the face of totally legitimate client direction.[339]

§ 11.09 Advance Consent

Reasonable Settlement Agreements

Q. Our firm does plaintiffs' personal injury work. Very lucrative. Very gratifying. We just love the luxury of being self-righteous. All the time. But in reviewing our last year we find that more and more our clients are accepting lowball settlement offers rather than taking the case to trial (or act prepared to) to get their just deserts. We've decided one way to solve the problem

339. RLGL § 21 (A client may "instruct" a lawyer during the representation, subject to the lawyer's reasonable belief that the action taken is "required by law." § 21 comment d adds that although a lawyer is not required to carry out instructions contrary to professional rules or other law, "or which the lawyer reasonably believes to be unethical or similarly objectionable, . . . a lawyer may not continue a representation while refusing to follow a client's continuing instruction."). On representing a criminal defendant who disagrees with a lawyer's advice, see Monroe H. Freedman & Abbe Smith, Understanding Lawyers' Ethics § 3.07 (5th ed. 2016).

is to rewrite our standard agreement. The client is permitted to settle only if we agree the settlement is reasonable. Seems like the only way to save our clients from themselves. This will give them some backbone.

A. What a great idea. Why not just cut out the client altogether. Write the agreement to provide that you will decide whether, when, and at what amount the client will settle. That way clients will always act in their best interests.

Q. That sounds even better.

A. But it isn't. In fact, it simply compounds the problems inherent in your proposal. Under our rules, the client gets to decide about settlement. You can advise. You can say what you would do. But the client gets to decide. And an agreement like this would be viewed in a particularly jaundiced way because you are representing the client on a contingent-fee matter in which lawyers have been accused of overreaching, forcing clients to go for the big bucks when an early, modest, and certain settlement would have been in the client's best interests. We know that myth is the product of those who oppose plaintiffs' trial lawyers. We also know that our friends in the plaintiffs' bar suggest that more often than not the reverse is true, that is, clients with unwarranted visions of sugarplums in their dreams turn down settlements that their lawyers recommend. But that does not change the rule that the client does get to decide. And any restriction on that right would not only be void but could subject you to discipline for seeking such rule-violating authority.[340]

§ 11.10 Negotiation Strategy

What Does the Client Know?

Q. We are in negotiations to settle a professional malpractice case against an engineering firm. They really did screw up the design of our client's new manufacturing plant. It has taken

340. *In re* Lansky, 678 N.E.2d 1114, 1115 (Ind. 1997) (lawyer suspended for 30 days for violating Rule 1.2(a) by including provision in retainer agreement that authorized lawyer to settle "for any amount he determines is reasonable without further oral or written authorization"). In addition to agreements explicitly conferring all settlement authority to the lawyer, courts have also "generally held that the lawyer may not burden the client's ability to make settlement decisions by structuring the representation agreement so as to allow the lawyer to withdraw, or to ratchet up the cost of representation, if the client refuses an offer of settlement." Nehad v. Mukasey, 535 F.3d 962, 971 (9th Cir. 2008).

months and millions of dollars to resume regular production. The other side has admitted fault, but the big debate is over damages. Defendant's counsel offered a million dollars plus complete reimbursement of all out-of-pocket expenses. The client wants to go back with a $25 million offer to settle, even though the client would be happy to take $5 million. I tell the client $25 million will end negotiations with no settlement, but the client insists. I tell you, what clients don't know about negotiations would fill a library.

A. You have identified an important issue. Clients have complete control over whether to settle, but the rules say that the means to achieve those client objectives are to be subject to consultation with the client. You did that, but now the client insists on a strategy that you think is doomed to failure. If you cannot persuade the client to go your way, we think you must follow the direct instructions your client has given you, as unavailing as they might be. Just make sure you put your advice to the client in writing to help avoid later recriminations.

§ 11.11 Lawyer Authority

Lawyers have absolute authority and a direct responsibility to say "no" if asked to participate in unlawful client acts.[341] Neither the client's power to control the goals of the representation nor the lawyer's obligation to obey the client's directives allows either to violate the bounds of the law. Every legal representation requires that lawyers understand these bounds, communicate them to clients,[342] and pursue the client's goals in a lawful manner. If your client seeks to use your services to pursue illegal activity, you must disentangle yourself and refuse to participate.

Lawyers also have implied authority to act for clients in matters before a tribunal.[343] This authority becomes inherent and absolute when the legal system's procedures require an immediate decision without time to consult the client. But when the lawyer reasonably can foresee that an important decision will need to be made at trial, the lawyer should consult with the client before the exigent circumstance occurs. If

341. MR 1.2(d); RLGL § 23.
342. MR 1.4(a)(5).
343. RLGL § 25.

the client gives advance instructions, the lawyer should honor them, as long as permitted by court rules or professional obligations.[344]

Your ability to bargain with your client about the objectives and means of the representation ends when either your client or you are about to embark on illegal or fraudulent activity. If you can't talk your client out of pursuing a criminal or fraudulent action, you *must* withdraw and refuse to be involved in the matter.

§ 11.12 Lawyer or Client?

Lawyer Accepts an Offer

Q. We took all your learning about the client getting to decide to heart. I was at a settlement conference before Judge Grady. You know how tough she can be. So, she finally gets the plaintiff to offer 250. I've got authority to settle for 300 and, after I try to be a hero by going for 200, I accept, ever so reluctantly, the 250, thinking how happy my client will be.

A. So far we see no problem.

Q. Neither did I. But when I called my client with the good news, he shocks the hell out of me. He rejects the 250. Says he won't agree to a dime over 150. I didn't know what to do.

A. We hope you called the judge.

Q. Oh, right away. And do I get an earful. She says we had a deal. That she already notified court administration that the case was concluded. I then remember what you taught me. Only the client can decide whether to settle. Even cite Rule 1.2(a). But nothing mollifies her. She suggests she's going to hold me to the deal. I've got the judge on one side; the client on the other. Help!

A. It is a dilemma. And there is not one answer. Generally it is said that an agreement by a lawyer to a settlement is not binding on the client until the client ratifies it.[345] Everyone in the settlement process—judge, opposing counsel, counsel—knows about exclusive authority here, and, therefore, no authority exists to settle the case simply because a client asked a lawyer to negotiate. In agency terminology, the lawyer must have

344. *Id.* § 23 cmt. d.

345. Cole v. Myers, 21 A.2d 396, 398 (Conn. 1941) ("Either precedent special authority from the client or subsequent ratification by him is essential in order that a compromise or settlement by an attorney shall be binding on his client."); Makins v. District of Columbia, 861 A.2d 590, 593 (D.C. 2004) ("Agency principles are applied to determine whether the attorney or agent had authority to bind his principal to the settlement contract.").

express authority (the client said so), implied authority (the client's conduct, beyond sending the lawyer to negotiate said so), or apparent authority (the client's holding out to the third party said so).[346]

But that is not the case in some jurisdictions. In Michigan, for example, unless the lawyer disclaims authority the client is stuck with the lawyer's acceptance of the deal. And if the client is injured by that result, the client's recourse is not to escape the agreement of the agent, but to make a claim against that lawyer.[347]

Q. Ouch!

A. And it gets worse for you, my friend. It sounds like your settlement was part of an official court process—perhaps a court-ordered settlement session? If that is the case, in many jurisdictions the lawyer's authority before a court is implied or inherent due to the client's engagement of that lawyer.[348] So, you can see, if it's not too painful for us to say it, that it is simply critical that when you deal with settlement on behalf of a client to be absolutely clear about your authority, never to exceed it, and, in any event, to the greatest extent possible, hedge your bets by making it clear you still must confirm the deal with the client before the deal becomes the "real deal." And all of this becomes even more essential in court-annexed or court-ordered proceedings.

§ 11.13 Exclusive Lawyer Control

The Lawyer's Prerogative

Q. Well, what is a better example of when the lawyer gets to decide?

A. The general category is the client cannot direct us as lawyers to violate the law or violate a rule of professional conduct. So, for example, if the client told us the client was prepared to give

---

346. Robertson v. Alling, 351 P.3d 352 (Ariz. 2015) (clients bound to an agreement despite email to lawyer revoking a settlement offer; client's prior authorization to keep settlement offer open for two days created apparent authority that lawyer had authority to reoffer the same settlement days after the deadline expired).

347. Capital Dredge & Dock Corp. v. City of Detroit, 800 F.2d 525, 530 (6th Cir. 1986).

348. Koval v. Simon Telelect, Inc., 693 N.E.2d 1299 (Ind. 1998) (client is not bound by the lawyer's agreement absent a specific authorization, but in the circumstance of a court-required proceeding, including mediation, lawyers have implied or "inherent" authority to bind the client because, if required, the mediation constitutes a proceeding before a tribunal).

informed consent to a nonconsentable conflict of interest, that would not give us permission to do so. Similarly, if the client told us that we could decide when to disclose confidential information for the client, that open-ended authority would be too broad, and clearly not given on informed consent. Other examples abound, but you get the idea.

§ 11.14 The Middle Ground: Client-Lawyer Consultation

When considering how to implement the client's goals, a wise lawyer consults with her client. Decisions not within the sole discretion of client (goals of the representation) or lawyer (bounds of the law) are best thought of as delegated discretion. Within this sphere of shared authority, clients have the power to instruct lawyers, and may wish to delegate all authority, prefer to cede none, or choose to rely on the lawyer for some matters but wish to be consulted about others. Lawyers and clients are free to contract ahead of time about these matters, and absent specifics, the lawyer is empowered to pursue the client's goals by any lawful means. All of this delegated discretion is subject to the lawyer's duty to consult with the client.

Here, the lawyer's duties of communication and to obtain informed consent remain prominent. The lawyer must reasonably consult with the client about the means to be used to achieve the client's goals, keep the client reasonably informed about the status of the matter, promptly respond to client requests for information, and provide enough information to enable the client to make informed decisions regarding the representation, such as retaining other counsel, limiting the scope of the representation, and any informed consent to waive a client obligation such as confidentiality and conflicts of interest.[349]

The negotiated scope of a client's control and the lawyer's authority also impacts the client's relationship with third parties. A lawyer-agent who acts within this scope legally binds the client-principal.[350] An unauthorized lawyer who causes harm can be liable to both client[351] and any third person who reasonably relies on the lawyer's authority.[352]

349. MRs 1.2(a), 1.4.
350. RLGL § 26.
351. *Id.* §§ 49 (breach of fiduciary duty), 55 (breach of contract).
352. *Id.* §§ 30, 56.

§ 11.15 Litigation Strategy

Who Knows Best?

Q. I really face a dilemma. This is an automobile case. My client is the plaintiff and the facts are much in dispute. But the other side has a witness prepared to testify that my client ran the red light. The witness is old. Her glasses are Coke-bottle thick. I could probably put her testimony into significant doubt, but the woman is charming, and she is going to appeal to the jury. I know that.

A. Don't tell us. Your client wants you to cross-examine her.

Q. You are so correct. She thinks that little ol' lady's testimony is devastating, and the only way to win is to rigorously challenge the witness's eyesight, her age, and her infirmities. I am convinced that will backfire, and any cross-examination will simply create sympathy for the witness and, perhaps, disdain for me, and will reflect badly on my client. But my client is insistent.

A. These disputes arise all the time. Clients don't have the benefit of your experience with juries. You have properly learned this lesson the hard way, perhaps with some results you deeply regret.

Q. You can say that again. But the client is adamant.

A. We do not believe this is something about which the client can insist. You have had a good discussion. You have consulted with the client. We are sure you considered it from every angle. This is one of those issues that falls into the middle ground under Rule 1.2, and we believe your obligation is to use your best judgment and proceed accordingly. There are so many matters where lawyers have to make judgments without the ability to consult the client. But, when you can consult the client, certainly that is preferable. However nothing in the rule instructs you to follow the client's instruction on a topic where your expertise is so vast and the client's so limited.

§ 11.16 Limited Scope Agreements

Clients usually hire lawyers to handle specific cases or matters. Lawyers generally prefer the client who wants that lawyer to handle all legal matters. Increasingly common is the client who seeks or the lawyer who offers the opposite: "Unbundled" legal services which limit the scope of the representation, by breaking down legal services into discrete tasks, such as drafting, negotiation, or court representation, or by providing service only for a particular legal issue, such as custody or property valuation.[353]

Model Rule 1.2(c) and the Restatement both approve of these contractual bargains, but only if the limitation is reasonable and the client gives informed consent.[354] Here, the reasonableness standard is determined from the viewpoint of the client, not the professional, so consider whether the benefits of the limitation to your client (reduced fee, able lawyer) would outweigh the risks (inadequate or incomplete legal advice or service).

The bookends are clear: Just as you cannot agree to limit your client's right to settle a matter or whether to plead guilty in a criminal case,[355] you cannot agree to conduct a "preliminary" investigation that does not provide an opinion on which the client can rely.[356] Be especially aware of specialty areas of practice: A bankruptcy court has held that a lawyer representing a Chapter 7 debtor may not limit the scope of representation and must represent the debtor in all aspects of the bankruptcy case.[357] And don't forget lesson number one: Identify your client. For example, if you are retained by an insurance company, duties to your client-insured mean that the insurer may not limit your obligation to the insured by requiring prior approval of depositions, research, and motions.[358]

On the other hand, agreeing to offer short-term legal services via a legal services hotline,[359] to handle a trial but not an appeal,[360] to advise about one transaction or claim but not others,[361] or to provide a quick legal opinion about a proposed mediated settlement without additional factual investigation,[362] all are reasonable as long as your client gives informed consent. Informed consent requires that the client understands the alternatives, especially those that other lawyers might

353. Forrest S. Mosten, Unbundling Legal Services: A Guide to Delivering Legal Services a la Carte (2000).

354. RLGL § 19.

355. Jones v. Barnes, 463 U.S. 745 (1983) (fundamental decisions to plead guilty, waive jury, testify, or appeal are for defendant); *In re* Lansky, 678 N.E.2d 1114 (Ind. 1997) (fee-agreement provision which gave up client's right to settle civil matter violated Rule 1.2(a)).

356. MR 1.2 cmt. [7].

357. *In re* Egwim, 291 B.R. 559 (Bankr. N.D. Ga. 2003).

358. *In re* Rules of Professional Conduct, 2 P.3d 806 (Mont. 2000) (insurance defense counsel may not abide by agreements to limit the scope of representation that interfere with their duty to insured client).

359. MR 6.4.

360. Young v. Bridwell, 437 P.2d 686 (Utah 1968).

361. Delta Equip. & Constr. Co. v. Royal Indem. Co., 186 So. 2d 454 (La. Ct. App. 1966).

362. Lerner v. Laufer, 819 A.2d 471 (N.J. Super. Ct. App. Div. 2003).

include in the same representation.[363] So, for example, a lawyer may be acting reasonably in limiting a representation to a worker's compensation claim alone, but only if the client understands that other lawyers could be retained who would be free to identify and pursue additional tort actions against third parties.[364]

The more complex the legal matter, the greater the need for explicit informed consent from your client to limit the scope of your representation. A good engagement letter provides you with an opportunity to clarify which legal services you do and do not intend to provide. Be sure to specify alternatives that you will not pursue to make it clear that, if the client desires those services, the client should seek them elsewhere.[365]

§ 11.17 Insurance Defense Control

Insurance Intermeddlers

Q. These damn guidelines. We love the fact that our insurance company clients send us books of business. Stay on their good side and you can assure yourself constant work. But the demands are impossible. Take this one. We have a serious product liability case. Our defense will require a nationally recognized metallurgical expert, and we could use that person right now as we develop the defense. But the insurance company has an absolute rule: No experts may be hired until six weeks before trial. They say it cuts down on a lot of needless costs. But their savings are not cost free. You cannot shape your case anew six weeks before trial. What shall we do?

A. This is a classic. The insurance company certainly has a legitimate interest in your defense, but your client is the insured, even if the insurance company claims it is also a client. And

363. Barnes v. Turner, 606 S.E.2d 849 (Ga. 2004) (lawyer who perfected client's security interests by filing UCC financing statements also undertook duty to renew statements after five years or inform client of need to do so).

364. Greenwich v. Markhoff, 650 N.Y.S.2d 704 (N.Y. App. Div. 1996).

365. SCB Diversified Mun. Portfolio v. Crews & Assocs., No. 09-7251, 2012 WL 13708 (E.D. La. Jan. 4, 2012) (law firm retained to verify validity and tax implications of bond sale had no obligation to identify environmental issues); Janik v. Rudy, Exelrod & Zieff, 14 Cal. Rptr. 3d 751 (2004) (class member could allege legal malpractice for failure to pursue cause of action not specifically approved in class certification order as long as cause of action arose out of the same facts and class members would reasonably expect it to be considered); Barnes v. Turner, 606 S.E.2d 849 (Ga. 2004) (lawyer who perfected client's security interests by filing UCC financing statements also undertook duty to renew statements after five years or inform client of need to do so); Flatow v. Ingalls, 932 N.E.2d 726 (Ind. Ct. App. 2010) (law firm that agreed to provide client unbundled services in particular litigation had no obligation to client in other litigation).

if the insured has any exposure here, either monetary or reputational, then your individual client's views and needs are critical. You either have to use your remarkable powers of persuasion to get the insurance company to relent, give your client-insured an opportunity to foot the bill, at least temporarily, or write an appropriate letter to the insurance company explaining how the insured may very well have a claim at the end of the day, in whole or in part, because of the failure to hire this expert at the present time.[366]

Q. What an uncomfortable solution.

A. We wish we could make the practice of law totally comfortable but, from time to time, it is anything but, and lawyers are often faced with situations where for the benefit of their clients they have to take principled stands to make sure their client's best interests are served, even if it hits the pocket book.

§ 11.18 Chart: Lawyer's Authority to Act for Client

<table>
<tr><td></td><td colspan="2">Actual Authority:
RLGL §§ 26, 30
Restatement (Third) Agency §§ 2.01, 2.02</td><td>Apparent Authority:
RLGL §§ 25, 27
Restatement (Third) Agency § 2.03</td></tr>
<tr><td>Definition</td><td colspan="2">Lawyer's act within the scope of authority granted by client or client ratifies lawyer's act
RLGL § 26</td><td>Lawyer's act within scope of apparent authority due to third party's reasonable belief based on client's manifestation that lawyer is authorized
RLGL § 27</td></tr>
<tr><td>Examples</td><td>Express (specific authorization)
RLGL § 26 cmt. a</td><td>Implied (express authority arising out of general delegation of power to act)
RLGL §§ 26, 27</td><td>Presumed before a tribunal
RLGL § 25</td></tr>
</table>

366. Univ. of Miami v. Great Am. Assurance Co., 112 So. 3d 504 (Fla. Dist. Ct. App. 2013) (insurer had obligation to pay for separate lawyers to defend two insureds that blamed each other for an accident and was required to reimburse defendant that retained its own lawyer instead of proceeding with the conflicted defense).

Agency Power	Agent's acts designated or implied in principal's manifestations and acts necessary to achieving principal's objectives as agent reasonably understands them Restatement (Third) Agency § 2.02	Power of an agent due to third-party's reasonable belief agent has authority traceable to the principal's manifestations Restatement (Third) Agency § 2.03
Result	Client bound by authorizing lawyer either specifically or generally to achieve an objective, unless lawyer misrepresents authority RLGL § 30	Client not bound simply by retaining lawyer without actual or apparent authority RLGL § 27 comment c

CHAPTER 12

Communication

§ 12.01 Introduction: The Foundation of the Six Cs

Communication is essential to every aspect of the client-lawyer relationship. It defines the initial terms of the relationship and is required to make each of the six Cs work properly. Without communication, you cannot identify your clients with confidence. Nor can you act competently without understanding what the client hopes to accomplish and how you can assist the client in getting there. Clients cannot identify or control the goals of the representation without information about feasible options. Conversation also provides you with the obligation and opportunity to educate clients about the limits of the law. You must receive client informed consent before disclosing confidential information. And you must search for and disclose conflicts of interest in order to resolve them properly.

The key to understanding your foundational fiduciary duty of communication is to remember that you must initiate the conversation.[367] When you do, you will be in a position to know your client's identity, what your client both wants and expects, whether your client is willing to disclose confidences, and whether your client understands and wishes to give informed consent to proceed despite a conflict of interest. When you do not initiate these conversations, you can breach more than one basic fiduciary duty designed to protect your client whose

367. MR 1.4; RLGL § 20.

interests you have agreed to further. Because the duty to communicate is so fundamental, it is formulated broadly.

In certain well-defined instances, the law governing lawyers requires more than just communication. Informed consent, which requires specified disclosures and usually a written confirmation of client instructions, is required as a precondition to your receiving instructions about the goal of the representation from your client,[368] to limiting the scope of a representation,[369] to disclosing or using confidential or attorney-client privileged information,[370] and to resolving conflicts of interest.[371]

§ 12.02 Informed Consent

In specified situations, the Model Rules require "informed consent."[372] When this occurs, you must begin the process by communicating information and explaining it sufficiently so that clients from whom consent is sought fully appreciate the significance of the decision they are being asked to make. To do so, they also must understand the alternatives to the course of conduct you propose. For example, if prospective clients seek to establish a joint representation from you, you should inform them of their right to consider separate lawyers and explain the benefits of that alternative. And in every joint client representation you should provide sufficient information to secure informed consent about the impact of the joint representation on your handling of the confidential communications of the parties involved.

Many Model Rules also require that the informed consent be "confirmed in writing,"[373] which means that you can either provide a written document complete with disclosures for the client to sign or confirm a previously obtained oral consent in a timely post-decision document. Many jurisdictions also require a writing with specific disclosures for certain kinds of conflicts, such as business transactions with clients.[374] Even if not required, a writing confirming the discussion and the client's consent, preferably countersigned by the client, is the very best way of protecting not only the client but also the lawyer, who might find that the lengthy and quite informative conversation regarding this topic is remembered quite differently (if at all) should the client become disgruntled.

The law governing lawyers relies heavily on the notion of informed consent as a means to enable clients to maintain control and to prevent

368. MRs 1.2(a), 1.4.
369. MR 1.2(c).
370. MRs 1.6(a), 1.9(a), 1.18(d).
371. MRs 1.7(b)(4), 1.8–1.12, 2.3(b).
372. MR 1.0(e).
373. MR 1.0(b).
374. MR 1.8(a).

lawyers from breaching fiduciary duties. The notion that lawyers must obtain "informed consent" parallels a similar doctrine that governs the conduct of physicians and other health care providers.

The law of informed consent reflects the belief that persons make meaningful choices only if they have (1) understood the information, (2) appreciated the consequences of each choice, and (3) used reason to evaluate this information. As a means of promoting the autonomous choices of those you serve, the law of informed consent imposes two obligations on you: an obligation to provide information and deference to the client's choice.

The first obligation, disclosure, requires that the lawyer communicate "adequate information and explanation about the material risks of and reasonably available alternatives to the proposed course of conduct."[375] To determine what constitutes "reasonably adequate information" you should think about it from your client's point of view, including the client's experience, or lack thereof, in similar legal matters, as well as the complexity of the matter itself.[376]

Once the client has received information about alternatives and risks, the client's informed consent requires an affirmative response. Silence does not indicate consent, but consent may be implied from the client's other conduct.[377] In many situations where the lawyer must obtain informed consent, the consent must be "confirmed in writing." This can be achieved either by a written document your client signs or by a prompt transmittal of a writing that confirms an earlier oral informed consent.[378]

§ 12.03 Informed Consent: When?

Bad News

Q. The irony of this one is not lost on us. We were bringing a legal malpractice claim against our client's former lawyer. Our complaint sounds in negligence and breach of contract, or at least it did. The court just threw out our negligence claim on the ground that we missed the statute of limitations.

A. That is not irony; that is tragedy.

Q. Yes, we know that. But we figure we are actually in pretty good shape. We still have the breach of contract claim, and we figure the case is such a good one we are just as likely to win

375. MR 1.0(e); RLGL § 20.
376. MR 1.0 cmt. [6].
377. MR 1.0 cmt. [7].
378. MR 1.0(b) & cmt. [1].

on that basis as we would have on negligence. The good news is the client does not know. We figure there was no reason to get him upset.

A. Well, you certainly do not want an upset client. But that is not the standard for communication. Even if the client is going to get upset, you have an obligation to convey any material bad news.[379] And you and we both know that the client's case is not as strong today as it was before the dismissal. Moreover, you missed a statute, and that means there is a conflict between your client and you. It might be a consentable conflict if an independent lawyer advises the client that the client is well off to continue with your services. But the client has to know that you missed the statute, if for no other reason than it speaks volumes about your ability to handle the case.

Q. Oh, we won't make any more mistakes.

A. We hope that is true, but that does not answer the question regarding what you have to do now. And the first thing you have to do now is communicate with the client, tell the client of the problem, explain the conflict, urge the client to contact another lawyer for advice, and abide by the client's decision as to how to proceed. The client does not have to ask. You have to tell. And, as painful as it is, it is the only way you can fulfill your fiduciary duty to communicate and identify conflicts of interest.

§ 12.04 Reasonable Consultation

The Profitable Summary Judgment Motion

Q. Trial in this huge case is scheduled in a month. But we are convinced that will never occur. This case is so ripe for the grant of summary judgment. There are no disputed facts and no reason to burden the courts with a 12-week trial. So, we put together this beautiful summary judgment, so persuasive, and a set of exhibits three inches high. Off it went yesterday to the court, opposing counsel, and the general counsel of our client. I should say our former client.

A. Former?

---

379. MR 1.4(a)(b); ABA Comm. on Ethics & Prof'l Responsibility, Formal Op. 481 (2018) A Lawyer's Duty to Inform a Client or a Former Client of a Lawyer's Material Error ("[MR] 1.4 requires a lawyer to inform a current client if the lawyer believes that he or she may have materially erred in the client's representation . . . an error is material if a disinterested lawyer would conclude that it is (a) reasonably likely to harm or prejudice a client; or (b) of such a nature that it would reasonably cause a client to consider terminating the representation even in the absence of harm or prejudice.").

Q. That is what it looks like. General counsel fired us ten minutes ago. Says we wasted valuable time on a summary judgment motion that is sure to be denied. I explained our theory, how clever it was. She responded that no judge is going to take the time to go through three inches of exhibits with less than a month to go before trial. There is no likelihood it would be granted, she insists. "I am sick and tired of outside counsel running their meters on summary judgment motions that are doomed to failure," she screamed. "You didn't even have the courtesy to tell me you were planning it."

A. General counsel has a point, a very good point. This again is one of those issues that must be addressed with the client before any action is taken. Everyone thinks a summary judgment is the solution, but the statistics are a disaster. Those motions are rarely granted, and the client is entitled to undertake a cost-benefit analysis before money is spent on a summary judgment motion, or any other major initiative. Remember, we are the agents of our client, not the other way around. And while clients can and should defer to us, it is best if that deference is secured after there has been a full explanation and discussion with the client.

§ 12.05 Keeping the Client Reasonably Informed

Client Consultation

Q. My ears are still ringing from the dressing down I just received. We were handling this consumer class action for a major manufacturer of high-end electronics. The great issue is whether the product had an inherent defect or the problem arose due to customer misuse. We hired an expert from MIT, very expensive and very worth it. She issued a report that exonerated our client and blamed the consumer. Perfect defense. Except such reports do not come cheap. This one cost $200,000. And with our latest invoice to the client including that expert's charges, it launched the tirade I just endured.

A. Your client objected to the price of the expert?

Q. The client objected to our hiring an expert. The client did not know we had done that. The client claimed his in-house people could have been just as effective in defending the product. He employs three MIT engineers of his own, or so he claims.

A. Let us hope he calms down. But this could be a lesson for you. When you are going to make a decision to hire an expert and the client is on the hook for expert's fees, you must consult the client beforehand, even if you think the expert is absolutely necessary. First, the client may wish to use his own employees. Not as effective, but far cheaper. Or the client may have an alternative expert in mind. Or the client may prefer to go without an expert, a decision the client can make so long as you explain the risks involved. In any event, this kind of expenditure requires client communication and approval, even if you are convinced you are doing the right thing.[380]

§ 12.06 Reasonable Alternatives

ADR

Q. We had this terrific case we defended for a small manufacturer. We thought our defense was fantastic, and we had the best expert one could find. But, alas, after settlement discussions broke down, we went to trial and lost. Three weeks later the client gives me a call. "You never told me about mediation." Turns out the client, now disgruntled, was talking to a lawyer friend at a cocktail party. This officious intermeddler asked the client why he didn't settle. "Didn't your lawyer tell you trying a case like this is a crap shoot?" When the client tells her that they tried to settle, she asks whether they tried mediation. The client said "no, I don't even know what mediation is." Now the client called me and wants to know why we never mentioned mediation. This other lawyer told our client, "That is the best way to get settlement."

A. Interesting you should ask that question. The Ethics 2000 Commission that rewrote the Model Rules was asked to mandate discussions about mediation. Of course, the request came from the mediation bar. Ethics 2000 rejected that idea on the grounds that the rules would become unwieldy if we mandated various means of which mediation is but one.

Which does not mean you are off the hook. You are supposed to consult with the client about the means to obtain the client's objectives. All it takes is some expert to say that under the circumstances of your defense of this client the standard of care was to recommend or, at least consider, mediation. You will certainly have a defense if you thought mediation was not

380. *See also* § 24.03 in this book.

appropriate, too expensive, or so unlikely to produce a positive result that it was not worth the effort. But then some jury is going to decide who is correct about the standard of care.[381]

§ 12.07 Hiring Another Lawyer

Hiring Reinforcements

Q. We agreed to take on a patent infringement case. We never did one before, but we hired this MIT computer science genius last year whose precise expertise is at the center of this litigation.

A. Sounds like a good start. If he knows what he is talking about.

Q. She. It's a woman. Anyway, she is very diligent and eager, but I am uneasy. This is a big case. I figure we would be well-served to run the case by a friend who has been doing this work for decades.

A. A great idea. Just call the client . . .

Q. Not so quick. We do not want the client to know of our doubts. We might lose the case entirely. Can't we simply consult on the q.t.?

A. The answer is almost certainly no. Though Rule 1.6(b)(4) permits you to consult a lawyer outside the firm without consulting your client when the question relates to professional responsibility matters, you are not otherwise free to share confidential information with lawyers outside your practice setting unless the client provides informed consent. The client is entitled to know with whom you plan to speak, draw whatever conclusions need be drawn from your need to do so, and grant or withhold consent as the client chooses.

Q. We'd better not then.

A. We think just the reverse. If you feel the need to find additional expertise to provide the kind of service the client deserves, bringing in a wise counselor is precisely what you should do. Indeed, Rule 1.1, the competence rule, explicitly suggests such consultation as a way to assure you fulfill the competence requirement. We know you will do the right thing.

---

381. Colo. R. Prof'l Conduct 2.1 (2018) ("In a matter involving, or expected to involve litigation, a lawyer shall advise the client of alternative forms of dispute resolution which might reasonably be pursued to attempt to resolve the legal dispute or to reach the legal objective sought."); *see also In re* Cohen, 82 P.3d 224 (Wash. 2004) (lawyer suspended for one year for deciding to pursue arbitration of case without informing client that losing arbitration would result in client's liability for opponent's lawyer's fees).

§ 12.08 Chart: Eight Events That Trigger a Lawyer's Duty to Communicate with a Client

1. Initially, to agree on a fee arrangement and to define the scope of the representation, both of which should be explained in an engagement letter.

2. When decisions require client consent about the objectives of the representation, such as the decision to settle or appeal a matter.[382]

3. When you must obtain the client's informed consent, including when you seek to:

    a. Limit the scope of a representation.[383]

    b. Obtain an exception to a fiduciary obligation owed your client, especially the duties of confidentiality and loyalty (conflicts of interest resolution).[384]

    c. Obtain an exception to a fiduciary obligation owed to a prospective client.[385]

    d. Provide an evaluation for use by a third person that is likely to adversely affect the client's interests.[386]

4. When decisions require client consultation about the means to be used to accomplish the client's objectives, such as whether to litigate, arbitrate, or mediate a matter; stipulate to a set of facts; or consult with another lawyer.[387]

5. When necessary to update clients periodically on the status of a matter, including information about important developments in the representation itself, as well as changes in the lawyer's practice, such as a serious illness of the lawyer or a merger with another law firm.[388]

6. When a lawyer makes a significant mistake in the matter.[389]

7. When a client requests information.[390]

8. When the law imposes limits on conduct that a client expects you to undertake.[391]

382. MR 1.2(a); RLGL § 22.
383. MR 1.2(c); RLGL § 19.
384. MRs 1.4(a)(1), 1.6–1.12; RLGL §§ 20, 60–62, 121–135.
385. MR 1.18; RLGL § 15.
386. MR 2.3; RLGL § 95.
387. MRs 1.2(a), 1.4(a)(2), 2.1; RLGL § 21.
388. MR 1.4(a)(3); RLGL § 20 cmt. c.
389. MR 1.4 (a)(3); RLGL § 20 CMT. C.
390. MR 1.4(a)(4); RLGL § 20 cmt. D.
391. MR 1.4(a)(5); RLGL § 22 cmt. c.

CHAPTER 13

Confidentiality

§ 13.01 Introduction: The Never-Ending Obligation

Although lawyers often use the words "confidentiality" and "privilege" interchangeably, they are, in fact, quite different concepts. Your duty of confidentiality is a fiduciary obligation that arises from your loyalty obligation in agency law and is now enshrined in the Rules of Professional Conduct.[392] It protects prospective,[393] actual, and former clients, and never ends.[394] This fiduciary obligation has always protected nearly all client information, requiring you to keep confidential all information learned in the course of a representation from any source. Exceptions are narrow and tend to be discretionary, although a few go so far as to require disclosure of what would otherwise be confidential.

The privilege, on the other hand, is a rule of evidence that governs what you may be forced to disclose if you are called to testify or produce documents.[395] Privileged information is a subset of the category of confidential information.[396] Like the fiduciary duty, it too lasts forever.[397] The evidentiary privilege has never protected all client confi-

392. MR 1.6; RLGL § 60.

393. MR 1.18; RLGL § 15.

394. MR 1.9; RLGL §§ 60 cmt. e, 132; State *ex rel.* Counsel for Discipline v. Tonderum, 840 N.W.2d 487 (Neb. 2013) (fired defense lawyer suspended for at least three years for disclosing to prosecutor names of witnesses who could be used to prove her former client's guilt).

395. RLGL § 68.

396. MR 1.6 cmt. [3]; RLGL § 59 cmt. b.

397. RLGL § 77; Swidler & Berlin v. United States, 524 U.S. 399 (1998).

dences, and has developed a number of widely accepted exceptions. Exceptions are broader than those found in the Rules of Professional Conduct and, when applicable, require disclosure. Both doctrines protect organizational as well as individual clients.

Confidentiality can be traced historically to the nineteenth-century developments of the fiduciary duty of loyalty in agency law as well as the recognition of the attorney-client privilege in the law of evidence. Shortly after World War II, the law of evidence also began to protect lawyer work product from discovery, including witness statements, as well as lawyer opinions and mental impressions formed in representing the client in anticipation of litigation.[398]

Confidentiality encourages clients to communicate fully with lawyers so that they can be effectively represented. Without all the facts, lawyers will not be able to give competent and complete legal advice, which will, in turn, disserve clients seeking to follow the law and undermine the ability of lawyers to promote compliance with the rule of law. Confidentiality also promotes a primary value of the legal system—respect for human rights—by promoting trust and privacy in the client-lawyer relationship. The lawyer's obligation to protect this private sphere becomes especially important when the government seeks to invade it through compulsion. The following chart compares these two bodies of law.

§ 13.02 Chart: Source and Scope of Client Confidentiality Obligations

	Ethical/ Fiduciary Obligation	**Evidentiary Rules**
Source of Law	Agency Law; Model Rules 1.6, 1.8(b), 1.9, 1.18	Statute; Common Law of Evidence
Definition	MR 1.6 (a): Information relating to the representation of a client	Attorney-Client Privilege: A communication made between privileged persons in confidence for the purpose of obtaining or providing legal assistance. RLGL § 68 Work-Product Immunity: Material prepared by a lawyer in reasonable anticipation of litigation. RLGL § 87

398. RLGL § 87.

§ 13.03 Scope of the Confidentiality Protection

The fiduciary obligation of lawyer confidentiality attaches to all client representations and protects all "information relating to the representation" regardless of its source; it is not limited to matters the client requests you to keep confidential.[399] Lawyers may not disclose or use such information without the informed consent of the client or some other clear exception to the protection. Information relating to the representation includes your client's identity and any oral, written, electronic, or other information obtained from any source, whether client, witness, public record, document, or the like.

Confidentiality attaches whether or not the communication is privileged, whether the client pays a fee, whether the information was obtained by the lawyer or an agent of the lawyer, and whether others know about or can uncover the information.[400] Even if publicly available, if you came across the information because of the client representation, the information and its location are protected.[401] Unless the client directs otherwise, lawyers may share confidential information within their law firms.[402] Lawyers also may use hypotheticals to discuss issues relating to client representations, as long as the facts shared present "no reasonable likelihood that the listener will be able to ascertain the identity of the client or the situation involved."[403]

§ 13.04 Client Identity and Public Documents

Client identity and public documents you come across in representing a client are protected by confidentiality, which means you cannot disclose them without client informed consent.[404] The Restatement purports to exclude "information that is generally known," but cabins the meaning of this phrase to public documents only if "obtainable through publicly available indexes and similar methods of access."[405] It further warns that "[a] lawyer must not justify adverse use or disclosure of client information simply because the information has become known to

---

399. MR 1.6(a), 1.6 cmt. [1].

400. RLGL § 59 cmt. d.

401. MR 1.6 cmt. [3]; RLGL § 59 cmt. b.

402. MR 1.0(c), 1.6 cmt. [5]

403. MR 1.6 cmt. [4].

404. MR 1.6; RLGL § 59; *In re* Diaz, 288 P.3d 486 (Kan. 2012) (former military lawyer disbarred for anonymously releasing classified list of Guantanamo Bay detainees to human rights lawyer).

405. RLGL § 59 cmt. d.

third persons, if it is not otherwise generally known."[406] Similarly, public documents by definition do not constitute generally known information within the meaning of the lawyer's confidentiality obligation to former clients.[407]

In the context of creating exceptions to the attorney-client or work-product privileges, however, many courts force disclosure of these bits of information. Client identity, though clearly confidential, generally is not privileged because it does not constitute a "communication." The fact that a particular client retained a particular lawyer usually does not communicate anything about the content of the client's communication. In circumstances where disclosing client identity might disclose the nature of the client's underlying concern, courts are willing to extend the privilege, for example, to consultation with a criminal defense lawyer that would reveal that the client committed a specific crime.[408]

Remember that the privilege is not the sole definition of the scope of your obligation of confidentiality to clients. A public document found in the course of representing a client may not be privileged but certainly is subject to the fiduciary duty of confidentiality. So is your client's identity and the fact that she retained you. If you *don't* disclose what clients tell you, what you learn about them, or the advice you give, and you *do* claim the appropriate privilege if the information is sought in litigation, you will be in great shape. Of course, you also should be aware of relevant exceptions to confidentiality, which can allow or on occasion mandate disclosure.[409]

---

406. *Id.; see also* Matter of Anonymous, 654 N.E.2d 1128 (Ind. 1995) (lawyer reprimanded for use of information gained during initial consultation with prospective client, despite the fact the information was readily available from public sources).

407. ABA Comm. on Ethics & Prof'l Responsibility, Formal Op. 479 (2017) The "Generally Known" Exception to Former-Client Confidentiality (The "generally known" exception to the duty of former-client confidentiality in Rule 1.9 (c)(1) is limited. . . . Information is not "generally known" simply because it has been discussed in open court, or is available in court records, in libraries, or in other public repositories of information.).

408. RLGL § 69 cmt. g; Dean v. Dean, 607 So. 2d 494 (Fla. Dist. Ct. App. 1992) (lawyer bound by attorney-client privilege not to disclose client's identity because client sought lawyer's advice about how to return stolen property). The authors would be more inclined to protect client identity where the client's interests would be prejudiced. *See, e.g.,* MR 1.6(b)(7) (confidentiality exception "to detect and resolve conflicts of interest for conflicts arising from the lawyer's change of employment or from changes in the composition or ownership of a firm, but only if the revealed information would not compromise the attorney-client privilege or otherwise prejudice the client").

409. Barton v. U.S. Dist. Ct., 410 F.3d 1104 (9th Cir. 2005) (online law firm questionnaire filled out by eventual plaintiffs in class action that sought information about drug injury but warned that questionnaire was not a request for legal advice not privileged); Prudential Ins. Co. v. Massaro, 47 F. App'x 618 (3d Cir. 2002) (former inside counsel who incorrectly believed that former employer's misconduct fell within crime-fraud exception to the privilege permanently enjoined from disclosing any additional privileged information).

§ 13.05 Client Information in Public Records

Currying the Favor of the Press

Q. I give background information on high-profile cases I've heard about whenever the press calls. Of all the ideas I've had for promoting my practice, none works like currying the favor of reporters. You do them a favor; they'll do one for you. I explain the importance of cases. The significance of certain decisions. You get the idea.

A. Educating the public is one of our responsibilities. You get high marks from us for such civic commitment. Even if you're doing it for the wrong reason.

Q. Wrong? Are you kidding me? Every time I get quoted, I get phone calls from folks. Most are not matters I would take. Lots of crackpots. But then amidst the coal are a few diamonds. Terrific matters. Nothing wrong with that, right?

A. We suppose so. You are at least not soliciting these potential clients.[410]

Q. But here's my problem. One of my favorite reporters has been covering a matter I am handling. Lots of coverage. Public figures in a fight over control of the family company.

A. So far so good.

Q. Better than that. I've even been interviewed on Action News. That's not what's got me worried. This reporter friend called me up and asked me a question. I told her I'd get back to her. I was worried about my confidentiality duty to my client. It turns out the answer to her inquiry can be found in one of the 23 volumes of deposition transcripts filed in the courthouse. I figure I can tell her the volume and page number—and garner her undying gratitude—since it is a public record. Not confidential then, is the way I figure it.

A. We have a question. Will the disclosure of this information help your client?

Q. Well, not really. It's actually a little embarrassing. But these facts are going to come out sometime, so why not be the source and get some credit?

A. On this one you are wrong. Even if the argument can be made that, under our rules, this information is not confidential, you should be the last person who should be handing this info to page six of the *New York Post* or its gossip equivalent in your

410. MR 7.3(a).

hometown. If you don't think you could recommend the disclosure to benefit your client, you shouldn't even be considering disclosure.

Q. But it's on file in the courthouse.

A. That may be so. But that does not render the information not confidential. Some ask how it can be confidential when it's been on the front page of the local newspaper—above the fold. But importantly, the Model Rule contains no exception for publicly available information, even "above the fold."[411] The Restatement of the Law Governing Lawyers talks about a limited exception for that which is "generally known," a view rejected by most jurisdictions.[412] Yet, by definition, this information is not generally known or this reporter would not be in your debt because you revealed it to her.[413] Although an occasional state has exempted public filings from the definition of confidential information,[414] the far better and vast majority view is significantly broader than that. And while the Internet has certainly improved the accessibility by the public (and the press) to what otherwise would be considered hidden information, even if there really were an exception for "generally known," we certainly don't think that term should be stretched beyond its accepted definition to apply, without the informed consent of your client, to what might be found on a clever Google search, much less something buried in a transcript that's only available from the courthouse.

---

411. MR 1.6 cmt. [3] ("The confidentiality rule . . . applies not only to matters communicated in confidence by the client but also to all information relating to the representation, whatever its source.").

412. RLGL § 59.

413. *Id.* § 59 cmt. d (Information that has become generally known to a relevant sector of the public is not confidential, but not if a person who seeks the information can find it only "by means of special knowledge or substantial difficulty or expense."); *In re* Peshek, 798 N.W.2d 879 (Wis. 2011) (reciprocal discipline based on Illinois suspension for blogging about cases and clients as a public defender, lawyer revealed details that would allow those familiar with her cases to identify them, even though she subjectively believed she had maintained client confidentiality).

414. MINN. R. PROF'L CONDUCT 1.6(b)(2) (2018) (non-privileged information may be disclosed but only if the lawyer reasonably believes the disclosure would not be embarrassing or likely detrimental to the client).

§ 13.06 Client Identity and Client Matters

The Law-Firm Website

Q. Our firm is going to develop a redesigned website with more information, more details, fewer platitudes about what a jovial place our firm is, and less about our wonderful history. That's what sells in today's cutthroat world, or so we've been told by the marketing gurus.

A. Great idea. You want to remain competitive. For sure.

Q. We are going to list our clients. We figure we've done work in the last ten years for 30 of the Fortune 100 companies.

A. Funny. We don't think of your firm as playing in that league.

Q. Oh, you are right in one respect. Most of what we've done has been small potatoes. Serving subpoenas, providing a conference room, filing pleadings.

A. Have you asked these former clients for permission to disclose this information?

Q. No. Why should we? Our ethics guy told us that the identity of your clients and former clients is not privileged. So we can list Ford, Merck, or Walmart without asking them. Besides they might say no.

A. Who you represent is not considered privileged. That is generally true, unless the fact of representation might carry with it a communication about the substance of the interaction between lawyer and client.[415] Think of the disclosure of the identity of the client that Larry Lawyer represented, on whose behalf Larry Lawyer turned into the police the proceeds of a bank robbery. The mere fact of the representation would disclose the content of the client-lawyer discussions.

Q. Well, that's not the case here. No one's going to know what we did for Conoco Philips if we list them as a client.

A. True enough. But the issue is not privilege. Privilege is a rule of evidence that establishes when anyone may refuse to produce documents or testify about certain communications between lawyer and client that meet the precise standards of the privilege. But your website is not a deposition. You are not being forced to list these present and former clients on your website. As a result, the applicable legal doctrine is the fiduciary duty of confidentiality, which tells lawyers when they are obliged to refuse to disclose information relating to the representation

415. RLGL § 69 cmt. g.

on a voluntary basis, what information they cannot share with their spouses or their buddies at the 19th hole, or the person on the next Stairmaster. And the fact that you are representing company X is a piece of confidential information that you may not disclose unless the client has agreed to such disclosure. Moreover, companies jealously guard this information. Not just anyone may list General Electric as a client, even if G.E. has hired the firm to do some legal work. So, before you list "representative clients" anywhere, including on your own firm's website, get your present or former client's permission to do so, preferably in writing.[416]

Q. Well, actually we go much further than that. We like to describe our successes in some detail. We've achieved some terrific verdicts, appeals, decisions, and settlements over the last decade.

A. That kind of disclosure cries out even more for client permission. What may be viewed by you as a giant victory may be an organizational or individual client event that remains a source of embarrassment or worse. But even if it were a complete triumph for the client, one still must get permission. And one more thing.

Q. You are making this impossible.

A. You'd better follow your local jurisdiction's rules on advertising.

Q. But this is a website.

A. Precisely. Almost all regulations consider a firm website to be simply an electronic billboard subject to all the rules governing lawyer ads.[417] As a result, your website may have to be labeled "advertisement," your description of your successes may be scrutinized for any statements that are remotely misleading, and you may be forced to include a disclaimer that explains that these reputed triumphs may not be comparable to the prospective client's matter and that these "achievements" are no guarantee of future success for new clients of the firm. For example, you may have settled a case for $50 million, but how is the prospective client going to be able to determine whether that result exceeded reasonable expectations or reflects a totally mediocre recovery in a case that should've resulted in

416. MR 1.0(e) & cmt.[6]; RLGL § 62 & cmt. c.

417. ABA Comm. on Ethics & Prof'l Responsibility, Formal Op. 10-457 (2010) Lawyer Websites.

a recovery four times that amount?[418] Or that the result was achieved in just one of ten similar cases the firm handled with respect to the same defective product?

§ 13.07 Using Confidential Information

The Great Opportunity

Q. We are representing Disney in acquiring a huge tract of land for a new Disney Theme Park, as yet unnamed except as Project X. We are using straw parties to act as purchasers. So far the secret is secure. I am even handling a specific performance claim against a seller who refuses to go to settlement. She changed her mind. Anyway, that's really beside the point.

I got this great idea. I heard from my brother-in-law—he's an architect—that a 35-acre plot abutting the future Disney park is on the market. My brother-in-law has no idea about Disney's plans. He merely thought, if our siblings purchased the land, we could finally have the vineyard we have always dreamed about. I figure my firm should buy it—we put up a hotel and end this billable-hour grind once and for all.

A. Are you going to tell Disney?

Q. Why should I do that? When we started the project, they made it quite clear they only wanted the land within prescribed metes and bounds.

A. But that was then, and this is now. And just as you ought to communicate with your client any new offers from the other side—even when you think your client will reject them—you should tell Disney about the availability of this opportunity.

Q. Then, if they reject it, are we free to proceed with Plan Ritz Carlton?

---

418. *In re* Anonymous, 932 N.E.2d 671 (Ind. 2010) (lawyer's obligation of confidentiality attached once prospective client asks for a referral; subsequent disclosure to friends about client's marital difficulties violated Rule 1.9 (c)(2)); *In re* Diaz, 288 P.3d 486 (Kan. 2012) (lawyer for Guantanamo defendants who released classified information about clients without authorization to a human rights organization was convicted of four military felonies and disbarred for violating Rules 1.6(a) and 8.4(b)); Disciplinary Counsel v. Cicero, 982 N.E.2d 650, 653 (Ohio 2012) (lawyer who disclosed prospective client's criminal activity to Ohio State football coach to warn coach of "possible association" of team members with prospective client violated Rule 1.18 and suspended for one year); Perez v. Kirk & Carrigan, 822 S.W.2d 261 (Tex. App. 1992) (former lawyers liable for breach of fiduciary duty for disclosing confidential information to prosecutor, even where the information probably was not privileged because the client's father and uncle were present when Perez communicated with his lawyers; claims based on the state deceptive trade practices act and conspiracy to violate the state insurance code also upheld).

A. Very funny. What do you think?
Q. I thought we could do it without ever telling them.
A. Don't you see any problems with not telling them?
Q. I see only opportunity.
A. Well, for starters, your firm will suddenly have a very big (and undisclosed) stake in Disney going forward with the project.
Q. So? Our interests will be perfectly aligned.
A. Not if it turns out you think it's in Disney's best interests to abandon or narrow the project. Or to pursue only certain parcels first.
Q. Anything else?
A. Well, you are setting yourself up to be a business competitor of your client. For sure, Disney is going to have hotels. Don't you think this valuable client is entitled to know that fact and evaluate how it might affect the representation? Moreover, Disney should know your firm is entering into this business venture so it can decide whether such a venture will simply be a distraction that will affect the quality of your legal work.
Q. That's it?
A. Naturally, we saved the best for last. The truth is our rules explicitly prohibit the use of client confidential information adverse to the client.[419] Now it may be, it just may be, that Disney won't view this to be a violation of Rule 1.8(b) because it is not adverse. But that is not a risk you should run. If you really are serious about abandoning your concentration in law to chase this entrepreneurial dream, you must notify Disney of the land's availability and, if Disney is not interested, you then must discuss your pipe dreams with them and get their consent to what you plan. Otherwise, there may be hell to pay when Disney learns the developer of the new Ritz Carlton is Disney's own law firm, dashing their plans for the Fantasy Land Four Seasons.[420]

---

419. MR 1.8(b); RLGL § 60.

420. Oasis West Realty, LLC v. Goldman, 250 P.3d 1115 (Cal. 2011) (lawyer's use of client confidential information to oppose client's project after lawyer ended the representation establishes cause of action for breach of fiduciary duty, professional negligence, and breach of contract); David Welch Co. v. Erskine & Tulley, 250 Cal. Rptr. 339 (1998) (no expert testimony required to show that law firm that used client's confidences to set up a competing business breached a fiduciary duty; firm was required to disgorge its gains in a constructive trust); *In re* Coggs, 14 P.3d 1123 (Kan. 2000) (lawyer indefinitely suspended for using information about client's trust assets to borrow from the trust); Meinhard v. Salmon, 164 N.E. 545 (N.Y. 1928) (agent who used client information to buy adjoining property had to hold property in constructive trust for principal).

§ 13.08 Advanced Waivers of Confidentiality

Don't Bother the Client

Q. I explained to the client the importance of confidentiality and how it was up to the client to decide whether confidential information could be disclosed to third parties. Frankly, I don't think the client was impressed. She does not want to be bothered. Just wants the matter to go away. I got this great idea. Why not add a clause to our engagement letter, a standard clause that delegates to our firm the discretion to decide when it is in the client's best interest to disclose. After all, we are experienced in such matters.

A. We are sure your idea springs from good will and maybe a little attempt to streamline the representation. But there can be no open-ended prospective consents of the client's right to confidentiality. Remember, any waiver must be an informed consent. That standard is as serious as it sounds. Taken right from the practice of medicine. And consent can never be informed if either the content of the disclosure or the recipient of the information is unknown.[421]

Q. But we were going to promise to proceed in this way only if we determine it will benefit the client.

A. How will you be prescient enough to know what is in her best interests?

Q. Because we pride ourselves on our ability to protect our clients.

A. Even when you may not understand their real wishes?

§ 13.09 Informed Consent or Waiver?

Confidentiality Waivers

Q. Why do you speak of informed consent instead of confidentiality waivers?

A. Because one of the most critical of your fiduciary duties to your clients is the duty of confidentiality. Everything learned in the course of the representation comes within the rule. Unlike the

421. MR 1.0(e) & cmt. [6]; RLGL § 62 & cmt. c; People v. Issac, 2016 WL 6124510, No. 15 PDJ 099 (O.P.D.J. 2016) (lawyer who posted client's confidential information on internet without client's informed consent in response to client's negative consumer review suspended for six months); Commonwealth v. Downey, 842 N.E.2d 955 (Mass. App. 2006) (new trial granted to murder defendants whose lawyers wore body microphones during trial at the request of a television production company because lawyers failed to explain potential pitfalls of such an arrangement).

old ABA Code which covered only client secrets, information that, if disclosed, would harm the client and other information the client asked you to keep confidential. So, if you have an inclination to disclose confidential information, you must seek and receive the informed consent of your client to do so. This requires a discussion with the client that identifies the confidential information to be disclosed, the pros and cons of disclosure, and alternatives to disclosure; and, ideally, should be confirmed in writing lest there be any misunderstanding later about the lawyer's authority in this regard.[422]

Q. I thought the rule said that the disclosure by the client can be impliedly authorized?

A. It is true that some disclosures might be impliedly authorized, if necessary to carry out the representation. Disclosures required by the rules of civil procedure governing discovery come within that construct. But even there it is important that the trial lawyer explain to the client the discovery process in litigation so that the client fully understands not only the scope of these obligations but also that much of the information that will have to be disclosed would otherwise be protected from disclosure absent the litigation process. That way the client can decide whether the game is worth the candle. Dropping the litigation to avoid disclosure is always a possibility.

Q. This description of my confidentiality obligation really gives me pause.

A. Why?

Q. Well, the way you describe it, a lot of my conversations with reporters about my clients' cases violate the rule. Worse than that, my bragging about my cases at cocktail parties puts me in jeopardy, if my clients ever find out.

A. Your obligation under the confidentiality rule should not be defined by whether your clients uncover your boasting at a libation-filled social event. You have an obligation to refuse to discuss these matters, even if there is no chance your clients will discover your transgressions. Find another area of endeavor—golf, marathons, politics, whatever—about which to make yourself the most interesting dinner partner and keep

422. MR 1.0(e) & cmt. [6]; RLGL § 62 & cmt. c.

your clients' affairs to yourself no matter how fascinating you think your stories are.[423]

§ 13.10 Chart: Confidentiality Duties to Current, Former, and Prospective Clients

	Current Clients	Former Clients	Prospective Clients
Definition	RLGL § 14: C & L agree that L will provide legal services or C agrees and L fails to object, and client reasonably relies	1.9(a): Formerly represented a client in a matter	1.18(a): Consults with a lawyer about the possibility of forming a client-lawyer relationship with respect to a matter
Duty	1.6(a): No disclosure of information relating to the representation AND 1.8(b): No use of such information to the disadvantage of the client	1.9(a), (b): No subsequent materially adverse representation in the same or substantially related matter AND 1.9(c): No use to client's disadvantage unless generally known and no disclosure of information relating to the previous representation	1.18(c): No subsequent materially adverse representation in the same or substantially related matter if information received could be significantly harmful AND 1.18(b): No use or disclosure of information learned in the consultation
Exceptions	1.6(b)	1.9(c):1.6 exceptions	1.18(b) (c) & (d): 1.6 exceptions

423. Banner v. City of Flint, 99 F. App'x 29, 36 (6th Cir. 2004) (lawyer sanctioned for breaching both Rule 1.6 and attorney-client privilege by deposing former client without explaining attorney-client privilege including "advantages and disadvantages of revelation in language the client can understand"); *In re* Koeck, 178 A.3d 463 (D.C. App. 2018) (lawyer who improperly disclosed confidences of her former client to newspaper reporter and governmental officials suspended for 60 days).

§ 13.11 Confidentiality in Joint Representations

Multiple Clients/Multiple Secrets/Former Clients

Q. I've been representing father and son in bitter litigation against uncle and three cousins over control of a family business. The good news is that the business remains quite successful, so there's plenty of money to fund the army of lawyers on each side.

A. Sounds like a godsend in these perilous times. What's the problem?

Q. Well, I met with son yesterday. Alone. He drops his voice and starts with those words no lawyer wants to hear, "I know you won't tell dad, but. . . ."

A. Uh oh.

Q. You can say that again. Then he continues, "but I am in discussions with one of my cousins to lend my shares to their side in return for an agreement that will make me CFO and heir apparent when my uncle reaches 65."

A. What does your engagement agreement say about confidential information?

Q. Engagement? We have no such agreement. This grew directly out of our representation of the company. And that started so long ago, we weren't even using engagement letters back then. Why do you ask?

A. Well, one way of dealing with this not-so-rare problem is for the lawyer to sit with the two clients and discuss with them how confidential information should be handled. Will you always share such information? Will you never? That way, all clients know the ground rules and, if one of the clients then shares information with you, the client will be warned in advance of the implications of that.[424]

Q. But there was no discussion. In fact, I started representing dad v. uncle 18 months before the next generation got embroiled in this family feud.

A. That is not unusual. In the ideal world, a joint representation begins as a joint representation with plenty of time to go over matters like this. But for trial lawyers, the joint representation often grows out of an individual representation that morphs. The company asks you to represent an employee, and the corporation is added as a defendant. Or vice versa. Or you start out representing one alleged victim of employee discrimination, and others are added as plaintiffs later.

424. MR 1.7 cmt. [31].

Q. I get that it's common. But what do I do?

A. Now you have to determine what the default rule is in your jurisdiction. It all depends on that jurisdiction's confidentiality exceptions.[425] Many have not addressed the topic. The Restatement of the Law Governing Lawyers concludes that you may share—in situations consistent with its recognized confidentiality exceptions.[426] In any event, all agree on one thing.

Q. What is that?

A. Even if you cannot disclose, if the information you learn from the one client creates a conflict of interest, you must withdraw from both representations unless . . .

Q. Unless what?

A. Unless the conflict is consentable *and* the client sharing the information gives you permission to disclose it in order to seek the informed consent necessary to continue on behalf of one or both clients.[427] Which means you will have former clients to whom you also owe confidentiality.[428]

Q. I guess I have some research to do.

A. That and a great lesson on why, even as to joint representations that arise after the commencement of a matter, you should use an engagement letter to address these potential problem situations long before the consternating confidential information gets shared.

Q. You can say that again.

§ 13.12 Prospective Client Confidentiality

The Juicy Tidbit from a Prospective Client

Q. I got a call yesterday from Small & Company. Potential new client. Wants our firm to bring a RICO claim against Colossus. This is big. Maybe hundreds of millions. I am drooling. I circulate a conflicts memo. I already know we don't represent Colossus or any of its 200 subs. I am pretty sure we can take it. Only problem is client wants us to do it on a contingency.

Then I am surprised by a call from one of our banking guys. He is breathless. "What's the problem?" I ask. He's

425. A. v. B., 726 A.2d 924 (N.J. 1999) (discretionary exception in N.J. Rule of Professional Conduct allowed lawyer to disclose husband's illegitimate child to wife to rectify a fraud in estate plan lawyer drafted for both husband and wife).

426. RLGL § 60 cmt. l.

427. MR 1.7 cmt. [31].

428. MR 1.9.

thrilled we got this call. Then I can take it, I announce. Not at all, he responds. But he is about to go to a closing—just ten days from now—on a loan from Big Bank to Colossus. He'll be some hero when he tells the bank this important piece of information. I was so sad, but I guess at least some good will come from Small's inquiry. Even if I will not get credit for it.

A. You told him he could tell the bank?

Q. No. I told him I would call you guys to see if there was any way we could represent Small once we told the Bank. Can I?

A. Let's put that question aside for a moment. Where did you learn about this lawsuit?

Q. From Small.

A. And what is Small?

Q. A prospective client.

A. And does a prospective client have any rights?

Q. Not when it comes to a contest with Big Bank. Big Bank sends us dozens of loans. They chisel on rates, but still . . .

A. That might be how your firm feels, but the truth is, as a prospective client, Small is entitled to full confidentiality for any information it shares with a prospective lawyer.

Q. Even when Big Bank desperately needs to know about the lawsuit? It could ruin Big Bank's loan.

A. Even then. Without Small's consent you may not disclose.

Q. Don't think we'll get that. It's in Small's interest that the loan go through. After all, while Small might hate Colossus, the one thing Small wants is for Colossus to survive and thrive—to pay that big judgment Small dreams about.

A. Rule 1.18 is relatively new. And it does not really change the law. It merely emphasizes for lawyers that even though they owe prospective clients very little, they do owe them a duty of confidentiality. And we have to offer such protection or else prospective clients would be in jeopardy simply by pursuing the totally legitimate process of seeking a lawyer.

Q. I hear you, but it sounds like that rule could create quite a bit of mischief. Wife goes around talking to every star divorce lawyer in town. Gives them confidential information. Then when her husband tries to find someone to represent him, everyone is conflicted out.

A. Some clients have thought just that way. The courts have addressed this. If a prospective client abuses the protection otherwise available, the protection is lost, and wife may find herself facing off against a lawyer who knows her secrets.[429]

429. MR 1.18 cmt. [2].

Q. So, if we can't disclose to Big Bank, can we at least take on Small's case? It's certainly not directly adverse to Big Bank. And since when do we have to worry about whether any of our clients are creditors of the company we are suing? We'd never be able to take on any new matters.

A. It is true you generally do not worry about the secondary effects on creditors of your outstanding trial lawyer skills leaving these creditors' counterparties trembling in their boots. But this case is different. First, the lawsuit is a huge one. And we take it the loan by Big Bank is of similar size. This is not a question whether Colossus will be able to pay its electric bill. Add to that the fact that it is your firm that is working on the loan, and you are presented with a situation where it is highly likely a reasonable lawyer (the applicable objective standard)[430] would conclude that your firm's dedication to Big Bank would create a material limitation on the ardor with which you attack Colossus.

Q. Are you kidding me? I'm ready to go after Colossus hammer and tong.

A. That may be so. Precisely why the rule is written the way it is. The rule drafters recognized how unhinged enthusiastic trial lawyers can get when they have a new opportunity put before them. So, they insisted that the standard for determining whether a material limitation exists was an objective one.

Q. I guess I'll turn down Small, sad as that is. Thanks, I think.

A. Do you think you are done?

Q. Done and disappointed.

A. Not quite. What're you going to do about Big Bank?

Q. We have to do something?

A. We think so. Your firm is representing Big Bank. About to close a big loan to Colossus. A loan Colossus might not close if it knew about the Small lawsuit.

Q. All true.

A. And you can't tell Big Bank about it. Or try to figure out another way for Big Bank to "learn" about the possible contingent liability. Indeed, you are the one firm in the world that cannot deal with this important issue.

Q. But if we withdraw from the matter, the next firm will never discover it.

A. That may be so. But at least that firm is free to search. And search they may.

Q. Why would they ever think of doing that?

430. MR 1.7(b)(1); RLGL § 122(2).

A. Because of your firm's withdrawal. You can't disclose the fact of the lawsuit, but you are free, indeed required, to tell Big Bank that you must withdraw. That perfectly permissible disclosure might raise some red flags, and Big Bank and its new counsel may redouble their due diligence. Nothing certain, but at least a real possibility.

Q. So, one phone call, a juicy bit of information, and we cannot take on the new matter; we cannot continue with the old matter; and we cannot tell our valuable client something it would be dying to know.

§ 13.13 Chart: Client Confidentiality Exceptions

	Evidentiary Rules	Ethical/Fiduciary Obligation
Client consent	Waiver. RLGL §§ 78–80 (implied by disclosure to any non-privileged third person)	Client informed consent, express or implied. MR 1.6 (a)
Physical harm	Future and continuing crime or fraud. RLGL § 82	To prevent reasonably certain death or substantial bodily harm. MR 1.6 (b)(1)
Financial harm	Future and continuing crime or fraud. RLGL § 82	To rectify, or mitigate future crime or fraud using the lawyer's services reasonably certain to result in substantial financial loss. MR 1.6(b)(2)(3)
Seeking advice	None	To secure legal advice about compliance with Rules of Professional Conduct. MR 1.6(b)(4)
Lawyer self-defense	Lawyer self-protection. RLGL § 82	Lawyer self-defense. MR 1.6 (b)(5)
Required by law or court order	Invoking the privilege. RLGL § 86	Required by law or court order. MR 1.6 (b)(6) Comments 19, 20
Conflicts Checking	None	To detect and resolve conflicts arising from a lawyer's change of employment if not protected by privilege or would otherwise prejudice the client.

§ 13.14 Confidentiality Exceptions

Defending Yourself . . . Cleverly

Q. I've been threatened with malpractice over my failure to include a non-compete clause in a contract for the employment of a new CEO. I don't remember them asking. They claim they did.

A. Did you suggest one?

Q. I . . . no, I didn't. Frankly, I forgot.

A. That could be the malpractice. All it takes is some geeky expert opining that the standard of care is asking your client whether it wants such protection.[431]

Q. Look, I don't think this CEO would have accepted one. She did not have one before. That's how we were able to steal her in the first place. Besides I am not really all that worried.

A. Because we're going to represent you?

Q. I hope that's true, but your skills are not as valuable as my own brilliant idea.

A. Dazzle away.

Q. Our firm is doing some product liability work for this client. Only we know that the client had a guy in the lab whose warnings about those ignition locks proved correct. But the other side has not uncovered him yet. We have a barely colorable privilege claim.

A. What's that got to do with the employment agreement?

Q. Nothing, but if they sue us for malpractice, we will be free to disclose the confidential information about the locks. It says so right in the rules you supposedly know so much about.

A. There is such a provision but threatening to use it would be extortion. That's blackmail. And using it would violate the rule.

Q. No way. I read the Rule. 1.7.

A. Actually 1.6, but it makes no difference. You are only allowed to disclose confidential information related to your defense. And all of the exceptions to confidentiality in Rule 1.6 hinge on one significant limit: The lawyer may disclose "only to the extent the lawyer reasonably believes necessary." As you admit, one matter is unrelated to the other. So, your desire is unreasonable; yes, unethical. If we were you, given a choice between going to jail

431. Russo v. Griffin, 510 A.2d 436 (Vt. 1986) (lawyer liable for malpractice, with appropriate expert testimony, for failing to tell his clients about the option of a covenant not to compete, probably because they were all family members working in the family business).

and/or being disbarred and calling your carrier . . . we would pick the last alternative, living for another day.[432]

§ 13.15 Confidentiality Exceptions: Threats of Substantial Bodily Harm or Death

Client Threats

Q. I have a matrimonial practice. And a cast iron stomach. The things clients say. And what they would do to their estranged spouse. You would never know these two enjoyed a honeymoon. At least they had one for the duration of that first trip to Hawaii. But this one is different. The decibel level is higher. I think both are seriously unbalanced. Mine I am told by others is bipolar. Anyway, when I tell her hubby's last offer on alimony—a pittance—she trembles, then stiffens, races out of my office promising violence to the scoundrel. "I'll use his prized ceremonial sword," she announces. What do I do?

A. Well, you can't go calling the police every time a client threatens mayhem.

Q. Oh, that's for sure. If I did that, half my clients would be in jail.

A. Well, the rule is clear. If you reasonably believe that your client is about to cause substantial physical harm to another, every jurisdiction—even California—now permits you to disclose what is clearly confidential information to prevent death or substantial bodily harm.[433]

Q. Do I have to?

A. Great question. In a few states this exception to Rule 1.6 requires you to take certain steps.[434] And there is some case

---

432. Fla. Bar v. Knowles, 99 So. 3d 918 (Fla. 2012) (lawyer suspended for one year for filing withdrawal motions that alleged criminal activity by the client and informing prosecutor that client planned to lie at an upcoming immigration proceeding after a fee dispute); Iowa Sup. Ct. Attorney Disciplinary Bd. v. Marzen, 779 N.W.2d 757 (Iowa 2010) (lawyer suspended for six months for being accused in highly publicized disciplinary complaint of sexual relationship with client while candidate for county attorney position, and for unilaterally disclosing to press that client had earlier sued her probation officer for similar sexual misconduct; disclosure improper even if information in the public domain); State *ex rel.* Counsel for Discipline v. Wilson, 634 N.W.2d 467 (Neb. 2001) (lawyer suspended for two years for threatening to disclose confidential information to INS and reopen client's divorce unless client paid disputed fee after client began a relationship with lawyer's estranged wife).

433. MR 1.6(b)(1); RLGL § 66.

434. *See, e.g.*, Ill. R. Prof'l. Conduct 1.6(c) (2016).

law that suggests an unknowing potential victim of your client's violence should be warned under *Tarasoff* principles.[435]

Q. *Tarasoff*?

A. That's the seminal California case that concluded a psychiatrist had a duty to warn unknowing potential victims of a patient's anticipated violent criminal conduct. But in almost all jurisdictions, the decision is up to you.

Q. This is no time to be told I have discretion. I would feel awful if something happened to the husband. But I sure don't want to get my client in trouble. I well remember telling her how absolutely critical it was that she tell me the truth. And I, in turn, promised her everything she told me would remain between us. Now my testimony might put her in jail or force her into a mental institution.

A. You might not have to worry about that.

Q. Why not? I call the police. Even if her conversation with me was privileged, haven't I waived the privilege by disclosing part of the contents?

A. First, you are not authorized to waive the privilege. That belongs to her. And, heaven knows, she hasn't given you informed consent. Moreover, the case law is pretty good. To encourage lawyers to act in these situations, the courts have been very sympathetic to the notion that the lawyer who breaches confidentiality for this purpose should not be forced to testify about either the conversations with the client or the warning that the lawyer delivered to the police. Any conviction of the client must come from independent evidence.[436]

---

435. Tarasoff v. Regents of Univ. of Cal., 551 P.2d 334 (Cal. 1976) (relationship of psychotherapist to either patient or intended victim sufficient to establish duty to warn or take other appropriate action to prevent patient from killing another); Hawkins v. King Cnty., 602 P.2d 361 (Wash. Ct. App. 1979) (lawyer's obligation to warn "must be permissive at most, unless it appears beyond a reasonable doubt that the client has formed a firm intention to inflict serious personal injuries on an unknowing third person"). *But see* RLGL § 66(3).

436. Purcell v. Dist. Attorney for the Suffolk Dist., 676 N.E.2d 436 (Mass. 1997) (Rule 1.6 of Model Rules of Professional Conduct allowed lawyer to warn about client's arson threat, but prosecutor's subsequent attempt to evade attorney-client privilege not justified by crime-fraud exception to privilege absent non-privileged information sufficient to trigger an in camera hearing); Newman v. State, 863 A.2d 321 (Md. 2004) (client's threats to kill husband made in lawyer's office during meeting that included client's friend not admissible under crime-fraud exception because client was not seeking legal advice about the crime; client did not waive privilege because friend participated in the meeting at lawyer's behest); *In re* Gonnella, 570 A.2d 53 (N.J. Super. Ct. Law Div. 1989) (lawyer who warned of client's threat against co-defendant's lawyer after client told him to do so required to testify about client's statements both because they fall within the crime-fraud exception and because client waived the privilege).

Q. Thanks, but I still don't know what to do. It's nice to know I won't be disciplined, and my client won't be convicted based on what otherwise was a privileged conversation. But turning in your client is unacceptable, and it'll ruin my reputation.
A. Well, you'd better decide soon, or the issue may become moot.

§ 13.16 Confidentiality Exceptions: Wrongful Conviction

The Shoe Pinches

Q. I can't sleep.
A. Why's that?
Q. I've had no trouble being a criminal defense lawyer with all the ethical demands that entails. But this one has me unhinged.
A. You?
Q. Yes. My client told me he was the perpetrator of a crime for which someone else has been convicted and is serving time. The dilemma has me torn. How can I let an innocent person spend one more day in Graterford Prison?
A. But your client is entitled to confidentiality.
Q. That may be so about his legal matter. But this disclosure has nothing to do with that. I didn't ask him for this information dump, and he had no business sharing it with me.
A. Its irrelevance to your matter is irrelevant. Your confidentiality obligation extends to everything you learn in the course of a representation. Everything. Including information like this. So, in order to disclose, you have to find an exception under Rule 1.6. Don't think you can find one.
Q. How 'bout serious bodily harm? Conditions in Graterford are abominable.
A. That might work, or at least the Restatement says so.[437] Your argument has been weakened by the fact that Massachusetts has promulgated a specific exception to permit disclosure

437. RLGL § 66 cmt. c.

when someone is wrongfully incarcerated, even though Massachusetts has the exception for serious bodily harm.[438]

Q. But it seems so unfair. Talk about injustice.

A. In one way it is. But look at it this way: if you had not promised your client confidentiality, you never would have learned this information. You obviously earned your client's trust. That creates a sound and likely successful representation. And that *is* a desirable result.[439]

§ 13.17 Confidentiality Exceptions: Seeking Advice

Getting Advice Outside Your Firm

Q. I wish our general counsel were around so I could put this problem firmly in her lap.

A. You can't talk to us about it?

Q. I don't think so. But that is why I am calling. I have a problem with a client that I would love to have your help solving, but it requires my sharing my client's confidential information with you. And that would breach confidentiality. I don't want to compound one ethical violation with another.

A. Does your problem raise questions under the Rules of Professional Conduct?

Q. Precisely. That is why I wanted to talk to the GC.

A. If it involves your seeking guidance to conform your conduct to these rules, then there is a specific exception to the confidentiality rule, Rule 1.6(b)(4). It says that without the permission of your client you may breach confidentiality to seek advice. This specific rule was adopted to encourage lawyers to go outside their firms for guidance because so often the ethical issues that have arisen involve client conduct. It is our clients that too often get us in trouble.

Q. Well, that is precisely my case. My client insists I call a particular individual as a witness, and I don't want to.

438. Mass. R. Prof'l Conduct 1.6(b)(1) (2016) ("A lawyer may reveal confidential information . . . to prevent the commission of a criminal or fraudulent act that the lawyer reasonably believes is likely to result in death or substantial bodily harm, or in substantial injury to the financial interest or property of another, or to prevent the wrongful execution or incarceration of another.").

439. State v. Macumber, 544 P.2d 1084 (Ariz. 1976) (two lawyers who were prepared to testify that their now-deceased client had confessed to the murders for which another person was incarcerated were precluded from doing so when the prosecutor raised the attorney-client privilege).

A. Then you have come to the right place, and we will be glad to listen to your predicament and help you solve it. As long as we don't have a conflict.

§ 13.18 Confidentiality Exceptions: Lawyer Self-Defense

The Turncoat Lawyer

Q. We agreed to handle a habeas claim on behalf of a death-row inmate. Case is a mess. We met with trial counsel. You could smell the whiskey. Took the case for the money and Montgomery County pays next to nothing.
A. Sounds like a great ineffective assistance of counsel claim.
Q. That was the least of it. He hired no experts. Didn't even consider them. And no investigation on mitigation. Never interviewed a family member.
A. What's the problem?
Q. The problem is this guy is so offended that we would accuse him of incompetence that he's been meeting with the AG's office, helping them defend against our claim! Sharing all kinds of client confidential info. When I confronted him, he laughed. Now he's an ethics maven. Tells me there's an exception to confidentiality for lawyers' defending themselves. Even gives me a number. Rule 1.6(b)(5). Can this be right?
Q. It is correct that lawyers may use confidential information to defend themselves. But this lawyer is not a party to the habeas. No charges or claims have been brought against him.[440] The authors believe that what he is doing is not only a sin—cooperating with those who would execute his former client—but also a violation of Rule 1.6.[441] We recognize that the DC Bar

---

440. *Compare* Meyerhofer v. Empire Fire & Marine Ins. Co., 497 F.2d 1190 (2d Cir. 1974) (lawyer's release of previously executed affidavit containing client confidential information justified to defend himself against charges of securities law violations when plaintiffs named him as a defendant in a subsequent lawsuit).

441. Cross v. United States, 2016 WL 4766490 (S.D.W.Va.) (lawyer accused of ineffective assistance of counsel may disclose information required by a court order requiring the submission of an affidavit and redacted documents in a court proceeding but may not speak to prosecutors outside of court proceeding); ABA Comm. on Ethics & Prof'l Responsibility, Formal Op. 10-456 (2010) Disclosure of Information to Prosecutor When Lawyer's Former Client Brings Ineffective Assistance of Counsel Claim ("It is highly unlikely that a disclosure in response to a prosecution request, prior to a court-supervised response by way of testimony or otherwise, will be justifiable.").

> Committee has concluded otherwise. That opinion, in our view, is wrong, has been roundly criticized, and should not be followed.[442]

Moreover, under no circumstance should the lawyer be free to decide unilaterally that a confidentiality exception has been triggered. To go behind the client's back and consort with the other side is unforgiveable.[443]

§ 13.19 Confidentiality Exceptions: Law or Court Order

Can You Trust the Trustee?

Q. Our client is the next friend of a group of minor foster children suing the Department of Social Services for injuries suffered at the hands of foster parents. The suit also named a number of individuals as defendants. Their cases were settled for $800,000, and those funds were put in a trust account of the next friend, with specific instructions from the judge not to disburse the funds until all the proceedings were concluded.

A. Sounds terrific.

Q. It would be, but it turns out our dedicated client did not exactly follow those instructions. She decided on her own that the children should not have to wait for money they need right now. "It's their money," she explained. And she is right. But she violated the judge's order. And we know it.

---

442. D.C. Ethics Op. 364 (2013) Confidentiality Obligations When Former Client Makes Ineffective Assistance of Counsel Claim (When a former client challenges a criminal conviction or sentence on the grounds of ineffective assistance of counsel (IAC), D.C. Rule 1.6(e)(3) permits the lawyer to disclose client confidences and secrets only insofar as reasonably necessary to respond to the client's specific allegations about the lawyer's representation. Where appropriate, the lawyer should take steps, such as seeking a judicial protective order or entering into an agreement with the prosecutor, to limit the use of such disclosures to the IAC proceeding). But see ABA Formal Op. 10-456 (2010) Disclosure of Information to Prosecutor When Lawyer's Former Client Brings Ineffective Assistance of Counsel Claim.

443. Fla. Bar v. Knowles, 99 So. 3d 918 (Fla. 2012) (lawyer suspended for one year for filing withdrawal motions that alleged criminal activity by the client and informing prosecutor that client planned to lie at an upcoming immigration hearing after a fee dispute); *In re* Skinner, 740 S.E.2d 171 (Ga. 2013) (lawyer who responded to a client's negative reviews on the Internet by disclosing personal and confidential information should receive stronger sanction than reprimand); State *ex rel.* Counsel for Discipline v. Wilson, 634 N.W.2d 467 (Neb. 2001) (lawyer suspended for two years for threatening to disclose confidential information to INS and reopen client's divorce unless client paid disputed fee after client began a relationship with lawyer's estranged wife).

A. This is so unfortunate. She was doing a good deed. But she disregarded a lawful order. And you have no choice. You must report it to the judge. You can plead for mercy . . . good intentions . . . whatever. But Rule 3.3(b) requires disclosure. It provides for the lawyer of a client who has engaged in criminal or fraudulent conduct to take reasonable remedial measures. In this situation, with the money disbursed, disclosure to the tribunal is required.[444]

§ 13.20 Confidentiality Exceptions: Law or Court Order

Is This a Tribunal?

Q. I spend weeks preparing my client for an upcoming mediation. I am not sure why we pursue this step with such enthusiasm. It would be less expensive simply to litigate the case. But, alas, it is a trend that we litigators cannot escape.

A. You can say that again.

Q. But let me tell you my present problem. After all that rehearsing, we are in a caucus session with the mediator when the mediator observes that our liability case is pretty weak. Before I can disabuse him of that notion, my client pipes in, "But we have hired Dr. Schwartz, that famous metallurgist from MIT. The jury will love him."

A. Nothing wrong with that. Sounds like a good comeback.

Q. Oh, it would be, but the problem is that we have never contacted Dr. Schwartz. We have no idea what he will say.

A. So, did you tell the mediator?

Q. Are you kidding me? And disclose my client as a liar? Did I have to?

A. That is the question of the hour. First, you must consider whether you were before a tribunal. This sounds like it was private mediation, and so the rules governing a tribunal would not apply. But if this were a court-annexed mediation,

444. Lane's Case, 889 A.2d 3 (N.H. 2005) (lawyer justified by future fraud exception to disclose information about a former client to another lawyer which implicated former client in litigation to remove former client as trustee of his mother's trust).

the argument that you were before a tribunal is considerably stronger.[445]

Q. What difference does that make?

A. If you are before a tribunal, Rule 3.3 gets triggered. And while your client was not under oath, an argument can be made that the judicial process was corrupted by your client's false statement, which would significantly change the view the mediator had of the strength of your case. You might have an obligation to disclose.

Q. But what if it wasn't a tribunal?

A. Then you have to look at Rule 4.1 and Rule 1.2. Under Rule 4.1, you have to determine whether you are making a misrepresentation to a third party by virtue of your continued participation in these proceedings after your client lied. Under Rule 1.2(d), you have to determine whether your continued participation aids and abets a client fraud, which then requires you to determine whether what your client did was a fraud. The Rules of Professional Conduct define fraud according to the substantive and procedural law of the applicable jurisdiction with a purpose to deceive.[446] So, a trip to the books (oops, some computer research) will be required.

§ 13.21 Confidentiality Exceptions: Law or Court Order

Staying Out of Jail

Q. I am willing to do a lot for my clients but going to jail seems a bit much.

A. Without more, that sounds like an important and correct statement.

Q. Let me tell you the problem. We are claiming privilege for a document which our client, unfortunately, shared with a third party. We argued strenuously that that sharing did not waive the privilege. But sad to say, we lost that argument, and the judge has given my client ten days to turn it over or else he

445. RLGL ch. 7, Introductory Note (Chapter 7, Representing Clients in Litigation, applies in contested arbitration and similar trial-type proceedings but not to a mediation, unless the mediation is in the form of a contested proceeding.).

446. MRs 1.0(d), 1.0 cmt. [5].

will hold me in contempt, something about my being an officer of the court. I tell my client we have to comply, but my client insists that we appeal. I have tried one hundred times to explain to my client that the order is not appealable; it is interlocutory. He won't take no for an answer. What can I do?

A. A lawyer in that situation has an obligation if the client insists to exhaust all of the possibilities. If defying the court order would give your client an opportunity to seek mandamus from the appeals court (thus avoiding the limitation on appeals) we think you are obliged to do so. Lawyers regularly take that one additional step. But they are only required to do so if it is clear that the lawyer will not be imprisoned until the mandamus petition is heard. It is one thing to put yourself at de minimus risk in order to get another hearing. It is another for the lawyer to be incarcerated while the issue gets litigated. No one thinks the lawyer owes her client that level of dedication. Lawyers, of course, from time to time place themselves in that position, that is, go to jail rather than produce privileged information, but your duties to your client do not comprehend a diet of bread and water for two weeks.

§ 13.22 Rule 1.6 Exceptions to Client Confidentiality by State

Jurisdiction	Express Authority	Implied Authority Entities (E) Clients with Diminished Capacity (DC)	To Prevent Future Crime (CR), Fraud (FR), Death Subs. Bodily Harm (D/SBH), or Subs. Financial Harm (SFH)	To Secure Legal Advice	Lawyer Self-Defense	To Comply with Law or Court Order Fraud on Tribunal Assisting Client Fraud	To Detect Conflicts of Interest Due to Lawyer's Employment Change
ABA Model Rules	1.6(a) May	1.6(a) May 1.13(c) May (E) 1.14(c) May (DC)	1.6(b)(1) May (D/SBH) 1.6(b)(2)(3) May (CR/FR & SFH)	1.6(b)(4) May	1.6(b)(5) May	1.6(b)(6) May 3.3 Must. 4.1(b) Must if 1.6	1.6(b)(7) May
Alabama	1.6(a) May	1.6(a) May 1.14(c) May (DC)	1.6(b)(1) May (CR & D/SBH)		1.6(b)(2) May	1.6 comment 3.3 Must. 4.1(b) Must if 1.6	

Jurisdiction	Express Authority	Implied Authority Entities (E) Clients with Diminished Capacity (DC)	To Prevent Future Crime (CR), Fraud (FR), Death Subs. Bodily Harm (D/SBH), or Subs. Financial Harm (SFH)	To Secure Legal Advice	Lawyer Self-Defense	To Comply with Law or Court Order Fraud on Tribunal Assisting Client Fraud	To Detect Conflicts of Interest Due to Lawyer's Employment Change
Alaska	1.6(a) May	1.6(a) May 1.13(c) May (E) 1.14(c) May (DC)	1.6(b)(1) May (D/SBH) 1.6(b)(2)(3) May (CR/FR & SFH or wrongful execution or incarceration of another)	1.6(b)(4) May	1.6(b)(5) May	1.6(b)(6) May 3.3 Must 4.1(b) Must if 1.6	

Jurisdiction	Express Authority	Implied Authority Entities (E) Clients with Diminished Capacity (DC)	To Prevent Future Crime (CR), Fraud (FR), Death Subs. Bodily Harm (D/SBH), or Subs. Financial Harm (SFH)	To Secure Legal Advice	Lawyer Self-Defense	To Comply with Law or Court Order Fraud on Tribunal Assisting Client Fraud	To Detect Conflicts of Interest Due to Lawyer's Employment Change
Arizona	1.6(a) May	1.6(a) May. 1.14(c) May (DC)	1.6(b) Must (CR & D/SBH) 1.6(c) May (CR) 1.6(d)(1) May (CR/FR & SFH)	1.6(d)(3) May	1.6(d)(4) May	1.6(d)(5) May 3.3 Must 4.1(b) Must if 1.6	1.6(b)(7) May
Arkansas	1.6(a) May	1.6(a) May 1.13(c) May (E) 1.14(c) May (DC)	1.6(b)(1) May (CR) 1.6(b)(2)(3) May (CR/FR & SFH)	1.6(b)(4) May	1.6(b)(5) May	1.6(b)(6) May 3.3 Must 4.1(b) Must if 1.6	1.6(b)(7) May

Jurisdiction	Express Authority	Implied Authority Entities (E) Clients with Diminished Capacity (DC)	To Prevent Future Crime (CR), Fraud (FR), Death Subs. Bodily Harm (D/SBH), or Subs. Financial Harm (SFH)	To Secure Legal Advice	Lawyer Self-Defense	To Comply with Law or Court Order Fraud on Tribunal Assisting Client Fraud	To Detect Conflicts of Interest Due to Lawyer's Employment Change
California	1.6(a) May		1.6(b) May (CR & D/SBH)				
Colorado	1.6(a) May	1.6(a) May 1.13(c) May (E) 1.14(c) May (DC)	1.6(b)(1) May (D/SBH) 1.6(b)(2) May May (CR/FR & SFH)	1.6(b)(5) May	1.6(b)(6) May	1.6(b)(8) May 3.3 Must 4.1(b) Must if 1.6	1.6(b)(7) May

Jurisdiction	Express Authority	Implied Authority Entities (E) Clients with Diminished Capacity (DC)	To Prevent Future Crime (CR), Fraud (FR), Death Subs. Bodily Harm (D/ SBH), or Subs. Financial Harm (SFH)	To Secure Legal Advice	Lawyer Self-Defense	To Comply with Law or Court Order Fraud on Tribunal Assisting Client Fraud	To Detect Conflicts of Interest Due to Lawyer's Employment Change
Connecticut	1.6(a) May	1.6(a) May 1.13(c) May (E) 1.14(c) May (DC)	1.6(b) Must (CR & D/SBH) 1.6(c)(1)(2) May (SFH)	1.6(c)(3) May	1.6(d) May	1.6(c)(4) 3.3 Must 4.1(b) Must if 1.6	1.6(c)(5) May
Delaware	1.6(a) May	1.6(a) May 1.14(c) May (DC)	1.6(b)(1) May (D/SBH) 1.6(b)(2)(3) May (CR/FR & SFH)	1.6(b)(4) May	1.6(b)(5) May	1.6(b)(6) May 3.3 Must 4.1(b) Must if 1.6	1.6(b)(7) May

Jurisdiction	Express Authority	Implied Authority Entities (E) Clients with Diminished Capacity (DC)	To Prevent Future Crime (CR), Fraud (FR), Death Subs. Bodily Harm (D/ SBH), or Subs. Financial Harm (SFH)	To Secure Legal Advice	Lawyer Self-Defense	To Comply with Law or Court Order Fraud on Tribunal Assisting Client Fraud	To Detect Conflicts of Interest Due to Lawyer's Employment Change
District of Columbia	1.6(e) (1) May	1.6(e)(4) May. 1.14(c) May (DC)	1.6(c) May (CR & D/SBH) 1.6(d)(1)(2) May (CR/FR & SFH)	1.6 (e)(6) May	1.6(e)(3)(5) May	6(e)(2) May 3.3 Must if 1.6 4.1(b) Must if 1.6	
Florida	4-1.6(a) May	4-1.6(c)(1) May 4-1.13(c) May (E) 4-1.14(c) May (DC)	4-1.6(b)(1) Must (CR) 4-1.6(b)(2) Must (D/SBH)	4-1.6 (c)(5) May	4-1.6(c)(2)(3)(4) May	4-1.6 (c)(5) 4-3.3 Must 4-4.1(b) Must if 4-1.6	4-1.6(b)(6) May

Jurisdiction	Express Authority	Implied Authority Entities (E) Clients with Diminished Capacity (DC)	To Prevent Future Crime (CR), Fraud (FR), Death Subs. Bodily Harm (D/SBH), or Subs. Financial Harm (SFH)	To Secure Legal Advice	Lawyer Self-Defense	To Comply with Law or Court Order Fraud on Tribunal Assisting Client Fraud	To Detect Conflicts of Interest Due to Lawyer's Employment Change
Georgia	1.6(a) May	1.6(a) May 1.13(c) May (E) 1.14(c) May (DC)	1.6(b)(1)(i) May (CR & SFH) 1.6(b)(1)(ii) May (D/SBH)	1.6(b)(3)(iv) May	1.6(b)(1)(iii) May	1.6(a) May 3.3 Must 4.1(b) Must if 1.6	
Hawaii	1.6(a) May	1.6(a) May May (E) 1.14(c) May (DC)	1.6(b)(1) May (CR/FR & D/SBH/SFH) 1.6(c) Must (C/F & SFH)	1.6(b)(3) May	1.6(b)(4) May	1.6(b)(6) May 3.3 Must 4.1(b),1.6(b) Must	1.6(b)(7) May

Jurisdiction	Express Authority	Implied Authority Entities (E) Clients with Diminished Capacity (DC)	To Prevent Future Crime (CR), Fraud (FR), Death Subs. Bodily Harm (D/SBH), or Subs. Financial Harm (SFH)	To Secure Legal Advice	Lawyer Self-Defense	To Comply with Law or Court Order Fraud on Tribunal Assisting Client Fraud	To Detect Conflicts of Interest Due to Lawyer's Employment Change
Idaho	1.6(a) May	1.6(a) May 1.13(c) May (E) 1.14(c) May (DC)	1.6(b)(1) May (CR) 1.6(b)(2) May (D/SBH) 1.6(b)(3) May (SFH)	1.6(b)(4) May	1.6(b)(5) May	1.6(b)(6) May 3.3 Must 4.1(b) Must if 1.6	1.6(b)(7) May
Illinois	1.6(a) May	1.6(a) May 1.13(c) May (E) 1.14(c) May (DC)	1.6(c) Must (D/SBH) 1.6(b)(1) May (CR) 1.6(b)(2)(3) May (CR/FR & SFH)	1.6(b)(4) May	1.6(b)(5) May	1.6(b)(6) May 3.3 Must 4.1(b) Must if 1.6	1.6(b)(7)

Jurisdiction	Express Authority	Implied Authority Entities (E) Clients with Diminished Capacity (DC)	To Prevent Future Crime (CR), Fraud (FR), Death Subs. Bodily Harm (D/SBH), or Subs. Financial Harm (SFH)	To Secure Legal Advice	Lawyer Self-Defense	To Comply with Law or Court Order Fraud on Tribunal Assisting Client Fraud	To Detect Conflicts of Interest Due to Lawyer's Employment Change
Indiana	1.6(a) May	1.6(a) May 1.13(c) May (E) 1.14(c) May (DC)	1.6(b)(1) May (D/SBH) 1.6(b)(2)(3) May (CR/FR & SFH)	1.6(b)(4) May	1.6(b)(5) May	1.6(b)(6) May 3.3 Must 4.1(b) Must if 1.6	
Iowa	1.6(a) May	1.6(a) May 1.13(c) May (E) 1.14(c) May (DC)	1.6(b)(1) May (D/SBH) 1.6(c) Must (Imminent D/SBH) 1.6(b) (2) (3) May (CR/FR & SFH)	1.6(b)(4) May	1.6(b)(5) May	1.6(b)(6) May 3.3 Must 4.1(b) Must if 1.6	

Jurisdiction	Express Authority	Implied Authority Entities (E) Clients with Diminished Capacity (DC)	To Prevent Future Crime (CR), Fraud (FR), Death Subs. Bodily Harm (D/SBH), or Subs. Financial Harm (SFH)	To Secure Legal Advice	Lawyer Self-Defense	To Comply with Law or Court Order Fraud on Tribunal Assisting Client Fraud	To Detect Conflicts of Interest Due to Lawyer's Employment Change
Kansas	1.6(a) May	1.6(a) May 1.14(c) May (DC)	1.6(b)(1) May (CR)	1.6(b)(2) May	1.6(b)(3) May	1.6(b)(4) May 3.3 Must 4.1(b) Must not	1.6(b)(5) May
Kentucky	1.6(a) May	1.6(a) May 1.13(c) May (E) 1.14(c) May (DC)	1.6(b)(1) May (D/SBH)	1.6(b)(2) May	1.6(b)(3) May	1.6(b)(4) May 3.3 Must 4.1(b) Must if 1.6	

Jurisdiction	Express Authority	Implied Authority Entities (E) Clients with Diminished Capacity (DC)	To Prevent Future Crime (CR), Fraud (FR), Death Subs. Bodily Harm (D/SBH), or Subs. Financial Harm (SFH)	To Secure Legal Advice	Lawyer Self-Defense	To Comply with Law or Court Order Fraud on Tribunal Assisting Client Fraud	To Detect Conflicts of Interest Due to Lawyer's Employment Change
Louisiana	1.6(a) May	1.6(a) May 1.13(c) May (E) 1.14(c) May (DC)	1.6(b)(1) May (D/SBH) 1.6(b)(2)(3) May (CR/FR & SFH)	1.6(b)(4) May	1.6(b)(5) May	1.6(b)(6) May 3.3 Must 4.1(b) Must if 1.6	1.6(b)(7) May
Maine	1.6(a) May	1.6(a) May 1.13(c) May (E) 1.14(c) May (DC)	1.6(b)(1) May (D/SBH) 1.6(b)(2)(3) May (CR/FR & SFH)	1.6(b)(4) May	1.6(b)(5) May	1.6(b)(7) May 3.3 Must 4.1(b) Must if 1.6	1.6(b)(6)

Jurisdiction	Express Authority	Implied Authority Entities (E) Clients with Diminished Capacity (DC)	To Prevent Future Crime (CR), Fraud (FR), Death Subs. Bodily Harm (D/SBH), or Subs. Financial Harm (SFH)	To Secure Legal Advice	Lawyer Self-Defense	To Comply with Law or Court Order Fraud on Tribunal Assisting Client Fraud	To Detect Conflicts of Interest Due to Lawyer's Employment Change
Maryland	1.6(a) May	1.6(a) May 1.13(c) May (E) 1.14(c) May (DC)	1.6(b)(1) May (D/SBH) 1.6(b)(2)(3) May (CR/FR & SFH)	1.6(b)(4) May	1.6(b)(5) May	1.6(b)(6) May 3.3 Must 4.1(b) Must	
Mass-achusetts	1.6(a) May	1.6(a) May 1.13(c) May if 1.6, 3.3, 4.1 or 8.3 (E) 1.14(b) May (DC)	1.6(b)(1) May (CR/FR & D/SBH or wrongful execution or incarceration of another) 1.6(b)(2)(3) May (CR/FR & SFH)		1.6(b)(2) May	1.6(b)(4) May 3.3, 1.6(b) Must 3.3(e) Must not (criminal defense) 4.1(b) Must if 1.6	1.6(b)(7) May

Jurisdiction	Express Authority	Implied Authority Entities (E) Clients with Diminished Capacity (DC)	To Prevent Future Crime (CR), Fraud (FR), Death Subs. Bodily Harm (D/SBH), or Subs. Financial Harm (SFH)	To Secure Legal Advice	Lawyer Self-Defense	To Comply with Law or Court Order Fraud on Tribunal Assisting Client Fraud	To Detect Conflicts of Interest Due to Lawyer's Employment Change
Michigan	1.6(c)(1) May	1.6 comment 1.13(c) May (E)	1.6(c)(4) May (CR) 1.6(c)(3) May (CR/FR)		1.6(c)(5) May	1.6(c)(2) May 3.3 Must May if 1.6	
Minnesota	1.6 (b)(1) May	1.6 (b)(2)(3) May 1.13(c) May if 1.6 (E) 1.14(c) May (DC)	1.6(b)(6) May (D/SBH) 1.6(b)(4), (5) May (F & SFH or CR)	1.6(b)(7) May	1.6(b)(8) May	1.6(b)(9) May 3.3 Must May if 1.6	1.6(b)(11) May

Jurisdiction	Express Authority	Implied Authority Entities (E) Clients with Diminished Capacity (DC)	To Prevent Future Crime (CR), Fraud (FR), Death Subs. Bodily Harm (D/SBH), or Subs. Financial Harm (SFH)	To Secure Legal Advice	Lawyer Self-Defense	To Comply with Law or Court Order Fraud on Tribunal Assisting Client Fraud	To Detect Conflicts of Interest Due to Lawyer's Employment Change
Mississippi	1.6(a) May	4-1.6(a) May 1.14(c) May (DC)	1.6(b)(1) May (D/SBH) 1.6(b)(2)(3) May (CR/FR & SFH)	1.6(b)(4) May	1.6(b)(5) May	1.6(b)(6) May 3.3 Must 4.1(b) Must if 1.6	
Missouri	4-1.6(a) May	4-1.6(a) May 1.14(c) May (DC)	4-1.6(b)(1) May (D/SBH)	4-1.6(b)(2) May	4-1.6(b)(3) May	4- 1.6 (b)(4) May 3.3 Must 4.1(b) Must if 1.6	1.6(b)(5) May
Montana	1.6(a) May	1.6(a) May 1.14(c) May (DC)	1.6(b)(1) May (D/SBH)	1.6(b)(2) May	1.6 (b)(3) May	1.6(b)(4) May 3.3 Must 4.1(b) Must if 1.6	

Jurisdiction	Express Authority	Implied Authority Entities (E) Clients with Diminished Capacity (DC)	To Prevent Future Crime (CR), Fraud (FR), Death Subs. Bodily Harm (D/SBH), or Subs. Financial Harm (SFH)	To Secure Legal Advice	Lawyer Self-Defense	To Comply with Law or Court Order Fraud on Tribunal Assisting Client Fraud	To Detect Conflicts of Interest Due to Lawyer's Employment Change
Nebraska	1.6(a) May	1.6(a) May 1.13(c) May (E) 1.14(c) May (DC)	1.6(b)(1) May (CR or D/SBH)	1.6(b)(2) May	1.6(b)(3) May	1.6(b)(4) May 3.3 Must 4.1(b) Must if 1.6	
Nevada	1.6(a) May	1.6(a) May 1.13(c) May (E) 1.14(c) May (DC)	1.6(b)(1) May (D/SBH) 1.6(c) Must (CR&D/SBH) 1.6(b)(2)(3) May (CR/FR & SFH)	1.6(b)(4) May	1.6(b)(5) May	1.6(b)(6) May 3.3 Must 4.1(b) Must if 1.6	1.6(b)(7) May

Jurisdiction	Express Authority	Implied Authority Entities (E) Clients with Diminished Capacity (DC)	To Prevent Future Crime (CR), Fraud (FR), Death Subs. Bodily Harm (D/SBH), or Subs. Financial Harm (SFH)	To Secure Legal Advice	Lawyer Self-Defense	To Comply with Law or Court Order Fraud on Tribunal Assisting Client Fraud	To Detect Conflicts of Interest Due to Lawyer's Employment Change
New Hampshire	1.6(a) May	1.6(a) May 1.13(c) May (E) 1.14(c) May (DC)	1.6(b)(1) May (D/SBH) 1.6(b)(1) May (CR & /SFH)	1.6(b)(2) May	1.6(b)(3) May	1.6(b)(4) May 3.3 Must 4.1(b) Must if 1.6	1.6(b)(5) May
New Jersey	1.6(a) May	1.6(a) May 1.13(c) May (E) 1.14(c) May (DC)	1.6(b)(1)(2) Must (CR/FR & D/SBH/SFH)		1.6(d)(2) May	6(d)(4) May 1.6 (b)(2), 3.3 Must 4.1(b) Must	1.6(d)(5) May

Jurisdiction	Express Authority	Implied Authority Entities (E) Clients with Diminished Capacity (DC)	To Prevent Future Crime (CR), Fraud (FR), Death Subs. Bodily Harm (D/SBH), or Subs. Financial Harm (SFH)	To Secure Legal Advice	Lawyer Self-Defense	To Comply with Law or Court Order Fraud on Tribunal Assisting Client Fraud	To Detect Conflicts of Interest Due to Lawyer's Employment Change
New Mexico	16-106 (A) May	16-106(A) May 16-113(C) May (E) 16-114(C) May (DC)	16-106(B)(1) May (D/SBH) 16-106(B) (2)(3) May (CR/FR & SFH)	16-106(B)(4) May	16-106(B)(5) May	16-106(B)(6) May 16-303 Must 16-401 Must if 16-106	1.6(b)(7) May

Jurisdiction	Express Authority	Implied Authority Entities (E) Clients with Diminished Capacity (DC)	To Prevent Future Crime (CR), Fraud (FR), Death Subs. Bodily Harm (D/SBH), or Subs. Financial Harm (SFH)	To Secure Legal Advice	Lawyer Self-Defense	To Comply with Law or Court Order Fraud on Tribunal Assisting Client Fraud	To Detect Conflicts of Interest Due to Lawyer's Employment Change
New York	1.6(a)(1) May	1.6(a)(2) May 1.14(c) May (DC)	1.6(b)(1) May (D/SBH) 1.6(b)(2) May (CR) 1.6(b)(3) May (CR/F & reliance on lawyer's previous opinion)	1.6(b)(4) May	1.6(b)(5) May	1.6(b)(6) May 3.3 Must 1.6(b)(3) May if reliance on lawyer's previous opinion	

Jurisdiction	Express Authority	Implied Authority Entities (E) Clients with Diminished Capacity (DC)	To Prevent Future Crime (CR), Fraud (FR), Death Subs. Bodily Harm (D/SBH), or Subs. Financial Harm (SFH)	To Secure Legal Advice	Lawyer Self-Defense	To Comply with Law or Court Order Fraud on Tribunal Assisting Client Fraud	To Detect Conflicts of Interest Due to Lawyer's Employment Change
North Carolina	1.6(a) May	1.6(a) May 1.13 (c) May if 1.6 (E) 1.14(c) May (DC)	1.6(b)(2) May (CR) 1.6(b)(3) May(D/SBH) 1.6(b)(4) May (CR/FR)	1.6(b)(5) May	1.6(b)(6) May	1.6(b)(1) May 3.3 Must 1.6(b)(4) May	1.6(b)(8) May
North Dakota	1.6(a) May	1.6(a) May 1.13(c) May (E) 1.14(c) May (DC)	1.6(b) Must (D/SBH) 1.6(c)(1)(2) May (CR/FR & SFH)	1.6(c)(3) May	1.6(c)(4) May	1.6(c)(5) May 3.3 must not if client Must if nonclient 1.6(c)(1) (2) May	1.6(b)(7) May

Jurisdiction	Express Authority	Implied Authority Entities (E) Clients with Diminished Capacity (DC)	To Prevent Future Crime (CR), Fraud (FR), Death Subs. Bodily Harm (D/SBH), or Subs. Financial Harm (SFH)	To Secure Legal Advice	Lawyer Self-Defense	To Comply with Law or Court Order Fraud on Tribunal Assisting Client Fraud	To Detect Conflicts of Interest Due to Lawyer's Employment Change
Ohio	1.6(a) May	1.6(a) May 1.13(c) May if 1.6 (E) 1.14(c) May (DC)	1.6(b)(1) May(D/SBH) 1.6(b)(2) May (CR)1.6(b)(3) May (CR/FR & SFH)	1.6(b)(4) May	1.6(b)(5) May	1.6(b)(6) May 3.3. Must 4.1(b) Must	1.6(b)(7) May
Oklahoma	1.6(a) May	1.6(a) May 1.13(c) May (E) 1.14(c) May (DC)	1.6(b)(1) May (D/SBH) 1.6(b)(2)(3) May (CR/FR SFH)	1.6(b)(4) May	1.6(b)(5) May	1.6(b)(6) May 3.3 Must 4.1(b) Must if 1.6	

Jurisdiction	Express Authority	Implied Authority Entities (E) Clients with Diminished Capacity (DC)	To Prevent Future Crime (CR), Fraud (FR), Death Subs. Bodily Harm (D/SBH), or Subs. Financial Harm (SFH)	To Secure Legal Advice	Lawyer Self-Defense	To Comply with Law or Court Order Fraud on Tribunal Assisting Client Fraud	To Detect Conflicts of Interest Due to Lawyer's Employment Change
Oregon	1.6(a) May	1.6(a) May 1.13(c) May (E) 1.14(c) May (DC)	1.6(b)(1) May (CR) 1.6(b)(2) May (D/SBH)	1.6(b)(3) May	1.6(b)(4) May	1.6(b)(5) May 3.3 Must 4.1(b) Must if 1.6	1.6(b)(6) May
Penn-sylvania	1.6(a) May	1.6(a) May 1.14(c) May (DC)	1.6(c)(1) May (D/SBH) 1.6(c)(2)(3) May (CR & SFH)	1.6(c)(5) May	1.6(c)(4) May	1.6 cmts. [18], [19] 3.3 Must 4.1(b) Must if 1.6	1.6(b)(7) May

Jurisdiction	Express Authority	Implied Authority Entities (E) Clients with Diminished Capacity (DC)	To Prevent Future Crime (CR), Fraud (FR), Death Subs. Bodily Harm (D/SBH), or Subs. Financial Harm (SFH)	To Secure Legal Advice	Lawyer Self-Defense	To Comply with Law or Court Order Fraud on Tribunal Assisting Client Fraud	To Detect Conflicts of Interest Due to Lawyer's Employment Change
Rhode Island	1.6(a) May	1.6(a) May 1.13(c) May (E) 1.14(c) May (DC)	1.6(b)(1) May (CR & D/SBH)	1.6(b)(3) May	1.6(b)(2) May	1.6(b)(4) May 3.3 Must 4.1(b) Must if 1.6	
South Carolina	1.6(a) May	1.6(a) May 1.13(c) May (E) 1.14(c) May (DC)	1.6(b)(1) May (CR) 1.6(b)(2) May (D/SBH) 1.6(b)(3)(4) May (SFH)	1.6(b)(5) May	1.6(b)(6) May	1.6(b)(7) May 3.3 Must 4.1(b) Must if 1.6	1.6(b)(8) May

Jurisdiction	Express Authority	Implied Authority Entities (E) Clients with Diminished Capacity (DC)	To Prevent Future Crime (CR), Fraud (FR), Death Subs. Bodily Harm (D/SBH), or Subs. Financial Harm (SFH)	To Secure Legal Advice	Lawyer Self-Defense	To Comply with Law or Court Order Fraud on Tribunal Assisting Client Fraud	To Detect Conflicts of Interest Due to Lawyer's Employment Change
South Dakota	1.6(a) May	1.6(a) May 1.13(c) May (E) 1.14(c) May (DC)	1.6(b)(1) May (CR & D/SBH)	1.6(b)(2) May	1.6(b)(3) May	1.6(b)(5) May 3.3 Must 4.1(b) Must if 1.6(b)	1.6(b)(6) May
Tennessee	1.6(a)(1) May	1.6(a)(2) May 1.13(c) May if 1.6 & 4.1 (E) 1.14(c) May (DC)	1.6(b)(1) May (CR) 1.6(c)(1) Must (D/SBH)	1.6(b)(4) May	1.6(b)(5) May	1.6(c)(2) Must Must if 3.3 Must if 4.1(b)(c)	1.6(b)(6) May

Jurisdiction	Express Authority	Implied Authority Entities (E) Clients with Diminished Capacity (DC)	To Prevent Future Crime (CR), Fraud (FR), Death Subs. Bodily Harm (D/SBH), or Subs. Financial Harm (SFH)	To Secure Legal Advice	Lawyer Self-Defense	To Comply with Law or Court Order Fraud on Tribunal Assisting Client Fraud	To Detect Conflicts of Interest Due to Lawyer's Employment Change
Texas	1.05 (c)(1) May 1.05 (c)(2) May	1.05(d) May	1.05(c)(7) May (CR/FR) 1.05(e) Must (CR & D/SBH)		1.05(c)(5)(6) May 1.05(d)(2) May	1.05(c)(4) May 3.03 Must 4.01(b) Must	
Utah	1.6(a) May	1.6(a) May 1.13(c) May (E) 1.14(c) May (DC)	1.6(b)(1) May (D/SBH) 1.6(b)(2)(3) May (CR/FR & SFH)	1.6(b)(4) May	1.6(b)(5) May	1.6(b)(6) May 3.3 Must 4.1(b) Must if 1.6	1.6(b)(7) May

Jurisdiction	Express Authority	Implied Authority Entities (E) Clients with Diminished Capacity (DC)	To Prevent Future Crime (CR), Fraud (FR), Death Subs. Bodily Harm (D/SBH), or Subs. Financial Harm (SFH)	To Secure Legal Advice	Lawyer Self-Defense	To Comply with Law or Court Order Fraud on Tribunal Assisting Client Fraud	To Detect Conflicts of Interest Due to Lawyer's Employment Change
Vermont	1.6(a) May	1.6(a) May 1.13(c) May (E) 1.14(c) May (DC)	1.6(b)(1) Must (CR & D/SBH) 1.6(c)(1) Must (CR/FR & SFH)	1.6(c)(2) May	1.6(c)(3) May	1.6(c) May 3.3 Must 1.6(b)(3) Must	
Virginia	1.6(a) May	1.6(a) May 1.14(c) May (DC)	1.6(c)(1) Must (CR) 1.6(b)(3) May (if related to subject matter of representation)		1.6(b)(2) May	1.6(b)(1) May 1.6(c)(2) 3.3 Must 4.1(b) Must	

Jurisdiction	Express Authority	Implied Authority Entities (E) Clients with Diminished Capacity (DC)	To Prevent Future Crime (CR), Fraud (FR), Death Subs. Bodily Harm (D/SBH), or Subs. Financial Harm (SFH)	To Secure Legal Advice	Lawyer Self-Defense	To Comply with Law or Court Order Fraud on Tribunal Assisting Client Fraud	To Detect Conflicts of Interest Due to Lawyer's Employment Change
Washington	1.6(a) May	1.6(a) May 1.13(c) May (E) 1.14(c) May (DC)	1.6(b)(1) May (D/SBH) 1.6(b)(2) May (CR) 1.6(b)(3) May (CR/FR & SFH)	1.6(b)(4) May	1.6(b)(5) May	1.6(b)(6)(7) May (inc. b/fid duty) 3.3 Must if 1.6 4.1(b) Must if 1.6	1.6(b)(7) May
West Virginia	1.6(a) May	1.6(a) May 1.13(c) May (E) 1.14(c) May (DC)	1.6(b)(1) May (D/SBH) 1.6(b)(2)(3) May (CR/FR & SFH)	1.6(b)(4) May	1.6(b)(5) May	1.6(b)(6) May 3.3 Must 4.1(b) Must if 1.6	1.6(b)(7) May

Jurisdiction	Express Authority	Implied Authority Entities (E) Clients with Diminished Capacity (DC)	To Prevent Future Crime (CR), Fraud (FR), Death Subs. Bodily Harm (D/SBH), or Subs. Financial Harm (SFH)	To Secure Legal Advice	Lawyer Self-Defense	To Comply with Law or Court Order Fraud on Tribunal Assisting Client Fraud	To Detect Conflicts of Interest Due to Lawyer's Employment Change
Wisconsin	20:1.6(a) May	20:1.6(a) May 20:1.13(c) May (E) 20:1.14(c) May (DC)	20:1.6(b) Must: Client (CR/FR & D/SBH/SFH) 20:1.6(c)(1) (2) May (D/SBH/SFH)	20:1.6(c)(3) May	20:1.6(c)(4) May	20:1.6(c)(5) May 20:3.3 Must 20:4.1 must if 20:1.6	20:1.6(c)(6) May
Wyoming	1.6(a) May	1.6(a) May 1.13(c) May (E) 1.6(b)(8), 1.14(c) May (DC)	1.6(b)(1) May (CR) 1.6(b)(2) May (FR & SFH)	1.6(b)(4) May	1.6(b)(5) May	1.6(b)(6) May 3.3 Must 4.1 Must if 1.6	1.6(b)(7) May

CHAPTER 14

Privilege and Work Product

§ 14.01 Introduction: The Privileges: Scope of the Protections

The attorney-client and work-product privileges recognize two subsets of the broad world of confidentiality designed to protect from forced disclosure information, otherwise admissible, for important public policy reasons. Because the adversary process requires access to and disclosure of facts to adjudicate disputes, absolute privileges or immunities from disclosure could destroy the value of fact-based adjudication. On the other hand, some confidentiality protection is necessary to encourage clients to disclose even embarrassing facts to lawyers, and to encourage lawyers to treat what witnesses tell them with healthy skepticism and think creatively. All of which, in turn, facilitates adequate representation. Although the privileges create tension with the search for truth, they also promote client trust by preventing lawyers from being forced to testify against clients and by enabling lawyers to advise clients candidly about relevant legal limits related to a client's past, ongoing, or future conduct.

Given this delicate balance, courts apply the attorney-client privilege only when a communication occurs between privileged persons (including the agents of clients and lawyers), in confidence, for the purpose of obtaining legal assistance.[447] Courts distinguish these com-

447. RLGL § 68.

munications from underlying facts, which can be sought through appropriate discovery.[448] Unlike the fiduciary duty of confidentiality, which automatically attaches to all information learned in the course of representing a client, a client or lawyer must claim the protection of the privileges when the evidence is sought or the client could lose the protection.[449]

Further, not all information is protected. The limitation to "communications" protects some but not all documents and does not protect from discovery the underlying facts contained in the communication. If the client is otherwise subject to the court's jurisdiction, the knowledge of the client can be probed during testimony.[450] "What happened on March 31?" is a proper question. "What did you tell your lawyer about what happened on March 31?" is the objectionable question.

The requirement that the communication occur only between "privileged persons" includes only the client, the lawyer, or their agents.[451] For organizations, this includes agents acting within the scope of their employment.[452] The limitation to communications made "in confidence" means that no one other than client and lawyer and their agents were privy to the communication. Disclosure to an unprivileged person before or after disclosure to the lawyer waives the privilege.[453] Finally, the communication must be for the purpose of offering or obtaining legal assistance. If a lawyer works in a dual capacity, say board member and lawyer, or friend and lawyer, the privilege may not attach, unless it can be established that legal assistance was the purpose of the communication.[454] Exceptions to the privilege parallel, but do not exactly mimic, those of the fiduciary obligation of confidentiality.

---

448. *Id.* § 69 cmt. d; *In re* Grand Jury Investigation, 22 N.E.3d 927 (Mass. 2015) (if client cannot be compelled under Fifth Amendment to produce underlying facts, lawyer, who stands in shoes of client, likewise cannot be so compelled).

449. RLGL § 86.

450. *Id.* § 69.

451. *Id.* § 70.

452. *Id.* § 73; Upjohn Co. v. United States, 449 U.S. 383 (1981). Governmental organizations and their employees also are protected. RLGL § 74; *In re* Lindsey, 158 F.3d 1263 (D.C. Cir. 1998).

453. RLGL §§ 71, 79.

454. *Id.* § 72; *In re* Riehlmann, 891 So. 2d 1239 (La. 2005) (Prosecutor/friend told another lawyer/friend of a violation of Brady v. Maryland, (a violation of Rule 3.8(d)), triggering lawyer/friend's obligation to disclose violation to the grievance authority under Rule 8.3).

§ 14.02 Privileged Communications

Privilege or Pretense

Q. Our client is a major pharmaceutical company. You can imagine how heavily regulated it is. The client can't operate any aspect of its business without consulting its lawyers. Right?

A. We get that. Look at the ridiculous fine type no one reads on the back of an ad for Lipitor in *People* magazine. They couldn't write that without lawyers.

Q. Our point exactly. We have this product liability case. Bad unanticipated side effects. And we list on our privilege log all the memos back and forth regarding ads, the package circular, the FDA application—every document on which the lawyers were copied. We should win, right?

A. You may be a bit overconfident. We take your point that the lawyers' work is essential. And the copying of the lawyers might be for the purpose of seeking legal advice. Memos directly to the lawyer would be more persuasive evidence of that. But depending on how many people were copied and who they were, the privilege claims might be compromised.

Q. How can that be? I thought everything within the company was sheltered by the privilege.

A. The privilege protects communications between privileged persons for the purpose of giving or receiving legal advice. "Privileged persons" include the client, the client's lawyer, and agents of either who facilitate the communication.[455] As applied to entities, agents of the organization are limited to those who reasonably need to know of the communication to act for the organization. Lawyers can communicate with other employees about everything from the deli menu to the grammar of the company's advertising. These communications would not be for the purpose of receiving legal advice.

Q. But in a heavily regulated company, every activity takes place against an elaborate legal background.

A. You are correct. There is a larger issue here. There is case law out there that suggests a client—no matter how heavily regulated and how much it needs lawyer advice in all aspects of its business—cannot shield its operation from discovery

455. RLGL §§ 70, 73.

in litigation by hiding all of that activity behind a claim of privilege.[456]

Q. That view has to be wrong, because the more an entity needs a lawyer, the more the benefit of the privilege should apply.

A. One of us agrees with you, the other is not so sure. But you should know this antipathy to the privilege is abroad in the land—like so many other examples—reflecting a jaundiced view by some judges to assertions of the privilege in general. Their attitude reflects the fact that the privilege is an evidentiary rule. Because it blocks the admissibility of otherwise relevant evidence, some courts construe its scope very narrowly.

Q. Is anything clear?

A. Two things are certain: First, the privilege is more limited in scope than the fiduciary obligation of confidentiality embodied in Rule 1.6, which protects all "information relating to the representation" and regulates the lawyer's obligation to the client in all contexts. Second, the fiduciary obligation of confidentiality is automatic; the client does not need to assert anything (other than the fact he/she or it is a client) to receive this fiduciary protection. On the other hand, the privilege is anything but automatic. The client does have to "claim" the privilege in litigation, and also has the burden of proof to establish its protection for each communication or document if the privilege assertion is challenged.[457]

§ 14.03 Privileged Persons

Sometimes You Don't Want Privilege

Q. I have always cherished the privilege. I recognize how valuable it is for my client. I'm in-house GC. Two years ago, my company did a secondary stock offering. These things are

456. *In re* Vioxx Prods. Liab. Litig., 501 F. Supp. 2d 789 (E.D. La. 2007) (heavily regulated business cannot claim privilege on all documents sent to legal counsel, company must claim privilege and document elements of privilege for each document or email).

457. *Id.* Smithkline Beecham Corp. v. Apotex Corp., 232 F.R.D. 467 (E.D. Pa. 2005) (Fed. R. Civ. P. 26(b)(5) requires parties to claim privilege expressly and describe documents covered by a claim of privilege, including identification of documents' authors, to determine any involvement by agents of lawyers or client; routine documents transferred or routed through a lawyer not privileged unless client identifies with specificity nearly every person who received each document); *In re* Seroquel Prods. Liab. Litig., No. 6:06-md-1769-Orl-22DAB, 2008 WL 1995058 (M.D. Fla. May 7, 2008) (when business chose to mix legal consultation with many other sources for creating final documents, most claims of privilege cannot be sustained because it is nearly impossible to establish that the primary purpose of the lawyer's involvement was to provide legal rather than business advice).

tricky. We engaged outside counsel. We got Caldwell & Moore. Everyone says they are the best. Anyway, they gave us advice that turned out to be a disaster. I got sued, the company got sued, so did the CEO.

A. Sounds like a real mess!

Q. It is, but it just got worse. I relied entirely on Caldwell for advice. That's my defense.

A. Sounds perfect!

Q. It would be if I could use it.

A. Don't tell me!

Q. Yes, I have to tell you. They take my deposition. I explained my total reliance on Caldwell & Moore. But my company is represented by separate counsel; that counsel interposed an attorney-client privilege objection and did not plead advice of counsel. She says the company has not waived the privilege and I was not the client; the company was.

A. Sadly, we are afraid you are in a trap. If your company were the only client, it is its privilege to waive. If it were a joint representation, you still must get co-client's waiver or the privilege stands.[458] Either way, you are barred from disclosing the advice you received and, therefore, your defense has disappeared.

Q. And here I thought the privilege was my friend.

A. Most, but not all, of the time.

The Consulted Accountant

Q. We've been handling the defense of this large antitrust claim brought by our client's dealers. Something about assigning exclusive territories. The exposure is big but we have great defenses. Anyway, our client calls us. The accountants are giving him fits. He wants me to send them our last memo to the board. We say sure.

Now we have to update our privilege log. We put down that memo. List a copy going to the CPA's. Suddenly, we're hit with a challenge to our privilege and work-product claim. Worse than that, lawyers for the dealers argue there's been subject-matter waiver. We respond there can't be waiver because we kept it all in the family. We're right, right?

458. RLGL § 75.

A. Not exactly. A "privileged person" is an agent of the client or lawyer who facilitates the communication for the purpose of the client's receipt of legal advice. Any subsequent communication to non-privileged persons constitutes a privilege waiver, even if unintended as such.[459]

Q. But I know that some jurisdictions recognize an accountant-client privilege, so we should all be under the same umbrella, correct?

A. In some states there is an accountant-client privilege. That might keep it "in the family" in state courts in those few states. But most states, and the federal courts, don't recognize that privilege. And, unlike lawyers, whose main duties are to their clients, accountants' duties—when they are auditing—run to the public. Sharing the information with them almost surely waives the privilege, particularly because you shared your "privileged" memo with them for purposes of their auditing the company's financial statements.

Whether such a waiver also acts as a complete subject-matter waiver and how broadly the subject matter will be defined are separate questions. You certainly can argue that the document was self-contained, and no other documents address the same topic (the status of the lawsuit at a given point in time) but don't be surprised if your adversaries argue they now get to see all communications with the board, or all assessments of the litigation. Good luck.[460]

§ 14.04 Employee Email

It's Our Computer

Q. Ten employees have sued our client for age discrimination. Bogus case.

459. *Id.* §§ 70, 79.

460. United States v. Ruehle, 583 F.3d 600 (9th Cir. 2009) (privilege does not protect communications between CFO and outside counsel because CFO knew communications would be disclosed to company's outside auditors); United States v. Ackert, 169 F.3d 136 (2d Cir. 1999) (conversation between corporate inside counsel and investment banker not privileged, even though important to the lawyer's representation of the client); United States v. Schwimmer, 892 F.2d 237 (2d Cir. 1989) (accountant hired by lawyer to assist in preparation of criminal defense after government's investigation began was lawyer's agent, where lawyer told client to speak to accountant; the communication was for the purpose of preparing the defense and therefore privileged); Cavallaro v. United States, 153 F. Supp. 2d 52 (D. Mass. 2001) (because accounting firm was not hired for the purpose of facilitating legal communication between closely held corporation and its law firm, but rather simply collaborated with the law firm, documents created or reviewed by the accounting firm were not protected under the attorney-client privilege and must be produced to the IRS). *See also* § 23.07 in this book.

A. Of course.

Q. Anyway, we just met with general counsel. He's a bit of a nut. But maybe he is right on this one. His bet is that these employees have been communicating with their lawyers on the company's computers. Since we own 'em, he says, we should conduct a little surveillance. Learn what they are up to.

A. What did you say?

Q. We asked him how he could justify this. After all, he's talking about attorney-client communications. His response was the employee manual warns employees that their email is subject to review. On page 27 of a single-spaced document, he admitted.

A. Of course.

Q. What do you think?

A. This a hard one. We have competing interests. Clients should be able to communicate with their lawyers. Everyone, without exception, uses his or her employer's computer for personal messaging, to play solitaire, and to order from Amazon. In that way, it is like using your work phone to call the childcare provider. No one would tap a phone line. But because email never disappears, it is available for inspection. And the employer does have the right to inspect under certain conditions.

Q. Can we, or can't we?

A. Let's start with a caveat. Unless the applicable jurisdiction has clear law on the topic, the lawyers involved proceed at their own peril. That is because Rule 4.4(a) tells us that you cannot invade a third-party's attorney-client privilege. Third parties include your client's adversaries.

Q. Doesn't that end the inquiry?

A. Not really. The argument runs that this email is not privileged because it is accessible by individuals other than the lawyer and client.

Q. How do we determine whether that assertion wins the day?

A. Your question brings us back to the beginning. In some jurisdictions, the mere warning in an employee manual that email is subject to surveillance waives the privilege. In others, more than a warning buried on page 27 is required. The employees must be on actual notice that the employer is, in fact, conducting an email review in an open and notorious way. Otherwise, the employees can assume their communications are private. Last, there are cases that conclude that reviewing otherwise privileged email is never permitted, despite warnings and actual periodic review.

Q. Not helpful.

A. Only helpful in spurring you to do the required research. And to warn you of the pitfalls of viewing this email without either clear precedent or the securing of a court ruling that it is fair game.[461]

§ 14.05 Privilege and Shareholders

The Derivative Suit

Q. We are handling a derivative suit brought by one of those extortionate lawyers. Our client lost a huge patent infringement suit. Paid nine figures and suspended an entire product line. Now this guy brings a suit in the name of the company seeking damages, payable to the company, from the CEO, other officers, and the head of research. Alleges—correctly—that the company would never bring the lawsuit itself. Claims the entire board is biased in favor of CEO.

A. Sounds tough.

Q. That it is. But the real problem is the plaintiff's lawyer sought a zillion documents. We, of course, asserted privilege. But the son-of-a-gun claims there is no privilege as to this claim because, for this purpose, he represents the company! Can you imagine such a ridiculous idea? He's the last person to have the company's best interests in mind. All you have to see is how upset the board is.

A. It might be a surprising result. But, there is precedent for it. In the seminal case of *Garner v. Wolfinbarger*,[462] the court concluded that in this situation, where the plaintiff stands in the shoes of the reluctant company, the privilege will not apply because it belongs to the company, whose interests the minority shareholder seeks to vindicate. While that is not a unanimous view, it has been followed fairly often.[463]

461. *In re* Info. Mgmt. Servs., Inc. Derivative Litig., 81 A.3d 278 (Del. Ch. 2013) (email from senior officers of company who face breach of fiduciary duty claims to private lawyers using office email accounts not privileged).

462. Garner v. Wolfinbarger, 430 F.2d 1093 (5th Cir. 1970).

463. *See, e.g.*, Pittsburgh History & Landmarks Found. v. Ziegler, 200 A. 3d 58 (Pa. 2019) (rejecting *Garner* despite its having been followed by a majority of courts).

Q. He can look through our dirty underwear? Read all the internal memos regarding the merits of the defense?

A. That's correct. He's now part of the family, even if he's not invited for Thanksgiving. This is yet another reason why we constantly remind lawyers that they should be circumspect, even when they are creating documents they think will remain privileged forever. You never know when the client will waive the privilege, or the client will get bought and change management, or go into bankruptcy, or . . . be the subject of a derivative suit.

Q. So, does this mean that when we defend these shareholder class actions we also cannot assert the privilege on behalf of the corporation?

A. That is different.

Q. I don't see why. If all the shareholders are suing, aren't they the corporation for purposes of deciding questions of privilege?

A. No. When lawyers represent an entity (even if they do so directly through a shareholder suing in the name of the company) the entity is the client. Not its constituents, its officers, directors . . . or its shareholders. Thus, the company may assert—with some confidence—the privilege in a plaintiffs' class action shareholder suit.

§ 14.06 Creating Work Product

The Investigation

Q. There was an explosion at our client's plant. No deaths, but a number of serious injuries. The next day they hired an engineering firm to get to the cause. They operate similar plants in six states. Engineers came in, did a great job, identified the problem, and recommended an inexpensive fix. We were retained six weeks later when the first litigation was threatened.

A. We know where this is going.

Q. Right. We've received a document request. It clearly seeks the engineers' report. We explained that to the client who asked us if we cannot label it attorney work product to keep it out of the plaintiff's hands.

A. This is a tough one. If the report has been requested by you and the investigation conducted under the lawyers' supervision and control, it would clearly be work product. To label it that way after the fact is clearly an improper misrepresentation of what occurred.

Q. We're in a trap.

A. You have one out if you are in federal court or a state with a similar view. Rule 26(b)(3) of the Federal Rules of Civil Procedure stipulates a broader definition of work product to include matters the client undertook in anticipation of litigation, even if not done under the direction and control of a lawyer. It defines work product as documents "prepared in anticipation of litigation or for trial by or for another party or by or for that other party's . . . attorney, consultant, . . . insurer or agent."

Q. Then there's a chance?

A. So long as you describe the basis of the claim in a truthful way.

Q. Of course.

§ 14.07 Work-Product Protection

The work-product privilege protects the lawyer's response to the client and encourages lawyers to prepare adequately for litigation. Like the attorney-client privilege, it will be lost if not timely asserted.[464] Work product protects everything lawyers prepare for clients in anticipation of litigation other than underlying facts.[465] It is broader than the privilege, including materials obtained from persons other than the client, but also is narrower because it applies only to materials prepared in anticipation of litigation, not to all legal representations. Although the privilege absolutely bars the admission of evidence, work product creates an "immunity" that can be overcome with a proper showing of necessity. Your mental impressions, notes, legal theories, and opinions form the core of "opinion" work product, which is immune from discovery absent some clear exception.[466] Statements of witnesses prepared from lawyer interviews also are protected as "ordinary" work product, which may be a bit easier to obtain if substantial equivalent testimony is unavailable, for example, the witness died.

464. RLGL § 90.

465. *Id.* § 87; Hickman v. Taylor, 329 U.S. 495 (1947).

466. RLGL § 89.

§ 14.08 Investigations

The Supervised Expert

Q. So, if I supervise an expert's investigation into the cause of my client's paper mill explosion, then my notes will be privileged forever, right?

A. Not so fast, my friend. No matter how well we maintain all of the indicia of the privilege, there is one wild card we can never control.

Q. What's that?

A. The client can always decide that it is in its best interest to waive the privilege, to disclose your notes, memoranda, and other privileged materials.[467] Think about a company that changes management.[468] Or one that decides to cooperate with the SEC. Or a corporate client that wants to cut a deal with an aggressive unrelenting prosecutor. The lesson from all of this is never let down your guard in the care with which you write simply because it has the words "privileged and confidential" emblazoned in red ink on each page. In fact, assume that everything you write may someday appear on the front page of the *Wall Street Journal*. Then you may be dismayed that others are reading your work product. But you won't be embarrassed. The truth is lawyers too often put in writing matters that are best left unstated, and if they must be stated at all, can be just as effectively stated orally. The proliferation of email has only aggravated this problem and given the world some of the most outrageous examples of intemperate client-lawyer dialogue.

§ 14.09 Ordinary and Opinion Work Product

What Is Ordinary about Ordinary Work Product?

Q. I thought I did everything by the book. I remembered that you had said to label work product appropriately so that our interviews with possible witnesses and others would never have to be disclosed. We were interviewing a number of key witnesses to this alleged stock fraud and each lawyer in my

467. *Id.* §§ 78, 79.

468. Tekni-Plex, Inc. v. Meyner & Landis, 674 N.E.2d 663 (N.Y. 1996) (successor corporation controlled attorney-client privilege).

office religiously followed the protocol and labeled every page "attorney work product." But now one of the individuals we interviewed died unexpectedly. The other side asked if we had interview notes of that person, and we refused to answer until the judge ruled otherwise. Then we admitted we had interviewed the individual, and we had notes, but still refused to turn them over.

A. That sounds right.

Q. Well, now the other side has filed a motion to compel our production of those interview notes. Claims necessity since the individual is deceased. The last thing we want to produce in this case are those notes.

A. Your obligation to hand them over will likely turn on a different point. Interview notes certainly are work product. And if all you did was record the answers to the questions asked of the witness, it may be that you will be forced to produce them. But, if you can argue that this is opinion work product because you have interlineated into your notes your impressions, you may still be able to withstand the request. But this is a good lesson for the future. It is not enough to fully protect work product unless you do your level best to make it opinion work product, which is much more likely to be protected by a court.

Q. Well, I hope we will know better for the next time. I'm afraid we have a very weak argument on this set of notes.

§ 14.10 Privilege and Work-Product Waivers

Who Has the Right to Waive?

Q. Years ago, we handled takeover litigation for Magna. Those were the swashbuckling days when secret raids were fashionable. Now, it is derivative litigation brought in the name of the company against the old directors and officers, claiming they engaged in reckless conduct that cost the company huge sums.

A. What has that got to do with you?

Q. Well, of course, we are not handling that litigation. But my deposition has been noticed.

A. What are you worried about?

Q. I met with new CEO yesterday. He has decided the best interests of the company are for the company to waive the privilege and permit me to testify to any and all matters relating to the original takeover litigation. New CEO tells me, "I don't think old CEO is liable here, but I see no reason to shield an inquiry into his reckless conduct, so I am going to waive the privilege for the company."

A. You certainly have your marching orders. It is the client's right to waive, and the CEO certainly has the right to do so on behalf of the company. 'Fraid you are going to have to sit for a deposition.

Q. I know that. What worries me is that old CEO is a defendant in the derivative case. While I tried to make it clear back then that I only represented the company, it is not unlikely that old CEO thinks I represented him as well.

A. Why might he think that?

Q. Well, our firm did prepare estate plans for the C-suite executives, and I represented the CEO's son on a DUI.

A. That could do it. If there is any reasonable doubt about CEO's view of your role, you must notify old CEO that you have been told to testify to privileged matters. Urge him, under the circumstances, to consult his own counsel and have that counsel inform you whether old CEO plans to assert the privilege. If so, you will be a bystander while he takes whatever steps are appropriate to assert that the company's waiver is not enough to free you to testify to privileged matters.

Q. New CEO is not going to be very happy.

A. That is not your problem. One of the characteristics of joint representation is that, if there is to be a waiver of the privilege, the waiver must be by all affected clients.[469] You must wonder why: If in every joint representation one of the clients could waive the privilege for all, no one would be willing to be a client in a joint representation and give the other client or clients the right to waive. Yet there are times when join representations are appropriate and offer legitimate financial savings to the parties involved. But they do come with limitations, and this is one of them.

§ 14.11 Waiver by Sharing

The Nosy Accountants

Q. Damn accountants.

469. RLGL § 75.

A. We know. They always tell you that you owe Uncle Sam more than you ever expected.

Q. That too. But what I'm complaining about is those auditors' letters. There's that agreement that all we need say is that the chance of an unfavorable outcome in the litigation is neither probable nor remote.

A. That's our understanding.

Q. But you know that's often not enough. The auditors want to know more.

A. And you worry whether what you tell the auditors could be considered privileged.

Q. Worse than that. It could result in a subject-matter waiver, forcing the client to disclose a lot more privileged communications in the very litigated matter we are handling.

A. You can't do that.

Q. But the client is worried that he can't get an unqualified opinion from the auditors. How about if we get another law firm to represent the client for purposes of giving the accountants an opinion?

A. Same problem. As soon as the opinion is shared with the auditors, any privilege could be deemed waived. And it's probably not work product either.

Q. Could the auditors hire a lawyer?

A. Of course. But the issuer cannot share any privileged information with that lawyer and conversations between the auditors' lawyer and the issuer also will be subject to discovery.[470] Not privileged; not work product. Moreover, because of the auditors' duties to the public, these conversations might be discoverable in the same way as the auditors' work papers have to be produced.

§ 14.12 Waiver by Reliance on Legal Advice

Advice Regarding Advice

Q. What was I thinking?

A. Hard to rely on mental telepathy.

470. Eagle Harbor Holdings, LLC v. Ford Motor Co., No. 3:11-cv-05503, 2013 WL 6173761 (W.D. Wash. Nov. 25, 2013) (litigant who shared legal advice with third persons who shared a joint business interest waived attorney-client privilege; joint business interest does not qualify as a common legal interest).

Q. Sorry to be obtuse. But I am kidding myself. I was defending our client in an SEC investigation. The SEC is challenging the disclosure by our client in a recent convertible debenture offering. The claim: We should've disclosed the tentative results in the human trials of the client's new anti-psychotic drug. We were too negative. Imagine that; criticized for being conservative. I thought the only way to really get in trouble is to be too enthusiastic.

A. It goes both ways.

Q. But one way much more often. Anyway, in responding to one of the SEC interrogatories we wrote an admittedly long-winded, drop-this-case defense. I got carried away and I wrote that the client had consulted us and that we had given the company our view that it was fair disclosure.

A. An advice-of-counsel defense?

Q. You got it. We really did not focus on that at the time. But that's precisely what the Commission argues.

A. They want the opinion letter.

Q. There is no letter. It was oral, and it was privileged.

A. Not the end of the story.

Q. Hardly. They want the deposition of the corporate partner in charge. They want our entire file. And they reserve the right to take more lawyer deps. It's a frontal assault on the sacred privilege.

A. We agree with you there. But, alas, the Commission has a good argument.

Q. Can't we just agree not to assert the advice-of-counsel defense?

A. We're afraid that genie is out of the bottle.

Q. But all our documents? And more depositions?

A. The Commission is going to claim waiver by asserting an advice-of-counsel defense. You cannot go down that path without waiving the privilege.[471] Then it will assert subject-matter waiver. It will assert that you cannot get away with providing just the opinion letter or the testimony regarding the oral opinion. That the Commission is entitled to all of your firm's work product behind the opinion. Then the judge will decide just how broad or narrow the subject-matter waiver should be.

Q. We really didn't even need to disclose our opinion. What a mistake.

---

471. Seneca Ins. Co. v. W. Claims, Inc., 774 F.3d 1272 (10th Cir. 2014) (insurer's reliance on advice of counsel to justify its settling with its insured waived privilege in subsequent suit against an adjuster for equitable indemnity).

A. Only if there are damaging privileged communications.

Q. My bet is there are. Once lawyers start writing documents they believe are privileged, any brake on overstatement or good taste disappears.

A. Precisely why we repeatedly warn lawyers to assume that even the most likely privileged matter will end up on Facebook. Then put their toned-down thoughts on paper.[472]

§ 14.13 Selective Waiver

Beware Selective Waiver

Q. I know I shouldn't've listened to the damn government lawyers. We needed their help, but not at this cost.

A. You are going to have to stop talking in riddles.

Q. This is the story. We were representing Colossus in an SEC investigation. Something about overbroad patent claims putting the client's key product in jeopardy. We convince the stuffed shirt AUSA to let us conduct an internal independent investigation. Hire a former regional director, now at Big Law.

A. So far so good.

Q. Oh, we went a lot longer thinking all was copacetic. To keep it independent we were ordered not to interfere. Then we get their report. Can those guys bill. But the report is mostly helpful. Not perfect, mind you, but good enough to keep the constabulary at bay. Then we made the fatal mistake.

A. We can feel your pain already.

Q. The AUSAs insist on the report. We, of course, say no way. First rule of survival: Don't share privileged material. In response, they tell us our concerns are not well founded, that if we choose to share the report with them, they will see to it that the judge issues one of those orders concluding that our sharing with the government is not a waiver as to anyone else. Sounds great to us, so we agree. Judge gives us a fully certified, original signature document and all is well with the world until . . .

Until we get sued by some of our shareholders. Omission of material facts is alleged. And they ask for any investigative

472. RLGL § 80.

reports. We identify the internal investigation, the report, and the privileged sharing with the SEC.

A. Privileged?

Q. Sure. That is what the order says. We were privileged to share it with the SEC and that we are privileged in the future to refuse to produce it.

A. But the plaintiffs don't accept that response.

Q. I'll say. They announce that the order isn't worth the paper it is written on, that sharing with the government, our adversary, broke the privilege, and that the document must be produced unredacted.

A. We agree. Though some courts have recognized a selective waiver, most will not. And an uncertain privilege is no privilege at all. Two lessons: First don't put anything into a privileged memo that you don't want to become public; sometimes conversations are far superior to writings. Second, if at all possible, don't turn over any privileged communications, and, if you must, remember that the subject-matter waiver doctrine may result in a broader loss of the privilege than you ever contemplated.

§ 14.14 Lawyer's Authority to Waive the Client's Privilege

Does Breaching Confidentiality Waive the Privilege?

Q. I handle a large number of matrimonial disputes. Usually, I represent husbands. They love being represented by women. They think we female lawyers take away the sympathy advantage that wives have in such proceedings. So, I have heard a lot of threats, mayhem, even death has been a topic. But I always attribute it to the high stakes emotions involved in such proceedings and refuse to act. But this time it was different. My client seemed so agitated, and he is ex-military and an avid hunter. So, when he threatened his spouse as he raced out of my office, I picked up the phone and called the police. They, in turn, arrested him, and now the D.A. wants to charge him with attempted murder. I have been called before the Grand Jury, and I know that I am going to be asked about the conversation in my office and then my phone call to the police. Do I have to testify?

A. You should not have to; the case law is much in your favor. In order to encourage lawyers, under very limited circumstances, to report their clients, the courts have held that your phone call does not waive the privilege, because, of course, your client was never consulted on your disclosure, and waiving privilege is a decision to be made by the client. The courts do not want to compound your compromise of your duty of confidentiality by also forcing you to testify against your client. As a result, you should invoke the privilege.

Q. But the conversation we had, such as it was, about murdering my client's wife, had nothing to do with legal advice. So, how do I invoke the privilege?

A. The case law covers that as well. If you were not aiding and abetting the potential crime (and you weren't), then the entire conversation was privileged because the crime-fraud exception does not apply. It would only apply if you gave him advice about how to carry out the crime.[473]

Q. Well, I certainly did not do that.

§ 14.15 The Crime-Fraud Exception: Innocent Client

Visiting the Sins of the Lawyer on the Client

Q. We made a terrible mistake. Out of an excessive burst of enthusiasm. No evil intent, trust me.

A. Sometimes the best of intentions gets our lawyers in trouble. But remember: Many of our rules do not require proof of intent to result in discipline. Nor is ignorance a defense. Lawyers are expected to know the rules that regulate their conduct. But we'll credit your statement. After all, we want to help. So shoot.

Q. We handle asbestos cases for old shipyard workers. This occurred decades ago. And we have settled with most of the manufacturers. But Colossus has refused to settle. We have dozens going to trial. It's an assembly line operation.

A. And?

473. Purcell v. Dist. Attorney for the Suffolk Dist., 676 N.E.2d 436 (Mass. 1997) (Rule 1.6 of Rules of Professional Conduct allowed lawyer to warn about client's arson threat, but prosecutor's subsequent attempt to evade attorney-client privilege not justified by crime-fraud exception to attorney-client privilege absent non-privileged information sufficient to trigger an in camera hearing).

Q. One of our young associates was worried that the clients would not remember whose asbestos they used in 1945. He came up with an aide memoir.

A. Using French won't help.

Q. Probably not. But she had each client fill in a questionnaire. When she got to the manufacturer part she wrote, "Now remember, the packaging was bright yellow."

A. Sounds close to the line.

Q. Would not have been a problem, if we had not inadvertently produced a completed questionnaire to the other side at the deposition of one of our clients.

A. We feel your pain.

Q. Yes, the counsel for Colossus has filed a disciplinary complaint against all of our lawyers handling asbestos claims. Worse still, they want to be able to introduce the questionnaires at trial to disparage our client. Don't know how we can stop them. These folks have good claims and, but for our inadvertent production, we are sure they would receive their just deserts.

A. Not so fast. You claimed attorney-client privilege, right?

Q. Of course. And work product too. But the Colossus lawyers screamed crime-fraud. I'm afraid they are right.

A. Actually, it is not dispositive. The crime-fraud exception to the privilege applies when the client engages in one or the other, rendering the lawyer an instrumentality of the actionable client conduct.[474] If the client is innocent, then the lawyer may have some serious accounting to do, but the privileged communications should remain protected.[475] Here, it sounds like the clients are both innocent and injured. If so, the documents should remain privileged.

§ 14.16 The Crime-Fraud Exception: Innocent Lawyer

The Duped Lawyer

Q. I am so embarrassed. I was completely duped.

---

474. Olson v. Accessory Controls & Equipment Corp., 757 A. 2d 14 (Conn. 2000) (court may engage in in camera review of allegedly privileged information to determine applicability of crime-fraud exception to attorney-client privilege only if party seeking to invoke crime-fraud exception presents lawfully obtained evidence that has not been adjudicated to be privileged sufficient to support good faith belief that client intended to perpetrate crime or fraud and that the communications sought in discovery were made in furtherance of that crime or fraud).

475. *See also* § 26.09 in this book.

A. How's that?

Q. The client belonged to the Downtown Club. I had known him for years. Okay, maybe he drank too much, but he never seemed drunk. Besides, he went to Princeton.

A. Keep going.

Q. He started a new business. Buying and selling McDonald's franchises. Those things are very profitable. More profitable than you think.

A. So far so good.

Q. Until we discovered that the franchises did not exist. Early investors made money, only to reinvest even more. He even stole our stationary to write nasty letters to McDonald's, which was his excuse to his customers why their payments were delayed.

A. What brings you to us?

Q. Well, the FBI is investigating. They want us to turn over all our files. We say they are privileged. They respond: crime-fraud. But that can't apply here. We had no idea. Like I said, our former client went to Princeton!

A. We are afraid you are wrong on this one. The crime-fraud exception applies to client fraud. The lawyer had better be completely innocent of the fraud. If not, there is a lot more to worry about than the waiver of the privilege.

Q. So, we have to turn it over?

A. Not until you attempt to defend the production on privilege grounds.

Q. And if we fail?

A. You might have to hire counsel yourself because, if Mr. Orange & Black turns out to be impecunious, the losing investors may cast a broader search for deep pockets.[476]

Q. Oh no.

---

476. United States v. Chen, 99 F.3d 1495 (9th Cir. 1996) (reasonable cause to believe lawyer's services were used to further an unlawful scheme despite lawyer's lack of knowledge of crime found in disclosures outside attorney-client communications); Purcell v. Dist. Attorney for the Suffolk Dist., 676 N.E.2d 436 (Mass. 1997) (factual basis to allow judge's discretion to conduct in camera review of the evidence to establish whether crime-fraud exception applies limited to non-privileged information); Disciplinary Counsel v. O'Brien, 899 N.E.2d 125 (Ohio 2008) (lawyer suspended for six months for disbursing $64,000 of former client's money in office trust account on eight occasions while bankruptcy was pending when he reasonably suspected former client had not disclosed the asset in the bankruptcy proceeding; lawyer's belief that attorney-client privilege prevented disclosure of former client's bankruptcy fraud, and reliance on expert who agreed, did not excuse lawyer's active complicity).

§ 14.17 The Crime-Fraud Exception: Ignoring Legal Advice

Irresponsible Clients

Q. Clients are so irresponsible. I repeatedly warned my wealthy client that deducting his daughter's wedding was impermissible, even if he had invited a few business friends to attend. But all he wanted to know were his chances of getting caught, and I refused to give him the answer.

A. Sounds like you did the right thing.

Q. So far so good. But now I have been subpoenaed to testify at my former client's trial on tax fraud. I called up the prosecutor to see how I could possibly be a witness. His answer is he is sure I warned my client not to do that. He knows what a straight arrow I am, and that is the testimony that he wants to elicit.

A. And your response?

Q. I told him it had to be privileged. But his response was crime-fraud exception. Is that right?

A. No. The crime-fraud exception applies to communications between a client and a lawyer in which the client is seeking and receiving assistance—unwitting assistance—in the commission of a crime. What you were doing was telling the client to obey the law. That type of communication remains privileged, and the prosecutor may not enhance his chances of success by calling the accused's lawyer to the stand to admit the lawyer warned the client. You may stand your ground.[477]

§ 14.18 The Testamentary Exception

Does the Privilege Die?

Q. I understand that my confidentiality obligation as well as my duty to protect the attorney-client privilege lasts past the end of the representation. But there must be some limit. Can the truth be hidden forever? Past death?

A. What prompts your inquiry?

---

477. United States v. Bauer, 132 F.3d 504, 510 (9th Cir. 1997) (no crime-fraud exception when lawyer advised client to obey the law and client did the opposite because it is "impossible to discern a causal connection or functional relationship between the advice given by [lawyer] and the actions taken by [client]").

Q. My client lived a lie. He appeared to be a happily married heterosexual. Lovely wife. Three kids. But he also had a partner. A friend from his college days. I'd known for years. But somehow he kept the secret. Sad, really.
A. A lot for you to keep a secret.
Q. Especially because I am pretty sure his suicide last year was the result of his friend's tragic death in a boating accident. . . .
A. And?
Q. And the fact that his widow, who I also represent, has been blaming herself for the suicide. When she had nothing to do with it.
A. So, you want to tell her?
Q. I do. It will relieve her pain to know she is not at fault.
A. And to know her husband was living a lie.
Q. Well, there is that. But I thought she'd still be better off knowing.
A. Fortunately, your deceased client made that decision for himself . . . and for you. You must honor his entitlement to confidentiality by not disclosing his other relationship voluntarily and, if you are ever under subpoena to testify regarding these matters . . . ever, and we mean ever, you must assert the privilege.[478]

---

478. RLGL § 77; Swidler & Berlin v. United States, 524 U.S. 399 (1998) (notes of client interview made shortly before client's death protected by attorney-client privilege; knowing that client's communications will be privileged posthumously encourages client to communicate fully).

CHAPTER 15

Conflicts of Interest

§ 15.01 Introduction: Your Loyalty Obligation

This chapter explores the fiduciary duty of loyalty, which can be traced back several centuries in the law of agency.[479] Fiduciary obligations arise out of relationships where one person must share confidential information with, and trust and depend upon, another. Loyalty imposes an obligation on lawyers to act for the benefit of clients by recognizing and responding to any influences (conflicts of interest) that may interfere with loyalty to the client's interests.

In what has been viewed as a classic description of the fiduciary duty of loyalty, then Chief Judge Cardozo explained:

> Many forms of conduct permissible in a workaday world for those acting at arm's length are forbidden to those bound by fiduciary ties. . . . Not honesty alone, but the punctilio of an honor the most sensitive, is then the standard of behavior.[480]

Agency law recognizes that lawyers derive power from clients, but at the same time, also possess the superior knowledge and skill to overpower client interests.[481] The loyalty obligation ensures effective client representation by obligating lawyers to avoid harm to clients. You accomplish this by recognizing and responding to any influences (conflicts of interest) created by others, including the interest of another current, former, or prospective client of your law firm, the interest of a

479. RLGL ch. 8, Introductory Note; Restatement (Third) of Agency § 8.01 (Am. Law Inst. 2006).

480. Meinhard v. Salmon, 164 N.E. 545, 546 (N.Y. 1928).

481. Restatement (Third) of Agency § 1.01 (Am. Law Inst. 2006).

third person, or your own interest that may interfere with your obligation to act in the client's best interests.[482]

The next section outlines a four-step process that the law governing lawyers requires to properly resolve conflicts.[483] All of these obligations continue throughout the course of the representation, as law, facts, and the relationships of the clients and lawyers can shift. Nearly all conflicts of an individual lawyer are imputed to the lawyer's firm.[484] When you encounter a new or more clearly defined conflict, the identification, consentability, and informed-consent process begins anew.

Failure to properly identify and resolve conflicts can create overlapping remedies for clients. A client can seek tort relief for harm caused[485] and injunctive or disqualification relief when harm is threatened.[486] Proceeding with a representation without disclosing a conflict also can result in fee disgorgement,[487] the establishment of a constructive trust, or professional discipline.[488]

---

482. MR 1.7 cmt. [1]; RLGL § 121 cmt. b.

483. MR 1.7 cmt. [2].

484. MRs 1.8(k), 1.10; RLGL § 123.

485. Ellis v. Davidson, 595 S.E.2d 817 (S.C. Ct. App. 2004) (client stated cause of action for breach of fiduciary duty and legal malpractice against lawyer who took 60 percent interest in client company that lawyer set up); Anderson v. O'Brien, No. CV-044003913, 2005 WL 3624382 (Conn. Super. Ct. Dec. 8, 2005) (client stated cause of action for legal malpractice, recklessness, and violation of state unfair trade practices act for failure to protect seller's interests while simultaneously representing buyers in a real estate transaction).

486. Maritrans GP Inc. v. Pepper, Hamilton & Scheetz, 602 A.2d 1277 (Pa. 1992).

487. Burrow v. Arce, 997 S.W.2d 229 (Tex. 1999).

488. Monco v. Janus, 583 N.E.2d 575 (Ill. App. Ct. 1991) (contract with client voidable due to undue influence despite lawyer's proof of numerous hours of unpaid legal services in setting up the business); Liggett v. Young, 877 N.E.2d 178 (Ind. 2007) (contract with client voidable due to influence where lawyer-consumer drafts contract).

§ 15.02 Chart: Five Steps to Resolving Conflicts of Interest

1. Identify the client(s): RLGL §§ 14, 96.
2. Determine whether a conflict of interest exists. Seven categories:
A. Personal Interests of a Lawyer
General Rule: MR 1.7
Specific Rules: MR 1.8(a) Business transactions with clients
MR 1.8(b) Use of client information
MR 1.8(c) Client gifts to lawyer
MR 1.8(d) Literary rights
MR 1.8(e) Financial assistance to client
MR 1.8(h) Limitation of liability to client
MR 1.8(i) Proprietary interest in litigation
MR 1.8(j) Lawyer/client sexual relationship
MR 3.7 Lawyer as witness
B. Interests of Another Current Client
General Rule: MR 1.7
Specific Rules: MR 1.8(g), 1.13(g)
C. Interests of a Third Person
General Rule: MR 1.7
Specific Rules: MR 1.8(f), 5.4(c), 1.13(a)
D. Interests of a Former Client
General Rule: MR 1.9
E. Interests of a Prospective Client
General Rule: MR 1.18
F. Government Lawyers
General Rule: MR 1.11
Specific Rule: MR 1.12
G. Imputed Conflicts
General Rule: MR 1.10
Specific Rules: MR 1.8(k), 1.11, 1.12
3. Decide whether the conflict is consentable: MR 1.7(b)(1)–(3), 1.8.
4. If it is, consult with affected clients and obtain informed consent, in writing: MR 1.7(b)(4); 1.8.
5. Consider remedies if the conflict is not properly resolved: RLGL §§ 5, 6.

§ 15.03 Conflicts-Control Systems

Once you have identified your clients, you need to identify whether a conflict of interest exists. To do this, you need a conflicts-control system, which will allow you and your law firm to search for a potential adverse interest that may arise from either your own interests or the interests of others.

Conflicts arise from the interests and clients of individual lawyers, and are imputed to your "firm," a defined term that encompasses all associations that practice law, including legal services organizations, inside legal departments, and shared office facilities without reasonably adequate measures to protect client confidentiality.[489]

When a prospective client arrives, you need to be sure that neither your firm nor you already represent any other parties to the matter, that third persons who are not clients will not interfere with your independent professional judgment, and that you do not have a conflicting personal interest.

Your conflicts control system should include two steps:

1. Searching a series of lists in a database that correspond to legally recognized conflicts, including prospective clients, current clients, former clients, third-party payers of the firm, and lawyer personal interests.
2. Sending an individual new client memorandum to all lawyers in the firm that ferrets out any information omitted or incorrectly placed in the list database.

All conflicts detection and avoidance practices should be institutionalized by written policies and procedures that require compliance with these two steps by all law firm personnel. Law firms should establish a committee or designate a partner with responsibility to implement and supervise the conflicts control system. When potential conflicts are discovered, the partner or committee should have authority to decide how to respond. Law firm policy should include the requirement that any member of a law firm ethics committee potentially involved in any conflict remove herself from considering its resolution. The partner or committee in charge of conflicts also should make clear that deviations from law firm policies are serious concerns that, if not followed, could result in appropriate penalties.

We outline these procedures in the following list. Following them will not prevent conflicts, but it will put you in a position to know about them and respond appropriately. If you have searched the database and found no matches, and no one in your firm has responded to your new client memo, you can proceed to take what, at least initially, is a conflict-free representation, subject to your continuing duty of diligence.

Never rely on your memory for a conflicts check. Don't even rely on a computer database. Your innocent forgetfulness or less than full due diligence will be no defense to any of the myriad remedies a client may seek, and some, such as fee forfeiture, constructive trust, and

489. MRs 1.0(c), 1.0 cmts. [2]–[4], 1.10; RLGL § 123.

professional discipline, can be imposed even if the client suffers no harm beyond the breach of loyalty. Concisely, your conflicts-control system should include these steps:

1. Identify your clients, prospective clients, former clients, and third-party payers.
2. Identify the nature of the matter for each client, prospective client, former client, and third-party payer.
3. Build a database of lists that correspond to legally recognized conflicts, including current clients, prospective clients, former clients, third-party payers, and law firm lawyer personal interests.
4. Use your data base as a conflicts-control system each time you propose to take on a new matter or client. Your system should include two steps:
   a. Searching each list in a database for any matches to the prospective new client or any other interested parties (including co-plaintiffs and defendants).
   b. Sending an individual new client memorandum to all lawyers in the firm that ferrets out any information omitted or incorrectly placed in the list database.
5. Develop a written policy and procedure that requires compliance with these two steps by all personnel. Law firms should establish a committee or designate a partner with responsibility to implement and supervise the conflicts control system.
6. Designate and empower a senior lawyer or committee with responsibility to implement and supervise the conflicts-control system, authority to decide how to respond to conflicts, and power to address any deviations from law-firm policies.
7. Respond to conflicts by determining:
   a. Whether the conflict is consentable.
   b. If it is, obtaining proper informed consent from all affected clients, confirmed in writing.
   c. If allowed, establish an effective screen.

§ 15.04 Zero-Sum Situations

Double the Clients, Double the Fun

Q. There is an open TV channel in New York City. One of our partners received a call from Viacom to represent it before the FCC in the competition for the channel. That was two days ago. Today, I got a call from Disney. Guess what? They want us to represent them in competing for the same channel. We just had a firm meeting to decide how to deal with this abundance of riches, and one of our partners brilliantly suggested that we should form two teams and represent each of them. Of course with their consent. But given how outstanding our FCC practice is, we think it just might yield us double the pleasure.

A. Keep those visions of sugarplums in your dreams, but don't start spending the double fees quite yet.

Q. I know. We still have to ask the clients.

A. No. It is more than that. Do you really think you would be allowed to take on the representation of both? What's the Disney team going to do?

Q. I am going to lead that team. We will demonstrate why Disney is the very best candidate. Our client's reputation is so much better than Viacom's.

A. What did you just do?

Q. I demonstrated my zealous advocacy on behalf of Disney.

A. You certainly did. But part of your zealous advocacy was trashing Viacom's CEO. And what will Viacom be under your planned bonanza?

Q. A client of the firm, I suppose.

A. Precisely. In representing Disney, you are going to promote Disney and disparage Viacom. Your other team is going to do the reverse. While there might not be any versus in a caption, you would be taking a position directly adverse, not only to a client of the firm, but a client in the firm that is a party to the same proceeding. Under the applicable rule, that conflict is not consentable, because you cannot provide competent and diligent representation to both clients.[490] And that is what you would be prevented from doing. You would also be entering engagements where the best you would do is bat .500. That, of course, is a splendid batting average in baseball, but for lawyers to start a representation where they know one client will win and one client will lose is a nonstarter.[491]

---

490. MR 1.7(b)(1).

491. Murray v. Vill. of Hazel Crest, No. 06-C-1372, 2006 WL 3589969 (N.D. Ill. Dec. 7, 2006) (lawyer disqualified from representing four plaintiffs, each of whom claimed employment discrimination and sought the same job as deputy chief of the police department). *Compare* RLGL § 121 cmt. c ("In most instances [of representing competitors for the same broadcast license], informed consent of both A and B would not suffice to allow the dual representation.").

§ 15.05 Continuing Obligation

Prosecutorial Control

Q. The EPA is investigating this family-controlled public company when things get more complicated with the launch of a parallel SEC investigation. I am asked by the company to represent two of the family members on the board. They want to save money and cannot imagine how either could be involved in this distracting sideshow.

A. Did you take it on?

Q. I met with them individually. Based on what we know, I could not see any conflict. I have met with the SEC lawyers a number of times. Produced some documents. Answered some questions. So far so good.

A. It would seem. But you are calling us.

Q. Yes. The SEC started mumbling to company counsel about possible criminal charges. While I still thought my clients were okay, shivers ran through the company, discombobulating my clients. Things got worse when both clients received subpoenas to testify. We decided to resist, announcing both would take the Fifth. Only prudent thing to do when flying blind.

A. Still sounds copacetic.

Q. The collar got tighter three weeks later. I get a call from the SEC. One of my clients is now a "subject" of the investigation. They don't want his deposition. But they want the other brother to testify. I asked why, given my understanding that he was not involved in any way. When the SEC lawyer refused to tell me anything, I advised the client to invoke the Fifth, he agreed, and so I informed the government.

A. Good for you.

Q. Not so fast. The SEC lawyer tells me that I have a conflict and must withdraw from representing the non-subject brother. If I don't, they will move to disqualify me. That's ridiculous. I know a conflict when I see one.

A. We love it. Whenever the prosecution types raise conflicts issues you wonder whether it has less to do with ethics and more to do with tactical advantage.

Q. That's why I came to you. Is their motion to DQ just a hollow threat?

A. Not really. They are going to argue that you are not free to recommend strenuously that brother #2 testify because of your representation of brother #1.

Q. But I did.

A. We have no doubt, but the situation of the client representation, without sharing your privileged conversation with the second brother, could have affected the dialogue.

Q. Does that mean I must withdraw from the representation of brother #2?

A. You might be able to avoid it. You can get truly independent counsel for the second brother to counsel him on whether to testify. Get someone who will be viewed as truly independent and experienced. Have that person review what you know and give his or her best advice to the client. If the client decides to testify, this person can represent him. If not, you have a very strong argument why the joint representation can continue. No guarantees, but it's the best you can do.

§ 15.06 Simultaneous Adverse Representation in Unrelated Matters

Not Solving the Problem

Q. What if we were asked to represent Viacom and just Viacom in the television channel dispute, but Disney was a client of our firm for labor law matters? Could we represent Viacom in that situation?

A. Not without Disney's consent. You would still be taking a position directly adverse to Disney. And our Rules of Professional Conduct bar lawyers from being directly adverse to their present clients on totally unrelated matters without the client's consent.[492] We already described why the representation of Viacom would be directly adverse to Disney, and Disney is clearly a present client of the firm. The only way you could do this is if you got the consent in writing from Disney to undertake the conflicting representation. Even then, some might assert you could not do that because there is no way a reasonable lawyer would conclude that he or she could trash a present client of the firm in order to zealously represent a competing bidder of that present client.

492. Eastman Kodak Co. v. Sony Corp., Nos. 04-CV-6095, 04-CV-6098, 2004 WL 2984297 (W.D.N.Y. Dec. 27, 2004) (law firm disqualified from case it took on after former client was acquired by opposing party in other litigation).

Q. But there is really very little risk. We're not opposing them in litigation, so we don't have to worry about disqualification.

A. Ever heard of injunctive relief?[493] What about malpractice or breach of fiduciary duty?[494] Fee forfeiture?[495] Professional discipline?[496]

§ 15.07 Losing a Client by Disqualification or Injunction

The last problem identified multiple remedies that the law of agency has made available to clients whose lawyers breach fiduciary duties of loyalty or confidentiality. In the past half-century, courts have examined most conflicts of interest in the context of motions to disqualify lawyers.[497] Often these cases present circumstances where harm is threatened but has not yet occurred. Clients, former clients, and other litigation participants can seek to prevent harm by using a disqualification motion in a matter pending before a court. Outside of court, clients and former clients can seek injunctive relief to prevent the representation of other clients in transactional representations.

Disqualification motions originated over a century ago as requests for court orders addressed to the inherent power of a court.[498] The motion to disqualify may be made by the lawyer's client, former client, or any other party to the litigation, and judges are also empowered to raise the conflict issue sua sponte.[499] Although a few courts initially

493. Maritrans GP Inc. v. Pepper, Hamilton & Scheetz, 602 A.2d 1277 (Pa. 1992) (law firm enjoined from taking on new clients in adverse substantially related representations to prevent breach of loyalty).

494. Kilpatrick v. Wiley, Rein & Fielding, 909 P.2d 1283 (Utah Ct. App. 1996) (breach of fiduciary duty claim against lawyers who represented multiple clients interested in acquiring a television station).

495. So v. Suchanek, 670 F.3d 1304 (D.C. Cir. 2012) (lawyer violated Rule 1.7 by simultaneously representing two clients in a contract matter, providing an opinion letter to one client that undercut claims under the contract against the other client; lawyer's subjective belief that his conduct was appropriate was unreasonable and constituted a breach of fiduciary duty warranting fee forfeiture).

496. G.D. Searle & Co. v. Pennie & Edmonds LLP, 801 N.Y.S.2d 233 (N.Y. Sup. Ct. 2004) (law firm violated conflicts rule when, without seeking either client's consent, it simultaneously represented two different patent clients in connection with related, though not necessarily identical patent applications with knowledge of the likelihood that one client would sue or attempt to license the other).

497. Franklin v. Callum, 782 A.2d 884 (N.H. 2001) (both parties granted disqualification of the other side's lawyer on different legal theories).

498. *Id.* Appellate courts review disqualification decisions of trial courts using an abuse of discretion standard. People *ex rel.* Dep't of Corps. v. Speedee Oil Change Sys., Inc., 980 P.2d 371, 378 (Cal. 1999).

499. FED. R. CRIM. P. 44(c) (federal district courts required to inquire into any proposed joint representation); Cuyler v. Sullivan, 446 U.S. 335 (1980) (trial judge has important role in assuring fairness of trial of joint defendants).

thought they had no such power, litigation over the past 50 years has left no doubt that courts can, and should, disqualify lawyers when their conduct threatens the fairness of a judicial proceeding.[500] Disqualification is sought to prevent a lawyer or former lawyer (and that lawyer's current law firm) from representing another client. When granted, disqualification can ensure that the case will be presented without conflicting loyalties or that confidential information of a former client will not be used against that client in the current matter.[501]

Injunctive relief provides a similar equitable remedy for breaches of statute or common-law fiduciary duty. It is only to be granted when there is an urgent necessity to avoid injury and no adequate legal remedy exists, such as the harm threatened by a law firm's use of a former client's extensive business secrets to benefit its current client in the same competitive industry. If injunctive relief were not available in such a case, the former client would be forced to wait until it lost all or part of the company's business before claiming a remedy.[502]

Although disqualification and injunctions provide relief from real or serious threats to client loyalty or confidentiality, unlike other remedies, they can impose costs on other parties to a proceeding. When the motion to disqualify comes from the opposing party or the court, a client can be deprived of a chosen lawyer, and that client must be afforded additional time to retain new counsel.

Courts recognize that motions to disqualify can be used as a litigation tactic by opposing parties and have responded in three ways to this potential for misuse of the court's power. First, courts are careful to scrutinize the facts and law offered in support of disqualification motions. Second, courts increasingly use the doctrine of laches, estoppel, or waiver to deny motions to disqualify when they have not been timely made.[503] Third, orders granting or denying disqualification

500. Ennis v. Ennis, 276 N.W.2d 341, 348 (Wis. Ct. App. 1979). Administrative law judges also exercise this power in appropriate circumstances. Prof'l Reactor Operator Soc'y v. United States NRC, 939 F.2d 1047 (D.C. Cir. 1991); SEC v. Csapo, 533 F.2d 7 (D.C. Cir. 1976); Pour Le Bebe, Inc. v. Guess? Inc., 5 Cal. Rptr. 3d 442 (Cal. Ct. App. 2003) (court will not overrule denial of disqualification motion by arbitration panel unless party to arbitration can show clear and convincing evidence that a conflict existed and that it had substantial impact on the panel's decision); *In re* Scioto Broadcaster, 5 FCC Rcd. 5158 (1990). Arbitrators also consider motions to disqualify. Biedermann Indus. Licensing Inc. v. AVMAR M.V., 570 N.Y.S.2d 33 (N.Y. App. Div. 1991) (application to disqualify counsel in arbitration proceeding is within exclusive jurisdiction of the courts).

501. RLGL § 6 cmt. i.

502. Maritrans GP Inc. v. Pepper, Hamilton & Scheetz, 602 A.2d 1277 (Pa. 1992).

503. Universal City Studios, Inc. v. Reimerdes, 98 F. Supp. 2d 449 (S.D.N.Y. 2000).

usually are not appealable until a final judgment on the merits.[504] This means that when disqualification is denied, the targeted lawyer may continue the representation, but the other side can raise the issue on appeal. On the other hand, if the motion is granted, the client represented by the now-disqualified lawyer is forced to find new counsel.[505] If that client settles or wins the case, the disqualified lawyer has no independent right to appeal. Only if the client loses the case can the issue be raised on appeal.

In assessing whether a lawyer should be disqualified, courts begin with the conflict of interest rules in the applicable Rules of Professional Conduct, statute, or case law.[506] The moving party has the burden of proving the violation. If a rule of professional conduct has been violated, disqualification commonly follows. A few courts require more: that the violation would "taint" the court proceeding.[507] More typical are courts that explicitly reject this "hands-off approach," finding motions to disqualify counsel to be "the proper method for a party-litigant to bring the issues of conflict of interest or breach of ethical duties to the attention of the court."[508]

One issue likely to arise when a law firm seeks to defend a disqualification motion is whether it can charge its current client for the defense. Some clients in this position may agree to fight the motion. Others may agree, but only if pursued at the firm's own expense.[509] Others may not be willing to defend at all, especially if the issue is close, and the client faces a real risk of losing your services.

Whenever your firm or you are subject to a disqualification motion, remember that a court order of disqualification means you have breached a fiduciary duty, thereby setting up a client's partial or complete defense to the payment of legal fees.[510] If the conflict has affected the representation from an earlier date, your now former client also may seek disgorgement of fees already paid.[511]

---

504. Richardson-Merrell Inc. v. Koller, 472 U.S. 424 (1985); Flanagan v. United States, 465 U.S. 259 (1984); Firestone Tire & Rubber Co. v. Risjord, 449 U.S. 368 (1981). State courts are split on this issue. *See* David B. Harrison, *Appealability of State Court's Order Granting or Denying Motion to Disqualify Attorney*, 5 A.L.R. 4th 1251 (1981).

505. Successor counsel will usually be allowed to use the disqualified lawyer's work product if it does not contain impermissible client confidential information. RLGL § 6 cmt. i.

506. *In re* Leslie Fay Cos., 175 B.R. 525 (Bankr. S.D.N.Y. 1994).

507. European Cmty. v. RJR Nabisco, Inc., 134 F. Supp. 2d 297 (E.D.N.Y. 2001) (reviewing Second Circuit decisions).

508. *In re* American Airlines, Inc., 972 F.2d 605, 611 (5th Cir. 1992).

509. Padco v. Kinney & Lange, 444 N.W.2d 889 (Minn. Ct. App. 1989).

510. *In re* Bonneville Pacific Corp., 196 B.R. 868 (Bankr. D. Utah 1996); Sheppard, Mullin, Richter & Hampton, LLP v. J-M Manufacturing Co, 425 P. 3d 1 (Cal. 2018).

511. *In re* Fountain, 141 Cal. Rptr. 654 (1977).

§ 15.08 Personal Injury Plaintiffs

Father and Son

Q. What a great case! Or so it seemed. Adult son was driving; dad in the passenger seat. An intersection collision with a 17-year-old driving the family Mercedes. Clearly the kid's fault. The police charged him with speeding. He pled guilty. And there's plenty of insurance.

A. Sounds perfect.

Q. That's what I thought. Then things began to unravel. I'm preparing Son for his deposition. I ask him where he was before he picked up Dad. He drops his voice, "At Scott's pub. Downing a few with the boys." I ask, "Does Dad know that?" "Why would I tell him?" Son responds. "Has nothing to do with the accident. That kid was speeding, and I swear he was high on something."

A. Uh oh!

Q. You can say that again.

A. Uh oh! What are you going to do?

Q. Well, I agree with Son. His drinking is irrelevant. So, I'm going to ignore it.

A. How long do you think that will last?

Q. Maybe they won't be as inquisitive as I?

A. Highly unlikely. How did you tell your clients you would handle confidential information?

Q. I told 'em I would keep everything they told me confidential. Just like I tell every client.

A. And if one of them told you something damaging?

Q. I didn't tell them anything.

A. Well, isn't Dad entitled to know about Son's drinking?

Q. I don't think so.

A. Unless you told the clients you would not share information like that with the other client, you have to do so.

Q. Why?

A. Because Dad has a better claim than Son. In fact, he may have a claim against Son. The teenage kid may defend based on that fact. Even counterclaim against Son. In any event, Dad needs to know so he can get independent advice.

Q. From me?

A. Hardly. Dad needs a lawyer who considers suing son. If you represent Dad, you would have to consider a claim against Son, which would be taking a position directly adverse to a former client in the same matter. If you represent Son and not Dad, you would have similar problems because you would be defending Son against a claim by Dad or at least having to represent Son in considering that claim. We are afraid that your interest in representing both may very well turn out to be representation of neither.

Dad may choose to ignore this little fact. It is his son, after all. But you can't advise Dad. What looked like a concurrent representation without a conflict now appears to be just the opposite. Each of your clients now has significantly different interests.

Q. And what if I had agreed with the clients not to share confidential information? What then?

A. Under those circumstances, you would be forced to withdraw from representing either because of the conflict between them. In silence.

Q. From two clients to none. In this great case. When they call those fees contingent, they aren't just kidding. Even when liability is clear.

A. But you would have been in trouble even if Son had imbibed Poland Spring.

Q. How can you say that?

A. Because of the speeding teenager's second form of speeding.

Q. That makes liability even clearer.

A. Oh, that's true, alright. But it puts insurance coverage of the speeding teenager in jeopardy. With no insurance, you have two clients with outsized claims competing for a limited pot of gold. In short, you have conflict problems. Your enhancing Dad's injury claim can hurt Son, and vice versa. So, unless the two clients can reach some way of proceeding that eliminates the competition, you face another obstacle to securing your pot of gold.

Q. Quickly turning to cast iron.

A. And, we hasten to add, such an allocation decision made pre-litigation may not be enforceable. Imagine if Dad and Son reached such an agreement here. And then Dad found out about Son's visit to the taproom. Dad could certainly assert that all bets were off. Dad now may be unhappy with the 60/40 agreement. Dad may want to settle. Dad may have a claim against Son, and Son certainly does not want to settle for zero, or so we assume.

Q. But they're family.

A. That may be true. But lawyers cannot represent families. Every time they try that approach, they can get into real trouble.

Because in representing a family the lawyer is actually representing individuals, autonomous individuals, each of whom is entitled to determine his or her own objectives, counseled by a lawyer who is dedicated to conflict-free representation, even if that requires eight lawyers. This is one time when father does not know best, at least for family members capable of determining their own objectives.

§ 15.09 Employer and Employee

Investigating the Company Accident

Q. We represent a big beverage distributor. One of their employee truck drivers was involved in a terrible accident with a school bus that killed more than 20 children. We visited the employee in the hospital, told him the employer sent us to represent him, and took his statement, all witnessed by his dad and uncle. Once we learned that the employee failed to follow company policy about checking the truck brakes, we withdrew and got him his own lawyer.

You can imagine our small community's pain caused by this accident. The prosecutor was threatening to subpoena our record of the employee's statement. To be good citizens, we handed it over without a fight. The grand jury indicted the employee for involuntary manslaughter. He was acquitted three years later. Turns out the brakes had nothing to do with the accident. Now he is suing us for turning over that statement. All we did was cooperate in the investigation of a horrible tragedy. And the statement wasn't even privileged, because the presence of his dad and uncle waived it. We should be safe, right?

A. We think not, not by a long shot. First, you should have advised the employee that his dad and uncle's presence would waive the privilege. Second, your fiduciary duty of confidentiality extends to all information relating to the representation, whether privileged or not. Third, you had a conflict of interest when you turned his statement over to the prosecutor, because you were now favoring the employer's interests. Why didn't you ask his new lawyer whether he would recommend that his client consent to the disclosure?

As a matter of civil liability, we advise settlement. You have breached a core fiduciary duty, confidentiality. This breach is so obvious that it will not require expert testimony to prove. In terms of harm caused, it cost your former client three years of misery while he waited for the trial. His damages easily can include emotional distress as well as any other economic loss.[512]

§ 15.10 Entities and Affiliates

Corporate Family Redux

Q. We're in big trouble. Two ways. We were asked to bring a RICO claim against a local stockbroker who invested his client's money with that guy Naidoff. We ran a conflicts check. Nothing showed up. So we fired away. Ten days later we get a nasty gram from the lawyer for the broker. In the form of a motion to disqualify. He tells us the broker is a third-tier subsidiary of Commerce Bank. We do employment discrimination cases for the bank. Have for years. But we had no idea. Besides, representing the bank doesn't make the broker our client. How could it?

A. Let's take it one step at a time. Today, in our consolidating corporate world, we think the standard of care is for you to know who owns whom. You can buy a service from Dun & Bradstreet, maybe others, that will tell you all your client's affiliates. Even if not required, having this information will avoid incidents like this.[513]

Q. But why do we care? Our client is Commerce Bank. Isn't that all we have to worry about?

A. Not really. Some think that should be the case. Others think quite the opposite. If an entity is a wholly owned part of a corporate family that includes your client, they believe there is no basis for suing your client's parent, subsidiary, or sibling. The Model Rules adopt a middle ground. The Restatement and a comment to Rule 1.7 require a fact-specific inquiry that looks into such factors as officers, common line of business, common

512. Sanford v. Commonwealth of Virginia, 687 F. Supp. 2d 591 (E.D. Va. 2009) (lawyers for sets of defendant/employees disqualified despite clients' earlier conflicts consent when facts and law created alternatives for each defendant that would harm jointly represented parties); Perez v. Kirk & Carrigan, 822 S.W.2d 261 (Tex. App. 1991) (lawyers liable for breach of fiduciary duty for turning over joint client-employee's statement to prosecutor without client's consent).

513. MR 5.1 cmt. [2]; RLGL § 11 cmt. g.

location, common offices, and common in-house counsel to determine whether you have to treat the nonclient affiliate as a client for conflict of interest purposes.[514] You haven't told us enough facts yet to permit us to say whether you can thread the Model Rule needle here. They are in two different, albeit related, businesses, that is, the bank and the broker, but we need to know more.[515] One thing you should also check is whether when the bank retained you it gave you instructions on how to treat its affiliates. Many of the more sophisticated corporate families do. They say they might grant a conflict waiver, but don't go suing our affiliates without asking first. You said you were in trouble two ways?

Q. Oh, yeah. Our client suing the broker is really upset. She signed a contingent-fee agreement with us. Now she's making noises about holding us responsible for her losses.

A. Well, that is a bit much. But if you withdraw or choose to litigate and lose the motion to disqualify, and then your client cannot find alternative counsel on the same basis, you may find yourself underwriting the lawyer.[516]

Q. Well, at least we can get a share of the new firm's fee—for our effort.

A. We don't think so. If you cannot handle the case because of a conflict of interest, it is impermissible for you to collect a fee.[517]

514. MR 1.7 cmt. [34] (lawyer who represents organization does not necessarily represent corporate affiliates unless the affiliate of client should also be considered a client or there is understanding between lawyer and client); RLGL §§ 14 cmt. f, 121 cmt. d (whether lawyer for an organization also represents affiliate is a question of fact; relevant factors include financial loss or benefit to affiliate that will have a "direct adverse impact on client," "loyalty of lawyer would be compromised due to the lawyer's relationship with another client or person whose interests would be adversely affected by the representation," significant control of the nonclient by the client," and an obligation to hold information confidential to the nonclient").

515. Certain Underwriters at Lloyd's London v. Argonaut Ins. Co., 264 F. Supp. 2d 914, 924 (N.D. Cal. 2003) (parent corporation and its subsidiary, even if wholly owned, are generally regarded as separate entities for conflicts purposes, unless an exception applies—where the relationship between the entities are such they have a "unity of interests," such as relatively direct financial relationship or common management, including supervision, over the legal affairs of both entities); Eastman Kodak Co. v. Sony Corp., Nos. 04-CV-6095, 04-CV-6098, 2004 WL 2984297 (W.D.N.Y. Dec. 27, 2004) (wholly owned subsidiary same client as parent company for conflict of interest purposes where close relationship exists due to interlocking board members, corporate officers, and shared legal department).

516. RLGL § 37 cmt. d.

517. Silbiger v. Prudence Bonds Corp., 180 F.2d 917 (2d Cir. 1950); Crawford & Lewis v. Boatmen's Trust Co., 1 S.W.3d 417 (Ark. 1999).

§ 15.11 Entity-Created Conflicts

The Client Merger

Q. We have been representing Paragon Corporation in an antitrust suit against NewTech. We are three years into the case, and trial is scheduled for three months from now. But I just read in *The Wall Street Journal* that NewTech is being bought by General Amalgamated. Actually, it is technically a merger, though Paragon will be the surviving company.

A. And?

Q. Well, here is the problem. General Amalgamated is a client of our firm. We do lots of work for them, though not their corporate work. Suddenly we are going to find ourselves on both sides of the "v." What a horrible conflict of interest.

A. You have identified that correctly.

Q. I didn't need you to tell me that. What I need to know is what are we supposed to do. Trial is three months away. It would be impossible for new counsel to get up to speed. But my guess is that we have to withdraw from both representations.

A. Under the general analysis of conflicts of interest that is exactly what would happen. When you end up with clients on both ends of a dispute, unless one consents to the continuation against it, you have to withdraw.

Q. No one is going to consent to this conflict.

A. We understand. That is why the Model Rules adopted a comment for what we call "thrust upon conflicts."[518] That is what we have here. Neither you nor your present client had anything to do with this conflict. As a result, this comment gives you a choice. You may choose to represent Paragon, or you could choose to represent General Amalgamated, but not both. You would think you would be required to represent the client that would suffer the greatest hardship from your withdrawal, but actually you are going to be free to choose the client you most want to represent. You can drop Paragon and continue to represent General Amalgamated.

Q. In the lawsuit against Paragon?

A. No, no, not in that lawsuit. But, generally, you do not have to stop representing General Amalgamated. It is your choice.

---

518. MR 1.7 cmt. [5]; RLGL § 121 cmt. d.

Q. Sounds unseemly to me, but I will talk to my partners. I will fight to continue to represent Paragon, but my guess is that General Amalgamated is a better long-term business bet for our bottom line–obsessed law firm.

§ 15.12 The Corporate Family

The Wholly Owned Subsidiary

Q. I cannot believe my good fortune. I got a call from Lord Silversmith, the British takeover tycoon. He wants me—me!—to represent him in a takeover of Target, not Targeé, the fashionable discount store, but Target the conglomerate. No one's going to think my productive days are over.

To make sure my partners were appropriately impressed, I didn't just use the email conflict form. Instead, I sent around the conflict clearance form in sealed envelopes with those little blue "confidential" stickers. No responses for two days. Then I get a call from a new real estate partner in our Miami office. Guy was supposed to be a big producer. But you wouldn't know it from his current billings or the matter he called me about.

He starts by saying he's "sure" this won't be a problem, but he is representing Movies Unlimited, a third-tier wholly owned subsidiary of Target, in the leasing of one of those 300-square-foot kiosks that rent movies, this one in a Coral Gables shopping center. He just wanted to let me know.

A. Now you know. What are you going to do about it?

Q. I think nothing. How could this insignificant representation create a conflict?

A. Are you worried about anything?

Q. Well, we would be adverse to Target. Target's not our client.

A. Are you sure?

Q. Yes, I checked our database. Target's not in there.

A. And the engagement letter from Movies Unlimited?

Q. Why do I need to consult that?

A. Because sometimes sophisticated companies will tell their lawyers in a client-to-lawyer engagement letter that the law firm has to treat all the affiliates of the client as clients for conflicts purposes. And if you didn't object at the time, that communication will control how you can proceed.

Q. Let's assume they did. Can't we get a conflict waiver? Maybe we'll just call Movies Unlimited. See if they mind. If they're like some subsidiaries, they probably hate the parent and will be thrilled we would be suing Target.

A. Can you do that?

Q. Just a phone call. Worst comes the worst, they say no. Doesn't mean we can't come up with another argument why we can sue Target.

A. You're missing one key problem.

Q. Now what could that be? We seek waivers all the time.

A. We're sure you do. But there is a fundamental point you ran right past. Unless Lord Silversmith has changed his ways, he likes to move at night by stealth; surprise the object of his latest flirtation. In any event, you need Lord Silversmith's permission to disclose to Movies Unlimited his intentions. That is because those intentions represent clearly confidential information of Lord Silversmith. And only he has the authority for you to disclose it, even if it is information you need to disclose to clear the conflict.

This confidentiality obligation is not limited to the good Lord. It applies to all prospective clients. Before you seek to take on a new matter that raises a possible conflict, you have to get the permission of the prospective client on the new matter to make that key phone call. Our bet: Lord Silversmith won't give you permission.

Q. You are undoubtedly right. But is this really a conflict? As we discussed, Movies Unlimited is our client. For all we know they'll welcome the Lord's assault on the company's ultimate parent.

A. Some at Movies Unlimited might welcome your takeover. But you don't get to decide whether this takeover is in the best interest of Movies Unlimited. Nor do the folks you deal with there. That decision is reserved to those who govern Movies Unlimited, and something tells us that with 100 percent ownership of this company, what's in the best interests of Movies Unlimited is in the hands of Target.

Q. I guess you are right.

A. But you do raise a great question. There are two points of view here. Some, including one of the authors, have taken the position that a position adverse to any member of a 100 percent corporate family, like Target and its subs and subs of its subs, is an attack on all of them.[519] Whatever else can be said about how a conglomerate came to be structured the way it is—undoubtedly at the advice of lawyers to limit liability or for regulatory reasons—at the end of the day it is one economic enterprise that consolidates its results and therefore a $10 million loss in a third-tier sub has just as great an effect on the bottom line as if it occurred in the parent. And that same $10 million loss will (1) affect the stock price of the parent, which issues the only shares that the subs can use to reward their employees and (2) equally affect the ability of the parent to raise funds by borrowing or the issuing of new shares, not only for the benefit of the parent but for the subs as well. As a result, a reasonable argument can be made that taking a position directly adverse to the parent could have a directly adverse effect on the sub, in this case Movies Unlimited.

Q. That's not very helpful.

A. We know. And the good news for you may be that the ABA Model Rules have a comment that provides that there could be situations in which you can take a position adverse to your client's affiliate—be it a parent, a sub, or a sibling—under certain circumstances.[520] The analysis turns on whether there are facts or circumstances that would require you to consider the affiliate a client.[521] One fact would be what the engagement letter provides for, as we already discussed. Another might be special circumstances that have arisen in the course of the representation of the one affiliate that would make another affiliate reasonably conclude it, too, should be considered a client. Third, the nature of the relationship between the two entities—lines of business, geographic location, common personnel, and particular interdependence—might be such that the law firm representing one cannot take a position adverse to the other.

Q. Doesn't sound very clear.

A. That is true. It will be the rare situation in which the lawyer who wants to undertake a representation adverse to an affiliate of a client can predict with certainty how a court will rule. The offended client will certainly muster all the arguments it can why the law firm should be disqualified from the new representation.

519. Stratagem Dev. Corp. v. Heron Int'l N.V., 756 F. Supp. 789 (S.D.N.Y. 1991) (law firm was per se ineligible to represent plaintiff when the firm had not clearly terminated its representation of defendant's wholly owned subsidiary before preparations for the instant litigation began).

520. *See* MR 1.7 cmt. [34].

521. Ramada Franchise Sys., Inc. v. Hotel of Gainesville Assocs., 988 F. Supp. 1460 (N.D. Ga. 1997).

The law firm, defending its decision, of course, will argue separateness, and the court in its infinite wisdom will rule.

Q. What if we decide that the Target representation is so removed from the Movies Unlimited representation that there is no basis to disqualify us from taking on the career-saving Lord Silversmith representation? Can we just go ahead?

A. What do you think?

Q. I sure want to.

A. Aren't you forgetting something really important? Stop thinking about yourself and start thinking about your prospective client.

Q. That's who I am thinking about. He's going to be so lucky to hire me.

A. Well, he won't be very lucky if a motion to disqualify is brought. Win or lose, such a motion could knock his plans into a cocked hat. Delay can be death to tender offers. So, even if you think you have a basis to proceed, you must communicate with your client the real possibility that a motion will be filed. You are obliged to tell the client of the risk. The client gets to decide if he will accept it. You can only get in trouble if you say nothing.

Q. That avenue sounds problematic. What else can we do? How 'bout if we get rid of Movies Unlimited? It's a minor representation. Maybe we can finish the work really quickly.

A. Two thoughts. First, if in fact you can really provide Movies Unlimited with the services it requires competently and quickly, there's nothing wrong with being efficient. Then Movies Unlimited would be a former client. And the conflict analysis then would be conducted under Rule 1.9, which provides that the only matters you may not undertake as to the former client are those that are substantially related to the matters you handled for the former client.

Q. There's certainly no relationship between a kiosk and a takeover of the kiosk owner's grandparent.

A. That would appear to be the case. But Rule 1.9(c) contains another prohibition: you cannot take on a matter in which you could use confidential information of the former client in the new representation. Even if the matters are unrelated.

Q. Can't imagine that. How would we know confidential information about Target?

A. Unlikely. But that fact would not necessarily stop Movies Unlimited from arguing precisely that point, alleging that your partner knows the innermost secrets of his client and that Movies Unlimited is an outsized segment of Target's many business lines. Just working on a single lease for a kiosk would be unlikely to generate that kind of information, but in the business of former client conflicts, there are no guarantees.

Q. But what if we can't finish the lease quickly enough? That pathetic new partner has already spent three months on the damn thing. The truth is, it would pay for our firm to buy Movies Unlimited its own kiosk to get to represent the good Lord. Can we just resign the representation of Movies Unlimited? Make 'em a former client?

A. That you cannot do. You would be violating the "hot potato" rule. That rule provides that you may not drop a conflicting client like a hot potato to make the client a former client so you can take on what would otherwise be a conflicting representation. You can drop a client at any time for no reason at all. But the case law is uniform. The courts find such conduct unseemly, despite the willingness of some commentators (but not the authors) to condone this conflict-clearing method.[522]

Q. What can we do? How about if we fire the damn partner? He's such a disappointment.

A. That would work. If this lawyer were to leave and take the client with him, the imputation rule, Rule 1.10—which, so long as he is with you, imputes this conflict to everyone in your firm (as well it should)—operates quite differently upon his departure. The client, Movies Unlimited, becomes a former client of the firm. Rule 1.9 then applies to the firm's, but not the former partner's, conflict analysis.

As a result, the only argument Target can make is that it's a former client and the new matter is substantially related.[523] And as to that, you have two responses: Target was never a client; even if it were, the matter you are now undertaking is not substantially related. You, however, have to convince your firm to fire the partner. That's not ethics, but it could be messy firm management.

Q. What a tour of the Rules of Professional Conduct. Let me just hope one of these alternatives permits me to undertake the representation.

---

522. Unified Sewerage Agency v. Jelco, 646 F.2d 1339, 1345 n.4 (9th Cir. 1981); Santacroce v. Neff, 134 F. Supp. 2d 366, 367–71 (D.N.J. 2001); Universal City Studios, Inc. v. Reimerdes, 98 F. Supp. 2d 449, 453–54 (S.D.N.Y. 2000); Local Union 1332 v. Int'l Longshoremen's Ass'n, 909 F. Supp. 287, 293 (E.D. Pa. 1995); Stratagem Dev. Corp. v. Heron Int'l, N.V., 756 F. Supp. 789, 794 (S.D.N.Y. 1991); Picker Int'l Inc. v. Varian Assocs., Inc., 670 F. Supp. 1363, 1365–66 (N.D. Ohio 1987), *aff'd*, 869 F.2d 578 (Fed. Cir. 1989); Eastman Kodak Co. v. Sony Corp., Nos. 04-CV-6095, 04-CV-6098, 2004 WL 2984297 (W.D.N.Y. Dec. 27, 2004); Truck Ins. Exchange v. Fireman's Fund Ins. Co., 8 Cal. Rptr. 2d 228, 232 (1992).

523. *See* MR 1.9(a).

§ 15.13 Insurance Defense

Settling Within Limits

Q. Do you know how much work I do for insurance companies? Without them I would be flipping hamburgers. But sometimes they drive me crazy. The other side has offered to settle for a million dollars. That is just under my client's policy limits. I talked to my client, who is positively thrilled. I think it is a fair settlement. But when I called the insurance company, they said "no way." They think the case has maximum exposure of $250,000. They tell me not to settle. Who do I listen to?

A. Well, whether they are treated as a client or not, you can't settle without the insurance company's money. You need their contribution. But your exclusive or sole client here is the insured, who is perfectly happy to settle for that number.

Q. She is worried sick to think that any judgment might be higher than her coverage.

A. The best thing you can do is to create a record recommending the settlement so that the insured will have an excellent claim against the insurance company for excess verdict should one come down.

Q. The insurance company certainly will not like that.

A. That is precisely why we think lawyers are well-served to have only one client, the insured. But sometimes we lawyers just have to be courageous. If our client is insured and the client is entitled to the settlement, we have to demonstrate our professional independence, as painful as that might be.[524]

§ 15.14 Nonconsentable Conflicts

Suing Your Current Client

Q. We just received a call. Start-up Co. wants us to sue Conglomerate for a RICO violation. Case sounds great. Only problem: we represent Conglomerate. But I figure we call Conglomerate and see if the company will waive the conflict.

A. Do you actually think they will?

---

524. Paradigm Ins. Co. v. Langerman Law Offices, P.A., 24 P.3d 593 (Ariz. 2001) (rule that in the absence of a conflict, the lawyer has two clients, the insurer and the insured, is too absolute. In some cases, the potential for conflict is strong from the beginning, for example, in a case of questionable liability against an insured who is covered by limits much lower than the injury alleged. When such a conflict arises, the lawyer's duty is exclusively owed to insured and not the insurer.).

Q. Who knows. Worth a try. The assistant general counsel we deal with hates the company. Maybe we'll get an informed consent to the conflict.

A. But are you allowed to?

Q. What do you mean? They consent, I am home free.

A. That's a little too glib. The applicable rule, Rule 1.7(b)(1), is quite clear. It provides that before a lawyer even seeks an informed consent (not a "waiver," that's what happens when you fail to claim a privilege in court), the lawyer must "reasonably believe that the lawyer will be able to provide competent and diligent representation to each affected client." Can you say you could do that?

Q. Well, my partner who wants to sue our client for the RICO violation "relishes" the opportunity.

A. Wow! What an interesting expression of loyalty to your firm's existing client. "Relishes!" But would a "reasonable" lawyer conclude the same thing? Is it reasonable to think that a lawyer in your firm would be able to go hammer and tong against a client whose fees he shares, a client represented by his partners, on such a serious charge?

One of your authors believes that, except as to obligatory cross-claims in Superfund litigation or something similar in outsized cases such as bankruptcy, no lawyer can ever conclude that the standard of 1.7(b)(1) can be met in any situation in which the client is asked to give informed consent to a conflict that arises because the firm plans to sue its present client for any claims, let alone a claim for a RICO violation. An informed consent that allowed you to be adverse in a transactional matter, however, depending on the circumstances, could be okay.[525] But to sue your current client will rarely if ever meet the 1.7(b)(1) standard, in the view of one of us.[526]

525. Van Kirk v. Miller, 869 N.E.2d 534, 541–43 (Ind. Ct. App. 2007) (concurrent conflict of interest consentable when purchaser-client and vendor-client asked lawyer to draft terms of agreement that they had independently negotiated).

526. W. Sugar Coop. v. Archer-Daniels-Midland Co., 98 F. Supp. 3d 1074 (C.D. Cal. 2015) (law firm merger conflicts check which missed current representation of client now opposed in unrelated litigation created conflicts of interest that required firm's disqualification as counsel; lack of informed consent not cured by withdrawal, advance waiver, or subsequent attempt to screen tainted lawyer).

§ 15.15 Business Transactions with Clients

Timely Business

Q. I've waited for my chance to outdo those corporate types. They look down on us litigators like we were unrefined rugby players. So highfalutin with their Hermés ties and Armani suits. But now I've got the opportunity that will put them in their place.

A. We are all ears.

Q. We are handling this SEC investigation. If all goes well (and it should) we can make 'em go away. The client says, if that happens, the client, in lieu of our fee, will give our firm 5 percent of its next stock offering. We're talking the next Google.

A. You are doing business with your client?

Q. No. Just an intriguing contingent fee.

A. We better slow down.

Q. And ruin our chances for glory?

A. No. Assure your "ticket" stays intact.

Q. We know how to handle the SEC.

A. That may be so. What we want you to do is handle the Rules of Professional Conduct. Rule 1.8(a) addresses the requirements for entering into a business transaction with a client. And that is what this is. The case law is clear. Any time you negotiate an unconventional fee like this one, you must satisfy both the fee rule, Rule 1.5, and Rule 1.8(a).

Q. What do they require?

A. Let's take 1.8(a) first. It requires that the transaction be entirely fair to the client, that it be in writing in a way that is easily understood, that the client be given both the advice and an opportunity to consult independent counsel, and the client must consent to the transaction in writing.[527]

527. Fla. Bar v. Ticktin, 14 So. 3d 928 (Fla. 2009) (lawyer suspended for 91 days for taking control of client's business after client announced change in a press release; lawyer, not client, must prepare written documentation required by Rule 1.8(a)); Iowa Supreme Court Bd. of Prof'l Ethics & Conduct v. Fay, 619 N.W.2d 321 (Iowa 2000) (lawyer suspended for 30 days for failing to provide full disclosure and recommend another lawyer for advising client on business matters and then leasing his own property to client for client's business; lawyer also civilly liable for negligent misrepresentation because client had regularly relied on lawyer for legal services); *In re* Snyder, 35 S.W.3d 380 (Mo. 2000) (lawyer suspended for failing to comply with Rule 1.8(a) for making fee agreements that included acquiring an interest in clients' residential properties indefinitely); *In re* Hibner, 897 N.Y.S.2d 489 (N.Y. App. Div. 2010) (lawyer suspended for four years for having clients convey title to their home to him to prevent a foreclosure sale and subsequently seeking to evict them); Stark Cnty. Bar Ass'n v. Buttacavoli, 775 N.E.2d 818 (Ohio 2002) (lawyer-financial planner suspended for six months for failing to comply with business transactions with clients rule by billing clients for legal work, but not disclosing commissions when he sold them other investments).

Q. And 1.5?

A. Rule 1.5 forbids a lawyer from contracting for, charging, or collecting an unreasonable fee. That same language regarding reasonableness is repeated in Rule 1.8(a).

Q. This is certainly reasonable. If the client is unsuccessful, they pay nothing. Dealing with the SEC is always risky, and we are only receiving 5 percent of the net offering, which is not even guaranteed to occur. How could anyone challenge that as overreaching? Our corporate colleagues do that all the time.

A. You are likely right. But there are those who believe that you do not just judge reasonableness going in. They argue that the client gets a "look back." If the next Google turns into a repeat of Google stock price-wise, you may have your fee challenged on that basis.

Q. Yet another risk.

A. Precisely. One more thing. Is this a criminal investigation?

Q. No. Not yet. Why do you ask?

A. Because it is impermissible to charge a contingency fee in a criminal case.

Q. You are piling on.

A. No. But if you are going to join the Gucci loafer crowd, we want you to be fully informed. Our ties come from Marshall's.

§ 15.16 Personal Conflicts and Undue Influence

Lawyer-agents who breach duties of obedience, loyalty, or confidentiality lose their entitlement to contractual rights because they have violated a basic fiduciary obligation essential to rendering the contract enforceable.[528] Courts begin by applying relevant Rules of Professional Conduct or agency law requirements to determine whether a breach of fiduciary duty occurred. Once that is established, they apply the agency presumption of undue influence both to protect individual clients and to create an incentive for lawyers to fulfill fiduciary duties. In

528. *In re* McIntosh, No. 13-11774 AJ, 2015 WL 241130 (Bankr. N.D. Cal. Jan. 16, 2015) (lawyer who breached duty of loyalty by undermining his client's legal arguments in a subsequent fee dispute after being fired by client forfeits all fees including those previously paid; lawyer cannot switch sides for any reason, even if lawyer believes the position previously asserted was wrong).

many cases, the lawyer is unable to rebut the presumption and loses the benefit.[529]

Lawyers can lose a contractual benefit when they sue a client to enforce the contract's terms, or when they sue to collect a fee and the client alleges breach of fiduciary duty in a counterclaim. If the contractual benefit has already been received, the client can seek return of the benefit through other equitable remedies, such as a constructive trust or fee forfeiture. Lawyers have been forced to account for, return, or hold in constructive trust specific property acquired because of the improper use of confidential information.[530] Another example denies the lawyer's entitlement to client gifts of property when the lawyer has breached fiduciary duty by drafting the document of gift.[531]

§ 15.17 Media Rights

Being Famous

Q. You know we have maintained a successful country practice. They know us in Norristown, but we are anonymous to the rest of the world. That is, until now.

A. What happened?

Q The nut job heir to a huge fracking field up-county shot his wife and her lover at their trout fishing cabin, and my partner, an assistant D.A. years ago, gets hired. Hasn't done criminal work in a decade. Now our firm name is in the papers daily. That's what gave us the idea.

A. What idea?

Q. Instead of charging a fee, we got the client to assign us the media rights to his story. We get him off, and the movie rights could give us a great pay day. To say nothing of the novel.

A. Your enthusiasm is palpable.

Q. Wouldn't you like to be famous?

---

529. Passante v. McWilliam, 62 Cal. Rptr. 2d 298, 298 (1997) (lawyer who "came through in the clutch" by raising money for client's business not able to enforce client's promise to pay him three percent of the company's stock); Monco v. Janus, 583 N.E.2d 575 (Ill. App. Ct. 1991) (lawyer who provided hundreds of hours of legal services to business startup unable to rebut presumption of undue influence when he sought to dissolve the corporation); Liggett v. Young, 877 N.E.2d 178 (Ind. 2007) (contract with client voidable due to influence where lawyer-consumer drafts contract); Petit-Clair v. Nelson, 782 A.2d 960 (N.J. Super. Ct. App. Div. 2001) (lawyer who secured payment of legal fees with mortgage on client's house unable to foreclose on mortgage).

530. RLGL § 6 cmts. d, e.

531. Comm. on Prof'l Ethics v. Randall, 285 N.W.2d 161 (Iowa 1979) (lawyer made himself sole beneficiary of client's will); *In re* Putnam, 177 N.E. 399 (N.Y. 1931) (gift to lawyer reflected in document lawyer drafted presumed to be the product of undue influence).

A. We certainly would. But not for getting disbarred.
Q. We win this case, the bar will be giving us justice awards.
A. Would that it were so. But bargaining for the literary rights to your client's story is a prohibited transaction. As tempting as it is, and as consistent with the client's interest as it might seem at first blush, the conflict that the contract creates is profound.[532]
Q. We're going to fight as hard as we can.
A. You might. But what we worry about is that you will fight for your literary rights at the expense of your client. After all, if your client pleads guilty to a lesser charge, your literary rights are worthless. You need (1) a highly publicized trial and (2) a victory. That may not be what your client needs.
Q. Oh well. We never were famous. Why start now?

§ 15.18 Financial Assistance

The Client Needs Help: Can the Lawyer Do So?

Q. It is wrenching. My heart breaks. We have this wonderful medical malpractice practice. Referrals abound. The problem is those damn deep pocket defendants. No matter how meritorious the case, they have one modus operandi. Take every case to the eve of trial unless the plaintiff accepts a ridiculous lowball offer.
A. Makes it easy to reject.
Q. That's what you think. Our clients are, by and large, impecunious. They live, just barely, paycheck to paycheck—if they work at all after the defendants get done with them. Then these malefactors compound their original sin by dangling a pathetic sum in front of these beleaguered folks.
A. Surely they don't fall for that.
Q. That's the thing. To our clients the offers seem like the answer to their prayers. When they hear $10,000, it's as if they think they will become millionaires.
A. You have to persuade them to reject it.
Q. We try. But it is hard. Often they'll say, "You want me to wait, then help me out until the trial."

532. Commonwealth v. Downey, 842 N.E.2d 955 (Mass. App. Ct. 2006) (new trial granted to murder defendants, whose lawyers wore body microphones during trial at the request of a television production company, because lawyers failed to explain potential pitfalls of such an arrangement); Harrison v. Miss. Bar, 637 So. 2d 204 (Miss. 1994) (lawyer disbarred for signing media rights contract and engaging in a pattern of dishonesty toward the court).

A. And you tell them you're not allowed.
Q. That's what you taught us. No loans. No living expenses. Frankly, we like that rule, but sometimes you wish there were an exception.
A. The problem is lending money to the client changes the relationship. Changes your stake in the matter, creates its own conflicts. Lawyers in D.C. and California are permitted to advance funds.[533] But nowhere else.[534]
Q. Then we'll have to continue relying on our persuasive powers to forestall acceptance of these inadequate offers.
A. Always remembering it is the client's decision.

§ 15.19 Outside Financial Assistance

Litigation Funders—A Mixed Blessing

A. Depending on your jurisdiction's champerty statutes, you could introduce your client to a litigation funder.
Q. Tell me more.
A. These companies will buy an interest in the proceeds of your clients' cases in return for advancing funds to give your clients the wherewithal to get to trial.
Q. How much help? How much interest in the case?
A. It depends. But to generalize, if what they charged were interest, which they say it is not because the client only pays if the case is successful, you would be shocked at the percentage they receive. But they are taking a risk.
Q. I'll bet they only take on really good cases.
A. They certainly conduct due diligence to determine whether to proceed.
Q. How's that work? Can I talk to them about the case?
A. Your concern is well warranted. They are not your client. And you don't want them to become one. The plaintiff must remain

533. Cal. R. Prof'l Conduct 1.8.5 (2018); D.C. R. Prof'l Conduct 1.8(d)(2) (2015).

534. MR 1.8(e); RLGL § 36; Lorain Cnty. Bar Ass'n v. Stuart, 984 N.E.2d 1041 (Ohio 2012) (lawyer did not violate Rule 1.8(e) by agreeing to pay half of a client's settlement because of lawyer's errors in the matter); Office of Disciplinary Counsel v. Lombardi, 770 N.E.2d 1013 (Ohio 2002) (lawyer suspended for two years for loaning client substantial sums of money to assist client while she was in contempt of court); State *ex rel.* Okla. Bar Ass'n v. Smolen, 17 P.3d 456 (Okla. 2000) (lawyer suspended for 60 days for loaning $1,200 to client whose house had been destroyed by fire because clients may have based their decision to retain counsel on improper inducements); Disciplinary Bd. v. Nessel, 769 S.E.2d 484 (W. Va. 2015) (lawyer reprimanded for violating absolute requirement of Rule 1.8(e) for claiming he gave small amounts of money to imprisoned clients out of kindness and denying seeking referrals).

your sole client with complete Rule 1.2(a) autonomy to decide whether and when to settle and all other client questions. As a result, if you discuss the case with the funder you run the risk of waiving the attorney-client privilege. Can't afford to let that happen.

Q. I'll say. How 'bout work product? Can I share that?

A. An even more interesting question. You don't waive work product by sharing with nonclients, like experts, who are on your side. But at the time the funder wants the most information, the interests of the funder and your client are directly adverse. The funder wants the biggest piece of the pie for the least amount of money advanced and vice versa. So, unless there is clear law in your jurisdiction on waiver, you may only share what the funder could uncover on its own.[535]

§ 15.20 Joint or Aggregate Settlements

The Lawyer's Job

Q. Today is a banner day for our firm. We have been representing ten employees of an oil company who were all badly injured in a refinery fire five years ago. We are suing the designer of the facility. They have just offered us $15 million to settle all claims, but they insist everyone settle or they will not proceed. Can they do that?

A. Yes, it is proper to condition an agreement to settle on everyone accepting the terms. That is because if just one claimant does not settle, the defendant still is forced to defend the case through the inevitable appeals.

Q. Well, then it is our job to persuade everyone to accept the settlement.

A. No, it is your job to counsel with your clients about the proposal, keeping in mind the whole time that each client is an individual who gets the final say. This is an aggregate

535. Fausone v. U.S. Claims, Inc., 915 So. 2d 626 (Fla. Dist. Ct. App. 2005) (client who borrowed $30,000 from a litigation funding company required to pay arbitrator's award of $102,007 for principal, interest, and company's attorney's fees; court asked legislature to consider imposing limitations on litigation loans).

settlement.[536] You must be very careful. No overreaching. Just be your persuasive self, but also respect the clients' wishes.

Q. I think we can do that. What will help is we get to decide what each plaintiff gets based on how serious the injuries are. To make sure the clients go along with our approach, we will not tell any client what the other clients will be receiving. And we won't tell them the total either. They will just hear their own big number.

A. No you won't! The aggregate settlement rule, Rule 1.8(g), is quite clear. When you are given the authority, as you have been here, you must tell each client two things: the total amount received and the amount each individual is receiving. That way the client can make an individual determination whether the settlement is fair. As you say, you will be more likely to get approval if you don't share that information. But the first casualty of that approach is informed consent. And the result of uninformed consent can be professional discipline, malpractice, and fee forfeiture for your breach of loyalty.[537]

§ 15.21 The Equity of Fee Forfeiture

The remedy of fee forfeiture can be traced back three centuries.[538] Unlike legal remedies such as malpractice, it does not require proof of causation or damages but only that the client or former client shows a clear and serious breach of fiduciary duty.[539] The more serious the breach, the greater the fee forfeited to the former clients.

Breaches of the core agency duties of obedience (client control), disclosure, confidentiality, and loyalty usually qualify as clear and serious breaches, although the source of the duty can be civil law (for example, legal malpractice) or criminal law (for example, fraud or unauthorized

536. Booth v. Davis, 57 F. Supp. 3d 1319 (D. Kan. 2014) (malpractice plaintiffs who allege breach of fiduciary duty in an aggregate settlement do not need to prove they would have won at trial; proof that a substantial settlement would have been achieved in the absence of the lawyer's misconduct will satisfy the malpractice causation requirement); *In re* Gatti, 333 P.3d 994 (Or. 2014) (aggregate settlement occurs whenever resolution of individual clients' claims are interdependent); Principles of the Law of Aggregate Litigation § 316 (2009).

537. Ky. Bar Ass'n v. Helmers, 353 S.W.3d 599 (Ky. 2011) (lawyer disbarred despite reliance on senior lawyer's direction to lie to clients and violate aggregate settlement rule); Burrow v. Arce, 997 S.W.2d 229 (Tex. 1999) (cause of action for fee forfeiture of $60 million contingent fee stated against law firm for violating aggregate settlement rule).

538. Woods v. City Nat'l Bank & Trust Co. of Chi., 312 U.S. 262 (1941); Silbiger v. Prudence Bonds Corp., 180 F.2d 917, 920 (2d Cir. 1950).

539. RLGL § 37.

practice) as well.[540] Most common are conflicts of interest, such as representing a client's wife in a divorce,[541] failing to disclose that the law firm employed the opposing party's adjuster,[542] pressuring a client to change a fee contract,[543] or settling a client's case without consent.[544]

The first factor, whether the violation was "clear," is determined by an objective standard: whether "a reasonable lawyer, knowing the relevant facts and law reasonably accessible to the lawyer, would have known that the conduct was wrongful."[545] For example, the lawyers in one case were not able to claim they had no idea Model Rule 1.8(g) regulated aggregate settlements.[546] The second factor, whether the violation was "serious," may be established by proof of a single breach,[547] or when multiple breaches of fiduciary duty occur in the same case.[548] Inadvertent breaches, such as the failure to fully explain the terms of a settlement when the trial judge explained them to the client, do not rise to the level of a clear and serious breach.[549]

Once a clear and serious breach of fiduciary duty has been shown, total fee forfeiture is presumed.[550] Most courts recognize that partial fee forfeiture may be more appropriate when the misconduct can be separated in time from other valuable services the lawyer has performed. Factors such as the willfulness of the violation, its effect on the client, and the adequacy of other remedies, as well as "the public interest in maintaining the integrity of attorney-client relationships," all will be relevant.

Thus, when the breach of fiduciary duty permeates the entire relationship, the grounds for total fee forfeiture are found. This explains why so many of the full fee forfeiture cases involve a conflict of interest that tainted the entire representation. On the other hand, when the

---

540. *Id.* § 37 cmt. c; Birbrower, Montalbano, Condon & Frank P.C. v. Super Ct., 949 P.2d 1 (Cal. 1998) (law firm that engaged in unauthorized practice in violation of state statute rendered fee agreement unenforceable).

541. Jeffry v. Pounds, 136 Cal. Rptr. 373 (1977).

542. Rice v. Perl, 320 N.W.2d 407 (Minn. 1982).

543. Searcy, Denney, Scarola, Barnhart & Shipley, P.A. v. Scheller, 629 So. 2d 947 (Fla. Dist. Ct. App. 1993).

544. Francisco v. Foret, No. 05-01-00783-CV, 2002 WL 535455 (Tex. App. Apr. 11, 2002).

545. RLGL § 37 cmt. d; Hardison v. Weinshel, 450 F. Supp. 721 (E.D. Wis. 1978) (lawyer who withdrew from case shortly before trial because he mistakenly believed client would not prevail forfeits all fee); Conant v. O'Meara, 117 A.3d 692 (N.H. 2015) (lawyer who lied under oath about former clients' agreement to his fee in a fee arbitration proceeding had clear conflict of interest requiring disgorgement of $837,000 arbitrator's award under fraud-on-the-court doctrine).

546. Burrow v. Arce, 997 S.W.2d 229 (Tex. 1999).

547. Gammon v. Hodes, No. 03-13-00124-CV, 2015 WL 1882274 (Tex. App. Apr. 24, 2015) (lawyer forfeited all right to legal fees by entering into an "unconscionable" contingent-fee agreement that gave him a 50 percent interest in his client's home).

548. Piro v. Sarofim, 80 S.W.3d 717 (Tex. App. 2002).

549. Hoover v. Larkin, No. 14-00-00427-CV, 2001 WL 1046266 (Tex. App. Sept. 13, 2001).

550. RLGL § 37 cmt. e.

conflict materializes during the representation, the lawyer may be reimbursed for services provided before she was obliged to respond to the conflict.[551]

Finally, note that liability insurance usually will pay a damage award, but rarely will be available to cover a fee forfeiture claim. One court has analogized fee forfeiture to punitive damages and concluded that insurance covering a lawyer's individual breach of fiduciary duty was contrary to public policy, but coverage for a law firm's vicarious responsibility was not.[552]

Fee forfeiture also can occur pursuant to statute. Most prominent are criminal statutes that provide for forfeiture of the fruits of criminal activity, including lawyer's fees.[553] Forfeiture statutes provide for civil forfeiture of the client's funds traceable to criminal activity, on the theory that they passed to the government at the time of the crime. The government can seize all assets of a defendant at the point of indictment on a showing of probable cause to believe that the assets will ultimately be found to be subject to forfeiture.[554] If the criminal case determines that the assets are the proceeds of the crime, they are permanently forfeited to the government.

The Supreme Court has held that these statutes are intended to reach lawyer's fees, as well as other assets of the defendant, and that using this statutory power to freeze cash paid to a lawyer does not violate a client's rights.[555] The practical reality created by these cases is that a lawyer retained by a defendant where such a statute applies takes a risk of nonpayment. Further, because the statute exempts a "bona fide purchaser for value" of property otherwise subject to forfeiture, lawyers essentially must audit the source of the client's money in order to assure themselves of payment.[556]

551. Hill v. Douglass, 271 So. 2d 1 (Fla. 1972) (lawyer did not forfeit fee until he should have known he would be a witness).

552. Perl v. St. Paul Fire & Marine Ins. Co., 345 N.W.2d 209 (Minn. 1984).

553. 21 U.S.C. §§ 848, 853 (2012).

554. United States v. Monsanto, 924 F.2d 1186 (2d Cir. 1991) (en banc).

555. Caplin & Drysdale v. United States, 491 U.S. 617 (1989); United States v. Monsanto, 491 U.S. 600 (1989); *compare* Luis v. United States, 136 S. Ct. 1083 (2016) (pretrial restraint of a criminal defendant's legitimate, untainted assets (those not traceable to a criminal offense) needed to retain counsel of choice violates the Sixth Amendment).

556. A "bona fide purchaser for value" is a person who "was reasonably without cause to believe that the property was subject to forfeiture" when he took the property. 21 U.S.C. § 853(c) (2012). *See also* United States v. McCorkle, 321 F.3d 1292 (11th Cir. 2003) (burden of proof on lawyer F. Lee Bailey to identify the portion of the fee collected while he was a bona fide purchaser for value).

§ 15.22 Lawyer-Client Sexual Relationships

Sex with Clients

Q. I say it is no good deed goes unpunished. Poor Sarah Snyder. She is a star associate in our litigation department. But she has no life. So, none of us was surprised that the rumor mill went into overdrive when Sarah began dating the general counsel of Big Bank. What better way to cement the relationship, as it were, than to have Sarah's social life coincide with our business interests.

A. You wouldn't teach that, would you?

Q. No. But if nature takes its course, that is not such a bad thing. Or so we thought. But then someone reminded us that there is a rule about sexual relationships.

A. And there certainly is.

Q. Well, we thought that rule would apply to the evil matrimonial lawyer taking advantage of the helpless, dependent wife.

A. In a situation like this where parties are more or less equal, the rule is quite clear. Unless the relationship predated the legal representation, the ongoing relationship is prohibited.[557] Sarah Snyder must stop working for Big Bank. At first blush, that might seem quite draconian. But when you think about it you can see how the relationship could interfere with the ability of the lawyer participant to provide the objective advice that the client—in this case, of course, Big Bank, not general counsel—so desperately needs.[558] The silver lining is that Sarah's conflict is personal and, therefore, not imputed to the rest of the firm.[559]

§ 15.23 Related-Lawyer Conflicts

Adam's Rib

Q. The situation is right out of that famous movie, *Adam's Rib*. Our firm represents Acme Corporation in litigation against Zenon, Inc. For the last year, the senior associate on the case has been Adam Jones. Zenon is represented by Caldwell & Moore, and Adam's wife just joined that firm and has been

557. MR 1.8(j); Iowa Supreme Court Attorney Disciplinary Bd. v. Monroe, 784 N.W.2d 784 (Iowa 2010) (lawyer suspended from practice for 30 days for sexual relationship with client, although client initiated relationship).

558. MR 1.8 cmt. [19] (sexual relationships when client is an organization).

559. MR 1.8(k).

assigned to this case. I was worried that this presented a difficult conflict of interest. But Adam says he thinks it will be a great challenge and at least someone in his family will win. What do you think?

A. There is no absolute rule covering husband/wife conflicts anymore. Nonetheless, you can definitely see how "pillow talk" could be a problem. Similarly, the spouses might pull their punches because of the identity of the lawyer on the other side. As always, the question is whether a reasonable lawyer would conclude that this relationship created a material limitation on the representation. If it would not, and if you also conclude that you can provide competent and diligent representation despite the conflict, then you may seek informed consent of both clients.

But it is one thing for married lawyers to be in law firms that are adverse. It is quite another for the spouses themselves to be adverse. We think it is far better to leave such plot lines to Spencer Tracy and Katharine Hepburn. We would urge the wife to reconsider.[560]

§ 15.24 Issue Conflicts

Inconsistent Legal Arguments

Q. We are representing a law firm that just went through a divorce. Ugly. Recriminations. And fights about money. The traitors took a huge malpractice case. Settled it ten days later after client signed a new engagement agreement. Our guys are claiming the contingent fee. Say all the work was done before the secession. The new firm asserts our folks just get their hourly rate, one-tenth of the contingent fee.

A. Sounds like you have the better of the argument.

---

560. Petrovic v. Amoco Oil Co., 200 F.3d 1140 (8th Cir. 1999) (lawyer disqualified in class action because two class representatives were husband and sister-in-law to his partner); People v. Jackson, 213 Cal. Rptr. 521 (1985) (conviction reversed where defense counsel did not disclose to defendant a dating relationship with the prosecutor in defendant's case); Commonwealth v. Stote, 922 N.E.2d 768 (Mass. 2010) (no actual or potential conflict from defense lawyer's intimate but non-cohabiting relationship with appellate division lawyer in prosecutor's office who had no part in the appeal, but lawyer should have told client about the relationship); Disciplinary Counsel v. Owen, 30 N.E.3d 910 (Ohio 2014) (lawyer suspended for one year due to his affair with wife of criminal defense client on trial for murder; lawyer's actions created an inherent and impermissible conflict of interest that deprived the client of his constitutional right to undivided loyalty from his lawyer); Ariz. Op. 2001-10 (rules about married lawyers apply to prosecutor and public defender who live together, the lawyers may not take cases against each other without the clients' consent).

Q. Oh, we would alright. But we just learned partners in our new Pittsburgh office, just across the state, have taken a similar case, but they are representing the breakaway group. These clients assert that the clients followed their group because they were so disgruntled with the old firm. If old firm is entitled to anything, it's $85 per hour.

A. Ouch!

Q. You said it.

A. One thing is clear. You don't want to lose both cases. But we doubt you can handle the second. This is a conflict of interest. The decision in the earlier decided case is going to be cited against the laggard. Your briefs in one case may even be quoted against your colleagues in the other case. If it is not directly adverse, it sure is indirectly adverse. Which makes it a material limitation. A real issue conflict.

Q. How far does this go? We argue inconsistently all the time. In the morning, I argue the other side's discovery requests are a fishing expedition. In the afternoon, I try to justify my own Orvis moment. Am I violating the conflict rules?

A. Not really. Issues like that are really fact specific. And the legal standard is well-trod territory.[561] That is not true of the real-life example your law firm faces. The entitlements to fees of predecessor and successor counsel are all over the place. Some say quantum meruit entitlement turns on relative contribution. Others say it is limited to a reasonable hourly rate. And the law varies state by state, and state court versus federal court. The real question the affected lawyer has to ask is whether the decision in either case would likely be cited to or by the court in the other case. That won't happen in your scope of discovery example. But it is likely to occur in these two fee disputes. It is because issue conflicts are real that so many lawyers end up only representing personal injury plaintiffs, or just labor, not

561. Fiandaca v. Cunningham, 827 F.2d 825 (1st Cir. 1987) (lawyer who argued for one client that a state facility should be used for an expanded prison while simultaneously arguing for another client that same facility should be used for mental health treatment should have been disqualified; new trial ordered on tainted portion of case); Williams v. State, 805 A.2d 880 (Del. 2002) (lawyer's motion to withdraw granted with commendations to both defense counsel and the state in criminal appeal where defense counsel faced positional conflict created by prior appellate argument to the same court on behalf of a different client regarding the weight to be given jury instructions); ABA Comm. on Ethics & Prof'l Responsibility, Formal Op. 93-377 (1993) Positional Conflicts (if a court's determination in one case is likely to have a significant impact on the determination of another case and would impair the lawyer's effectiveness, the lawyer should not accept the second representation, unless both clients consent after full disclosure of the potential ramifications of the lawyer's continuing to handle both matters).

management, or officers and directors, not shareholders. And why some clients—the best example is accounting firms—insist that lawyers who represent them never take positions adverse to similarly situated competitors. Don't want their lawyers making bad law.

Q. Let's just hope following your advice doesn't result in a split of our firm!

§ 15.25 Former Client Confidentiality Obligations

Summer Associate Blues

Q. I was a summer associate at a Big Law firm's D.C. office. Great summer. Among other interesting experiences, I worked on a securities case. Did basic research. Fascinating question. Gave the partner plenty of case support for our client's side.

A. I see no issues.

Q. Not yet. When I came back to school, I joined a securities litigation seminar. Need to write a paper. Publishable if possible. I returned to the topic of that memo.

A. Gave you a leg up.

Q. Sure did. And the more I thought about it, the more I thought the case law was wrong. The better public policy goes the other way. My professor loved the analysis. She thinks my essay could be a great candidate for publication. A real feather in my cap.

A. We can understand your enthusiasm. But there is a serious problem.

Q. That's what my teacher was worried about. Why I contacted you.

A. We don't want to know the name of your former client. Let's call it Colossus. Would Colossus be happy to read your article?

Q. I doubt it.

A. Is it likely that, if published, your article would be cited against Colossus?

Q. Could be. But I don't think they would connect the article with my work this summer.

A. Let's get one thing straight. That the client won't realize your conflict is no defense.

Q. Conflict?

A. Yes, the conflict is clear. What is Colossus vis-à-vis you?

Q. Have no idea.

A. It's your former client. And in writing this article, what are you doing?

Q. Commenting on an issue in the case?

A. More than that. You are taking a position directly adverse to your client in the same matter.

Q. But I am not a lawyer.

A. As a subordinate employee of a lawyer and as a law student you are required to follow the Rules of Professional Conduct. You were paid by the law firm to do the research on this issue and presumably the law firm charged the client for your time. But payment is irrelevant. Even if you were an unpaid intern and the client never paid a dime for your services, the result would be the same.[562]

Q. No publication?

A. No publication. Or posting on Facebook, without the consent of Colossus. Just the satisfaction of what we hope is a good grade.

§ 15.26 Conflicts and Confidentiality

The Confidentiality Trap

Q. We've been asked by Colossus Insurance Company to bring an antitrust claim against the Happy Valley Health System. Seemed like no problem. Right in our wheelhouse. So much so, we hired the former Happy Valley General Counsel years ago. Her specialty is antitrust. And seven years is a long time. We decided there could be no conflict because of the passage of time. We told Colossus we had no conflict. What a great new engagement!

A. You aren't here because you love legal ethics.

Q. That's right. Colossus on its own brought up former GC. They were surprised we had not mentioned that "little" fact ourselves. We explained that our ethics committee concluded we had no conflict. But that did not satisfy them. They worry that Happy Valley may not take the same view. They asked

562. Jun Ki Kim v. True Church Members of the Holy Hill Cmty. Church, 236 Cal. App. 4th 1435 (2015) (lawyers who had represented joint clients that became adverse barred from cross-examining officials of one faction); Oasis W. Realty, LLC v. Goldman, 250 P.3d 1115 (Cal. 2011) (lawyer's use of client confidential information to oppose client's project after lawyer ended the representation establishes cause of action for breach of fiduciary duty, professional negligence, and breach of contract).

to interview the former GC, so they can decide whether they were willing to proceed without a waiver. What do you think?

A. It may be okay to sue your former client, which is what Happy Valley is by virtue of former GC's presence in your firm. Her conflicts are also yours. The real problem here is former GC explaining her role at the hospital complex to Colossus. That information remains confidential. In perpetuity. Unless your jurisdiction has adopted the Model Rule exemption to Rule 1.6,[563] the confidentiality rule, you are barred from sharing any confidential information—any—with Colossus. And even if that exception has been adopted, it would be hard to conclude the conversation you want to have is not prohibited. In any event, if Happy Valley finds out about it, you can be assured they will so argue. We think Colossus will have to simply hire you and take its chances. Or look elsewhere for counsel. But before it gets to decide, your firm must decide—as does your client—whether it wants to risk a motion to disqualify. Some firms wear being on the receiving end of such motions as a badge of honor. The authors find them more a matter of shame.

§ 15.27 Former Client Conflicts

Hiring the Former General Counsel

Q. This one's got us flabbergasted. We saw the health care growth early on. Figuring it out, we recruited the GC of the largest regional hospital complex as our perfect entrée into this field. But now it's looking like a huge mistake.

A. How could that go wrong?

Q. Conflicts, conflicts. Every time we take a position adverse to GC's former employer, we are met by a motion to disqualify. Is that fair?

A. Well, that depends. As you know the questions are (1) are the matters substantially related to matters former GC handled; and (2) does the conflict-creating lawyer, in this case the former GC, possess confidential information that could be used to the former client's detriment.

Q. That's what they are always asserting. They say she knows the hospital's playbook. She knows the personalities. She knows the philosophy. She knows their business practices.

563. MR 1.6(b)(7).

A. Usually that won't do it. The party seeking disqualification is supposed to demonstrate a particular connection. The problem is that "substantial relationship" is a litigator's dream, giving advocates on each side a colorable argument why the movant can or cannot succeed. Alas, we have not come up with a better test. We certainly don't want the affected client to have to disclose the confidential information in order to protect it.[564]

Q. But the former client rule gives the former client too much power.

A. Actually, the reverse is true. The amount of loyalty owed to former clients is shockingly parsimonious. The day after a representation ends, the former lawyer can sue the hell out of yesterday's client for a RICO violation, a qui tam claim, treble damages, even punitive damages, or a claim that could give rise to criminal charges. And it's even gotten worse.

Q. How's that?

A. Well the Model Rules and over one-half the states have rewritten Rule 1.10, the imputation rule, to permit people like your

564. Madukwe v. Del. State Univ., 552 F. Supp. 2d 452, 455 (D. Del. 2008) (law firm that represented university as outside counsel for 25 years in numerous employment and labor matters disqualified from representing plaintiff in subsequent employment discrimination suit; legal issues governing former and current representation "entirely identical"); *In re* N. Am. Deed Co., 334 B.R. 443 (Bankr. D. Nev. 2005) (the presence of playbook information confirms existence of a substantial relationship between prior representation of debtor in a wide array of matters and current adversarial representation of debtor's individual officers); Guzewicz v. Eberle, 953 F. Supp. 108 (E.D. Pa. 1997) (lawyer who was General Counsel to corporations not disqualified in subsequent representation of minority shareholders against majority shareholders and corporations, because corporations were nominal defendants); Mitchell v. Metro. Life Ins. Co., No. 01-CIV-2112(WHP), 2002 WL 441194 (S.D.N.Y. Mar. 21, 2002) (lawyer who defended Met Life in a number of lawsuits while employed at her former firm, learned company policies, playbook information, and personally interviewed managers whose testimony would be relevant in subsequent action personally disqualified in subsequent suit and conflict imputed to new law firm; screening measures were not initiated until two months after lawyer joined firm); *In re* Carey, 89 S.W.3d 477 (Mo. 2002) (en banc) (lawyers who billed Chrysler over 500 hours on products liability and consumer fraud matters and later formed a new law firm that took on plaintiffs as clients in a national products liability class action against Chrysler violated Rule 1.9 and were indefinitely suspended, with leave to reapply for admission after one year because (1) the subsequent matters involved the same former client and the same type of case; (2) the lawyers deposed several of Chrysler's expert witnesses in the past; (3) the lawyers knew Chrysler's roadmap in defending and settling similar products liability cases; (4) the lawyers had access to detailed confidential information about a government investigation that was the subject of the litigation); Jamaica Pub. Serv. Co. v. AIU Ins. Co., 707 N.E.2d 414 (N.Y. 1998) (former inside counsel for insurer on Canadian professional liability insurance matters not disqualified in subsequent representation of insured against insurer in coverage dispute not involving same or similar matters); *In re* Basco, 221 S.W.3d 637 (Tex. 2007) (disqualification of hospital's lawyer required because lawyer would have to challenge advice given by former partner in a previous case); ABA Comm. on Ethics & Prof'l Responsibility, Formal Op. 99-415 (1999) Representation Adverse to Organization by Former In-House Lawyer ("[F]act that the lawyer had represented his former employer in similar types of matters or that the lawyer had gained a general knowledge of the strategies, policies, or personnel of the former employer is not sufficient by itself to establish a substantial relationship," but courts have diverged when answering "whether the lawyer has protected information depends on the facts and circumstances of each particular case.").

peripatetic GC to come to your firm without creating any conflict problems whatsoever.

Q. In Florida we don't have anything like that.

A. True. Many states have the old rule. When a new lawyer comes to firms in these states, that lawyer brings all her conflicts with her. Full imputation. But in others, the rule, sadly, is quite different.

Q. Sadly?

A. Well, your authors believe the relaxed rule in those jurisdictions is quite unfortunate. The Model Rule essentially provides that the transferring lawyer brings none of her conflicts with her.

Q. How does that magic occur?

A. It is said that regardless of the role the transferring lawyer played—could've been lead counsel—so long as the lawyer is screened, that lawyer's presence in the new firm, *mirabile dictu*, will not disqualify the new firm from continuing to be directly adverse to the new partner's former client.[565]

Q. But that lawyer switched sides.

A. Indeed.

Q. And that lawyer knows all the confidential information.

A. You got that right.

Q. How can they justify such a rule? The former client must be a wreck.

A. That is the regrettable aspect. Without being given a choice, all the former client is told is that there is a screen. Take it or leave it.

Q. What good does that do? What's a screen?

A. Screens are a legal fiction. The word itself proves the point. Screens are those things we put into our windows in the spring. They keep out the bugs, but otherwise let in air, sound, and light. These screens operate the same way. They say the screen protects the former client's confidential information. They talk about locked file cabinets and computer firewalls. But none of that can stop the side-switching lawyer from spilling the beans, intentionally or inadvertently. All the former client gets when told that a screen is in place is the admonishment, "Trust me." But that trust is being sought by a lawyer who abandoned the client for greener pastures. Not very confidence building.

565. MR 1.10(a)(2).

Q. Talk about putting the interests of the lawyer ahead of the client.

A. Exactly. The proponents wrapped themselves in the story of the oppressed associate, shackled to her desk, billing 2,500 hours per year, desperate for a more humane law firm. But the rule, as written, applies to any lawyer going over to the other side regardless of the lawyer's rank (could be a first chair partner) or the extent of the lawyer's knowledge.

Q. Yeah, I might see it as okay if it were a junior lawyer who worked on just one motion.

A. That more restricted formulation of permissible screen is the rule in about half of the jurisdictions. They permit nonconsensual screening while recognizing that lawyers who had a substantial role or received significant confidential information from the former client cannot be screened. Unlike other conflicts where the client gets to decide whether to give informed consent to the conflict one way or the other, this rule removes all decision making from the former client. We'll discuss other examples of the creeping malignancy of involuntary screening next.

§ 15.28 Screening

Screens: Not the Ones We Put Up in the Spring

Q. I hear folks talking about screens all the time. Sometimes they call them Chinese walls. Say they solve all kinds of conflicts problems that way. I'd do just about anything to avoid sending business away. It's competitive enough out there. Tell us, ethics geeks, how can we add screens to our arsenal?

A. Your war analogy is appropriate. Screens have definitely become a weapon in the guerilla conflict between lawyers and clients over how much loyalty we have to provide our clients.

Q. Well, it is ridiculous. I want to bring in a new client. But one of my partners in a different department in a different office halfway around the world represents the party who this prospective client would like to sue. In a totally unrelated matter. Not even the same area of law. Can we just screen my "partner," the guy in Singapore from me and vice versa to solve the problem?

A. No. No. No. Not yet.

Q. Soon?

A. Your authors hope not. What we are addressing is the imputation principle found in Model Rule 1.10. That rule makes the conflicts of one lawyer in a firm the conflicts of every lawyer. If your Singapore colleague cannot sue her own client, then you cannot either. Unless the conflict is consentable and the Singapore client gives informed consent.

Q. Oh, we won't get that.

A. Of course not. And since that is so, many have argued that you should be able to set up involuntary screens between different offices, different departments, even different floors. So far no jurisdiction has approved it. If the client is willing to give informed consent to the conflict—voluntarily—many will offer to put up a screen to help convince the client the arrangement will at least protect the client's confidential information. That is far different from an involuntary screen.

Q. Why should we have imputation across the globe? I don't even know my partner in Singapore. We may never meet.

A. Undoubtedly true. But you gleefully share the profits of the Singapore office.

Q. True enough. Actually, it's one of only two foreign offices that is profitable. I keep telling management "Enough already!"

A. And you tout on your firm's website that clients who come to Caldwell & Moore receive the benefits of a worldwide organization, drawing on the globe-girdling talent of 1,850 lawyers in 20 financial capitals.

Q. True enough. But it still bothers me.

A. And your authors. But notwithstanding our dim view of screens, it is only fair that we tell you when screens—involuntary screens—are available to you to avoid what would otherwise be conflicts of interest that would preclude representation.

§ 15.29 Prospective Client Screens

Prospective Client Solutions . . . Maybe

Q. I now know that Rule 1.18 requires lawyers to maintain confidentiality for prospective clients. If the engagement is not taken on, confidentiality is nonetheless required of all that was learned before a decision was made.

A. That's right. When a client calls, you need to learn some confidential information—even some embarrassing information—before you can decide. Before the client can decide.

Q. Correct. You also would not want the law firm to end up representing the adverse party in the matter.

A. Also correct.

Q. But that's not what the rule provides. It says that the firm can represent the opponent in the same matter so long as the lawyers in the firm who learned the otherwise disqualifying information are screened.

A. Yes.

Q. Screened! Another involuntary screen?

A. Yes.

Q. Even if the lawyers spent hours with the prospective client before the decision was made?

A. Well, there's a raging debate there. Some say you can only take advantage of this little "gift" if the conversation is quite short. But the language of the rule says it applies if the conversation is limited to what is required to take on the matter. The authors thought that was simply information related to any conflict from the client's perspective. It certainly should be. But some firms take the view a screen is acceptable in the case of a far-ranging conversation, that is, from the lawyer's perspective.

Q. What a horrible result.

A. It certainly does not inspire the confidence of the former prospective client.

Q. Particularly when it comes with no warning. But could you get the prospective client to agree in advance that whatever the client discloses, the law firm can take on an otherwise conflicted representation if the lawyers with the confidential information are screened?

A. That would certainly be vastly better than the screen solution. The client would at least have a warning.[566] But as you know, we are highly skeptical of all prospective "waivers" no matter how "sophisticated" the prospective client, because no one can give informed consent when they do not know what confidential information will be shared after the prospective consent is snared. Sophistication does not mean clairvoyant.

566. Clark Capital Mgmt. Grp., Inc. v. Annuity Investors Life Ins. Co., 149 F. Supp. 2d 193 (E.D. Pa. 2001) (phone conversation did not disqualify law firm where it was clear that conflicts check needed to be done and lawyer to whom prospective client spoke was screened for any participation in the case); Jimenez v. Rivermark Cmty. Credit Union, No. 3:15-cv-00128-BR, 2015 WL 2239669 (D. Or. May 12, 2015) (law firm's associate's warning that firm did not take cases like the one described by a prospective client and frequently represented opposing parties sufficed as reasonable measures to prevent disqualification under Rule 1.18(d)).

§ 15.30 Chart: Comparison of Former Client, Former Government Client, and Former Adjudicator Conflict-of-Interest Provisions

	Former Client	Former Government Representation	Former Judge, Arbitrator, Mediator or Other Third-Party Neutral
Prior Representation	Formerly represented a client in a matter	Government employee or public officer	Judge, arbitrator, mediator, or other third-party neutral
Subsequent Disqualification	Same or substantially related matter & Materially adverse interests	"Matter" [1.11(e)] & Personal and substantial participation as Government Employee/Officer & 1.9(c)	"Matter" & Personal and substantial participation as a Judge, Arbitrator, Mediator or other Third-party Neutral
Except	Informed consent of former client	Informed consent of agency	Informed consent of all parties to the proceeding
Firm	1.10	1.11(b)	1.12(c)

§ 15.31 Government Lawyers

The First Screens

Q. How did the profession go down this treacherous road?

A. Screens probably began as a condition of client informed consent. The first approval of involuntary screening to avoid imputation in the Model Rules applied to government lawyers who wished to return to the private world. The suggestion was made that to encourage lawyers to work for the government it would be a great idea to permit those lawyers, when entering or rejoining the private world, to not bring to their new place of employment what would otherwise be conflicts that might discourage private employers from hiring them. And the way to accomplish that piece of legerdemain was to screen the government-abandoning lawyers.

In some ways it made sense. The private firms most likely to hire these lawyers were the firms that handled litigation (or non-litigation matters) adverse to the agencies for which these lawyers worked. The firm, for example, most likely to hire an AUSA was a firm with a burgeoning practice adverse to the U.S. Attorney's office in the lawyer's city. It also did not hurt that it was the government that would be the "client" that would run the risk that the departing lawyer might betray the former client.

There were those, including the authors, who worried that this was just the beginning of an attempt to compromise the imputation principle on a wholesale basis, but a screening rule—an involuntary screening rule—was adopted, and its growing power has proved more robust than even the worst pessimists could have imagined.

Q. This history makes sense. An SEC enforcement lawyer who wants to join our firm is exactly the kind of lawyer we seek out regularly. Clients love to know they are represented by someone who previously worked for the enemy.

A. But if that person came to work for your firm, you can imagine how many problems that would create.

Q. Not sure.

A. When that person leaves the agency she brings with her all the conflicts of all the representations she had for the government. By virtue of Rule 1.10, her conflicts would be imputed to the entire firm. She would be like Typhoid Mary, spreading her conflicts to your San Paulo office.

Q. But we screen her?

A. Yes, Rule 1.11 provides that so long as she is timely screened from any matters your law firm is handing vis-à-vis the agency where she worked, and the agency is timely notified, her conflicts are not to be imputed. The ABA concluded it was more important, as a matter of public policy, to make it easier for government lawyers to leave for private practice after their public service ended (and, therefore, made it easier for the government to recruit talent) than enforce imputation under these special circumstances.

Q. Wow! That is terrific. Can I push the envelope?

A. You can try.

Q. What if she comes to us from a federal agency and our firm is on the same side as she? Imagine, for example, she was handling an SEC investigation against Lehman Brothers' old management, and we represent a class of plaintiffs suing the same Lehman officers for their huge stock losses arising from the same events. I hope then we would not have to screen her. She could help us.

A. You are close. Those facts present a different situation. If the agency consents, then there is no need to screen her.

Q. Why does the agency get involved at all?

A. Because as a government lawyer armed with the special powers of that status, she was likely privy to much information that a private litigant could never secure. The rule gives the agency a chance to decide, as a public policy matter, whether its former lawyer may actually participate in the related civil action, even though her participation is on the side that the government might very well favor. That puts the decision in the correct hands. If no permission is forthcoming, the plaintiffs' case can go on. Just not with help from the screened former government lawyer.[567]

§ 15.32 Screening Former Judges

Judges, Arbitrators, and Mediators: Which One Does Not Belong?

Q. There are other permissible screens?

A. An ever-growing, increasingly dismaying number. Rule 1.12 permits the screening of judges, arbitrators, and mediators. At the same time as Model Rule 1.11 was adopted, Rule 1.12 came along. This one permitted a revolving door between the judiciary and the practice of law, some would say an unfortunate development since the image of an end-of-career judgeship to cap a lifetime in the trial trenches—an ideal, if unrealistic, model—has gone by the wayside.

Q. What's wrong with that? It was certainly my hope.

A. Well the first two certainly make sense. Neither judges nor arbitrators come to practice with former clients. Therefore, they have no client confidential information that could be used against the parties adverse to the parties represented by the judge's new law firm. And, theoretically at least, the adverse

---

567. San Francisco City & Cnty. v. Cobra Solutions Inc., 135 P.3d 20 (Cal. 2006) (lawyer who left private practice to head government law office disqualifies entire office in substantially related matters); Walker v. La. Dep't of Transp. & Dev., 817 So. 2d 57 (La. 2002) (lawyer who defended state in road hazard cases for ten years not disqualified from later representing plaintiffs in road hazard cases against the state involving different roads, absent proof by the state that lawyer had access to relevant confidential information); *In re* FINRA Arbitration, 909 N.Y.S.2d 285 (N.Y. Sup. Ct. 2010) (former government lawyer not adequately screened due to 20-lawyer firm's failure to exercise special care and vigilance in maintaining screen; size of firm and anything less than complete isolation from lawyers participating in screened matter ineffective).

parties know exactly what the judge knows from the proceedings before the judge.[568]

Same with respect to arbitrators. Even though not robed and not called "Your Honor," a screened arbitrator was still a neutral, only learned information that both sides of the case knew, assuming again no ex parte contacts. And we certainly think there is some benefit to having practicing lawyers act in this role from time to time, without being deemed to have as "clients" the parties who appeared before them then.

Q. But mediators "do not belong"?

A. Correct, because mediators, as an inherent part of the mediation process, learn information from one party they promise to keep confidential from the other side. Indeed they encourage such disclosure.

Q. Well how did mediators get added to Model Rule 1.12?

A. Because many argued that it was important to let mediators join or remain in law firms without creating so many conflicts. The authors disagreed, but many states have adopted Rule 1.12 to include mediators. Our personal views aside, in those states, former mediators can be screened to avoid imputation of the conflict. And the affected mediation participants are left relying solely on the integrity of the mediator who has joined the adverse law firm.

Q. Looks the same to me. All this ADR stuff we real trial lawyers are forced to endure. Even dragooned into acting as mediators when all we really want to do is deliver riveting closing arguments. Screening the former mediator should be just as acceptable.

A. Well, think about it. Every year you litigate on behalf of the electric company the price your client will pay Charleston Coal under that crazy formula they put in the requirements contract they negotiated 40 years ago.

Q. It is like an annuity for our firm.

A. But remember last year you mediated it before Ol' Grey Head.

Q. We did.

---

568. Monument Builders of Penn. Inc. v. Catholic Cemeteries Ass'n, Inc., 190 F.R.D. 164 (E.D. Pa. 1999) (former judicial clerk's disqualification due to participation in settlement conference in case not imputed to firm because former clerk could be screened from participating in the matter); *In re* Sofaer, 728 A.2d 625 (D.C. 1999) (lawyer who served as legal advisor in the U.S. State Department in the government's investigation of the 1988 bombing of Pan American Flight 103 over Lockerbie, Scotland, subject to informal admonition for later undertaking representation of the government of Libya in connection with criminal and civil disputes arising out of the same incident, without seeking the consent of his former agency).

A. Did he do a great job?

Q. Well, it took four days. But we reached a settlement. Client was happy enough to hire us again.

A. Now suppose we told you Ol' Grey Head was now working at the firm that represents the coal company. How would you feel?

Q. It's not how I'd feel. It's how my client would feel.

A. How's that?

Q. They would really be upset. Ol' Grey Head learned a lot about our operation, our strategy, our bottom line—which was actually more than we ended up paying. And he wrenched that information out of us by assuring us of his commitment to confidentiality. Now his firm is representing the other side.

A. True. But I'm telling you he's been screened under Model Rule 1.12.

Q. That's what they say. But my client won't find that much comfort. Frankly, I don't either. One short conversation and Ol' Grey Head could destroy us. And we trusted him.[569]

§ 15.33 Side Switchers

The Recent Addition

Q. Are there other screens?

A. There is one that, in the authors' view, is the most controversial. It has been adopted by about one-quarter of the jurisdictions and, importantly, has been inserted into the Model Rules.

Q. Worse than the mediator example?

A. Definitely. This one permits a lawyer representing client A in A v. B to switch sides, go to work at the law firm of B and, so long as the participating lawyer is screened, B's law firm is

569. Fields-D'Arpino v. Rest. Assocs. Inc., 39 F. Supp. 2d 412 (S.D.N.Y. 1999) (law firm that failed to obtain informed consent of parties to a prior mediation and failed to screen a partner who previously mediated a dispute disqualified from later representing one party to the mediation against the other); Poly Software Int'l, Inc. v. Su, 880 F. Supp. 1487 (D. Utah 1995) (mediators should be governed by Rule 1.9's substantial-relationship test, as well as Rule 1.12's same-matter test, because mediators receive significant confidential information); Matluck v. Matluck, 825 So. 2d 1071 (Fla. Dist. Ct. App. 2002) (law firm whose lawyer acted as mediator for the parties in the same action disqualified from subsequently representing one of the parties in order to preserve the confidences of parties to the mediation and to protect the integrity of the mediation process itself); State Bar of Tex. Prof'l Ethics Comm. Op. 583 (2008) (Rule [1.12(b)] prohibits a lawyer from agreeing to serve both as mediator between parties in a divorce and as a lawyer to prepare the divorce decree and other necessary documents to effect the agreement resulting from the mediation).

not infected with Mr. Greener Pastures clear conflict of interest and his treasure trove of A's confidential information.[570]

Q. Amazing!

A. Some would say that. Others would decry this screening opportunity as a fundamental assault on loyalty. The former client has no choice, yet think how that former client would feel? This is why most jurisdictions impute the conflicts of side-switching lawyers to the new firm and do not permit curing the conflict with a screen.[571]

Q. Betrayed comes to mind. Sabotaged. Worried.

A. Yet the proponents say that the turncoat lawyer may be screened.

Q. Not much comfort. The lawyer is telling the former client: "Trust me, even though I just abandoned you to join the law firm that A and A's former lawyer found untrustworthy."[572]

§ 15.34 Adequate Screens

Is It Really Adequate?

Q. We've talked a long time. But we have not addressed what is required to establish a screen.

A. Before we do that, let us make one more point. All the trappings of a screen are just that. There is no way to police the side-switching lawyer, former mediator, government lawyer, or prospective client consulter from divulging all the confidential information he or she possesses. And if the lawyer has integrity all the trappings may be unnecessary.

Q. But I've heard that courts will disqualify law firms if they are not satisfied that the screen meets certain criteria.

---

570. MR 1.10(a)(2).

571. CSX Transp., Inc. v. Gilkison, No. 5:05-CV-202, 2006 WL 3203419 (N.D. W. Va. Nov. 3, 2006) (overlap in parties, potential witnesses, and facts and circumstances from which alleged physical injuries or lack thereof arose created substantial relationship and warrant disqualification which cannot be cured by screening); City Nat'l Bank v. Adams, 117 Cal. Rptr. 2d 125 (2002) (collecting cases); Twenty-First Century Rail Corp. v. N.J. Transit Corp., 44 A.3d 592 (N.J. 2012) (no screen allowed without former client's consent in subsequent adverse representation in same matter); Kala v. Aluminum Smelting & Refining Co., 688 N.E.2d 258 (Ohio 1998) (screens not allowed in side-switching cases despite availability of such a remedy in other former-client conflict situations).

572. Hempstead Video, Inc., v. Inc. Vill. of Valley Stream, 409 F.3d 127 (2d Cir. 2005) (screen appropriate to cure any conflict of lawyer who became "of counsel" to firm solely to transition several of his clients to new firm upon his retirement); Krutzfeldt Ranch LLC v. Pinnacle Bank, 272 P.3d 635 (Mont. 2012) (lawyer who did not overtly end a client representation before joining a new firm deemed to continue representing client; new firm disqualified from its representation of opposing client in litigation and could not establish a screen; migrating lawyer should have delayed move to new firm until trial was over or asked client and court for permission to withdraw before moving to new firm).

A. You are more than correct. There are some essential aspects to a screen. First, the screen must be timely, that is, when the firm knew or should have known of the issue. Waiting until a motion to disqualify is filed is too late.

Q. So, no substitute for an adequate and timely conflicts-checking system.

A. Without a doubt. And second, the affected former client must be promptly given a written notification including a description of the firm's screening procedures and an affirmative statement of the firm's willingness to promptly respond to any written inquires or objections.

Q. Hadn't thought about the fact our firm needs written screening procedures. But I guess we can do that. Now, we are finished?

A. No, the third requirement necessitates certifications of compliance with the screening procedures at reasonable intervals when the affected client requests them in writing. New lawyers (and others) join the team. People forget. Periodic reminders are critical.

Q. Ok, I get it, plenty of paper documentation.

A. And fourth, the affected lawyer should be banned from access to physical and electronic files and cannot participate in the fee that comes from the screened matter. You might wonder why go to this bother when what the screen is trying to protect is disclosure by the screened lawyer of what that lawyer knows because keeping that screened lawyer away from those on the case prevents inadvertent breaches. Some also think it is wise to have the affected lawyer certify that the screen has not been breached. But in the end the ethical screen must serve its purpose: to isolate the lawyer who possesses confidential information from opportunity to share it. Of course, to be truly effective, the good character and care of the participant lawyers will be absolutely required as well.[573]

573. Silicon Graphics, Inc. v. ATI Techs., Inc., 741 F. Supp. 2d 970 (W.D. Wis. 2010) (screening appropriate in side-switching case, even if lawyer performed substantial work on matter, where lawyer will not have contact with lawyers in another city working on the matter and will not attend any meetings on any subject with any lawyer who has worked on the case); Norfolk S. Ry. Co. v. Reading Blue Mountain & N. R.R. Co., 397 F. Supp. 2d 551 (M.D. Pa. 2005) (screen not adequate because no affidavit that firm will not share its fee with screened lawyer or indication of strong sanctions if screen is breached, as well as no time lapse between former and current representations, substantiality of former lawyer's involvement, and ten-lawyer size of new firm, despite timely implementation of screen and restrictions on new lawyer's access to case and prohibition on discussing case with new lawyer); Martin v. AtlantiCare, No. 10-6793, 2011 WL 5080255 (D.N.J. Oct. 25, 2011) (screen not adequate where no details of screen were included in certification to former client, firm had no written screening policy, and no indication tainted lawyer was physically separated from former client's file, and no notification to new firm of screening measure before tainted lawyer joined firm).

§ 15.35 Checklist for Effective Screens

Screens may be available to resolve some former-client conflicts,[574] either as part of the informed-consent process,[575] or if otherwise recognized by the Rules of Professional Conduct[576] or common law.[577] When allowed, courts agree that the screen also must be legally adequate.[578]

Model Rule 1.0(k) defines "screened" as "isolation of a lawyer from any participation in a matter through the timely imposition of procedures within a firm that are reasonably adequate under the circumstances to protect information that the isolated lawyer is obligated to protect under these Rules or other law." [579]

To meet this standard, courts require law firms to:

- Determine whether the firm is large enough to establish an effective screen;[580]
- Implement a written screening policy; [581]

574. MR 1.10(a); D.C. Bar Legal Ethics Comm., Formal Op. 349 (2009) (although joint defense agreements do not create former "clients," such agreement can give rise to a conflict that requires a timely screen to avoid disqualification).

575. MRs 1.7, 1.8, 1.9; State v. Smith, 761 N.W.2d 63 (Iowa 2009) (the screen was one factor to be considered, along with client's waiver of conflict, in deciding whether the conflict was actual or potential, serious or speculative).

576. MRs 1.11(b)–(c) (former government employees), 1.12(c) (former judges, arbitrators, and mediators), 1.18(d) (prospective clients).

577. RLGL § 124; Kirk v. First Am. Title Ins. Co., 108 Cal. Rptr. 3d 620 (2010) (screening allowed in prospective client case where lawyer was in different office of large law firm and possessed only a small amount of confidential information); Meza v. H. Muhlstein & Co., 98 Cal. Rptr. 3d 422, 429 (2009) (screening not allowed in a side-switching case where disqualification is due to lawyer's representation of the opposing side during the same case).

578. Several empirical studies indicate that lawyers do not often understand these requirements. SUSAN P. SHAPIRO, TANGLED LOYALTIES: CONFLICT OF INTEREST IN LEGAL PRACTICE 411–12 (2002) (screens do not always meet the specifications found in ethics codes and case law and reinforce a double standard between clients with clout and one-time less powerful clients); Lee A. Pizzimenti, *Screen Verite: Do Rules About Ethical Screens Reflect the Truth About Real-Life Law Firm Practice?* 52 U. MIAMI L. REV. 305, 333 (1997) (study found the majority of firms take conflicts seriously, but that they "are hampered by flawed conflicts detection, flawed systems for maintaining screens and, to some extent, an adversarial rather than fiduciary analysis of screen issues").

579. MR 1.0(k).

580. Intelli-Check, Inc. v. TriCom Card Techs., Inc., No. 03-cv-3706, 2008 WL 4682433 (E.D.N.Y. Oct. 21, 2008) (screen upheld where firm consisted of 420 lawyers and screened lawyers were separated geographically and technologically); United States v. Pelle, No. CRIM-05-407-JBS, 2007 WL 674723 (D.N.J. Feb. 28, 2007) (ten-lawyer firm too small for effective screen because accidental exposure to the matter is likely).

581. Tucker v. George, 569 F. Supp. 2d 834, 841 (W.D. Wis. 2008) (implementation of a formal mechanism to isolate the tainted lawyers required to prevent a mere "de facto screen that occurred by happenstance").

- Establish the screen before the screened lawyer joins the firm, or if the lawyer is already in the firm, as soon as the conflict has been timely detected;[582]
- Acknowledge in writing that the screened lawyer will not communicate with any firm lawyers about the matter;
- Notify all law-firm personnel about the screen, indicating they may not communicate with the screened lawyer about the matter;
- Quarantine all law firm files about the screened matter. Electronic files should be available only with a proper password, and paper files should be kept in an area not available to the screened lawyer;[583]
- Establish bookkeeping procedures that ensure the screened lawyer does not share in the fee revenue from the case;[584]
- Give prompt notification to all clients, former clients, or other parties that the screen has been established;[585]
- Create law firm mechanisms that periodically remind screened lawyers of their obligations and inquire about the maintenance of proper screening procedures; and
- Promptly notify the affected clients and former clients if the screen is breached.[586]

---

582. Lutron Elecs. Co. v. Crestron Elecs., Inc., No. 2:09-CV-707, 2010 WL 4720693 (D. Utah Nov. 12, 2010) (screen was timely when created as soon as firm was notified that one of its lawyers had worked for the opposing party at his former firm); Chinese Auto. Distribs. of Am., LLC v. Bricklin, No. 07-cv-4113, 2009 WL 47337 (S.D.N.Y. Jan. 8, 2009) (screen was not timely when set up three months after lateral joined firm when firm knew about conflict at the time lateral joined but determined there was no conflict). *See also* Lucent Techs., Inc. v. Gateway, Inc., 509 F. Supp. 2d 912 (S.D. Cal. 2007) (screen was not timely when lateral listed former client upon joining the firm, but firm did not screen until after it made appearance in new case one month later).

583. Papyrus Tech. Corp. v. N.Y. Stock Exch., Inc., 325 F. Supp. 2d 270 (S.D.N.Y. 2004) (sealing of firm's document management system so that only members of the team working on the case could access electronic documents held to be effective); Graham Co. v. Stanton T. Griffing and Connor Strong Cos., No. 08-1394, 2009 WL 3646348 (E.D. Pa. Nov. 3, 2009) (screen should include restrictions on access to billing records of the matter at issue).

584. Gerald v. Turnock Plumbing, Heating & Cooling, LLC, 768 N.E.2d 498 (Ind. Ct. App. 2002) (screened lawyer was a partner and would receive a portion of firm's fees; disqualification granted).

585. MRs 1.10(a)(2)(ii) (former clients), 1.11(b)(2) (former government officers and employees), 1.12(c)(2) (former judges, arbitrators, and mediators), 1.18(d)(2)(ii) (prospective clients).

586. Steel v. Gen. Motors Corp., 912 F. Supp. 724 (D.N.J. 1995) (inadvertent breach in screen required disqualification); Spur Prods. Corp. v. Stoel Rives LLP, 153 P.3d 1158 (Idaho 2007) (valid malpractice claim presented by client for failure of law firm to inform client of breach in a screen, causing client to agree to settle the underlying litigation client would not otherwise have agreed to if it had known about screen breach); Prince Jefri Bolkiah v. KPMG [1999] 2 AC (HL) 222 (disqualification required where lawyers in accounting firm disregarded screen in favor of team approach to prelitigation services).

§ 15.36 Chart: State Rules of Professional Conduct Screening Provisions

Jurisdiction	Former Clients	Former Government Officers and Employees	Former Judge, Arbitrator, Mediator, or Other Third-Party Neutral	Prospective Clients
				Other
ABA Model Rules	1.9(a), 1.10(a); yes	1.11(b), (c); yes	1.12(c); yes	1.18(d); yes
Alabama	Only with former client consent, 1.9(a), 1.10(d)	1.11(a), (b); yes	1.12(c); yes	
Alaska	Only with former client consent, 1.9(a), 1.10(c)	1.11(b), (c); yes	1.12(c); yes	1.18(d); yes
Arizona	1.9(a), 1.10(d); yes	1.11 (a), (b); yes	1.12(c); yes	1.18(d); yes
Arkansas	Only with former client consent, 1.9(a), 1.10(c)	1.11(b), (c); yes	1.12(c); yes	1.18(d); yes
California	1.9(a), 1.10(a)(2); yes	1.11(b), (c); yes	1.12(c); yes	1.18(d); yes
Colorado	1.9(a), 1.10(e); yes	1.11(b), (c); yes	1.12(c); yes	1.18(d); yes
Connecticut	1.9(a), 1.10(a); yes	1.11(a), (b); yes	1.12(c); yes	1.18(d); yes
Delaware	1.9(a), 1.10(c); yes	1.11(b), (c); yes	1.12(c); yes	1.18(d); yes
District of Columbia	1.9(a), 1.10(b); yes	1.11(c); yes	1.11(c), 1.12 (c); yes	1.18(d); yes
Florida	Only with former client consent, 4-1.9(a), 4-1.10(d)	4-1.11(b), (c); yes	4-1.12(c); yes	1.18(d); yes

Jurisdiction	Former Clients	Former Government Officers and Employees	Former Judge, Arbitrator, Mediator, or Other Third-Party Neutral	Prospective Clients
				Other
Georgia	Only with former client consent, 1.9(a), 1.10(c)	1.11(a), (b); yes	1.12(c); yes	
Hawaii	1.9(a), 1.10(c); yes	1.11(a), (b); yes	1.12(c); yes	1.18(d); yes
Idaho	1.9(a), 1.10(a); yes	1.11(b), (c); yes	1.12(c); yes	1.18(d); yes
Illinois	1.9(a)(1), 1.10(e); yes	1.11(b), (c); yes	1.12(c); yes	1.18(d); yes
Indiana	1.9, 1.10(c); yes	1.11(b), (c); yes	1.12(c); yes	1.18(d); yes
Iowa	Only with former client consent, 1.9(a), 1.10(c)	1.11(b), (c); yes	1.12(c); yes	1.18(d); yes
Kansas	Only with former client consent, 1.9(a), 1.10(c)	1.11(a), (b); yes	1.12(c); yes	1.17(d); yes
Kentucky	1.9(a), 1.10(d); yes	1.11(b), (c); yes	1.12(c); yes	1.18(d); yes
Louisiana	1.9(a), 1.10(c); yes	1.11(b), (c); yes	1.12(c); yes	1.18(d); yes
Maine	Only with former client consent, 1.9(a), 1.10(a)	1.11(b), (c); yes	1.12(c); yes	1.18(d); yes
Maryland	1.9(a), 1.10(c); yes	1.11(b), (c); yes	1.12(c); yes	1.18(d); yes
Massachusetts	1.9(a), 1.10(d); yes	1.11(a), (b); yes	1.12(c); yes	1.18(d); yes
Michigan	1.9(a), 1.10(b); yes	1.11(a), (b); yes	1.12(c); yes	
Minnesota	1.9(a), 1.10(b); yes	1.11(b), (c); yes	1.12(c); yes	1.18(d); yes

Jurisdiction	Former Clients	Former Government Officers and Employees	Former Judge, Arbitrator, Mediator, or Other Third-Party Neutral	Prospective Clients Other
Mississippi	Only with former client consent, 1.9(a), 1.10(d)	1.11(a), (b); yes	1.12(c); yes	
Missouri	Only with former client consent, 4-1.9(a), 4-1.10(c)	4-1.11(b), (c); yes	4-1.12(c); yes	1.18(d); yes
Montana	1.9(a), 1.10(c); yes	1.11(b), (c); yes	1.12(c); yes	1.20(d); yes
Nebraska	Only with former client consent, 1.9(a), 1.10(c)	1.12(b), (c); yes	1.12(c); yes	1.18(d); yes 1.9(e); yes (Support persons)
Nevada	1.9(a), 1.10(e); yes	1.11(b), (c); yes	1.12(c); yes	1.18(d); yes
New Hampshire	1.9(a), 1.10(c); yes	1.11(b), (c); yes	1.12(c); yes	1.18 (d); yes
New Jersey	1.9(a), 1.10(c); yes	1.11(b); yes	1.12(c); yes	1.18(c); yes
New Mexico	16-109(A), 16-110(C); yes	16-111(B), (C); yes	16-112 (C); yes	16-118 (D); yes
New York	Only with former client consent, 1.9(a), 1.10(a)	1.11(b), (c); yes	1.12(c); yes	1.18(d); yes
North Carolina	1.9(a), 1.10(c); yes	1.11(b), (c); yes	1.12(c); yes	1.18(d); yes
North Dakota	1.9(a), 1.10(b); yes	1.11(b), (c); yes	1.12(c); yes	1.18(d); yes
Ohio	1.9(a), 1.10(d); yes	1.11(b), (c); yes	1.12(c); yes	1.18(d); yes

Jurisdiction	Former Clients	Former Government Officers and Employees	Former Judge, Arbitrator, Mediator, or Other Third-Party Neutral	Prospective Clients
				Other
Oklahoma	Only with former client consent, 1.9(a), 1.10(a)	1.11(b), (c); yes	1.12(c); yes	1.18(d); yes
Oregon	1.9(a), 1.10(c); yes	1.11(b), (c); yes	1.12(c); yes	1.18(d); yes
Pennsylvania	1.9(a), 1.10(b); yes	1.11(b), (c); yes	1.12(c); yes	1.18(d); yes
Rhode Island	1.9(a), 1.10(c); yes	1.11(b), (c); yes	1.12(c); yes	1.18(d); yes
South Carolina	Only with former client consent, 1.9(a), 1.10(c)	1.11(b), (c); yes	1.12(c); yes	1.18(d); yes
South Dakota	1.9(a), 1.10(c); yes	1.11(b), (c); yes	1.12(c); yes	1.18(d); yes
Tennessee	1.9(a), 1.10(c); yes	1.11(b), (c); yes	1.12(c); yes	1.18(d); yes
Texas	1.09, Only with former client consent	1.10(b), (c); yes	1.11(c); yes	
Utah	1.9(a), 1.10(c); yes	1.11(b), (c); yes	1.12(c); yes	1.18(d); yes
Vermont	1.9(a), 1.10(a); yes	1.11(b), (c); yes	1.12(c); yes	1.18(d); yes
Virginia	Only with former client consent, 1.9(a), 1.10(c)	1.11(b), (c); yes	1.12(c); yes 1.10(a), 2.10(e); no (M)	1.18(d); yes
Washington	1.9(a), 1.10(e); yes	1.11(b), (c); yes	1.12(c); yes	1.18(d); yes
West Virginia	Only with former client consent, 1.9(a), 1.10(c)	1.11(a), (b); yes	1.12(c); yes	1.18(d); yes

Jurisdiction	Former Clients	Former Government Officers and Employees	Former Judge, Arbitrator, Mediator, or Other Third-Party Neutral	Prospective Clients
				Other
Wisconsin	20:1.9(a), 20:1.10(a); yes	20:1.11(b), (c); yes	20:1.12(c); yes	1.18(d); yes
Wyoming	1.9(a), 1.10(a); yes	1.11(b), (c); yes	1.12(c); yes	1.18(d); yes

PART FOUR

The Limits of the Law

When You Should or Must Say "No": Boundaries

Up to this point, we have examined the contours of loyalty to your client, zealous representation, fiduciary duty, or the Six Cs: client identification, competence, control, communication, confidentiality, and conflict of interest resolution. Put another way, we have explored what it means to say "yes" to your clients, and how to avoid under-identification with your clients' goals.

At the same time, every agency relationship is subject to one significant limitation: neither your client's power of control nor your obligation of loyalty allows either of you to violate the limits or bounds of the law.[587] As autonomous legal persons,[588] both your client and you remain responsible for the consequences of your conduct. In other words, there are times you must say "no" to clients; lawyers have always been in the business of advising clients to avoid illegality.[589]

Many times in this book we have discussed limits and boundaries. Some are easy to recognize; others turn on how a standard like "reasonable" gets interpreted after the fact as a condition of consent or follow-on litigation. Sometimes we need to go to the edge. Sometimes our own client is goading us to do so. Sometimes we do it in the heat of the

587. MR 1.2(d); RLGL § 23(1).

588. Restatement (Third) of Agency § 1.01 cmt. f (1) (Am. Law Inst. 2006).

589. MRs 1.2(d), 2.1; RLGL § 94. Former ABA President Elihu Root famously said, "About half the practice of a decent lawyer consists in telling would-be clients that they are damn fools and should stop." Philip C. Jessup, 1 Elihu Root 133 (1930).

moment without first taking a deep breath. At all times, however, we should examine the "good-lawyering" point. We can do X, but should we? If the answer to that threshold question is "no," then you should reexamine what you have planned.

The limits of the law include several familiar bodies of law, such as crime, fraud, and procedural rules, which are explicitly incorporated into the Rules of Professional Conduct. This incorporation extends the reach of these bodies of general law into the scope of professional discipline. In addition, the range of sanctions a lawyer or client may be forced to endure is increased by a court's substantial inherent power to provide equitable relief for conduct that violates these bodies of law. As a result, lawyers can face legal and equitable remedies, such as procedural sanctions, civil and criminal accountability, and equitable relief, as well as professional discipline for the same conduct.

Chart: Sources of Legal Limits and Corresponding Model Rules

Law	Legal Penalties	Corresponding Model Rule(s) (Professional Discipline)
Crime (approximately 4,000 federal and 1,000 state provisions)	Fines, imprisonment	1.2(d), 3.4(a), 8.4(b)
Tort (e.g., fraud)	Damages, Loss of a Contractual Bargain	1.2(d), 3.3, 4.1, 8.4(c)
Evidence (privileges)	Contempt, sanctions	3.4
Court Orders (inherent power of the court)	Disqualification, injunctive relief, court-ordered counsel	3.4(c)
Procedural Rules (e.g., Fed. R. Civ. P. 11, 26, 37, 60)	Sanctions, injunctive relief	3.1, 3.4
ADR Rules (arbitration or mediation codes or procedures)	Disqualification	1.12, 2.4
Administrative Regulations (e.g., Sarbanes-Oxley)	Disbarment	1.6(b)(6), 1.13
Federal and State Conflict-of-Interest Provisions	Criminal penalties	1.11, 1.12

CHAPTER 16

Getting Out: When You Must or May Withdraw from a Representation

§ 16.01 Introduction: Legal Grounds for Withdrawal

Subject to the permission of a tribunal,[590] there are times you must get out. Three general circumstances require involuntary withdrawal from a client representation, even if you do not want to or your client wants you to continue the representation:

- Your continued representation of a client would result in a violation of the Rules of Professional Conduct. This could occur if you lack the competence to complete the matter. Or, a conflict of interest could become nonconsentable. Worse, your client might insist that you engage in or assist the client in engaging in criminal or fraudulent conduct during the course of the representation.
- Your physical or mental condition materially impairs your representation of a client.
- Your client fires you. Clients have the absolute right to fire lawyers at any time for any reason or no reason at all.

Beyond involuntary mandatory withdrawal, you also have voluntary discretion to withdraw in a wide variety of circumstances (subject to the permission of a tribunal), including:

590. MR 1.16; RLGL § 32.

- If withdrawal can be accomplished without an adverse effect on a client's interests, you may withdraw for no reason (subject to approval required by a court). But if you decide to withdraw, you must take steps to protect your client's interests by providing reasonable notice, time to employ substitute counsel, surrendering any papers to which the client is entitled, and refunding any advance fee payment not earned. You also need a disengagement letter to properly inform your client.
- Even if the withdrawal might adversely affect the client's interests, when you reasonably believe (but do not yet "know") that your client persists in criminal or fraudulent conduct and your client has used your services to perpetrate a crime or fraud, or your client insists upon action that you consider repugnant, or the client has otherwise rendered the representation unreasonably difficult, you can seek to withdraw. But you still need to protect your client's interests, as just described.
- Similarly, if your client substantially fails to fulfill a financial obligation after you have given a reasonable warning that you will withdraw unless the obligation is met, the representation imposes an unreasonable financial burden on you, or if any other good cause for withdrawal exists, you can seek to withdraw. Again, you will need to protect your client's interests, as just described.

Courts do not construe all of the circumstances that appear to justify withdrawal at face value. For example, it is very difficult to show an "unreasonable financial burden" or "repugnance" in many jurisdictions. If you have more than one reason to withdraw, be sure you investigate cases in your jurisdiction to determine which ground will best support your instincts.

§ 16.02 Being Fired

The Nerve

Q. I really wanted this case. From the beginning I made the mistake of counting my chickens . . .

A. Dangerous business. Low expectations avoid disappointment.

Q. Easy enough to say. Anyway, I represent the plaintiff. Great claim: one-third of the recovery (before deducting costs and disbursements) is mine. Could be a million-dollar judgment.

A. Good for you.

Q. Well it was good. But now the client has fired me. Seems his brother-in-law just joined a big law firm. Wants to help the guy out. Just when we had a real breakthrough in the deposition of defendant's CEO. I tried to persuade him not to switch horses in the middle of a ballgame, but he is determined. And as you have told me, the client can fire the lawyer at any time for any reason or no reason at all.

A. True enough. But you do have one arrow left in your quiver.

Q. I do? I tried everything.

A. Rule 1.16(c), the withdrawal rule, contains the caveat that any withdrawal from a litigated matter must be consistent with the rules of the court. And almost every court has a rule that court permission is required before you withdraw. The closer to trial and the more likely your client's legitimate or illegitimate desire to replace you will interfere with the judge's schedule, the more likely your client's wish to jettison you will not be granted.

Q. So I should sabotage the client's demand?

A. You can't do that; the client is entitled to a fair presentation of his wish. But the judge still might deny the request.

Q. And if not? Have I lost my huge investment?

A. No. But your vision of sugar plums may disappear. In some jurisdictions, if the former client is successful, you can collect your hourly rate times the number of hours you spent. In others you might get even more as fair value or quantum meruit, but only if your successor counsel succeeds.[591]

§ 16.03 Firing the Client

The Profession's Dirty Little Secret

Q. I've had enough with this client. Can I just get out?

A. It's our profession's dirty little secret. We spend so much time and energy trying to snare new clients. We grovel, we importune, we participate in beauty contests, we speak, we write, we get involved in community affairs, we shamelessly fawn over in-house counsel, we get active in the bar, all to bring work in the door. We pontificate about successfully carrying out the engagement. Far less time and thought addresses the firing of

591. RLGL §§ 39, 40.

clients, an act that is sometimes required and, far more often, is simply the exercise of good judgment.

§ 16.04 Withdrawing from Litigation

You Need the Judge

Q. I understand that point. You hate to lose the business so conscientiously snared, but that inner voice tells you to cut your losses, get out of the representation. We have one such case right now. We just sent the client a letter, ending the relationship.

A. We hope you mean announcing your intent to do so.

Q. No. We've made up our minds. We're outta here.

A. Not so fast. Our transactional brothers and sisters can withdraw from a representation if the rules permit. But trial lawyers have a different problem.

Q. It's a small price to pay not to be bored to tears drafting trust indentures, but don't the rules apply to all lawyers?

A. They do, but the "firing your client" rules have a little extra gift for litigators. They require a minor detail—getting the permission of the court—before you can withdraw.

Q. Those judges.

A. Well, we all know how they like to protect their dockets. So, motions to withdraw too close to the time of trial are unlikely to be granted, unless new counsel are available and prepared to swear on a stack of Bibles that they will stick to the court's schedule. But without substitute counsel, the courts are particularly reluctant to grant such a motion. You know how judges hate to deal with pro se litigants. The requirement of seeking judicial approval also gives the client a chance to object and even challenge whether the lawyer has grounds for the requested relief.[592]

---

592. Brandon v. Blech, 560 F.3d 536 (6th Cir. 2009) (law firm that gave timely warning it would withdraw if client continued not to pay allowed to withdraw; danger of prejudice low because case was inactive and client had time to secure new counsel); Fidelity Nat'l Title Ins. Co. v. Intercounty Nat'l Title Ins. Co., 310 F.3d 537 (7th Cir. 2002) (motion to withdraw granted where clients' interests were protected by lawyers who finished discovery in case despite $470,000 in unpaid legal fees and lawyers gave clients adequate warning); United States v. Heron, 513 F. Supp. 2d 393 (E.D. Pa. 2007) (lawyer's fear of not being paid in the future insufficient to support withdrawal); Haines v. Liggett Group, Inc., 814 F. Supp. 414 (D.N.J. 1993) (motion to withdraw denied even though financial burden on lawyers had become substantial because lawyers had agreed to advance the costs of the litigation, client was unable to find another lawyer, and her interest would be prejudiced); United States v. Hutchins, 69 M.J. 282 (C.A.A.F. 2011) (separation from active duty not always good cause for military lawyers' withdrawal).

§ 16.05 Mandatory Withdrawal

You Gotta Get Out

Q. Well, we know Judge Jones will grant this one.

A. Such remarkable confidence.

Q. Look, our client wants us to put a witness on the stand we know is lying. Client says maybe he'll fool the jury. We explain it doesn't work that way. But the client persists. Our only choice is to withdraw.

A. How are you going to do that?

Q. We'll file a motion.

A. And what are you going to write?

Q. That we have grounds to withdraw.

A. Anything more?

Q. Not unless I have to.

A. Good for you. Your grounds for withdrawal are client confidential. As a result, you should do everything in your power to disclose as little as possible.[593]

Q. Is it okay if we just tell the judges?

A. It is true that you should minimize the injury to the client. One way to do that is to begin with another heart-to-heart with the client. Explain the following procedure, which might cause the client to relent. If not, you could file something ex parte, denying information to the other side that could be used against your client. But if the judge learns the basis for your withdrawal, that won't do your client any good either. Your duty is to see if you can use the vaguest of descriptions like "irreconcilable differences" to describe your grounds. At the end of the day you may have to disclose more, but that should be a last resort.

§ 16.06 Confidentiality and Successor Counsel

Should We Alert Our Successor?

Q. Do we have to worry that if we withdraw and our client gets new counsel, that counsel won't know what we know? Should we alert our successor?

A. You can't do that. Your confidentiality obligation precludes your sharing client confidences with your successor without former client's informed consent. And once you have

593. MR 3.3 cmts. [11], [12].

withdrawn, the anti-fraud exceptions in Rule 1.6 don't apply unless the client used your services to further a fraud. Since your client has not yet put the witness on the stand, you have no duty to rectify anything that has not yet occurred. Of course, successor counsel will be on notice that you are not free to share this information, which just might put successor on notice that something is awry.

But the fact is that new counsel may never know, will put that witness on the stand in ignorance, and if cross-examination doesn't unearth the problem, the false testimony will not be revealed to the jury. But you will know that your ethical duties have been fulfilled by your remonstrations with the client and your timely withdrawal.

Q. That was a mandated withdrawal, correct?

A. Yes. Under Rule 1.16(a), a lawyer, subject to court approval, is required to withdraw when continuing the representation would result in a violation of the Rules of Professional Conduct.

Q. For example?

A. Your firm failed to identify a conflict of interest.[594] Or your continuing the representation would aid and abet a client fraud.[595] Or you're going to have to be a witness for your client on a controverted matter.[596] Or, your client insists on your pressing a frivolous argument or pleading a frivolous claim in violation of Rule 11 of the Federal Rules of Civil Procedure.[597]

Q. Anything else?

A. You are fired by the client. You are physically or mentally unable to continue with the representation.

Q. Like I fell before my opening statement? Or didn't sleep well last night?

A. Not quite.

---

594. Sanford v. Virginia, 687 F. Supp. 2d 591 (E.D. Va. 2009) (counsel has a responsibility to withdraw when a conflict arises after the representation has begun).

595. MRs 1.2(d), 4.1(b); *In re* Sharp, 802 So. 2d 588 (La. 2001) (lawyer suspended for one year for failing to withdraw when client asked him to prepare receipt and release that assisted client's attempts to encourage noncompliance by key witness in criminal trial); *In re* Potts, 158 P.3d 418 (Mont. 2007) (lawyer subject to discipline for failing to withdraw when his client insisted on nondisclosure of a material fact that "propelled the lawyer's services into the realm of assisting a client fraud").

596. MR 3.7; Neumann v. Tuccio, No. DBDCV-07-5002831-S, 2009 WL 2506357 (Conn. Super. Ct. July 17, 2009) (lawyer disqualified as a necessary witness once client claimed advice of counsel as a defense).

597. MR 3.1.

§ 16.07 Permissive Withdrawal

Discretion to Desist

Q. Is that it?
A. For mandatory withdrawal, yes.
Q. The rest is up to me?
A. No, you are not completely free to drop any matter. But often lawyers can find themselves in the middle ground. They have grounds for withdrawal but are not obliged to do so.
Q. And your view?
A. Before thinking about the rule, there is a good-lawyering point to consider. Permissible grounds for withdrawal are red flags. They should make the concerned lawyer pause, take some time to think whether this is a representation one wants to continue, even if it would not violate the rules to do so.

§ 16.08 Permissive Reasons

No Reason at All

Q. Someone told me we don't even need a reason.
A. That is true. If there is no substantial prejudice to the client from the withdrawal—and a court approves—you need no grounds. You can get up one morning, announce that life is too short and proceed with the withdrawal process.
Q. I have this med-mal case. We haven't filed yet—that avoids the court permission issue. And we got an expert but not at all what we had hoped for. Frankly, the case is a dog. A good chance we'll lose a jury verdict after a time-intensive trial. I'd like to send our client a note, tell her we are dropping some of our med-mal cases, give her a copy of the expert report, and the names of a few other med-mal lawyers.
A. You forgot one thing.
Q. What's that?
A. When does the statute of limitation run?
Q. We still have a few months. We'll tell her to follow up soon.
A. You have to do more than that to avoid prejudicing her case. What if she is out of town when the note arrives? Does she know the exact date the statute runs? You may have to file the

case to avoid harming her. And that, of course, means that the court will have to approve any subsequent withdrawal.[598]

§ 16.09 Solving a Conflict by Withdrawal

Taking Advantage of an Opportunity

Q. That gives me a great idea. Sometimes we get a great opportunity. A $100,000 case. And lo and behold, we've got a present client who creates a conflict. Fees from that client: two dollars and fifty cents. If you are right, we can fire that little client for no reason.

A. You are too clever by half. It's true you can withdraw for no reason. But that does not permit you to withdraw from one client, turn that client into a former client, then take on a more lucrative engagement. Though some commentators have suggested to the contrary, the case law is virtually uniform that lawyers may not drop a client like a "hot potato" to solve a conflict of interest presented by a prospective engagement.[599] It is not only unseemly but most importantly, reflects the very opposite of the loyalty we owe our clients.

Q. But if I can withdraw for no reason, why do we have all these grounds for firing the client in the rules?

A. Because if you have no reason to withdraw you must demonstrate that there is no prejudice to the client from the withdrawal. If in fact you have other permissive grounds for withdrawal, even if the withdrawal will have a material adverse effect on the client, you may proceed to invoke them.

§ 16.10 Client Fraud

Not Sure

Q. This is a hard one. I think the client is lying. I'm not sure. But I feel really uncomfortable. I know you told me I had to withdraw if the continuing representation would result in a

598. Gilles v. Wiley, Malehorn & Sirota, 783 A.2d 756 (N.J. Super. Ct. App. Div. 2001) (former client stated cause of action against lawyers who withdrew at the last minute without adequately warning her by certified mail that the statute of limitations was about to run on her medical malpractice case).

599. Universal City Studios, Inc. v. Reimerdes, 98 F. Supp. 2d 449 (S.D.N.Y. 2000); Eastman Kodak Co. v. Sony Corp., Nos. 04-CV-6095, 04-CV-6098, 2004 WL 2984297 (W.D.N.Y. Dec. 27, 2004).

violation of the Rules of Professional Conduct. In this case that is far from clear, yet I am reluctant to get to the bottom of it if I don't have to do so. Could I escape this representation?

A. Rule 1.16(b)(2) allows you to withdraw if the client persists in a course of action involving your services that you "have reason to believe" is criminal or fraudulent. That's your situation: Your services are going to be used to put a lying witness on the stand. Okay, you're not sure; but you certainly have a "reasonable belief" that is the case. Again, the only real difficulty is how to escape without violating your duty of confidentiality to your client. Even if you could make an argument that the Model Rule 1.6 exceptions for disclosure of confidential information could permit disclosure, there is no reason for you to make that disclose as part of your withdrawal, unless you are forced to do so.

Q. What if I prepared answers to interrogatories for the client and, a year later, I learn that these answers were false? This happened to one of my partners. She was furious. Could she withdraw?

A. Absolutely. Rule 3.3 requires "reasonable remedial measures" including withdrawal when the lawyer learns of a client fraud on the court. Rule 1.16(a) further requires withdrawal if the representation will involve a violation of the rules. Here, Rule 3.3 requires "reasonable remedial measures" including withdrawal. The problem may be that withdrawal alone may not be enough to correct the record.

Q. But what if I'm not sure, just worried?

A. Rule 1.16(b)(2) provides that if the lawyer reasonable believes her services have been innocently used to perpetrate a completed fraud, the lawyer may, but is not required to, withdraw. This contrasts with what would happen if a lawyer found herself part of a then ongoing fraud; withdrawal would have to be sought immediately and without discretion.[600]

Note, again, the interplay between the withdrawal rules and confidentiality. In most cases, trial lawyers are called on to defend clients for past conduct and, no matter how fraudulent the client's past conduct, the lawyer may not breach confidentiality. But once the lawyer's services are or have been used, the lawyer may be free upon withdrawal to disclose the otherwise

600. MRs 1.2(d), 4.1(b); Calley v. Woodruff, 751 So. 2d 599 (Fla. Dist. Ct. App. 1998) (lawyer who withdrew because he suspected client would commit perjury in a civil case not entitled to legal fees because lawyer made no effort to confirm his suspicion or to dissuade client from offering false testimony).

confidential information to prevent, mitigate, or rectify the effects of the fraud. Moreover, if the fraud is on the tribunal, the lawyer's duty to disclose is mandatory. But in other jurisdictions the disclosure rules in this situation range from mandatory to impermissible. The conscientious lawyer must know what her jurisdiction's rules governing confidentiality provide.[601]

§ 16.11 Moral Repugnance

A Lawyer's Dismay

Q. I know you'll help me on this one. We have a contingent-fee case. The client's injuries are serious but not nearly as worthy of a high damage award as the client thinks. And liability is far from certain. Especially when you consider how unsympathetic our client will appear. Just a nasty old man. Anyway, we were shocked. The other side offered $100,000, in a case where our bet was a $50,000 verdict. We were thrilled. But you guessed it, not our client. He thinks he'll get $500,000. Un … believable. So, we decide to withdraw based on our client's repugnant course of action. We're right, right?

A. Sorry. You are justifiably outraged. But the case law is clear. Lawyer's dismay at client's settlement decisions does not rise to the level of moral repugnance. Particularly when our ethics rules bend over backwards to make it clear that the decision to settle is exclusively that of the client. If we say the client gets to decide, we simply cannot say it is morally repugnant when the client does so.[602]

Q. OK, what is morally repugnant?

A. There's not much case law on this section, but the black letter does add to moral repugnance a client action "with which the lawyer has a fundamental disagreement." We suppose it could be the refusal of a client to permit us to point out an error to the other side that will result in wife receiving enough for child support. Or insisting on interposing a technical defense to an otherwise valid claim. Situations where the retained lawyer might say to the client that client is entitled to take a certain course of action but that this lawyer will not do it.

---

601. MR 1.6(b)(2)–(3); *see* § 13.22 in this book.

602. MR 1.2(a). *See also* State v. Jones, 923 P.2d 560 (Mont. 1996) (client's decision to accept plea bargain and waive jury trial does not constitute grounds for withdrawal).

§ 16.12 Unpaid Fees

Booting the Deadbeat

Q. Morally repugnant may be ambiguous, but refusing to pay fees on a timely basis—that's a mortal sin. Certainly, that gives a lawyer grounds to withdraw?

A. We hear your pain. The case starts out small. You represent a minor defendant. But before you know it, you've blown through the initial retainer, and you forgot to bill a couple of months. You call up the client, determined to set things right. And the ingrate responds shocked at how high the bill is, convinced you told him the initial retainer equaled the first year's fees, refusing to pay more to defend this frivolous case.

Q. Then I withdraw. Oops, I mean ask the court if I can withdraw. We don't do involuntary pro bono for individual defendants in Rule 10b-5 cases.

A. Not so fast. It is true Rule 1.16(b)(4) provides as a discretionary ground for withdrawal the failure of the client to fulfill an obligation of the representation. Lawyers always assert paying the bill is the most important example under that subsection. The courts, however, have not been so inclined. They talk about the client's obligation to cooperate in the case, supplying documents, making themselves available for depositions, that sort of thing.

Q. But it's an obligation.

A. We offer no guarantees. But you can definitely strengthen that argument if, in your engagement letter, you make two things clear: first, payment for professional invoices is an obligation; second, failure to pay on a timely basis is grounds for your seeking withdrawal from the court. In the end, of course, the judges will exercise discretion, and the hallways of courthouses around the land are crowded with lawyers who could not get out, who tried the big case for no compensation at all.[603]

---

603. Hasbro, Inc. v. Sarafino, 966 F. Supp. 108 (D. Mass. 1997) (motion to withdraw denied despite significant lack of payment by client where client had paid considerable fees to date and would be lost in a maze of litigation if unrepresented); Gibbs v. Lappies, 828 F. Supp. 6 (D.N.H. 1993) (motion to withdraw denied where counsel not paid by insolvent insurer; obligation to pay was not client insured's, withdrawal would prejudice client's case, and lawyer had not shown unreasonable financial burden or any other grounds for withdrawal); Hammond v. T.J. Litle & Co., 809 F. Supp. 156 (D. Mass 1992) (motion to withdraw granted where client's nonpayment extended over a substantial period of time, lawyer agreed to cooperate fully with new counsel and to subordinate attorney's lien to successor counsel's lien, and client-lawyer relationship irretrievably broken down).

Q. Assume I have grounds. What do I have to worry about then?

A. Great question. Grounds are not enough. First, you must communicate with your client your intention to resign and your grounds. The client may be happy. Whether happy or determined to stop you in your tracks, the client is entitled to know as soon as your intention is formed. As with a conflict of interest, the notice must be timely so the client can absorb his or her huge disappointment and decide how to respond.

Q. That'll be uncomfortable.

A. We never said withdrawal was a walk on the beach. Next you have to prepare your motion to withdraw. This raises the confidentiality issues already mentioned. The less said the better. And if, as a last resort, anything has to be disclosed that could injure the client, the disclosure should be made in camera and still with as little detail as possible.

Q. So, I am done?

A. Well, not quite. Rule 1.16 provides some guidance on the appropriate procedure the lawyer must follow in seeking to withdraw from a representation. According to subsection (d), a lawyer who seeks to terminate his representation of a client must give the client reasonable notice of the lawyer's desire to withdraw, including, in most cases, a copy of the submissions the lawyer files with the court in support of a motion to withdraw. The lawyer must also allow time for the employment of substitute counsel and be prepared to help bring substitute counsel up to speed on the case. Finally, Rule 1.16(d) requires the lawyer to give back to the client what rightfully belongs to the client—most often, papers, property, and unearned fees—and take any other steps geared toward protecting the client's interests.[604]

Q. Maybe we should just sue the deadbeat for the unpaid fees.

604. Bell & Marra v. Sullivan, 6 P.3d 965 (Mont. 2000) (law firm that withdrew because contingent fee would not be sufficient to cover the costs of protracted litigation did not have good cause to withdraw that would justify a fee award); Sage Realty Corp. v. Proskauer Rose Goetz & Mendelsohn, L.L.P., 689 N.E.2d 879 (N.Y. 1997) (client who fires lawyer with no legal fees outstanding is entitled to access entire client file, including lawyer work product, citing RLGL § 43); ABA Comm. on Ethics & Prof'l Responsibility, Formal Op. 471 (2015), Ethical Obligations of Lawyer to Surrender Papers and Property to Which Former Client Is Entitled.

A. Unless you wait until you have finished the suit without breaching any of your duties to the client, you would then compound your problems. Surely you recognize that suing a client while representing him represents the ultimate breach of your loyalty obligation.[605]

605. *In re* Simon, 20 A.3d 421 (N.J. 2011) (filing suit seeking fees against a client creates an untenable conflict under Rule 1.7 between lawyer's duty to client and lawyer's personal interest in collecting the fee).

CHAPTER 17

Supervisory and Supervised Lawyers

§ 17.01 Introduction: When to Defer to Another Lawyer's Judgment

Life would be simplified if we could rely on the judgment of an identified sage. But because even the wisest lawyer can miss an issue, a nuance of fact, or the meaning of a legal doctrine, you may find that you occasionally differ with another lawyer whose judgment you trust (or know nothing about). If so, the first step is to figure out why. It may be because one of you knows more about the facts, the law, or the application of the law to the facts.

When you discover why you disagree, then you need to identify if the issues you confront include questions of legal ethics as well as questions about the application of "other" law. We have seen, for example, that the Rules of Professional Conduct read other laws into their provisions, including criminal law, the law of fraud, and procedural rules. If your disagreement touches on any of these areas of law, more is at stake than just your client's conduct. You need to be clear about the legal limits to your conduct as well.

Once you identify why you disagree and the implications under the law governing lawyers, you need to ask if the answer to your question is arguable. If it is not, you may not rely on another lawyer's judgment. One way to make this clear to yourself and others is to write a memo that explains the law governing the matter and why the proper response is not arguable. Offer your work product to the lawyer with whom you disagree or ask another experienced lawyer to consider it. Do the same for the law governing lawyers issues and implications of the matter. Be sure to mention relevant and potentially overlapping penalties that conceivably could occur, such as professional discipline, malpractice, disqualification, fee forfeiture, or litigation sanctions. And ask another experienced lawyer for advice; you also may want to call a bar hotline, find a relevant ethics opinion, or request an opinion from a grievance authority or bar association, either of which can assist you in understanding local Rules of Professional Conduct.

If you are not in a position to make what you believe to be the only correct decision and are still uncomfortable with another lawyer's resolution of the issue, decide whether you must do something about it (tell the client, a court, or the bar; or withdraw from a representation). Ultimately, such a choice might also include looking at whether you want or are able to continue to practice law at that law firm.[606] Remember, criminal activity cannot be justified by relying on the views of your supervisor.[607] Nor could that activity be justified by failing to correct your senior partner's lie to a court during an ex parte hearing.[608] If you are the supervisory lawyer, failing to properly supervise your associate to be sure the work is done in a timely and competent manner also constitutes an independent breach of the professional rules.[609] The same can occur when you know of the conduct at a time when its consequences can be avoided or mitigated but you fail to take reasonable remedial action.[610]

---

606. Kelly v. Hunton & Williams, No. 97-CV-5631 (JG), 1999 WL 408416 (E.D.N.Y. June 17, 1999) (lawyer who reported partner's billing fraud several times within the firm entitled to cause of action for wrongful discharge where firm conditioned a favorable job reference on his silence because firm placed him in a position of choosing between continued employment and the consequences of failing to report the partner's conduct to the bar); Pane v. Goffs, No. 07-P-1929, 2009 WL 1119480 (Mass. App. Ct. Apr. 28, 2009), *rev. denied*, 914 N.E.2d 331 (cause of action for wrongful termination stated by lawyer who was fired after he refused to destroy images discovered on client's computer that evidenced illegal activity where law required disclosure to authorities).

607. People v. Casey, 948 P.2d 1014 (Colo. 1997) (lawyer who assisted his client in committing the crime of criminal impersonation was not relieved of responsibility because he was assigned to the matter by his senior partner and consulted with his senior partner about the case).

608. Daniels v. Alander, 844 A.2d 182 (Conn. 2004) (associate who failed to correct partner's false statement to a court witnessed by associate during an emergency custody hearing violated Rule 3.3).

609. *In re* Wilkinson, 805 So. 2d 142 (La. 2002) (lawyer suspended for 60 days for failing to supervise law school graduate not admitted to the bar); Attorney Grievance Comm'n v. Ficker, 706 A.2d 1045 (Md. 1998) (lawyer suspended for 120 days for conducting high volume practice failed to properly supervise inexperienced and overburdened associates so as to avoid incompetent representation); *In re* Sheridan's Case, 781 A.2d 7 (N.H. 2001) (lawyer whose associate was handling a probate estate had duty to see that work was done properly and, because his misconduct occurred mainly before injuries that might have been protected by the ADA, public censure was proper); *In re* Myers, 584 S.E.2d 357 (S.C. 2003) (supervising prosecutor who failed to supervise deputy prosecutors privately reprimanded for violating Rule 5.1).

610. MR 5.1(c).

§ 17.02 Subordinate and Supervisory Lawyers

Juniors and Seniors

Q. I can't tell you how good it is to chat today. I couldn't sleep last night.

A. Why?

Q. We're in trial. Third week. I had gone from gut-wrenching excitement to boredom. When our client's in-house counsel shows up with a new document. Actually old, but new to us. He claims he just found it. The document is really damaging. Undercuts the contract interpretation we've been asserting. Big time.

A. Well, I am hoping it's privileged.

Q. That's just it. It's from old CEO to former GC. Clearly asking advice.

A. What's the problem?

Q. There are actually two. First, the partner, who is otherwise a really good guy—even taught ethics as an adjunct once—does not want us to amend the privilege log. He says we are in the middle of the trial; it's clearly privileged so they are not entitled to it; and the act of amending the privilege log will unnecessarily arm the other side with an opportunity to create mischief. Allege wrongdoing. Give them a chance to get the document in front of the judge.

A. And the second problem?

Q. Oh that! It seems CEO sent the document to our outside auditors. Not sure why. But he did. Last time I checked that destroyed the privilege.

A. I see.

Q. Well, not exactly. I told partner my views. Told him we had no choice but to identify the document. That our duty to identify the document did not end with the selection of a jury. That's what I learned. His response? I'm a second-year associate. He's in the American College of Trial Lawyers. It is his decision to make, and he is not opening that can of worms. Then he mumbled something about if I want to make partner.

A. The rules give us the answer. Rule 5.2 says that a junior lawyer is free to defer to a supervisory lawyer on an arguable question of law.[611] Lawyers' views often differ. So long as both sides of the matter are making good faith assertions, the supervisor can

611. MR 5.2; RLGL § 12.

pull rank. For example, you might think it is not privileged because a copy was sent to a third party; but the partner might assert that the client can claim the third party was an agent for the purpose of the representation and therefore sending the copy to that individual did not break the privilege.[612]

Q. Not much help to me.

A. You've taken the time to research it?

Q. At first, I didn't think I needed to. But because he was so adamant, I decided I'd better. The law is clear on both points that the privilege was waived by sending the document to the outside auditors, and that means we have to turn over the document.

A. Then you have an obligation to go back at him one more time. But explain this time that, if he does not act, you will. It may cost you a partnership (or your job), but it will preserve your license.

The only way our system of justice fulfills the ethical requirements is if lawyers follow the rules, even when subordinate lawyers might flirt with the notion that the senior lawyers' determination to withhold the document is your "excuse." For if it ever comes out that you knew and did not act, Rule 5.2 violation will be clear. And partners don't have a monopoly on wisdom. As difficult as it may be, you must now take responsibility.[613]

A first step should be consulting someone in your practice setting. Perhaps your firm has a designated ethics counsel or an ombudsman with whom you could chat. Whatever the possibilities, this is no time to resolve the question yourself, even if it means going outside your firm to counsel with a former professor or a lawyer who specializes in advising lawyers.

§ 17.03 Supervisory and Subordinate Lawyers

Trust the Juniors

Q. I can't believe the rules of the game have changed just when I got to an exalted spot.

A. What's that mean?

612. MR 3.4(d); RLGL §§ 70 cmt. e, 105.

613. People v. Casey, 948 P.2d 1014, 1016 (Colo. 1997) (associate subject to discipline despite consulting with senior lawyer for failing to correct client's lie to the court because duty not "arguable"); Daniels v. Alander, 844 A.2d 182 (Conn. 2004) (associate reprimanded for failing to correct supervisory lawyer's false statement to a court made when associate was present).

Q. All my career I looked up to my elders. They were the experienced ones. The revered ones. The mentors. The client gatherers. Now I am the right age. But the world is not my oyster.

A. How so?

Q. It's this new technology. First email. Then the Internet. Now social media. Facebook. Twitter. You name it, and trial lawyers have been reduced to combatants in a videogame called electronic discovery. All of which leaves me totally dependent on first-year associates and paralegals, though I've been told that if I really want to succeed I should be supervised by my ten-year-old granddaughter. It's not fair.

A. It's not only not fair. It is not enough. You cannot delegate your supervisory responsibilities simply because you and social media are strangers and search terms make your eyes glaze over. Just as if Congress had passed a new statute governing environmental enforcement, Silicon Valley has passed a new way of processing information that we all must master—even those superannuated lawyers over 30![614]

§ 17.04 The Conciliatory Supervisor

Trouble . . . Everywhere

Q. I hoped this would never happen!

A. Lawyers get to say something like that all the time.

Q. Fortunately, not for this reason. I'm a senior associate. "In the window" as they say. The partners are now asking me on a regular basis what I am doing to bring in new business.

A. We all know about those campaigns. A brave new world.

Q. Not why I went to law school. Anyway, you need to know what's on the line. We have this huge case. Bet the company. Lots of discovery. I'm the senior associate. It's a billable-hour giving tree. No problem reaching my quota this year.

A. Sounds problem free.

Q. It would be. Until I was reviewing the bills going out last month. My hours—over 230—were billed at the partner's rate. $750. Instead of $400. Then I look back and saw the same as far back as April. I contacted the partner; went to see him.

614. *In re* Trahant, 108 So. 3d 67 (La. 2012) (lawyer suspended for six months for failing to detect staffer's house flipping scheme due to running a very busy, overwhelming, and voluminous real estate closing practice that he entrusted to an associate and a few nonlawyers).

A. And?

Q. He told me he would look into it. He mumbled the words "coding errors." When I did not hear anything more from him for a week, I dropped by and inquired again. His answer: it was a mix-up. Something about the pressure around here. He's on a medication for his depression.

A. And the bills? Are they corrected?

Q. I don't know.

A. We're afraid your responsibilities have not ended. While Rule 5.2 permits you to accept a supervisory lawyer's resolution of an arguable question, here there is theft, and you do not know whether the overbilling has been resolved.[615] You also do not know if the partner is fit to be practicing law. The only good news is that you do not have to resolve this problem all by yourself. You are a lawyer at a large firm. You must run both issues—possible billing fraud and the partner's health problems—to ground but only to the extent of enlisting the other partners in the firm to address these matters. Not a pleasant assignment, but even associates are lawyers and lawyers, all lawyers, must look out for their clients and their colleagues. The rules require it.[616] And further action on your part will only be required if your discreet referral does not result in appropriate action.[617]

Q. But the case goes to trial in a month.

A. Even that exigency cannot excuse a failure to act now. The trial itself could be in jeopardy.

---

615. Conn. Ethics Op. 96-20 (billing statements contained false and misleading communications about the lawyer and the lawyer's services in violation of Rule 8.4(c) when lawyer claimed to perform services that lawyer in fact did not).

616. MRs 5.1(c)(1), 5.2.

617. ABA Comm. on Ethics & Prof'l Responsibility, Formal Op. 03-429 (2003) Obligations with Respect to Mentally Impaired Lawyer in the Firm (If a lawyer's mental impairment is known to partners in a law firm or to a lawyer having direct supervisory authority over the impaired lawyer, steps must be taken that are designed to give reasonable assurance that such impairment will not result in breaches of the Model Rules. If violations have already occurred, an obligation may exist to report the violation to the appropriate professional authority. If the impaired lawyer resigns or is removed from the firm, the firm may have an obligation to discuss with the client the circumstances surrounding the change of responsibility. The obligation to report a violation of the Model Rules by an impaired lawyer is not eliminated by departure of the impaired lawyer.).

§ 17.05 The Departing Associate

The Mistaken Associate

Q. I only did it to protect the clients.

A. Did what?

Q. Gave the clients a far better alternative.

A. Alternative to what?

Q. It's a little complicated to explain. I've been at Caldwell & Moore for almost a decade. Still a senior associate. Plaintiffs' work. We take them all. The owners, I mean partners, really run an advertising colossus. We're on billboards, late night TV, the backs of buses. The associates do all the legal work for nothing while the big shots take cruises in the Mediterranean.

But we are so busy taking in new cases, we don't really treat the files with the care the clients deserve. The business model is to get the clients something as quickly as possible. Then take the next case. I have 100 files or more. Think of an assembly line running 12, 15 hours a day. When they didn't make me a partner this year I decided to act. I could give these clients what they deserve. I picked 75 files, worked on each from my home computer, told the clients I was leaving, and got them to sign engagement letters. No more assembly line. I would treat them right. And all but two signed up.

A. And then?

Q. Then I told the managing partner. I knew he wouldn't be happy. But I never envisioned what happened next. I figured I had the absolute right to leave: non-competes of lawyers are not enforceable, and the clients have an absolute right to switch lawyers. Add that up and I was on the ethical high road.

A. You may have been on the ethical high road, but you were definitely on the fairness low road.

Q. Well I knew law partners owed each other fiduciary duties. But I decidedly am not a partner, as I am reminded every month.

A. That is correct, but there still are obligations your employer and you owed the client. The partners can sue you for civil theft, for deceitful conduct while still in their employ, for signing up clients without giving the present counsel an opportunity to persuade them to stay before your former colleagues were presented with a fait accompli.[618]

Q. And they have. All of that. What I really hate is that I gave them a chance to be self-righteous. I guess I should've looked into it further before I jumped.

A. These situations are classic examples of why lawyers should not necessarily represent themselves.

618. Fla. Bar v. Winters, 104 So. 3d 299 (Fla. 2012) (two associates suspended from practice despite reversal of civil theft jury verdict against them due to lack of evidence that theft caused any client to leave firm, for unilaterally copying and taking law firm's files to use in setting up a new law practice and violating criminal theft statute); *In re Smith*, 843 P.2d 449 (lawyer who took client files to new law firm and only then informed them they had a choice about continuing counsel suspended for four months for deceitful conduct toward old law firm); Meehan v. Shaughnessy, 535 N.E.2d 1255 (Mass. 1998) (lawyer/partners had statutory right to dissolve partnership at any time, but law firm stated cause of action for breach of fiduciary duty to partners based upon departing lawyers' immediate communication with clients without notifying former partners about which clients departing lawyers intended to solicit until two weeks after their announcement to leave, by which time they had obtained authorization from a majority of the clients); Co. Bar Formal Ethics Op. 116, Ethical Considerations in the Dissolution of a Law Firm or a Lawyer's Departure from a Law Firm (2007).

CHAPTER 18

Court Orders and Court Rules

§ 18.01 Introduction: The Power of a Court

Courts have inherent power to control the conduct of matters before them, including the conduct of lawyers, parties, and witnesses. These orders can require a lawyer to represent a client,[619] enjoin[620] or disqualify[621] a lawyer from further representation of a client, impose sanctions for disregard of obligations to the court,[622] and find a party to litigation in contempt for refusing to obey a court order.[623]

Your role as an advocate is subject not only to the limit of procedural rules that govern litigation, but also to specific orders of the court, such as judicial rulings about the admissibility of evidence and the application of an evidentiary privilege. Once the order is made, a lawyer must obey (and potentially appeal), or risk a contempt citation. Civil contempt allows a judge to impose fines or imprisonment until a person complies with the court order. Criminal contempt punishes refusal to comply and requires elaborate procedural guarantees, similar to those in criminal trials.

This power of court orders is recognized in several key provisions of the Model Rules, such as Model Rule 1.6(b)(6), which allows lawyers to

619. Bothwell v. Republic Tobacco Co., 912 F. Supp. 1221 (D. Neb. 1995).

620. Maritrans GP Inc. v. Pepper, Hamilton & Scheetz, 602 A.2d 1277 (Pa. 1992).

621. Merits Incentives, LLC v. Eighth Judicial Dist. Court, 262 P.3d 720 (Nev. 2011).

622. United States v. Shaffer Equip. Co., 11 F.3d 450 (4th Cir. 1993).

623. Hughes v. Meade, 453 S.W.2d 538 (Ky. 1970) (enforcing a trial court contempt finding if lawyer does not testify on remand).

disclose client information when "required by law or court order," and Model Rule 3.4(c), which requires lawyers to obey the rules of a tribunal, including court orders.[624] These provisions recognize and integrate the legal limit of a court order into the requirement of a professional obligation.[625] They also presume that lawyers have a clear fiduciary and procedural obligation to properly raise and protect client interests. For example, lawyers have an obligation to assert the attorney-client privilege on a client's or former client's behalf whenever a nonfrivolous claim against disclosure or limitation of the scope of disclosure can be made.[626] Failure to do so could result in legally effective waiver of the privilege by the lawyer, especially when a court can later characterize the lawyer as acting with apparent authority as the client's agent.[627] Any harm that results from such a nonconsensual disclosure could then subject the lawyer to claims of malpractice or breach of fiduciary duty.[628]

Court orders also can be sought to assist your advocacy on behalf of a client. Model Rule 3.5(b) and (c) prohibits contact with jurors, unless authorized by law or court order, and Model Rule 4.2 recognizes that court orders can justify contact with represented parties.

§ 18.02 Court Orders

Contempt

Q. You know how difficult it is to get judges to understand the scope of the organizational privilege. Now we are defending a partnership against a claim by its disgruntled limited partners. Anyway, we did a pre-suit investigation. Talked to a dozen partnership employees—salespeople who peddled the limited partnerships. The plaintiffs demanded the interview notes. We claimed both privileges, citing *Upjohn*. This wrong-headed judge rejected the claim. If they are limited partners, she wrote, they are entitled to see all. We tried a mandamus

---

624. RLGL § 105; Ausherman v. Bank of Am. Corp., 212 F. Supp. 2d 435 (D. Md. 2002) (lawyer sanctioned $8,649.25 and referred to disciplinary committee for continuing to assert privilege after court ordered him to answer interrogatories and making untruthful statements in return for settlement of the case).

625. Hirschfeld v. Super. Ct., 908 P.2d 22 (Ariz. Ct. App. 1995) (lawyer convicted of criminal contempt for continuing to verbally assault a party opponent after being admonished to stop by the judge); Stark Cnty. Bar Ass'n v. Ake, 855 N.E.2d 1206 (Ohio 2006) (lawyer suspended for six months for violating several court orders during his own divorce).

626. MR 1.6 cmt. [15]; RLGL § 86; ABA Comm. on Ethics & Prof'l Responsibility, Formal Op. 94-385 (1994).

627. RLGL § 77.

628. *Id.* § 63 cmt. b.

with no success. The documents are due tomorrow, and we sure don't want to produce them.

A. Well you now have a way to get appellate review. But it'll be painful. You can refuse to turn them over. Argue irreparable injury and an entitlement to judicial review. But don't be surprised when the other side moves for contempt. And succeeds in getting such a finding.[629] But think of it this way: You'll join a long line of courageous lawyers who fell on their respective swords to defend important principles.[630] If you lose at the next level, it will be time for you to cure the contempt and turn the documents over. As painful as that might be. We don't want any lawyers in civil prison defending the privilege, no matter how wrong the judiciary gets it.

§ 18.03 Statutes of Limitation

Going All Out for the Client

Q. Our prospective client came to us with a marvelous medical malpractice claim and very serious damages. Only one problem: The statute of limitations has run. But we feel so sorry for the woman we wonder if we are free to file a complaint under those circumstances and see what happens.

A. If you have to make a representation to the court that you are within the statute, you may not do so. But if the statute of limitations is an affirmative defense, then there is nothing ethically improper about filing that complaint. Maybe the other side won't pick up on it, though that is quite unlikely. But the fact that an expired statute of limitation is an affirmative defense gives you a chance to see if your client gets lucky.

Q. And what of our reputation at the courthouse? Won't we look silly filing a complaint on this late date?

A. Well, you are not going to burnish your reputation with the court, but sometimes it is critical in effectively representing

---

629. *Id.* § 105 cmts. d, e.

630. Mohawk Indus., Inc. v. Carpenter, 558 U.S. 100 (2009) (district court orders that reject claims of privilege are not immediately appealable under the federal collateral order doctrine); Maness v. Meyers, 419 U.S. 449 (1975) (lawyer who advised a client to refuse to obey a court order to testify in order to trigger immediate appellate review of the issue and to protect the client's Fifth Amendment rights could not be punished where procedural rules provided no other means to test the validity of the trial court's ruling and the lawyer believed in good faith that disclosure of the information tended to incriminate the client); *In re* Grand Jury, 705 F.3d 133 (3d Cir. 2012) (party that wants immediate appeal of disclosure order has to suffer contempt sanctions and risk having them upheld on appeal).

a client to take measures that don't necessarily enhance your standing with the judiciary. But this slight blemish, caused by dedication to your client, should not be a reason not to try. One word of caution: make sure your client understands what a long shot this is.[631]

§ 18.04 Frivolous Lawsuits

If you are competent, you won't file a frivolous lawsuit. If you aren't careful, you can be surprised by at least two well-defined bodies of law that govern frivolous court filings:

1. Procedural rules such as Rule 11 of the Federal Rules of Civil Procedure, federal and state statutes, and the inherent power of a court, all of which can provide for monetary sanctions against errant lawyers or clients;[632] as well as professional discipline.[633]
2. Several provisions of the Model Rules prohibit frivolous suits in parallel language and further prohibit lawyers from knowingly violating the rules of a tribunal.[634] This means that the imposition of sanctions also can result in professional discipline, and vice versa.[635] Claims and assertions must be supported by a good faith basis in law and in fact, including a good faith argument for an extension, reversal, or modification of existing law.[636] You should presume that fact and law investigation are required before you file. Do not assume you are freed by notice pleading rules to allege a few facts and wait for discovery to find your cause of action.[637]

---

631. ABA Comm. on Ethics & Prof'l Responsibility, Formal Op. 94-387 (1994) Disclosure to Opposing Party and Court That Stature of Limitations Has Run (no violation of MR 3.1 or 3.3 occurs if a lawyer files a time-barred claim "so long as this does not violate the law of the relevant jurisdiction").

632. FED. R. CIV. P. 11.

633. Iowa Supreme Court Bd. of Prof'l Ethics & Conduct v. Ronwin, 557 N.W.2d 515 (Iowa 1996) (lawyer disbarred for filing frivolous lawsuits and making false accusations of criminal conduct against lawyers and judges); Attorney Grievance Comm'n v. Zdravkovich, 762 A.2d 950 (Md. 2000) (lawyer indefinitely suspended for a FED. R. CIV. P. 11 violation for failing to read a federal statute that would have made it clear that removal was not allowed); *In re* Blasi, 660 N.Y.S.2d 151 (N.Y. App. Div. 1997) (lawyer suspended for five years for filing a number of meritless law suits to settle personal disputes with a neighbor); *In re* Wood, 526 N.W.2d 513 (Wis. 1995) (lawyer suspended for 60 days for filing small claims suits against a former client to harass her).

634. MRs 3.1, 3.4(c); RLGL §§ 107, 110.

635. *In re* Blasi, 660 N.Y.S.2d 151 (N.Y. App. Div. 1997) (lawyer sanctioned for filing meritless lawsuits and suspended from practice five years).

636. MR 3.1; RLGL § 110.

637. Ashcroft v. Iqbal, 556 U.S. 662 (2009); Bell Atlantic Corp. v. Twombly, 550 U.S. 544 (2007).

If you represent a criminal defendant, you certainly may passively defend the case requiring every element of the case be established beyond a reasonable doubt, even if your investigation otherwise leads you to believe that the defense is "frivolous."[638] In criminal appeals, *Anders* briefs require you to disclose "anything in the record that might arguably support the appeal."[639]

§ 18.05 Procedure and Sanctions

Assert Any Claim, Offer Any Defense?

Q. I know I am in real trouble. But surely you have time to help a now-self-confessing sinner.

A. We are equal opportunity advice givers (just as long as you understand we are not your lawyers; you are not our client; and we are engaged in this dialogue to provide general information, not legal advice).

Q. Got it. Anyway, I took on the representation of this client. He claimed he invented the computer mouse. Showed us a dated picture from 1959 that was describing a device that provided features like the mouse we use today.

A. So, you filed suit?

Q. We did. And undeterred by the defendant's extensive informal attempts to persuade us we were wrong, and egged on by our client, we pressed on until the defendant's motion for summary judgment was granted and Judge Greenspan awarded costs to the defendant. He never does that.

A. You think that was unfair?

Q. We did until the judge then invited the defendant to file a Rule 11 motion. The defendant had already raised Rule 11 by sending us repeated notices about what they called our "frivolous" actions. Which we, of course, threw in the circular file.

A. And the Rule 11 motion?

Q. Motions. Oh they were granted. Seven in all. Attacking the complaint, the testimony, the exhibits, discovery abuses. The book was thrown at us. Do you think that was fair? We thought we were doing the Lord's work, getting this fellow his day in court. Now we owe the defendant a half million.

---

638. MR 3.1; RLGL § 110(2).

639. Anders v. California, 386 U.S. 738 (1967).

A. Fair is not our area of expertise. But we do see one line of attack. Rule 11 can only be used to sanction written documents, such as pleadings, motions, and other papers signed and filed by lawyers. So you may be able to get the sanction reduced. If some of it was based on conduct rather than written filings, the court overreached.[640]

But you are not out of the woods yet: While Rule 11 addresses frivolous signed papers, Rule 3.1 of the Model Rules of Professional Conduct is violated by frivolous conduct of the lawyer in any respect. Lawyers may proceed (1) without having substantiated every necessary fact or (2) if the lawyer plans to develop vital evidence in discovery. But once it becomes obvious that those tasks will go unfulfilled, and there is no basis for seeking an extension, modification of reversal of existing law, the lawyer must take appropriate action.

Q. What a one-two punch.

A. It does not end there. The presiding judge has even more in her arsenal if the lawyer engages in advocacy beyond established limits. It is not at all unusual for a trial judge to invoke 28 U.S.C. § 1987, a federal statute that authorizes the imposition of excess costs, expenses, and lawyer fees if the lawyer "multiplies the proceedings in any case unnecessarily and vexatiously," a standard that could permit the trial lawyer's tenacity and enthusiasm on behalf of what is considered by the court a frivolous cause.

Q. Is that all?

A. We hate to ruin your day, but there is at least one more. It is said that the courts have inherent authority beyond the civil procedure rules, the Rules of Professional Conduct, and any statutory authority. This inherent authority may be exercised upon a finding that "counsel's conduct constituted or was tantamount to bad faith."[641]

Q. So if I lose the case, I have to wait for another shoe (or shoes) to drop?

---

640. Christian v. Mattel, Inc., 286 F.3d 1118 (9th Cir. 2002) (Rule 11 sanctions limited to "papers" signed in violation of the rule; conduct in depositions discovery meetings of counsel, oral representations and behavior in proceedings do not fall within the ambit of the Rule); *In re* Tutu Wells Contamination Litig., 120 F.3d 368 (3d Cir. 1997).

641. Chambers v. NASCO, Inc., 501 U.S. 32 (1991); Christian v. Mattel, Inc., 286 F.3d 1118 (9th Cir. 2002).

A. That should not be the case. The test is based on a frivolous standard. But as you imply with your question, it is harder for the conscientious lawyer dedicated to his client's cause to get the perspective that a judge is expected to have as a neutral in the proceeding.

§ 18.06 Procedure and Statutes of Limitations

Procedural Rules: The Last-Minute Client

Q. Client comes to me with a med-mal claim. I listen patiently. Don't even see the key question. The injuries sound serious and negligence a plausible cause. But then I inquire, seeking details. Like when all this occurred. Turns out the statute of limitations arguably will expire in less than a week.

A. You are in the nick of time.

Q. Not really. In our state the law is pretty clear. Tort reform has won the day. In order to file, I need an expert prepared to testify to the violation of the standard of care. Needless to say, that is impossible. What do I do? This might be a big deal.

A. It is not your fault the client waited too long. Might not be his either. Lay people rarely understand statutes of limitation. As a result, most states will waive the normal requirements for a pre-suit investigation of some kind when the statute is about to expire.

Q. Great. Then I'll file away and plead the emergency situation. Thanks for the guidance.

. . .

Q. I took your point and filed without an expert lined up. But my search for an expert has gone on now for six months with no luck. Everyone is sympathetic with the plaintiff's plight, but to a person they say there was no negligence. Now what do I do?

A. It is time to withdraw the complaint.

Q. That is not the answer I was looking for. We took it on a contingency. I've put in dozens of hours. And my client is counting on me. I can't abandon her now. I'd be better off losing.

A. But that may not be an alternative.

Q. Why not? At least she'll get her day in court. And maybe a jury will feel sorry for her. She's quite sympathetic.

A. The problem is *you* are more likely to get your day in court.

Q. Me?

A. Yes, you. Violating the rule requiring an expert opinion may be okay if you are in an emergency to avoid the statute of limitations. But now you've had six months and, by your own admission, you've found no one. But even if that requirement were waived, there are potential sanctions that await the lawyer who pursues a claim once she knows it is meritless.[642]

§ 18.07 Procedural Rules: Continuing Obligations

An Accumulation of Difficulties

Q. We brought a claim against this physician for medical malpractice. The newborn child's injuries were profound, requiring a lifetime of care likely to cost eight figures. I had never seen such a sympathetic case. Though we hadn't been able to locate an expert witness who could assign the child's condition to some error in the delivery room—all we had was the 36 hours of labor—we thought that was enough.

A. Then what happened?

Q. The physician moved for dismissal of the complaint. His lawyer alleged it was frivolous, that an expert witness was required, and we had not located one. Nor did we find one before the motion was to be decided, yet the case cried out for relief.

A. We take it the judge did not agree.

Q. That is correct. The judge dismissed the complaint and assessed lawyers' fees to be paid by us for the cost of the physician's motion to dismiss.

A. A double insult.

Q. That is not the whole of it. Today we received a disciplinary complaint from the constabulary. Proceedings have been brought against us by those folks alleging a violation of Rule 3.1. Haven't we suffered enough?

A. It certainly sounds like you have, but this situation demonstrates a very important point. Even though there are other ways lawyers can be sanctioned under the Rules of Civil

---

642. Zamos v. Stroud, 87 P.3d 802 (Cal. 2004) (cause of action for malicious prosecution stated against lawyer who properly commenced a lawsuit then continued to prosecute it after learning it was not supported by probable cause); Jandrt *ex rel.* Brueggeman v. Jerome Foods, Inc., 597 N.W.2d 744 (Wis. 1999) (complaint was not frivolous when filed close to statute of limitations, but became so when a lawyer reasonably should have discovered the lack of causation by consulting an expert witness).

Procedure or similar statutory provisions, a disciplinary complaint also can be brought for the exact same behavior. It may sound like double jeopardy but, in fact, just as some claims can be brought under state law and also federal law, so too can lawyers be sanctioned in different forums for the same conduct. Your case is an excellent example. Rule 11 of your procedural rules may have been the basis for your sanctions in the court proceeding, but that same conduct can be found to violate Professional Conduct Rule 3.1. One may not necessarily follow the other, but it could. It is time to hire yourself a talented disciplinary lawyer to defend this proceeding.[643] We are sorry for the bad news.

The same kind of "double jeopardy" can arise in other contexts. For example, you are obliged to follow the rules governing discovery, complying with your obligations and insuring that your clients comply with theirs. But the Rules of Civil Procedure are not the only source of this obligation. Rule 3.4(c) requires you to comply with court orders. That term has been interpreted to include obligations under the Rules of Civil Procedure. So, if you fail to fulfill some obligation under the procedural rules, do not be surprised if the disciplinary folks take their own interest in that violation and bring a claim that the lawyer should be further disciplined under the Rules of Professional Conduct. Indeed, it is not unheard of for judges also to make direct referrals to the disciplinary authorities as well of those lawyers who have run afoul of the civil procedure rules.

§ 18.08 The Power of Court Sanctions to Control Discovery

Courts have a variety of procedural rules, statutes, and inherent powers to impose monetary sanctions against lawyers, clients, and law firms who file frivolous lawsuits or evade applicable discovery obligations. These rules are important for two reasons: first, violation of the rules can result in court sanctions. Second, a court determination that a

643. Shaohua He v. Holder, 781 F.3d 880 (7th Cir. 2015) (lawyer's misuse of a motion to reconsider which forfeited his client's chance for appeal on the merits referred to lawyer disciplinary committee for review); Bd. of Prof'l Responsibility v. Stinson, 337 P.3d 401 (Wyo. 2014) (lawyer publicly reprimanded for filing frivolous answer and counterclaim when information available to lawyer indicated he had reason to doubt client's veracity; no expert testimony needed to prove a violation of Rule 3.1).

lawyer has violated a relevant procedural rule also can result in professional discipline for violating Model Rules 3.1 or 3.4.[644]

Procedural rules, like Rule 11 of the Federal Rules of Civil Procedure, require lawyers to perform due diligence; that is, a reasonable inquiry into both facts and law before filing a pleading, written motion, or other paper. If the complaint is legally or factually baseless from an objective perspective and the lawyer has not conducted a reasonable inquiry into the law or facts, sanctions can follow.[645] Sanctions may include court directives of a nonmonetary nature, orders to pay a penalty into the court, and orders directing payment of reasonable attorney's fees to the movant for expenses incurred as a direct result of the violation.

With respect to discovery abuse, Federal Rule of Civil Procedure 26(g) requires discovery requests to be signed with a certification similar to Federal Rule of Civil Procedure 11, and Federal Rule of Civil Procedure 37 provides for sanctions that parallel those in Federal Rule of Civil Procedure 11 for certifications made without substantial justification. Rules of appellate procedure include similar provisions.[646]

Each of these provisions extends to specific conduct. For example, Federal Rule of Civil Procedure 11 and similar state provisions do not extend to conduct other than conduct reflected in written documents, such as oral deposition abuses or oral misstatements to a court. But beyond these procedural rules, courts have inherent power to control such conduct as long as they make explicit findings that the conduct is the equivalent of bad faith.[647] Inherent power sanctions can include fines, disqualification, discipline, and claim or defense preclusion. They do not include the "wielding of legislative power," such as the power to order parties to pay fines outside of the litigation.[648]

Federal courts also can rely on 28 U.S.C. § 1927, which authorizes them to impose "excess costs, expenses, and attorneys' fees" on a lawyer

---

644. People v. Spangler, 676 P.2d 674 (Colo. 1983) (lawyer suspended for abusing discovery in a federal court); *In re* Boone, 7 P.3d 270 (Kan. 2000) (lawyer subject to two-year probation for violating Rules 1.3, 3.1, 3.2, 3.4, and 8.4(d) for filing motions for additional time, failing to meet deadlines, and failing to respond to discovery requests); State *ex rel.* Okla. Bar Ass'n v. Patmon, 939 P.2d 1155 (Okla. 1997) (lawyer suspended for two years for, inter alia, failing to pay sanctions for discovery abuse); *In re* Anonymous Member of S.C. Bar, 552 S.E.2d 10 (S.C. 2001) (law firm partners and other lawyers who directly or indirectly supervise other lawyers could be sanctioned and subject to discipline for failing to mitigate the known misconduct of another lawyer in discovery and depositions, failing to make reasonable efforts to supervise, even without knowledge of misconduct, or failing to put systematic procedures in place to prevent misconduct); Lawyer Disciplinary Bd. v. Smoot, 716 S.E.2d 491 (W. Va. 2010) (lawyer suspended for one year for removing narrative portion of medical report before giving it to opponent).

645. Christian v. Mattel, Inc., 286 F.3d 1118 (9th Cir. 2002).

646. Matter of Hendrix, 986 F.2d 195 (7th Cir. 1993) (Federal Rules of Appellate Procedure allow for imposition of sanctions and discipline for failing to cite relevant law).

647. Chambers v. NASCO, Inc., 501 U.S. 32 (1991).

648. *In re* Tutu Wells Contamination Litig., 120 F.3d 368 (3d Cir. 1997).

who "multiplies the proceedings unreasonably and vexatiously," a standard that also requires what is essentially a finding of bad faith. If bad faith is found, other remedies such as state tort law actions for malicious prosecution might follow, at least when the plaintiff can show the institution of an action without probable cause, with the presence of malice (which can be inferred by lack of probable cause), and termination of the action in favor of the plaintiff.[649] Of course, any finding of a procedural rule violation also can result in professional discipline for violating Model Rules 3.1 or 3.4.

§ 18.09 Discovery Abuse

The Damaging Documents

Q. The bad news is my client unearthed some very damaging documents. They really will hurt my client's case. The good news is I think I've found the perfect defense to producing them. These documents came out of the warehouse of my client's subsidiary in Puerto Rico. We'll just respond that it's too burdensome for us to search for documents at any subsidiary and far too burdensome to search outside the mainland United States. No judge is going to let them go on such a fishing expedition.

A. You could get lucky and the other side could accept your objection. Or on motion practice the judge could rule your way. The problem is that you are misstating to the court and the other side the burden of producing these documents. You've already identified them. A similar ploy was tried on the *Fisons* case. Somehow the documents came out. And then the wrath of the court fell on the lawyers. Interposing such an objection was viewed harshly. And precipitated a very expensive sanction ($325,000).[650]

When it comes to the discovery process, good lawyering often trumps clever objections. Even if you can assert some basis for delaying production of certain information, the question we lawyers must always ask is whether the approach is best for the client in the long run.

---

649. Mattel, Inc. v. Luce, Forward, Hamilton & Scripps, 121 Cal. Rptr. 2d 794 (2002) (upholding a cause of action for malicious prosecution following sanctions for the same conduct in Christian v. Mattel, Inc., 286 F.3d 1118).

650. Washington State Physicians Ins. Exch. & Ass'n v. Fisons Corp., 858 P.2d 1054 (Wash. 1993).

How will the judge view the objection? What if the documents otherwise surface? Pyrrhic victories are rarely touted on law-firm websites.[651]

§ 18.10 Access to Privileged Information

Informal Discovery

Q. I'm sitting in a deposition. My client's CEO is being deposed. It's noon and we take a lunch break. Opposing counsel leaves his briefcase thrown against the credenza. No sooner does he leave than my client leans over and asks me to see what's in the briefcase.

A. And you're telling us this, why?

Q. I'm not sure I did the right thing.

A. What did you do?

Q. I told my client that was impermissible.

A. Good for you.

Q. But I am not sure. I learned in law school we have to protect privileged information like the crown jewels.

A. That's certainly true. Our ethical obligation is to ensure as much of our communication with our clients is privileged; and the privilege can be lost so easily. Let a nonclient sit in on a privileged conversation and, assuming the nonclient is not there to facilitate the privileged discussion—think interpreter, guardian, you get the idea—you lose the privilege. Send a privileged email to those who do not have a need to know, same result.

Q. Isn't that what my opponent did? If he wants to protect the contents of his briefcase, he should take it with him.

A. You can make that assertion. But we don't think it overcomes the fact that when he put the papers in his briefcase, he had an expectation of privacy. Do we really want a profession where we cannot trust each other, rifle each other's briefcases, or hack electronic communications? You would be clearly using

---

651. Rimkus Consulting Grp., Inc. v. Cammarata, 688 F. Supp. 2d 598 (S.D. Tex. 2010) (adverse inference instruction that evidence destroyed can be presumed to be prejudicial, reasonable sanction for intentional spoliation of adverse relevant email); Pension Comm. of Univ. of Montreal Pension Plan v. Banc of Am. Sec., LLC, 685 F. Supp. 2d 456 (S.D.N.Y. 2010) (failure to issue a written litigation hold constitutes gross negligence warranting adverse inference instruction that spoliating party failed to preserve evidence after its duty to preserve arose, allowing a presumption that lost evidence was relevant and would have been favorable to opposing party); Allstate Ins. Co. v. Dooley, 243 P.3d 197 (Alaska 2010) (tort of fraudulent concealment of evidence, not spoliation, is appropriate cause of action when evidence is intentionally concealed until after expiration of Alaska Civ. R. 60(b) time period for relief).

improper methods to invade the rights of another, in this case, your client's adversary. That would violate Rule 4.4 and could result in serious sanctions against your client and you; even dismissal of your client's case.[652]

Q. Does that mean we could've looked if the lawyer had left the papers on the conference room table?

A. Not really. Think of a trial. Papers strewn everywhere. No one has the energy or the time to store that stuff under lock and key even once a day, let alone five or six times. The honor among thieves is that no one looks at the other side's table. The same rule should apply here.

Q. How about if the lawyer on the other side crumpled up his notes and threw them in the wastebasket? Can I get my associate to dive in?

A. We notice you're not going to dirty your hands, you delicate thing.

Q. Partnership has its prerogatives.

A. This is a harder case. Thinking about the Fourth Amendment, one can say the lawyer has no expectation of privacy in the tossed foolscap. On the other hand, we are supposed to respect the other side's privilege. The trashcan hypo would be a perfect topic for litigators to hone their motion practice skills. You would have an argument that you were entitled to get your associate covered in coffee grounds. What we do for our clients.

§ 18.11 Insider Disclosure

Authority to Waive

Q. You've been very helpful, but I have one more question. I got a call. Weird guy. Says his name is Max. He's got info I'd find "very" interesting. I'm intrigued and tell him so. Seems it involves a big theft of trade secrets case against Colossus. How our client would love to nail them.

A. You agreed to meet?

Q. I did. He told me he'd be at the bar at The Pierre Hotel. Goofy guy. Says he'll be wearing a bow tie.

652. Jablow v. Wagner, No. A-4202-13T4, 2015 WL 1541011 (N.J. Super. Ct. App. Div. Apr. 8, 2015) (lawyer properly disqualified from case for keeping for several months and using opponent's privileged documents received from unidentified source).

A. And?
Q. And there he is. Sitting at the bar. A dog-eared manila envelope in front of him. He pushes it to my place. Asks for nothing from me. My use of the documents will be his reward, or so he says. We each order a drink, discuss the hapless Mets and off he went.
A. You didn't find out who he is?
Q. Max!
A. We know that, or maybe we don't, but you asked him no questions?
Q. Didn't want to learn too much. And no, I haven't opened the envelope. Doesn't mean I'm not anxious to do so. You think I can?
A. We don't know enough. If they are privileged documents of your client's adversary, it is highly unlikely Max has the authority to waive that party's privilege. And, of course, if you review purloined privileged documents, you could be in real trouble. Your client, too. Just too risky.
Q. What if I got you to review them? You're not in the case. You could tell us whether we have any claim to them. Maybe they are non-privileged documents, wrongfully withheld in discovery.
A. A taint team?
Q. If DOJ claims it can do that, why not me?
A. We think that'll work, but if you cannot find someone to do that for you, don't do it yourself. Such informal discovery could be your undoing.

§ 18.12 The Power of Disqualification

Help Behind the Scenes

Q. I only wanted to help.
A. If that's all there is, we are sure you did nothing wrong.
Q. I was handling this patent infringement suit. Good stuff. When our client's adversary was purchased by Acme, a client of our firm.
A. Then what did you do?
Q. We resisted a motion to disqualify. Argued no conflict because Acme is in a different line of business than its new sub. But the judge wasn't buying. Something about one integrated enterprise. He disqualified us.

A. Well you fought the good fight.

Q. Not exactly past tense. We withdrew our appearance. Our client hired new counsel. One of our former associates. At our suggestion. We knew he would work well with us.

A. He what?!!!

Q. Promised to work with us. We would have to be behind the scenes. The judge wouldn't know.

A. Don't tell us. The judge found out?

Q. It was ugly. New counsel was arguing a technical point. To support his argument he asserted that our firm assured him the argument was a winner. The judge dropped his pen, stared off onto the distance and summoned our firm to be in his chambers in 20 minutes, a deadline we could never have met. We show up in an hour. Our office is 20 miles from the courthouse. Then matters turned really ugly. He accused us of misrepresentation, violating a court order, contempt of court, and he referred us to the disciplinary authorities. Even though we never appeared in court, took no depositions, stayed away from the mediation.

A. You have to remember that the Rules of Professional Conduct are rules of reason. They focus on substance, not form. You were disqualified. That means you could have no role in the matter. No crossed fingers. No hidden participation. Your conflict infects the representation either way, in plain sight or behind a curtain and to the same effect.

Q. And all we wanted was to protect our client.

A. Your former client.

Q. True.

A. And collect a fee.

Q. Also true. We had already budgeted 100K per month in fees. And that disqualification order cut that in half.

A. Other than a temper tantrum, did the judge do anything else?

Q. Oh yes. He fined us $25,000 and referred us to the Ohio legal police. We have our hands full.

A. We wish you good luck. Your lesson will not be lost on anyone.

CHAPTER 19

Crime and Fraud

§ 19.01 Introduction: The Criminal Law and Professional Obligation

Lawyers have no special immunity from the criminal law, either in representing clients or in their own personal conduct outside of law practice. You need to be aware of the contours of the vast scope of the criminal law (constituting thousands of federal and state crimes) both to avoid committing crimes yourself and to provide competent counsel to clients. Courts typically impose severe disciplinary sanctions on lawyers convicted of serious crimes, including all felonies, and any misdemeanors that reflect adversely on the lawyer's fitness to practice, such as misrepresentation, fraud, deceit, bribery, extortion, theft and misappropriation, and crimes involving interference with the administration of justice.[653]

---

653. MR 8.4(b); RLGL § 5; ABA Model Rule for Lawyer Disciplinary Enforcement, Rule 19; Fla. Bd. of Bar Exam'rs *Re* Castro, 87 So. 3d 699 (Fla. 2012) (lawyer who paid kickbacks and bribed a judge engaged in such egregious conduct that no evidence of subsequent rehabilitation would ever be enough to allow readmission); *In re* Keaton, 29 N.E.3d 103 (Ind. 2015) (lawyer disbarred for pursuing a stalking, harassment, and intimidation campaign of revenge against daughter's college roommate who ended intimate relationship with him); Ky. Bar Ass'n v. Maze, 397 S.W.3d 891 (Ky. 2013) (former county attorney disbarred for crimes including vote buying and perjury, as well as violation of Rules 3.4(a) and 3.5(b) for misconduct related to jury tampering, although he was investigated for but not charged with jury tampering in his criminal case); *In re* Braunstein, 42 A.3d 153 (N.J. 2012) (lawyer suspended for one year for being convicted of attempted coercion based on his threat to file a discrimination lawsuit and accuse his supervisor of theft if he was not promoted and paid $750,000); Disciplinary Counsel v. Calabrese, 36 N.E.3d 151 (Ohio 2015) (lawyer disbarred for committing more than two dozen felonies including corruption, bribery, fraud, and racketeering); Disciplinary Counsel v. Pappas, 21 N.E.3d 260 (Ohio 2014) (lawyer suspended two years after being convicted of making false

The Model Rules also require that you refrain from knowingly counseling or assisting a client crime and, if necessary, withdraw to prevent this from happening.[654] You cannot avoid this through stupidity or willful blindness. "Knowingly" means that you know of the client's activity, not that you "know" it constitutes a fraud or crime.[655] Further, your knowledge of the facts can be inferred from the circumstances.[656] If you fail to discover the crucial fact you hoped did not exist, you have disserved your client, who could have avoided the crime, and you may have set yourself up for a malpractice suit as well.

In short, you cannot commit a crime, and you cannot counsel or assist your client to do so. Remembering the following four-step analysis can help you avoid both.

- First, be competent. Know the law and facts of a matter sufficiently to provide competent legal advice. Criminal law has reached into corners where you might not expect it, and a change in what your client does may push the conduct from legal into illegal territory (or vice versa).[657]
- Second, communicate criminal law boundaries to your client and make clear that you do not counsel and cannot assist conduct that crosses those lines.[658]
- Third, if you know that your client's conduct is yet to occur or is continuing and, after your heart-to-heart, your client will not desist, you must withdraw to avoid assisting the crime.[659] And, if you have a reasonable belief, but do not have enough facts about the conduct to know whether it constitutes a crime or fraud, you may withdraw.[660]

statements to federal authorities); Disciplinary Counsel v. Dann, 979 N.E.2d 1263 (Ohio 2012) (lawyer suspended six months after being convicted for misdemeanors for paying two employees under the table and filing false financial disclosure forms while attorney general).

654. MR 1.2(d); RLGL § 23.

655. *In re* Bloom, 745 P.2d 61 (Cal. 1987) (lawyer could not defend disciplinary charge by arguing he did not know client's transport of plastic explosives to Libya was unlawful); Fla. Bar v. Brown, 790 So. 2d 1081 (Fla. 2001) (lawyer who failed to consider legality of assisting client's criminal campaign reimbursement scheme should have known scheme was criminal or fraudulent).

656. MR 1.0(f).

657. MR 1.1.

658. MRs 1.2(d), 1.4(a)(5); Stichting Ter Behartiging Van de Belangen Van Oudaandeelhouders In Het Kapitaal Van Saybolt Int'l B.V. v. Schreiber, 327 F.3d 173 (2d Cir. 2003) (cause of action for legal malpractice stated against lawyers who gave flawed advice about whether entity's action was bribery of a foreign official, even though company later pled guilty to crime); *In re* Sharp, 802 So. 2d 588 (La. 2001) (lawyer suspended for one year for assisting client in attempting to bribe a witness to drop the charges in client's criminal case by drafting receipt for client to give witness); *In re* Breslin, 793 A.2d 645 (N.J. 2002) (lawyer whose client attempted to bribe the police commissioner censured because he should have advised client that lawyer could not participate in illegal activity).

659. MRs 1.2(d), 1.16.

660. MR 1.16(b)(2).

- Finally, if your client's future conduct threatens serious physical or financial harm, or if your client is an organization, check the exceptions to confidentiality in your jurisdiction to determine if you have discretion (or an obligation) to take action including disclosure to prevent or rectify harm.[661]

Be especially careful about the criminal law when you represent a heavily regulated client, or when you represent a client in a matter where you have had little experience. Lawyers have been disciplined for helping clients commit crimes of which the lawyer was totally unaware.[662]

Lawyers who do not directly violate a criminal provision but advise clients who do so may be accountable as accomplices or co-conspirators. Further, lawyers who know that their clients are paying them with the fruits of the crime also risk a charge of aiding and abetting the crime or other criminal accountability, such as a charge of receiving stolen property.

Typical accomplice statutes prohibit the purposeful or intentional aiding, abetting, advising, assisting, counseling, or encouraging the criminal act of another.[663] The *mens rea* (mental state) of these provisions roughly parallels the knowledge requirement of Model Rule 1.2(d), and the "counsels or assists" prohibition in the Model Rule roughly parallels the *actus reus* (conduct element) of these criminal statutes. Lawyers convicted of aiding and abetting usually face professional discipline for violating this provision as well as Model Rule 8.4(b).[664]

Lawyers who intend to commit a serious crime (*mens rea*) and agree to aid the client in committing it (*actus res*) also can become entangled in client crimes as co-conspirators.[665] Unlike accomplice liability, conspiracy to commit a crime constitutes a separate crime, even if the underlying crime is not completed. To be found guilty of conspiracy, a lawyer need not aid, abet, or assist the client's crime as long as she pur-

---

661. MRs 1.6(b)(1)–(3), 1.13(c).

662. People v. Casey, 948 P.2d 1014 (Colo. 1997) (lawyer suspended for 45 days for entering an appearance and getting a case dismissed for a client who had given the police a false name and, therefore, assisted the client in committing the crime of criminal impersonation, despite good faith but unsuccessful attempt to bring his ethical dilemma to a supervising lawyer's attention).

663. Wayne R. LaFave, Substantive Criminal Law § 13.2 (4th ed. 2003); Model Penal Code § 2.06 (Am. Law Inst. 1962).

664. *In re* REFCO Secs. Litig., No. 07-CV-6767, 2010 WL 3911780 (S.D.N.Y. Sept. 28, 2010) (lawyer was disbarred and subject to damages in a civil RICO action following criminal conviction for conspiracy in client's securities fraud); *In re* DeRose, 55 P.3d 126 (Colo. 2002) (lawyer disbarred who pleaded guilty to aiding and abetting a client's illegal structure of financial transactions to evade reporting requirements).

665. *In re* Palmer, 835 So. 2d 410 (La. 2002) (lawyer convicted of conspiracy to defraud and disbarred for furthering entity client's sham transactions by backdating documents, despite testimony of U.S. Attorney that convictions of principals would not have been possible without lawyer's cooperation.)

posely promotes the criminal act and agrees with the client that one of them will commit it.[666] Like accomplices, lawyer co-conspirators often face professional discipline as well.[667]

§ 19.02 Crime

Political Assistance

Q. What a quandary. Our client, the Illuminating Company, does a lot of business with the Commonwealth of Virginia: lobbyists galore, bundling political contributions; you get the idea. Now there's a big tribute dinner to fund the next campaign. They say if they can buy two tables, they are sure their application for a new facility will be looked upon with favor. But the company has maxed out. They want our firm to buy a table. Ten thousand bucks. For the Local People's Party. We would certainly earn the undying affection of Illuminating.

A. Clients lean on lawyers all the time. Chamber of Commerce dinners, Boys Club testimonials honoring the CEO, galas for the orchestra. And lawyers certainly succumb to client imprecations. They have no choice. But here, the question is the legality of the "contribution." If Illuminating were reimbursing you for the cost ("charge us what you wish"), it would be illegal, probably criminal.[668] If the contribution were a bribe, a quid pro quo, that too would be criminal. And lawyers may not engage in criminal conduct.[669] On the other hand, simply currying the favor of politicians is an ancient and hoary

666. Model Penal Code § 5.03 (Am. Law Inst. 1962); 18 U.S.C. § 371 (2012).

667. *In re* Petition of Anderson, 851 S.W.2d 408 (Ark. 1993) (lawyer convicted of conspiracy with client to possess cocaine with intent to distribute failed to gain readmission to the bar); *In re* Lee, 755 A.2d 1034 (D.C. 2000) (lawyer convicted of conspiracy with client to launder money disbarred).

668. Fla. Bar v. Brown, 790 So. 2d 1081 (Fla. 2001) (lawyer suspended 90 days for assisting client in violating campaign finance laws); *In re* Convery, 765 A.2d 724 (N.J. 2001) (lawyer suspended for 6 months for pleading guilty to a federal misdemeanor of promising employment in return for political activity when he was discovered to have used his local political position and influence to pressure a local zoning board to grant a variance for his client); Disciplinary Counsel v. Conese, 812 N.E.2d 944 (Ohio 2004) (lawyer Board of Elections member convicted of a misdemeanor and suspended for two years for threatening to fire a Board of Elections employee unless the employee agreed to contribute 100 percent of his salary to the county Democratic party).

669. *In re Convery*, 765 A.2d 724 (lawyer suspended for six months for pleading guilty to a federal misdemeanor of promising employment in return for political activity when he was discovered to have used his local political position and influence to pressure a local zoning board to grant a variance for his client); Disciplinary Counsel v. Conese, 812 N.E.2d 944 (lawyer Board of Elections member convicted of a misdemeanor and suspended for two years for threatening to fire a Board of Elections employee unless the employee agreed to contribute 100 percent of his salary to the county Democratic party).

American tradition. Your assignment is to spend a little time assuring yourself that your firm's $10,000 is the latter, not the former. If not, you'll have to find a different excuse for not succumbing to your client's imprecations.

§ 19.03 Extortion

The Appropriate Threat

Q. I can't believe it. Our client was defrauded. The swindler on the other side knows it. His lawyer does too. But these guys know my client is desperate for the money and our slow docket means the case won't be heard for three years. They offer a pittance in the hopes of squeezing the poor widow. I've been looking for some leverage. We already added punitive damages. I thought of a class action but I don't think we really have an identifiable class—this guy swindled so many different ways. Then I thought I'd threaten criminal prosecution. But something tells me that's not permitted.

A. It wasn't permitted in the old days. But that provision has been repealed. There's an ABA opinion on point.[670] You can now threaten a criminal complaint on two conditions. The first is that you must have a good faith basis.

Q. No problem there. This was white collar highway robbery.

A. And the second is that the threatened criminal prosecution is related to the civil claim.

Q. This is the same thing. What he did is a sin . . . and criminal, too.[671]

---

670. ABA Comm. on Ethics & Prof'l Responsibility, Formal Op. 94-383 (1994) Use of Threatened Disciplinary Complaint Against Opposing Counsel (a lawyer's use of the threat of filing a disciplinary or criminal complaint against opposing counsel to obtain an advantage in a civil case is constrained by the prohibitions in MRs 8.3, 8.4 (b), 4.1, 3.1, and 4.4. Such a threat may not be used as a bargaining point when the subject misconduct raises a "substantial question" under MR 8.3, and would also be improper if the misconduct is unrelated to the civil claim, is not well-founded in fact and in law, or if the threat has no substantial purpose other than to embarrass, delay, or burden opposing counsel or his client, or prejudice the administration of justice). *See also In re* Kenny, 217 P.3d 36 (Kan. 2009) (lawyer disciplined for using the threat of a disciplinary complaint to assist his clients in obtaining a fee refund from his clients' former lawyer; lawyer violated Rules 4.4, 8.3, and 8.4 because his letters had no substantial purpose other than to coerce a refund of the attorney's fee (Rule 4.4(a)), because he believed he had knowledge of a violation of the rules and did not report (Rule 8.3(a)), and because his demand letters constituted conduct prejudicial to the administration of justice (Rule 8.4(d)); State v. Hynes, 978 A.2d 264 (N.H. 2009) (lawyer who demanded $1,000 from hair salon to avoid a baseless lawsuit committed theft by extortion).

671. Iowa Supreme Court Disciplinary Bd. v. Stowers, 823 N.W.2d 1 (Iowa 2012) (lawyer suspended for 90 days for sending threatening email that could be deemed extortionate to director of charity lawyer's wife was suing).

A. Then you can threaten away. Extortion is a crime. But threatening to seek the assistance of the constabulary to concentrate your opponent's mind is perfectly okay.[672]

§ 19.04 Criminal Aiding and Abetting

Legitimate Advice

Q. We do a lot of tax work at this firm. Even do some tax litigation. We represent our clients zealously but keep in mind our obligations to assure ourselves that our clients are complying with the law, which brings me to the present problem. One of my colleagues represents an extremely wealthy couple. We do their tax returns. And this year, as usual, my partner met with the clients just last week. When discussing business expense deductions, the couple included what my colleague knew to be their daughter's wedding party. The reason: She and her husband attended the event. When my partner raised this issue with the clients, they immediately temporized. Then began the hard part. They asked my partner if they deducted this expense what were the chances of getting caught. My partner immediately informed them that we could not participate, when husband announced, "No, we'll take care of the tax return this year. Just tell us the answer to the question. May we?"

A. One point is clear: You may not aid and abet an income tax fraud. But the tax return has now been taken out of your hands. Is the client now entitled to the information he seeks? It would seem the only reason you are being questioned is because they plan to deduct that wedding. Giving them the correct answer, if you know it, may encourage or discourage them from doing the right thing. We think they are entitled to the answer, but it should be accompanied by yet one more warning of the consequences of engaging in such criminal conduct.[673]

---

672. Tessier v. Rockefeller, 33 A.3d 1118, 1132 (N.H. 2011) (cause of action for fraudulent misrepresentation and negligent infliction of emotional distress by lawyer's spouse against another lawyer who allegedly threatened to report her husband to the disciplinary office and to file criminal charges against him unless the plaintiff agreed to execute a reverse mortgage on, and release her homestead interest in, the family home; fraud allegedly occurred when lawyer notified the disciplinary board despite promise not to do so if money was released; negligent infliction of emotional distress because the defendants' scheme coerced plaintiff into "doing an action that she could not be legally bound to do").

673. Estate of Trompeter v. C.I.R., 111 T.C. 57, 69 (T.C. 1998) (Swift, J. concurring) ("I note that under current law and ethical guidelines, tax return preparers may no longer consider the audit lottery when evaluating the 'reasonableness' of tax return positions."). *See* Regulations Governing Practice Before the Internal Revenue Service, 31 C.F.R. pt. 10 (2014).

§ 19.05 Generally Applicable Law: Treasury Regulation 8300

Obeying the Law

Q. When I started a criminal law practice, I knew that some days my collar might get very tight. But I did not expect this one. New client calls me up. He has been charged with embezzlement and wants to hire me. I tell him I require a $15,000 retainer. "No problem," he replies, and insists on a meeting that afternoon.

A. Smart move getting that retainer.

Q. Not so fast. This is what happened. He shows up with a large duffle bag and promptly lays out $15,000 in cash on my desk in $10 bills. Fifteen thousand dollars is a lot of money. I am aghast, and I tell him, "You know I am going to have to report this." His response, "My last criminal lawyer told me he would keep everything confidential. Don't you follow the same rules?"

A. We feel your pain. Your client surprised you with a cash payment before you could warn him of the consequences. Now you have received a fee of $15,000, all in cash. Over 20 years ago, one brave lawyer challenged the federal statute that requires the reporting of cash transactions. Argued, for good reasons, it should not apply to lawyers. But he lost.[674] And so we are afraid you are going to be required to report the transaction or else violate that statute.

Q. Can I just return the money to him?

A. Read the Regulation, it applies to you.

674. Lefcourt v. United States, 125 F.3d 79 (2d Cir. 1997), *cert. denied,* 524 U.S. 937 (1998) (criminal defense lawyer's unsuccessful challenge to Treasury Regulation 8300 as applied to lawyers; lawyers are not exempt from disclosing a client's name on a Treasury Form 8300 required for the receipt of cash transactions over $10,000); Office of Disciplinary Counsel v. Massey, 687 N.E.2d 734 (Ohio 1998) (lawyer suspended for six months for conduct involving dishonesty and conduct prejudicial to the administration of justice for attempting to assist client in structuring transactions to evade IRS Form 8300 filing requirement); *In re* Vanderveen, 211 P.3d 1008 (Wash. 2009) (criminal defense lawyer disbarred for willfully violating federal cash reporting laws for not reporting accepting two paper bags containing $20,000 in cash).

§ 19.06 Generally Applicable Law: Fair Debt Collection Practices Act

Debt Collection

Q. We just got a new client that should really help our bottom line.

A. Congratulations, tell us more.

Q. The state AG is tired of debt collection. They assigned the cases to us as "special counsel" to collect debts.

A. And?

Q. We got creative. We used AG letterhead to send our dunning letters, and we marked up each claim by 50 percent so we could cover our fees. The taxpayers should be happy.

A. But then you found out that lawyers are covered by the federal Fair Debt Collection Practices Act?[675]

Q. How did you know? But we read the law and there is an exemption for "officers" of the state. We figure we must qualify.

A. At least one court has said you do not—only those specifically authorized to act for the state by state statute are covered. And we are also the bearers of more bad news.[676]

Q. Are you kidding me? The AG has been so happy with us.

A. But the AG doesn't control federal law that applies to all debt collectors, including lawyers. And charging 50 percent more, unless it amounts to something like a transcription error, seems to be a prohibited practice under the federal statute.[677]

Q. If we change our practices, are we home free?

A. Except for penalties under the act in cases you have already filed. And if your 50 percent markup was not just a mistake but a misrepresentation, then discipline could follow as well.[678]

---

675. Heintz v. Jenkins, 514 U.S. 291 (1995) (FDCPA applies to lawyers who are regularly engaged in consumer debt collection on behalf of a creditor client).

676. Gillie v. Law Office of Eric A. Jones, LLC, 785 F.3d 1091 (6th Cir. 2015) (although authorized by the state attorney general to collect state debts, private lawyers were independent contractors and did not act as officers of the state so as to qualify for exemption from act's requirements).

677. Powell v. Palisades Acquisition XVI, LLC, 782 F.3d 119, 128 (4th Cir. 2014) (law firm that overstated debt due by more than 50 percent liable under act unless it could justify a "bona fide error" defense).

678. MR 8.4(c).

§ 19.07 Crime or Fraud

The Good-Deed Crime

Q. We planned it for months. Talked about it even longer. We had been at Richards Richards & Richards for almost a decade. That's where chumps in the middle of their class at no-name law schools end up. Working at plaintiffs' mills. High volume; small injuries. Ads on the subway. The back of buses. Runners monitoring police radios. Churning them out. Barely on the right side of the ethics line.

A. Violating the rules?

Q. We didn't worry about that much. We were associates. We finally realized we would always be associates. Unless we married a partner's daughter. And none of them would stoop to marry low-lifes like us.

A. You know associates are lawyers, too. Rule 5.2.

Q. We remembered that, but we always figured the bar police would come after the partners. Took a chance to keep our jobs. If we had rocked the boat, we would have been replaced by clones of us, only at even lower salaries.

Then we decided to go out on our own. We could do this better. And treat the clients the way they deserve to be treated.

A. You left.

Q. Not before we planned very carefully. We lined up the clients, got new engagement letters, and found space.

A. Without telling anyone?

Q. Of course. How else could we succeed?

You taught us that clients can fire their lawyers at any time for a good reason or no reason at all. That was enough for us. We were supporting client autonomy. And they all followed. None of them had ever met a Richards. Those guys were too busy flying their Gulfstream between family resorts. Made it easy.

A. And when they discovered you had absconded with their clients?

Q. Our clients. And we did not abscond. We gave them a choice. They chose wisely.

A. Why are you here?

Q. We've been sued. For deceitful conduct. For theft. Even the district attorney is investigating. And we have been slapped with a disciplinary complaint. All because we did what was in the best interests of our clients.

A. You were right about the client's rights. But what you forgot is that you also are subject to other law. In this case, you owed some duties to your employer. Inconsistent with them was a future plan to quit and take all the clients before the partners had any notice. Partners of course owe each other fiduciary duties. But associates owe duties too. You ran afoul of all of them.

§ 19.08 The Law of Fraud and Professional Obligation

The law of fraud limits the legally acceptable conduct of lawyers and clients. If your client commits fraud, civil or criminal remedies could result. If you do so, you face the same consequences plus a third possibility: professional discipline.[679] Moreover, if you assist your client or fail to warn him off, you also may be subject to tort liability as well as professional discipline.[680]

The Model Rules contain four provisions that effectively incorporate all of the law of fraud, deceit, dishonesty, and misrepresentation into a professional obligation. Lawyers can be disciplined if they make false statements of material fact to tribunals or third persons while representing clients, even if the statement is not relied on and does not cause harm.[681] Lawyers also can be disciplined for any conduct (representing a client or not) "involving dishonesty, fraud, deceit or misrepresentation."[682] Beyond your own conduct, you can be disciplined for knowingly counseling or assisting your client's fraudulent or criminal conduct.[683]

The vast scope of the modern law of fraud reflects its common occurrence and often disastrous consequences. Liars are "free riders": Persons who hope to gain an advantage from everyone else's honesty while benefiting from their own deceit.[684] Deceitful practices can undercut competition, raise the price of goods, and cause loss of confidence

679. *In re* Herman, 348 P.3d 1125 (Or. 2015) (en banc) (lawyer disbarred for diverting funds from a company he established with nonlawyer partners to other businesses the lawyer controlled).

680. Thomas Lee Equity Fund V, L.P. v. Mayer Brown, Rowe & Maw LLP, 612 F. Supp. 2d 267 (S.D.N.Y. 2009) (cause of action stated for common-law aiding and abetting a fraud against law firm for partner's repeating of client's intentional misstatements during due diligence in a leveraged buyout); *In re* REFCO Secs. Litig., No. 07-CV-6767, 2010 WL 3911780 (S.D.N.Y. Sept. 28, 2010) (same lawyer was disbarred and subject to damages in a civil RICO action following criminal conviction for conspiracy in client's crime).

681. MRs 3.3(a)(1) (making false statements of fact to a tribunal), 4.1(a) (making false statement of material fact to a third person).

682. MR 8.4(c).

683. MRs 1.2(d), 3.3(a)(3), 3.3(b), 4.1(b).

684. Sissela Bok, Lying: Moral Choices in Public and Private Life 23 (2d ed. 1999).

in the market system by diminishing trust in its mechanisms. In some cases, fraud can chill faith in individual relationships and social ties. Your advice can play a central role in avoiding these massive personal and social costs.

The law of fraud includes hundreds of criminal provisions as well as extensive tort liability. Dishonest conduct also creates a defense to otherwise valid claims, and invalidates an otherwise lawful consent in tort, property, and contract law. In short, fraud vitiates everything, even court orders and judgments.[685]

To sum up: You cannot lie, and if your client does, you probably have to do something about it. Lies short of actual fraud or crime do not trigger a duty to remedy a client lie, but if your client or you are close to the line, remember the four steps to identifying and responding to the limits of the law:

- Competence requires that you know just how close to which legal line the conduct or proposed conduct creeps.[686]
- Communication demands that you tell your client so, in clear terms.[687]
- If the conduct is over the line of crime or fraud, you must withdraw.[688] If it makes you worry, and you have a reasonable belief it might constitute a crime or fraud, you may withdraw.[689]
- If your client will not desist from questionable conduct, you need to identify if your withdrawal from the matter prevents your assistance in the matter. If it is not enough, check to determine whether your jurisdiction's confidentiality exceptions require or allow disclosure to prevent, mitigate, or rectify the harm. If an exception exists, you also may also have an obligation to disclose if doing so is reasonably necessary to prevent assisting the client's crime or fraud.[690]

---

685. Sydney E. Williams, Kerr on Fraud and Mistake 4 (1928).

686. MR 1.1.

687. MR 1.4(a)(5).

688. MRs 1.2(d), 1.16(a); *In re* Potts, 158 P.3d 418 (Mont. 2007) (lawyer subject to discipline for failing to withdraw when client fraudulently induced other parties to enter into a settlement agreement).

689. MR 1.16(b)(2).

690. MR 4.1(b); RLGL § 98.

The law of fraud also includes the tort of misrepresentation, which forms the basis for understanding the potential for liability far beyond a client-lawyer relationship.[691]

In tort, "fraud" includes both intentional as well as reckless misstatements. To be liable, the defendant does not have to intend harm to the plaintiff, but only has to know he is lying, or recklessly ignoring the truth.[692] This distinction is important, because the lawyer's liability for fraud extends to all foreseeable third persons who reasonably rely on the false information.[693] If the lawyer's material misrepresentation is merely negligent, liability usually extends to a more limited group of persons identified at the time the statements were made.

Although the tort of misrepresentation usually requires an affirmative misrepresentation, there are a few occasions when failure to speak can create liability as well. Fiduciary duties create obligations to disclose, which means that lawyers, who owe fiduciary duties to clients, have affirmative duties to disclose material information to them.[694] A duty to disclose also may arise when previous statements have become untrue, misleading, or material.[695] For example, a lawyer may have a duty to disclose tax liens to a prospective purchaser at a foreclosure sale if the buyer was induced to bid by the lawyer's incomplete prior representations.[696]

Whenever you state a fact orally or in writing that you expect another will rely on, do not depend solely on your client for determining the

---

691. The Restatement (Second) of Torts §§ 525–552(c) provide the basic elements of a cause of action for misrepresentation: (1) Making a false representation (by words or actions), or failing to speak when (a) a fiduciary obligation exists, or (b) previous statements made have become untrue, misleading or material; (2) Concerning a presently existing material fact; (3) Which the representor knows to be false or is made recklessly, knowing that there is insufficient knowledge upon which to base the representation, or which is made negligently; (4) For the purpose of inducing another to act; (5) The other party reasonably relies on the representation; and (6) To his injury or damage.

692. Slotkin v. Citizens Cas. Co. of N.Y., 614 F.2d 301, 307 (2d Cir. 1979) (insurance defense lawyer liable for fraud for settling medical malpractice case after stating that "to the best of his knowledge" there was no excess insurance coverage, when lawyer's file indicated otherwise); Fire Ins. Exch. v. Bell, 643 N.E.2d 310 (Ind. 1994) (plaintiff's counsel had right to rely on insurance defense counsel's representation of policy limits even though plaintiff's lawyer could have used discovery to ascertain limits).

693. RLGL § 56 cmt. f; Restatement (Second) of Torts § 531 (Am. Law Inst. 1977); Ultramares Corp. v. Touche, Niven & Co., 174 N.E. 441 (N.Y. 1931).

694. Baker v. Dorfman, 239 F.3d 415 (2d Cir. 2000) (lawyer liable for fraud, including compensatory, emotional distress, and punitive damages for lying about the extent of his legal experience and failing to disclose all relevant facts to a client).

695. Restatement (Second) of Torts § 551 (Am. Law Inst. 1965). *See also In re* Alcorn, 41 P.3d 600, 604 (Ariz. 2002) (trial lawyers who made a secret agreement with opposing counsel to dismiss action against their client fined and disciplined for failing to disclose agreement to trial judge who indicated he did not want any sweetheart deals or anything "crafted" that "would be misleading" to him); People v. Rolfe, 962 P.2d 981, 982 (Colo. 1998) (lawyer censured for violating Rule 3.3(a)(1) for stating that a social worker had "begun" her investigation of the matter, but failed to inform the court about the existence of social worker's letter that concluded no abuse could be substantiated).

696. Gerdin v. Princeton State Bank, 371 N.W.2d 5 (Minn. Ct. App. 1985).

truth of the matter. Lawyers have been held liable for fraud and negligent misrepresentation to third parties when they believed their client's lie and innocently (they thought) repeated it.[697]

Lawyers accustomed to the six Cs easily can assume that their only responsibility is to their clients. The law of fraud is but one example of potential liability to others beyond your clients.

If your client or you invite a third party to rely on your work, and if you negligently produce it causing harm to the third party, you can be held liable to both your client and the third party.[698] One example is an invitation to rely on your legal opinion (which may be required by the third party as part of a transaction).[699] You may avoid this reliance by making clear that your opinion or representation is intended for the client only, or by making clear that you are relying on the client's provision of facts without an independent investigation.[700] Similarly, if you invite a nonclient to rely on your services, for example, by offering to record a deed at a real estate closing, and the opposing party suffers harm as a result of your deficient performance, that party will have a cause of action against you if you fail to follow through competently with the task you undertook.[701]

You also owe duties of competence to third-party beneficiaries of your client (such as intended beneficiaries of your client's will or trust) regardless of their reliance on your work.[702] Here, everything depends on the clarity of your client's intent.

Beyond intended beneficiaries, most courts impose a duty to prevent economic harm only when liability for misrepresentation or its statutory equivalents, such as securities fraud, can be established.[703]

---

697. Greycas, Inc. v. Proud, 826 F.2d 1560, 1562 (7th Cir. 1987) (lawyer liable for fraud and negligent misrepresentation to lender when client defaulted on loan for stating that he had "conducted a UCC, tax and judgment search" but instead relied on client's statements that no liens existed on farm property).

698. RLGL § 51.

699. MR 2.3; RLGL § 95.

700. RLGL § 51 cmt. e.

701. Nelson v. Nationwide Mortgage Corp., 659 F. Supp. 611 (D.D.C. 1987) (lawyer volunteered to answer questions and explain document); Kremser v. Quarles & Brady, L.L.P., 36 P.3d 761 (Ariz. Ct. App. 2001) (corporation's lawyers undertook responsibility to perfect nonclient creditor's security interest).

702. *In re* Guardianship of Karan, 38 P.3d 396 (Wash. Ct. App. 2002) (minor child has cause of action against mother's lawyer who set up child's trust to allow pilfering of the estate); Lucas v. Hamm, 364 P.2d 685 (Cal. 1961) (intended beneficiaries of a will could recover from lawyer whose negligence in drafting document caused them to lose their testamentary rights).

703. Rubin v. Schottenstein, Zox & Dunn, 143 F.3d 263 (6th Cir. 1998) (en banc) (lawyer who represented seller in a securities transaction assumes a duty to provide complete and nonmisleading information with respect to subjects on which he undertakes to speak under 17 C.F.R. § 240, 10b-5); Orshoski v. Krieger, No. OT-01-009, 2001 WL 1388037 (Ohio Ct. App. Nov. 9, 2001) (prospective buyers who relied on negligent misrepresentations of lawyer for developer concerning subdivision's restrictive covenants could sue for negligent misrepresentation, but not for legal malpractice).

This duty stems from the fact that once you have undertaken a duty to speak, you must do so with care. If you make the misrepresentation intentionally or recklessly, your liability extends to all persons who might foreseeably rely on it. Although a few jurisdictions extend liability for negligent misrepresentation this far as well,[704] most hold lawyers liable for negligent misrepresentation only to a limited class of persons for whose benefit and guidance the lawyer intends to supply the information or those third persons to whom the lawyer knows the recipient intends to supply the information.[705]

§ 19.09 Discovery Deception

Facebook Discovery

Q. We heard about this personal injury plaintiff who was claiming serious back problems, but posted on Facebook triumphant pictures of having climbed the Eiffel Tower. We decided we should friend the plaintiff in our case: could be a treasure trove; nothing to lose.

A. Other than your license.

Q. This woman has 700 friends. What difference does one more make?

A. Because one more, if he or she is the adversary's lawyer, is violating two rules.

Q. With 700 friends it's hardly confidential.

A. True enough. But Rule 4.2 says you may not communicate with a represented party.

Q. Then I'll get a paralegal to do it.

A. But Rule 8.4(a) says you cannot do through the acts of another what you cannot do yourself.

Q. How about an independent contractor?

A. Same result. May be independent in that he is not an employee, but he is still your agent. Besides, there is another problem.

Q. You are piling it on.

---

704. Molecular Tech. Corp. v. Valentine, 925 F.2d 910 (6th Cir. 1991); Mehaffy, Rider, Windholz & Wilson v. Cent. Bank Denver, N.A., 892 P.2d 230 (Colo. 1995) (lawyer who issued a legal opinion in connection with a municipal bond offering may be liable to third-party investors under RESTATEMENT (SECOND) OF TORTS § 552 for negligent misrepresentation).

705. RLGL § 51; RESTATEMENT (SECOND) OF TORTS § 552(2) (Am. Law Inst. 1965); Vega v. Jones, Day, Reavis & Pogue, 17 Cal. Rptr. 3d 26 (2004) (fraud claim stated by acquiring shareholder against law firm which did not expressly undertake to disclose financing transaction in merger but provided disclosure schedules that did not include material terms of the transaction).

A. No. Just giving you fair warning. If you seek to friend the plaintiff, you would also be violating Rules 4.1 and 8.4(c).
Q. Like I know what that is.
A. These are rules that prevent you from engaging in fraud or dishonesty. Posing as a friend when you are anything but is a big lie.[706] But I'm sure you know that you can seek all of this Facebook information in discovery. No guarantees, and a bit more time and money, but it will save your license.

§ 19.10 Fraud: Mistake of Law

Other Side's Mistake

Q. Big real estate dispute. Partner versus Partner. We try to settle. At the end of the day, other side suggests we divide up the partnership assets. Several shopping centers. Some vacant land. Other side starts by asking if his guy can receive the property near I-91. "Since it's already zoned commercial, we can have it shovel ready in weeks." My client tells me confidentially that is wrong. Property is industrial. Does not permit a strip mall. But don't tell the other side. Right?
A. You had nothing to do with the mistake?
Q. Nothing.
A. But you have no video of the conversation.
Q. True enough.
A. If that's the case you certainly have no duty to correct the other side's error. But you must warn your client of the risk.
Q. Risk?
A. Sure. When the other side recognizes the error, they will be furious.

---

706. *In re* Faraone, 722 A.2d 1 (Del. 1998) (lawyer suspended for six months for violating Rule 4.1(a) and (b) for knowingly assisting an unscrupulous client in taking advantage of third parties in real estate transactions, by misleading them into believing that they were protected from further liability); Hansen v. Anderson, Wilmarth & Van der Maaten, 630 N.W.2d 818 (Iowa 2001) (once a lawyer responds to a request for information in an arm's-length transaction, lawyer had a duty to the lawyer requesting the information to give it truthfully; breach of the duty gives rise to a claim for equitable indemnity by the defrauded lawyer against the defrauding lawyer); State *ex rel.* Neb. State Bar Ass'n v. Addison, 412 N.W.2d 855 (Neb. 1987) (lawyer's silence construed as a misleading statement during a settlement negotiation where lawyer settled client's hospital bill without telling hospital about an insurance policy that might cover some of client's expenses); Cleveland Bar Ass'n v. McMahon, 872 N.E.2d 261 (Ohio 2007) (lawyer suspended for six months for fabricating testimony from a nonexistent transcript in letter to insurer to persuade it to enter into settlement negotiations); *In re* Gallagher, 26 P.3d 131 (Or. 2001) (lawyer suspended for two years for committing acts of dishonesty for attempting to accept a settlement offer when he knew opposing counsel had made a mistake and for repeatedly lying to the bar about the matter).

Q. Furious at their lawyer?

A. Maybe, but you can't be sure. That errant lawyer will be embarrassed. That might translate into misremembering. And a lawsuit against your client and you.[707]

Q. I owed them no duty.

A. If you spoke and they relied, maybe you did. They may argue there was no reason to check since you already did. And there's no videotape.

Q. Well maybe we can get a representation that each side relied on its own lawyer, and we made no reps and warranties.

A. That would help.

Q. It better because my guy is never going to let me disclose the error. He is high risk. He'll take his chances.

A. Not with your license.[708]

§ 19.11 Fraud: What Is a Tribunal?

The Tax-Fraud Interview

Q. We were handling a tax fraud investigation initiated against our longtime real estate client. They are always walking close to the edge. The IRS asked to interview one of the two brothers who control the operation. After a great deal of angst, we agreed, and the IRS agents showed up at our office for the little conversation.

A. We take it "little" is facetious.

Q. It is. The interview goes on for hours. Three different properties are discussed. Focusing on whether expenses are legitimate. Our clients would run their kids' weddings through the company's books, if they could get away with it.

A. And then?

Q. Silence. Heard nothing for a year. But when we did, the explosion was deafening. The clients were indicted for tax

707. Burds v. Hipes, 763 S.E.2d 887 (Ga. Ct. App. 2014) (affirming summary-judgment motion in favor of lawyer dismissing misrepresentation claims).

708. *In re* Mintz, 317 P3d 756 (Kan. 2014) (lawyer suspended indefinitely for lying and withholding information from police who investigated his romantic partner's death, even though lawyer corrected misstatement two days later); ABA Comm. on Ethics & Prof'l Responsibility, Formal Op. 94-387 (1994) Disclosure to Opposing Party and Court That Statute of Limitations Has Run (no duty to inform the other side in negotiations that the statute of limitations has run on the claim, as long as a lawyer does not make "any affirmative misrepresentations about the facts showing that the claim is time-barred, or suggest that she plans to do something to enforce the claim (e.g., file suit) that she has no intention of doing.").

fraud—phony write-offs, trumped up losses, unreported cash, lying to the IRS. You name it.

A. Sounds like a challenging case, assuming your clients can still afford to pay you.

Q. Oh, it would be that alright. But there is a bigger problem. They have accused us of aiding and abetting. We had nothing to do with their returns. To make matters worse, the IRS made a referral to the disciplinary authorities.

A. What's that about?

Q. They accuse us of violating Rule 3.3(a)(3), "offering evidence" we know to be false when our clients met with the IRS agents.

A. It will take more discussion to determine if you've got other concerns, but you did not violate Rule 3.3(a). When you were meeting with the IRS agents, the IRS was not acting as a tribunal. It was simply a party to an investigation, just another litigant, albeit a powerful one. And your clients were not testifying. They were not under oath. There was no adjudication.[709]

Q. Are we fine then?

A. Not quite so fast. It's a good start. But lying to IRS agents probably violates some other law. And if you knew that was occurring, you had an obligation to determine whether anything you did aided and abetted a crime or fraud. That topic will require research into positive law. Remember Rule 1.2(d) prohibits your aiding and abetting a client crime or fraud, but you must look elsewhere for definitions of those words. They vary from state to state. The same is true of Rule 4.1. You cannot lie, and you cannot aid and abet your client's lie; but Rule 1.6, the confidentiality rule, trumps any disclosure obligation under Rule 4.1, unless your jurisdiction has adopted Rules 1.6(b)(2) or (b)(3), subsections that permit disclosure in the case of a client fraud. Which brings us back to the definition of fraud!

Q. And that's good news?

A. Well, you don't have to worry about 3.3.

§ 19.12 Fraud: Mistake of Fact

Scrivener's Error

Q. We brought an employment discrimination claim against our client's former employer based on age discrimination. One of

709. MRs 3.9, 3.9 cmt. [3].

the terms of our oral agreement is our client will agree to a non-compete. That was the last sticking point in the negotiations.

A. Sounds okay so far.

Q. It was until they sent me an agreement to sign in which they omitted the non-compete. You can imagine how delighted my client was, and he instantly signed it and returned it to me. Do I have any obligation to correct?

A. The law on this topic is mixed. Some might treat it as a fraud to sign an agreement you know omitted a critical fact. Courts are especially likely to do this if the error is numerical. It is your job to conduct some research in your jurisdiction to determine how you proceed, but do proceed with caution.[710]

§ 19.13 Aiding and Abetting a Client Fraud

Duties to Others

Q. We know two principles of lasting importance. First, we owe our fiduciary duties to our clients. The law goes out of its way to narrow any area where our duties run otherwise. If we don't follow this precept, we'd be in a perpetual state of conflict. Someone buys from our client; their lawyer takes care of them. We do what's in our client's interests to achieve the client's objectives.

A. You're teaching us, go on.

Q. Second, our clients get to exercise their business judgment. We might think the choices the client makes are ill-advised, and we are free to share our candid views, even if those views have nothing to do with law. But the client gets to decide, for example, to merge, to buy, and to sell.

A. Sounds like you know exactly what you are doing.

710. Stare v. Tate, 98 Cal. Rptr. 264 (1971) (reformation of a divorce settlement agreement ordered due to one lawyer knowingly taking advantage of a mistake of fact in calculations by the opposing lawyer in preparing a counteroffer); Sumerel v. Goodyear Tire & Rubber Co., 232 P.3d 128, 136–38 (Colo. App. 2009) (settlement agreement based on unilateral numerical error unenforceable because one party could not exploit error of the other "to gain a windfall of over $550,000 more than the jury in the case awarded to them . . . the proper course was obvious . . . counsel should have called [opposing counsel], identified the discrepancy, and concluded the matter without further delay."); Fire Ins. Exch. v. Bell, 643 N.E.2d 310 (Ind. 1994) (plaintiff's counsel had right to rely on insurance defense counsel's representation of policy limits even though plaintiff's lawyer could have used discovery to ascertain limits); Restatement (Second) of Contracts § 153(a) (Am. Law Inst. 1981) (unilateral mistake does not permit avoidance of a contract unless it amounts to an unfair advantage due to an obvious mistake in numbers or an arithmetic error).

Q. Well, it turns out, not quite. We specialize in IPOs. The digital revolution has been a dream come true. We were asked to do one for Giggle, a start-up that provides a digital clearing house for jokes, stand-up comics, anyone interested in filling the world with laughter. All protected by a series of IP patents, design patents, and some trade secrets. Who knew? Anyway, they had a first-rate investment banker represented by one of our peer firms. Looked really good. All systems go. Raising a million dollars. Before the company has made one red cent. Hard to believe.

A. You may have been on the wrong side of the transaction.

Q. We always are. Fortunately, not the wrong side we are on now.

A. Talk to us.

Q. All systems were go. We even had a very expensive pre-closing dinner. Opus One poured like it was water. Then on the way out, the CFO, more than a bit inebriated, turns to me and announces in a stage whisper, "Sure am glad we did not have to disclose that darn letter." "What letter?" I reply, suddenly a lot more sober than the CFO. He tells me it was from Giggle's chief competitor, Comicon, claiming we infringed one of their patents. I ask the CFO whether this creates problems. His response: "Only if we do not go forward with the IPO. We need that cash this week."

A. Sounds troubling.

Q. I did nothing that night, but first thing in the morning I call the CEO. He assures me it's a frivolous attempt to derail the IP by a competitor. Frivolous claim, he says.

A. What did you do then?

Q. What do I know about this IP stuff? Giggle has a CEO who went to Cal Tech. I let it go. It's the CEO's decision.

A. Was it a success?

Q. For nine months. Oversubscribed, the stock was up 40 percent when the other shoe dropped. Comicon sued for patent infringement, the price fell ten points, and it was not a week later when the first shareholder suit was filed, naming our law firm and me. And of all things, claiming we "aided and abetted" our client's fraud. I say to go against us is a violation of Rule 11. Don't you agree?

A. Not entirely. Your firm was counsel for the IPO. The offering memorandum identifies your firm's role. And if you knew of the fraud and assisted it, you have aided and abetted as well.

Q. The offering does define our role. But we represented the company. We did not owe any duty to the future shareholders. That was the role of the underwriters and their counsel.

A. That's the argument. But you know about the threatened patent claim. You did not change the disclosure.

Q. We were told it was frivolous.

A. By clients who wanted the IPO to go forward without delay. You did no due diligence yourself. As far as you knew, the company did not do any diligence either. If your client was right that the claim was meritless, all should be okay. But if not, then you knew a potentially material fact that no patent litigator at your firm evaluated. The client may have omitted a material fact. That could be a fraud on your client's part. And your firm, it will be argued, aided and abetted it by not conducting any investigation and leaving the firm name in the offering memorandum. This is one of those special situations where you owed duties to third parties as well as your client. You could be in trouble to the shareholders.

Q. Let us hope the claim gets thrown out or there will nothing very funny about the whole episode.

CHAPTER 20

Bias

§ 20.01 Introduction: The Enduring Problem

Bias remains a persistent and endemic problem in the legal profession, the courts, and in our society. With respect to lawyers, courts have responded in a number of ways, imposing sanctions for litigation misconduct using their inherent powers.[711]

Beyond monetary and other court-ordered sanctions, disciplinary authorities have successfully sought professional discipline against lawyers who display biased behavior.[712] Some of these cases rely on the general language of Model Rule 8.4(d) (conduct prejudicial to the

711. Lee v. Am. Eagle Airlines, Inc., 93 F. Supp. 2d 1322, 1325 (S.D. Fla. 2000) (statutory attorney's fees reduced 40 percent due to counsels' repeated misconduct during trial, including disrespect for trial judge's rulings, "trash talk" common to sporting events used outside the judge's hearing, and wrongful accusations of improper conduct against opposing counsel; court also forwarded its opinion to disciplinary counsel); Mullaney v. Aude, 730 A.2d 759 (Md. Ct. Spec. App. 1999) (protective orders and attorney's fees to obtain it awarded to plaintiff who did not prevail, but was subject to insults by opposing party and his lawyer); Principe v. Assay Partners, IRO Int'l Ltd. 586 N.Y.S.2d 182, 184 (N.Y. Sup. Ct. 1992) (sanctions against a lawyer who in a deposition said to opposing counsel: "I don't have to talk to you, little lady," "What do you know, young girl," "Be quiet, little girl," and "Go away little girl.").

712. Fla. Bar v. Norkin, 132 So. 3d 77 (Fla. 2013) (lawyer suspended for two years due to his "rude and antagonistic behavior," which included accusing a mediator of criminal conduct, engaging in denigrating and humiliating behavior toward 71-year-old opposing counsel who was suffering from Parkinson's disease, and disrupting court hearings by yelling at judges); *In re* Barker, 993 N.E.2d 1138 (Ind. 2013) (lawyer suspended six months for referring to opposing counsel's client as someone who doesn't understand laws and court orders, "probably because she's an illegal alien to begin with"); *In re* O'Dwyer, 221 So. 3d 1 (La. 2017) (lawyer disbarred for vile and racially derogatory communications made to judges and other lawyers and threat in his own bankruptcy proceeding to creditors ("Suppose I might become homicidal?")); *In re* Griffith, 838 N.W.2d 792 (Minn. 2013) (lawyer suspended for at least three months because of his sexual harassment of a student he taught as an adjunct law professor).

administration of justice) or 4.4(a) (using means that have no purpose other than to embarrass or burden a third person).[713]

Increasingly, various jurisdictions have added specific nondiscrimination provisions to Rule 8.4, and the ABA recently added its own recommended version.[714] Some track the general law against discrimination, requiring proof of a "discriminatory act," "harassment," or "unlawful discrimination."[715] The broad coverage of these laws gives you an incentive to treat others in the litigation process with respect. This wide range of remedies for biased conduct nevertheless indicates that biased behavior continues. One thing is clear: Sanctions and professional discipline are especially likely to occur when a lawyer engages in a pattern of biased practices that effect, taint, or limit the fair participation of parties, witnesses, lawyers, or court personnel.

§ 20.02 Bias

The Courtroom Bully

Q. Betty's very upset. The lawyer on the other side was oppressive, kept referring to her as a "girl lawyer," and referred to her hemline, repeatedly, while the judge seemed delighted; he certainly didn't do anything. What can we do? She is really upset.

A. Bias in the courtroom is a lingering problem. Many courts have established task forces to identify and ameliorate such conduct. Some have specifically amended their Rules of Professional

---

713. Fla. Bar v. Martocci, 791 So. 2d 1074 (Fla. 2001) (sexist, racial, and ethnic insults in a divorce case constituted conduct prejudicial to the administration of justice because it further exacerbated relationships among opposing parties, counsel, and the court in an already difficult case); Idaho State Bar v. Warrick, 44 P.3d 1141, 1143 (Idaho 2002) (county prosecutor suspended for 30 days for violating Rule 4.4(a) by writing "waste of sperm" and "scumbag" next to inmate's name on an inmate control board not seen by inmate); Attorney Grievance Comm'n v. Marcalus, 112 A.3d 375 (Md. 2015) (lawyer disbarred for sexting pro se litigation opponent); *In re* Charges of Unprofessional Conduct, 653 N.W.2d 452 (Minn. 2002) (lawyer's request to exclude disabled judicial clerk from trial violated state provisions against disability discrimination and constituted conduct prejudicial to the administration of justice); *In re* Vincenti, 704 A.2d 927 (N.J. 1998) (lawyer disbarred for making insinuations about a witness' sexual orientation, harassing, and intimidating her); *In re* Monaghan, 743 N.Y.S.2d 519 (N.Y. App. Div. 2002) (race-based abuse of opposing counsel at a deposition was conduct prejudicial to the administration of justice and unlawful discrimination).

714. MR 8.4(g) (2016) (prohibiting conduct that the "lawyer knows or reasonably should know is harassment or discrimination on the basis of race, sex, religion, national origin, ethnicity, disability, age, sexual orientation, gender identity, marital status or socioeconomic status in conduct related to the practice of law").

715. RLGL § 106 cmt. d; CAL. R. PROF'L CONDUCT 8.4.1(2018); MICH. R. PROF'L CONDUCT 6.5 (2019); ILL. R. PROF'L CONDUCT 8.4 (j) (2010); MINN. R. PROF'L CONDUCT 8.4(g) (2018); N.Y. R. PROF'L CONDUCT 8.4(g) (2018); OHIO R. PROF'L CONDUCT 8.4(g) (2017); TEX. DISCIPLINARY R. PROF'L CONDUCT 5.08 (2019).

Conduct to prohibit various forms of discriminatory conduct. There is no excuse for such behavior. It diminishes the system of justice to have lawyers disparage their colleagues, and it is up to the judge, if the conduct occurs in the courtroom, to correct the situation.

You can help the court by pointing out that lawyers have been sanctioned, forfeited fees, and been professionally disciplined for bias.[716] Your colleague should ask the court, on the record, repeatedly if necessary, to instruct such oppressive adversaries to call her by her name. You might consider a phone call to the court as well, and, perhaps, it is time for this particular court to take a more institutional approach to the problem. You should cite the Code of Judicial Conduct, which explicitly prohibits judges from manifesting bias or prejudice and requires them not to permit others subject to the judge's direction to do so.[717]

§ 20.03 Bias and Immigration Status

Using an Improper Advantage

Q. I represented a dad in a dissolution matter. Poor guy, hasn't seen his baby in over a year, despite a court order to the contrary.

A. So far, you are on the side of angels.

Q. That's what I thought. I wrote a letter to former wife's lawyer stating these facts. Then I realized that the mom may not realize the importance of a court order. I added for emphasis: "Your client doesn't understand the importance of what laws and court orders mean, probably because she's an illegal alien. I want you to tell her in whatever language she understands that we'll be demanding she be put in JAIL for contempt of court. I'm filing a copy of this letter with the court to document the seriousness of this problem." Then I sent a copy of my letter to the presiding judge in the case. I knew that would get their attention.

A. We bet it did. Then what?

716. *See* § 20.01.

717. MCJC Rule 2.3.

Q. Instead of justice, I got a disciplinary complaint. Some allegation about bias and harassment. This is legitimate advocacy in my book.

A. Not if you used tactics that have no purpose other than to harass. Or if your reference to her immigration status, even if true, demonstrates bias rather than relevant advocacy about your client's parental rights. If your jurisdiction has a specific provision about bias in your Rules of Professional Conduct, you need to find defense counsel for yourself.[718]

§ 20.04 Bias in Jury Selection

Getting the Jury We Want

Q. My nostalgia for the good old days knows no bounds.

A. Before air conditioning?

Q. No. The practice of law. Jury trials, picking the panel. We used to get to question the venire. For ten minutes each. Really probe. Now we're lucky to watch as some court clerk asks perfunctory questions and we get to observe. Guess who we want by what they are wearing. What they are reading. Looking at their watches for clues.

A. You'll never go back.

Q. We're resigned to that. But we still hire jury consultants. They test our case. Give us guidelines. But even those are less helpful than they should be.

A. Shocked to hear that. But don't tell me you are relying on factors such as race. Aren't you the guy who brought the class action challenging de facto segregation in the local schools?

Q. That was our firm. But there are times when I know my client will be better served by the racial composition—one way or the other—of the panel. And the consultants confirm that.

A. But there is the law of the land. Constitutional law.[719]

Q. That's why I will never strike, for example, all Hispanics. That way I insulate my politically incorrect decision by including at least one when I am trying a case in Bridgeport, for example.

---

718. *In re* Barker, 993 N.E.2d 1138 (Ind. 2013) (lawyer suspended from practice for 30 days for writing letter in this problem, which court found violated both Rule 4.4(a) (prohibiting tactics that have no real purpose other than to embarrass or burden a third person) and Rule 8.4(g) (prohibiting bias or prejudiced conduct in a professional capacity based on a list of factors, including national origin, that is not legitimate advocacy).

719. Batson v. Kentucky, 476 U.S. 79 (1986).

A. That's not good enough. And you know it. The Supreme Court recently reaffirmed *Batson*, holding that the Constitution "forbids striking even a single prospective juror for a discriminatory purpose."[720] If you struck other Hispanics because they were Hispanics, leaving the last Hispanic on the venire is not good enough. If the venire is 40 percent of one racial or ethnic group, a token selection will not, and should not, protect you. Your job is to convince a constitutionally selected jury of the merit of your client's cause. To do otherwise compromises your bona fides and perpetuates unconstitutional conduct we can't condone. Can't we appeal to the better you?

Q. I know you are right. There are fair limits. But I so want my clients to have every advantage. Trial work is the assembling of thousands of pieces.

A. Within the limits of the law.

---

720. Flowers v. Mississippi, 139 S. Ct. 2228, 2242 (2019) (upholding *Batson* challenge based on finding that a prosecutor's peremptory strike of a black juror under all the relevant circumstances was "motivated in substantial part by discriminatory intent").

PART FIVE

Representing Clients Pretrial

Legal Ethics in the Context of Pretrial Representation

Up to this point, we have examined the contours of fiduciary duty, or the six Cs: client identification, confidentiality, competence, control, communication, and conflict of interest resolution, that is, what it means to say "yes" to your clients. We have also taken some time to identify the one significant limitation to your fiduciary duty: the limits or bounds of the law.[721]

In Part Five, we explore the application of these two basics in the context of pretrial representation. Here, the first C, identification of your client or clients, is crucial. You begin any litigation with an entry of an appearance for a client; court rules alone mean that you need to clearly identify that client. Then, you continue to owe your client or clients the six Cs. You must competently research both fact and law and competently identify applicable causes of action and relevant defenses. Your client controls whether to bring the litigation, and how and whether to settle the matter. You remain responsible for reasonably consulting and keeping your client reasonably informed about the status of the matter and explaining significant issues in the matter to enable your client to make decisions and give you informed consent where necessary. As

721. MR 1.2(d); RLGL § 23(1).

with any representation, you owe your client a duty of confidentiality, including the obligation to claim the attorney-client or work-product protection when privileged information is sought. Your duty of loyalty requires continued vigilance during pretrial, where changing facts or legal rights can create new conflicts.

Significantly, you fulfill all of your fiduciary duties to clients within well-defined limits of the law, which include procedural rules, civil and criminal accountability, as well as the significant power of a court to use equitable relief where lawyer or client conduct violates legal boundaries. Nearly all of these bounds of the law are explicitly incorporated into the Rules of Professional Conduct for lawyers. As a result, lawyers can face legal and equitable remedies, such as procedural sanctions, civil and criminal accountability, and equitable relief, as well as professional discipline for the same conduct.

CHAPTER 21

The Investigation

§ 21.01 Introduction: The Ethics of Proper Investigation

The lawyer's duty of competence and to avoid frivolous allegations requires a proper investigation of facts. You, of course, will begin with your client, but an adequate investigation requires that you confirm client narratives by looking at physical evidence, documents, and communicate with other persons.[722]

Failing to ascertain a reasonable fact basis for your client's claim or defense in fact and in law can result in court sanctions[723] and

722. Douglas R. Richmond, Brian S. Faughnan, & Michael L. Matula, Professional Responsibility in Litigation, 25–35 (2011). Special obligations exist regarding physical evidence of a client crime. RLGL § 119; People v. Belge, 372 N.Y.S.2d 798 (Onondaga Cnty. Ct. 1975), *aff'd*, 359 N.E.2d 377 (N.Y. 1976) (lawyer who observed but did not alter, destroy, or take possession of evidence of client crime not subject to criminal indictment); *In re* Original Grand Jury Investigation, 733 N.E.2d 1135, 1140 (Ohio 2000) (physical evidence must be turned over to the grand jury and lawyer "is obligated to relinquish that evidence to law-enforcement authorities").

723. Gurary v. Nu-Tech Bio-Med, Inc., 303 F.3d 212 (2d Cir. 2002), *sanctions on remand*, Gurary v. Winehouse, 270 F. Supp. 2d 425 (S.D.N.Y. 2003) (claims deemed frivolous under Fed. R. Civ. P. 11 constitute ground for full sanctions under 1995 Private Securities Litigation Reform Act's mandatory sanctions provision where the inclusion of nonfrivolous claims are not weighty enough to prevent the suit as a whole from being nonabusive; sanctions of $215,050.83 awarded); Kalwasinski v. Ryan, No. 96-CV-6475, 2007 WL 2743434 (W.D.N.Y. Sept. 12, 2007) (sanction of dismissal proper where serious death threats were directed at opposing party); Jandrt *ex rel.* Brueggeman v. Jerome Foods, Inc., 597 N.W.2d 744 (Wis. 1999), (complaint that was not frivolous when filed became so when lawyer reasonably should have discovered the lack of causation by consulting an expert witness, subjecting lawyer to sanctions under Wis. R. Civ. P. 11).

professional discipline[724] for filing a frivolous claim. Extreme disregard for facts can result in tort liability for abuse of process or malicious prosecution.[725] You are not required to believe your client will prevail, but you are required to inform yourself about the facts and the law in the case to determine that you can make a good faith argument to support your client's position.[726]

Speaking to witnesses raises other issues. If you know the witness is represented in the matter, you may not speak to them except through counsel or formal discovery procedures.[727] If the witness is unrepresented, you may speak to that person directly, but may not "state or imply" disinterest.[728] Further, you must correct any misunderstanding about your role in the matter, and not offer legal advice, except the advice to seek counsel if the witness's interests conflict with your client's interest.[729] You also must respect any confidentiality obligation that a witness has to a party. You cannot use an informal conversation to delve into information protected by other law.[730]

§ 21.02 The Investigation

Protecting the Privilege

Q. I am so proud of myself. I am general counsel of Excelsior. We own paper plants in 12 states. Twenty-five facilities altogether. We were having a C-Suite meeting—the CEO, the CFO, the CIO, and me. The chiefs brought up our ongoing compliance with enumerated rules. One of our competitors just got hit with big fines. The CEO suggested we get the head of our QC lab . . .

---

724. Iowa Supreme Court Bd. of Prof'l Ethics & Conduct v. Ronwin, 557 N.W.2d 515 (Iowa 1996) (lawyer disbarred for filing frivolous lawsuits and making false accusations of criminal conduct against lawyers and judges); Attorney Grievance Comm'n v. Zdravkovich, 762 A.2d 950 (Md. 2000) (lawyer indefinitely suspended for, inter alia, a FED. R. CIV. P. 11 violation for failing to read a federal statute that would have made it clear that removal was not allowed); *In re* Rios, 965 N.Y.S.2d 418 (N.Y. App. Div. 2013) (lawyers suspended for nine months due to inducing a personal injury client to misrepresent a key fact in the case by explaining the importance of the fact and the law before asking her version of the incident); *In re* Blasi, 660 N.Y.S.2d 151 (N.Y. App. Div. 1997) (lawyer suspended for five years for filing a number of meritless law suits to settle personal disputes with a neighbor).

725. Zamos v. Stroud, 87 P.3d 802 (Cal. 2004) (cause of action for malicious prosecution stated against lawyer who properly commenced a lawsuit but continued to prosecute it after learning it was not supported by probable cause); Mattel, Inc. v. Luce, Forward, Hamilton & Scripps, 121 Cal. Rptr. 2d 794 (2002) (cause of action for malicious prosecution upheld against lawyers who brought a copyright infringement action without probable cause, and the underlying case terminated in favor of the opposing party; malice could be inferred by the lack of probable cause).

726. MR 3.1 cmt. [2].

727. MR 4.2; RLGL § 99.

728. MR 4.3.

729. MR 4.3; RLGL § 103.

730. RLGL § 102.

A. QC?

Q. Quality control. To conduct an investigation.

I said, why not have me conduct with my team. Then it will be privileged. Keep any bad results out of the hands of the damn regulators. The CEO thought that was a great idea. Anything that'll improve my bonus. A team player.

A. Brilliant!

Q. I knew you'd say that.

A. I was being facetious. You may have promised more than you can deliver.

Q. Look, I know how to conduct an investigation.

A. We are sure you do. It's the privilege part. Remember to be privileged one of the requirements is that the communications, in this case your report to the CEO, has to be for the purpose of giving or receiving legal advice. You can certainly include such advice based on your findings. But that won't stop some adverse party, for example, the EPA, from arguing that the only reason the company had the lawyers conduct the investigation was to shield from public scrutiny an investigation the company had to undertake for business purposes and placing lawyers in meetings or activities that the company has to do anyway will not create privilege. By the way, what's your title?

Q. What's that got to do with anything? Executive vice president and general counsel. Why do you ask?

A. That's another reason your privilege claim may fail. Your adversaries will argue you wear two hats. And when you conducted the inspection you were acting as the EVP, not the GC.

Q. Well, I hate to hire outside counsel. They are so expensive. And when you ask them to do an investigation, they get all uppity and independent. Won't use our billing task codes. Interview too many people.

A. Theoretically, hiring outside counsel should not change the equation. If they are doing the same investigation for the same client under the same circumstances the privilege equation should be the same. It's either legal advice or it isn't. But the courts are much more willing to conclude that in-house counsel's work is not privileged. Indeed, in *Vioxx*, Judge Fallon, in adopting the analysis of Professor Paul Rice, gave total privilege protection to outside counsel's claim of privilege.[731] We call it the outside counsel full employment act.

731. *In re* Vioxx Prods. Liab. Litig., 501 F. Supp. 2d 789 (E.D. La. 2007).

Q. Well, if we can't claim attorney-client privilege, can we claim it's work product? Refuse to turn it over on that basis?

A. You are clever to think of another basis. It is our duty to conduct a representation to maximize to the greatest extent possible that which we have to turn over to our clients' adversaries. But . . .

Q. There you go again.

A. You can only claim work product for endeavors undertaken in anticipation of litigation. We didn't hear that in your question.

Q. We are always under fire. Anticipation of Litigation "R" Us.

A. But you weren't anticipating litigation on these issues at that time. At least as you described it, which leads to a critical ethics lesson.

Q. Am I in trouble?

A. No. We are keeping you out, we hope. We lawyers certainly have an obligation to claim privilege whenever we have a good faith claim. But we also must not either claim the wrong privilege (attorney-client when its work-product), nor may we willy-nilly assert privilege when we know the privilege does not apply.[732] Wholesale claims of every privilege as to every document on a privilege log will not only result in loss of credibility with the court; it also could result in the sanction of striking a privilege log in its entirety.[733]

Q. I know that's wise counsel. I've seen lawyers at all levels get overly enthusiastic about such assertions. Sometimes it is hard to talk them out of it.

A. Just remind them of these sanction cases—smelling salts for lawyer prizefighters.

Q. I like that.

§ 21.03 Interviewing Client Employees

The Problematic Interview

Q. So, I am asked to investigate concerns about possible side effects of our new arthritis drug. The claim is that it's causing dangerous palpitations. Our guys say 10 percent of our user profiles exhibit the same symptom. Not our drug, they say. Anyways, an investigation is requested.

732. Advanced Display Sys., Inc. v. Kent State Univ., 212 F.3d 1272 (Fed. Cir. 2000).

733. Wachtel v. Health Net, Inc., 239 F.R.D. 81 (D.N.J. 2006).

A. You've done them before?

Q. Of course. That's why Pharma's CEO picked us. Anyway, I have to talk to the head of the lab. I know the guy well. He is the inventor on some of Pharma's best patents, patents our law firm handled at the PTO.

A. So, no problem.

Q. Actually, big problem. Dr. Panipento—that's our guy's name—greets me warmly; I ask him his opinion. He first tells me it's nothing to worry about. But then he drops his voice. "I know you won't tell anyone," staring straight at me, "but I've had back problems, started taking these painkillers for the spasms, and I think I got hooked. I've been a little fuzzy lately. Maybe the tests weren't thorough enough."

A. You got a lead.

Q. I got a problem. Dr. Panipento thinks I am his lawyer. And I will keep his confidences. But how can I?

A. You did not give him the warnings?

Q. The warnings?

A. Yes. That you only represented the company, not him. That everything he told you would be shared with the company.

Q. Oh, I couldn't do that. If I had read him some kind of *Miranda* warnings, he likely would have clammed up. I needed to get to the bottom of it.

A. You are at the ethical bottom, that's for sure. The company has to know about his condition. But you tell them, and Dr. Panipento may become Dr. Plaintiff. He'll claim that you had a client-lawyer relationship. And you did nothing to clarify the situation.

§ 21.04 Privilege Waiver: Criminal Defense

Settlement by Waiver

Q. Our client wants to turn over to the Feds our recent investigation of their compliance with air pollution guidelines. Some investigation; we have 30 coal-fired plants, plant superintendents, even janitorial employees. The Feds say they will indict if we don't disclose. But they assure us they will give us a letter stating that turning the investigation report over to them should not be a waiver as to anyone else.

A. How generous of them. Where to begin? It is outrageous that the Feds would use such tactics. No decision on whether to indict should turn on waiver of the privilege. That "waiver" is anything but voluntary, and it is one thing to seek underlying information, quite another to seek privileged information.[734] We thought such thug-like tactics had been laid to rest.[735]

Next the letter is worthless. It binds neither future litigants against your client nor future judges who will be called on to adjudicate the waiver question.

If your client, nonetheless, feels that it must cooperate this much, you still must make sure that none of the individuals you interviewed have any basis for asserting an individual privilege like poor Dr. Panipento. If you used the proper warnings and have a written record that you did so, you should be okay in that regard.

§ 21.05 Privilege Waiver: Civil Cases

Insistent Auditors

Q. We conducted an investigation of our client's sales practices. Interviewed dozens. Insiders, customers, you name it. Great report.

A. Why call us?

Q. Because somehow, I don't know how, after all our warnings, the auditors learned of the work we did. They insist on securing our report. Won't sign off with a clean opinion until they do. Something about contingent liabilities. CEO says we cannot afford to be tardy on filing the 10-K.

A. But showing the report to the auditors is likely to waive the attorney-client privilege. You knew that.

Q. I do. Don't know why. But I know it's a problem.

A. Attorney-client privilege requires the advice be in confidence. Showing it to a third party destroys that.

Q. Even though they are our auditors?

A. Yes. Auditors owe primary duties to the public. They are independent of your client. But you still might be saved.

Q. How's that? Any shelter in the storm.

---

734. RLGL § 69 cmt. d; Upjohn Co. v. United States, 449 U.S. 383 (1981) (privilege protects what client's agent told lawyer but not underlying facts).

735. *9-28.000—Principles of Federal Prosecution of Business Organizations*, U.S. DEP'T OF JUST., https://www.justice.gov/usam/usam-9-28000-principles-federal-prosecution-business-organizations (last visited June 7, 2017).

A. It depends of course on the facts. But if this investigation was undertaken in anticipation of litigation, then it would qualify as work product.

Q. Was it ever. The company is worried this could be worse than our last vaccine debacle.

A. When it comes to work product, there is no waiver of the protection if the work product is shared with a party that is not likely to divulge it further.[736] We think the auditors should qualify. Of course we make no representation how the auditors will react to the contents. However, if waived in one matter, the waiver may be deemed a universal waiver, that is, one that triggers a requirement to produce in all other cases that follow where the documents or communications are relevant.[737]

---

736. RLGL § 91 cmt. d; *In re* Gen. Motors LLC Ignition Switch Litig., No. 14-MD-2543 (JMF), 2015 WL 221057 (S.D.N.Y. Jan. 15, 2015) (interview materials compiled by outside lawyers conducting a corporate internal investigation remain protected by work-product and attorney-client privilege even if company publicly released the lawyers' report).

737. *In re* Qwest Commc'ns Int'l, 450 F.3d 1179 (10th Cir. 2006) (company that waived attorney-client privilege and work-product protection on 220,000 pages of materials by disclosing documents to SEC and DOJ also waived protections for all other purposes, where it knew that other securities case was pending; doctrine of selective waiver rejected by most circuits and most state courts).

CHAPTER 22

Contacting Nonclients

§ 22.01 Introduction: Legal Regulation of Third-Person Contact

These rules are simple but not always intuitive. You may not contact a person represented by counsel in a matter about the subject of the representation without permission from his or her lawyer. Clients cannot give informed consent to this contact, which is designed to protect the relationship of that other client and lawyer and prevent you from interfering with that relationship.[738]

Courts can allow such contact or determine the scope of your responsibility, especially when the represented "person" is an entity.[739] When you deal with unrepresented nonclients, including witnesses, you may not mislead the nonclient about your identity and the fact that you represent an opposing party; you must refrain from giving them legal advice except the advice to seek independent counsel, and if you reasonably should know that they misunderstand your role in the matter, you have an affirmative duty to correct the misunderstanding.[740] Of course, if procedural rules limit your access to a witness, such as an expert, you must abide by those limitations.

---

738. MR 4.2; RLGL § 99.

739. Messing, Rudavsky & Weliky, P.C. v. President & Fellows of Harvard College, 764 N.E.2d 825 (Mass. 2002).

740. MR 4.3; RLGL § 103; *In re* Gamble, 338 P.3d 576 (Kan. 2014) (lawyer who represented biological father suspended for six months for sending private Facebook messages to unrepresented biological mother designed to induce guilt for giving up baby for adoption; unnecessary to decide whether lawyer deceived mother or violated Rules 4.3 or 4.4 because egregious misconduct was conduct prejudicial to the administration of justice, violating Rule 8.4(d)).

§ 22.02 Communication with Represented Persons

What's a Settlement?

Q. Here I was minding my own business. We've got this big case. Plaintiff sued the hospital. Liability is a problem. So are damages. We just say it's not our fault. We relied on the lab. Anyway, had a mediation the other day. I thought we were close to settlement. You could just tell the plaintiff was drooling at the numbers. But her damn lawyer. So stubborn. It was clear his client wanted to settle. And don't the rules say the client—not the lawyer—gets to decide?

Anyway, like I said, I didn't do anything but stew until my phone rings. I pick it up, bark my name, and lo and behold it's the plaintiff. Such a sweet woman. I know that's all beside the point. But she complains about her lawyer and says she'd be happy to settle for just $100,000 more than we last offered. Now I'm drooling. I tell her she's doing the right thing. How glad I am she called me. How she could lose in front of a jury.

I can't wait to tell my client. Another $100K is still a million less than my authority. For good measure I record the conversation, so I have proof of our agreement. Tell her to come in tomorrow to sign the papers and get her check. I could tell how relieved she was. "You're such a fine young lady," is how she ends the call.

I'm waiting for her this morning. When instead I am greeted by her creepy lawyer. Enraged. Calls me unethical. Me. He says I've violated Rule 4.2. What does he know? He's the rule violator. He tells me we have no deal, he's going to report me to the judge and the discipline folks. The nerve.

A. Let's just calm down. He has a point.

Q. A point. She called me. She wanted to escape the clutches of that shyster lawyer. She was so unhappy 'til she got to share her troubles with me.

A. That may all be true. But we must consider Rule 4.2. It doesn't just prohibit you from contacting a represented person. It prohibits communication with a represented person.

Q. But she wanted to talk.

A. The rule is designed to protect people like her.

Q. From me? I was so nice to her.

A. You may have been nice. But after you realized who she was and why she was calling, you should have ended the call.[741] By being nice after that, you actually demonstrated the reason for the rule. She trusted you. And you gave her advice, something that is forbidden, even if she were not represented. And all that time you weren't acting in her best interest. You were taking advantage of your superior knowledge. You were overreaching even if you were a model of good manners. You were acting solely in your client's interest. You saved your client almost a million bucks. That's a million bucks that this woman, properly represented, might have snared. Still might, as it turns out. The rule says you cannot talk to a represented person without the permission of the lawyer.

Q. He would have never given that, the scoundrel. Can't she decide she doesn't want her lawyer?

A. Of course she can.

Q. Then I should've told her if she wants to talk to me, she had to fire her lawyer.

A. No. No. No. That's another reason for the Rule. We can't have lawyers giving advice to the client on the other side. And we don't want opposing counsel to interfere with our client-lawyer relationships.

Q. Could I have told her I cannot talk to her so long as she is represented?

A. That would be okay so long as you added "or with your lawyer's permission."

Q. I'm in trouble.

A. You could be. The opposing counsel doesn't have to turn you in. And he can't do so without his client's permission, because any reporting of your alleged misconduct would include client confidential information.[742]

Q. And the settlement?

A. We are afraid it's back to the negotiating table.[743]

---

741. Zaug v. Va. State Bar *ex rel.* Fifth Dist.—Section III Comm., 737 S.E.2d 914 (Va. 2013) (lawyer who briefly remained on phone line with opposing party after she realized who was calling did not violate Rule 4.2; lawyers must disengage when contacted by represented parties but are not required to be discourteous or impolite).

742. MR 8.3(c).

743. Hopkins v. Troutner, 4 P.3d 557 (Idaho 2000) (lawyer who advised opposing unrepresented party that case was only worth $3,000 to $4,000 inappropriately offered legal advice, creating grounds for a Idaho R. Civ. P. 60(b) motion to set aside prior release and dismissal with prejudice).

§ 22.03 Distinguishing Represented from Unrepresented Persons

Firing the Jerk

Q. I am in trouble. But it seems so unfair. I am sure you'll defend me.
A. Let's have it and no commitments.
Q. Well, I am defending an employment discrimination suit. Actually, a meritorious claim. But we got a real break.
A. What was that?
Q. The plaintiff's lawyer is a jerk. The judge hates him. We had a conference last week and the judge nearly held him in contempt. The jerk falsified the privilege log.
A. Sounds good so far.
Q. Oh it gets better. I'm in my office when I get a call. It's the plaintiff.
A. Uh oh!
Q. Not what I thought. She is fed up with her lawyer. Says she fired him and before she finds another she asks me if we can't just settle. She tells me what a gentleman I've been. I sat up in my chair and straightened my tie.
A. And then?
Q. And then we settled for $50,000. My client was thrilled. So was the plaintiff. All's well that ends well.
A. Let us guess. It did not end well?
Q. You got that right. Two hours later the phone rings. It's the jerk.
A. Why are we not surprised?
Q. He says I violated Rule 4.2 by talking to his client. I say, "no way, your client called me."
A. You are in trouble. The rule says you cannot communicate. Makes no difference who places the call.
Q. But she fired her lawyer.
A. That's what she said. But the lawyer obviously had no idea he was out of a job. You should have talked to the jerk first. Now you are at his mercy.
Q. That is what he said. He said if we don't settle at his number, he'll report me.
A. Now that's a break. He cannot threaten disciplinary action to gain a litigation advantage. That violates the rules.[744]

---

744. ABA Comm. on Ethics & Prof'l Responsibility, Formal Op. 94-383 (1994) Use of Threatened Disciplinary Complaint Against Opposing Counsel (a lawyer's use of the threat of filing a disciplinary

Q. What do I do now?

A. See if you can settle. But no threats and no promises not to report. You have to decide whether to report him, but before you do so, your client has to approve the referral. The information of his violation is client confidential. Disclosing it requires your client's informed consent.[745] Which means your client and you can decide. It may be better just to settle the damn case. Dealing with scoundrels is a dangerous business.

Q. And my transgression?

A. Hope he doesn't report you and, if he does, you'll hire a good lawyer.

Small Claims

Q. My client gets sued all the time. In small claims court. I don't even remember this claimant, but I am sure part of her story was correct.

A. Which part?

Q. I call up the pro se claimants and offer to settle. It is cheaper for our client to pay a few shekels than pay for representation in small claims. A lawyer could spend hours waiting for a ten-minute Judge Judy treatment.

A. You settled this?

Q. The complaint says for $900. Like I said, there are so many.

A. And the problem?

Q. I am now being sued to overturn the settlement. Now she has a lawyer. And her complaint alleges I gave her advice to settle. In violation of one of those rules.

A. 4.3?

Q. Yeah, That one.

A. And did you?

---

or criminal complaint against opposing counsel to obtain an advantage in a civil case is constrained by the prohibitions in MRs 8.3, 8.4 (b), 4.1, 3.1, and 4.4. Such a threat may not be used as a bargaining point when the subject misconduct raises a "substantial question" under MR 8.3, and would also be improper if the misconduct is unrelated to the civil claim, is not well-founded in fact and in law, or if the threat has no substantial purpose other than to embarrass, delay, or burden opposing counsel or his client, or prejudice the administration of justice). *See also In re* Kenny, 217 P.3d 36 (Kan. 2009) (lawyer disciplined for using the threat of a disciplinary complaint to assist his clients in obtaining a fee refund from his clients' former lawyer; lawyer violated Rules 4.4, 8.3, and 8.4 because his letters had no substantial purpose other than to coerce a refund of the attorney's fee (Rule 4.4(a)), because he believed he had knowledge of a violation of the rules and did not report (Rule 8.3(a)), and because his demand letters constituted conduct prejudicial to the administration of justice (Rule 8.4(d)).

745. MR 8.3.

Q. Well that's just it. I always tell them the offer is fair. Is that advice, or am I being an advocate? This lawyer alleges I "charmed" his client. I AM nice to them.

A. Nothing wrong and everything right about being polite. It is a little minefield, but you should be successful in defending your conduct unless . . .

Q. Unless what?

A. She recorded the conversation and you misremembered.[746]

§ 22.04 Client Communication with Represented Persons

Unforwarded Settlement Offers

Q. Like all clients, my client is convinced he could settle this nasty employment discrimination suit if opposing counsel would just forward our generous offers to the plaintiff. Since we know opposing counsel is obliged to forward our offers, my client wants me to cure opposing counsel's misconduct with a letter to the client, informing the client directly.

A. But that would be a communication with a represented person.

Q. Well I thought we could get around that silly rule by sending a copy of the letter to opposing counsel, just as a courtesy. If we get lucky, the client will accept the offer before her lawyer even knows we sent the letter.

A. But it's still a violation of Rule 4.2.

Q. Maybe, if you say so, but this one cures that lawyer's transgressions.

A. We don't think so. The rule is designed so that clients never have to receive one of those scary registered letters in a law firm's envelope that starts your hand trembling even before you get to see the contents. All those communications go to the lawyer instead.

Q. How do we cure the other side's rule violation?

A. Well there is nothing to stop your client from writing the plaintiff.

746. *In re* News Am. Publ'g Inc., 974 S.W.2d 97 (Tex. App. 1998) (sanctions should have been imposed against lawyer who contacted opposing party who initiated contact and told opposing counsel he had terminated his relationship with his lawyer; lawyer was obligated to confer with opposing party's lawyer before responding to the contact).

Q. Hadn't thought of that. I can write a withering letter, let my client sign it and send it to the plaintiff. That way the lawyer doesn't ever know. What a great idea!

A. Slow down. For sure you can tell your client that she can contact the other side. But remember the other basic rule. Lawyers cannot do through the acts of another what they can't do directly themselves. If we can't contact the client on the other side, we can't send a paralegal or investigator to do so.

Q. But this is the client doing the contacting.

A. Whether there is an exception to the indirection rule for client conduct is a source of controversy. Some assert that since the lawyer is an agent of the client the client cannot be turned into an agent of the lawyer and, therefore, if what the lawyer instructs the client to do is something clients are entitled to do, that is the end of the inquiry.[747]

Others (such as the authors) believe the purposes of the rule are undermined just as much if the lawyer scripts or masterminds the client's conduct. Our transactional colleagues say they script client contacts all the time. That's their stock in trade, they claim. And maybe their custom and practice argument can protect them. But for us trial lawyers, we think the far better view is for you to instruct your client about the availability of client-to-client contact, but not turn your client into your puppet bringing your wily lawyer ways to how that contact should be scripted.[748]

---

747. N.Y. City Bar Op. 2002-3 (where the client conceives the idea to communicate with a represented party, client's lawyer may advise the client concerning the substance of the communication so long as the lawyer does not assist the client inappropriately to seek confidential information or invite the nonclient to take action without the advice of counsel or otherwise to overreach the nonclient).

748. S.F. Unified Sch. Dist. *ex rel.* Contreras v. First Student, Inc., 153 Cal. Rptr. 3d 583 (2013) (lawyers may advise clients about direct communication with opposing parties; no evidence that lawyers coached clients about what to say or prepared binding legal documents for client to ask other party to sign); *In re* Pyle, 91 P.3d 1222 (Kan. 2004) (lawyer censured who tried to circumvent Rule 4.2 by drafting affidavit and advising client to give it to opposing party); Bd. of Prof'l Responsibility v. Melchoir, 269 P.3d 1088 (Wyo. 2012) (lawyer publicly reprimanded for crafting a divorce settlement agreement for client to present to represented spouse absent the knowledge of spouse's lawyer); ABA Comm. on Ethics & Prof'l Responsibility, Formal Op. 92-362 (1992) Contact With Opposing Party Regarding Settlement Offer (lawyer who has made settlement offer may not contact opposing party to see if offer has been communicated, but may advise his own client about the latter's ability to contact the opposing party).

§ 22.05 Communication with Employees of Represented Entities

Economical Discovery

Q. Formal discovery's useless. Depositions are endless and the witnesses have been so beaten up in preparation you get the same meaningless answers you receive from serving interrogatories or requests for admission. And the clients hate it because the bills are over the top. Plenty of billables for the lawyers, but no satisfaction for the bill payer and little help for the case. What I like are those informal interviews. You find your adversary's employees at a bar, a convention, outside the factory gate. You schmooze 'em a little bit, maybe buy 'em a libation. Before you know it, you've got the skinny on what really happened, the unvarnished truth, the cost is minimal, and the other side doesn't even know what you know. That's discovery the old-fashioned way, discovery you can believe in.

A. You do this often?

Q. Every case. Oh . . . we take some deps so the other side thinks they are getting the upper hand with their rehearsed answers and near prevarications. But then we surprise them with who's on our witness list. And they don't receive that until it's too late.

A. Do you worry about who you are contacting?

Q. Hell no, we don't touch the big guys. They're lawyered up. What we do is totally ethical.

A. Well not quite. It sounds like you may be violating some very important rules.

Q. Haven't been caught yet.

A. And we don't want you to be caught. But we also don't want you to break the rules. That's why we're here. To give you clear guidance.

Q. I'm listening. Just don't cramp my style.

A. Well the rules we have to worry about are 4.1, 4.2, and 4.3.

Q. Now we are in trouble.

A. No. No. Hear us out. We are worrying about who you can contact without going through counsel when the adversary party or parties are organizations.

Q. That's what we do. Sue the malefactors of great wealth.

A. Then you must know who is (and who is not) fair game for your taproom chats. Rule 4.2 prohibits contacting represented persons. But when the represented person is a legal fiction, an organization, it is Rule 4.2 that tells you which of the organization's constituents—a big word for officers, employees, and agents—you may contact.

Q. Shoot.

A. Well the first group you cannot contact is any member of the control group, the group that counsels with the lawyer on the matter to determine how the representation will proceed.

Q. You mean the "big shots." Told you we never talk to them.

A. Well the persons in this category are not necessarily big shots. It's whomever the lawyer is assigned to consult with. Could be the CEO.

Q. Not talking to him.

A. Could be the general counsel.

Q. For sure we would never contact that gal. We're not stupid.

A. But it could be the plant superintendent. Or some employee in the lab.

Q. How would we know?

A. You've identified the problem.

Q. But I came to you for solutions.

A. Of course. And the solution here is that if you're going to contact an employee on the other side, and you are not sure of that person's position vis-á-vis the matter, it's your burden not to conduct a substantive discussion with the object of your desire until you satisfy yourself that Rule 4.2's prohibition does not apply. And the risk of a mistake is on you.[749]

Q. Hardly fair.

A. That is true. In the battle between those who want informal discovery and those who want to protect the organizational client, there is a little tilt toward the latter, with uncertainty having some chilling effect on your free-wheeling ways.

Q. I can't talk to the big shots. Anyone else?

A. The present version of the Model Rules has one more. You may not contact any constituent of the organization whose

---

749. Gifford v. Target Corp., 723 F. Supp. 2d 1110 (D. Minn. 2010) (law firm disqualified for receiving confidential information from a managerial employee of opposing company); Faison v. Thornton, 863 F. Supp. 1204 (D. Nev. 1993) (lawyers disqualified and ordered to pay $46,000 in fees for engaging in ex parte communications; evidence also excluded); Kaiser v. AT&T, No. 00-724-PHX-JWS, 2002 WL 1362054 (D. Ariz. Apr. 5, 2002) (lawyer disqualified for engaging in ex parte contacts with a high-ranking former manager who was a critical witness in the case); *In re* Bilbe, 841 So. 2d 729 (La. 2003) (lawyer suspended from practice for three years for, inter alia, engaging in ex parte contact with employees of represented company); ABA Comm. on Ethics & Prof'l Responsibility, Formal Op. 06-443 (2006) Contact With Inside Counsel of an Organization Regarding a Matter When the Organization Is Represented in the Matter by Outside Counsel (MR 4.2 allows a lawyer who represents a client in a matter involving an organization to communicate with the organization's inside counsel about the subject of the matter without first obtaining consent of the entity's outside counsel).

conduct may be imputed to the organization for purposes of liability. To put it simply, you can't contact the employees who allegedly screwed up.

Q. But if someone is a mere witness?

A. If they're not in either of the two groups we've identified, there's no problem. Say you're suing a company because its driver hit your car. You can't talk to the reckless driver. But you can talk to any company employee who is a passenger.

Q. Do I get this right? If we're suing Colossus on a product claim, I can't talk to the designer, but I can talk to anyone else?

A. That would be so if your theory of the case is that the designer is the only person responsible.

Q. Well, at an early stage we hardly know that. Why do you think we are conducting our little investigation?

A. Then you would not be able to talk to anyone involved in the design or manufacture. And maybe if product descriptions are implicated, anyone involved in drafting those. You get the idea.

Q. Oh, I get it alright. But I am not happy.

A. And don't forget that when you talk to mere witnesses, you have Rule 4.3 obligations if they are unrepresented by counsel. You may not pretend to be disinterested. If the person misunderstands your role as counsel for the opposing party, you must clarify. And you must remain vigilant to the possibility that the interests of your witness may be in conflict with your client's interests. If this occurs, you also may not give any legal advice like "the law protects you if . . ." except the advice to secure counsel.[750]

§ 22.06 Communication with Former Employees of Represented Entities

The Disgruntled Former Employee

Q. We've got a new case. What a winner. And the really good news is that we've been in contact with a disgruntled former employee. I have no idea how we got so lucky. He's agreed to meet with us next week. The other good news is, we checked the Model Rules. They say Rule 4.2 doesn't apply to former employees, so the coast is clear, right?

750. MR 4.3; RLGL § 98.

A. A little too fast. This one comes with an exception and a caveat.
Q. Wouldn't you know it.
A. No, seriously, the Model Rule comment says former employees are fair game. But not every jurisdiction agrees. You just have to check to make sure you are not in one of those dissenting jurisdictions that includes former employees within the Rule 4.2 protections.
Q. I take it that's the exception.
A. Indeed.
Q. You and your damn warnings. It is enough to make a grown man cry. What's the caveat?
A. Even if you are free to chat with a former organizational constituent, some areas of inquiry are off limits. For sure you cannot inquire into privileged communications with present or former employees. Beyond that, Model Rule 4.4 says you may not use methods of obtaining evidence that violate the legal rights of a third person, including the adverse party. The Restatement limits this prohibition to rights that arise by operation of law.[751] But the Model Rule comment observes that it is "impractical to catalogue all rights," and one of your authors thinks you may not tortiously interfere with contractual rights of confidentiality such as those found in employment agreements. Nor may you induce a breach by the individual of a fiduciary duty the contracted constituent owes its present or former employer.
Q. Well, that seems wrong. For sure I can get that information at a deposition.
A. Maybe you can. But in a deposition the lawyer for the organization can object and take other measures to restrict your inquiries. She might succeed; she might fail. But at least she knows what's being sought. With your ex parte contact, the organization doesn't stand a chance.
Q. Precisely why we conduct ourselves as we do.
A. We didn't hear that. One more thing. Even if the coast is otherwise clear, there may be some employees or former employees you just don't want to bother contacting. This situation would arise if by the nature of the matter and the employee's role in it, disclosure of privileged information is an inevitable result of the conversation you seek. For example, if the issue is the company's tax return and the employee you want to contact is

751. RLGL § 102.

known to you to be the person who interfaced with counsel on its preparation, preparation that is the issue in the matter, then contact would be unwise.

Q. Sounds pretty restrictive to me. The good thing is it's nice and ambiguous. Worst case scenario, we just apologize.

A. Apologies might not do it, our friend. Lawyers have been disqualified for invading the privilege, for violating Rule 4.2.[752] And barred from talking to the successor counsel. Forcing the client to start all over and successfully seeking a return of fees previously paid.[753] Plus there are the disciplinary folks. They get lots of reports of Rule 4.2 violations.

Q. Why so many?

A. Because there is always a really pissed off lawyer on the other side ready, willing, and able to turn in the miscreant once the surreptitious contact gets disclosed.

Q. This is serious stuff.

A. That's what we've been trying to tell you.

Q. Of course, I don't limit my informal discovery to former employees of these malefactors of great wealth. There is a whole treasure trove of great information I can snare from present employees, believe you me. So many unhappy employees; so much to learn.

A. Present employees are fair game—that's true. But you have to be even more careful there.

Q. There you go again showing your corporate mentality.

A. You can say that, but what we really are trying to protect is you. Some present employees are forbidden territory.

Q. I know, I know. But most are not.

A. That depends on the size. But that is certainly true of large organizations.

Q. I just have to avoid the forbidden areas. But I must say you guys haven't made it easy.

A. Well, the categories are clear.

Q. Not really. These people don't present with a Rule 4.2 protective hat on.

A. That is correct. Which emphasizes one important point: it's your obligation—the contracting lawyer—to make the requisite determination before a substantive comment is made.

Q. There's that chilling effect again.

A. True enough. But more often than not, you'll have no trouble.

752. *Faison*, 863 F. Supp. at 1204.

753. Featherstone v. Schaerrer, 34 P.3d 194 (Utah 2001).

Q. I know I can't contact the big shots.

A. That is correct. If by that you mean the people on the organizational chart who deal with the lawyer on this matter such as the board, the CEO, the plant superintendent, the head of the lab, or some combination of folks. Don't contact them.

Q. Beyond that it seems tricky.

A. Well, under the Model Rule, you can't contact those whose conduct is to be imputed to the corporation for purposes of liability. If it's an insider trading case against a company, people who allegedly engaged in the trades would be protected from your wily ways. And anyone up the ladder who may have authorized them would be protected too. If it's a product liability case, it could be a whole range of employees, from engineers to purchasing agents to the designers of the assembly line to the marketing folks.[754]

Q. Doesn't that just prove my point?

A. A few jurisdictions retain a prohibition on anyone whose testimony will act as an admission on behalf of the company. Though this is ambiguous because, broadly construed, it could reach nearly any employee.[755]

Q. Of course.

A. But those in positions of authority as to the litigated matter whose admissions could bind the company clearly are protected.

§ 22.07 Authorized by Law Exception

Government Lawyers

Q. I won't use expletives, but I cannot tell you how outraged I am. The EPA started snooping around our client, something about compliance with the Clear Water Act. Just an investigation. So, I call up EPA counsel, introduce myself, tell 'em we are representing Excelsior and all contacts with our "very cooperative" client should be through our firm. Lawyer on the other side thanks me. And we sit back, waiting to hear where this is going.

A. Good for you.

754. MR 4.2 cmt. [7].

755. *See, e.g.*, Messing, Rudavsky & Weliky, P.C. v. President & Fellows of Harvard College, 764 N.E.2d 825 (Mass. 2002) (discussing various court tests).

Q. Not so fast. So, it's a Saturday morning. Quite early. I'm sleeping in when my hope for some weekend catch-up is shattered. It is Excelsior's general counsel. He just learned that EPA lawyers showed up at the homes of three Excelsior employees, maybe more, inquiring about our compliance with the act.

A. Who did they contact?

Q. We know it was the QC director, the plant superintendent, and a janitor in the paper mill's filtration plant. Weren't they supposed to go through me?

A. You told him you were representing the company. And the rules provide that, based on that organizational representation, certain employees are off limits. The employees the lawyers consult for guidance in handling the representation. And employees whose conduct could give rise to company liability fall within those rules.

Q. So, does that include these three?

A. It certainly could. We would need to know more.

Q. Well, the plant superintendent is the person we contact to get instructions as to the investigation into his facility.

A. He was definitely protected.

Q. Actually, it's a she.

A. And the head of the QC lab?

Q. That's the person who established all of our pollution control standards. Great employee. Really smart.

A. And probably he's protected as well. If he erred, Excelsior could be in trouble.

Q. You got the gender right this time. The janitor?

A. Do we know enough? If he or she is just a witness to what was happening, they were entitled to contact the janitor. If the janitor is alleged to have screwed up some maintenance work, the janitor, too, is protected.

Q. Well, this careful analysis sounds correct, but when I screamed at the EPA lawyer for gross violations, he told me that I didn't understand, that since this was an investigation and the EPA has the duty to enforce our country's pollution laws (flag waving, please), the EPA lawyers were not bound by Rule 4.2.

A. Such statements recall a fight of yesteryear that we thought was settled. When Dick Thornburgh was attorney general under Bush I, he issued a memo that purported to exempt DOJ lawyers from compliance with Rule 4.2 because of the language in the rule "Unless authorized by law." To prove this was a bipartisan attack on our rules, when Janet Reno became attorney general under Clinton, she did Thornburgh one better by issuing regulations, regulations that were declared invalid by the Eighth Circuit.[756] This did not stop New Mexico from disciplining a DOJ lawyer admitted in that state[757] and McDonnell Douglas from securing a decision of the Eighth Circuit that there was no grant from Congress to DOJ sufficient to authorize violations of Rule 4.2, striking the regulations.[758]

Q. So we won.

A. Oh, it gets better. See, when you shoot the king, you better kill him. And in this case DOJ went after Congressman McDade of Pennsylvania on criminal charges. Only problem: McDade was acquitted. And he turned out to be a vengeful member of the House, with DOJ firmly in his sights. As a result, after McDade retired, Congress passed what was instantly labeled the McDade amendment, requiring all DOJ lawyers to abide by their applicable rules of professional conduct.[759]

Q. So, these EPA lawyers transgressed.

A. If they violated 4.2, they did. And you can report them for discipline and seek relief from the courts.[760] Quash any indictment, suppress any information so secured, force DOJ to bring in new lawyers. All are worth a try.

Q. Sounds like more aggravation. To protect the company, I should've done what I originally planned. I should've notified the employees and instructed all of them not to talk to DOJ.

A. Glad you didn't. How could you ever represent all the employees? How many do they have?

Q. Two thousand or so.

A. And you don't see the problem? All the conflicts? Just the logistics of interviewing that many people?

Q. Well, maybe I wouldn't represent them all. Just tell them not to talk to DOJ.

---

756. United States *ex rel.* O'Keefe v. McDonnell Douglas Corp., 132 F.3d 1252 (8th Cir. 1998).

757. *In re* Howes, 940 P.2d 159 (N.M. 1997) (assistant U.S. Attorney responsible for violating MR 4.2 despite reliance on advice of supervisory DOJ lawyers).

758. *O'Keefe*, 132 F.3d at 1252.

759. 28 U.S.C. § 530B (2017).

760. United States v. Koerber, 966 F. Supp. 2d 1207 (D. Utah 2013) (evidence suppressed because it was disclosed to federal prosecutors who violated state rule 4.2, the target's constitutional rights, and the McDade Amendment by instructing FBI and IRS agents to interview target without notifying his lawyer).

A. That's trouble, too, we're afraid. Some, DOJ folks in particular, might argue that is obstruction of justice. It is okay to remind folks they don't have to talk to DOJ. That you'll get them a lawyer. It's another to bar them from doing so.[761]

761. Terra Int'l Inc. v. Miss. Chem. Corp., 913 F. Supp. 1306, 1317 (N.D. Iowa 1996) ("(A)n employer cannot unilaterally create or impose representation of employees by corporate counsel. Such an automatic representation rule would serve no useful purpose, but would instead impede the course of investigation leading to or following the filing of a lawsuit."); ABA Comm. on Ethics & Prof'l Responsibility, Formal Op. 95-396 (1995) Communications with Represented Persons (general counsel cannot assert blanket representation of all employees).

CHAPTER 23

Discovery

§ 23.01 Introduction: Legal Regulation of Discovery Abuse

Litigators do not have to be reminded of the importance of good faith in the document production process. As the real world of document creation, storage, review, and production has gone from carbon copies to the copy machine to the digital revolution, the lawyer's involvement, focus, dedication of hours, and responsibility has only increased. So have the obligations of lawyers as officers of the court to ensure that their clients produce that which is required.

It never was easy to insist that clients produce all requested documents, no matter how damaging to the client's case the production may be. But now with the wholesale use of email that provides clients the opportunity to write and send intemperate messages to half the civilized world in a fraction of a second and determining whether documents are, for example, privileged in light of how widely distributed and redistributed they are and the need to ensure that documents are not destroyed that are required to be preserved when they might be found on cell phones or home computers or iPads, the obligation has become both more critical and more difficult to achieve.

As a result, counsel's responsibility has been revisited by both the case law and the rules committees, in a conscientious but nonetheless incomplete way. Suffice it to say the lawyer has a heavy responsibility in situations in which their clients are unlikely to be "caught," as well as those situations where omissions would be easily uncovered another way.

Like frivolous lawsuits, discovery rules such as Federal Rules of Civil Procedure 26 and 37,[762] combined with state and federal statutes and the inherent power of the court regulate how and when you must disclose information.[763] In serious cases of discovery abuse, the common law of spoliation of evidence also provides remedies.[764] Several provisions of the Model Rules incorporate these procedural rules, subjecting you to professional discipline if you violate the procedural rule, or otherwise unlawfully obstruct another party's access to evidence or alter a document.[765]

§ 23.02 Inadvertent Document Receipt

Inadvertent Email

Q. Let me ask you a different question. We're preparing for trial. Eight-figure damages. One of those frivolous product liability claims.

A. Oh, we know about those.

Q. No, no. This one really is far-fetched. Complaining about air bags exploding. But the other side survived a *Daubert* challenge to their expert. Anyway, it is two days before trial, and we are handed this great gift. The plaintiff sent us an email that was addressed to all defense counsel, and it included a juror profile prepared by Decision Quest, giving the results of potential juror research for this particular case. Those guys are good. You get what you pay for. But we paid nothing. Sure helped us know who to strike. Really made our peremptories pay off.

762. Parsi v. Daioleslam, 778 F.3d 116, 118 (D.C. Cir. 2015) (court invoked Fed. R. Civ. P. 37 and inherent power to impose $183,000 sanction for "disturbing pattern of delay and intransigence" in discovery).

763. Jimenez v. Madison Area Technical Coll., 321 F.3d 652, 657 (7th Cir. 2003) (lawyer's failure to verify authenticity of falsified documents after opposing party denied authorship justified sanction of dismissal with prejudice because filing of baseless claim amounted to "veritable attack on our system of justice"); Pilot v. Focused Retail Prop. I, LLC, 274 F.R.D. 212 (N.D. Ill. 2011) (although a showing of inadvertence prevents subject-matter waiver under Fed. R. Evid. 502, the rule also requires proof that the party took reasonable steps to prevent the disclosure and to rectify the error; failing to take any screening steps during discovery and failing to assert the privilege when the inadvertently disclosed document was used at the party's deposition constitutes failure to act reasonably, waiving the privilege); Rambus, Inc., v. Infineon Techs. AG, 220 F.R.D. 264 (E.D. Va. 2004) (filing of an incomplete privilege log waives privilege as to inadequately described documents).

764. Surowiec v. Capital Title Agency, Inc., 790 F. Supp. 2d 997 (D. Ariz. 2011); Zubulake v. UBS Warburg LLC, 220 F.R.D. 212, 216 (S.D.N.Y. 2003).

765. MR 3.4(a)–(c); RLGL § 118–20.

We were so excited when the email arrived. It was the eve of trial, and we were representing a plaintiffs' class of individuals who bought cars with the brake defect.

A. You used it?

Q. We certainly did. It was really helpful, and we got just the jury we wanted. But opening statements are tomorrow, and some of our colleagues are getting cold feet. They are worried that if the other side ever discovers that we had that jury report, the judge might declare a mistrial or we could lose on appeal. I don't know what we should do.

A. Without telling the other side?

Q. Look, we didn't steal it. They sent it to us. Was that wrong?

A. The answers to those questions are all over the place. Where to begin? Years ago the ABA Ethics Committee was asked this question. One of us worked on it. Cobbling together the importance of the privilege, the law of missent property, the Golden Rule, and yours truly's expectation that he was more likely to send than receive, the opinion established two principles. If it is privileged, the sender must be notified; the recipient must abide the instructions of the sender or else get the court to adjudicate any claim to which the recipient is entitled.

Not much later, the Philadelphia Bar Association issued an opinion endorsing what you did. Asserting that the privilege was waived in the sending. That opinion gave carte blanche to use without notification.[766]

When the Ethics 2000 Commission of the ABA rewrote the rules and comments, it struck a middle ground. It still required notice to the sender. But it punted on what happened next. Instead of taking an affirmative position, the ABA left it to state law to determine whether there were any other obligations.[767] One important lesson here: The receiving lawyer acts at the lawyer's peril, if the sender claims a right to return and threatens sanctions or worse if you have or plan to read beyond what was required to establish a credible claim of privilege. But that rule really applies across the board. When privilege is asserted, await adjudication of the question or render yourself vulnerable to being charged with a Rule 4.4 violation and the sanctions that can follow.

The one thing you cannot do is let things proceed as they are. Rule 4.4 tells us that the receipt of that document, clearly

766. Philadelphia Bar Ass'n Op. 94-15 (1994).
767. MR 4.4(b) cmt. [2].

not intended for you, required you to notify the other side of its receipt. Obviously, you did not do that. But if you had, defense counsel would at least have known what you knew and could have taken further action.

Q. What kind of further action?

A. The law on notification is clear. After that the obligation of the lawyer varies from jurisdiction to jurisdiction. Some agree with the original ABA opinion on this topic, which requires both notification—reading only so much of the document as to determine that it is privileged or work product—and abiding by the instructions you receive from the sender. Rule 4.4, as adopted, only requires the notification, but that of course permits the sender to at least attempt to retrieve the document and seek whatever relief might be appropriate under the circumstances, at the same time permitting the receiver to argue (1) the sending was a waiver, and (2) the receiver was entitled to keep and use the document. In any event, your worried colleagues have justifiable concerns. Though the notice to the sender will be tardy, as they say, better late than never.[768]

§ 23.03 Electronic Documents

Regret at Leisure

Q. I have a problem. What was I thinking? My client is suing for gender discrimination. She was passed over for promotion in favor of a guy who got the promotion solely because he's a good ol' boy. Same colleagues as the CEO.

A. Sounds like a great case.

Q. It was. Surely it was. You see, before we had the case, I went on my client's Facebook page. It was my teenage daughter's

768. Salmeron v. Enter. Recovery Sys. Inc., 579 F.3d 787 (7th Cir. 2009) (counsel's promise to opposing counsel to keep sensitive document confidential until court could enter a protective order meant that giving the document to a member of the press was more than sufficient to support the finding of willfulness as the basis for dismissing the case with prejudice); Perna v. Elec. Data Sys., Corp., 916 F. Supp. 388 (D.N.J. 1995) (party who obtained unauthorized access to and photocopied opposing party's documents required to pay opposing party's fees incurred in connection with the motion to dismiss as well as suffer dismissal of party's action with prejudice); State v. Lenarz, 22 A.3d 536 (Conn. 2011) (case dismissed where prosecutor was inadvertently exposed to defendant's privileged communications with counsel, unless state can establish lack of prejudice to defendant or that some other remedy will suffice); Merits Incentives, LLC v. Eighth Judicial Dist. Court, 262 P.3d 720 (Nev. 2011) (lawyer who receives documents in a case from an anonymous source must notify opposing counsel or risk being in violation of ethical duties and subject to disqualification).

idea. Well, not her idea. But when she told me what her friends posted, I got worried. What was on my client's page?

A. And …

Q. It was bad. Real bad. Pictures of her and her friends living it up. Smoking. Something other than tobacco. From a water pipe. Hadn't seen one of them in 25 years.

A. Kids will be kids.

Q. She's 38. In any event, I told her to take that stuff down. Before we filed. So it would not come back to haunt her.

A. And she did?

Q. Yep. But now the other side has asked to see all entries on her Facebook page for the last four years. But so much of it is gone. When I told the other side, they deposed her, and she blurted out that I instructed her to do it. Then they moved to dismiss her complaint because of the spoliation. And reported us for discipline. Violations of a slew of rules.

A. What were you thinking?

Q. That Facebook did not count. That only friends were allowed to see it. Her employer could never be a friend. They're the enemy.

A. There is no magic here. While it is true you cannot fake friendship to see someone's page, the contents are just as discoverable as any other non-privileged items. Unless what is on there is irrelevant to the proceeding, the other side can see it. And if that is so, then you cannot destroy it once the duty to preserve is triggered.[769]

Q. So, what do I do now?

A. Explain to your client you have made a mistake and may have a conflict. Urge her to get new counsel. And notify your carrier. Maybe it'll turn out she did not have a very good claim.[770]

Q. Even if I told her the opposite?

A. You were wrong.

---

769. N.Y. State Bar Ass'n, Social Media Ethics Guidelines § 4A (2015), *available at* https://www.nysba.org/Sections/Commercial_Federal_Litigation/Com_Fed_PDFs/Social_Media_Ethics_Guidelines.html.

770. ABA Comm. on Ethics & Prof'l Responsibility, Formal Op. 481 (2018), A Lawyer's Duty to Inform a Client or a Former Client of a Lawyer's Material Error ("[MR] 1.4 requires a lawyer to inform a current client if the lawyer believes that he or she may have materially erred in the client's representation . . . an error is material if a disinterested lawyer would conclude that it is (a) reasonably likely to harm or prejudice a client; or (b) of such a nature that it would reasonably cause a client to consider terminating the representation even in the absence of harm or prejudice.").

§ 23.04 Destroyed Documents

The Deleted Files

Q. We are conducting document discovery and, as we interview various key employees, we learn that one of them stripped his electronic files of hundreds of documents related to this matter as soon as he learned the lawsuit had been filed. Thought he was doing the employer a favor because he thought some of them were "ambiguous." Now we are making production and, as requested, we are producing all of the documents in our possession or control that are responsive to the request. It may be that this includes the documents that were destroyed, but we can't tell for sure. One of my colleagues thinks we have to tell the other side. I said no way.

A. We are afraid your colleague is right. When you produce documents there is an implied representation by the lawyers that they are producing all responsive documents. It is the obligation of the lawyers to satisfy themselves that they have conducted a diligent search of all files, electronic and otherwise. You actually know that some documents were destroyed. As a result, you cannot produce the documents you have in silence because that implied representation is incorrect. Your duty as an officer of the court is to inform the other side of as much information as you have about the missing documents, including the steps you took to retrieve them. It is painful. But just remember one thing: It was your client's employee. Your job is to minimize the harm but, before you do, that full disclosure is required.[771]

Who Knew?

Q. Our client processes chicken for fast food restaurants. It has supplied Chicken King since 1975. Back then the feed was enhanced with a chemical designed to speed weight gain. They reduced the time from egg to mature chicken of the required weight.

Five years ago this couple in Indiana brought a lawsuit claiming their child's brain tumor was caused by that chemical supplement. They claimed Chicken King was the only place

771. Fed. R. Civ. P. 26(g).

the kid would eat. And Chicken King settled the case quietly under seal.

A. So far, so good.

Q. That was when we got this great idea. The case was an aberration. No one expected another one. So the company decided to destroy all the documents relating to the case and the development of the additive. That way even if another nut job brought a lawsuit, there would be no need for expensive document discovery. With no other specific cases pending or threatened we knew the coast was clear. And we so advised the clients.

A. "Coast was clear."

Q. Something like that. But now this class action was brought against Chicken King attacking the chemical as the cause for other children's illnesses. Class counsel served a document request. Basically, we told them there were no documents. "None?" they asked. "Yes, all that material was so old. We can't clutter our hard drives with 20-year-old records." With no records they could not proceed, and the case was dismissed.

A. A great result.

Q. It was until somehow—we don't know how—but somehow, the plaintiffs' counsel found out about the first case and the document dump; and they have sued us, the lawyers, for aiding and abetting spoliation. Can you believe that? It can't be spoliation if there was no litigation pending.

A. Sad to say that is incorrect. You may not destroy documents, indeed you must preserve them, if you anticipate litigation. It need not be actually pending.

Q. We didn't anticipate litigation either. There had been this one frivolous case. It was dismissed. And sealed. Can't get better than that.

A. Then why did your client—with your blessing—destroy all the documents?

Q. They were so old.

A. You can try out that argument. It might prevail. But we would not count on it. And if it doesn't, your client may suffer the consequences. An assumption that the missing material would have reflected actual knowledge by your client that the chemical was dangerous to human health.

Q. We did not destroy anything.

A. You may as well have. Your firm, because of its permission to the client, may be responsible to the class as an aider and abettor and to your client for malpractice.

§ 23.05 Manufactured Documents

What to Do?

Q. It is the weekend before trial. I am prepping my key witness. He owns a construction company and is suing a customer for failing to pay for extras that were added to the construction project after the original contract was signed. He has produced dozens of work orders reflecting the requests for these extras and plans to introduce them to the jury through this witness. I show him the first document and ask him if it was prepared on or about the date it bears. He hesitates and then, dropping his voice, answers, "No, I prepared these documents a couple of months ago, but I won't testify to that on Monday."

I would never have thought the documents were back-dated. Moreover, they have been listed on our pretrial order with exhibit numbers. What do I do?

A. Lawyers may not offer false testimony. By the same token, they may not introduce 12 forged documents. You, of course, are not going to use the documents on Monday. The question is whether that is enough.

Q. I sure hope it is.

A. We don't think so. We think it is now relevant that your client prepared these documents, and you have represented to the court and opponent that they are genuine. They are entitled to know what happened.

Q. Do I have to tell the court?

A. What you have to do is take reasonable remedial action.[772] We think you could tell your opponent and see if it is possible to settle the matter once the opponent knows this critical piece of information. But, failing that, we believe you have no alternative but to tell the court as well, because of the implicit representation you made about the genuineness of the documents.

Getting It Right

Q. I am in such trouble. And I was only trying to make sure the record was accurate.

A. A worthy goal, don't you think?

Q. It was a terrible case. But three things happen. Doctors cannot cure everyone.

772. MR 3.3(a)(3), (b), and cmt. [10].

A. You are sounding like a med-mal defense lawyer.

Q. You got that right. Obstetrics case. The infant was jaundiced at birth. My client, the doctor, saw the yellowing on a visit the second day. It was limited to the chest area. But the nurse entered into the chart "yellowing to the waist." If that were so, extraordinary action was required. But the doctor was certain of his finding, so he asked the nurse to correct her report. She did that. Wrote a second accurate report.

A. Not sure but could be okay.

Q. That's what we thought. We substituted the correct report and destroyed the original. No reason to confuse the record. The case got tried, defense verdict, of course. Our doc did nothing wrong.

A. We're feeling uncomfortable, but that can't be the end.

Q. Not at all. Two years pass. Someone sends the deceased's parents a copy of the incorrect report, the one we thought was destroyed. Now we are being sued. Can you imagine? We were only making sure no one was misled by the incorrect nurse's report.

A. Such good Samaritans. In fact, you know—you have to know—what you did was wrong. Maybe criminal. Certainly fraud. If the doctor consented to create a second properly dated report that was one thing. But substituting one for the other is worse than spoliation. It is changing testimony. It is destruction of evidence.[773] You'll find no sympathy here, I am afraid to say.

§ 23.06 Privilege Logs

Privilege Log Rolling

Q. This makes no sense. The case involves thousands of documents that are privileged. That's the way we do business in our regulated world. Lawyers review every aspect of our operation.

A. That does make sense.

Q. Oh, sure, claiming the privilege makes plenty of sense. But now the other side insists we create a privilege log. That'll take 100 hours. Maybe more. Why don't we just agree that we will turn over all the documents and claw back any documents we think are damaging? Get the other side to agree that production of a

773. MR 3.4(a)–(c).

few privileged documents is not a waiver. Frankly the documents I have seen don't hurt us.

A. The problems abound. You never want the judge, let alone your opponent, to see your client's privileged documents. It could not possibly help your case. Plus, any agreement you have with the other side would not bind a third party who wanted to claim that sharing documents here is a waiver for all.[774] Finally, if you produce all these documents the effect will be to waive the privilege, not only as to the documents listed, but also as to the subject matter of all those documents. That could easily lead to the wholesale depositions of you and all your colleagues as well.[775]

Q. Sounds like false economy to me.

A. We would not be quite that polite. Start preparing the log.[776]

§ 23.07 Accuracy in Privilege Logs

Just One Document

Q. We've been battling with our client's GC for week. They've been sued in a consumer class action. Turns out a memo we wrote addressing the strengths and weaknesses of the case that was addressed and reviewed by the board of directors was shown by one of the directors to his stockbroker. Not turned over; just shown.

A. Could be trouble.

Q. Just wait. We have to prepare a privilege log. And we do. We list this document, and we show that a copy went to the broker. The GC hit the ceiling. Screaming, he insists we delete that reference. He wasn't *sent* the memo. He was shown the memo. Therefore, GC insists we delete the cc: entry.

A. Too clever by half. You might be able to come up with some dubious argument that you can still claim privilege despite the cc: entry, but you cannot pretend the sharing did not take place.

Q. GC says the board member did not have authority to do that. Therefore, it's okay.

774. RLGL § 78.

775. *Id.* § 79.

776. *In re* Vioxx Prods. Liab. Litig., 501 F. Supp. 2d 789 (E.D. La. 2007).

A. You could very well use that argument if a disgruntled employee, a whistleblower, an extortionist, did that. But this memo was addressed to the director.

Q. GC agrees that she will take the heat for the decision if it doesn't work out.

A. You know how serious the responsibility is to be as accurate as humanly possibly on a privilege log. Otherwise the ramifications can be profound. At the very least, a court could find waiver of the incorrectly described documents.[777] Courts have stricken an entire privilege log for inaccuracies.[778] The judges observe, correctly, that the integrity of the entire litigation process depends on lawyers being both honest and conscientious in this connection. Claims and defenses have been dismissed for transgressions in this area.[779] In the end, the lawyer who takes responsibility for this play could be irrelevant to the judge's sanctioning of the client. Moreover, you are the lawyer before the court. As a result, if the GC is willing to take responsibility for the misdeed, that only means you may get to share a jail cell with your former friend.[780]

Q. GC did ask me what the chances of getting caught were.

A. We can't wait to hear your response.

Q. I did not know what to do. I do think the chances are very slim, but I was afraid if I told her that, it would merely encourage her to insist we submit an inaccurate privilege log.

A. This is a hard question. The client is probably entitled to the information. Tax lawyers face this dilemma all the time. Client wants to deduct as a business expense the cost of daughter's wedding. Tax lawyer says it's illegal. Client then asks how likely it is that the IRS will ever pick up on the deduction. One thing is clear. If you know and you tell the client the answer, you better accompany the tempting advice with a stern lecture on the obligation to be honest with the IRS and the serious, really serious, consequences if you are caught.[781]

---

777. Rambus, Inc. v. Infineon Techs. AG, 220 F.R.D. 264 (E.D. Va. 2004) (filing of an incomplete privilege log waives privilege as to inadequately described documents).

778. *E.g.*, SEC v. Yorkville Advisors, LLC, 300 F.R.D. 152 (S.D.N.Y. 2014).

779. *E.g.*, Brown v. Katz, 868 N.E.2d 1159 (Ind. Ct. App. 2007).

780. *See also* § 14.03 in this book.

781. MR 1.2(d); RLGL § 94.

CHAPTER 24

Dealing with Experts

§ 24.01 Introduction: The Importance of Experts

Expert witnesses can be helpful and are often crucial to competent client representation. Lawyers learn about the importance of legal and factual issues from experts and rely on them to articulate the standard of care, calculate damages, or establish causation.[782]

Perhaps because they are so often used, the conduct of experts also is highly regulated. Courts use their inherent power and multifaceted procedural rules to control the admissibility and scope of expert-witness testimony and to respond to allegations of conflict of interest.[783] These rules have been folded into the Model Rules,[784] making violations of expert-discovery provisions grounds for professional discipline as well as procedural sanction.

From start to finish, your work with expert witnesses can present not only strategic challenges but also ethical challenges. Client counseling, confidentiality, competence, conflicts, candor to the tribunal, observing limits on communications with both represented and unrepresented persons—these ethical considerations and others may be implicated along the way. It is good to chart the straight and narrow path—and to stay on it. The reality of your expert may never be as good as your dream. But you certainly do not want to make it a nightmare.

782. Douglas R. Richmond, Brian S. Faughnan, & Michael L. Matula, Professional Responsibility in Litigation 369–70 (2011).

783. Fed. R. Civ. P. 26(e)(2).

784. MR 3.4; RLGL §§ 116, 117.

§ 24.02 The Dream Expert

The Big Case

Q. I have a dream case. It's a "big" one. Our firm is thrilled to be handling it and I am a hero for bringing it in. Lots of documents. Close questions. Depositions galore. And a need for expert witnesses to wow the jury with the merits of my client's position.

A. Do not wake up yet.

Q. I locate the preeminent expert in the field. The expert is charming, presents well, is good-humored, and has a curriculum vitae (CV) that knocks your socks off: not a pretentious bone in his body. Speaks clearly. Just enough gray hair.

A. Still dreaming?

Q. And the expert endorses my position; no, he actually reinforces it using a line of analysis neither my client nor I ever considered.

The expert prepares a report. Comprehensive. Understandable. To the point. Letter perfect. Just what the doctor ordered to bring the other side to its knees in the upcoming mediation. Alas, that does not work. The opponent just does not get it. They will be sorry later.

The deposition prep lasts mere minutes. The testimony is better than expected. Still no settlement. But I need a good trial to get my sea legs back and my expert is our ace in the whole.

No need for trial prep. Just a slight tutorial for my benefit. And the jury loves my expert. No jargon. Great eye contact. Stands at the easel and teaches the "class." Even the judge asks questions that help my case along.

Only cross-examination can go wrong now, but, true to form, my expert remains calm, turns each question into an opportunity to reinforce the points made on direct, and returns to the easel to give a perfect summation. If I lose this case, it will be in spite of the dream expert.

A. Now open your eyes. We know that is what we seek to achieve. But we also know that it never happens quite that way. The path for lawyer and expert, from identifying the right person (always flawed in some respect) to the final cross-examination in a windowless courtroom (featuring a cantankerous judge and a bored-to-tears jury, as well as two or three concessions you could do without), is a roadway filled with potholes, speed bumps, and detours, requiring enormous energy and good judgment, an activity that can present ethical challenges as well as strategic ones.

Others are filling this book with strategic guidance. This chapter aims to help you meet the professional responsibility requirements that pervade the expert-witness process.

§ 24.03 Client Approval

Do Not Forget the Client

Q. I decided I needed an expert in a tax case. An accountant who could bless my client's challenged deductions. I needed him to testify. Heaven knows, I need him just as much to educate me. I picked up the telephone and called an expert I thought would be ideal. Told her all about the case. Now I've hired her for $750 an hour. Glad to snare such a star.

A. But not so fast! Did you forget something? It is the client's case. And it is the client's money you are about to spend. You are not a free agent (pun intended). You have ethical and fiduciary duties to communicate with the client, collaborate on the decision whether to hire an expert and who that expert should be, and accept the client's direction about how to proceed.[785] Your client can reject the use of an expert. Or have strong views on who should fill that role. And, of course, clients foot the bill for the expert's fees, which can be pretty steep. They need to know what is in store.

Q. OK, OK, I should've asked the client.

A. It's more than that. What about client confidentiality?[786] In talking to this prospective expert, you shared confidential information. But you, of course, are required to preserve the client's confidences—not just what you learned from the client but everything else "relating to the representation"—that is, unless your client gives you "informed consent" to disclose them.[787]

Q. I'm sure my client wanted me to share.

A. Do not be tempted here to say that the client has "impliedly authorized" you to disclose confidences to the expert "to carry out the representation." This is no time to rely on the client's implied consent. Your client might not recognize that disclosing client confidences is part of the process of choosing an

785. MRs 1.2(a), 1.4(a), 1.4(b).
786. MR 1.6.
787. MRs 1.0(e), 1.6(a).

expert and how extensive the disclosure may have to be for you to accomplish the necessary work. Do not proceed into the expert-witness terrain without your client at your side giving approval along the way.

§ 24.04 Finding the Best Expert

Shopping for the Right Expert

Q. I have to worry about the client before I start expert shopping? Am I home free once I have the client's permission?

A. Hardly. You want someone with the right credentials, knowledge, experience, demeanor, presence, and personality. And, crucially, you want someone whose opinions will help your client's case. But as you conduct the beauty contest and vet the potential expert, you want to proceed in a manner that never comes back to haunt you. The ethical imperatives to be competent and maintain confidentiality call on you to take precautions to prevent disclosures. The last thing you want to come out is the fact that you approached 11 different potential experts before you found the one you needed—even if you rejected the first ten not because of their opinions, but because they were total geeks, brilliant, and hopeless candidates for witnesshood.

Q. Can I keep my initial screening confidential?

A. With respect to experts who are not also lawyers, the best you can do is try, but there are no guarantees. Your own screening efforts will be protected by the work-product immunity, meaning that your role in the process of vetting potential experts should not be the subject of inquiry by the opposing party. But there is nothing you can do to prevent a potential expert who is never hired from disclosing to the lawyers on the other side (should they later happen upon him) that you contacted him first.

Q. Is there anything I can do?

A. Well, when the time comes to convey the news that there will be no second date, you may deliver a parting admonition that you hope the proposed expert will not tell anyone that you spoke. But the jilted expert is not duty bound to comply with your stern instruction. If the prospective expert is contacted to testify for the other side, the individual may have to disclose the contact to prevent these new lawyers from getting into trouble.[788] A lawyer-expert, on the other hand, will have an ethical duty to maintain the prospective client's confidences,[789] a duty that will ordinarily continue unless and until she is designated as a testifying expert.[790]

§ 24.05 Vetting the Opinion

Shopping for the Right Opinion

Q. I get a great expert. Credentials are perfect. But I cannot be sure the expert will really help me. How do I proceed to learn if this expert is a keeper?

A. At an early stage, you are probably not ready to vow to use this expert as a trial witness. Returning to the dream world, it is sometimes possible to decide on the expert's "witnessability" before the hiring has occurred. Maybe it is obvious, based on her prior writings, that she can support your position. Or maybe the issue in the case is easy enough to describe that the expert can evaluate it and reach at least a tentative conclusion before the engagement starts. But far more often the expert will have to learn a lot more about the case and undertake other research before reaching a tentative opinion. And that will generate not only fees for your client to pay but also communications, both written and oral, that could later become grist for the other side's mill.

Q. Can I do anything to stop that?

A. Well, you can certainly try.

There are two confidentiality concerns regarding your communications with the potential testifying expert. The first arises if, alas, he is never designated to testify. Anticipating that possibility, you want to take steps to ensure that the expert's work remains subject to the protection of the work-product doctrine to the greatest extent possible. This is likely to be so if the expert undertakes her work subject to your direction and control and neither of you share it with anyone aside from your firm, your client, and those with whom you have a joint-representation agreement. It also will require labeling documents generated by the expert as work product and limiting

788. *See* § 24.06 in this book.

789. *See* MR 1.18.

790. ABA Comm. on Ethics & Prof'l Responsibility, Formal Op. 97-407 (1997), Lawyer as Expert Witness or Expert Consultant.

their distribution to those whose receipt of the documents will not destroy the assertion of work-product immunity. In addition, you should ensure that the consulting expert contractually agrees that she recognizes the privilege, will not disclose any information relating to the matter unless you approve, and will notify you if she is contacted by anyone seeking information on the matter.

Q. But what if I decide to use this expert?

A. Completely contrary to the simple edifice one can erect to protect all with respect to the consulting expert, once the expert becomes a testifying expert all bets are off. In many state courts (although no longer in federal court),[791] absent a contrary agreement between or among the parties, most or even all preparatory work by a testifying expert is subject to wholesale discovery. This includes notes, research, documents reviewed, conversations, email and other written communications, drafts of reports or opinions, and materials reviewed and relied on. As a result, unless you know that the expert you are consulting will never testify or you are in a jurisdiction that has adopted a narrower approach to expert discovery, it matters little that the expert's preliminary work initially might have work-product protection.

Q. How confusing!

A. To be sure and, as a result, you must learn the rules of the jurisdiction in which you are litigating. This is absolutely key. And the rules governing expert discovery are all over the place. Some allow just expert reports to be discovered. Some allow drafts. Some allow all documents relied on. Some allow all documents reviewed. Some allow all documents received. Some allow every communication between lawyer and expert. The rules on discovery are also ever changing.

Q. What a balancing act!

A. Precisely. Your responsibility is to protect as much information as possible and at the same time advise the expert what her retention and production responsibilities are likely to be. If expert discovery is freewheeling, let your expert know that from the start, so that she can understand the need to conduct herself as if everything put in writing will be published on the front page of the *New York Times* (above the fold). If required under your rules, also advise whether the expert must keep

791. Fed. R. Civ. P. 26(a)(2)(B) (disclosure of expert reports required, depositions of experts in federal civil proceedings allowed, disclosure of drafts not required).

every shred of paper. But note that the expert is under no obligation to write things down. And there may be more protection available in your jurisdiction for work the expert undertakes that is not shared with counsel than that which is. You and your expert should be careful about the extent and content of your communications, particularly written communications that are most easily turned into a *cause célèbre*, effective in the centerpiece of a withering cross-examination.

Stating the proposition from a professional responsibility point of view, the lawyer should deal with the expert in a way that maximizes privilege protections while minimizing the amount of discoverable communications. But the lawyer must do so in a manner consistent with the obligation of the lawyer to act competently in dealing with the expert. In other words, as in so many situations, wise judgment is the order of the day.

§ 24.06 Experts and Conflicts

Hiring an Opposing Expert from a Different Pending Case

Q. My client is on the wrong end of a superfund case. Lots of experts are needed. Turns out our client is particularly enthusiastic about a remediation expert who helped my client at another site reduce the client's contribution by half. Hire him, I was urged. But then I remembered that this same expert is testifying against another client of our firm in a dispute between a seller and buyer over which entity is contractually responsible for some recently uncovered arsenic drums found in a junk pile down by the river. Can I follow my client's recommendation?

A. Not without difficulty. The cases may be totally unrelated. Nothing that happens in one will affect the other. That is, unless your colleague's cross-examination of this expert in the acquisition case materially undermines his ability to help your present client in the superfund matter. As a result, it would be best to suggest an alternative expert.

Q. What if the client insists on using the expert?

A. Then you have a hard question to answer. Are you reasonably certain that your firm will still be able to competently represent both the client in the superfund case and the client in the contract action?[792] Or will you be operating under a material limitation within the meaning of Model Rule of Professional

792. MR 1.7(b)(1).

Conduct 1.7(a)(2)? This means that you must be objectively convinced that your partner in the contract action will not pull punches to avoid creating a record that could be used to undermine the expert's credibility in your own case. Conversely, you must be objectively convinced that your partner will not have a need to create a devastating record of impeachment material that would later lead your client to complain that your firm prejudiced it. If you are satisfied that neither client will be harmed, you still need the informed consent confirmed in writing of both clients.[793] This will require three important considerations. First, you will be required to share the respective clients' confidential information. Second, to do that, you will be required to get each client's consent to that sharing. As a result, none of this may be achievable unless you manage to get permission from each client to disclose to the other its confidential information regarding both its case and its plans for expert assistance. And third, these client-informed consents must be confirmed in writing.

Q. What if I have hired a pristine remediation expert, one who has never previously testified in our neck of the woods, but, lo and behold, she is later designated as the expert by the opposing party in another case our firm is handling?

A. Same problem. Can you anticipate and avoid it? Certainly. You can make it a term of the expert's retention agreement that until your case is over she will not accept engagements in cases in which your firm is on the other side. If she agrees, you avoid the conflict. If not, this may be a red flag about the expert's commitment to the engagement. In addition, even if the expert has a plausible explanation for objecting to the term, you will assume some risk by hiring the expert, and you have to decide whether the expert is so good that it is a risk worth running.

---

793. MR 1.7(b)(4). "Informed consent" means "the agreement by a person to a proposed course of conduct after the lawyer has communicated adequate information and explanation about the material risks of and reasonably available alternatives to the proposed course of conduct." MR 1.0(e).

§ 24.07 Former-Employee Experts

Hiring the Turncoat as an Expert

Q. My client knows of a disgruntled former employee of his adversary who can testify as an expert on adhesives. He just knows this expert will stick it to his old company.

A. Putting aside that a jury may not consider a disgruntled employee to be particularly objective and that the jury may be distracted from the genuine credentials of this supposed expert, one must tread very carefully when contacting former employees, much less when hiring them. Some jurisdictions restrict communications with former key employees of the opposing organizational party. They subject these communications to Rule 4.2, which forbids communications with represented persons.[794] In many jurisdictions, you are free to speak to former employees without running afoul of this rule. But even if you are free to contact this person, you still must proceed with caution. You may not invade the other side's attorney-client privilege.[795] You also may not tortiously interfere with any confidentiality agreement the employee has with the former employer.[796] Moreover, you must not induce the former employee to breach any fiduciary duties that he owes the old employer.[797] Rule 4.4(a) requires you to respect the rights of third parties—including adversaries.[798]

§ 24.08 Hiring the Other Side's Former-Prospective Expert

The Undisclosed Consult

Q. I hired a superb expert. Everything was going well. I was on the cusp of producing her expert report. How I would devastate the other side! Then, in a final conversation, the expert mentioned my opposing counsel. I did not remember mentioning him before. "How do you know him?" I ask. "Oh, I met with him a couple of weeks before you called me. Paid me

---

794. MR 4.2; RLGL § 99.

795. *See* RLGL § 102.

796. *See* MR 4.4 cmt. [1] ("(I)t is impractical to catalogue all such rights, but they include . . . unwarranted intrusions into privileged relationships, such as the client-lawyer relationship.").

797. *Id.*

798. MR 4.4(a); RLGL § 102.

$5,000. A lot of money for me to tell him I couldn't help." "And you didn't tell me?" I exclaimed. "You never asked," was her response. The first lesson is, of course, I should've asked that question early on. If, however, I didn't and end up in this situation, may I go ahead and retain her?

A. Your expert is obviously the expert of choice. The problem is, she's been chosen twice. And in her first engagement, she may have learned the other side's privileged information. That means that your expert could very well be disqualified. The expert may have spoken to opposing counsel only briefly, but you can imagine how that will be characterized in the other side's disqualification motion.

Q. And if the other side revealed its privileged and work-product information to this expert before deciding not to hire her, they will claim—and a court may be inclined to assume—that she disclosed this information to you after you did hire her. Communications between a prospective expert and a potential-hiring lawyer can be considered privileged by the court and should be protected from disclosure under the work-product privilege. For instance, in *Shadow Traffic*,[799] the lawyers who hired an expert interviewed by the opposing party as a potential expert were disqualified, as was their entire firm.[800] If you knowingly elicited the other side's privileged information, you will subject yourself to serious discipline.[801] But even if you did so unintentionally and unwittingly, you still run the risk of being disqualified to prevent you from using what you learned.[802]

§ 24.09 Hiring All the Available Experts

Disqualifying by Shopping

Q. I've hired the very best of the available experts, but there are still several very good ones out there. I would not be thrilled to see any of them on the other side. What about this idea?

---

799. Shadow Traffic Network v. Super. Ct., 29 Cal. Rptr. 2d 693, 700 (1994).

800. *Id.* at 705.

801. MR 4.4(a).

802. Cordy v. Sherwin-Williams Co., 156 F.R.D. 575, 581–82 (D.N.J. 1994) (an expert who had billed 28 hours and received confidential information could not act as a witness for the opposition); Connors v. Dawgert, 38 Pa. D. & C. 4th 367, 381 (C.P. 1998) (an expert who did not remember a solicitation letter by the plaintiff that contained information in the public record could act as an expert witness for the defense).

I identify the other four or five leading experts on the issue, contact them for possible retention, give them lots of confidential information, maybe even pay each one something, and that way our adversaries will either have to settle for second best or go far afield in search of their expert witness.

A. It's a creative idea. Yet contacting experts just to make them unavailable to the other side would probably be a waste of money and effort and, worse yet, might violate the Rules of Professional Conduct. As the court observed in *Paul v. Rawlings Sporting Goods Co.*[803] if the courts make it too easy to disqualify an expert, "unscrupulous attorneys and clients may attempt to create an inexpensive relationship with potentially harmful experts solely to keep them from the opposing party."

§ 24.10 Compensating Your Expert

The Contingency Fee

Q. My client has a great claim. I took it on a contingency fee, in part because the client had no cash. Now I've found the ideal expert witness—a leader in the field of fluid dynamics. Nothing stands in the way of hiring him. He has never spoken to the other side. He has never been hired by one of our other opponents. Well, maybe there is one impediment: money. The best do not come cheap. $850 per hour! And now our firm's cash is running low, too. I explained our plight to the expert and, what a nice guy, he sympathized. "No problem," he replied. "You took the case on a contingency. I will too. Promise me 5 percent of any recovery by the client. That is how much I think is fair."

A. You are entering more than treacherous terrain. You have solved your cash flow problem. But you have created a bigger one. It is unethical to pay testifying experts a contingent fee. The Restatement (Third) of the Law Governing Lawyers prohibits paying a witness a fee contingent on the outcome of the litigation or on the content of his testimony. Otherwise, an expert may be paid for expenses he incurs as a result of testifying and a non-contingent fee.[804] While the Model Rules are a

803. Paul v. Rawlings Sporting Goods Co., 123 F.R.D. 271, 281–82 (S.D. Ohio 1988).

804. RLGL § 117.

bit oblique in their discussion regarding expert-witness fees,[805] almost all jurisdictions prohibit the payment of contingency fees to experts.[806]

The only proper way to proceed is to pay the expert for his time, without regard to the content of his testimony or the result of the proceeding. Even if it were not contrary to the ethical rules to make an expert's compensation contingent on the outcome of the trial, the arrangement would be bad lawyering. What credibility will your expert have once it is disclosed that his compensation is tied to victory? Juries start off viewing party-retained experts with some suspicion. Undermining your expert's credibility by entering into a contingent-fee arrangement would border on malpractice—or cross that border—even if it were otherwise permissible.

§ 24.11 Influencing the Expert's Opinion

Shaping Conclusions

Q. My case has multiple defendants. We represent one of them. Our job is to shift blame to the others. To support this effort, we've hired a renowned metallurgy expert—a professor from the M.I.T. of our state. But the good professor came back with a tentative opinion that was not quite as helpful as we would have hoped. It left open the question of whether our client's product could have played a role, albeit minor, in the ultimate disaster that prompted the high-stakes litigation. Then our client reviewed the expert's preliminary conclusions with dismay. Despite our expert's view, the client remains convinced that the catastrophe did not result from its product. The client says that the professor should go back to the drawing board. And the client wants us to help the professor see the light. Is it ethical for me to discuss with the expert matters he may have overlooked or might reconsider in an effort to shape his conclusions?

A. Of course it is. In the end, your obligation of competence requires that you put on the stand an expert who is at ease with her opinions. It is perfectly legitimate to help the witness

805. MR 3.4(b) explains, "A lawyer shall not offer an inducement to a witness that is prohibited by law . . . ."

806. MR 3.4 cmt. [3]; RLGL § 117 cmt. d; D.C. R. Prof'l Conduct 3.4 cmt. 8 (2015) (allowing experts to be paid contingency fees but prohibiting the fee to be based on a percentage of any recovery).

get to that point by identifying facts the expert might have overlooked, subject areas the expert has not addressed, or theories that might support a different opinion. Your client has been living the case for years; you have been engaged in the matter for months yourself; and, as a result of the well-trodden path you both have walked 100 times, you both may be able to help the expert.

But remember this. Your expert must maintain her credibility and integrity. That does not mean your expert must be cloistered from your influence, a monk who takes your client's original problem and returns, after an unguided journey to a sheltered-expert temple, with some irrefutable truth. Push if you wish. The good expert will refuse to leave her comfort zone but could very well be persuaded to revisit initial opinions and address additional topics suggested by your client or you.

These discussions could form the basis of cross-examination so, of course, that's one issue you must consider. But having your expert admit that, with the receipt of additional information, the expert's opinion was modified is far better than failing to have your expert address an important topic, allowing your expert to proceed from a flawed premise, or having your expert remain ignorant of some new development in her field of expertise.

§ 24.12 Ghostwriting the Expert's Report

The Draft Disaster

Q. My expert's a certified genius and his report (if I can call it that) fully supports our side, but the draft report is a disaster. No one without a PhD in biochemistry and 20 years of research lab experience sponsored by the National Institutes of Health could understand it. Can I rewrite his report? Is that ethical?

A. In many cases you may, and, if you are being competent, perhaps you must. It is your responsibility to work with the expert to achieve a clear, concise, and comprehensive report. Translating his overly technical language into something the judge, jury, and opponents will understand is critical. Maybe in some dream world your expert's report is letter perfect from the first draft. But in the real world, the expert's first draft will often need editing, even heavy editing. And, in some cases, the expert is simply incapable of producing a cogent report. You can write away with three huge caveats.

Q. You and your caveats.

A. First, you had better assure yourself that you are writing or rewriting a report that accurately reflects your expert's opinions. The touchstone of the rules is not whether the expert prepares the report in isolation from the lawyer but whether the report accurately reflects the expert's opinions and findings.[807]

Second, the Federal Rules of Civil Procedure require that expert witnesses "prepare" their reports.[808] A lawyer may aid an expert witness in preparing his testimony, but the expert must substantially participate in the preparation.[809] If the lawyer prepares the expert's report from whole cloth and then asks the expert to sign the report, the expert fails in his duty to prepare the report.[810] Furthermore, if the lawyer prepares and submits a report that does not reflect the expert's actual opinion, then the lawyer violates Federal Rule of Evidence 702.[811] Consequently, a lawyer may participate in the preparation of an expert report, but the ultimate document must reflect the actual opinion of the expert.

Third, you have to be prepared for your role in editing, rewriting, or writing your expert's report to be disclosed in testimony. Only you can make the call whether this is all worth it. But there is certainly nothing unethical about your role as author, that is, as long as your expert later answers questions truthfully about your invaluable assistance.[812]

§ 24.13 Preparing Your Expert

Practice, Practice, Practice

Q. I was so worried I spent days preparing my expert's testimony for deposition—girding the expert for cross-examination—videotaping the entire event and showing it to the expert and to

---

807. *See* Standing Comm. on Legal Ethics of the Va. State Bar Op. 1726 (1998) (A lawyer may prepare a medical report for a physician who is his expert witness to review, and the lawyer may also sign it if it accurately reflects the physician's own findings and opinions.).

808. Fed. R. Civ. P. 26(a)(2)(B).

809. Trigon Ins. Co. v. United States, 204 F.R.D. 277, 292–93 (E.D. Va. 2001).

810. *Id.* at 293.

811. Fed. R. Evid. 702 (an expert witness may testify if "the witness has applied the principles and methods reliably to the facts of the case"); *Trigon Ins.*, 204 F.R.D. at 294.

812. Resolution Trust Corp. v. Bright, 6 F.3d 336 (5th Cir. 1993).

my jury consultant, too, since the stakes are so high, and our client can afford it. Was that unethical?

A. Not at all. Your job is to prepare witnesses. It is your ethical obligation. Letting an unprepared witness on the stand might border on malpractice. This upcoming trial is a crucial event. Entering a courtroom is an intimidating experience. If your expert is new at this, you might even want to have walked the expert down to the courthouse to watch a trial or two at least to get the feel of the place. More important, it was crucial that you prepare the expert witness, this $1,000 per hour genius, to deliver the truthful opinion testimony that is critical to your case in a way that is totally understandable to judge and jury.

Q. I get to shape his testimony?

A. Try "clarify." You can accomplish witness clarity only through extensive preparation. Jettison the jargon. Simplify the sentences. Turn the lofty research professor on the cusp of a Nobel Prize into a junior high school teacher who makes no assumptions and delivers the key information in an accessible and understandable way. Does this take time? Of course it does. Does this take patience? Sure. But, the important lesson is that it is perfectly proper to so proceed.

Q. What about his charts? They are equally opaque.

A. If your expert's testimony might be conveyed, in part, through demonstrative evidence, it is perfectly acceptable not only to suggest but also to assist the expert in developing such material. Decisions, for example, on how slick or folksy to make the expert's graphs and charts are perfectly appropriate topics for discussion between lawyer and expert witness.

Q. I have free reign?

A. Of course not. All of this comes with two caveats, but they are the same caveats that apply to most witness preparation. First, the preparation of the expert, though arguably work product, may turn out to be an appropriate topic for cross-examination—and perhaps an embarrassing one. (You rehearsed how many times?) As with so many judgments the ethical lawyer must make, striking the right balance is a consideration that deserves careful attention. Second, and this is absolutely critical, you may not counsel the expert (or any other witness, for that matter) to testify falsely or allow him to do so.[813]

813. RLGL § 116 cmt. b ("In preparing a witness to testify, a lawyer may invite the witness to provide truthful testimony favorable to the lawyer's client. Preparation consistent with the rule of this Section may include the following: discussing the role of the witness and effective courtroom

§ 24.14 An Expert Who Is Also Your Client in Another Matter

Squaring Off Against Your Client

Q. The other side just identified its damages expert. An economist we know well. Indeed we admire this individual's work with which we are way too familiar. Why the treasure trove of information? Because this expert—the person hired to force our client to pay triple any reasonable amount if our client loses—is our firm's client. As is his little consulting business, which our firm incorporated. How cozy is that?

A. You have a conflict of interest. Actually, two. Without his informed consent, you may not cross-examine your firm's own client, even if he is just a third-party witness. How could you ever tear into his exaggerated credentials or accuse him of offering the best opinion money can buy? He is entitled to take offense. You may not act directly adverse to a client without his informed consent and attempting to impeach your client on cross-examination is an example of direct adversity.[814] That is the first conflict.

Q. And the second?

A. The second is that to spare the client-expert's feelings and reputation there is a risk that you will pull your punches in cross-examining him. That is a problem for the party you represent in the lawsuit. You owe that party zealous, not half-hearted, advocacy. Even if you are confident that your cross-examination of the client-expert will be first rate, you may not conduct it without the informed consent of the client for whom you are litigating.

Q. I hope this doesn't mean I will have to give up the case?

A. It is certainly a development you will have to discuss right away with your client in the litigation. Perhaps there will be no way around withdrawing from the representation so that the client can hire a new lawyer who has nothing standing in

---

demeanor; discussing the witness's recollection and probable testimony; revealing to the witness other testimony or evidence that will be presented and asking the witness to reconsider the witness's recollection or recounting of events in that light; discussing the applicability of law to the events in issue; reviewing the factual context into which the witness's observations or opinions will fit; reviewing documents or other physical evidence that may be introduced; and discussing probable lines of hostile cross-examination that the witness should be prepared to meet. Witness preparation may include rehearsal of testimony. A lawyer may suggest choice of words that might be employed to make the witness's meaning clear. However, a lawyer may not assist the witness to testify falsely as to a material fact.").

814. MR 1.7(a)(1); ABA Comm. on Ethics & Prof'l Responsibility, Formal Op. 92-367 (1992).

the way of a devastating deposition and cross-examination of the opposing expert. But wait! The client wants you to remain on the case. All that time and money has been invested in educating you. And you are such a great trial lawyer. A switch now would work a severe hardship. The client happily will give informed consent to the conflict.

Q. That, of course, only solves half the equation. Can I actually ask the expert client to give informed consent to the conflict as well?

A. Rule 1.7(b)(1) certainly suggests the answer could very well be no. It provides that, before you even ask for an informed consent, you must conclude that each representation will be able to proceed with diligence and competence. That is a difficult conclusion to reach when any objective observer would conclude that your cross-examination of your own client must be circumscribed by your continuing loyalty to the client.

Q. I don't understand that. I am very capable of loyalty to my client and razor-sharp cross examination.

A. It's an objective standard, not a subjective one. Not unlike asking a client for an informed consent to sue it for a Racketeer Influenced and Corrupt Organizations Act (RICO) or securities fraud violation or for punitive damages. Yet one could imagine a case in which the nature of the testimony (and more important, the nature of the anticipated cross-examination) might make the seeking of an informed consent a legitimate possibility, though if you proceed that way, you must keep in mind that the informed consent may be limited only to the circumstances you now anticipate. If those circumstances change, a new informed consent may need to be sought or, more likely, another solution found at that later date.

Q. Can I put an end to my representation of the opposing expert as a client?

A. That may be hard. Courts do not like it when you drop one client like a hot potato to represent another client.[815] Here, you might plead, the representation of the party to the lawsuit was well under way when the conflict arose. And you could not have anticipated it. The court may be sympathetic, especially if it thinks the client-expert will be harmed less than the party to the lawsuit if the former has to lose his lawyer of choice.[816]

Q. And if not?

---

815. Harte Biltmore, Ltd. v. First Pa. Bank, N.A., 655 F. Supp. 419 (S.D. Fla. 1987).

816. MR 1.7 cmt. [5]; *In re* Sandahl, 980 F.2d 1118 (7th Cir. 1992).

A. Maybe there is an even better solution. There is at least a suggestion in the previously cited ABA Formal Opinion 92-367 that new counsel could be brought in to cross-examine the expert whom you represent in another matter. It would require that the area of your client's expert testimony be a discrete part of the matter and that you would not only not conduct the cross-examination, but also not participate in any way in the preparation for the cross-examination as well as the direct examination of your side's expert. The conflict-of-interest rules apply with equal vigor to what is done behind the scenes as to what occurs in the conference or courtroom.

§ 24.15 Contact with Opposing Experts

Cozying Up to the Other Side's Expert

Q. I know the other side's expert. Our kids go to the same school. I see him at PTA meetings and school plays from time to time. If I took him out to lunch, I would have a chance to persuade him of the error of his ways. I have looked at Rule 4.2. It tells me that I may not contact represented persons. But he is not represented. He is a mere witness. I wonder, why not?

A. There are two "why nots." First, if you contact this proposed expert to talk about this case, you could be violating Rule 4.4(a), which requires you to respect the rights of third parties. This includes the rights of your adversary. And one of those rights is the right to work-product protection. Talking to the other side's expert would run an almost certain risk that you would be learning work product of the other side. Yet the meeting would be just a wasted, albeit pleasant, lunch, if you did not learn work product. Why else take the time?

Q. But if the other side's expert testifies at a deposition or at trial, this information will be discoverable anyway.

A. That is no excuse. First, the expert has not testified yet and may never testify. Second, if he does testify, it will be under circumstances that will permit the other side's lawyer to object and limit the inquiry. Many courts cabin the permissible areas of inquiry so that the only discovery of the other side's expert to which you are entitled is the discovery provided by the rules. In some jurisdictions, that means you get a report.[817] In

817. Pa. R. Civ. P. 4003.5.

others, you get a report and a deposition.[818] In still others, you get a report, a deposition, drafts, and all documents the expert received. Whatever the jurisdiction allows probably does not include a one-time ex parte lunch filled with intrusive or even subtle questioning and persuading.

§ 24.16 Preventing Contact Between Your Expert and Opposing Counsel

Preventing Cozying Up to Opposing Counsel

Q. Can I instruct my expert witness not to talk to the other side?

A. It makes sense that you can do so—at least in those jurisdictions that limit the available discovery from experts. If the other side is entitled only to your expert's report, the instruction simply helps prevent opposing counsel from surreptitiously undermining the discovery rule. But if the jurisdiction does not prohibit a party's lawyer from communicating ex parte with the other side's expert, the instruction may run afoul of Rule 3.4(f),[819] though you may inform your expert that there is no requirement that he chat with the other side.

Q. What about strategy?

A. It may be a strategic error to give the forbidden instruction. The jury may view your expert as overly partisan if it comes out on cross-examination that you instructed him not to talk with the opposing counsel. Still, you can at least warn your expert not to share any material with the other side that is covered by the work-product protection or the attorney-client privilege. Again, the fact that the expert may testify by deposition or in open court does not open the expert to these informal inquiries because the expert might not testify and, even were the expert to testify, certain areas of inquiry could be the subject of sustainable objections.

818. N.J. R. Civ. P. 4:10-2(d).

819. MR 3.4(f) ("a lawyer shall not . . . request a person other than a client to refrain from voluntarily giving relevant information to another party . . . ").

CHAPTER 25

Negotiations and Settlement

§ 25.01 Introduction: Negotiation Ethics

Lawyers are prohibited from knowingly making false statements of material fact and cannot assist a client's fraud in negotiation.[820] Any lawyer who has studied the law of fraud knows how difficult it can be to determine whether fraud is implicated in a concrete situation. False statements during negotiation can run the gamut from "puffing" to fraud. Failure to correct a lawyer or client's prior statement thought to be truthful but now known to be false can trap an unwary lawyer. If found to be material, or fraud, the lawyer can be subject to professional discipline, and the client's long-sought deal may not be enforceable.[821]

§ 25.02 Duty to Correct

Correcting Mistakes

Q. Representing companies, we're always in negotiation. Selling property. Employment agreements. New borrowings. You know how these things go. Back and forth. Conversations with the other side's lawyer. Meetings between clients and lawyer. Phone calls. Email. Faxes. It's endless.

---

820. MR 4.1; RLGL § 98.

821. MRs 4.1, 8.4(c).

That's what I get paid for. And I'm good. What worries me is when mistakes are made. By our side. When do we have to correct? When can we leave well enough alone?

A. Let's start from first principles, not rules, but good ethical lawyering. Any misstatement of fact by lawyer or client has the potential for causing mischief. It might not be deemed a misrepresentation.[822] And the other side may not have relied on it. But if it is recognized before the transaction closes, there are excellent reasons why the record should be corrected. For if the other side is disgruntled with the deal and discovers the error later, the risk that the mistake will form the basis for some claims is very high. So, regardless of duty, the conscientious lawyer will at least suggest that for good business reasons it pays to make full disclosure up front.

Q. I take your wise counsel. But what's the law? What do the rules require?

A. Let's take them one at a time. Suppose you tell the other side the property's zoned commercial. That's what your client told you. But you then learn it's still residential. You ask your client to correct the record, but she refuses. Says it'll kill the deal. What must you do?

Q. My misstatement was made totally unknowingly. I am not sure about my obligation to correct what I now know to be a misstatement of material fact.

A. You must consult Rule 4.1. You certainly did not violate Rule 4.1(a) when you spoke. But your failure to correct probably fits within the tort of misrepresentation, which means that your failure to correct the previous misstatement violates Rule 8.4(c).[823] Disclosure, being required by (tort) law, also creates an exception to client confidentiality under Rule 1.6(b)(6).

Q. Now suppose the same facts. What if my client makes the statement about zoning in my presence? It turns out my client was wrong, but she didn't know it at the time. I recommend client correct and she refuses.

A. If the client makes the disclosure you are in a different position. You have not yet misspoken, but your client has the same obligation to correct her misstatement that you did. For you, this inquiry is governed by Rule 4.1(b). It requires you to ask

822. Restatement (Second) of Contracts § 159(ff.) (Am. Law Inst. 1981); Restatement (Second) of Torts § 525(ff.) (Am. Law Inst. 1965).

823. RLGL § 98 cmt. d; ABA Comm. on Ethics & Prof'l Responsibility, Formal Op. 92-366 (1992), Withdrawal When a Lawyer's Services Will Otherwise Be Used to Perpetrate a Fraud.

many questions. The first is whether your failure to correct the misstatement is essential to avoiding assisting a criminal or fraudulent act by the client. That in turn requires an inquiry into whether your client was simply mistaken or affirmatively misled you. But it also requires a determination whether, even if your client knew he was supplying you with misinformation, the conduct is fraudulent, a question that then requires you to be familiar with the law of fraud. Did your client intend for the other side to rely on the misstatement? And even if the client did, was it reasonable for the other side to rely on that statement. Wouldn't a reasonable purchaser, particularly of commercial property, check on the applicable zoning? Of course by now you recognize that it is likely only after the fact that definitive answers to some of these questions will be forthcoming. Which might lead you to the view that you should disclose.

Q. Actually, I'd rather not. Confidentiality is sacrosanct.

A. You are correct that Rule 4.1(b)'s obligations to disclose to avoid assisting a criminal or fraudulent act by the client can only be evaluated in light of the applicable version of Rule 1.6 in your jurisdiction. If that rule, as the Model Rule, permits disclosure to prevent, rectify, or mitigate a fraud in which the lawyer's services have been used, then you must disclose. But if your jurisdiction prohibits disclosure with respect to client fraud, then you would be barred from making any disclosure, absent client consent. Back to remonstrating.

Q. And if my client won't allow me to speak?

A. Even if you don't disclose, you are certainly required to withdraw from the representation even if the closing is scheduled for the day after you learn of the error.[824] And if the other side draws some inference from the fact that you are no longer on the scene that is an acceptable result so long as all you disclose is the withdrawal itself.

For example, suppose your client intentionally tells the other side the wrong information. It's the only way we'll get our price, he announces. You hit the ceiling, demand a correction, but your client refuses and reminds you what you said regarding confidentiality. Here the client fraud is clear. The misstatement is not only intentional but designed to be relied on by the other side. If the other side finds out, it will back out of the deal. After unsuccessful remonstration, you must withdraw from the representation.

824. MRs 1.2(d), 1.16(a), 4.1 cmt. [3]; RLGL §§ 32, 94.

§ 25.03 Defining Material Fact

Puffing

Q. We are sitting in negotiations of a big med-mal case. My client is by my side. When the other lawyer disparages our case, my client blurts out, "How can you say that? We will have Dr. Gillespie from the Hospital of the University of Pennsylvania testify for us."

A. That sounds very impressive.

Q. Oh, it is impressive alright. Except the truth is we have not talked to Dr. Gillespie, and I just got off the phone with the lawyer on the other side. He tells me, in light of our success in finding an expert, his client is ready to settle this case for a million dollars. I think we are okay, but I just wanted to check with you.

A. Why do you think you are okay?

Q. Well, my client is just puffing and, under the rules, puffing is allowed.

A. Doesn't sound like puffing to us. It is one thing to say my client will never pay more than a million when, in fact, I think it is more than likely that it will, because that's an opinion not a material fact.[825] But when you make a representation about a fact of your case—you have hired the most prominent doctor in the field—that is a statement that the other side might very well have relied on, as it appears to have happened here.

Q. Does it make any difference that my client made the statement?

A. No. For sure you would never have made that statement, but it cannot be excused simply because a layperson made it. It was designed to be relied on. The other side appears to have relied on it, and that, my friend, could be fraud. Continuing in the case without correcting the record could be viewed as aiding and abetting, and you don't want to do that.[826]

---

825. MR 4.1 cmt. [2].

826. Ausherman v. Bank of Am. Corp., 212 F. Supp. 2d 435, 439–40 (D. Md. 2002) (lawyer personally sanctioned $8,649.25 under Fed. R. Civ. P. 37(b) and referred to court's disciplinary committee to investigate whether he had violated Rule 4.1, in response to settlement offer, for indicating that he had "made confidential arrangements" to obtain information when, in fact, he had not and later said it was "settlement bluster"); Hoyt Props., Inc. v. Prod. Res. Group, L.L.C., 736 N.W.2d 313, 319 (Minn. 2007) (lawyer who responded "There isn't anything" to opposing party's question, "I don't know of any reason how we could pierce the veil, do you?" made a material statement of fact; issue of fact exists as to whether lawyer made the representation without knowing whether the statement was true or false); Charles B. Craver, *Negotiation Ethics for Real World Interactions*, 25 Ohio St. J. on Disp. Resol. 299 (2010).

§ 25.04 The Client's Right to Settle

Settlement Negotiations

Q. I am sick and tired of having clients accept ridiculously low settlement offers. I put in thousands of hours of work and they settled for a pittance. I have this new idea. I am going to put in the engagement letter that the decision to settle be given to me because I am so much better informed than the client. I'll gussy it up with some good informed-consent language.

A. Sounds like a great idea. It certainly would solve two problems. Just one little hitch. It would violate the Rules of Professional Conduct. Rule 1.2 says the decision whether to settle and on what terms is exclusively the domain of the client.

Q. Well, how about if I say this: If the client accepts a settlement offer that I think is unreasonable, the client agrees to pay me $500 an hour instead of the contingent fee. At least that will give the client pause before she settles.

A. This solution is no better. You are now substituting your judgment for the client's by penalizing the client for exercising what Rule 1.2 tells the client is its exclusive domain.

Q. Well can I at least withdraw if the client doesn't accept one I think is great?

A. Wrong again. You are interfering with client decision making. You might have better judgment. But the rule is clear, clients are allowed to make mistakes.[827]

§ 25.05 Disclosing Offers

Touching Base

Q. I met with the client three weeks ago. She told me she would never take an offer of less than $1 million. I agree this case should not settle for less than that. But I just received an offer by phone from opposing counsel. He offered to settle for $750,000. I told him no way, that it was ridiculously low. Sure am glad I didn't have to call the client again.

A. Why is that?

Q. Because sometimes clients change their minds when they actually get offered real money.

827. *See supra* §§ 11.03, 11.04 in this book.

A. Precisely. Even if the client told you that morning the client would never accept less than $1 million, you have an obligation to tell the client of the new offer, for the very reason that you stated. It is one thing for the client to have a view in the abstract. It is another when a real-world offer is presented. No matter what the client told you earlier, your communication obligation requires you to disclose this important new fact.

§ 25.06 Offer Accepted Without Authority

Surprised Lawyer, Surprised Client

Q. I hope I am not in trouble. I thought I was doing exactly the right thing. I was in a conference with the court on some discovery issues—just my opponent, me, and the judge. She turned the discussion to settlement, which was not on the agenda. But out of the blue my opponent offered $2 million. I knew my client would be thrilled, or so he told me, with $500,000, and I was scared to death the offer would go away. I immediately told the judge we would take $2.5 million and, lo and behold, my opponent offered $2.25 million, which I accepted.

I was so delighted to call my client to share the good news, but the ingrate told me he was not satisfied. He wants $3 million. Talk about greed!

A. Your client refused to go along with the settlement.

Q. Yes, and I conveyed that to the court. But the court has concluded my client is "stuck" with the settlement. Now my client is threatening to sue me. What should I do?

A. The law is generally on your side. Everyone knows that settlement is in the hands of the client and there was no client in sight. Nor did you call your client during the course of these discussions. You have a great argument that you did not have apparent authority for that reason. As a result, your first line of defense is to formally challenge the judge's decision.

Q. I know Judge Jones is going to be furious, but I guess it is worth a try. I will move to strike the alleged settlement on the ground that I did not have authority. But what if I lose?

A. If you lose, your client can bring a claim based on your failure to communicate. But the client will have to prove that, if contacted, he really would not have accepted the settlement and, also, that he would have done better if the matter had gone to trial. The case will look a little bit like a trial within the trial, the client trying to prove whether he would have won more than $2.25 million, and you defending on the ground that $2.25 million was better than he could have done if he had taken that route.

It is a good lesson for us all. Even when we think we are being heroes, our clients' response may change as circumstances do. Before any offer, your client was thrilled to get a half a million dollars, but once he heard the number $2 million offered, he suddenly hoped to get three. Again, we have to communicate with our clients, even when we think our client would approve our decisions.

§ 25.07 Client Direction Not to Discuss Settlement

No Authority . . . Again

Q. I have this bitter case. My client is being sued. He thinks the other side's case is frivolous.

A. They always do.

Q. I certainly know that. Anyway, my client insists on a scorched-earth defense. We are pulling out all the stops—depositions ad nauseam, document disputes of epic proportions. The one thing the client keeps saying is I would rather pay you a fortune than settle with the other side for a dime.

A. That should be music to your ears.

Q. Well, it would be, but I know too often such brash behavior begets horrible remorse further down the line. In any event, the client insists that I never broach the topic of settlement. He calls it a sign of weakness, which doesn't mean I have not brought the topic up with him. I think it is my duty as a lawyer to continuously point out that his chosen course may not be in his best interest. But every time I deliver that little lecture, the client goes berserk.

A. Well, it sounds like you have fulfilled your obligations. I would say you have engaged in good lawyering.

Q. Thanks. But that doesn't solve my problem. I was meeting with plaintiff's counsel the other day, and he brought up the topic of settlement. Instead of shutting him down immediately, I asked him what he had in mind. He told me, and I must say it is a nominal sum of money given what my client is spending on defense costs. I call my client up and share the news the plaintiff will settle for $50,000.

A. Let us guess what happened next.

Q. No guessing needed. The client went ballistic, saying I have ruined his entire case. I should never have allowed the plaintiff's lawyer to mention the word "settlement." I have been fired, and the client has announced he is paying none of my outstanding bills which, by the way, now total $350,000. Am I in trouble?

A. You could be. A client's direction not to discuss settlement is a fair request; clients can demand that their lawyers refuse to engage in the topic. On the other hand, lawyers also have an obligation to explore all options if they think it is in the best interests of their client. Under the circumstances, it sounds to us like you really did not have a choice but to hear the offer. Your response hardly constitutes an expression of interest on your client's part.

§ 25.08 Confidentiality in Settlement

Disclosing the Offer

Q. I have been handling one of these cases against Pharma relating to its now notorious painkillers. My client and I had a meeting the other day where the defendant made a quite generous offer. Just today I received a call from a lawyer handling a similar case wanting to know whether we had had any settlement discussions. I, of course, happily disclosed what looks like a great starting offer. But now I am having second thoughts. Was I allowed to do that?

A. Settlement discussions are part of a representation, and everything you learn in the course of a representation is confidential. Telling another lawyer the facts of your discussions without your client's informed consent breaches the duty of confidentiality. Now you will have to explain to the client what you have done and deal with the consequences.

Q. Well, I didn't hurt the client by doing that.

A. That will be for the client to decide. You best recommend that your client consult other counsel. It may be that Pharma was only willing to go forward with your settlement if it was kept secret, which is why when one looks at the definition of confidential information, it is described in the broadest terms. We lawyers are put on notice.[828]

---

828. Young v. Achenbauch, 136 So. 3d 575 (Fla. 2014) (lawyers disqualified from representing flight attendants in individual lawsuits alleging misuse of funds by settlement-created entity following a class action settlement due to prior representation of named class representatives who now sit on board of settlement entity in the same case).

§ 25.09 Admissions During Settlement Discussions

The Apology

Q. Now I have the reverse problem. During settlement discussions among our adversary, the adversary's lawyer, my client, and me, the adversary stated how sorry he was for these unfortunate events and how guilty he felt. My client insists that I call the adversary to testify to admit that is what he said. Otherwise, my client says he will testify to it. I am not so sure.

A. Your concern is justified. What the other side tells you is not confidential if your client wishes to disclose it. But in many jurisdictions, settlement discussions are off the record. Whatever is said during those discussions may not be disclosed in the case on the merits. There is a great public policy reason for this. We want to encourage settlements, and we do not want the participants to worry that what they say during those negotiations will come back to haunt them if the case does not settle. You had better check the law in your jurisdiction because it does vary from state to state.[829]

§ 25.10 Mistakes of Fact

Dangerous Fact Mistake

Q. Strange case. There was an automobile accident, and plaintiff who was injured sued my client. The insurance company picked me. The plaintiff complained of back injuries so the insurance company had a physician examine the plaintiff. Turned out his back injuries were not that serious, but the plaintiff is suffering from an aneurysm. His doctor didn't pick it up, and the insurance company directed me not to disclose the news to the plaintiff lest the potential damages of the plaintiff's case be enhanced, and I have not. We have reached a very good settlement, but the problem is it has to be approved by the court. The plaintiff is a minor. The insurance company still insists I cannot disclose the aneurysm, but I am worried in approving the settlement, the judge is going to ask a lot of

829. *E.g., In re* Vitamins Antitrust Litig., 357 F. Supp. 2d 50 (D.D.C. 2004) (court would analyze admissibility of statements in settlement negotiations in light of interests of clients and public in maintaining their confidentiality, and competing public interest in access to materials submitted during litigation or judicial resolution of a dispute); Computer Commc'ns Specialists, Inc. v. Hall, 373 S.E.2d 63 (Ga. Ct. App. 1988) (state statute characterizes "admissions or propositions made with a view to a compromise" as "not proper evidence").

questions, some of which are going to be very hard to answer if I am prevented from disclosing the aneurysm. What do I do?

A. First, you can tell your clients if they want to avoid disclosure, they can try to avoid going forward with the settlement hearing. But if the client chooses to go forward, you must explain to the client that your answers to the court must be truthful and complete. If the court comes anywhere near eliciting the embargoed information, you will be obliged to disclose it. If the court does not ask, you may have an obligation to disclose because you will be jointly petitioning the court on behalf of the minor. The clients get to choose, but only up to the point of your obligation of candor to the tribunal.[830] And one more thing: an aneurysm could be life-threatening. If so, you have discretion to disclose to save a life.[831]

§ 25.11 Mistakes of Law

The Incompetent Opposing Lawyer

Q. I am handling a divorce case. The wife is represented by a young lawyer fresh out of law school. He has been doing a good job, but he just made a fatal mistake. He told me since we are having such difficulty agreeing on alimony, we should settle custody and child support and defer the alimony discussion until a later date. Sounds reasonable enough. But it turns out, proceeding as he proposes, will waive the wife's right to alimony. Should I correct him?

A. Well, the first place to go is to talk to husband. Tell him of this development. Despite his bitter battle with his spouse, it may be that he will not want you to take advantage of this . . .

Q. Oh no; he will want to capitalize on it. I know my client.

A. Nonetheless, you should run it by your client. But you have no obligation to the other side. And this mistake of law, sadly, will result in a malpractice claim against this new lawyer. However, that should not be your concern. You can remonstrate with your client, even remind your client that cutting his wife off from alimony will also be cutting off money from the mother of his children. But you have no obligation and, to

830. Spaulding v. Zimmerman, 116 N.W.2d 704 (Minn. 1962) (court exercised its authority to vacate settlement of a minor 18 months after court approval based on failure to disclose full extent of damages; defendant did not disclose aneurysm found by its expert but not found by treating physician).

831. MR 1.6(b)(1); RLGL § 66.

the contrary, must refrain from correcting this mistaken young lawyer because of your duty of confidentiality.[832]

§ 25.12 Aggregate Settlements

The Smart Advance

Q. We have been representing three passengers who were seriously injured in a car accident a few weeks ago. We just learned that the other car was driven by a company employee who ran a red light. The company has a $10 million policy and the insurer has offered the entire amount to be done with the aggravation. We have the standard contingency fee contract and are about to get rich. The reason: We were smart enough to get our three clients to agree up front to an even split in the proceeds.

A. When they agreed to those terms, was it clear how injured each person was?

Q. Of course not. That's what we wanted to avoid, having to work up each case when liability was so clear.

A. But you forgot that you have three clients, each entitled to an individual work-up of their damages. And the aggregate settlement rule prevents your reliance on the advance agreement to split evenly, unless and until each client has learned two things: the total amount received and the amount each individual is receiving. That way the client can make an individual determination whether the settlement is fair. As you say, you will be more likely to get approval if you can evade that obligation now by reminding them of their prior consent. But the first casualty of that approach is informed consent.

Q. Well, I suppose we could work up damages for each client based on how serious each person's injuries are.

A. And . . . all other relevant factors. Are they the same age? Same degree of disability?

Q. Are you telling me that I have to share these details about each client with the others if they ask?

A. Yes, and that's a good reminder why your initial engagement should have included a consent to the sharing of all information relating to the representation instead of a non-enforceable advance informed consent, reliance on which could also subject you to professional discipline and fee forfeiture.

---

832. Monroe H. Freedman & Abbe Smith, Understanding Lawyers' Ethics, 391–412 app. B (5th ed. 2016).

§ 25.13 Plea Bargains

The Exploding Offer

Q. I just became a public defender down here in Georgia, and I have got to say they don't do things like they did them back home.

A. What does that mean?

Q. Well, I am handling regular felonies now, and they have this strange procedure. They bring dozens of defendants into a courtroom. There are three defenders there, and the judge opens court, then announces that it is plea bargain time and that each of the defendants will be receiving a plea offer that they will have one hour to accept. If they don't accept the plea offer, the plea goes away. The defendants get into three lines, each in front of one defender, and one-by-one we walk them up to tell the court whether they accept or not. No time for discussions. No time for investigations. No time for conflict checks. No time for anything. And when I complained, the court told me they have been doing things this way forever; it's the only way they can handle the caseload. Can you believe that?

A. Now you have identified a new issue. Settlement discussions on the civil side don't have any constitutional dimensions. Absent fraud or criminal conduct, anything goes. But on the criminal side there is a thing called the Constitution that seems to be ripped apart by the procedure. Maybe the Rules of Professional Conduct, too. Your clients are entitled to a lawyer, but that is not what they are receiving. They are entitled to effective assistance of counsel. Here they are getting none. In order to be a competent lawyer, you have to investigate. You have to know whether the charges are justified. You have to explore any defenses. You have to be able to talk to witnesses, and you have to be able to counsel your client on a matter that is delegated to the client, specifically the decision whether to plead guilty. In short, this is a travesty of justice, and your complaints are well-founded. Other than litigation to stop the practice, we don't know what else you can do.[833]

833. Padilla v. Kentucky, 559 U.S. 356 (2010) (counsel's failure to correctly advise about deportation consequences of a plea agreement rendered satisfies first prong of *Strickland*, that counsel fell below an objective standard of reasonableness; remand for consideration of prejudice); *In re* Longacre, 122 P.3d 710 (Wash. 2005) (lawyer subject to 60-day suspension for violating Rules 1.1, 1.2(a), 1.3, and 1.4, despite no other pattern of misconduct, for failing to communicate several plea offers to a client and inform him of correct sentencing ranges).

§ 25.14 Settlements in Divorce and Dissolution of Marriage

Collaborative Law

Q. I handle matrimonial litigation. I understand how that proceeds. But my husband's client just came to me with a proposal he received from his spouse. She says they should proceed with collaborative law. Client wants to know whether that is a good idea.

A. What did you tell him?

Q. I told him I had no idea, but that I would look it up.

A. And did you?

Q. I did. And this is what I found. Under collaborative law, the parties and the lawyers sign a four-part agreement. The agreement provides that each side will provide all relevant information voluntarily. It also provides that should either side decide to withdraw from the collaborative deal, the lawyers presently handling the matter will withdraw.[834]

A. You have to withdraw? Because your client fires you?

Q. This is what they tell me. I have to withdraw no matter when the breakdown takes place, no matter how much time has elapsed, no matter how much the client has already spent paying me.

A. It's true you have to withdraw whenever your client decides to fire you, but this agreement seems to put your future involvement and the continuing value of your work in the hands of your client's adversary.

Q. That is what I thought, but they say this fosters settlement.

A. We think this agreement would be much fairer if it allowed either of the parties to walk away at any point in the negotiation. And we do not like the requirement about document production either. Who is to decide what is relevant? You need to have a heart-to-heart with your client about other alternatives. What about mediation?

You received a request. You have reviewed it correctly. Just say "no." Too many issues, ethical issues, to accept. Florida, although accepting collaborative process in general, has in fact specifically promulgated a new rule of professional conduct

834. Updated Executive Summary: Uniform Collaborative Law Rules and Uniform Collaborative Law Act (2011), *available at* https://globalcollaborativelaw.com/wp-content/uploads/2017/07/Updated_Executive_Summary_3-9-11.pdf.

significantly regulating the practice. It requires extensive written disclosures and protects the client's right to terminate the process at any time.[835]

And one more thing. If your client has been the subject of abuse in the relationship, this procedure will not be possible. The Florida rule requires lawyers to inquire about such a history and absolutely prohibits collaborative law in such situations.[836]

§ 25.15 Agreements to Limit Future Practice

The Buyout

Q. Another strange question. I represent plaintiffs in lemon law cases against various car manufacturers. I have been doing it all my life. This case is against Subaru, and it is the fifth one I have brought. Now Subaru's lawyer has called me and said the settlement of the most recent case, which I thought was worth about $100,000, could be settled for $1 million if I offer to never sue Subaru again. I am in a terrible situation. My client would love the million dollars, but . . .

A. I get it. They are trying to create a conflict between you and your client. That itself is clearly improper. But it is worse than that because Rule 5.6 says that it is an ethical violation to offer or accept as part of a settlement a limitation on the lawyer's right to practice. That is what they are doing.

Q. What if I avoid the conflict by asking Subaru to pay me $2 million as part of the settlement, and I will never sue them again?

A. That solves nothing. You have the same conflict because now you are bargaining away money your client would receive for money you would receive. And you are still violating 5.6.[837] But even worse, it sounds to us like you are taking a bribe.

Q. Oh, I would never do that. I just thought I would make it worth their while. How about if I would agree that after the case is over they would hire me for a million dollars over the next two years? Problem solved?

---

835. Fla. R. Prof'l Conduct 4-1.19 (2018).

836. *Id.* 4-1.19(c).

837. *In re* Hager, 812 A.2d 904 (D.C. 2002) (lawyer suspended for one year for, inter alia, agreeing not to represent any clients against settling defendant); Cardillo v. Bloomfield 206 Corp., 988 A.2d 136 (N.J. Super. Ct. App. Div. 2010) (lawyer violated Rule 5.6 for agreeing not to represent parties against same defendant while also negotiating an agreement to settle; agreement not enforceable).

A. Not at all. You are still bargaining at your client's expense. If it is part of the settlement, it is still a bribe and taking you out of the Subaru-slamming bar remains a violation of 5.6.[838]

Q. Is there no way out of this?

A. You have two choices: You can settle the case with no limitation and no promises and continue suing Subaru, or they can settle the case and, after the case is settled, with no winks involved, they can negotiate an engagement of your services that will make Subaru your client and prohibit you from taking any matters adverse to the company.

§ 25.16 Revoking Settlement Authority

Unreliable Clients

Q. I thought we were doing so well. Our client has a terrific antitrust claim against Giggle, the Internet darlings. We took the case on a contingent-fee basis and recently have been negotiating a settlement. After hours of discussion, the client agrees to settle for a one-time license fee. The client would get $10 million. I convey the offer to Giggle and, lo and behold, they accept it. But now I have gone back to my client for final approval, and he says $10 million is not enough. Frankly, I am ready to walk, and I have told the client that. We earned our fee, and he cannot change his mind.

A. It is a close case, but it is also a good object lesson. You obviously did the right thing in getting authority from the client, and you got an offer within that range. But the deal is not final, and, until it is, clients are free to revoke their authority at any time, for any reason, or for no reason at all. The other side, of course, may try to enforce the agreement. But you are not authorized to proceed with it, nor are you free to resign because the client changed his mind.

---

838. State *ex rel.* Verizon W. Va., Inc. v. Matish, 740 S.E.2d 84 (W. Va. 2013) (Rule 5.6 does not apply to a confidential settlement agreement that does not expressly preclude firm from representing future clients, but such an order or agreement may not be construed to preclude a lawyer from representing a client in a subsequent similar matter based solely upon the lawyer's obligations to maintain confidentiality of information subject to protective orders).

§ 25.17 Offering Settlement Advice

Should Anyone Care What Lawyers Think?

Q. Our client is in real trouble. The design defect in the client's new nine-speed transmission resulted in a series of fatal accidents—something about the shift from fifth to sixth gear. In any event, the client has insisted on a scorched-earth defense on these cases and maintains that the accidents were each caused by human error. Meanwhile, the client is getting blasted in the press; even members of Congress have spoken out against this all-American company. I go to see the CEO. It takes me weeks to get an appointment. My pitch: The client ought to be settling these cases. There aren't that many, and the negative publicity is tarnishing the company's very good name. I give my little sermon thinking the worst that can happen is he will just say no. That is not his reaction at all. He rises from his desk, red-faced, points a quivering finger at me and screams, "You are fired! We need lawyers who are dedicated to us. And I don't need to hear any preaching from you!" Did I act unethically?

A. The fact is you acted in the highest traditions of our profession. Although lawyers are never required to provide non-legal advice, Rule 2.1 certainly encourages that. Of course the client had the right to fire you, and such a response may chill future lawyers in similar positions from offering advice on non-legal topics, but unethical is the last way we would characterize your conduct. And who knows, there are lots of laps around the track, and you very well might be vindicated as events unfold.

Q. That may be true, but I am watching the game from the sidelines. That's for sure.

§ 25.18 Disparaging Clients as Settlement Strategy

Don't Tell My Clients

Q. I had this strange encounter with opposing counsel the other day. We had just had a pleasant meeting with the judge. Anticipating trial, the judge has sent us to a magistrate judge for settlement discussions. I said something about how optimistic I was that we could settle this matter. Opposing counsel replied,

"Forget about it. My client is crazy and so unrealistic. There is no way he will settle for any reasonable sum. Let me tell you, this is one of the worst representations of my life."

That got me thinking. Was he allowed to say that to me? It struck me as quite inappropriate.

A. Lawyers engage in such colloquy all the time. Sometimes it might be part of an actual strategy, sort of good cop/bad cop. But if it were not that, the impropriety is clear. It is undoubtedly the disclosure of client confidential information without the client's consent. The client would be appalled to learn his lawyer was trashing the client. Yet lawyers do complain to their adversaries all the time about the conduct of their clients. Which does not make it right. We should use this test: If the conversation with opposing counsel is one you would be happy to have the client overhear, you are in safe territory. But, if the conversation would be an embarrassment if the client found out, you should never proceed in that way.

§ 25.19 Secret Settlements

Public Disclosure Versus Private Gain

Q. I am feeling a little uncomfortable. We are settling a wrongful death case against a pacemaker manufacturer. Seems there was something wrong with the wire connections and the device failed. They have offered us lots of money, but one condition is that the record in this case—including the amount of the settlement—be sealed. I certainly want to accept the settlement, but it bothers me because there are thousands of these pacemakers in use today. Seems like the world should know about these problems.

A. You raise a very important public policy issue. Should settlements like this be subject to secrecy provisions? If you agree, you maximize your client's recovery. But, at the same time, you are perpetuating ignorance of the consuming public of what may be a serious problem. In some jurisdictions these settlements have been prohibited, and legislation has been proposed to prohibit them across the board. Your job is to find out what the applicable law is in your jurisdiction. Obviously, you cannot agree if such a provision is prohibited. If it is not, you owe your client the decision whether to agree to that term.

PART SIX

Representing Clients at Trial

The Lawyer's Role at Trial

It might come as a surprise that very little of this book addressing ethics for litigators would consider lawyer ethics at the heart of what litigators do: the actual trial of a matter. This is not a function of the fact that we live in an era of the disappearing jury trial. Rather, it is a reflection of the characteristics of the trial itself.

First, what happens at trial occurs in front of a judge and, more often as not, in front of a jury as well. To say that their presence has a chilling effect on conduct that might be considered unethical would be an understatement. The boorish behavior that too often mars the taking of depositions in large part disappears in the trial setting because, in fact, both the lawyers' and their clients' every move is being observed by those who will decide the case. This does not mean all misconduct disappears, but it does have a positive effect.

Second, the fact that there are opposing lawyers in the courtroom means that what otherwise might be viewed as unethical behavior often can be "cured" by the opportunity opposing counsel has to respond. Judges often take the view that the less judicial interference during the proceedings the better, encouraging opposing counsel to respond to inappropriate behavior by taking advantage of it as a way of "curing" minor transgressions, and permitting the proceedings to go forward at a reasonable pace, basically uninterrupted by the court.

Third, whatever conduct is taking place in the courtroom occurs in front of the judge. And judges do not hesitate in certain situations to handle unethical conduct in the courtroom at the very time it occurs by "punishing" the transgressing lawyer or client in front of the jury at that instant, rather than wait for a referral to disciplinary authorities to mete out the appropriate sanctions for the misconduct. Judges in the face of unethical conduct also will not hesitate at the conclusion of a proceeding to administer their own form of justice. They do this by imposing more formal sanctions, such as instructions to the jury or monetary assessments, as an expeditious way of not only punishing bad conduct but also sending a signal to future litigants and lawyers about what to expect if they go over the line in this particular judge's courtroom.[839]

Nevertheless, there are some issues of litigation misconduct that rise to the level of ethical violations as well. This Part explores those issues, which are regulated by Model Rules 3.1 to 3.9.

Overall, these provisions enhance your honesty obligations to third persons when you appear before a tribunal. Entering an appearance for a client triggers not only affirmative obligations not to lie but also responsibility to correct prior misstatements, to disclose directly adverse legal authority, to offer evidence not known to be false, and to correct false evidence or any other fraud on a court committed by any court participant.[840] When appearing ex parte, you also must disclose all material facts.[841]

In addition to your general obligation to adhere to the relevant procedural rules and court orders, special obligations regarding witnesses,[842] evidence,[843] comment on evidence,[844] and contact with judges and jurors also exist.[845] If you should become a witness, you may lose your ability to appear at trial, although your firm may be able to carry on.[846] These professional obligations apply to all lawyers, but prosecutors incur an additional set of obligations as ministers of justice.[847] The same obligations apply to you if you appear before a legislative body or administrative agency in connection with an official hearing or meeting to which you are presenting evidence or argument.[848]

The following dialogues provide a small sample of the situations governed by these rules.

---

839. *E.g.*, Surowiec v. Capital Title Agency, Inc., 790 F. Supp. 2d 997 (D. Ariz. 2011).

840. MR 3.3; RLGL § 120.

841. MR 3.3(d); RLGL § 112; *In re* Malmin, 895 P.2d 1217 (Idaho 1995) (lawyer privately reprimanded for appearing ex parte before magistrate and moving for entry of default judgment but not mentioning tentative agreement on the matter).

842. MR 3.4; RLGL §§ 116–118.

843. MR 3.4(b); RLGL § 118.

844. MR 3.4(e); RLGL § 107.

845. MR 3.5; RLGL §§ 113, 115.

846. MR 3.7; RLGL § 108.

847. MR 3.8; RLGL §§ 97 cmt. h, 109(2).

848. MR 3.9; RLGL § 104 cmt. d.

CHAPTER 26

Candor to the Tribunal: Frivolous Claims, Expediting Litigation, and Disclosure Obligations

§ 26.01 Introduction: The Wide Scope of Litigation Candor

Courts cannot adjudicate disputes without knowledge of the facts and applicable law. Lawyers have an affirmative obligation of candor, which enhances the honesty requirements beyond avoiding misrepresentations. These affirmative candor obligations begin when the lawyer enters an appearance before a court and continues throughout the proceeding. They include obligations not to assert a frivolous claim or defense,[849] obligations to expedite litigation,[850] and other affirmative obligations of candor. These include obligations not to lie, to correct prior misstatements of fact, to disclose directly adverse legal authority, to only offer evidence not known to be false, to seek reasonable remedial measures when a litigation participant commits a fraud on the court, and to disclose all material facts when appearing in a legally recognized ex parte proceeding.[851]

849. MR 3.1; RLGL § 110; Fed. R. Civ. P. 11.
850. MR 3.2.
851. MR 3.3; RLGL §§ 111, 112, 120.

§ 26.02 Entering an Appearance

Who Is My Client?

Q. I do a lot of DUI work. Represent a lot of teenagers. I like to think I help people in trouble. Now it is me that is in trouble.

A. What's the story?

Q. I was representing this client who was arrested on a DUI. It was only after we met for the first time that I learned she used a friend's driver's license when she was pulled over. So, the case is styled *Commonwealth v. McCarthy*, but my client's name is Olson. She says she has made a deal with her friend that she will pay her $500 if she is allowed to use her name throughout the proceedings. She doesn't want her parents to know that she was arrested. It would be the second time.

A. You told her she couldn't do that?

Q. No, I thought that would betray my client. Admitting she lied would be worse than the DUI. The whole thing seemed innocent enough. But now I am scared to death that the next time I appear in court someone will discover the switch in identity, and it will be me that is in trouble.

A. You certainly have that right. What you have done is misrepresent someone's identity from the beginning. You aided and abetted your client's falsehood before the tribunal.

Q. Well, she never testified. In fact, she never said a word.

A. That may be correct, but your standing by her knowing her name is Olson when the Court Clerk called out "McCarthy" was ratification that your client's name was McCarthy. Even though you said nothing and she said nothing, the Court has the right to believe that someone named McCarthy is in trouble for a DUI. And about to be convicted or plead guilty. That is a clear violation of Rule 3.3. It is time to correct the record and hope that in doing so no one comes after you for your conduct at that initial hearing. We zealously represent our clients, but there are limits, and this is one of them.[852]

852. People v. Casey, 948 P.2d 1014 (Colo. 1997) (lawyer suspended from practice for 45 days for violating Rules 1.2(d), 3.3(a)(1), and 8.4(c) and (d) for entering an appearance and appearing at a pretrial conference on behalf of a person whose identity was used by lawyer's client with the police); People v. Bauer, 80 P.3d 896 (Colo. App. 2003) (lawyer guilty of 20 counts of criminal impersonation for continuing to practice law after his license was suspended because his conduct amounted to assumption of a false or fictitious capacity for purposes of the statute); Fla. Bar v. Cox, 794 So. 2d 1278 (Fla. 2001) (prosecutor suspended for one year for lying to the court about the real identity of an informant); *In re* Gross, 759 N.E.2d 288 (Mass. 2001) (lawyer suspended for 18 months for having an alibi witness impersonate his client in court).

§ 26.03 Obligation to Disclose Adverse Legal Authority

The Uncited Case

Q. I always tell young lawyers this is as important as preparation to an effective trial lawyer: every once in a while, your adversary hands you a little gift, a gift more helpful than spending five hours practicing your closing argument.

A. And your good fortune was?

Q. It's on our motion for summary judgment. The other side is asserting strict liability for the design of the product. We say it doesn't apply to our widget. There's a not very helpful recent case. But the other side didn't cite it. Without that, the case law pretty much goes our way. Our answering brief will be devastating.

A. Might be a mixed blessing.

Q. How can that be?

A. Sometimes the failure of the other side to cite a case shifts the burden to us.

Q. I'm supposed to be the lawyer for my opponent?

A. Not quite. But when there is precedent in the controlling jurisdiction, even precedent going the wrong way, that is contrary to your position, you are required to bring it to the attention of the judge.

Q. Let the judge do his own research.

A. That could be the rule. But it's not. We say that as officers of the court, we have this relatively narrow obligation to make sure the court is well informed about the law. Not every judge has the luxury of multiple brilliant clerks from your august alma mater.

Q. But we could argue this isn't precedent. In fact, in our view, it's more dicta. The court stated a legal proposition but then said it didn't apply in the case before it.

A. Before we address your argument to get out from under the rule, let us ask you the good-lawyering point.

Q. Good lawyering? If I were a good lawyer, I'd tear this opinion out of the reporter . . . and delete it from Lexis, too.

A. Not so fast. Let's assume you don't cite it and the judge's eager clerk finds it. Then what?

Q. I'm sure she'll recognize it as dicta, too.

A. Can you be so sure? The fact is, if the court does uncover this case, you will want the court to know why you think it's dicta.

Why it was wrongly decided. Why the far better view is that reflected in the vast majority of the cases. But the court won't have your persuasive advocacy if you don't cite this case.

Q. But what if our client wants to run that risk?

A. You raise an interesting question. Is this an issue for the client or for you? The Rule 3.3 obligation is clearly yours. No client can block your fulfilling your duty of cantor to the tribunal. Assuming no 3.3 obligation, on the question of whether it is best to disclose and distinguish than not cite at all, we believe that, too, should be a lawyer decision but consultation with the client is always advisable.

Q. You still haven't told me whether I have to cite this case.

A. If it's truly dicta, then we think there is no obligation on the ground that it is not solid precedent for the damaging proposition.

Q. And what of the fact that it's a decision by an intermediate appellate court in a different judicial department?

A. Again, technically it's not controlling. But we are sure sister departments look to each other for authority. Which means you are really back to deciding how to be the most effective advocate you can be.[853]

§ 26.04 Obligation to Disclose Adverse Facts

The Misinformed Judge

Q. Talk about dumb luck. Listen to this one. I recommended my guy plead guilty to a minor felony charge. He agrees. We go to the sentencing, my guy stands up, acknowledges his plea, and the court gives a stern lecture, but then announces that because this is my guy's first offense he's going to fine him $500 and give him one-year probation.

A. That doesn't sound like luck. It sounds like excellent lawyering.

Q. Thanks, but there's this little problem.

A. What's that?

Q. My client has two priors. That's what he admitted to me. I stood there flabbergasted when the judge announced the sentence.

A. Did you contribute to the court's error?

---

853. *See also* § 28.01 in this book.

Q. Of course not. No one asked us anything and we didn't volunteer the misinformation. Must be some clerk's mistake. For one minute, I thought I could earn the undying respect and affection of the judge by correcting her error. "As an officer of the court, I want to let the court know my client actually has two priors." But then I remembered all that stuff about privilege and confidentiality. I shut up. But I am not sure that was so smart. After all, lawyers have that duty to tell courts about cases that go the wrong way.

A. You have identified an important distinction. When it comes to the law, we have the special affirmative duty to cite controlling precedent. But when it comes to the facts, so long as we haven't contributed to the mistake, we lawyers are free to leave the record uncorrected.

Q. I'm okay?

A. You are from a Rule 3.3 point of view. But that leaves the good-lawyering point. At a minimum, you should check with your client. Explain what might happen if the court later discovers the error. How outraged the judge might be. How your explanation to the judge about protecting privileged information, your duty of confidentiality, may not mollify an embarrassed, outraged judge who may or may not be able to review the sentence and who may re-sentence your client far more harshly than he would if you did what the judge will think was the honorable thing and save the court from this error. Given your client's current choice between no jail time and almost certain jail time, we would be shocked if your client instructed you to disclose, but at least your client will have been forewarned if it all hits the fan later.

§ 26.05 Obligation to Disclose a Client's Death

The Lost Client

Q. We've been handling a serious defamation action. The *Chronicle* sure damaged our client. Suggesting many infidelities when he is the model of a family man. We've got the *Chronicle* on the ropes. The source for the rumor turned out to be a disgruntled former employee. An anonymous source whose "story" was never investigated.

We had a settlement conference last week. The *Chronicle* started regaling the mediator with long speeches about our unfettered free press and its vital role in a democracy. The mediator wasn't buying. Went on and on about professional responsibility of journalists. Suggested a seven-figure settlement. The *Chronicle* lawyers left in a huff.

Then last night they offered $750,000. My client would've been thrilled. I called them this morning to accept.

A. Would've?

Q. Yes, alas, my client died last Thursday. Awful. Only 59 years old. A driving accident. Fortunately, their California lawyer didn't pick it up. And you know there's no way I'm telling them. I have duties of confidentiality, you know.

A. You sure do. But that won't work now.

Q. How can that be?

A. Do you still have a client?

Q. Of course I do. It's the estate.

A. Have they hired you?

Q. Not yet. But I'm sure they will.

A. And you don't even know who the executor is.

Q. True enough. But we gotta accept the offer before it goes away and with it my quarter of a mil fee.

A. That would be nice. But you're going to have to tell them.

Q. I thought I didn't have to correct the other side's mistake of fact.

A. That's true. But here, every day you are implicitly representing that you have a specific live client and that client continues to retain you. Remember that appearance for your client you entered? It's no longer true that you represent that client. Moreover, as you know, the fact that your client is deceased could end the case or at least dramatically affect the damage calculation.

Q. I gotta tell? And I can't accept the offer first?

A. We're afraid so. Rule 3.3 demands no less.[854]

854. Virzi v. Grand Trunk Warehouse & Cold Storage Co., 571 F. Supp. 507 (E.D. Mich. 1983) (settlement set aside due to lawyer's failure to disclose client's death during pretrial settlement conference); Ky. Bar Ass'n v. Geisler, 938 S.W.2d 578 (Ky. 1997) (lawyer publicly reprimanded for making a false statement of material fact in violation of Rule 4.1(a) for failing to disclose client's death during settlement negotiations); *In re* Forrest, 730 A.2d 340 (N.J. 1999) (lawyer suspended for six months for violating Rules 3.3(a)(1) and 3.4(a) by failing to disclose client's death unrelated to underlying matter); Kingsdorf v. Kingsdorf, 797 A.2d 206 (N.J. Super. Ct. App. Div. 2002) (divorce judgment set aside, and lawyer referred to disciplinary counsel for failing to inform court of client's death); *In re* Rosner, 127 A.D.3d 129 (N.Y. App. Div. 2015) (lawyer suspended for one year for settling lawsuit on the eve of trial without disclosing client's death which occurred one month earlier). *See also* § 8.02 in this book.

§ 26.06 Limited Appearances

Ghostwriting

Q. Our lawyers staff the pro se desk in the courthouse on a volunteer basis. The court instructs those we advise that we are not forming a client-lawyer relationship in trying to help these folks.

A. Good for you. It is a real public service. We are proud of your firm.

Q. Not so fast. One of our associates met with a particularly sympathetic woman. Her ex is way behind in his support payments. He offered to draft a complaint that she could file pro se.

A. That is treacherous terrain. Although we certainly appreciate your desire to go the extra mile, you better proceed carefully. Some courts are of the view that it is a misrepresentation to present a lawyer-drafted complaint as pro se. The lawyer must enter an appearance and handle the entire case or not get involved at all.

Q. What a shame. I thought this was called "unbundling" and that is a good thing.

A. Many would agree with you. In fact, a few jurisdictions allow limited scope appearances.[855] If yours does not, candor to the tribunal demands that you disclose your assistance. For example, if you ghostwrite a brief for a pro se litigant, you should add to the cover, after the litigant's name, "drafted with the assistance of [your name]." That way, the court knows what you did, and understands that the rest is pro se.[856]

---

855. *E.g.*, Ohio R. Civ. P. 3(B).

856. *In re* Fengling Liu, 664 F.3d 367 (2d Cir. 2011) (lawyer who ghostwrote pleadings not required to disclose his involvement; discusses circuit split); Chung v. El Paso Sch. Dist. #11, 115 F. Supp. 3d 1242 (D. Colo. 2015) (district court rule does not allow most types of limited-scope representations, including ghostwriting a pro se client's pleadings, and other filings); FIA Card Servs., N.A. v. Pichette, 116 A.3d 770 (R.I. 2015) (lawyers who ghostwrote pro se defendants pleadings not subject to sanctions for violating Rules of Professional Conduct or Rules of Civil Procedure, but in future, all lawyers must obtain client's written consent to limited-scope representation and sign filings, disclosing the extent of the lawyer's assistance). *See also* § 11.16 in this book.

§ 26.07 Improper Limitations

No Good Deed . . .

Q. I felt sorry for the fellow. Ever since his bike accident he has not been the same. They put a pin in his broken leg, but after all this rehab, he was left partially paralyzed. He wants to sue the doc but no one will take his case. Me? I'm an investment company lawyer. What do I know?

A. You got the competence issue down.

Q. I say to my neighbor, you can go pro se. Nothing to lose. I give him a form and tell him I'll look over his handiwork before he files.

A. Did you?

Q. Of course. Spent a couple of hours. Made it look professional. Even looked up a case.

A. And then?

Q. He filed and, instead of offering the poor guy $1,000 to go away, the insurance company moves for sanctions, counterclaims for malicious prosecution. You name it. My neighbor shows up alone for a conference regarding the pending motions, and he tells the judge he did the best he could. Even talked to me for advice. Well that ends the conference. Until I am dragged onto the carpet. Accused of incompetence. Misrepresentation. Failure to disclose my role. The judge even takes me apart for the little agreement I had with my neighbor making sure he knew I wasn't his lawyer and waiving any claim against me for malpractice. I was being so careful.

A. Our guess is the judge was not impressed.

Q. For sure. Said my agreement was a nullity. But it gets worse.

A How could it?

Q. Don't shoot me, but I did this work at a time when my ticket had been suspended for failing to complete my 12 hours of damn CLE. I was almost there, but not quite.

A. Sadly your good deed has catalogued a long list of issues. While suspended, any law practice is in violation of the suspension and, in fact, represents the unauthorized practice of law. A crime in this state. Many jurisdictions also require lawyers who ghostwrite to disclose that fact. Yours apparently is one of them. Others take the position that what you did was an improper scope limitation because what you agreed to do was too little to provide meaningful services for the client. Finally, your attempt to limit your liability is clearly improper because your "client" was not separately represented, and you cannot prospectively waive your responsibility. In fact the only violation you seem to have avoided is charging an unreasonable fee. But even there, the argument can be made that your client overpaid given the trouble you got him into.

Q. Trying to be the Good Samaritan I have bought myself all kinds of trouble.

A. Let us hope the lessons of your case will save some other unfortunate soul. We will represent you, of course, but we will charge more than $100.

§ 26.08 Obligation to Disclose Undiscovered Witnesses

The Mystery Man

Q. Next thing you know you'll tell me I have to tell the other side that the witness they've been trying to track down is sitting outside the courtroom.

A. We don't go that far. Unlike legal authority, this is confidential information. And you have no obligation to help the other side. So long as you avoid any misrepresentation about mystery man's whereabouts, you may remain silent and start praying that the mystery man's identity remains your secret until the trial is over (unless you're a prosecutor).[857]

§ 26.09 Witness Preparation

Refreshing Memory

Q. I am afraid I've overdone it.

A. Tell us more.

Q. The process of prepping witnesses has always bedeviled me.

A. You've certainly done enough of them.

Q. That's true. But it doesn't get any easier. On the one hand, I feel an obligation to do that.

857. Office of Disciplinary Counsel v. Wrenn, 790 N.E.2d 1195 (Ohio 2003) (prosecutor suspended for six months, stayed for failing to disclose relevant, exculpatory, and unprivileged information when asked by both defense counsel and the court, despite the fact that defendant's eventual conviction and sentence did not change as a result).

A. That ethical obligation is clear and beyond challenge. It's the negligent lawyer who doesn't take the necessary time to do it right.

Q. But, on the other, I can't suborn perjury.

A. I'll say.

Q. So follow this. Representing a bunch of shipyard guys—asbestosis claims. They settled with some of the manufacturers, but not all. This was 30 years ago. I know these guys don't remember whose asbestos they used so I ask the first client "do you remember what color the asbestos packaging was." He says blue, just like that, before I give him the choices. Chastened, when the next poor fellow comes for prep, I try a different tack altogether. I explain we have settled with three. The only one left in the litigation is Johns Manville and that company used pink packaging. Next, I ask him if he remembers the color of the asbestos he worked with.

A. Let us guess. He says pink.

Q. Smart fellow. You're both smart. But did I go too far?

A. Well, you are entitled to explain the case. You are entitled to refresh his recollection. You could have shown him the pink wrapping and asked him if that refreshes his memory. But you might have gone too far. And suborning perjury is not the only thing you have to worry about.

Q. What else?

A. You don't want to place your client on uncertain terrain. It is one thing to refresh recollection; it is another to create it. And any time your witness is creating memory, you are running the risk that even if it is true, it cannot come off that way. Your client will seem insecure. Searching the courtroom to remember what you told him. Getting that panicked "don't believe me, jury" look. The truth is firm footing. Nudging your client into terra incognita may not be unethical, but it may be the antithesis of good lawyering.

Q. Can I take my client through a mock examination?

A. That is clear. Giving your client the likely questions in advance is a good idea. One of us has often said if the client hears the question for the first time at a deposition, the lawyer fails the competence test.

Q. Can we discuss language? Word choice?

A. Of course you can. First, telling your client to drop the gratuitous use of "like" or "y'know" may be essential. Jurors—some jurors—find those expressions grating; like listening to crackling chewing gum. Or, worse yet, blowing bubbles. But don't try to make your school bus driver sound like he is auditioning for Richard II. This is no time for a makeover in which your sneaker-wearing high school teacher is figuratively (or literally) wearing Bruno Maglis.

Second, good language, so long as the client is comfortable with it, can avoid difficult cross. Suggest away . . . just so long as you are comfortable that your client is presenting the truth.

Q. Can I videotape a practice session?

A. That can be a great idea. None of us have any objective idea how we appear. We don't recognize our own tics. The "tells" we provide others when we are nervous. Videotape can be a mixed blessing. It can horrify the witness. But is also creates a level of self-awareness that can improve the witness's presentation. Just make sure you leave the prospective witness on terra firma.

And one more thing. While you are preparing, take your witness to the courthouse. Let him see the setup where he'll sit. Where the jury will be. If the courtroom is empty, have him sit in the witness box. All of that is legitimate preparation.

Q. And not subject to inquiry?

A. Should not be. This is classic work-product activity. And it should be.

Q. May I tell the witness not to volunteer? Y'know, just another yes or no if at all possible?

A. This instruction clearly has a proper side. Witnesses, especially lawyer witnesses, love to fill in the silences. And the experienced questioner knows she gets a lot further creating silences rather than interrupting. It can be a perfectly legitimate instruction. Make the lawyer wait for his answers.

But on the other hand, this instruction should not be used to suppress the truth. If the prospective witness takes the instruction as a way to avoid giving a truthful answer, the lawyer has gone over the line.

Q. What about "I don't remember"?

A. There's a theme here. If that is the honest answer the lawyer should recommend it. All of us—to a greater or lesser extent—want to please our questioner. We think we are still in school. To say we don't remember somehow is a mark of inferiority. As a result, recommending that answer—and removing the shame attached—is a healthy thing. "It's okay that you don't remember" is the lesson of the day.

But "I don't remember" is not a permissible answer when we do remember and just don't want to provide the unsettling facts the answer would provide. And we suborn perjury if we over-encourage its use for that reason. We also run the risk of destroying the witness's credibility when the witness tells judge and jury she doesn't remember a fact when, given the context, that fact would be seared in memory defying all attempts to sublimate it.

Q. Can the witness be urged to present the good facts and de-emphasize the bad?

A. Again, this is a fine line. Remember two things. First, the witness has sworn to tell the whole truth. Omitting a key fact could be viewed as perjury. Second, your witness will be cross-examined after your carefully rehearsed but seemingly complete representation of the facts pour out of your witness's mouth. And even a not so talented cross-examiner can make much of that which was omitted. The likely questions are too elementary to be repeated here. But even short of suborning perjury, burying bad facts can be a risky business indeed.

At the end of the day we have to be our own consciences when it comes to witness preparation. We are officers of the court. Just as we must disclose to the tribunal false testimony, even out of the mouth of our own client, we must avoid putting on false testimony that is the product of our "education" of our witnesses. Prep away but keep that fine line in the forefront of your considerations.

§ 26.10 Witness Inducements

Expensive Testimony

Q. Sure the letter could have been written better, but that does not mean we should be pilloried like this.

A. What letter?

Q. Our associate was responsible for lining up witnesses in this case brought against our public company client, its auditors, the usual suspects. We thought the former CFO would be helpful. So we sent this letter. Actually, we drafted it for the present general counsel to send. The CFO has been retired to Florida for years. The letter explained that if old CFO "could be helpful, we would fly him to New York, pay all his expenses and $500 per hour for his time."

A. Uh oh!

Q. Precisely. He spent a week with us. He took us through all the auditor's work papers. Helped us develop our defense and testified at a deposition. Unfortunately, and unbeknownst to us, he brought that letter to the deposition. Arguably work product, but too late to do anything about it. The other side says we suborned perjury, only paying former CFO $20,000 because he conformed his testimony to our needs.

A. If that was the result, you are in trouble.

Q. Of course not. But we understood we could pay him for his trouble. Even if he is retired, playing golf.

A. In most jurisdictions, but, importantly, not in all, fact witnesses can be paid for their time but not their testimony. It is admittedly a fine distinction. And even if retired, the witness can be paid for giving up a week of golf and good weather. But $500 per hour? How did you get there?

Q. Because when he retired, he was making over a million. He really didn't need the money.

A. That will help. But there are no certainties here. Particularly because of the ambiguous language. It must be clear you are paying the individual for his or her time and aggravation. Unintentionally, the letter provided a line of attack. And another reminder to all of us that even when we are sure a document is privileged or work product, it may well see the light of day. Lawyers cannot be too careful.

§ 26.11 Candor to the Judge

The Forced Mediation

Q. Damn judge. Insisted we mediate the case. Said his magistrate judge knew how to knock heads and keep the judge's docket a ghost town of pending matters. Asked if we agreed. My opponent seized on the offer like it was a lifeline. She's got such a weak case. Any face-saving exit will be welcomed. Me? I was very reluctant. We have a summary judgment motion pending. Ten to one says it'll be granted. Only bad thing is our client's a nervous nelly.

Anyway, my client and I strategize. Agree that we won't go higher than a hundred thousand. That's my authority.

A. That was good. It may sound counterintuitive, but in fact your client's willingness to talk settlement and any amount the client is willing to offer or accept is confidential. You must discuss this with the client and get the client's informed consent before any disclosure.

Q. So, I go to the conference. Clients only have to be available by phone. You can imagine how relieved my client was. We exchange pleasantries. The other side surprises me by offering to settle for $200,000. Maybe they're getting realistic—at long last. And I see a chance to be a real hero. When the judge asks me my authority, I quickly shoot back: "Your Honor, this case has only nuisance value to us. Twenty-five just to get rid of it."

The judge is not pleased. "I know you," he announces. "You're too smart,"—all that fake flattery—"to have told your client to offer so little. We'll never get anywhere this way. What's your client's phone number?"

Now I'm in a panic. The judge dials the number, doesn't put it on speakerphone, so all I hear is one side.

"Mr. Ellis, this is Judge Francis. I'm trying to help you settle this terrible case. Your lawyer here seems quite uncooperative. But I know how much you want to end this litigation nightmare and get back to running your business. What can I offer the other side to end this sad chapter?"

I hear nothing. But a big smile crosses the magistrate judge's face. This can't be good.

"Your client says he told you to go to $100,000. We'll address that later. But he told me he'd double that to get a deal today. I am pleased to announce we have a settlement. As to Mr. Ellis's lawyer, I think we have a little referral to the discipline folks. It's not acceptable to lie to the court."

Am I in trouble?

A. Well, let's start at the client meeting. It could've been handled far better. It is certainly true that Rule 4.1, the rule governing lawyer representations to third parties includes an exception for puffing. You can tell the other side their case is worthless when you think otherwise. You can tell the other side your client will never pay more than a dime when you know she's quite anxious to settle. But your scenario raises two different issues.

Q. I'm all ears.

A. First, do the puffing rules in Rule 4.1 disappear when you are in front of the court? The technical answer is no, because Rule 4.1 applies to all client representations. But the real answer needs a new question: Does Rule 3.3 apply as well? When the court is acting as a settlement master, you really are not in front of a tribunal.

Q. Tell that one to this magistrate judge.

A. Exactly where I was going. Though you might be correct analytically in asserting that the black robes do not make a difference, judges are judges, we call them "Your Honor" all day, whether we mean it or not, and you could incur their undeserved wrath if you didn't apply Rule 3.3 in your dealings. The problem is that the 3.3 comments don't mention "puffing." Rule 3.3(a)(1) requires a bit more candor than Rule 4.1(a), which brings us to the second point.

Q. That is?

A. You want to be very careful when you get near the puffing line. For example, you probably don't want to announce what your authority is since your authority may be viewed as a material fact. Amending your statements to say your client is only prepared to offer a certain amount can help. In addition, you may want to make sure that your "authority" going into negotiations is no higher than your planned first offer, again to avoid getting in trouble like you did here. And whatever you do, avoid making any material statements of fact in negotiations before or outside the presence of the judge. Don't brag, for example, that you've retained local U's most prominent physics professor if you haven't.

§ 26.12 Candor about Later-Discovered Fact

The Prevaricating Proctologist

Q. I was in the middle of defending a medical malpractice case. The plaintiff claimed that my client, a doctor, misread the films and missed colon cancer. My expert heads the radiology unit at State University Hospital. He is an impressive guy, and he obviously wowed the jury. I obtained a defense verdict, and now the case is up on appeal on a challenge to the jury instructions. I am not concerned. But wait! There is a problem with my expert's credentials. He is not board certified and has been masquerading as such for 20 years. Unfortunately, I did not discover this fact when vetting my expert. Fortunately, my side already won, right?

A. Wrong. The case is still pending, and your duty to correct your witness's false testimony under Rule 3.3 continues until it is over.[858] If this is materially false testimony, you have to supplement the record even now. Can you argue it is not material? We do not think so. Even if it were just one line on a 50-page CV, it is a material line. Board certified means something. And he was your witness. You undoubtedly elicited his exalted credential right at the beginning of his direct testimony. What a shame, but life is too short, and your obligation is too clear.[859]

Q. Just what we need. I'm representing my client. Showing my best trial lawyer stuff. Advocating for factual findings that will win the day. And you come along and rain on my parade. Suddenly I have to worry about the truth. How to ruin a trial lawyer's day.

A. We believe as much as anyone in zealous advocacy. We don't want to cramp your style. But all lawyers have a stake in the integrity of the system. As a result, lawyers have duties as officers of the court. And Rule 3.3 is where many of them reside. It is true some of these will require you to put the court's interests ahead of your client's, but we hope that (1) you will recognize the importance of the duties, and (2) you will consider some of your duties under Rule 3.3 consistent with good lawyering. Think of it as a fair fight.

§ 26.13 Lying in a Deposition

Recent Memory

Q. My client's V.P. of sales was deposed by the other side. Claim is price fixing. I, of course, spend days preparing him. This guy is key to our defense. So, I ask him if he attended an industry convention in Atlantic City. He admits he did but then clams up about any people he saw. Body language told me he was very uncomfortable. So, I moved on reminding him a couple of times that he would be under oath and have to tell the truth.

Of course at the deposition he's asked about the meeting in Atlantic City. His answer, "I don't remember an Atlantic City meeting." I don't break my pencil and fall to the floor writhing in pain. Instead, I play poker. And wait for a break. Take the client aside. Ask him what the hell he is doing. He tells me that he thought about it last night, and he now remembers that he

858. MR 3.3(c).

859. United States v. Shaffer Equip. Co., 11 F.3d 450 (4th Cir. 1993).

didn't attend any convention in Atlantic City. The good news is because it was just a deposition, it wasn't before a tribunal. I don't have to worry about it yet.

A. Not so fast, our friend. There once was a debate in the profession whether Rule 3.3 applied to events outside of the courtroom. But in many jurisdictions that issue has been put to rest. Because most cases settle—and public policy favors settlements—the importance of discovery in its own right and not as preparation for trial is more acute. Only through discovery untainted by false testimony can each side of a litigated matter fairly evaluate the strengths and weaknesses of the matter.

Q. You mean I can't settle this matter while that answer is uncorrected?

A. Not unless your Rule 3.3 duty of candor hasn't been triggered.

Q. Well, I hope to convince you that's the case. Even if it applies to depositions, we didn't elicit the testimony. Doesn't that help?

A. That argument's also been made. But the rule applies to client statements whether you asked the question or your opponent did.

Q. What's left to get me off the hook? I know one thing: I don't really know whether the guy lied. Maybe he did refresh his memory.

A. You are right the standard is "known." The lawyer can't offer testimony the lawyer knows is false.[860] Also has to correct testimony if the lawyer knows a witness has testified falsely. Which raises the question only lawyers would ask: What does "knows" mean? Rule 1.0 of the Model Rules tells us "knows" denotes actual knowledge.

Q. So far so good. I don't have actual knowledge of anything.

A. But then the rule goes a little further. "Knowledge," it says, "can be inferred from the circumstances."

Q. Oh boy. I get where you're heading. I know he changed his answer. I know he changed it in a backward way. I know he acted weird when I probed about the Atlantic City meeting. And I know this might be really important.

A. The last point reflects the final test. Was this material? You don't have to correct if the "q" and "a" were on an immaterial

---

860. MR 3.3(a)(3); RLGL § 120. If the lawyer only has a reasonable belief that the testimony is false, the lawyer may refuse to introduce the testimony, except for the testimony of a defendant in a criminal case. MR 3.3(a)(3).

point. Say, your guy was asked if he ever smoked marijuana in a case where that was irrelevant.

Q. Well, wouldn't the fact that he lied when he answered the question itself be material?

A. If the fact that he lied would make disclosure a requirement, then the materiality standard would be rendered meaningless.

Q. You think I have an argument this isn't material? Sure would like to avoid telling the judge about this little problem.

A. The judgment on materiality is up to you, but just this little contretemps argues for concluding its material. Good news: calling the judge is hardly required. At least as a first step. If you were still in the deposition, you certainly could have remonstrated with the client to go back in and correct the answer. Or wait until the end of the deposition and you could elicit the correct answer with, "Is there an answer you'd like to correct?" Even after the deposition you could have your client change the answer on an errata sheet. Those sheets are not limited to typographical errors. And only if all those benign methods prove unavailing do you have a personal obligation to correct. But even then, you can just tell the other side, but only after you take one last crack at remonstrating with your client.

§ 26.14 Obligation to Correct Crime or Fraud

Reasonable Remedial Measures

Q. The litigation has been bitter from the start. Claims. Counterclaims. Shouting matches. You would never know these two were business partners for 25 years.

Anyway, the other side got a restraining order barring my client from touching disputed funds he's holding in a retirement account at Big Bank. Two months ago my client threatened to share those funds. He needs the money and says, rightly, the money belongs to him. But I tell him the court order trumps any ownership rights he has. My warnings were met with silence. But I figure I've done my job.

A day later he calls me from Big Bank. Tells me he'll be paying my bill shortly. I repeat my warning. He says he'll take complete responsibility for his actions.

Needless to say, he closed out the account. And the money is gone. He's in big trouble. But guess what? So am I. The other side has added me as a defendant. And added a new claim that I failed to report my client's planned withdrawal. I say I had a confidentiality obligation. After all, I wasn't aiding and abetting anything.

A. That's true. But Rule 3.3 goes much further. It places an affirmative duty on a lawyer. It provides: A lawyer who represents a client in an adjudicative proceeding and who knows that a person intends to engage, is engaging, or has engaged in criminal or fraudulent conduct related to the proceeding shall take reasonable remedial measures, including, if necessary, disclosure to the tribunal. And as you know Rule 3.3's duty of candor trumps any Rule 1.6 obligation you might have to your client. You can defend by explaining that you didn't even know what your client would do. But under these circumstances, don't be surprised if the judge is unsympathetic. Integrity of court orders. Officer of the court. And all of that.[861]

861. United States v. LaPage, 231 F.3d 488 (9th Cir. 2000) (conviction reversed due to prosecutor's failure to immediately correct known perjury of chief witness whose perjury may have made a difference in the case. Reasonable remedial measures required interrupting direct examination and bench conference with judge and defense counsel about how to inform the jury immediately that the testimony was false); *In re* Potts, 158 P.3d 418 (Mont. 2007) (lawyer who knew his clients had negotiated a settlement in an estate and then improperly took money outside the agreement assisted a client fraud in violation of Rule 1.2(d), and lawyer's failure to disclose his client's improper conduct to the court violated Rule 3.3, which superseded his duty of confidentiality under Rule 1.6); Gum v. Dudley, 505 S.E.2d 391 (W. Va. 1997) (remand for consideration of sanctions short of ordering a new trial and referral to disciplinary counsel against lawyer who knew of a settlement in the case but failed to respond when asked by the trial court whether a settlement agreement existed); *In re* Estate of Shelton, O.C. No. 1569 DE of 1994, 2009 WL 8558393 (Phil. Ct. Com. Pl. June 29, 2009) (Lawyer who failed to take appropriate actions to prevent client-executor from improperly transferring estate assets contrary to express court order and who perpetuated his client's fraudulent acts by later signing a statement to the court that his client-executor was fulfilling his duties as required by law was subject to a personal surcharge for the $1.6 million in lost assets if his client failed to repay the amount. Repeated unsuccessful attempts to remonstrate with client was not a reasonable remedial measure under Rule 3.3, which would have required lawyer to notify bank official about court order to prevent improper transfer.); *In re* Rantis, Ill. Disciplinary Op. 09-CH-65 (Rev. Bd. Nov. 14, 2011) (lawyer who counseled client and did disclose updated parentage facts to opposing party took reasonable remedial measures as a matter of law because he reasonably believed his actions were sufficient to undo the effects of his client's false statements; earlier disclosure to the court at a preliminary stage of dissolution proceedings would not have made a difference); ABA Comm. on Ethics & Prof'l Responsibility, Formal Op. 98-412 (1998), Disclosure Obligations of a Lawyer Who Discovers That Her Client Has Violated a Court Order During Litigation (Lawyer who discovers that a client has violated a court order prohibiting asset transfer must withdraw and must reveal that fact to the court if necessary to avoid an affirmative misrepresentation to the court or to avoid assisting the client's fraud. After withdrawal, the lawyer must make disclosures sufficient to avoid continued reliance by the court on prior representations now known to be untrue.).

§ 26.15 Documenting Testimony

Creative Writing

Q. I know I am to blame. My client, the construction guy, was stiffed by his customer, the owner of this beautiful health club. My client bids the job, wins, finishes on time, and goes to collect the final payment. Owner reneges. Our client is worried the owner is smoking his fee. Comes to us to institute litigation. I meet with the client. During the discussion I ask the client whether he is owed more than the contract amount. For change orders. Extras. You get the idea. My guy says of course. The amount is about $100,000. I ask if he's got any documents. He responds, like what? Change orders? Memo requests, that sort of thing?

A. Okay so far.

Q. For sure. A month later we get a document request. We produce a lot of paper. Including seven change orders. Upgrading lighting. Nicer tile. Bigger parking lot. All of which we produce.

A. Still okay.

Q. Getting to the punchline. Eve of trial I am prepping the client's CEO. I show him the change orders. I ask him whether they were prepared at, on, or about the date they bear. The answer: "No, I made them up last week, but I won't say that on Monday."

A. Now what do you do?

Q. I asked him why he did that. Because I asked him for documentation is his response. I ask, "you mean you actually did the work?" Of course, he responds. Every one of these items was for extras. I get upset, as you can imagine, but the client says, "We don't have to use them." That's true enough, but we already listed them on the pretrial order. We just can't ignore them. My client, seeing how upset I am, tells me to do whatever I have to do. I figure since the claims are real, the documents are harmless error. We'll just go to trial and never refer to them.

A. We wish you were right. But we think you are too far into it. You've made a representation. You better be the first to correct it. But candor to the tribunal requires you to tell the other side and if that doesn't settle it, the court. You must correct the misrepresentation that these documents are genuine.[862]

862. MR 3.3; RLGL § 120.

CHAPTER 27

Tribunal Impartiality: Fairness, Ex Parte Contact, Publicity, and Lawyer as Witness

§ 27.01 Introduction: Tribunal Impartiality

Impartiality is the essential requirement of a fair hearing. For this reason, several rules of professional conduct require trial lawyers to assist tribunals in assuring impartiality in judicial proceedings. In this chapter, we address four other impartiality requirements: the obligation of fairness to opposing parties and counsel, the obligation to shun ex parte contact with judges and jurors, restrictions on trial publicity (within the guarantees of the First Amendment), and prohibitions on lawyers who are necessary witnesses also appearing as advocates at trial.

§ 27.02 Access to Evidence

The Draft Document

Q. The lengths some lawyers—good lawyers—go to in order to please clients is shocking. We had a med-mal case. Horrible facts. The newborn had been starved of oxygen and ended up disabled for life. We brought suit against the hospital and the physician. Asked for the medical records and thought we had them all. They were ambiguous as to the cause and the child's distress signs. We settled for less than half what the child deserved. Will need full-time care her entire life.

A. They are tough cases. You probably did the right thing.

Q. Oh we did based on what we knew. But then a gift from the litigation gods. There is fallout litigation between the hospital's carrier and the docs. More discovery. This time the hospital produces one page that had never been produced. Nurse's notes. Demonstrates gross negligence of just about everyone. We bring a new suit based on the document that was withheld, and what it revealed. Added a punitive damage count, too.

A. What is the defense?

Q. They say they did not produce the nursing document because it was not correct. They did not want to confuse the record with an incorrect document. They also argue it was not produced because we failed to request drafts.

A. Let us ask you a question. Did anyone testify about the records?

Q. Of course. We asked whether we had been given the medical records. We were told by both the nurse and the physician that we had been given the records.

A. Did anyone mention the draft document?

Q. Not a peep.

A. This is a classic violation of Rule 3.4(a). We are barred from unlawfully obstructing another party's access to evidence or unlawfully concealing a document.

Q. I know. But they say it wasn't unlawful. They had a duty not to produce it to protect their client.

A. Lawyers can be zealous advocates. But at the end of the day we are officers of the court, and compliance with the rules of discovery depends on our honesty and trustworthiness.

Q. You should see how their email reflects how pleased they were that they had escaped needing to produce the draft.

A. One more thing. It sounds like they also violated Rule 3.3. If the witnesses were asked whether the hospital records had been produced and the witnesses—the nurse and the doctor—answered yes, they were testifying falsely. About the key fact in the case. As a result, at a minimum, you should get your new trial. And our guess is that the defense counsel will be facing disciplinary charges.

§ 27.03 Court Orders

Too Clever by Half

Q. The guy is a thug.

A. Who?

Q. The plaintiff in this medical malpractice case. One of those harebrained motorcycle nuts who wears a bandana instead of a helmet. Gets himself into an accident by his own reckless conduct. Then she, our doc, saved his life, and he sues her for malpractice because she allegedly screwed up his arm so badly six surgeries were required. Maybe, just maybe, he caused the problem.

A. Sounds like an ingrate.

Q. Oh he is alright. And he belongs to one of those white supremacist groups. But he shows up in court looking like a choir boy. Beard gone. White shirt and tie. Totally misleading. Worse than that. His clever lawyer files a motion in limine barring us from mentioning his affiliation or its nefarious goals on the ground that it's irrelevant. Hell. It is the most relevant information we have. Proves how reckless he is.

A. You can't win 'em all.

Q. Maybe. But I wasn't going to take no for an answer. And I got lucky. Found a picture of the plaintiff from the day of the accident. The swastika on his leather jacket is front and center. I decide to wait and use it in my closing. I just lean it against our defense counsel table. Casual like. Never mention the word Nazi or anything about racism. Just the picture.

A. Uh oh.

Q. You can say that again. The judge goes ballistic. Declares a mistrial. Sanctions us $150,000 for the cost of the first trial. And refers me to the disciplinary folks. Outrageous. I complied with his order.

A. Maybe in a technical sense. But you knew precisely the conduct the judge intended to prevent. And you did an end run by publishing the picture without getting a ruling that the swastika was admissible.

Q. Did the judge have the authority to do that?

A. 'Fraid so. Ample authority.[863] And your recklessness matches that of your Nazi friend. You did the lawyer equivalent of

---

863. Ferguson v. Valero Energy Corp., No. 06-540, 2010 WL 2164493 (E.D. Pa. May 27, 2010); Allied Prop. & Cas. Ins. Co. v. Good, 919 N.E.2d 144 (Ind. Ct. App. 2010).

riding a big hog without a helmet. And your sophistry in erecting this argument only made matters worse.

§ 27.04 Court Orders: Confidentiality

Settlement Agreement

Q. We had this major IP case. Patent for analyzing digital x-rays. As in all cases like this, we entered into a confidentiality agreement. We agreed to share our source code under very tight restrictions. That's the mother lode, you know.

A. Sounds like you started off on the right foot.

Q. Oh, we did. Over the years we've tightened these agreements. They run pages and pages. But the right language only gets you so far.

A. What happened?

Q. The patent troll's lawyer has a second case against us. If we don't settle for plaintiff's demand in the first case, he will use the source code in the second case. His client in that one was "drooling," his exact word, when the lawyer showed him the once-secret code.

A. In other words, he admits he violated the agreement.

Q. With not a hint of shame or remorse.

A. I assume the court "so ordered" the agreement making the lawyer's conduct a violation of Rule 3.4(c). The breach of the agreement is also likely to be actionable. You could move in the first case for dismissal based on the breach. Or an order barring the other side from using the code in the trial of the matter. Moreover, you should be able to get the potential second action dismissed on the ground that is entirely premised on the fruits of the poisonous tree. But for the violation of the source code agreement, the litigation would never have been commenced. We do not mean to imply the relief will be available without a battle. Expect all kinds of after-the-fact justifications that excuse this conduct, but as described you should have the better of the argument.

§ 27.05 Witness Incentives

Meeting Demands

Q. I worry all the time. Not about myself. But so much of what we do is in the hands of others. We wish we were scriptwriters of the performance. But we are not. We only get to develop our questions. Our adversaries develop and hide theirs. And for our witnesses, we can do our best to rehearse and prepare, but when the curtain goes up the witness may go off script or stay on script but sound as insincere and rehearsed as one can imagine. So, we control freaks control what we can.

A. And what control freaking did you do here?

Q. We needed the testimony of old CEO. But he left the company under a cloud. We cut off his stock options. It was ugly. Anyway, he demanded $10,000 a day to testify. All expenses. First-class ticket. Room at the Ritz.

A. Pretty nice list.

Q. It was far less than he made as CEO. New CEO was happy to pay it. But then there was the worry.

A. That someone would think it was too extravagant.

Q. Not at all. We read the ABA opinion on paying fact witnesses. Even if retired, we could pay him for his time to go to the trouble of leaving Sarasota in March.

A. There is that, but not every jurisdiction agrees. In some you go to jail for paying that kind of fee.

Q. New CEO's worry was that our guy wouldn't testify in a helpful way. We paid him half the fee up front. He gets the other half after he testifies as described in the letter agreement.

A. You paid him for his testimony?

Q. Not at all. By the hour actually. But he lost half if he testified falsely.

A. You mean if he did not testify as directed.

Q. That too.

A. Then you paid him for his testimony.

Q. That's what the judge said.

A. How did it come out?

Q. He was asked on direct about his compensation. Like good litigators, we thought we would get it out up front. But then our guy went off script a little bit on cross. Mentioned the letter agreement. Which led to a demand that we produce it. We thought it was work product, but the judge disagreed. Before we knew it the letter became an electronic billboard on the big screen in the courtroom, our witness had been dismissed and the jury instructed to ignore his testimony that had been the result of a bribe, and we were on the wrong end of a disciplinary complaint that is quite serious.

A. No surprise there. You can pay a witness for time. You cannot pay for testimony. You did the latter. In writing. That is a violation of 3.4.

§ 27.06 Ex Parte Contact with Judges and Jurors

This one is easy: Don't have ex parte contact with judges or jurors without specific legal authorization.[864] And don't be misled if either tries to initiate the contact with you.[865] Judges are prohibited from doing so, just as you are.[866] If such contact inadvertently occurs, it usually can be cured with appropriate notice to the other side. When ex parte motions are allowed by law, remember that you have enhanced disclosure obligations to compensate for the lack of advocacy on the other side, including the duty to disclose all material facts, whether adverse or not, that will enable the tribunal to make an informed decision.[867]

Model Rule 3.5 and the Model Code of Judicial Conduct Rule 2.9 prohibit ex parte communications to or by a judge or the judge's staff absent specific legal authorization.[868] Lawyers should not seek improper influence or advantage,[869] and judges should not obtain information outside of the court record (or those facts that may properly be judicially noticed).[870] For both lawyers and judges, the prohibition applies regardless of who initiates the communication.[871]

Some ex parte communications, such as an application for a temporary restraining order or an in camera review of privileged documents, may be specifically authorized by law. If so, Model Rule 3.3(d) creates special disclosure obligations to the tribunal.[872] Lawyers who appear without opposition have an affirmative duty to inform the tribunal of all known material facts, whether or not adverse. The absence of counsel representing the interests of other parties obliges the appearing lawyer to provide information necessary to assist the court in making an informed and just result.[873]

---

864. MR 3.5; RLGL § 113.

865. Disciplinary Counsel v. Stuard, 901 N.E.2d 788 (Ohio 2009) (assistant county prosecutor publicly reprimanded for responding to judge's request to prepare a sentencing order via ex parte communications); *In re* Ragatz, 429 N.W.2d 488 (Wis. 1988) (lawyer disciplined for responding to ex parte communication of a judge).

866. State v. Roberts, 850 N.E.2d 1168 (Ohio 2006) (discipline against judge in Disciplinary Counsel v. Stuard, 901 N.E.2d 788); *In re* Aulik, 429 N.W.2d 759 (Wis. 1988) (judge who initiated contact with lawyer in *In re* Ragatz, 429 N.W.2d 488, suspended from the bench for 90 days for violating provision substantially the same as current MCJC Rule 2.9).

867. MR 3.3(d); RLGL § 112.

868. RLGL § 113.

869. *Id.* § 113(1); *In re* McCool, 172 So. 3d 1058 (La. 2015) (lawyer disbarred for using online petitions, blog posts, and Twitter messages to ask members of the public to "call the . . . judges and let them know they are 'watching' them and are 'horrified' by their rulings" related to a sensitive child custody dispute; messages were ex parte communications and a "viral campaign to influence and intimidate the judiciary," improperly violating Rule 3.5).

870. MCJC Rule 2.9(C).

871. RLGL § 113 cmt. c.

872. *Id.* § 112.

873. MR 3.3 cmt. [14].

Because the touchstone of improper ex parte communication is unfair advantage, some ex parte communication is allowed where the danger of improper influence appears low and the need to meet other objectives appears high. For example, routine administrative matters such as scheduling may be accomplished ex parte, as long as a judge "reasonably believes that no party will gain a procedural, substantive, or tactical advantage," and as long as the judge promptly notifies other parties of the substance of the communication and gives them an opportunity to respond.[874] Similarly, but only with the consent of all parties, judges may confer with them separately for the purpose of settling the matter.[875]

If improper ex parte communication about the substance of a matter does occur inadvertently, it can be cured by prompt notification to all parties of the substance of the communication and affording them an opportunity to respond.[876] Lawyers who inadvertently fall into the trap of communication with judges ex parte should either inform the other party or request that the judge do so.[877]

§ 27.07 Ex Parte Contact with Courts

The Emergency TRO

Q. It was an emergency. Our client's neighbor was threatening to remove two 30-foot hedges on the property line. The so-called tree expert company had their equipment on the property. We raced into court for a TRO, after calling the lawyer we were told was representing the neighbor. We showed up at 3. No opposing counsel. The judge says we should proceed ex parte. Sure enough she issues the injunction and the work grinds to a halt.

A. Good for you.

Q. Oh, we had a happy client alright. But we have a very unhappy judge. She claims that she asked me, after my introductory argument, whether there were any other facts of which she should be aware. I answered in the negative. I had given her a complete (and quite persuasive) description. But I didn't tell

874. MCJC Rule 2.9(A)(1).

875. MCJC Rule 2.9(A)(4).

876. MCJC Rule 2.9(B).

877. United States v. Microsoft Corp., 253 F.3d 34 (D.C. Cir. 2001) (disqualification mandatory for trial judge who engaged in improper ex parte contacts); *In re* White, 996 So. 2d 266 (La. 2008) (lawyer convicted of misprision of a felony and disbarred for acting as a go-between with judge and client's counsel while client's case was pending, failing to blow the whistle on the judge's corruption).

her there already was litigation pending between the Hatfields and the McCoys. If she had known that, she claims she would have made us present our request to that judge.

A. Not a ridiculous assertion.

Q. But my client told us that judge has threatened to sanction him. That's why we came up with the idea of starting a new case.

A. But you forgot or ignored the admonition in Rule 3.3(d). In an ex parte proceeding you have a special duty of candor to bring all material facts—importantly, including facts adverse to your position—to the attention of the court to ensure the fairness of a proceeding in which the other side is not present.

Q. But that fact had nothing to do with the hedge.

A. It had everything to do with whether seeking equitable relief from this judge was appropriate. You certainly could argue 3.3(d) was not triggered. But it is our sense that an apology would be much more effective. Proceeding ex parte is an extraordinary privilege. It comes with special responsibilities that challenge the mindset of the zealous advocate, yet that must be fulfilled.

§ 27.08 Ex Parte Contact with Jurors

The Postmortem

Q. We were sure we were going to win. So was our opponent. The case was a lay down. Or so it appeared.

A. Uh oh!

Q. You are right. Defense verdict. We were shocked. And we recommended our client turn down $500,000. We decided to find out where we went off the rails. We just wanted to learn.

A. Learn what?

Q. How we could have lost. We thought we would interview a few jurors. The judge excused them so quickly we had no chance to interview but a few.

A. And so you tracked the rest down?

Q. Yes, it was easy. Except our investigator offended one of them. That's for sure.

A. Sounds like trouble to us. The juror called the clerk?

Q. Worse, called the judge. We barely escaped without being jailed. She has, however, made a referral to the disciplinary authorities. Why? The case was over. We were not likely to appeal.

A. This is one where you need to know the territory. Some jurisdictions permit juror contacts so long as you made it clear it is voluntary. Others prohibit them. Still others set up special procedures. Those that allow post-discharge contact all require hands off at any point if the juror tells you she doesn't want to talk.[878]

Q. Wish we'd thought of that. Now the judge is furious. But the result seems so irrational. How're we going to learn to improve our presentations?

A. You mean challenge the verdict?

Q. Well . . .

A. We appreciate your frustration. But if there is any area where you want to fulfill the letter of the law, it is here. You can inquire of the judge once the result is final. You can ask court personnel to share observations. Even your opponent might give you her point of view. But when it comes to jurors it is hands off unless explicit permission is given, and, even then, one must be extremely careful. No court will tolerate disrespectful behavior. Part of the religion of a jury trial is preserving the dignity of jurors. We don't want them to be reluctant to serve again because of overreaching lawyers or litigants.

Q. I guess that's the source of our strict rules regarding communication with jurors while the case is pending. I won't talk to them, of course, but often I will look for a sign.

A. We all do that to a certain extent. Face it: Lawyers are neurotic, trying to read the tea leaves. Did that juror smile at me? Why did that juror look down when I walked into the elevator? But even this nonverbal communication must be avoided. Have faith in your case, your client, and your ability to persuade when you are the "star" giving your opening statement, your closing argument. And trust the system. Enough sermon.

Q. My view entirely.

A. Here, it might be time to hire a former disciplinary counsel. And polish those apology skills.[879]

---

878. MR 3.4(c).

879. *In re* Nelson, 750 S.E.2d 85 (S.C. 2013) (assistant prosecutor suspended for six months for repeated ex parte contacts with a cousin who had been chosen as a juror in a criminal trial handled by other lawyers in the prosecutor's office); N.Y. City Bar Op. 2012-2 (lawyers may use social media to gather information about jurors but must not "friend" them or sign up to receive their postings).

§ 27.09 Trial Publicity

Winning on the Evening News

Q. The first casualty has been the image of all policemen. But the second casualty has been the Rules of Professional Conduct.

A. You're speaking in riddles.

Q. We represent cops. Always have. You can imagine how busy we are. There have been some bad cases. But it is too easy to second-guess at leisure the conduct of police officers, action taken in seconds in the face of unknown danger, doing their jobs under the kinds of pressure no one should endure.

A. But the Rules of Professional Conduct? Cops are not lawyers.

Q. That's true. It is not my clients that are the problem. One of our police clients has got himself in the crosshairs of the district attorney. And I worry the case looks bad at first blush. But nothing could justify the highly publicized tirade. The DA called our client a madman, a terrorist. On television; on YouTube; who knows where else? The damn case is being tried and my client has been convicted before anyone's been indicted. Is there no limit on pretrial publicity?

A. Of course. We have an elaborate rule.[880] And the violation of the rule can and should result in discipline. But the rule is written against a backdrop of the First Amendment of the Constitution. Attempts by the profession to limit pretrial publicity have not escaped the attention and criticism of the Supreme Court. As a result, whether any given example of pretrial publicity represents disciplinable conduct turns on a multifaceted test, including the nature of the proceeding (which might be affected by the publicity), the content of the speech, the media coverage, and the timing. In this case, the DA certainly went beyond any safe harbor established by the rule. And he did so in a way guaranteed to make the news, a transparent effort to convict your client in the eyes of future jurors. But the trial is likely more than a year away. Memories do fade, but, of course, that depends on what additional histrionics the D.A. engages in. You certainly are justified in filing a disciplinary complaint now. And you have one more arrow in your quiver.

Q. What's that?

A. The rule on pretrial publicity now includes a right of reply. You are supposed to be measured in your approach. But equivalent reciprocal transgressions of the rule are permitted. As long as

---

880. MR 3.6.

there is no escalation. The press conference does not have to go unanswered. But only you can decide whether that is a good idea. Just because you can respond does not mean you should. What's in your client's long-term interest? A robust reply that draws a sur-reply? Or silence?

Q. A good-lawyering point.

A. Exactly.

§ 27.10 Lawyer as Witness

Lawyer for Everything

Q. I handled the defense of this huge securities fraud case. On the second day of deliberations by the jury, the parties settled. But then the damn insurance company refused to fund the agreed amount. Claims the case simply was not worth it. Accused me of wimping out.

A. You wouldn't do that.

Q. That's what I say. We sue the insurance company. I can't wait to get that claim adjuster on the stand. What a thug.

A. Wait a minute!

Q. You too?

A. Maybe. How can you be the trial lawyer in this case?

Q. I gotta be. I know it better than anyone. I lived it.

A. That's true enough. But that fact cuts the other way. Are you not going to have to be a witness? Explain to the jury why the settlement was a good one?

Q. We thought we could use the CEO of my client. She made the decision.

A. But she won't be as effective as you. You've been doing this your whole life. When you explain your view of the case, it will be against a long background of settlements.

Q. But then I can't try the case. Nobody would cross-examine that adjuster like I would.

A. But Rule 3.7 prevents it. Even if your client agrees not to call you, the other side will. Especially if you decide to announce you will be trial counsel.

Q. Well, at least I can handle that bastard at his deposition.

A. It is true that Rule 3.7 only prohibits an anticipated witness from trying the case. Pretrial participation is permitted.[881]

881. Jensen v. Poindexter, 352 P.3d 1201 (Okla. 2015) (lawyer disqualified due to "hijacking" the legal process by making himself a "forensic interviewer" in order to improperly question a child about suspected child abuse, making himself a necessary witness in the case).

Q. Great! Then I will get my licks in early.
A. Not so fast.
Q. But you just said . . .
A. We know what we said. But just because Rule 3.7 allows you personally to handle pretrial and allows your client to use your firm as trial counsel does not mean that is in the interests of the client.[882]
Q. But I already told you I knew the case better than anyone.
A. That may be true. But that is not the only consideration. What is involved is the defense of your services and advice. Maybe it would be better for the client to be represented by a new firm in this endeavor. Better not to have you questioned by your partner. We certainly do not know enough to give the answer. But this is one of those issues that should be decided by the client. Even better if the client consulted a different firm to help the client make this decision.[883]
Q. If we do that, they'll recommend themselves.
A. That is a possibility. But to ensure objectivity, they could be retained just to answer the question. In any event, do not go forward with the representation until the client has been consulted. That will protect the client and you.
Q. Thanks. I think.

---

882. United States v. Evanson, 584 F.3d 904 (10th Cir. 2009) (criminal defense lawyer disqualified for having firsthand knowledge of events during government's investigation of client because he would have "unsworn witness" advantage if events came up at trial; violation of Rule 3.7 not the only ground for disqualification); Stewart v. Bank of Am. N.A., 203 F.R.D. 585 (M.D. Ga. 2001) (lawyers disqualified because they were necessary witnesses for being eyewitnesses to and had personal knowledge of foreclosure transaction that was subject matter of litigation); World Youth Day, Inc. v. Famous Artists Merch. Exch., Inc., 866 F. Supp. 1297 (D. Colo. 1994) (lawyer disqualified for being sole negotiator for party because lawyer was likely to be a necessary witness since his testimony was relevant, material, and unobtainable elsewhere); Shaughnessy v. Ass'n of Apartment Owners of Moana Pac., No. 09-00051-ACK-LK, 2011 WL 613580 (D. Haw. Feb. 10, 2011) (lawyer who drafted provisions at issue in subsequent lawsuit was necessary witness; no substantial hardship due to foreseeability that lawyer would be a crucial witness one year before court's ruling); People v. Hagos, 250 P.3d 596 (Colo. App. 2009) (defense lawyer disqualified who interviewed witness alone making himself a witness in the case); State *ex rel.* Neb. State Bar Ass'n v. Neumeister, 449 N.W.2d 17 (Neb. 1989) (lawyer suspended for one year for taking no steps to withdraw either before or after he testified as a material witness while he was attorney of record in the case); Brill v. Friends World College, 520 N.Y.S.2d 160 (N.Y. App. Div. 1987) (lawyer who brought action to recover legal fees forfeits entire right to fee because he knew he was a necessary witness in the underlying matter when he initiated the lawsuit and properly disqualified from the matter); *In re* Kluge, 66 P.3d 492 (Or. 2003) (lawyer suspended for two years for representing an entity in an employment discrimination case where lawyer's conduct as general manager of entity was subject of lawsuit because his testimony in the case potentially prejudiced the client).

883. Norman v. Elkin, No. 06-005-LPS, 2014 WL 556081 (D. Del. Feb. 10, 2014) (law firm disqualified as counsel where lawyer in firm would be called as a witness and asked either to undermine client's credibility or expose himself to potential professional discipline).

§ 27.11 Lawyer as Unanticipated Witness

Lawyer Testifying at the Last Minute

Q. I am lead counsel in this outsized securities fraud case, pending in our district court. The case has dragged on for four years, and finally the pretrial orders have been filed, and the trial date looms. I am exhausted, and we haven't called the first witness yet.

A. We know the syndrome.

Q. Yes, but you don't know this part. Last week, when the defendants filed their joint pretrial order, they put at issue the genuineness of a document we plan to rely on. It was I who signed that document, and now it looks like I am going to have to testify. Not only that, but they have filed a motion to prohibit my participation in the trial because they contend I must be a witness. I know this is just a tactical move, and I am flattered that they went to the trouble. I know I am not allowed to be a witness in a case that I am trying, but I don't know how someone else can get up to speed on such short notice.

A. There are two remedies for your problem. First, you certainly can argue pretrial that the issue relating to the document is frivolous, designed to knock you out of the lead chair. Second, even if that does not succeed, you are still in a position to try the case. There is an exception to the rule that you don't have to step out of your prize role if that would work a hardship on your client. Losing you at this late date would certainly be that.

Q. Well, I hope that is the way the client views the matter.

A. By the way, there is another exception to that rule that might have applied here. If the lawyer is being called as a witness for a fact that will not be controverted, then that lawyer is free to continue in the case as trial counsel, even though the lawyer will be called to testify on that one topic. But, as always, even if the rule would permit you to do so, the client should be consulted on the desirability of having you proceed in that way. Any time lawyers are serving as witnesses, the situation is sufficiently risky that the topic is worthy of an informed discussion.

§ 27.12 Closing Arguments

Caring Too Much

Q. I admit. I got carried away. I was representing this long-suffering former patient of Doctor Percival Jones who ended up with a leg amputation because of the doctor's negligence. I had rehearsed my closing hundreds of times since I first met my client. The doctor was lying from the beginning. But I should not have said it.

A. Said what?

Q. That I had never seen a case like this where everyone on the defense side lied. I actually said, "lied through their teeth." Of course, it drew an immediate objection. I hate to have my rhythm broken. But I was wrong, though I don't think the judge had to go as far as he did. He told the jurors to ignore my remarks. He told them I was not allowed to take credibility determinations away from the jury, that my opinion was not relevant, that he would take care of me later. But then the coup de grâce. The jury might've found that the doctor lied. But they were not going to do the same as to the chief OR nurse. She was a nun. My client lost. And the judge made a referral to the disciplinary police. Violation of 3.4(e), the rule that bars personal opinions.

A. Right. Personal opinions as to the justness of the case, the credibility of a witness, the culpability of a civil litigant or the guilt or innocence of an accused (that you violated wholesale). All forbidden. Because you can't be cross-examined.

Q. All I can do is throw myself on the mercy of the bar police. I knew the rule. I just tossed away my script and got carried away.

A. Our guess is, worst comes to worst, you get a public sanction.

Q. Oh no. That will not be all. My client—former client—has sued for malpractice. If I violated a rule of conduct, I must be liable for his loss, he claims. He seeks $20 million and punitives. For the doctor's conduct, not for mine. But for my closing argument, he would've won.

A. That is certainly not true. The violation of a rule does not, in and of itself, give rise to a successful civil claim. Your client will have to prove you breached the standard of care *and* that was the cause of the loss. That gives you plenty of opportunity to prove there was another cause.

Q. That may be true as a technical matter. But I am afraid my enthusiasm for the case before the horrible verdict and my cries of the injustice of it all will come back to haunt me.

CHAPTER 28

Appeals

§ 28.01 Introduction: Ethics in Appellate Practice

All aspects of the litigation process implicate professional responsibility issues. This includes appeals. While there is definitely a characteristic of the appeals process that seems to limit the possibilities for ethical lapses and promotes, if nothing else, better manners, the lawyer who is engaged in appellate advocacy cannot let her ethical guard down.

The ethical obligations of client representation and the limits of the law apply equally to representing clients on appeal. The six Cs of client representation have interesting applications to appellate practice. You must of course be competent in your advice about whether to appeal, and in your preparation of the appeal itself.[884] Clients are empowered to control whether to appeal (the goal of the representation) but not necessarily which issues to raise or how to organize a brief (the means).[885] You must communicate with clients so that they understand these options.[886] Although most of the facts you will refer to will have been recorded in documents or testimony in the trial court, any other assertion of information relating to the representation of your client remains subject to Rule 1.6. Conflicts of interest can arise in joint appellate representations, and occasionally show up as "positional conflicts," those that occur when you take a legal position that could create an adverse appellate authority for another client.[887]

884. MR 1.1, RLGL §§ 52, 53.

885. MRs 1.2(a), 1.4; RLGL §§ 21, 22.

886. MRs 1.3 cmt. [4], 1.4; RLGL § 21.

887. MR 1.7 cmt. [24]; RLGL § 128 cmt. f.

The limits of the law include those that generally apply to courts, such as the obligation not to file a frivolous appeal, the obligation to abide by relevant rules of appellate procedure, and obligations of candor to the tribunal.[888] To the extent lawyers are critical of trial court judges on appeal, they must be careful to avoid knowing or reckless misstatements about the qualifications or integrity of that judicial officer.[889]

§ 28.02 Appellate Fees

Scope of the Representation

Q. We took the case on a contingency. What a mistake. If the client's CEO had only disclosed that the head of the Colossus Quality Control Department had warned the company of variations in the accuracy of the test equipment that was Colossus's best-selling product. We sued the supplier of the key crystal used in the device, after signing an engagement letter that gave us one-third of any recovery.

A. And you lost?

Q. The jury was out 45 minutes. Defense verdict. Bad enough.

A. That's why they are called contingent-fee cases.

Q. We don't need your reminder. That verdict was bad enough. But now the client insists we handle the appeal.

A. Not a surprise.

Q. Was to us. We did not agree to handle an appeal.

A. And you made that clear in your engagement letter?

Q. Not exactly. We thought we had. Our stomach for risk only goes so far. But . . .

A. What?

Q. The engagement states "Firm" that's us, "agrees to try the case for client based on the firm's typical contingent-fee rate of 30 percent of any recovery before deduction of costs and expenses." We say the word "try" means a trial; the client argues it must include any appeal.

---

888. Matter of Hendrix, 986 F.2d 195 (7th Cir. 1993) (failure to acknowledge adverse precedent violates Rule 3.3 and may provide grounds for damages for delay under Fed. R. App. P. 38 as well as discipline of lawyer under Fed. R. App. P. 46(c)); Lieberman v. Lieberman, 160 So. 3d 73, 74 (Fla. Dist. Ct. App. 2014) (lawyer disqualified for violating duty of candor by not conceding on appeal that opposing lawyer, who was a necessary witness at trial, was not precluded by plain meaning of applicable rule and case law from representing opposing party in other aspects of the litigation; lawyer also ordered to pay appellate attorneys' fees as a sanction for his failure to "acknowledge clear and unambiguous controlling law directly adverse to his client's position.").

889. MR 8.2; RLGL § 114; Douglas R. Richmond et al., Professional Responsibility in Litigation 683–704 (2011).

A. The client has a point. Certainly, is ambiguous.
Q. Exactly what the client says. If we wanted to exclude appeal, clear language to that effect would have been easy to land.
A. And since you are the drafters *and* you are lawyers, we think you are stuck.

The Ingrate Client

Q. We dropped everything. The client wanted our crackerjack team of lawyers formerly with the S.G.'s office to handle an emergency appeal of a devastating injunction disrupting the client's pipeline project. We turned them down. We were already fully engaged. Two days later they called back. "We're desperate. Name your fee and we'll pay it."
A. What an invitation!
Q. That's what we thought. We said "Fixed Fee. $50,000. Not a penny less."
A. Nice.
Q. Pretty nice. We were going to be stretched to the limit, as we told them, but they confirmed that we had a deal. In fact, they were thrilled. At the time.
A. Uh oh!
Q. Precisely. We won. They celebrated. Had a fancy dinner at the Capitol Grill. Who knows what the wine cost. But a month went by. No payment. And in our haste to meet the short deadline, we forgot to ask for an up-front retainer. Finally, I called the CEO. An awkward conversation. He praised our work, but when I asked for payment his voice almost cracked. We'd have to talk to his GC.
A. How'd that go?
Q. Bad to worse. He said the fee was unreasonable. Accused us of taking advantage of the client's plight . . . they called us, you remember. . . . Anyway, he guessed the fee worked out to $2,000 or more per hour.
A. Did it?
Q. We have no idea. We were so excited to have landed a fixed fee, we told everyone to forget about recording their time. We're still alright, aren't we?
A. This is a difficult one. The applicable rule, Rule 1.5, provides that lawyers may not contract for, charge, or collect an unreasonable fee. But in setting your fee, you are not acting as a fiduciary. This fee certainly looks reasonable from the beginning.

The real question is whether the client gets a "look back." One of your authors argues that no look back should be available unless the lawyer can "look back" and charge more if the matter turns out to be more difficult than anticipated. A one-way look back is totally unfair in that view. But others argue to the contrary. So it is not a lay down.

Q. Certainly should be. Look how well we did for them. It's almost like a contingent fee.

A. But if you lost, you would still argue for the full fee.

Q. True enough. But then I could forgive the client for the sucker punch; on these facts? No way.

§ 28.03 Conflicts of Interest

Material Limitation

Q. I am so insulted. Our firm should never have volunteered to take this capital case. And we thought we were doing the right thing. There is no right to counsel in state habeas. We were importuned, again and again, to take on the representation of one of the dozens sitting on death row with no counsel and the clock ticking. I convinced a reluctant management we could do it. And now this!

A. What has you so dismayed?

Q. We lost in state habeas. All the way to a "cert. denied." Then we timely filed a federal habeas petition. Our reward for that? A motion to disqualify us. By the same federal defenders who have been our "senior partners" all along.

A. That's so sad.

Q. Exactly what we thought. Something about the fact that this Supreme Court case—*Martinez v. Ryan*—held that a habeas petitioner in federal habeas can argue that state habeas counsel was ineffective in raising original counsel's ineffective assistance at trial and direct appeal. We thought that was a great development. Gave us a new argument. We sure needed all the support we could muster.

A. If we hear you right, that means that since you were state habeas counsel, you would have to argue that you were ineffective in raising the client's ineffective counsel claim against its trial counsel.

Q. Exactly.

A. You can't do that.

Q. You're siding with the Feds?

A. We're siding with the conflict rules. A lawyer cannot take on a representation in which the lawyer's ardor for the case is materially limited because of the lawyer's duty to a client, a third party, or a personal interest of the lawyer.

Q. But we aren't limited.

A. Yes, you are. As a matter of law, you are disabled from arguing your own ineffectiveness. You couldn't possibly be objective on the topic of your own performance in state habeas.[890]

Q. Do we have to withdraw? Our client would hate to lose us now. And vice versa.

A. Not necessarily. We have argued that you could bring in independent counsel to review the record to see if there is any substantial argument that you were ineffective. If none, that lawyer can explain to your client that he has a choice: He can waive that *Martinez v. Ryan* claim and keep you guys, or he can get new counsel who would be free to argue your firm's ineffectiveness. The approach has not been blessed by any court yet, but it should be.

Q. Sounds complicated and time-consuming.

A. It is, but it's the only way to address the conflict.

Thrust-Upon Grief

Q. We are handling an appeal for Colossus in a case it lost to Magna Corporation. Our brief is due in four weeks when we receive a lawyer letter from our long-time client, Acme, telling us Acme has purchased Magna and at the closing the two companies will merge. Acme will be the surviving entity. "Accordingly," Acme writes, "we insist you withdraw from your representation of Colossus because of the direct adversity of interest between Colossus and Acme." Can that be?

A. It certainly "can be" that you have a conflict of interest. We call this a "thrust-upon" conflict because neither your firm, nor your present client in this matter, is responsible for the ethical disaster situation created by the merger.

Q. Is that supposed to be make us feel good?

A. No, it just tells us analytically where you are. There is a special comment to the rules that addresses this situation. In the case of a thrust-upon conflict, comment [5] to Rule 1.7 provides

890. N. Kennebrew v. State, 480 S.E.2d 1 (Ga. 1996).

that, instead of dropping both matters, the lawyer may be able to choose which of the clients it wishes to continue to serve.

Q. Oh, that's great. I will want to stay with Colossus. I'm an appellate specialist, this appeal is winnable and the publicity will be very helpful.

A. Then what's wrong?

Q. My firm will want to drop Colossus and continue representing Acme. Acme is an ongoing client. We only have this one matter for Colossus. And as you can tell, Acme is on the move. This is its sixth acquisition this year.

A. You would think that the rule drafters got it wrong. If you give the law firm a choice, the firm will proceed as you guess your firm will react. Choose the more lucrative client. When in fact it is Colossus that is least culpable, that is most injured by this development, most in need of immediate services with four weeks to go before the brief on appeal is due.

Q. I agree.

A. There is a possible solution that will keep you in the game. Notwithstanding the fact that this conflict requires your withdrawal, in order to withdraw under Rule 1.16 you not only need grounds, which, of course you have, but also the permission of the court.[891] That permission is not always forthcoming. And it might not be forthcoming here. With only four weeks to go and the extraordinary delay that the hiring of a new lawyer might necessitate, the appellate judges might deny your request. But if not, it will be adieu to Colossus, unless you succeed in persuading your law firm colleagues to recognize the harm this creates for an innocent, and injured, Colossus.

Q. Would the result have been the same if Acme had purchased Magna and kept it as a wholly owned subsidiary? Someone told me it made a difference.

A. It could have. It depends.

Q. On what?

A. Great question. There is a comment to Rule 1.7, the concurrent conflict rule, that addresses conflicts in the corporate family.

Q. Corporate family?

A. Yes, what results when a parent company has spawned many subsidiaries and sister corporations. When a lawyer takes a position directly averse to a client's sub or sister corporation, must the lawyer recognize a conflict with the sub? The comment's

891. MR 1.16(c).

answer is that there are certain factual circumstances where this is likely okay if the comment is followed. It depends on a number of factors, including whether the family members are in the same business; in the same physical location; have the same officers, directors, and/or in-house counsel; and whether the original engagement letter addresses this issue. Many clients make it quite clear that no lawyer they retain should ever take any action adverse to their family members of the retaining client.

Q. Could we have solved this problem by asking for one of those prospective waivers I have read about?

A. You could have tried. Again there is a Rule 1.7 comment that endorses the use of prospective waivers, despite the fact waivers of conflicts generally are supposed to be on informed consent, a defined term that is supposed to be as stringent as it sounds.[892] The thinking by those who endorsed these waivers was that some clients are so sophisticated they understand that their consent is uninformed, but they are willing to accept the risk. It might have helped, though a challenge to the lawyer's reliance on a prospective waiver would not be a surprising development. We have seen many in-house counsel argue that they accepted the waiver, but they never thought it would be used to bring a RICO action, or some similarly reputation-destroying claim against a good client of the firm.[893]

All for One and . . .

Q. I specialize in securities litigation. We deal with fraud, inadequate disclosure, insider trading, you get the idea.

A. Fascinating stuff.

Q. Truly. And we have a great record of defending our clients from that overreaching SEC. But we have a problem now.

A. You lost?

Q. No. We won. The court granted summary judgment of the government's charge of trading on non-public information against the issuer and two key employees, the CFO and the director of sales.

A. Then pop the champagne.

Q. Oh we did that. Good stuff. But we might've been premature. The SEC appealed. Claimed the district court broke new

---

892. MR 1.7 cmt. [22].

893. *E.g.*, W. Sugar Coop. v. Archer-Daniels-Midland Co., 98 F. Supp. 3d 1074 (C.D. Cal. 2015) (law firm could not rely on advanced waiver of former and current clients; a second waiver was required because the original waiver insufficiently disclosed the nature of a subsequent conflict).

ground narrowing the definition of insider trading. Now we are before the Third Circuit.

A. What's all that have to do with ethics?

Q. Nothing on the merits. But CFO just called us in a panic. "Can we settle?" he asks. "Why would we do that. Our strategy worked perfectly," I responded.

A. Sounds right.

Q. You would think. But an unidentified employee has threatened the CFO that she will go to the SEC and reveal damaging information she possesses about other CFO misdeeds unless he pays her one-half of his gain.

A. Blackmail.

Q. You could call it that. But before we go anywhere with this, we need to figure out the conflict we now face.

A. And before you address that you have to worry about confidentiality.

Q. What do you mean?

A. You represent three clients.

Q. Check.

A. One of them just told you about a startling development.

Q. Check.

A. Now what do you do?

Q. Tell all three?

A. You hesitate.

Q. I do. I was going to call a meeting. Consult the clients like you taught me.

A. But can you do that? Did you discuss how you would handle this issue when the representation began?

Q. Who remembers?

A. Now you have a conflict, unless the client subject to the threat, after being properly counseled by someone other than you, agrees to share the information.

Q. What if permission is not forthcoming?

A. Then you must address the conflict.

Q. Even on appeal.

A. The rules apply to the entire course of a representation. Conflicts can arise on appeal. So that even if you get permission to share the confidential information, and it is agreed that the threatened fellow will get separate counsel, you still might have to withdraw if you find that the representation of the other two clients requires you to take positions directly adverse to the withdrawing client or there is some material limitation on what you can do because of the actions you have to take in representing the remaining clients.

We Have Met the Enemy and . . .

Q. We are in the Ninth Circuit. Great case. Our firm helped Giggle, the tech mega-company, defend itself against some swashbuckling takeover artist wanting to seize control of our board and force the company to distribute its cash, when we, I mean our client's present board, is sure we can put the cash to better use. We won below. The district court upheld the Delaware poison pill. Giggles is incorporated in Delaware. If we win the appeal, Caldwell & Moore will be the "go to" firm for what promises to be very lucrative bet-the-company litigation.

A. Sounds great.

Q. Oh it was alright. Until yesterday. One of our colleagues represents Lord Silversmith. It appears the powerful Lord has his sights set on Kumquat, the computer giant. They are incorporated in Utah. But they copied the Delaware poison pill provision, which, of course, they want us to challenge. The case will be brought in Florida. Kumquat is headquartered in Orlando.

A. We see. You are worried about a conflict.

Q. I didn't think I needed to be. Someone said this was an issue conflict that really did not count.

A. Somebody is wrong. There is no such exception for issue conflicts on the grounds they aren't real. They're real alright.

Q. But another fellow told me they count only if the contrary position is taken in the same court. Here we have the Ninth Circuit and Utah. Not even close.

A. The test for whether issue conflicts should be recognized was as you state it. But today the world has shrunk. Plus, you have the copycat bylaw language regarding the pill. Under these circumstances the test should be when a lawyer's successful advocacy in one courtroom could be detrimental to the interests of another firm client in a different courtroom. This won't apply, in our view, when you are alternatively advocating for broad discovery and, in another case, for narrowing the scope. Those arguments are case fact specific. But the idea that your firm would defend and attack the same poison pill provision in two different courtrooms certainly bears significant soul-searching before you jump. And one more thing.

Q. What's that?

A. If you take both, only lose one!

§ 28.04 Frivolous Appeals

It Never Occurred to Me

Q. I am in trouble with Judge Grim. Apparently, he is appropriately named.

A. You don't fit the profile of lawyers he goes after.

Q. Exactly what I thought. I was representing an animal rights group. They wanted to picket the circus. Not a new idea, but a first for His Honor. The group likes to punctuate their demonstrations by opening some cages. Their folks have gone to jail for this. But this time they planned to only release some birds. I convinced myself that the existing case law, going off on the danger the animals posed to humans, would not apply to parrots. I defended his dim view of my argument by asserting I believed I was making a good-faith argument.

A. He wasn't buying?

Q. I'll say. He emphasized that Rule 3.1 establishes an objective test.

A. It's a particularly dangerous test for trial lawyers who are famous for losing their objectivity. As soon as they learn which team they are on, they embrace the assignment with gusto, losing much if not all of their ability to step back and evaluate matters objectively but maintaining their conviction that they are totally grounded in reality. Which is why Rule 3.1 employs an objective standard.

Q. It's actually worse than that. The judge did not just invoke Rule 3.1. He mentioned Rule 11 of the Rules of Civil Procedure, 28 U.S.C. § 1927, and his inherent authority to "rule" in his domain.

A. The citations are correct. Judges have vast discretionary authority to evaluate and sanction conduct that occurs before them.

Q. Well he's done nothing yet in terms of actual sanctions. We are to appear next week.

A. Our view: contrition will go a long way toward putting this behind you.

Client Direction

Q. We are really torn on this one.

A. You've come to the right place.

Q. We hope so. We are not so far out of law school to have forgotten two principles emphasized by many of our teachers.

A. Remembering two might be a new indoor record. Tell us more.

Q. We were constantly being reminded that as lawyers for clients there were two roles we should avoid. One was to be a mere instrumentality of our clients, unquestionably following their direction.

A. And the latter?

Q. We must avoid being directors, substituting our best judgment for that of the client. Rather, we have to remember that the exclusive domain of the client, enshrined in our rules, was determining the objectives of the representation. We should provide our best advice, but the client gets to decide.

A. So far so good.

Q. Another was that the Rules of Civil Procedure are incorporated into the rules via Model Rules 3.1 to 3.4, one of which is the prohibition on frivolous conduct.

A. How does that play out here?

Q. Our client wants us to take an appeal. This client will gladly pay for the effort. And we'd love to do it. The client got a raw deal. Let's just say that a New Yorker didn't stand much of a chance in a Jackson, Mississippi, courtroom. But we can't find a single argument that passes the laugh test. We told the client to which he snapped back that we were his agents.

A. This is a professional minefield. Both principles are correct. We take direction, like all agents, from our clients. But we also may not pursue frivolous actions. And the latter trumps the former. Under Rule 1.2, the one area exclusively assigned to the lawyer is the obligation to conform the lawyer's conduct to the rules. And here the rule tells you that you are in ethical trouble if you pursue the appeal.[894]

The Merits

Q. There is one more problem

A. What's that?

Q. We cannot think of a basis for appeal. This was a factual dispute that was resolved by the jury's answers on the verdict sheet. Truth is we never really understood the factual issues relating to the master crystal.

---

894. Matter of Hendrix, 986 F.2d 195 (7th Cir. 1993) (lawyers who failed to cite case that made appeal frivolous may be sanctioned under Fed. R. App. P. 38 (damages for delay) and are subject to professional discipline under Fed. R. App. P. 46(c)).

A. You're sure you are not reaching this conclusion simply because you think the appeal arguments won't succeed?

Q. We think the client knows it's a frivolous appeal. But they figure, if their adversary is forced to spend some money defending the appeal, that will teach them a lesson.

A. If that is so, you have a defense to pursuing an appeal. Rule 3.1 of the Model Rules establishes that there must be a nonfrivolous basis for seeking a new trial. That could include a good faith argument for an extension, modification, or reversal of existing law. However, the comment to the same rule provides that if the primary purpose of the course of action, for example, an appeal, is to harass or maliciously injure the adverse party, it is frivolous.

Q. And if the appeal is not frivolous, but merely a loser?

A. We doubt the language of your engagement will help you. To limit the scope of a representation, you must state that limitation clearly. Any ambiguity will redound the benefit of your client. So do your level best. Maybe the appeal will look a lot more likely to succeed when you divert the energy you have used avoiding the filing of the appeal to pursuing it with the competence that prompts so many to hire your firm in the first place.

Q. Flattery does not lessen the pain of your advice.

§ 28.05 Candor to the Court

Pro Bono Ghosts

Q. I know I did the right thing.

A. Hard to tell so far.

Q. I was down at the courthouse sitting in the lobby. This woman approaches. She's carrying a well-worn manila envelope. Never a good sign.

A. But you stayed at your station.

Q. I did. Too awkward to get up. And out comes a tale of woe. Social security issue. She represented herself. The district judge denied relief. And as I listen to her depressing story, it sounds like the judge got it wrong. Not that I know much about social security. I urge her to file an appeal. She looks at me like I asked her to run a marathon. I explain that I can't take on her case, but I will help her represent herself. The smile on her face was reward enough.

A. What did you do?
Q. I did some research. Wrote a short insert for her brief addressing a statutory interpretation issue and she filed pro se, thankful for my assistance.
A. What a rewarding result.
Q. Not so fast. She is contacted by the clerk of the court. Wants to know who helped her. She enthusiastically identifies *moi*! And before you know it, a disciplinary complaint is filed against me. Show cause why I should not be sanctioned for misleading the court. I thought I was helping. Now I am in trouble.
A. The legal world is certainly of two minds when it comes to providing such assistance. On the one hand, we want lawyers to pitch in as you did. On the other, many courts see what you did—assist anonymously—as an affront to the lawyer's duty of candor. Obviously this court is not charitable. A few mea culpas and perhaps an entry of appearance and further active participation will solve the problem. But this is a great object lesson for us all. Before you try your hand at ghostwriting, find out the relevant court's view.[895] And follow it!

It's the Principle

Q. Not sure we need you.
A. But something's bothering you.
Q. How'd you know?
A. If you answer enough ethical inquiries you can hear the concern in the caller's voice. Spit it out.
Q. We just wanted to fulfill our client's instruction. We tried this antitrust case against client's biggest competitor. The victory at trial was a huge success. So much so that, after the other side filed their totally frivolous appeal, opposing counsel initiated settlement discussions. Opening bid: more than our client had authorized us to accept! We told them we had a deal and happily told client's general counsel. That's when all hell broke out. The client was happy with the cash. But they wanted the appeal to continue because the case, if decided correctly by the Ninth Circuit, would provide an invaluable in terrorem effect on other competitors.

---

895. *E.g.*, *In re* Hood, 727 F.3d 1360 (11th Cir. 2013) (lawyer who filled out a preprinted Chapter 13 bankruptcy petition for a client without putting their signatures on it did not "draft" it and therefore did not engage in prohibited ghostwriting; Duran v. Carris, 238 F.3d 1268 (10th Cir. 2001) (lawyer who "ghostwrote" former client's brief admonished by the court for misrepresentation; brief must be accompanied by lawyer's signature).

A. What did you do?

Q. We called our opponent. Accepted the money and they agreed they would pursue their appeal seeking a remand for a retrial. Even though they were going to pay our client the money and not reenter the field, even if they won.

A. Sounds perfect. What's troubling you?

Q. It leaves us uneasy. Are we going through a charade? Not letting the court know we have already settled.

A. We agree. There is nothing perfect about it. The fact that, whatever the court does, nothing will change, means there really is no case or controversy. The court, without knowing it, will be issuing an advisory opinion. And your opponent has very little reason to pursue the appeal with the resources required if nothing will change no matter which way the court comes out. Your client's desire to pursue this course is understandable. You, as officers of the court, must respectfully decline the invitation. Candor to the tribunal is critical here.

Defeat from the Jaws of Victory

Q. How sweet it was. The jury came back in less than one hour. Victory for our client. Damages exceeding our wildest expectations. And then an appeal by the other side that looked like a "Hail Mary" pass, a totally frivolous attempt to disparage a clean verdict, the trial judge protecting us from the beginning by substantially granting all of our opponent's objections and denying ours. We could already visualize the celebratory trip to Paris.

A. And then?

Q. You got it. And then I get this call from Experts, Inc. Their CEO on the phone. They supplied our expert biochemist who put the last nails in the defendant's coffin. Superb. Charming. Credible. Persuasive. You could not get a better performance.

A. And?

Q. And CEO lowers his voice, and intones, "We are sure this won't make any difference, but we just discovered that Dr. Stevens—our great expert—does not have a PhD. He is ABD."

A. ABD?

Q. All but dissertation. He never received a PhD. He forgot. Or so we are told. But the CEO tells us we don't have a thing to worry about because his testimony was so persuasive and, having had two other experts review it, they confirm it is all solid science. Then he thanks us for our business.

A. Nothing to worry about.

Q. Really?

A. No. We were being facetious. It is a disaster.

Q. But the trial jury has spoken.

A. Based on an expert whose credentials were vastly exaggerated.

Q. No. Everything else he said was correct. He did do graduate work at Yale.

A. Have you taken a look at the transcript of his testimony?

Q. Sure. I already told you our client's in-house geniuses say he was right on.

A. That may be so. How many times did you call him doctor?

Q. I didn't count. Probably before every question.

A. Did you point out his degree?

Q. I am sure. I always do.

A. Then we have trouble with a capital T.

Q. Even if the trial is over?

A. This is correct. Rule 3.3(a)(3) provides that your duty of candor lasts until the end of the proceeding. You are not there yet.

Q. The rule also requires materiality.

A. I thought we already put that issue to bed when we counted the number of times you called him doctor. If that isn't enough to persuade you, think about how material it would be if the jury knew that your expert was lying about this critical aspect of his resume.

Q. Hadn't thought of that.

A. We're not sure, however, that you should be quite as upset as you are. We think your client has a great malpractice claim against the expert and his employer. You have already proved what would have happened if the expert had the credentials he claimed. We do not know whether you have to retry the case with a new expert or otherwise how it will play out. What we do know: all is not lost, unless . . .

Q. Unless what?

A. Unless you knew the truth when you put that expert on the stand.

Q. How dare you!

A. Just making sure you are listening.

§ 28.06 Candor in Brief Writing: Legal Authority

Do We Have To?

Q. Representing a small boarding school. Nonprofit. Well regarded. Very prestigious. Wish my kids could go there. Anyway, all beside the point. They have this difficult case. Hints of sexual misconduct by a long-time teacher. We got the case dismissed on summary judgment. Now we're on appeal. Other side filed its brief two weeks ago. Ours is due in another two weeks. A new case was just decided. In another court. Not a controlling jurisdiction. Besides, we think it's dicta. I thought we should cite it. Client—oops, client's board chairman who is a lawyer—says no way. What do you think?

A. You've raised a number of issues. First, you have it right that you are only required to cite authority, even if ignored by the other side, in the controlling jurisdiction.[896] If you are right, that this is dicta—are you?—then there is no requirement that you cite to the case. Even if not dicta, if not in the controlling jurisdiction, you are off the hook for that reason.

Q. That's it?

A. No. Second, you said you thought you should cite it. We do not know whether your "should" was a "must" or just a desirable thing to do. Since it looks like Rule 3.3 does not require citation, this question becomes who between client and lawyer gets to decide whether to cite. In our view this is one where the lawyer certainly may consult the client, but in the end the lawyer should decide. If you find the chairman persuasive, follow his direction. If not, use your judgment. That's why you were hired.

Q. You said there were three points.

A. Precisely. The last is the good-lawyering one, a consideration that you may have already addressed. Even if you do not have to cite a case under the rules, there are so many reasons to do so. The other side may get around to citing it. Or the judge's

---

896. MR 3.3(a)(2); RLGL § 111; Precision Specialty Metals, Inc. v. United States, 315 F.3d 1346 (Fed. Cir. 2003) (Department of Justice lawyer publicly reprimanded for misquoting and failing to quote fully from two judicial opinions in a motion for reconsideration that she signed and filed); Chavez v. City of Albuquerque, No. 99-2359, 2000 WL 15088352000 (10th Cir. Oct. 10, 2000) (lawyer reprimanded and admonished for violating Fed. R. Civ. P. 11 for knowledge of controlling legal authority because he had raised and lost the issue in several previous cases); Brundage v. Estate of Carambio, 951 A.2d 947 (N.J. 2008) (lawyer's failure to disclose an unfavorable unpublished decision or its pending appeal, while it approached the bounds of unacceptable behavior, was not prohibited by the Rules of Professional Conduct and, therefore, does not warrant imposing a litigation sanction on the lawyer's client).

law clerk may unearth it. And if either of those events occurs, you certainly want the judge to have in hand why the bad language is dicta, why that case is distinguishable from your case, or why that case was wrongly decided. And none of those pearls of wisdom will be available to Her Honor unless you address the new case head on. Not a rules point but certainly a good-lawyering one.[897]

897. *See also* § 26.03 in this book.

CHAPTER 29

Judicial Ethics for Lawyers

§ 29.01 Introduction: The Importance of Judicial Ethics for Lawyers

Judicial ethics is an important topic for lawyers because most judges are lawyers, and because lawyers interact with judges, and are thereby "indirectly governed" by the law that governs judicial conduct.[898] A survey of judicial conduct rules thus provides an opportunity to review similar concepts in the law governing lawyers.

Of course, the lawyer's role is partisan; to represent the client's interests zealously, within the bounds of the law.[899] The touchstone ethic for judges is the opposite: impartiality, not partisanship. Like lawyers, judges have obligations of communication, competence, confidentiality, and conflict remediation, but these judicial obligations are intended to promote confidence in the independence, integrity, and impartiality of a public tribunal.[900] The lawyer's reciprocal obligation to respect the impartiality of a tribunal is set out in Model Rule 3.5.

Just as lawyers are subject to their jurisdiction's version of the ABA Model Rules of Professional Conduct, judges are governed by their jurisdiction's judicial code, patterned after the ABA Model Code of Judicial Conduct and promulgated by the highest court. These codes apply to all the activities of full-time judges and some activities of part-time

898. Ronald D. Rotunda & John S. Dzienkowski, Legal Ethics: The Lawyer's Deskbook on Professional Responsibility §§ 10.0–10.1 (2014–2015 ed.).

899. MR Preamble ¶ [8].

900. MCJC Canon 1 promotes this goal by requiring compliance with law, MCJC Rule 1.1; avoiding impropriety and the appearance of impropriety, MCJC Rule 1.2; and prohibiting abuse of power, MCJC Rule 1.3.

judges,[901] including justices of the peace, magistrates, court commissioners, special masters, referees, and administrative law judges.[902] Federal judges are subject to the Code of Conduct for Federal Judges, adopted by the U.S. Judicial Conference.[903]

As governmental employees, state and federal judges also are subject to statutory regulations. For example, federal statutes prohibit the practice of law by federal judges[904] and create standards for disqualification.[905] Both state and federal judges also are subject to criminal sanctions for violation of applicable statutory regulations.[906]

Judges who leave the bench are subject not only to lawyer code provisions, such as Model Rule 1.12, but also to court rules that regulate their subsequent practice.[907] Model Rule 1.12 regulates the conduct of former arbitrators and mediators as well as that of former judges. Lawyers who serve in these capacities also may be subject to more stringent standards under state law or the code of ethics of a private organization, such as the American Arbitration Association or the Society of Professionals in Dispute Resolution.[908]

Judicial disciplinary procedures begin by the filing of a complaint by another judge, lawyer, or any member of the public. Lawyer and judicial professional rules of conduct create an obligation to report another lawyer's or judge's impairment or misconduct to the appropriate authority.[909] Nearly every state has created a judicial disciplinary commission empowered by constitutional amendment or statute to discipline sitting judges.[910] Disciplinary sanctions range from private and public reprimands to deprivation of salary to removal from office.

In the federal courts, Article III judges can be removed from office only by impeachment, a seldom-used remedy.[911] In 1980, Congress created judicial councils in each circuit and empowered them to take

---

901. *See* ABA MCJC Application pts. II (Retired Judge Subject to Recall), III (Continuing Part-Time Judge), IV (Periodic Part-Time Judge), V (Pro Tempore Part-Time Judge).

902. The first Model, the 1924 Canons of Judicial Ethics, was promulgated in response to a scandal created by Judge Kenesaw Mountain Landis, who earned six times his federal judicial salary in the private practice of law while sitting as a federal judge. ROTUNDA & DZIENKOWSKI, *supra* note 898, § 10.0–10.2.

903. 175 F.R.D. 363 (1998). Supreme Court Justices are not governed by these rules.

904. 28 U.S.C. § 454 (2012).

905. 28 U.S.C. § 144 (bias or prejudice of a judge), § 455 (disqualification) (2012).

906. JEFFREY M. SHAMAN, STEVEN LUBET & JAMES J. ALFINI, JUDICIAL CONDUCT AND ETHICS § 14.11 (5th ed. 2013).

907. For example, U.S. Supreme Court Rule 7 prohibits law clerks from participating in any case before the Court for two years after they leave government service.

908. *See* MRs 1.12 cmt. [2], 2.4 cmt. [2].

909. MR 8.3; MCJC Rule 2.15. MCJC Rule 2.14 also requires judges to take "appropriate action" if they reasonably believe that the performance of another lawyer or judge is impaired.

910. SHAMAN, LUBET & ALFINI, *supra* note 906, § 1.03.

911. *See* MARY L. VOLCANSEK, JUDICIAL IMPEACHMENT: NONE CALLED FOR JUSTICE (1993).

disciplinary action short of removal from office.[912] Disciplinary sanctions range from private and public censure to temporary suspension of a judge's caseload. Judicial councils also can ask judges to retire and recommend impeachment to the Senate.[913]

Unlike lawyers, however, judges are absolutely immune from civil liability for their official duties, even if they act from improper motives.[914] Judicial immunity extends to intentional torts such as defamation and malicious prosecution as well as statutory civil rights actions.[915] The Supreme Court has created this common-law immunity to protect judicial independence, and to encourage judges to decide all contested and controversial cases without fear of later legal retribution from the parties. An independent judiciary also promotes public confidence in the courts and the rule of law.[916]

The ideals of impartiality and independence remain the primary goal of judicial ethics, embodied in both codes of judicial conduct and relevant statutory regulations. Judges should suspend judgment until all of the evidence has been introduced, and if they cannot act in an unbiased manner, they should disqualify themselves from the case.

§ 29.02 Judicial Competence and Diligence

The Duty to Sit

Q. This judge! Campaigned with vigor, got elected, and is never around. Undecided motions pile up, and phone calls to the clerk go unanswered. I think the judge prefers a walk on the golf course over a session on the bench.

A. We hear you. The judge's basic duty of competence[917] requires that the judge "hear and decide matters assigned to the judge."[918] Your first assignment is to document the problems in terms of the amount of delay from the time the issue was set for decision, the relative complexity of the case, any knowledge you have about the general workload of the judge and his or her time off, and any information about delays in other

---

912. Judicial Councils Reform and Judicial Conduct and Disability Act of 1980, 28 U.S.C. §§ 331, 332, 372, 604 (2012).

913. Shaman, Lubet & Alfini, *supra* note 906, § 1.04.

914. Mireles v. Waco, 502 U.S. 9 (1991); Stump v. Sparkman, 435 U.S. 349 (1978); Pierson v. Ray, 386 U.S. 547 (1967).

915. O'Bryan v. Chandler, 352 F.2d 987 (10th Cir. 1965), Garfield v. Palmieri, 297 F.2d 526 (2d Cir. 1962).

916. Shaman, Lubet & Alfini, *supra* note 906, § 14.01.

917. MCJC Rule 2.5.

918. MCJC Rule 2.7.

matters.[919] You also might glean some information from reports that judges in some jurisdictions are required to prepare with respect to cases and matters that languish too long.[920] Then, we suggest that you run your concerns by the chief administrative judge. Although state statutes that attempted to condition payment of a judge's salary on performance have been ruled unconstitutional, judges who chronically delay are subject to discipline.[921]

§ 29.03 Judicial Mediation

Coerced Mediation

Q. It's outrageous! It was a sensitive abuse case against a local church. At the first motion hearing, as soon as the judge learned the subject matter, he took the lawyers and parties into chambers. "You are not leaving these chambers until you settle the matter. My courtroom will not become a circus for the press. It's a lose-lose for everybody. Now get busy." My client was so intimidated, he caved.

A. The judge had every reason to encourage settlement, but no right to coerce it.[922] A judge who goes too far with fear and intimidation does not meet the requirement that judges be impartial[923] and deprives parties of the right to be heard.[924] You had the responsibility to make that point with the judge, and to urge your client not to consent to a settlement you truly thought not to be in your client's best interests. We know that requires courage, but if lawyers don't seek to have judicial conduct conform to the Code of Judicial Conduct, who will?

§ 29.04 The Judge's Responsibility

While performing judicial duties, judges must be mindful of their obligations to act impartially, competently, and diligently. Competence and diligence require that judges give priority to judicial duties,[925] exercise

919. *In re* Lee, 933 So. 2d 736 (La. 2006).
920. FLA. JUDICIAL ADMIN. R. 2.085(e); N.Y. UNIFORM JUST. CT. ACT § 1304; OHIO R. CT. 6.
921. *In re* Grady, 348 N.W.2d 559 (Wis. 1984).
922. MCJC Rule 2.6(B); Kothe v. Smith, 771 F.2d 667 (2d Cir. 1985).
923. MCJC Rule 2.2.
924. MCJC Rule 2.6(A).
925. MCJC Rule 2.1.

necessary skill in a prompt and timely manner,[926] and properly hire and supervise court staff.[927] It also requires that judges afford every litigant the opportunity to be heard.[928] Judges can encourage settlement, but cannot coerce it.[929] Judicial involvement in settlement of cases also must avoid the taint that arises from information that could influence the judge's subsequent decisions in the matter.[930] If that occurs, "disqualification [of the judge] may be appropriate."[931]

§ 29.05 Judicial Bias

Manifest Bias

Q. When I came to the attorney general's office, the other lawyers warned me that Judge Jordan uses sexist language. I thought they were kidding, until last week, just after he ruled in my favor, he winked and referred to me as "attorney generalette." I approached him in chambers and politely explained why his behavior was demeaning and inappropriate. The next time I appeared in his court, the judge twice called me "Portia." I've had it!

A. And you should put a stop to it. This behavior clearly violates the Code of Judicial Conduct's specific mandate not to "manifest bias or prejudice, or engage in harassment, including but not limited to bias, prejudice or harassment based upon race, sex, gender, religion, national origin, ethnicity, disability, age, sexual orientation, marital status, socioeconomic status, or political affiliation," and requires that judges exercise control over court staff to prevent the same.[932] Demeaning nicknames and attempted humor based on stereotyping are examples of prohibited conduct.[933] We're gratified (but saddened) to report that judges have been disciplined for similar behavior.[934] Your assignment is to follow the available method of lodging a complaint.

---

926. MRs 1.1, 1.3; MCJC Rules 2.5, 2.7.
927. MRs 5.1, 5.3; MCJC Rules 2.12, 2.13.
928. MCJC Rule 2.6.
929. MCJC Rule 2.6(B).
930. MCJC Rule 2.6 cmt. (3).
931. *Id.*
932. MCJC Rule 2.3(B).
933. MCJC Rule 2.3 cmt. (2).
934. *In re* Kirby, 354 N.W.2d 410, 413–14 (Minn. 1984) ("lawyerette" and "attorney generalette"); *In re* Barr, 13 S.W.3d 525 (Tex. 1998) (referring to female assistant district attorneys as "babes").

§ 29.06 Impartiality and Fairness

To promote impartiality, Canon 2 of the Model Code requires judges to "uphold and apply the law";[935] act without bias, prejudice, or harassment;[936] ensure each person the right to be heard;[937] act in a patient, courteous manner;[938] and avoid ex parte contact with parties[939] as well as extrajudicial statements on pending matters.[940]

A judge's impartiality obligation also reaches into his or her extrajudicial life. Judges must avoid participating in activities that can often lead to disqualification, or undermine their independence, integrity, or impartiality.[941] For example, judges cannot appear voluntarily before a legislative body or accept governmental appointments, except in connection with matters concerning the legal system or administration of justice.[942] Nor may they affiliate with discriminatory organizations.[943] To avoid misuse of judicial power or prestige, judges cannot voluntarily testify as character witnesses,[944] or use nonpublic information for a purpose unrelated to judicial duties.[945] To avoid disqualification, judges cannot accept fiduciary appointments,[946] serve as arbitrators or mediators,[947] practice law,[948] serve as an officer or director of any for-profit business entity, or engage in any other for-profit activities that will interfere with proper performance of judicial duties.[949] Service on nonprofit boards is allowed, as long as those organizations' activities do not frequently come before the judge or the court of which the judge is a member, or otherwise undermine the judge's impartiality.[950] To maintain judicial independence, a number of rules regulate extrajudicial compensation, basically limiting it to reasonable honoraria, reimbursement

---

935. MR 8.4; MCJC Rule 2.2.

936. MCJC Rule 2.3; Judges who are lawyers also are governed by the antidiscrimination provisions in MR 8.4(g) and cmt. [3].

937. MCJC Rule 2.6. Part (B) of this rule distinguishes between encouraging and coercing parties to settle a matter.

938. MCJC Rule 2.8.

939. MCJC Rule 2.9; *see also* MR 3.5(b).

940. MCJC Rule 2.10.

941. MCJC Rule 3.1.

942. MCJC Rules 3.2, 3.4.

943. MCJC Rule 3.6.

944. MCJC Rule 3.3.

945. MRs 1.6, 1.8(b), 1.9, 1.11(c); MCJC Rule 3.5.

946. MCJC Rule 3.8.

947. MCJC Rule 3.9.

948. MCJC Rule 3.10.

949. MCJC Rule 3.11.

950. MCJC Rule 3.7.

of expenses, or the acceptance of "ordinary social hospitality."[951] Public reporting of extrajudicial compensation also is required.[952]

§ 29.07 Ex Parte Communications

The Perfect Opportunity

Q. Talk about being in the right place at the right time. Drinking coffee in the courthouse cafeteria and Judge Fulsome walks by. He sits down at my table.

"My law clerk thinks your motion to dismiss is pretty weak tea."

Of course, I was delighted for the chance to set him straight; ten minutes of oral argument why his clerk was wrong. What an opportunity!

A. Except for one thing: You had an improper ex parte communication with the judge. He should not have spoken to you about the merits of the case,[953] and you should not have responded.[954] You're both subject to discipline.[955] Notice to the other side and an opportunity to be heard at least will mediate this unfortunate situation.

§ 29.08 Avoiding and Curing Improper Ex Parte Communications

Model Rule 3.5 and the Model Code of Judicial Conduct Rule 2.9 prohibit ex parte communications to or by a judge or the judge's staff absent specific legal authorization.[956] Lawyers should not seek improper influence or advantage,[957] and judges should not obtain information outside of the court record (or those facts that may properly be judicially noticed).[958] For both lawyers and judges, the prohibition applies regardless of who initiates the communication.[959]

---

951. MCJC Rules 3.12–3.14.

952. MCJC Rule 3.14.

953. MCJC Rule 2.9.

954. MR 3.5(b).

955. *In re* Ragatz, 429 N.W.2d 488 (Wis. 1988) (lawyer in same matter suspended for 60 days for responding to judge's improper communication); *In re* Aulik, 429 N.W.2d 759 (Wis. 1988) (judge suspended for 90 days for initiating ex parte contact regarding whether case was frivolous).

956. RLGL § 113.

957. *Id.* § 113(1).

958. MCJC Rule 2.9(C).

959. RLGL § 113 cmt. c.

Because the touchstone of improper ex parte communication is unfair advantage, some ex parte communication is allowed where the danger of improper influence appears low and the need to meet other objectives appears high. For example, routine administrative matters such as scheduling may be accomplished ex parte, as long as a judge "reasonably believes that no party will gain a procedural, substantive, or tactical advantage," and as long as the judge promptly notifies other parties of the substance of the communication and gives them an opportunity to respond.[960] Similarly, but only with the consent of all parties, judges may confer with them separately for the purpose of settling the matter.[961]

If improper ex parte communication about the substance of a matter does occur inadvertently, it can be cured by prompt notification to all parties of the substance of the communication and affording them an opportunity to respond.[962] Lawyers who inadvertently fall into the trap of communication with judges ex parte should either inform the other party or request that the judge do so.

§ 29.09 Judicial Disqualification and Recusal

The High School Classmate

Q. I'm representing a client in an appeal to Judge Jones from an adverse zoning hearing board decision. Client calls me up in a total panic. Out to dinner on a family vacation in Puerto Rico last week. As the family went to their assigned table in the dining room, they passed a table where Judge Jones and the Solicitor for the Township, and their spouses were seated, clinking champagne flutes. As my client walked past, Judge Jones awkwardly explained they were attending a county association mid-winter meeting. "We're all high school classmates, y'know."

A. You raise four square the importance of an "appearance of impropriety" standard. Even if this dinner for four, complete with champagne toasts, in fact does not interfere with the integrity of the judge's decision making, the effect on the confidence your poor client will have in the result (unless the matter goes 100 percent his way) undermines the public's confidence

960. MCJC Rule 2.9(A)(1).
961. MCJC Rule 2.9(A)(4).
962. MCJC Rule 2.9(B).

in the judicial process, Justice Scalia's angry defense of his conduct notwithstanding.[963]

First, if Judge Jones has "inadvertently" spoken to the Township Solicitor ex parte about the case, he must promptly notify the other parties.[964]

Second, Model Code of Judicial Conduct Rule 1.2 and Comment [5] maintain the objective "appearance of impropriety" standard that is essential to promoting confidence in the impartiality of the judiciary and relevant to the standard for judicial disqualification.[965] On the one hand, judges are entitled to engage in "ordinary social hospitality."[966] On the other hand, when off the bench, judges should not participate in activities that appear to "undermine the judge's independence, integrity, or impartiality."[967]

With this in mind, we believe you should consider whether to ask Judge Jones to disqualify himself. If he is biased for or against a party's lawyer, he must, and his obligation to disqualify is not waivable.[968] But this is a subjective standard, requiring some showing of favoritism or ill will and will be difficult to establish unless the judge is willing to admit it. More likely, disqualification will be urged on the basis that his social contact with a party's lawyer during the pendency of the proceeding reasonably "calls into question his impartiality," the standard found in Rule 2.11, which includes the appearance of impropriety standard in Rule 1.2. At a minimum, Judge Jones should follow the dictate of Comment [5] to Rule 2.11 by

---

963. Cheney v. U.S. Dist. Court for the District of Columbia, 541 U.S. 913 (2004); Lawrence J. Fox, *I Did Not Sleep with That Vice President*, 15 Prof. Law., Issue No. 2 (2004).

964. MCJC Rule 2.9(B).

965. MCJC Rule 2.11(A).

966. MCJC Rule 3.13(B)(3); Schupper v. People, 157 P.3d 516 (Colo. 2007) (mere existence of trial judge's friendship with a member of a prosecution team, where judge had little present social involvement with prosecutor and prosecutor made a single appearance in the case, did not create either actual bias or the appearance of impropriety).

967. MCJC Rule 3.1(C); United States v. Murphy, 768 F.2d 1518 (7th Cir. 1985) (reasonable question about judge's impartiality existed where judge's family and lawyer's family were about to vacation together immediately after sentencing in a case); Velardo v. Ovitt, 933 A.2d 227 (Vt. 2007) (judge should have disqualified herself where guardian ad litem was her sister; appearance of impropriety was substantial).

968. MCJC Rule 2.11(A)(1) and (C).

disclosing the Puerto Rico meeting on the record and explaining why it does not constitute a basis for disqualification.[969]

§ 29.10 Public Statements

A Previous Commitment

Q. I just found out that the judge in our case has been giving private interviews to the press during the trial, apparently in an effort "to explain the complex nature of the case to the public." First Amendment notwithstanding, there must be some limit to this conduct. I can't talk to the press, why should she?

A. The limit is clear: public statements that "might reasonably be expected to affect the outcome or impair the fairness"[970] of a pending matter are impermissible. If this occurs, the judge is subject to discipline[971] and disqualification.[972]

§ 29.11 Impropriety and the Appearance of Impropriety

Impartiality requires that judges disqualify or recuse[973] themselves whenever their "impartiality might reasonably be questioned."[974] Rule 2.11 identifies a number of recurring circumstances where this general rule applies, and is used as the standard for both judicial discipline and disqualification.[975] A majority of states and the federal government

---

969. ABA Comm. on Ethics & Prof'l Responsibility, Formal Op. 07-449 (2007), Lawyer Concurrently Representing Judge and Litigant Before the Judge in Unrelated Matters (judge must determine bias when presiding over a case in which a lawyer's firm for one of the parties concurrently represents the judge in an unrelated matter; if not biased, judge may continue presiding if the judge discloses the concurrent representation on the record and the parties unanimously agree to waive the judge's disqualification after considering the disclosure outside the judge's presence).

970. MCJC Rule 2.10(A).

971. *In re* Bourisseau, 480 N.W.2d 270 (Mich. 1992) (judge censured for newspaper statement about new abortion law that stated how judge was likely to rule).

972. United States v. Microsoft Corp., 253 F.3d 34, 107–17 (D.C. Cir. 2001) (judge disqualified for giving private interviews to the press during trial whose cumulative effect was to disclose judge's views on factual and legal matters at the heart of the case).

973. "Disqualification" and "recusal" are used interchangeably in the Model Code of Judicial Conduct. MCJC Rule 2.11 cmt. [1]. Historically, however, recusal meant voluntary withdrawal from a case; and disqualification referred to removal of a judge following the motion of a party. RICHARD E. FLAMM, JUDICIAL DISQUALIFICATION: RECUSAL AND DISQUALIFICATION OF JUDGES § 1.1 (2d ed. 2007).

974. MCJC Rule 2.11. The federal disqualification statute uses the same "impartiality might reasonably be questioned" standard. 28 U.S.C. § 455 (2012). If personal bias or prejudice is alleged, another judge should be assigned to decide the motion. 28 U.S.C. § 144 (2012). For an analysis of the federal cases, see ALAN HIRSCH & KAY LOVELAND, RECUSAL: ANALYSIS OF CASE LAW UNDER 28 U.S.C. §§ 455 & 144 (2002).

975. SHAMAN, LUBET & ALFINI, *supra* note 906, § 4.01.

also have adopted statutory standards for judicial disqualification.[976] A minority of states allow for peremptory disqualification based on the simple motion of any party, but most jurisdictions require that good cause be shown to require disqualification.[977] The Supreme Court has recently added a constitutional dimension to extreme cases where a probability of actual bias is caused by large campaign contributions.[978]

Substantively, good cause for disqualification requires a determination that a judge's impartiality "might reasonably be questioned."[979] This standard has been construed in hundreds of cases, the general nature of which is identified in Rule 2.11 of the Model Code of Judicial Conduct. A judge's impartiality might reasonably be questioned in the following circumstances, but the impartiality standard is not limited to the items on this list:

- Personal bias or prejudice concerning a party, the party's lawyer, or personal knowledge of the facts in dispute.[980] Many courts add that the source of bias must be extrajudicial, that is, personal, rather than originating in the judicial proceeding itself.[981]
- Relatives of the judge who are parties, managers of parties, lawyers in the proceeding, likely to be a material witness, or have more than a de minimis interest that could be substantially affected by the outcome of the matter.[982]
- Economic interests of the judge or judge's household in the subject matter of the proceeding.[983]

---

976. FLAMM, *supra* note 973, § 2.4.

977. *Id.* § 3.1.

978. Caperton v. A.T. Massey Coal Co., 556 U.S. 868 (2009).

979. MR 1.7(a); MCJC Rule 2.11(A).

980. MCJC Rule 2.11(A)(1).

981. Liteky v. United States, 510 U.S. 540 (1994) (judge's opinions did not amount to bias or partiality unless they displayed a deep-seated favoritism or antagonism that would make fair judgment impossible); United States v. Microsoft Corp., 253 F.3d 34 (D.C. Cir. 2001) (judge who gave private interviews to reporters that were very critical to the defense disqualified for lack of impartiality; extrajudicial source rule inapplicable); Farmer v. State, 770 So. 2d 953 (Miss. 2000) (trial judge who took guilty plea overturned on appeal not disqualified from case on remand absent showing of extrajudicial source of partiality or bias).

982. MCJC Rule 2.11(A)(2); *In re* Johnson, 532 S.E.2d 883 (S.C. 2000) (judge who failed to disqualify herself in grandson's criminal case publicly reprimanded).

983. MCJC Rule 2.11(A)(3); Huffman v. Ark. Judicial Discipline & Disability Comm'n., 42 S.W.3d 386 (Ark. 2001).

- Receipt of donations to the judge's election campaign made by parties or their lawyers in excess of a stated amount.[984]
- Prior public statements by the judge that appear to commit him or her to reach a particular result or rule in a particular way in a proceeding or controversy.[985]
- Prior service as a lawyer, judge, material witness, or government employee or agent in the same matter.[986]

Once a judge is subject to disqualification, two events can override such a result. First, the rule of necessity—that no judge has the requisite impartiality to decide the matter—can prevail over an otherwise substantive basis for disqualification.[987] If there is some other judge who can act in the matter, however, disqualification is required.[988] Second, a disqualification not based on personal bias may be waived by the parties as long as they make such a decision to waive outside the presence of the judge.[989]

---

984. MCJC Rule 2.11(A)(4); Caperton v. A.T. Massey Coal Co., 556 U.S. 868 (2009); Mackenzie v. Super Kids Bargain Store, Inc., 565 So. 2d 1332 (Fla. 1990) (reasonable persons would not perceive judge biased in favor of litigants based solely on fact litigants made a campaign contribution in a jurisdiction where state constitution requires election of certain judges); Barber v. Mackenzie, 562 So. 2d 755 (Fla. Dist. Ct. App. 1990) (judge's disqualification required where counsel who represented party in matrimonial action before judge were members of the committee to re-elect the judge whose campaign was vigorously opposed).

985. MCJC Rule 2.11(A)(5); Pub. Utils. Comm'n v. Pollak, 343 U.S. 451, 467 (1952) (sua sponte recusal by Justice Frankfurter in a case involving radio programs played on public transit in Washington D.C., because his feelings were "so strongly engaged as a victim of the practice in controversy"); United States v. Norton, 700 F.2d 1072 (6th Cir. 1983) (judge who opposed racism of Ku Klux Klan and Nazi Party not disqualified from actions where those groups are parties).

986. MCJC Rule 2.11(A)(6); Williams v. Pennsylvania, 136 S. Ct. 1899 (2016) (state supreme court Chief Justice who earlier approved death penalty specification as District Attorney violated due process by failing to recuse himself in later appeal from stay of execution); Lee v. State, 735 N.E.2d 1169 (Ind. 2000) (judge who gained information from prior proceeding involving accomplice not required to recuse); Village of Exeter v. Kahler, 606 N.W.2d 862 (Neb. Ct. App. 2000) (judge who gained information from an earlier proceeding involving the same party disqualified).

987. For example, if all members of an appellate court would be disqualified in a case that challenges legislative pay raises for judges, utility rate increases, or state bar actions, the rule of necessity would override disqualification. Williams v. United States, 48 F. Supp. 2d 52 (D.D.C. 1999) (recusal not required where federal judge ruled on meaning of statute that affected federal judicial salaries); SHAMAN, LUBET & ALFINI, *supra* note 906, § 4.03.

988. FLAMM, *supra* note 973, § 20.2.3.

989. MRs 1.7(b), 1.0(e); MCJC Rule 2.11(C); *In re* Platt, 8 P.3d 686 (Kan. 2000) (judge whose waiver procedure required nonconsenting parties to fire counsel or seek statutory disqualification publicly censured for improper coercive procedures).

§ 29.12 Judicial Campaigns

The Campaign Influence

Q. I'm involved in a state court appeal in a high profile case. Guess what? I calculate the likely swing vote on the court, who was just elected last year, received more than half of his campaign funds from the CEO of the company who lost to my client in the trial court. Can I get this judge disqualified?

A. In most jurisdictions, this reeks of personal bias (a non-waivable ground for disqualification)[990] or, at the very least, raises a more than serious issue about whether the judge's "impartiality might reasonably be questioned."[991] And even if some judge or court would not so find, we're happy to report that the Supreme Court has added a constitutional dimension to facts like this, holding that as a matter of due process, an objective inquiry was required "into whether the contributor's influence on the election under all the circumstances 'would offer a possible temptation to the average . . . judge to . . . lead him not to hold the balance nice, clear and true."[992] The court concluded that a state supreme-court judge should have recused himself because he was asked to "review a judgment that cost his biggest donor's company $50 million."[993] The court found that on such "extreme facts the probability of actual bias rises to an unconstitutional level."[994] So you've got both rule-based and constitutional arguments.

§ 29.13 Judicial Selection

The Successful Campaign

Q. During a local candidate forum for next fall's county elections, the moderator asked the judicial candidates, "What is your opinion on abortion?" Our candidate for the appellate bench replied: "If I had the right case come before me, I'd overturn *Roe v. Wade* in a minute. Worst decision in history," she continued, as the applause from half the attendees drowned out the rest of her speech.

---

990. MCJC Rules 2.11(A)(1), 2.11(C).
991. MCJC Rule 2.11(A).
992. Caperton v. A.T. Massey Coal Co., 556 U.S. 868 (2009).
993. *Id.* at 886.
994. *Id.* at 886–87.

A. The clash between judicial candidates' free speech rights and the public's right to know, on the one hand, and the impartiality of the judiciary, on the other, continues, even after the Supreme Court's decision in *Republican Party of Minnesota v. White*.[995] The public policy debate concerns not only the case's extra license to candidates to declare their general public views on matters that could (or worse never will, but, by implication, leading the public to think they will) come before them. It also naturally leads to a discussion of the merits of electing judges, notwithstanding the stubborn fact that judicial elections remain in a vast majority of states.

Although *White* found Minnesota's "announce" clause unconstitutional, it did not rule on the clause in the current Model Code of Judicial Conduct rule regarding "pledges, promises, or commitments."[996] Comments [11] to [15] of the rule distinguish making statements or announcements of personal views on legal, political, or other issues, which are protected First Amendment activity, from making promises or commitments to rule in other than an impartial manner. If the totality of the statement indicates a closed mind or a pledge to rule in a particular way, disqualification is required under Rule 2.11.

§ 29.14 Judicial Campaigns and Judicial Speech

Judicial selection is governed by federal and state constitutional and statutory provisions. The U.S. Constitution requires that federal judges be appointed for life with the advice and consent of the Senate.[997] Alexander Hamilton recommended life tenure as a means to insulate judges from the "encroachments" of Congress and the "occasional ill humors in the society."[998] States have preferred two other methods: merit selection and judicial election.

Canon 4 of the Model Code of Judicial Conduct regulates a judge's campaign activity in the majority of jurisdictions where judicial election is a reality. It allows judges to participate in legally approved campaign

---

995. Republican Party v. White, 536 U.S. 765 (2002).

996. MCJC Rule 4.1(A)(13).

997. U.S. Const. art. III, § 1.

998. The Federalist No. 78 (Alexander Hamilton), *available at* http://thomas.loc.gov/home/histdox/fed_78.html.

committees and activities,[999] but requires judges who become candidates for non-judicial offices to resign from the bench.[1000]

In campaigning for judicial office, judges are prohibited from using court staff to campaign or raise money, seeking endorsements from or making speeches on behalf of political organizations, and, most controversially, making "pledges, promises, or commitments that are inconsistent with the impartial performance" of judicial office.[1001]

The "pledges, promises, or commitments" language has been more narrowly interpreted after the Supreme Court relied on the First Amendment to overturn a state rule of judicial ethics that prohibited judicial candidates from announcing their views on disputed legal and political issues.[1002] The Court found the state prohibition was not sufficiently cabined to serve an otherwise legitimate state interest in the impartiality of judges, defined as lack of bias for or against particular parties in particular proceedings.

Comments [11] through [15] to Rule 4.1 are intended to "encourage adoption of an appropriately narrow interpretation" of the clause, which produces the result that a judicial candidate does not compromise impartiality by announcing personal views as long as the announcement does not "demonstrate a closed mind on the subject" or include "a pledge or a promise to rule in a particular way if the matter comes before the court."[1003] However, a judge who "commits or appears to commit" to a particular result about issues that later come before the court will be subject to disqualification.[1004]

---

999. MCJC Rules 4.2–4.5.

1000. MCJC Rule 4.5. Williams-Yulee v. Fla. Bar, 135 S. Ct. 1656 (2015) (Florida rule prohibiting judicial candidates from personally soliciting contributions subject to strict scrutiny but justified by compelling state interest in preserving public confidence in the integrity of the judiciary).

1001. MCJC Rule 4.1.

1002. Republican Party v. White, 536 U.S. 765 (2002).

1003. Citizens United v. Fed. Election Comm'n, 558 U.S. 310 (2009) (*Caperton*'s rule that Due Process might require a judge to be recused upheld, but the litigant's political speech cannot be banned).

1004. MCJC Rule 2.11(A)(5).

PART SEVEN

The Big Picture Redux

Zealous Representation Within the Bounds of the Law

In this book, we have examined the contours of your ethical responsibilities, or the six Cs: client identification, competence, control, communication, confidentiality, and conflict of interest resolution, that is, what it means to say "yes" to your clients. We have also identified the one significant limitation to your fiduciary duty: the limits or bounds of the law, that is, when you must say "no" to your clients.

Understanding the necessity of client identification, fiduciary duty, and the limits of the law is crucial in litigation. Your client can morph during the course of a litigated matter, and your obligations to competently research and prepare, appropriately consult with your client, and obtain informed consent continue.

We also have seen that you fulfill all of these fiduciary duties to your litigation clients within well-defined limits of the law, which include procedural rules, civil and criminal accountability, as well as the significant power of a court to use equitable relief where lawyer or client conduct violates legal boundaries.

Your honesty obligations to third persons are more enhanced when you appear before a tribunal. You are expected not to lie about fact or law, and also to assume responsibility to correct prior misstatements, to disclose directly adverse legal authority, to offer evidence not known to be false, and to correct false evidence or any other fraud on a court committed by any court participant.

In addition to your general obligation to adhere to the relevant procedural rules and court orders, you are subject to special obligations regarding witnesses, evidence, comment on evidence, and contact with judges and jurors. If you should become a witness, you may lose your ability to appear at trial, although your firm may be able to take over.

Nearly all of these bounds of the law are explicitly incorporated into various Rules of Professional Conduct. As a result, lawyers can face a wide array of legal and equitable remedies to clients, opposing parties, and the court. The same misconduct can produce procedural sanctions, civil and criminal accountability, equitable relief (including disqualification and fines), as well as professional discipline.

CHAPTER 30

Fair Fight: Legal Ethics for Litigators

§ 30.01 Introduction: Fighting Fair as an Ethical Litigator (Chapter 1)

Being an ethical litigator means fighting fair, the same as being an ethical lawyer. To fight, you should represent your clients zealously (the six Cs). To fight fair, you must do so within the bounds of the law. You begin with the first C: identifying your clients. You continue as a client's agent by observing the other five Cs: competence, deference to client control over the goals of the representation, communication, confidentiality, and resolution of conflicts of interest. Busy lawyers can forget these obligations, but a vast array of client remedies in law and equity serve as constant reminders. Lawyers who breach a "C" often underidentify with a client, presuming without verifying what the client wants, needs, or should have.

You continue your work as agent alert to the relevant limits or bounds of the law that bind both you and your client. You need to understand these limits to properly advise your client. Otherwise, the client may end up in unanticipated trouble, including civil and criminal penalties to third persons. At the same time, failing to recognize a legal limit to your own advocacy can result in a number of remedies to third persons. Counseling or assisting your client to engage in prohibited behavior can also make you an aider and abettor in client misconduct, or a co-conspirator. Lawyers who breach a limit of the law often overidentify with a client.

Finally, understanding the remedies available to clients and third persons will enhance the depth of your understanding of your obligations to advocate zealously for your clients within the bounds of the law.

§ 30.02 Who Is Your Client? The First of Six Cs (Chapters 2–8)

Knowing your client should be easy: You consult, agree to represent a client for a matter, and wrap it all up in an engagement letter. But some clients are not that express. They request legal services (including legal advice) and reasonably rely on you to follow through. Such reliance could be created when you consult with a prospective client, even if you both decide not to take the matter further, which explains why non-engagement letters are necessary. Completing a client matter similarly demands a disengagement letter to clarify that your work is complete and your current client is now a former client.

Courts can create client-lawyer relationships as well, by appointing you to serve, even without pay. Other clients have trouble finding lawyers due to cost or the unpopular nature of their claims. Serving such clients on a limited term or pro bono basis qualifies as a bona fide client-lawyer relationship.

A number of clients confuse lawyers because they come in a context that includes more than one person. Joint clients allow you to choose one or many, but without a clear indication, they may reasonably believe you represent them all. The same is true in insurance defense, especially when the interests of the insured and insurer conflict, which may require you to clearly announce your allegiance to the insured alone.

Entity and government clients necessarily act through agents. Dealing with those agents makes them seem like clients, even though they usually are not. Finally, clients can morph. Businesses merge and fail. If a client files for bankruptcy, a trustee may succeed to the interests of the person or company. Individual clients can have waxing and waning capacity. If they die, you have a new client.

Understanding the dynamic nature of clients will help you recognize the need to clarify who you represent and when. You begin at the first conversation and monitor throughout the representation. That way, you know the client to whom you owe the other five Cs, as well as the prospective, former, or nonclients, to whom you owe much more limited obligations.

§ 30.03 When You Agree to Represent a Client: Fees and the Other Five Cs (Chapters 9–15)

When you agree to represent a client, agency law and the Rules of Professional Conduct impose fiduciary duties. Overall, this means that the ball is in your court. You have the responsibility for competence, in three ways: competence in legal knowledge and skill, competence in factual investigation, and competence in identifying your client.

You further have the affirmative obligation to clarify your fee, the scope of the representation, the client's goals, and to communicate with the client throughout the matter. Your confidentiality obligations extend beyond relevant litigation privileges, but you need to know the latter well to properly protect your client. You also take on a continuing duty of conflict of interest identification and resolution.

§ 30.04 The Limits of Your Advocacy (Chapters 16–20)

When you agree to represent a client, you also expressly or impliedly agree to act within the bounds of applicable law. Most prominent are limitations found in criminal law and tort law, such as the law of fraud. But other limitations in litigation are equally important, especially those imposed by the applicable rules of civil, criminal, or appellate procedure.

Failing to identify a legal limit can mean liability for you and your client. It can mean accountability to third parties for both of you as well. Heavily regulated clients or matters require special attention to the limits of the law.

§ 30.05 Client Representation and the Limits of the Law in Litigation (Chapters 21–29)

You have enhanced honesty obligations to third persons and to a court. These obligations begin when you enter an appearance for a client. Once you are before the court, you owe affirmative obligations not to lie, including responsibility to correct prior misstatements. You must disclose directly adverse legal authority, offer evidence not known to be false, and correct false evidence or any other fraud on a court committed by any court participant. When appearing ex parte, you also must disclose all material facts.

Whether at trial or on appeal, you also must obey relevant procedural rules and court orders. At trial, you have special obligations regarding witnesses, evidence, comment on evidence, and contact with judges and jurors. If you should become a witness, your ability to remain as counsel of record may be lost. Prosecutors must meet an additional set of obligations beyond advocacy due to their obligations as public ministers of justice.

These obligations apply to you if you appear before a legislative body or administrative agency in connection with an official hearing or meeting to which you are presenting evidence or argument. Throughout the trial and appellate process, your criticism of judges must be careful to avoid knowing or reckless misstatements about the qualifications or integrity of that judicial officer.

§ 30.06 So What?

Lawyers can get in trouble by underidentifying or overidentifying with clients.[1005] Underidentification often precedes breaches of agency-based fiduciary duties to clients. Overidentification often precedes failure to recognize a legal boundary to a client's or a lawyer's conduct. Zealous representation within the bounds of the law, or fighting fair, is the morally and legally safe middle ground. So why should you care?

For one thing, most lawyers find the fair-fight role morally satisfying. These lawyers often collaborate with clients, viewing their professional roles as opportunities rather than as problems. They tend to create enough professional distance to offer objective advice, while fostering client-lawyer relationships that enable clients to articulate the goals of the representation and trust the lawyer's advice. They prefer this to complete reliance on the client's value system (overidentification) or complete confidence in their own (underidentification).

The other reason to care is consequential or utilitarian. Lawyers who underidentify or overidentify with clients can get in trouble. Those who gravitate toward extreme underidentification tend to want to direct the representation and may lose sight of an ethical obligation. Those who prefer extreme loyalty to clients may miss a clear limit that causes harm. Either of these extremes can trigger equitable and legal remedies,[1006] as well as the potential for professional discipline.[1007] Lawyers who fail to

---

1005. John T. Noonan Jr., *The Lawyer Who Overidentifies with His Client*, 76 Notre Dame L. Rev. 827 (2001).

1006. RLGL § 6.

1007. MR 8.4(a); RLGL § 5.

recognize or understand a legal limit imposed on unrestrained legal advocacy also may be accountable to third-party nonclients.[1008]

Client legal remedies include breach of contract,[1009] malpractice,[1010] and breach of fiduciary duty.[1011] Equitable remedies for breach of fiduciary duty allow clients to seek a constructive trust,[1012] disqualification,[1013] injunctive relief,[1014] fee forfeiture,[1015] or restoration of pre-breach contractual rights.[1016]

Nonclients can seek relief against you if they are identified third-party beneficiaries, invited by your client or you to rely on your legal services,[1017] or if you commit crimes or intentional torts against them.[1018] In an increasing number of situations, nonclients also seek relief for negligent misrepresentation[1019] or aiding and abetting a client's fraud or breach of fiduciary duty.[1020]

Many of these client and nonclient duties also have become part of Rules of Professional Conduct provisions, so that lawyers who violate them may be subject to professional discipline as well as legal and equitable remedies for the same conduct.[1021]

All of these remedies have been created to support lawyers who seek to fight fair in litigation practice. Zealous advocacy necessitates fiduciary duty, and fairness requires knowledge and limits on advocacy imposed by other law. If you understand and observe your six C fiduciary duties, you should not create grounds for client relief. Identifying and staying within the limits of the law also should keep you out of third-party trouble.

We hope that this volume has engaged you in an interesting reflection about your own practice. We also hope that it has clarified your legally safe role. We believe this is good lawyering: a fair fight by representing clients zealously within the bounds of the law.

1008. RLGL §§ 51, 56.
1009. *Id.* § 55(1).
1010. *Id.*§ 48.
1011. *Id.*§ 49.
1012. *Id.* §§ 6 cmt. a, 44 cmt. h.
1013. *Id.* § 6(8).
1014. *Id.* § 6(2).
1015. *Id.* § 37.
1016. *Id.* § 6(3)–(5).
1017. *Id.* § 51(2)–(3).
1018. *Id.* § 56.
1019. *Id.* §§ 51(2), 95 cmt. c.
1020. *Id.* §§ 51(4), 56 cmt. h.
1021. MRs 1.1 (competence obligation); 1.2(a), 1.4, 1.6, 1.7, 1.8, 1.9, 1.10 (control, communication, confidentiality, and conflict of interest resolution obligations); 1.2(d), 3.3, 4.1, 8.4(c) (duty to avoid fraud, dishonesty, deceit, and misrepresentation); 3.4 (procedural obligations in tribunals); 1.2(d), 8.4(b) (crimes).

Table of Authorities

Index